S0-BBG-166

DISCARD

HANDBOOK
TO LIFE IN THE
INCA WORLD

ANANDA COHEN SUAREZ

JEREMY JAMES GEORGE

Facts On File
An Infobase Learning Company

Handbook to Life in the Inca World

Copyright © 2011 Ananda Cohen Suarez and Jeremy James George

All rights reserved. No part of this book may be reproduced or utilized in any form or by any means, electronic or mechanical, including photocopying, recording, or by any information storage or retrieval systems, without permission in writing from the publisher. For information contact:

Facts On File, Inc.
An imprint of Infobase Learning
132 West 31st Street
New York NY 10001

Library of Congress Cataloging-in-Publication Data
Cohen Suarez, Ananda.
   Handbook to life in the Inca World / Ananda Cohen Suarez, Jeremy James George.
      p. cm.—(Handbook to life)
   Includes bibliographical references and index.
   ISBN 978-0-8160-7449-5
   1. Incas—History. 2. Incas—Social life and customs. 3. Incas—Intellectual life. 4. Incas—Colonization.
5. Peru—Civilization. 6. Andes—Civilization. I. George, Jeremy James. II. Title.
   F3429.S93 2011
   985'.019—dc22 2010032027

Facts On File books are available at special discounts when purchased in bulk quantities for businesses, associations, institutions, or sales promotions. Please call our Special Sales Department in New York at (212) 967-8800 or (800) 322-8755.

You can find Facts On File on the World Wide Web at http://www.infobaselearning.com

Excerpts included herewith have been reprinted by permission of the copyright holders; the authors have made every effort to contact copyright holders. The publisher will be glad to rectify, in future editions, any errors or omissions brought to its notice.

Text design by Cathy Rincon
Maps by Dale Williams
Composition by Hermitage Publishing Services
Cover printed by Yurchak Printing, Inc., Landisville, Pa.
Book printed and bound by Yurchak Printing, Inc., Landisville, Pa.
Date printed: June 2011
Printed in the United States of America

10 9 8 7 6 5 4 3 2 1

This book is printed on acid-free paper.

To the Incas

CONTENTS

LIST OF ILLUSTRATIONS

LIST OF MAPS

ACKNOWLEDGMENTS _____

This book was made possible through the assistance of many people and institutions. We would first like to thank our adviser, Dr. Eloise Quiñones Keber, for her encouragement, guidance, and unwavering support throughout the process. She generously offered her time, expertise, advice, and California walnuts during marathon research sessions. For this, we are enormously grateful.

We would also like to thank the New York Public Library, the libraries of the City University of New York, the Columbia University libraries, and the Biblioteca Guido Delran Cousy of the Centro Bartolomé de Las Casas (Cuzco, Peru) for their research materials. Research travel grants from the Graduate Center of the City University of New York allowed for the investigation and documentation of several Inca sites discussed in this book.

Special thanks to Michel Besson for his sensitively rendered illustrations and to Claudia Schaab, Alexandra Lo Re, Michael Axon, and Katherine Barnhart at Facts On File for their editorial support.

Ananda would like to thank Rafael Aponte; Maria, Arthur, and Nana of the Cohen clan; Andrea Coronil; Allison Curseen; Kitty, Javier, Norah, and Asier of the Garcia clan; Maya Jimenez; Jung Joon Lee; Madonna Sang Lee; Renee McGarry; Pedro Pérez-Cabezas; Penelope Ojeda de Huala; Jennifer Samuels; John Semprit; and all of her pre-Columbianist and Latin Americanist colleagues at the Graduate Center, without whose support this book would not have been possible. Jeremy would like to thank his Graduate Center colleagues, his family, Tess, and his friends.

INTRODUCTION

The greatness of the Inca Empire, which by most accounts lasted less than 100 years in imperial form, is reflected today in the growing number of scholars and students trying to uncover the mysteries of the state enterprise. Often, decipherment takes the form of questions: Who were the Incas? How did they manage to control so vast a territory? Why did they rise so quickly, and how did they fall so fast? How did they carve such monumental stones and build such beautiful sites? We have tried to answer these questions and others in as concise a manner as possible. We hope, too, to have raised some new ones in the minds of young scholars.

At the moment of contact with the Spanish, the Inca Empire was already on the decline. Arriving in the midst of a fractious civil war between two rivals to the Inca throne, the Spanish conqueror Francisco Pizarro and the retinue in his charge were able to manipulate these divisions and contrive a surprisingly rapid defeat of the remaining imperial forces. The Spaniards' control was tenuous, as they fought among themselves while trying to manage a fallen empire, even as some hopeful Incas exiled deep in the mountains sustained a revolt into the 1570s. Today's descendants of these Andeans maintain many of the traditions, customs, and beliefs discussed herein—they speak the same language, and the archaeological remnants of their ancestors still mottle the landscape, so it should not be forgotten that the Andean culture remains vibrant, vital, and alive.

A note is necessary here on the Inca language—Quechua—the same one spoken today by some 5 million indigenous people. Language and spelling are among the most confusing aspects of reading about the Incas, because there is no standardized orthography. The Incas never developed an alphabetic writing component to their language, and as a result people felt free to translate spoken Quechua according to their own variation, resulting in numerous spellings of the same word—such as Inca, Inka, Inga, Ynga, Inqa—with little or no consistency. We have made the choice here to try and stay close to the spellings found most often in the literature and those that would be least confusing for an English speaker to pronounce. Here we have opted for what is hopefully the easier route—*Inca* with a *c* instead of a *k*, for example—even though the latter spelling is becoming more common. Pronunciation, however, is obviously a more complicated matter than presented here; Quechua words are accented on the penultimate syllable—PachaCUti YuPANqui—and pronunciation of most letters is the same as in English. Combinations of letters that are common in Spanish, such as the *ll* and the *ñ*, follow the Spanish pronunciation.

Finally, the nature of the Inca Empire, as we understand it, conflated and intertwined among the many aspects of daily life and the culture of the state—with mythology informing religion, religion informing politics, politics informing art making, and art making informing the creation of Inca culture—is, to an extent, reflected in the organization of this book. We find that many topics and issues are inextricable from the themes as broadly outlined in the contents, so we have chosen to deal with them where they make sense and emphasize the discussion within the context of that chapter's theme.

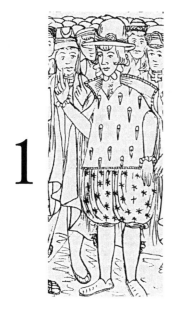

1

INCA CIVILIZATION AND ARCHAEOLOGY

INTRODUCTION TO THE INCA

The Inca Empire was an empire of superlatives: Covering nearly the entire expanse of western South America, Tawantinsuyu, the Quechua term for the Inca Empire, was the largest pre-Columbian civilization in all of the Americas. It had the longest ancient road system in the Western Hemisphere, totaling more than 30,000 kilometers (18,600 mi.) of roadway. The Incas built their empire along the rugged, often inhospitable terrain of the Andes Mountains, the longest mountain chain in the world. These accomplishments were carried out without the aid of horses, load-bearing animals, iron tools, the wheel, or an alphabetic writing system, and they were completed in just over a century.

Scholarly investigations of the Inca Empire differ considerably from those of the ancient Egyptian, Greek, and Roman, or any number of Old World empires. The absence of written records among the Incas means that it is much more difficult to capture the nature of the Inca Empire and the peoples it governed at the time of its apogee. It is therefore necessary to rely on histories of the Incas reconstructed after the Spanish conquest by Spaniards and indigenous descendants of the Incas. Another means of studying the Incas is through their archaeological remains. This chapter will look at the historiography of the Incas—how the ways of studying the Incas have changed over time—as well as current trends in Inca scholarship.

METHODS FOR STUDYING THE INCA PAST

Scholars have studied the Incas from a wide range of disciplinary standpoints. As a pre-Columbian civilization that was conquered by the Spanish about one century after its initial formation, the Incas have left behind both a material and a documentary record. The material record includes archaeological remains unearthed from the ground as well as objects produced by the Incas that remained in use or ended up in private collections after the Spanish conquest. The documentary record includes written documents composed in transliterated Quechua (the lingua franca of the Inca Empire), Aymara (the indigenous language of the peoples of southern Peru and Bolivia), Spanish, Latin, and other minor indigenous languages. Because the Incas lacked a written language, all of the documentary materials related to the Incas were produced after the conquest. Inca specialists have utilized these material and documentary remains in different ways, based largely on the dictates of their particular field of study. The primary fields of study used for examining the Inca past include anthropology, ethnohistory, and art history.

Anthropology

Anthropology is the study of human cultures, both past and present. A branch of the social sciences, anthropology is concerned with the way that the environment, biology, and culture interact with one another to shape human behavior. Two of its sub-disciplines are particularly useful for studying the Inca past: archaeology and ethnography.

ARCHAEOLOGY

Archaeology is defined today as the systematic study of material remains of human life. Material remains can include cultural artifacts such as ceramics, basketry, metallurgy, textiles, stone tools (also known as lithics), bone implements, and architectural structures, as well as physical remains such as animal bones, charred seeds or plants, and human skeletons or mummies. Archaeologists conduct their studies through mapping, survey, and excavation. Mapping consists of geographically defining the parameters and structural features of an archaeological site. Surveying requires systematically collecting artifacts at surface level within a given expanse of land to determine the extent of cultural or political power that the site exerted in the region. Excavation involves the systematic unearthing of material remains from the ground. Great care is taken to determine the coordinates of each object unearthed relative to the excavation plot. The stratigraphic placement of an artifact—the soil layer within which it is located—is also important for establishing its comparative age with other material remains in close proximity. This concept, which underlies all archaeological practice, is known by the Latin terms *terminus post quem* and *terminus ante quem*. *Terminus post quem*, literally the "limit after which," means that the stratigraphic layer within which a datable artifact is located must have been formed on or after the date of the artifact. *Terminus ante quem*, or the "limit before which," means that the stratigraphic layer beneath a datable object must be older than the object itself. At a broader level these terms refer to the idea that any artifacts found at a lower stratigraphic level tend to be older than those found closer to the surface. This rule of thumb is dependent on the fact that the stratigraphic layers in question are undisturbed by human intervention or natural disaster. The archaeological investigation of sites, artifacts, and architectural remains offers a wealth of insight to an understanding of the Incas.

ETHNOGRAPHY

Ethnography is the study of living cultures. It is conducted through a process known as ethnographic fieldwork. Ethnographic fieldwork involves the interaction between an anthropologist and individuals belonging to the culture under study. This fieldwork often requires "participant observation," which means that the anthropologist immerses him- or herself in the daily lives of his/her informants to the greatest extent possible. Ethnography is practiced both as a means of understanding contemporary cultures and of tracing the survival of ancient beliefs and traditions into the present day. Ethnographic fieldwork conducted with modern Andean populations has helped shed light on elements of Inca cultural practice that did not survive the archaeological or historical record but is preserved through the people who maintain it

today. For example, many modern Andeans continue to worship the same *huacas*, objects found in nature deemed to be sacred, and follow the same pilgrimage routes as their ancestors. An analysis of modern-day *huaca* worship and pilgrimage not only can reveal information relevant to the Inca past but stands as a testament to the enduring legacy of the Inca Empire nearly five centuries after its capitulation.

Ethnohistory

Ethnohistory refers to the use of historical documents to understand ancient cultures. Almost all studies of the Incas use an ethnohistorical approach to some extent, whether to support or contradict archaeological data or as the entire basis of one's study. Ethnohistorical documents used to reconstruct Inca society include 16th- and 17th-century conquest narratives, histories of the Inca Empire, statistical documents, and court testimonies. These types of documents are valuable for their potential to shed light on specific aspects of the preconquest past that would be otherwise unrecoverable. On the other hand, the fact that they were written after the conquest, some even up through the 18th century, means that much ethnohistorical research requires projecting colonial-period information onto a pre-Hispanic past. Given that cultures change over time, this method of inquiry can be problematic because of the vast temporal, cultural, and political gap between the Inca Empire and the Spanish colonial context within which these documents were generated. Nevertheless, when used carefully, this approach can be very effective in gaining a nuanced understanding of Inca society.

Art History

Art history is the study of human visual expression throughout history. One of the most important tools of art history is visual analysis. Visual analysis requires an examination of the different elements that make up an image or object. These elements include composition, color, size, shape, texture, line, medium (what it is made out of), technique, and style. An understanding of these different elements can help explain a number of issues such as the way that images and objects were produced, the types of symbols and motifs shared and mutually understood by a certain group, or the way that people visually described the physical and symbolic world they inhabited. Art history also looks at the various facets of artistic production: Was it organized into workshops or guilds? Were the workshops or guilds structured according to medium, type of object, or other criteria? Did artists and artisans submit their works as tribute payment to a centralized government or were they created for the general population? How were artistic styles and symbols disseminated?

Art has long been used as a tool for expressing social or political power, particularly among the Incas, who developed a specific "state style" that was immediately recognizable to its diverse inhabitants across the vast empire. Art historical analysis is useful for interpreting the wide range of Inca artistry, including ceramics, metallurgy, and textiles. As a civilization that lacked a written language, the Incas used the visual language of the arts as a means of expressing their beliefs and values. Historians studying the art understand that it is necessary to examine their crafts not simply as aesthetically pleasing objects but for their importance in spreading Inca ideas, values, and messages.

A Brief History of Archaeology in the Andes

Archaeology has been practiced in the Andes for 150 years. Study of Inca patrimony began in the 1860s, with the discovery of important archaeological sites by American and European scientist-travelers visiting South America. Several archaeologists from Peru, Europe, and the United States have proven instrumental in reconstructing Andean pre-

history through archaeological data. Many different schools of thought have impacted the way that the Andean past has been interpreted, resulting in the development of several subfields within the larger field of Andean archaeology. A specifically "Peruvianist" (*peruanista* in Spanish) approach developed in the 1930s alongside American and European techniques.

Early Explorers and Archaeologists

After Peru achieved independence in 1821, it welcomed outside visitors eager to explore a country largely unknown outside of South America. Explorers from North America and Europe traveled to South America, documenting its flora, fauna, geography, and archaeological sites and the customs of its inhabitants. Alexander von Humboldt, a naturalist from Prussia, was one of the most influential early explorers for his detailed studies and illustrations of the natural environment of South America. He was the first person to publish detailed descriptions of Inca ruins, in his 1810 text, *Vues des cordillères et monumens des peuples indigènes de l'Amérique* (Views of the cordilleras and monuments of the indigenous peoples of America). His work inspired a wealth of scientist-explorers to study the history and cultures of the Andes: Ephraim George Squier, Antonio Raimondi, Johann von Tschudi, and Charles Weiner all traveled to Peru and Bolivia in the 19th century and documented their findings in travel books, which provided information on the ancient and living inhabitants of Andean South America in the form of diagrams, illustrations, and detailed descriptions of their observations. Some of the illustrations of Inca archaeological sites are the only surviving documentation of now-disappeared or deteriorated sites. These early explorers were trained more as scientists than as formal archaeologists; stratigraphic excavations (measuring layers of soil to determine the length and relative date of site occupation) did not become fundamental to archaeological practice until the early 20th century.

Much of the archaeological fieldwork conducted in the Andes during the first half of the 20th century was focused on reconstructing the sequence of Andean cultures up to the Spanish conquest. Peruvian, North American, and European archaeologists alike were engaged in the project of tracing Andean prehistory. Particular emphasis was placed on the origins of Peruvian culture, which was tied in with nationalistic desires to cultivate a modern Peruvian identity. The archaeologists of the early 20th century approached excavation more systematically, with a keen eye for variations in artifact assemblages and architectural styles through space and time.

MAX UHLE (1856–1944)

Max Uhle was a German archaeologist who worked in Peru in the late 19th and early 20th centuries. The scientific precision with which he conducted excavations and analyzed artifacts was remarkable for his time. Uhle was the first prominent scholar in the Andean region to differentiate cultures based on stratigraphy, which is a branch of archaeology that focuses on how rocks and soil are layered. By examining variations in artifacts from the deepest layers of the soil (that is, the oldest) to the most superficial (the youngest), Uhle was able to distinguish between Inca culture and the Tiwanaku (Tihuanaco) culture that preceded it. Previously, scholars had lumped these cultures together because of their stylistic similarities. This discovery was important because it confirmed the veracity of postconquest historical documents about Tiwanaku civilization through concrete archaeological evidence. He was also well-known for his intensive study of Pachacamac, an Inca pilgrimage site near modern-day Lima, and Tambo Colorado, an Inca way station in the Pisco Valley to the west of Cuzco.

HIRAM BINGHAM (1875–1956)

Hiram Bingham, an American explorer, was the most important of the early explorers to make a lasting impact on Inca archaeology. Bingham was involved in a variety of different careers, including that of missionary, politician, aviator, and archaeologist. Deeply interested in Latin American history, he decided to retrace the great liberator Simón Bolívar's steps during his famous march from Venezuela to Colombia. He took a lectureship at Yale University to teach geography and South American history. After this first trip to South America Bingham returned several times on expeditions sponsored by Yale and the National Geographic Society to explore the vastly understudied cultural patrimony of the Andes. During a 1911 expedition Bingham discovered the site of Machu Picchu with the aid of local Peruvian guides. The discovery of this breathtaking site was instrumental in bringing the Incas to the forefront of scholarly attention. The success of Bingham's 1911 expedition inspired many scholars, both local and foreign, to conduct archaeological fieldwork in the Andes.

JULIO C. TELLO (1880–1947)

Julio C. Tello was one of the most important Peruvian archaeologists of his time and is considered the father of Peruvian archaeology. He was of indigenous descent and came from a humble background, born in the town of Huarochirí in the central highlands. Tello studied at the renowned University of San Marcos in Lima and pursued graduate work at Harvard on full scholarship. He is best known for his studies of Chavín, one of the earliest highland civilizations in the Andes, as well as the Paracas culture of the south coast. He eventually became the director of the National Archaeology Museum in Lima, for which he went on several expeditions to expand the museum's collection. During his directorship at the museum, Tello became involved in conservation projects on Inca archaeological projects. He also took an active role in designing exhibitions at the museum that communicated information about Inca sites to the general public in an accessible way. Furthermore, he introduced a major paradigm shift to the study of Peruvian prehistory. Unlike European archaeologists working in Peru such as Uhle, who believed Andean civilizations derived from Mesoamerican cultures that diffused into South America, Tello rightly argued that they developed independently in the highlands. Later in his career, he continued excavations that had been initiated by Uhle at the Inca site of Pachacamac. His work at this important pilgrimage site revealed earlier site occupations that had been left undiscovered by Uhle. Tello influenced an entire generation of Peruvian archaeologists, including Duccio Bonavia, Ramiro Matos, Rosa Fung, and Roger Ravines. His legacy was perhaps best continued by Luis E. Valcárcel, a Peruvian archaeologist who shared his commitment to engaging contemporary indigenous communities in the study of their cultural heritage.

LUIS E. VALCÁRCEL (1891–1987)

Luis E. Valcárcel pioneered a specifically "Peruvianist" approach to the study of indigenous cultures of the Andes. He studied literature, political science, and law at the Universidad de San Antonio Abad in Cuzco. While in Cuzco, he taught Peruvian history at his alma mater and founded the city's first museum of anthropology. Valcárcel succeeded Tello as director of the National Archaeology Museum in Lima in the 1930s. He was responsible for advocating a vested national interest in the pre-Hispanic past and the retention of indigenous cultural practices in the modern era. He contributed to the valorization of indigenous cultures in Peru through promotion of dramatic performances featuring Inca subject matter, such as the great colonial-era plays *Ollanta* and *Usca Paucar*. He promoted the study of these peoples through the disciplines of anthropology (the study of human cultures), archaeology, ethnography (the study of modern-day cultures), and ethnohistory (the study of native peoples and histories through examination of written documents). He wrote a wealth of important books on both Andean culture and archaeology and trained a number of Peruvian archaeologists, historians, and social scientists.

JOHN MURRA (1916–2006)

John Murra, an anthropologist trained at the University of Chicago, made an important contribution to the study of Andean economies before the Spanish conquest. He served as professor at several universities but made his biggest mark at Cornell, where he taught in the anthropology department up until his death. Murra's most famous contribution to the field was his characterization of the Andes as a "vertical archipelago." Unlike traditional archipelagoes, whose islands stretch outward across the sea, the Andes jut upwards in altitude, but in the same way that the chain of islands that make up an archipelago are connected by maritime trade, communities inhabiting different altitudinal levels of the Andes were economically interconnected through processes of exchange and reciprocity. Expanding on this concept, Murra proposed that the inhabitants of this special archipelago survived over the course of millennia through a strategy of "verticality." He argued that communities in the Andes traded goods cultivated in different altitudinal zones as a survival strategy; for example, maize producers in the lowlands could exchange their product for the potatoes cultivated by highland people, allowing for a more balanced and nutrient-enriched diet in both zones. This exchange was facilitated by the settlement of extended family units across this vertical landscape. Contingent to the verticality model was the idea of reciprocal relationships between different highland groups. Although scholars continue to debate the accuracy of Murra's theory, it continues to play an important role in understanding pan-Andean exchange systems, which would eventually become incorporated into Inca economic policy. Murra also wrote extensively about the economic and social value of textiles in the Inca Empire.

JOHN HOWLAND ROWE (1918–2004)

John Howland Rowe was one of the most influential Inca specialists of all time, publishing extensively on the Incas. He received his doctorate from Harvard in 1947 and began teaching in Cuzco at about the same time. During his stay in Cuzco he founded the archaeology department at the University of San Antonio Abad and became the director of the Museo Inca. His collaboration with Peruvian institutions paved the way for fruitful intellectual exchange between North American and Peruvian scholars. Rowe's most important early work was *Introduction to the Archaeology of Cuzco*, published in 1944. Two years later, he published the seminal article "Inca Culture at the Time of the Spanish Conquest," which detailed the various cultural, environmental, political, and economic elements that made up the Inca Empire. This article, published in the *Handbook of South American Indians*, remains even today one of the most consistently consulted sources for an overview of Inca culture owing to its comprehensiveness.

One of Rowe's most important contributions to the field was his solidification of a chronology of Andean civilizations based on artifacts collected by Uhle in the Ica Valley. Rather than assigning distinct terminology for each cultural phase (for instance, Preclassic, Classic, and Postclassic, as used in Mesoamerican and Maya archaeology), he grouped Andean cultures into "horizons" and "intermediate" periods. Horizons are defined as periods in which power is centralized and social organization is at the level of state or empire. Intermediate periods are characterized by decentralization of power and the rise of regionalism. The highest level of social organization usually achieved during intermediate periods is that of chiefdom or small state, as in the case of the Moche (0–700 C.E.) of the north coast. Over the course of his 60-year-long career, Rowe wrote more than 300 essays and articles. His indefatigable work at Berkeley to develop the field of Andean studies resulted in a flourish of both North American and South American scholarship.

Trends in Inca Archaeology

The way that the Incas have been studied archaeologically has evolved considerably over the past 100 years. Changes in archaeological field methods, the interpretation of sites and archaeological remains, as well as an increased interest in interdisciplinary approaches have helped to advance knowledge about the Inca Empire.

ARCHAEOLOGICAL METHODS

With the discoveries made by Bingham and other early archaeologists, the major concern in its nascent years was to excavate and identify major Inca sites. Before the advent of scientifically based excavation procedures, archaeological practice varied widely. The lack of systemization in field practices resulted in asymmetrical knowledge of Inca settlements and material culture. In the early years of Inca archaeology, typical practice was to unearth antiquities from the ground and uncover buried structures. Greater value was ascribed to complete objects over fragmented ones. Much of the archaeo-logical literature consisted of identifying and describing artifact types and attempting to reconstruct architectural features of the site under investigation.

With the development of codified archaeological field procedures and the application of scientific methods to the interpretation of artifacts, Inca archaeology began to move away from a merely descriptive approach to site and artifact analysis. Archaeologists became interested in interpreting artifacts as a means of reconstructing social organization, economy, and the political structure of the Inca Empire. Moreover, Craig Morris's excavations at the Inca provincial site of Huánuco Pampa and Timothy Earle and Terence D'Altroy's fieldwork in the Upper Mantaro Valley in the central highlands in the 1970s and 1980s paved the way for studies of Inca sites outside the imperial capital of Cuzco. Studies of so-called provincial Inca communities, sites, and artifacts are essential in understanding how the empire spread within the span of less than a century and how it governed its vast territories. An interest in regional variation in the construction, design, and style of architecture, settlement planning, and artifacts has provided an amplified view of the Inca state, moving away from a Cuzco-centric model to see the different ways that communities throughout the realm adapted and responded to Inca rule.

Technological improvements in the field of archaeology have also allowed for improved accuracy in the dating of sites and sourcing of materials. Aerial photography and global positioning systems (GPS) have allowed archaeologists to determine the layout and size of archaeological sites with unprecedented accuracy. Neutron activation analysis (NAA) provides qualitative and quantitative elemental analysis of artifacts, minerals, and biotic materials. Employing NAA onto a group of excavated materials such as ceramic fragments can identify the source of the clays and temper (crushed rocks or shells used to bind the clay together) to determine where the pots originated. If the clays and temper came from a nearby source, it can be assumed that they were produced locally; however, if they derived from distant sources, one can infer that the ceramics were imported. These kinds of details are important for understanding the way that a society was structured and the modes of exchange within which it was engaged.

THE SHIFT TO ARCHAEOLOGY

It was not until the mid-20th century that Inca archaeology could exist as a discipline in its own right, without recourse to the chronicles of the early colonial period. Archaeologists began to question the validity of the chronicler's descriptions of the Inca Empire. The individuals who wrote about the Inca Empire during the colonial period—conquistadores, Spanish friars, Christianized Indians, and mestizos (the product of Spanish and Indian unions)—wrote from a culturally and temporally distanced standpoint. Even the few indigenous chroniclers who actually experienced life under the Inca Empire before the Spanish conquest were writing about events from their childhood. Moreover, they had specific agendas of their own in characterizing the Inca Empire in an idealized way. As archaeologists began to focus more exclusively on Inca archaeological sites, it became evident that the archaeological record often tells a different story than the chronicles do. In fact, archaeological data often contradicts the early written sources, presenting a much more complicated picture of the Inca world than the historical narratives communicate. Archaeology also serves as an essential tool for understanding peripheral regions under Inca rule that are only scantily mentioned in the documentary record.

PROCESSUAL VERSUS HISTORICAL APPROACH

One of the biggest shifts in archaeological investigation of the Incas involved the application of processual approaches to the development of the Inca state in a field dominated by historical and ethnohistorical models. Processualism is an archaeological theory that states that cultural change and adaptation are contingent on large-scale factors such as the environment, subsistence activities, or population density. It differs significantly from historical or ethnohistorical approaches, which depend largely on texts about the Inca past that were produced after the conquest. Given that the construction of history requires the placement of past events

and historical figures into a sequence, it provides a version of the Inca past that sees the accomplishments of individuals as the main determinant of cultural evolution.

One of the major implications of this dichotomy lies in how scholars have explained the Incas' rise to power. The event-based, individual-centered perspective of the 16th- and 17th-century chronicles continues to filter into modern-day interpretations of the development of the Inca state. This historical approach, which accepts the model that empires are built and expanded by a few key heroic "players," was initiated by Rowe and perpetuated by many subsequent archaeologists and historians. In terms of Inca expansion, it sees the military victories of the rulers Viracocha Inca and his son, Pachacuti, as responsible for the expansion and consolidation of the empire. A processual approach to the development of the Inca state posits that empire-formation was a gradual process that was the result of economic and political ties forged between the major ethnic groups of the Cuzco region. Some of the proponents of this latter view include the archaeologists Brian Bauer, Dorothy Menzel, Terence D'Altroy, Craig Morris, Katharina Schreiber, and R. Alan Covey. Both approaches continue to be employed today, although the findings from excavations conducted in the Cuzco area increasingly point toward a much different story of the beginnings of Inca expansion than the versions provided by the chronicles of the 16th and 17th centuries.

INTERDISCIPLINARY APPROACHES

In recent decades more scholars have made efforts to integrate ethnohistorical, archaeological, and ethnographic data into their studies to gain a more well-rounded sense of the Inca past. The work of one Peruvian scholar in particular, María Rostworowski de Diez Canseco, demonstrates the success of such an approach. Rostworowski's proposal of the existence of two distinct Inca economies—one highland and one coastal—was able to come to fruition through her consideration of the importance and utility of each of these forms of data. Rather than relying on the methods of a single discipline, Inca scholars from a variety of fields, including anthropology, archaeology, literature, history, and art history, have begun to utilize a wealth of different sources and approaches to uncover the multifaceted nature of Inca civilization.

MATERIAL CULTURE STUDIES

Another subfield of archaeology that has gained currency in recent years is material culture studies. Material culture refers to objects produced and used by a culture, including anything from cooking pots to weapons to works of art. The difference between material culture and artifacts is that the former is an all-encompassing term that can pertain to living societies as well as ancient ones, while the latter only refers to the past remains of a society. Material culture studies examine the role that objects play in social interactions. It operates on the belief that material culture can simultaneously define and construct social relations. It also sees objects as having the power to communicate a set of common cultural values that become absorbed by their users through sustained usage. Material culture can communicate values through its practical function, its meaning, the symbols or motifs inscribed on it, the social and cultural contexts within which it operates, or a combination of all of these elements. The application of a material culture perspective on Inca objects such as ceramic serving and cooking vessels can reveal aspects of Inca life such as eating and drinking customs, domestic life, social status, or local traditions that are not as easily accessed through other methods of scholarly inquiry. For example, the morphology (shape) of a vessel, its decorations (or lack thereof), its function, and its method of manufacture can tell us something about the social situations that necessitated its use, whether of elaborate feasts or simple domestic meals. Material culture studies also facilitate a "bottom-up" rather than a "top-down" perspective, placing value on everyday objects typically produced by nonelite sectors of society and what they can tell us about the lives of their makers and users.

Problems from Looting

One unfortunate consequence of the rich archaeological record in the Andean region is the looting of sites, which has continued unabated since the Spanish conquest. After the Spanish discovered the vast quantities of gold and silver objects crafted by the Incas, they dug for "treasures" at Inca and pre-Inca archaeological sites and melted them down into bullion to increase the wealth of the Spanish monarchs. The looting and melting down of objects not only destroyed the objects themselves but the archaeological sites from which they came. Modern looters, known as *huaqueros* in Peru, do not melt objects down but instead sell them on the international black market to make a profit. Although looted objects sometimes make it to museums and galleries rather than private collections, they are irrevocably stripped of their archaeological context. Since archaeologists base much of their interpretation on the location of an object relative to the archaeological site, the absence of such information makes it difficult to discern the original cultural context within which the object was engaged. The loss of this valuable piece of an object's identity has led to erroneous claims of its significance.

THE WRITTEN RECORD

No alphabetic writing tradition existed in pre-Columbian South America. This does not mean that the Incas or the cultures that preceded them lacked language or methods for recording knowledge. In fact, the Incas developed a number of strategies for encoding information that functioned in much the same way as a written language. The quipu, made up of groups of knotted strings used for recording information, was an important device for delivering messages along great distances. Relay runners known as *chasquis* would pass quipus along a route until the message reached its final destination. Organized in a decimal system, with each knot representing a unit of 10, quipus contained information such as census tabulations and number or type of tribute payments. They also could be used to record histories, songs, and poetry. Oral tradition provided another mechanism for recording and preserving knowledge. In the absence of an alphabetic writing system, people relied heavily on the powers of memory, cultivating the skill through repetition. In addition, textiles were also interwoven with specific messages that would be recognized by its users. For example, the *tocapu* (repeating square patterns inscribed with geometric motifs) found on many Inca tunics probably served as a type of visual code that expressed information about its wearer.

The Spanish conquest of the Inca Empire in 1534, however, interrupted many of these traditions for recording and sharing information. The disintegration of the Inca imperial structure meant that Inca systems of communication would become supplanted by the alphabetic writing tradition used by the Spaniards. Despite the waning of Inca traditions, the transliteration of Quechua, Aymara, and other indigenous languages, along with the training of native Andeans in reading and writing Spanish and Latin, resulted in a flowering of literature after the conquest. Narratives of the conquest, histories of the Inca Empire, accounts of Inca customs, and illustrated chronicles with descriptions of Spanish abuses against native people are just some of the genres that developed in the colonial period. These written documents provide invaluable insights on Inca history from a variety of different perspectives. Their specificity provides impressive details in sequence of events, dates, and explication of cultural practice that cannot be found archaeologically, ethnographically, or through art historical inquiry.

Written documents, nevertheless, demand a cautious approach for the following reasons: First is the problem of temporal distance. The historical record reconstructs Inca culture after it had already been fundamentally altered by the Spanish conquest. Since the Incas did not leave behind records that could be deciphered by Spaniards, oral histories and the testimonies of native peoples who survived the conquest were the fundamental tools for reconstructing Inca history. For many of these individuals, the Inca Empire was a distant memory, with the added caveat that in the decades before the Spanish invasion, the empire was in crisis, possibly nearing the end of its peak, due to violent succession clashes between the half brothers Huáscar and Atahualpa. Second, the cultural distance that separated Inca forms of knowledge and Spanish written history was often vast. The transition from an oral history recounted in Quechua or encoded in a quipu to a written history in Spanish, Latin, or even transliterated Quechua often loses much of its original meaning. Inca forms of recording and disseminating knowledge were multisensory, requiring the use of sound, sight, and touch, whereas the written word is static and the act of reading only requires visual recognition. Thus, many specifically Andean or Inca concepts became lost in the transferral to written form. Third, whether the author of the text was Spanish, indigenous, or mestizo, he was always driven by an agenda, whether personal, political, moral, or any combination of these, that would invariably alter the form and content of the Inca history recounted. This is to say nothing of the fact that Inca practices of structuring, remembering, and narrating history from which the colonial chroniclers drew changed considerably over time, particularly when new rulers rose to power who wanted to associate themselves with important events and victories. For example, it was said that when Pachacuti came into power, he ordered the destruction of all quipus that told a story of the past that did not conform to his new vision of a strictly Pachacuti-centric history.

Types of Spanish Narratives

CHRONICLE (*CRÓNICA*)

Drawing from a medieval European tradition, the Spanish chronicle was a narrative device used to describe historical events in their sequence of occurrence, without any synthesis or interpretation. It was a straightforward, practical way to recount events that was often used when writing about the conquest. The chronicle was distinctive for its eyewitness, first-person perspective.

HISTORY (*HISTORIA*)

In this case *history* refers to the practice of recounting historical events, but unlike the chronicle, history involves the contextualization of historical events into an ideological framework. It requires one to synthesize past events and explain their relationship to the "bigger picture," whether to the history of the world, of a civilization, or of a place. However, despite the conceptual differences between these two writing genres, New World historians often drew from both traditions and used the terms interchangeably.

REPORT (RELACIÓN)

A *relación* is a legal report mandated by the Spanish Crown that described different aspects of colonial administration of indigenous populations in the New World. It was often written in the form of a letter, since it was directed to the king. The *relación* consists of factual information such as the imposition of labor regimes, the successes and failures of evangelization, or the founding of new towns and cities.

Chroniclers

The Spanish chronicles were used to recount the history of the conquest of Peru and were largely published in the decades succeeding the conquest in 1534. They are often written from a military perspective, since the chroniclers tended to be part of the military personnel of Francisco Pizarro, the conqueror of the Inca Empire. The chronicles provide a great deal of factual information about the conquest, although there are discrepancies as they were written by individuals with different levels of involvement in the conquest. Moreover, they were often composed several years after the event, during which some information can become lost.

FRANCISCO DE JEREZ (1497–1565)

Francisco de Jerez is credited with the first account of the conquest of Peru. His *Verdadera relación de la conquista del Perú* (True report of the conquest of Peru) was published in 1534. Jerez was a secretary for Francisco Pizarro and was thus writing about the conquest from direct experience. His work was incorporated into Gonzalo Fernández de Oviedo's *Historia general y natural de las Indias* (General and Natural History of the Indies), published a year later. Oviedo's work—and by extension, that of Jerez—

would have considerable influence on the later writings of Spaniards involved in the conquest.

PEDRO DE CIEZA DE LEÓN (1519–1554)

Pedro de Cieza de León's famous four-volume text, *La crónica del Perú (The Chronicle of Peru)*, published in 1553 and 1554, is the earliest comprehensive history of the conquest of Peru. He was born in Spain in 1520 and came to the Americas when he was about 13 years old. From the moment he arrived, Cieza was involved in military operations occurring throughout South America, but due to his young age he began as an apprentice, assisting soldiers when needed. While he did not participate in the early sieges of the Inca city of Cajamarca and Cuzco, Cieza was involved in civil wars that raged throughout Peru immediately after the conquest. He was appointed the official chronicler of the Indies, granting him the privilege of researching and writing about all subjects related to the New World. Cieza conducted interviews with descendants of Inca elites in order to piece together the genealogy of Inca kings. His *crónica* begins with an overview of the geography and inhabitants of South America and follows with a detailed description of the Inca Empire, aided by the interviews and field research he conducted. Cieza then describes the Spanish overthrow of the Inca Empire and the civil wars that ensued due to conflicts between the Pizarros and other Spanish factions. His *crónica* is one of the most important foundational texts for understanding Inca civilization and its conquest by the Spaniards. Cieza is credited for being the first to describe species of flora and fauna native to Peru. His vivid, first-person accounts are compelling and accessible and greatly impacted the format and content of the chronicles to follow.

AGUSTÍN DE ZÁRATE (1514–1560)

Agustín de Zárate's work, *Historia del descubrimiento y conquista de las provincias del Perú (History of the Discovery and Conquest of Peru)*, published in 1555, is a 300-page political history of the conquest. Zárate was sent to Peru as an accountant entrusted with managing the royal treasury. His text focuses primarily on the conflicts between the two principal groups of Spanish conquerors in Peru: Francisco Pizarro's army and the army of Diego de Almagro. Zárate's description of the Incas and other indigenous groups is heavily informed by European standards of culture and civility and therefore does not represent the Incas as accurately or perceptively as Cieza, Juan de Betanzos, and other contemporaries do.

JUAN DE BETANZOS (FL. 16TH CENTURY)

Juan de Betanzos's *Suma y narración de los incas (Narrative of the Incas)*, published in 1557, provides an account of Inca royal history unparalleled by his contemporaries in accuracy and detail. An expert in Quechua, he served as an official translator and interpreter in Peru. Betanzos married an Inca princess, Doña Angelina Añas Yupanqui, also known as Angelina Cusimaray. She was both niece of Huayna Cápac, the penultimate Inca ruler, and wife to his son, Atahualpa, the last legitimate Inca ruler. She then became Francisco Pizarro's mistress, bearing him two sons, and then married Betanzos in 1541 after Pizarro's death. Doña Angelina was the key to Betanzos's authorial success, providing him privileged access to royal records preserved in quipus, which she orally translated for his alphabetic transcription to written text. His text is especially strong in his discussion of Huayna Cápac and Atahualpa because of his wife's familial ties and knowledge of that history. Although much of Betanzos's *Suma y narración* comes from authenticated Inca sources, it is important to note that his exaltation of these members of the Inca royal lineage was also motivated by a desire to glorify his wife's lineage. Nevertheless, Betanzos's account stands out as one of the most authentic writings on the history of the Inca Empire and the events leading up to the conquest.

JUAN POLO DE ONDEGARDO (D. 1575)

Juan Polo de Ondegardo moved from Spain to Peru in 1545, where he enjoyed a career as a lawyer, tax collector, and magistrate. In addition to his bureaucratic pursuits, Ondegardo was deeply fascinated by Inca civilization. He was the nephew of Zárate, who published *Historia del descubrimiento y conquista de las provincias del Perú* in 1555. Ondegardo was commissioned by the viceroy Marqués de Cañete and the archbishop Fray Jerónimo de Loaysa to write a history of the Inca Empire based on information provided by native informants. His report, compiled in 1559, detailed Inca history, politics, economy, and religion. He was the first to undertake a systematic study of Inca social and political institutions, believing that it was necessary to understand the structures that made up the Inca Empire to successfully evangelize Indians and set up labor regimes in the new colonial state. Ondegardo's report was lost, but an excerpt of it, entitled *Tratado y averiguación sobre los errores y supersticiones de los indios* (Treaty and inquiry about the errors and superstitions of the Indians), was finally published by the Third Provincial Council of Lima in 1585. Fortunately, Ondegardo's section on religion was preserved through the writings of Father Bernabé Cobo, who borrowed liberally from his report.

PEDRO PIZARRO (CA. 1515–CA. 1602)

Pedro Pizarro was a cousin of Francisco Pizarro and participated in the conquest of the Incas. Although he was part of the original group of conquistadores, he did not publish his memoirs, *Relación del descubrimiento y conquista de los reinos del Perú (Relation of the Discovery and Conquest of the Kingdoms of Peru)*, until 1571. His work constituted one of the few eyewitness accounts of the conquest.

PEDRO SARMIENTO DE GAMBOA (1532–1592)

Pedro Sarmiento de Gamboa came to the New World in 1555, first residing in Mexico and settling in Peru a few years later. He was a sea captain and cosmographer for the Viceroyalty of Peru. Following in the tradition of acquiring information from native informants initiated by Betanzos and Ondegardo, Sarmiento sought to write an authentic history of the Incas. His *Historia índica (History of the Incas)*, published in 1572, synthesized accounts provided by indigenous scribes from Cuzco as well as the provinces of Jauja and Huamanga. He also interviewed professional *quipucamayos*, or quipu-readers, whose histories were incorporated into the text. Sarmiento's field research was facilitated by the newly appointed viceroy Francisco de Toledo, whom he accompanied on a royal inspection of all the major cities and settlements between Lima and

Cuzco. The *Historia índica* is composed of three sections: The first is a description of the geography of the Inca realm; the second consists of an overview of the Inca Empire, including detailed descriptions of the lives and deeds of the Inca kings; and the third section deals with the conquest and the imposition of colonial rule. Perhaps the most remarkable aspect about the *Historia índica* is that, in an effort to verify the veracity of the information collected, Sarmiento had his entire text read aloud to a group of 42 indigenous informants. Shortly thereafter, the manuscript, along with four painted canvases depicting the lineage of Inca kings, was to be sent to Spain to King Philip II but never made it due to logistical issues. The history is also of great significance because Sarmiento's text was one of the last to record Inca histories relayed by the first generation of Inca elites.

Indigenous and Mestizo Authors

In addition to Spanish writers, several indigenous authors wrote about the conquest and Inca-related themes. These authors came from diverse backgrounds; some were pure-blood descendants of Inca royalty, some were mestizos (of mixed Spanish and Indian descent), and others were Indians of non-royal descent. Despite their differences, however, what united these authors was a shared connection and familiarity with the Inca past, which endowed their writings with a unique perspective that distinguished them from their Spanish counterparts.

RELACIÓN DE CHINCHA

The *Relación de Chincha* (Report from Chincha) was compiled by two Spanish bureaucrats, Diego de Ortega y Morejón and Fray Cristóbal de Castro, in 1558. Although the compilers were Spanish, the manuscript is composed of testimonies given by the native inhabitants of Chincha, a *señorío*, or "chiefdom," on the southern coast of Peru. The *Relación de Chincha* provides an account of the Inca conquest of Chincha in the 15th century, when the Incas were in the process of consolidating their empire. It

describes the process by which the people of Chincha became subjugated by the powerful *cuzqueños* (people of Cuzco), which began as a process predicated on equality and transformed into an act of domination and exploitation. Highland relations with the Chincha lords who presided over their fishing society were originally commercial, rooted in pan-Andean notions of economic reciprocity. However, as the *relación* describes, the lords of Cuzco forcefully subjugated the people of Chincha into the rapidly growing Inca Empire, organizing the territory into a tribute-paying unit based on the decimal system, constructing roads, and erecting Inca administrative buildings. The *Relación de Chincha* is one of the few documents of the colonial period to describe Inca expansionism from a local perspective rather than from a "top-down" point of view. It contains valuable information about the dynamics between coastal societies and the highland Incas, a topic that is often ignored in the traditional chronicles. It also provides useful information about the customs and daily lives of the Chincha people at the time of the Inca conquest.

TITU CUSI YUPANQUI (CA. 1530–1571)

Titu Cusi Yupanqui was a grandson of Huayna Cápac, the penultimate ruler of the Inca realm. Titu Cusi himself was the penultimate ruler of the neo-Inca state, the last Inca holdout located in Vilcabamba, which was eventually defeated by Viceroy Toledo's forces in 1572. His manuscript, *Relación de la conquista del Perú (An Inca Account of the Conquest of Peru)*, written in 1570, is the earliest known book by a native Andean. Titu Cusi did not actually write the text but dictated his story orally in Quechua to an Augustinian friar, who then dictated his Spanish translation to a scribe.

Titu Cusi's manuscript stands as one of the only conquest narratives to recount the history of the conquest from the standpoint of Inca resistance. As head of the neo-Inca state, which successfully resisted Spanish rule for nearly 40 years, Titu Cusi saw Inca history as alive and present well after the conquest in 1534. Some of the details included in his description of the dynastic lineage are uncorroborated by any other written sources, particularly his claims of the deeds of his father, Manco Inca, the founder of the neo-Inca state in 1537. This has led scholars to suspect that his decision to write the manuscript was motivated by a desire to position himself as a legitimate heir to Inca power, since Titu Cusi was most likely one of Manco Inca's many illegitimate sons, in addition to the fact that Manco Inca was of questionable pedigree as well. However, his discussions of indigenous acts of adaptation and resistance to Spanish acts of subordination shed light on a largely ignored element of the conquest and are essential to a fuller understanding of the encounter between Incas and Spaniards. Moreover, Titu Cusi's manuscript itself is an act of adaptation and resistance; his use of Spanish rhetorical devices to produce a trenchant critique of Spanish policy against the Indians demonstrates one of the means by which indigenous peoples could attain power in the face of overwhelming Spanish domination. Some of the retentions of Inca ways of thinking and recounting history come through in Titu Cusi's account, particularly in his repetition of phrases four times when referring to Tawantinsuyu, the Quechua name for the Inca Empire, which literally means "the four parts together."

QUIPUCAMAYOS DE VACA DE CASTRO

The anonymous account *Quipucamayos de Vaca de Castro* (Quipu readers of Vaca de Castro) records the testimonies given by two witnesses who descended from the eighth Inca ruler, Viracocha Inca. The witnesses were *quipucamayos*, or record keepers who read and utilized the quipu, a system of knotted strings used to encode information. Part of the document was probably written during a legal investigation by a certain Vaca de Castro in 1542, but it was not completed until 1608.

HUAROCHIRÍ MANUSCRIPT

The *Huarochirí Manuscript* remains one of the most fascinating documents produced about indigenous peoples in the colonial period, both for its content and the circumstances of its creation. The *Huarochirí Manuscript* is an anonymous, undated, and untitled manuscript compiled by the Jesuit priest Francisco de Ávila around 1608. His reasons for creating this manuscript were deceit and revenge; after being jailed for illicit activities, he decided to

retaliate against the Indian community of Huarochirí that had spoken out about his wrongdoings. It is likely that he used the information he compiled pertaining to sacred rites and *huacas* to hunt down and extirpate these practices. It is thus called the *Huarochirí Manuscript* for its native oral authors from the central highlands.

What makes this manuscript most distinctive from the other chronicles is that it records a local, indigenous view of pre-Hispanic, Inca, and colonial history. The inhabitants of Huarochirí were neither Spanish nor Inca descendants but rather indigenous Andeans who had been conquered first by the Incas and then by the Spaniards. The *Huarochirí Manuscript* recounts their creation myth, which was accomplished by two sacred forces: Paria Caca, the mountain deity, and Chaupi Ñamca, the female coastal deity. Many aspects of pre-Inca and Inca belief systems are incorporated into the manuscript, such as *huacas* and the practice of llama sacrifice and divination. References are also made to the Inca Empire itself, describing its territorial divisions into *suyus* (quadrants). The hybrid nature of the *Huarochirí Manuscript* provides a glimpse into how different communities may have enmeshed Inca imperial ideologies with local beliefs and customs.

GARCILASO DE LA VEGA, "EL INCA" (1539–1616)

Garcilaso de la Vega, "El Inca," is credited with writing one of the most famous histories of Peru, *Comentarios reales de los incas (Royal Commentaries of the Incas)*. The first part was published in Lisbon, Portugal, in 1609, and the second part in Córdoba, Spain, in 1617. Garcilaso was born in Cuzco in 1539, five years after the conquest, and was a mestizo of royal descent on both sides of his family. His father was the Spanish captain Sebastián Garcilaso de la Vega y Vargas, and his mother was Ñusta Chimpu Ocllo (baptized to Isabel Ocllo), an Indian princess related to Huáscar and Atahualpa, the half brothers who competed for the throne before their eventual defeat by the Spaniards. Garcilaso spent his formative years in Cuzco but embarked for Spain in 1560 as a young man, where he spent the rest of his life devoted to writing the

Comentarios reales. As one of the first mestizos born in Peru, Garcilaso was uniquely privileged to shed a different light on the history of the Incas and the conquest in a way that had not been attempted by the Spanish authors.

El Inca Garcilaso's *Comentarios reales* is divided into two parts. Part 1 is composed of nine books, each containing between 25 and 40 chapters. It begins with a general description of the Andean region, followed by a genealogy of the Inca kings, and culminating with the violent clashes between Huáscar and Atahualpa. This compendious volume also covers an incredible range of subjects, including everything from astrological and astronomical knowledge and Inca poetry to the work of craftsmen. In addition, he discusses the social structure of Inca society, government administration, and religious festivities. Garcilaso accessed much of this information through communication with members of his mother's family. Part 2 deals with the Spaniards involved in the conquest and founding of the Viceroyalty of Peru. Much of Garcilaso's work, particularly Part 1, is concerned with elevating the Incas to a civilized people, believing the disparaging characterizations of them by Spanish authors were unfounded and stood in need of correction. However, Garcilaso's desires to challenge the writings of his Spanish contemporaries resulted in a largely idealized representation of the Inca Empire that reflected his own agendas more than an Inca reality. Nonetheless, his work is appreciated for its value as the first history of the Incas published by an American-born person of Inca descent.

JUAN DE SANTACRUZ PACHACUTI YAMQUI SALCAMAYGUA (D. AFTER 1613)

Juan de Santacruz Pachacuti Yamqui Salcamaygua wrote the *Relación de antigüedades deste reyno del Perú (An Account of the Antiquities of Peru)*, completed in 1613. It provided an account of Inca history and religion, with a strong focus on cosmology. Pachacuti Yamqui's *relación* is best known for his diagram of the Coricancha, the Sun Temple located in Cuzco, and its relationship to Inca religious cosmology.

FELIPE GUAMÁN POMA DE AYALA (CA. 1535–AFTER 1616)

Felipe Guamán Poma de Ayala was a native Andean, whose illustrated chronicle is arguably one of the most important sources on the Inca in existence. His work, *El primer nueva corónica* [sic] *y buen gobierno (The First New Chronicle and Good Government)*, completed in 1615, was an almost 1,200-page-long letter addressed to King Philip III of Spain intended to alert him of the achievements of the Peruvian people and of the injustices they suffered under colonial rule. The letter was hand-delivered to Lima and subsequently sent to Spain but never made it to the king. It was only rediscovered in 1908, when Richard Pietschmann found the manuscript at the Royal Museum of Copenhagen, where

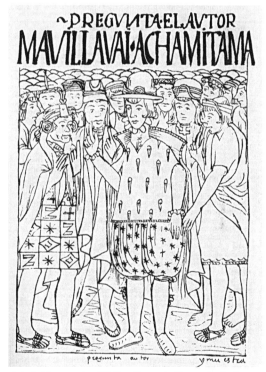

1.1 Self-portrait of Felipe Guamán Poma de Ayala, the author of El primer nueva corónica y buen gobierno *(1615). He is shown standing among his fellow native Andeans, inquiring about the history of ancient Peru.* (Felipe Guamán Poma de Ayala)

it remains today. Guamán Poma was born in Huamanga (present-day Ayacucho Province) to a mestizo father and an indigenous mother. He occupied a unique position in colonial Peruvian society as an *"indio ladino,"* or a Hispanicized and Christianized Indian. He served as a witness and interpreter at the court of Huamanga and later became involved in colonial administration of the provinces.

Guamán Poma's *crónica* begins with a history of the Andean peoples up through the rise of the Inca Empire. He continues with a detailed account of the conquest and spends the remainder of the letter enumerating the abuses and social inequalities that the Spaniards had inflicted on indigenous populations in the colonial period. The text contains a wealth of information not found in other sources, such as sections on different stages of life among the Incas, burial practices, and descriptions of the different festivals that occurred during each Inca month. Guamán Poma drew from written sources, interviews with native informants, and personal experiences to create his text. His description of the Inca Empire and the conquest differs in many ways from Spanish chronicles.

Perhaps most distinctive and impressive are the nearly 400 drawings that illustrate Guamán Poma's text. The illustrations he produced, executed in pen, constitute some of the only surviving authentic images of the Incas. The images illustrate Inca kings, queens, and princesses; different members of the Inca social stratosphere; maps; cityscapes; religious scenes, both Inca and Christian; images of the encounter between Spaniards and Incas; images of torture and abuse by the Spanish; and genre scenes of daily life in the colonial Andes. Guamán Poma's visual repertoire is unparalleled, granting visible form to aspects of Inca history that had only been illuminated through textual description. Indeed, many of his drawings are used to illustrate this book. His drawings combine European and Andean visual and symbolic conventions, providing a distinctly local, native vision of the Inca past.

Missionary Writings

There were a number of writings about the Incas by members of the missionary orders that settled in

Peru to convert the native population to Catholicism. While they held much disdain for Inca religion, which they perceived as idolatrous and inspired by the devil, the missionaries often took great interest in Inca history and cultural traditions. Many were trained in the European classical tradition and thus appreciated the archaeological heritage of the Incas for its contribution to universal knowledge. Moreover, as religious leaders in predominantly native communities, missionaries often acquired intimate familiarity with indigenous customs and belief systems. Indeed, some felt compelled to preserve knowledge about the Inca culture, which they saw at the brink of extinction. Paradoxically, their accounts of "idolatrous" Inca customs, which missionary writers described in great detail to illuminate their reasons for condemning them, ultimately helped preserve the history of Inca religion.

CRISTÓBAL DE MOLINA (D. LATE 16TH CENTURY)

Following in the tradition of Betanzos and Sarmiento of interviewing Inca elites and their descendants, Cristóbal de Molina wrote his most important treatise, *Relación de las fábulas y ritos de los incas (An Account of the Fables and Rites of the Incas)*, in 1575, but it remained unpublished until 1913. Molina was a hospice priest for a community of Indian parishioners in Cuzco and developed an interest in Inca civilization. His *relación* described Inca ritual and religion, which heavily influenced Bernabé Cobo's work, published nearly a century later. He was particularly interested in Inca religious festivals, such as Inti Raymi and Cápac Raymi, and agricultural festivals. He also described Inca ritual sacrificial practice, which spawned great debate among later chroniclers over the veracity of this claim. The accuracy of his vivid descriptions of the Cápac Hucha (child sacrifice) ceremony was later confirmed by archaeologists who excavated mummified children deposited at mountaintop shrines.

MARTÍN DE MURÚA (CA. 1525–CA. 1618)

Martín de Murúa was a Mercedarian friar who settled in Peru in 1550. He spent more than 50 years in Peru, involved in missionary work mainly in the Lake Titicaca area, Cuzco, and Arequipa. His manuscript, *Historia general del Pirú* (General history of Peru), was completed in 1613. It is composed of three books: 1) on the origin and descent of the Incas, 2) on the Inca government, their rites, and ceremonies, and 3) the major cities, towns, and settlements of the Inca Empire. It is one of only three surviving illustrated manuscripts of the Incas and the conquest of Peru. The 38 hand-colored illustrations accompanying Murúa's text were probably done by Guamán Poma, based on stylistic similarities to his illustrated manuscript. The illustrations consist mainly of Inca kings, queens, and warriors and stand as some of the earliest authentic artistic representations of Inca historical figures. However, despite the similarities between the drawings in Murúa's and Guamán Poma's texts, they illustrated very different types of narratives. While Guamán Poma's *El primer nueva corónica* offered a humanizing take on Inca history and the colonial period from an indigenous perspective, Murúa's text cast the Incas in a foreign, exotic light, as a culture radically different from his own. Murúa had a wealth of published and unpublished manuscripts on Inca history and the conquest. His text synthesizes many of the conquest narratives written by the early chroniclers and historians.

JOSÉ DE ARRIAGA (1564–1622)

José de Arriaga, a Spanish Jesuit priest, served as a religious inspector to assess the successes and failures of Catholic indoctrination among Indian populations in and around Lima. Arriaga wrote *La extirpación de la idolatría en el Perú (The Extirpation of Idolatry in Peru)*, published in 1621, based on his field research conducted a few years prior. Arriaga's text describes a variety of 17th-century ritual, religious, and superstitious practices observed by indigenous populations. Occurring nearly a century after the conquest, many of these practices combined Inca and Christian sacred beliefs, while others were Inca rituals that had survived nearly intact. Arriaga structures his descriptions of sacrificial practices, shamanism, divination, and *huaca* veneration in a narrative format, periodically interjecting personal observations or quoting infor-

mants. The second part of his text speculates on the reasons for the persistence of "idolatry" in Peru and provides guidelines for other missionaries wishing to assess and eradicate idolatrous practices in other Indian communities. Arriaga's study is valuable for understanding not only Inca religion but also the elements of it that continued to play an active role in the daily lives and belief systems of Indians living in colonial society.

FERNANDO DE MONTESINOS (1593–1655)

Fernando de Montesinos was a cleric who lived throughout Peru, serving as a rector, secretary, chaplain, and judge for the ecclesiastical court during his nearly 20-year stay. He wrote two histories of Peru: *Anales o memorias nuevas del Perú* (Annals or new memoirs of Peru) and *Ophir de España*. *Memorias antiguas historiales y políticas del Perú* (Ancient historical and political memoirs of Peru), published in the 1640s. Although his first publication was well received as a history of the Incas that followed conventions set by the earlier chroniclers, his second publication was received with much disdain. Decidedly polemical, his *Memorias antiguas* made several audacious claims about Inca history. Unlike earlier authors who traced the beginnings of Inca expansion to around 1400, Montesinos claimed that the empire was thousands of years old before the Spanish conquered it and that there existed almost 100 Inca rulers instead of the usually cited 12. These claims were likely a compilation of folklore and mythology relayed to Montesinos orally and transcribed in documents located in Jesuit archives to which he had access. Although Montesinos's *Memorias antiguas* was originally derided as outrageous and a work of pure fiction, it began to capture the attention of 20th-century archaeologists interested in long-term processes of cultural change. His idea of an Inca empire that extended thousands of years into the past was probably a conglomeration of many of the earlier Andean cultures into a unitary civilization. Although this does not reflect the "official" chronologies, Montesinos's text provides an interesting view of how the Incas may have conceived of their relationship to the rest of Andean prehistory.

BERNABÉ COBO (1582–1657)

Bernabé Cobo, a Jesuit priest from Spain, wrote the *Historia del Nuevo Mundo* (History of the New World) in 1653, which consisted of 43 books divided into three parts. The first part focuses on the geography and natural history of the New World, followed by a section on Inca beliefs and customs. The second part consists of a description of the Spanish conquests of Peru and the West Indies. The third part is devoted to New Spain (modern-day Mexico). All that survives today of Cobo's *historia* is the first part (the first 14 books, published as *Inca Religion and Customs* and *History of the Inca Empire*) and three books from the second part. Cobo had an extensive knowledge of the land and the peoples of the former Inca Empire, having traveled on foot throughout almost all of central and southern Peru. He also traveled along the Inca roads that ran between Cuzco and Lima. He was fluent in Quechua and Aymara, allowing him to freely converse with native inhabitants of the Andes who did not speak Spanish.

Books 11 through 14 are the most applicable to studies of the Inca, detailing origin myths, religious beliefs, and customs. Books 11 and 12 deal with the history of the Inca Empire. Book 13 discusses Inca religion in 38 short chapters. He writes about Inca creation beliefs, cosmology, and deities. He provides a description of famous religious sites such as the temple of Copacabana and Pachacamac. The ceremonial calendar is described in vivid detail. Perhaps one of the most important contributions to Book 13 is his enumeration of all of the *huacas* (sacred shrines) of Cuzco and its vicinities. Book 14 contains information not found elsewhere on the daily lives of the Incas and the 17th-century peasants that Cobo encountered during his fieldwork. Some of the topics covered include marriage ceremonies, games and entertainment, shamanism, households, dress and personal hygiene, and medicine.

In terms of sources, Cobo's work is a combination of personal observations, interviews with native informants, and use of earlier sources, both published and unpublished. Cobo consulted Ondegardo's now-lost 1559 report for his section on Inca religion. Molina's *Relación de las fábulas y ritos de los incas* also served as an important source for Cobo.

The section on *huacas* was likely taken from an unknown source about whose origins Cobo is mute. He also borrowed heavily from two published sources in circulation: José de Acosta's *Historia natural y moral de las Indias* (1590) and El Inca Garcilaso de la Vega's *Comentarios reales de los incas* (1609).

Natural History Treatises

Not all Inca sources focus on the history of the empire or the Spanish conquest. Some texts, produced mostly in the decades immediately following the conquest, focus on the natural world. With unique flora, fauna, environment, and ecology, the Americas truly seemed like a "new world" to the Spaniards. The efforts undertaken to visually and textually document the natural world allow us to "see" the New World through Spanish eyes. These authors also provide some of the earliest descriptions of native populations in the historical literature.

JOSÉ DE ACOSTA (1540–1600)

José de Acosta was a Spanish Jesuit who traveled throughout the New World. He incorporated his observations and experiences into the *Historia natural y moral de las Indias (The Natural and Moral History of the Indies)*, published in 1590. It is divided into seven books. The first book speculates on the origins of the indigenous inhabitants of the Americas and how they migrated to the continent. The second book focuses on the geography of the New World, with special emphasis on the lands encompassed by the Aztec and Inca Empires. The third and fourth books are dedicated to discussions of flora, fauna, minerals, and geology. The fifth, sixth, and seventh books provide the "moral" history of the Indies, focusing on the history, culture, and religion of the Aztecs and Incas. However, like many accounts of Inca religious ritual written by Spanish missionaries, Acosta's motivations behind providing a detailed account of Inca religious ritual was to alert other missionaries of idolatrous practices so they could take the proper actions to eliminate them. His *Historia natural y moral* also provided descriptions of the Aztec and Inca calendar, which Acosta praised for their accuracy. He was impressed by Inca administration and indeed is the first author to describe the Inca "postal system" comprised of relay runners known as *chasquis*. Acosta's discussion of Inca history, however, is scant in comparison to the attention and detail devoted to the Aztecs. Despite his lack of attention to Inca history, this work is important to Inca scholars for its firsthand documentation of the natural environment, flora, and fauna of the lands conquered by the Incas. For example, he comments on specifically Andean features of the natural environment such as the coca leaf and special farming techniques used in the high-altitude mountain regions. Translated into six European languages within three years of its initial publication, Acosta's work helped to garner outside interest in the Americas and its indigenous peoples and remained the authoritative source on natural history and geography of South America until Alexander von Humboldt's writings in the 19th century.

Court Documents

Native litigation in the colonial courts can provide important information about the Inca past. Many indigenous Andeans utilized the Spanish legal system for any number of issues, although some of the most common lawsuits were over property rights. They were able to use native sources of information, such as quipus and local oral histories, as "proof." Much of native litigation referenced "illegal" acts committed against local communities before the conquest and thus is of great value to historians and archaeologists attempting to grasp intercommunity relations under the Inca Empire.

Inventories, or itemized lists of a deceased person's possessions, along with wills are also important documents for understanding Inca life. These texts enumerate an individual's or family's lands, residences, and personal objects such as clothing, prized possessions, and household items. The inventories and wills of Inca royal descendants often contain descriptions of specifically Inca objects, particularly textiles, as well as lands acquired before the Spanish conquest. They are especially of use for those with an interest in the material lives of Inca royalty and elites.

READING

Methods for Studying the Inca Past

Jonathan D. Hill, ed., *Rethinking History and Myth: Indigenous South American Perspectives on the Past* (Urbana: University of Illinois Press, 1988).

Juha J. Hiltunen, "Knowing the Inca Past." In *Andean Archaeology*, edited by Helaine Silverman, 237–254 (Oxford: Blackwell, 2004).

Matthew Johnson, *Archaeological Theory: An Introduction* (Oxford: Blackwell, 1999).

Catherine Julien, "Finding a Fit: Archaeology and Ethnohistory of the Incas." In *Provincial Inca: Archaeological and Ethnohistorical Assessment of the Impact of the Inca State*, edited by Michael Malpass, 177–233 (Iowa City: University of Iowa Press, 1993).

W. David Kingery, ed., *Learning from Things: Method and Theory of Material Culture Studies* (Washington, D.C.: Smithsonian Institution Press, 1996).

A. Bernard Knapp, ed., *Archaeology, Annals, and Ethnohistory* (Cambridge: Cambridge University Press, 1992).

Katharine Martinez and Kenneth L. Ames, eds., *The Material Culture of Gender, the Gender of Material Culture*, 1st ed. (Winterthur, Del.: Henry Francis du Pont Winterthur Museum, 1997).

Esther Pasztory, *Thinking with Things: Toward a New Vision of Art* (Austin: University of Texas Press, 2005).

David S. Whitley, ed., *Reader in Archaeological Theory: Post-Processual and Cognitive Approaches* (London: Routledge, 1998).

A Brief History of Archaeology in the Andes

Hiram Bingham, *Machu Picchu, a Citadel of the Incas: Report of the Explorations and Excavations Made in 1911, 1912 and 1915 under the Auspices of Yale*

University and the National Geographic Society (New Haven, Conn.: Yale University Press, 1930).

Richard L. Burger, "An Overview of Peruvian Archaeology (1976–1986)," *Annual Review of Anthropology* 18 (1989): 37–69.

Timothy K. Earle et al., *Archaeological Field Research in the Upper Mantaro, Peru, 1982–1983: Investigations of Inka Expansion and Exchange*, Monograph 28 (Los Angeles: Institute of Archaeology, University of California Press, 1987).

John Hyslop, *Inkawasi: The New Cusco*, BAR International Series 234 (Oxford: British Archaeological Reports, 1985).

"Inca Culture at the Time of the Spanish Conquest." In *Handbook of South American Indians*. Vol. 2, edited by Julian H. Steward, 183–330 (Washington, D.C.: Smithsonian Institution, 1946).

Michael Moseley, "Andean Archaeology: New Light on the Horizon," *Review of Archaeology* 15, no. 2 (1994): 26–41.

Gustavo G. Politis, "Introduction: Latin American Archaeology: An Inside View." In *Archaeology in Latin America*, edited by Gustavo G. Politis and Benjamin Alberti, 1–14 (London: Routledge, 1999).

María Rostworowski de Diez Canseco, *History of the Inca Realm*. Translated by Harry B. Iceland (Cambridge: Cambridge University Press, 1999).

John H. Rowe, "Absolute Chronology in the Andean Area," *American Antiquity* 10 (1945): 265–284.

Richard P. Schnaedel and Izumi Shimada, "Peruvian Archaeology, 1946–80: An Analytic Overview," *World Archaeology* 13, no. 3 (February 1982): 359–371.

Ephraim George Squier, *Peru: Incidents of Travel and Exploration in the Land of the Incas* (New York: Harper Brothers, 1877).

Donald E. Thompson and Craig Morris, *Huánuco Pampa* (London: Thames & Hudson, 1985).

Max Uhle, *Pachacamac: Report of the William Pepper, M.D., LL.D., Peruvian Expedition of 1896* (Philadelphia: Department of Archaeology, University of Pennsylvania, 1903).

Luis E. Valcárcel, "Cuzco Archaeology." In *Handbook of South American Indians*. Bureau of American Ethnology, bulletin 143. Vol. 2, edited by Julian Steward 177–182 (Washington, D.C.: Smithsonian Institution Press, 1946).

Charles Wiener, *Pérou et Bolivie. Récit de voyage suivi d'études archéologiques et ethnographiques et de notes sur l'écriture et les langues des populations indiennes* (Paris: Hachette, 1880).

The Written Record

José de Acosta, *The Natural and Moral History of the Indies*. Edited by Jane Mangan and translated by Frances Lopez-Morillas (Durham, N.C.: Duke University Press, 2002).

Rolena Adorno, "Cultures in Contact: Mesoamerica, the Andes, and the European Written Tradition." In *The Cambridge History of Latin American Literature*. Vol. 1, *Discovery to Modernism*, edited by Roberto González Echevarría, 33–57 (Cambridge: Cambridge University Press, 1996).

———. *Guamán Poma: Writing and Resistance in Colonial Peru* (Austin: University of Texas Press, 1986).

Pablo José de Arriaga, *The Extirpation of Idolatry in Peru*. Translated by L. Clark Keating (Lexington: University of Kentucky Press, 1968).

Ralph Bauer, *An Inca Account of the Conquest of Peru by Titu Cusi Yupanqui* (Boulder: University Press of Colorado, 2005).

Juan de Betanzos, *Narrative of the Incas*. Translated by Roland Hamilton and Dana Buchanan (Austin: University of Texas Press, 1996).

Jorge Cañizares-Esguerra, *How to Write the History of the New World: Histories, Epistemologies, and Identities in the Eighteenth-Century Atlantic World* (Stanford, Calif.: Stanford University Press, 2001).

Francisco Carrillo Espejo, *Enciclopedia histórica de la literatura peruana* (Lima, Peru: Editorial Horizonte, 1989).

Pedro de Cieza de León, *The Incas of Pedro Cieza de León*. Translated by Harriet de Onís (Norman: University of Oklahoma Press, 1976).

Father Bernabé Cobo, *Inca Religion and Customs*. Translated by Roland Hamilton (Austin: Texas University Press, 1990).

Inca Garcilaso de la Vega, *Royal Commentaries of the Incas and General History of Peru, Parts 1 and 2*. Translated by H. V. Livermore (Austin: University of Texas Press, 1966).

Felipe Guamán Poma de Ayala, *Letter to a King: A Picture-History of the Inca Civilisation by Huamán Poma*. Translated by Christopher Dilke (London: George Allen & Unwin, 1978).

———. *El primer nueva corónica y buen gobierno*. 1615. Reprint (Mexico City: Siglo Veintiuno, 1980).

James Higgins, *The Literary Representation of Peru* (Lewiston, N.Y.: Edwin Mellen Press, 2002).

Juha J. Hiltunen, *Ancient Kings of Peru: The Reliability of the Chronicle of Fernando de Montesinos: Correlating the Dynasty Lists with Current Prehistoric Periodization in the Andes* (Helsinki: Finnish Historical Society, 1999).

Alexander von Humboldt, *Vues des cordillères, et monuments des peuples indigènes de l'Amérique* (Paris: F. Schoell, 1813).

Cristóbal de Molina (el Cusqueño), "Relación de las fábulas i ritos de los Ingas. . ." In *Fábulas y mitos de los incas*, edited by Enrique Urbano and Pierre Duviols, 47–134 (Madrid: Historia 16, 1989).

Susan A. Niles, *The Shape of Inca History: Narrative and Architecture in an Andean Empire* (Iowa City: University of Iowa Press, 1999).

Juan de Santacruz Pachacuti Yamqui, *An Account of the Antiquities of Peru*. Translated by Clements R. Markham (Boston: Massachusetts Historical Society, 1916). Biblioteca de Autores Españoles, vol. 209. 1613. Reprint (Madrid: Atlas, 1968).

Pedro Pizarro, *Relación del descubrimiento y conquista del Perú*. 1571. Reprint (Lima: Pontífica Universidad Católica del Perú, 1978).

———. *Relation of the Discovery and Conquest of the Kingdoms of Peru*. Translated by Philip Ainsworth Means (New York: Cortes Society, 1921).

Kathleen Ross, "Historians of the Conquest and Colonization of the New World: 1550–1620." In *The Cambridge History of Latin American Literature*. Vol. 1, *Discovery to Modernism*, edited by Roberto González Echevarría, 101–142 (Cambridge: Cambridge University Press, 1996).

Frank Salomon, Jorge Urioste, and Francisco de Avila, *The Huarochirí Manuscript: A Testament of Ancient and Colonial Andean Religion* (Austin: University of Texas Press, 1991).

Agustín de Zárate, *The Discovery and Conquest of Peru* (London: Penguin, 1968).

2

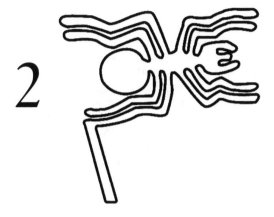

EVOLUTION OF ANDEAN CIVILIZATION

Summary of Major Pre-Inca Periods

The following is an overview of the major Andean civilizations from the earliest introduction of humans in South America up to the period of the Incas. The span presented here suggests continuities in cultural development that were borrowed and amended from one tradition to the next over vast amounts of time. Some of these traditions persisted until Inca times, and in this sense the Incas simply represented the next evolution in a particular style. Yet, given the quirks of history, the Inca contribution came to represent the climax of purely indigenous development. The dates offered here should be understood as tentative at best, especially for the earlier periods; given advances in technology and ongoing archaeological research, the periods themselves are continuously reevaluated and redefined. Cultures on the decline tend to fade out gradually. Therefore, it is very difficult for modern observers to pinpoint with certainty the end of one culture and the rise of another, especially when considering cultures from thousands of years ago. For this reason, the periods listed here tend to overlap. Nevertheless, what follows is a modest attempt to place in context the vast span of pre-Inca Andean cultural development.

A note on terminology: The terms *period* and *horizon* are used in Andean studies to indicate the ebb and flow of influence. *Period* is understood as a time span where no particular culture found widespread, imperial expression. By contrast, *horizon* is used to classify those spans when one or more cultures found widespread influence in an imperial manner—where their influence, in effect, "spans the horizon." These classifications are represented here.

Lithic Period
(CA. 20,000–3000 B.C.E.)

Twenty thousand years ago South America's Andean region was a very different place than it is today. The mountains were heavily glaciated, and the sea level was more than 100 meters (328 ft.) lower, exposing many miles of shore. As glaciers melted, shores rose and advanced inland, marine and meteorological currents shifted north, and natural habitats gravitated upward. Humans entered the scene at least 12,000–13,000 years ago. By 10,000–11,000 years ago distinct ways of life had evolved in desert, tropical lowland, sierra, puna (high-altitude treeless basin), and altiplano (extensive, high-plateau grassland). Adaptive plant cultivation occurred about 9,000–11,000 years ago, and sometime thereafter people began domesticating animals. The Lithic (stone) Period coincides with these developments, ending around 5,000 years ago, at which point the sea level stabilized and present-day climate and ecological zoning established itself, setting in place the broad ecological spectrum within which Andean civilization eventually developed.

Late Pleistocene/ Paleo-Indian Period
(ca. 9000–7000 B.C.E.)

The date of human arrival in South America is still a matter of debate, but the traditional migration theory holds that hunter-gatherers crossed Berengia—the "land bridge" between Asia and Alaska—on the trail of big game animals, moved slowly southward, then made their way across the Isthmus of Panama and into South America until finally reaching the continent's southernmost limits. Following mammoth and possibly mastodon, horse and giant sloth, and increasingly bison, these early migrants are believed to have entered North America at least 12,000 years ago, though some scholars allege the presence of humans at a much earlier date. Their descendants reached the southern tip of Chile about a thousand years later. Retracing and piecing together their advance across the vast landscape of the Americas rests largely on archaeology and the presence, or absence, of lithic artifacts such as fluted points and bifacial knives and scrapers—that is, the earliest hunting tools. A parallel theory of migration holds that early humans traversed Beringia via boat—there is archaeological evidence

Pre-Inca Andean Civilizations

ECUADOR

COLOMBIA

Gulf of Guayaquil

Amazon R.

Marañón R.

Batán Grande (Lambayeque)

SECHURA DESERT

BRAZIL

Lambayeque R.

Sipán (Moche)
Pampa Grande (Moche)
Huaca Prieta
Moche R.
Viracochapampa (Wari)
Chan Chan (Chimú)
Caballo Muerto
Huaco del Sol and Huaca de la Luna (Moche)
La Galgada
Huallaga R.
Cerro Sechín
Chavín de Huantár (Chavín)

Ucayali R.

Kotosh

Aspero

El Paraíso
Rimac R.
Huaca La Florida

Urubamba R.

PACIFIC OCEAN

Wari

Chancay
Apurimac R.
CUZCO BASIN
Pikillacta (Wari)

Paracas
Ica
Nazca R.
Nazca

Pukara

BOLIVIA

Chanca

Lake Titicaca

Tiwanaku

Lithic Period through Initial Period (ca. 20,000–1300 B.C.E.)

Early Horizon (ca. 1500–200 B.C.E.)

Early Intermediate Period (ca. 400 B.C.E.–540 C.E.)

Middle Horizon (540–900)

Late Intermediate Period (900–1438)

(Moche) Affiliated culture

Note: Map shown with modern borders.

0   200 miles
0   200 km

© Infobase Learning

Lake Poopó

Chinchorro

CHILE

Map 1 The Pre-Inca Civilizations of Andean South America

in Australia, Melanesia, and Japan dating boats between 25,000 and 40,000 years ago—and then traveled south along the coast, advancing much more rapidly than if by foot. This theory postulates that migrants could have reached southern South America in as little as 500 years. However, all signs of an exploratory route along the Pleistocene coastal shelf are now submerged; consequently, there is no direct archaeological evidence to support a coastal migration route.

GUITARRERO CAVE (CA. 8000 B.C.E.)

Guitarrero Cave is an important archaeological site in the Callejón de Huaylas in northern Peru. The Callejón de Huaylas is one of the great Andean basins and the only one that empties into the Pacific. One of the few highland sites known from this period, the cave lies at about 2,500 meters (8,200 ft.) above sea level at the base of the Cordillera Negra and is strategically located near mountain passes, abundant flora and fauna, and water. The cave is roughly 100 square meters (1,076 sq. ft.). Numerous stone flake tools were excavated there, including scrapers and hammerstones. Plants and organic materials preserved there suggest an Archaic (ca. 7000–6000 B.C.E.) date. Human remains at the site date it to around 11,000 to 9,000 years ago. Animal remains suggesting food sources include rabbit, the rabbitlike viscacha, birds, and deer. Some of the oldest known cultivated plants were found at Guitarrero Cave, many of which were utilized medicinally, as vital to health, or as industrials, used in clothing, containers, weapons, bedding, and shelter.

The abundance of plant material is important because it indicates a technology dominated by fiber as opposed to wood, especially in the production of netting and textiles. Guitarrero Cave thus stands at the beginning of a major Andean tradition focused on fiber technology, later adapted to domesticated plants (cotton) and animals (alpaca), that made textiles an extremely important element of statecraft. This Andean characteristic is unusual because in most civilizations ceramic production preceded other crafts. Another important development at Guitarrero Cave, and thus far the first known instance, was the discovery of a stone tool

wrapped in an animal hide and tied with a cord, thereby initiating the long-standing pan-Andean tradition of protecting, consecrating, even animating—or symbolically giving life to—objects through the act of wrapping them in material or fiber. This tradition is found in many Andean civilizations, including the Inca. It directly correlates with the ancient Andean mummification tradition.

Early Archaic Period (ca. 6000–3000 B.C.E.)

Paleo-Indians were very narrowly specialized hunters and gatherers constituting a fairly small population. Though it is difficult to distinguish Paleo-Indian cultural patterns from Archaic patterns, after 9,000 years ago, in the transition to Archaic peoples, Paleo-Indians evolved into generalized hunters and gatherers in combination with, eventually, agriculture and animal husbandry (the production and care of domestic animals). Populations at this time began to rapidly increase. Permanent villages based on rich maritime resources developed along the coast, and evidence from the highlands supports agricultural dates as early as 11,000–12,000 years ago. Over a span of many generations Archaic peoples began "settling in," tying themselves to resources within a region in permanent or semipermanent settlements. In general, sedentism (settling down) and village formation occurred at the end of the Archaic and have been seen as correlates of agriculture and as harbingers of a later Formative period (in the Andes this period is also referred to as the Pre-Ceramic Period), during which civilization emerges. However, in Peru it is likely that coastal communities anchored to maritime subsistence patterns "settled in" at about the same time. Evidence suggests that coastal community subsistence was based primarily on seafood, especially the resource-rich fishery of the Humboldt Current that circulates just off the Peruvian coast, and was probably supplemented with inland hunting and gathering.

One trait that connects the Paleo-Indian to the Archaic is wall paintings in caves and rock shelters. In general they show hunting scenes or scenes combining human and animal elements. Most animals seem to be camelids and deer, which were hunted extensively in both Paleo-Indian and Archaic times. Cave art has been widely reported in southern Chile's Patagonia, and it has wide Archaic-age distribution in the southern and central Andes and in northeast Brazil.

CHINCHORROS (BEGUN CA. 5000 B.C.E.)

Long before the Egyptians, the world's first instance of artificial mummification occurred at Chinchorros, in northern Chile, around 5000 B.C.E. Settled along the coast in modest communities based on the economies of fishing, the inhabitants of Chinchorros developed a cult of the dead whose notions of the afterlife included the preservation of the deceased via mummification, as the body must be intact in order to enter the afterlife. The majority of the mummified remains were of children and adolescents. Chinchorros morticians disassembled the bodies, removed internal organs, reassembled the bodies with implanted reed supports, and modeled facial details in clay. Recovered corpses display a range of interventions, some elaborately interred, or buried in a tomb, and others not at all. The variation probably reflects social differences and inequalities.

Cotton Pre-Ceramic/ Late Archaic (ca. 3000–1800 b.c.e.)

Between about 5,000 and 3,000 years ago simple foraging groups, or bands, evolved into sizable nucleated (clustered) communities in permanent settlements with monumental architecture, innovations in craft technology, and elaborate regional art styles. For the first time, pottery vessels came into use at some sites, and loom-woven textiles appeared by the end of the period. Settlements consisted of small dwellings—essentially large rooms—centered on plazas. Burials commonly were richly fur-nished, with children's burials more elaborate than those of adults. Intensive maize agriculture is not yet known, and subsistence centered on fishing and hunting—fishing along the coasts and the hunting of deer and camelids in the highlands. Cotton is so commonly found at sites in this period that it is thought that coastal peoples moved inland to cultivate cotton on alluvium (material deposited by running water), hence the cultural period designator "Cotton Pre-Ceramic."

Art production becomes more elaborate toward the end of the period. Increased ceramic production, advances in textile manufacture, and greater architectural decoration are common. Stylized paired animal images in textiles, such as one known from La Galgada, Peru, of a paired bird and a snake, stand out. Many of the new elements are shared throughout the region but there is no indication of a widespread cultural "horizon" similar to that known a thousand or so years later during the Chavín horizon. In terms of organization and administration it appears that systems of families and local community groups handled most activities, with evidence of hierarchical rulership arising only toward the end of the period.

Huaca Prieta (begun ca. 3000 b.c.e.)

Huaca Prieta was a modest fishing village along the coast north of Lima, the modern-day capital of Peru. Huaca Prieta's inhabitants lived in subterranean homes built of beach cobble set in mud mortar. While its architecture is perhaps unexciting, thousands of cloth fragments have been found there in shades of white, brown, and tan, many of which were twined while others were looped and knotted. The complicated textile manufacture is among the earliest in the world. The reconstruction of one twined textile shows the image of a raptor with a snake in its stomach, displaying a concern with composite or multiple beings. Another Huaca Prieta textile displays a crab transforming into a snake. Given the level of technology, both textiles are extremely complex and intricate examples of artistic visualization.

2.1 Reconstruction of a textile fragment from Huaca Prieta; Cotton Pre-Ceramic Period, ca. 3000 B.C.E. (Drawing by Michel Besson)

Áspero (begun ca. 2800 B.C.E.)

South of Huaca Prieta, the monumental site of Áspero, located near the coast in the Supe Valley north of contemporary Lima, covers roughly 13 hectares (32.5 acres), making it one of the largest Pre-Ceramic sites in Peru. It was also one of the first excavated, in 1941, at a time when it was thought that complex societies with monumental architecture developed only in tandem with maize agriculture. However, large public ceremonial architecture built at Áspero appears largely as a result of intensive fishing. The monumental constructions there emphasized large flat-topped platform pyramid mounds, some of which are U-shaped arrangements

around sunken courts, a design that later becomes common throughout the region. The elevated portions indicate the differentiation and segregation of sacred space. This arrangement is conscious of public orientation and is considered a sort of public stage for large audiences. Two of the larger ceremonial constructions are the Huaca de los Sacrificios and the Huaca de los Ídolos. Both are ceremonial platform mounds with simple summit structures.

THE HUACA DE LOS SACRIFICIOS AND THE HUACA DE LOS ÍDOLOS

The Huaca de los Sacrificios is so-named because two burials, one for an infant and one for an adult, were found there. The body of the infant, accompanied by a gourd bowl, was completely wrapped in a cotton textile and placed in a basket, which was itself wrapped in a textile around which was a cane mat tied with strips of white cloth. The elaborate preparation suggests the child was of exceptional importance. The Huaca de los Ídolos, covering an area of 20 meters by 30 meters (65.5 × 98 ft.), is a higher platform mound with summit structures that contain an entry court and smaller interior compartments, one of which had an altarlike bench and niches in the wall and circular fire pits. It derives its name from unbaked human figurines found in a cache in one of the summit compartments. The cache also contained twined baskets, matting, plant material, and animal fur. Of the many figurines found in the cache, one was a buried female infant effigy (an image of a person) wrapped in matting and textiles. The elaborate material culture and monumental architecture suggest either a politically centralized chiefdom society or a corporate (organized or unified) residence. Since many of the above elements are known to both chiefdom and corporate cultures, it cannot be definitively stated that Áspero was the site of an elite hierarchical chiefdom.

El Paraíso (ca. 2000 B.C.E.)

El Paraíso is a well-known Pre-Ceramic site with eight to nine large and small complexes of stone rooms; the largest room covers 300 meters by 100 meters (984 × 328 ft.). It is the largest Pre-Ceramic site and covers more than 50 hectares (125 acres). It is estimated that workers there moved 100,000 tons of stone. The two largest mounds are more than 300 meters (984 ft.) long, run parallel to each other, and define a central plaza area of more than seven hectares (42 acres). There are two irregular platforms at the south end, forming a U-shape—an early, perhaps the archetypal, instance of what is referred to descriptively as U-shaped ceremonial complexes. One of the smaller structures stands eight meters (26 ft.) high, measures about 50 meters (164 ft.) on each side, and has two separate flights of stairs leading to a central chamber with circular fire pits. The fire pits certainly involved rituals using fire, as did the summit court of the Huaca de los Sacrificios. The arms of the U are oriented toward the mountains, perhaps, as the Andean archaeologist Michael Moseley has surmised, as a symbolic invitation to the rising sun and a literal turning of the back to the sea. If this indeed was the case, it suggests the deeper implication of a cultural transition away from maritime subsistence to inland agriculture.

Kotosh (ca. 2450–800 B.C.E.)

In the northern highlands Kotosh represents a major cultural tradition linked to many sites. This highland tradition persisted into the Initial Period (ca. 1800–1300 B.C.E.). Kotosh sites are conspicuous by their location at the edges of the valleys and by the presence of large mounds composed of successive layers of entombed temples carefully preserved in fill that are in turn surmounted by numerous chambers built of masonry. The continued reuse of one site rather than rebuilding at another site underscores the sanctity of the spot and its connection to ancestors interred in previous building layers. The chambers, for their part focused around a central fire pit, served as the setting for a ritual tradition involving fire and burned offerings. The mounds are surrounded by and overlook large residential areas of mud and fieldstone houses, a pattern that makes it seem urban in nature.

In the Kotosh tradition ceremonial practice does not appear to have been limited to an elite class, as ritual rooms interspersed with the residential structures suggest communal facilities. Similarly, all

Kotosh sites have ceremonial architecture, further indicating egalitarian ritual practices. The most elaborate chamber measured about nine meters (29.5 ft.) on a side, was built of cobblestones set in mud mortar, and had thick plaster walls with niches on the interior. Below the niches opposite the entrance were sculpted clay images of crossed human hands, causing its excavators to name the structure the Temple of the Crossed Hands. It is noteworthy that niches appear here and along the coast and continue into Inca times, when they find expression as symbols of, or at least a recurring motif in, state and religious architecture.

LA GALGADA

Occupied ca. 2400–1900 B.C.E., La Galgada is one of the best-preserved sites connected to the Kotosh religious tradition. This highland center is located at about the 1,000-meter (3,281-ft.) elevation on the Tablachaca River. Several oval mounds located there are surmounted by ritual chambers, which resemble the kiva of the southwestern United States. These rooms were entered from above, had sunken hearths for burned sacrifices, benches, and niches for display or storage. They were perhaps ceremonial meeting places for descent groups such as extended families. Later the tops of the mounds accommodated a larger, but singular, U-shaped sunken ritual structure. At this time, too, pottery, the heddle loom, and images familiar to the later Chavín horizon culture are introduced. One of the more distinct images is the raptorial bird paired with a snake, which is similar to the paired images found at Huaca Prieta. Eventually, after many years of use and careful maintenance the ritual chambers were transformed into burial tombs. Each was closed, surrounded by fill, and eventually superimposed by another chamber, thereby continuing the pattern.

INITIAL PERIOD (CA. 1800–1300 B.C.E.)

During the Initial Period coastal peoples settled inland parts of valleys, lived in larger settlements, produced pottery on a large scale, and built spectacular ceremonial complexes. Along the coast, fishing continued to supplement the inland growing of chili peppers, maize, and beans, and irrigation agriculture provided a foundation for ongoing civic development and for the transition from maritime-oriented to agriculture-oriented societies. In the mountains transhumance, or the seasonal migration of herds, took on added importance. Three related but distinctive systems of public architecture developed along the coast, and highland architecture remained similar to the Kotosh tradition. U-shaped mounds were favored in the central coastal region of Peru, in the Lurín, Rímac, Chillón, Chancay, and Huaura Valleys; rectangular mounds and circular forecourt complexes were common in the Supe, Casma, and Nepeña Valleys; and along the north coast low-lying civic-ceremonial complexes were found from Virú to Lambayeque and are called Cupisnique, after the associated pottery style. The highland sites favored sunken circular courts combined with rectangular platforms, themselves surmounted with sunken rectangular plazas. Highland settlements during this period were widely dispersed between northern Peru and the Titicaca Basin.

Abundant data in this period shows sustained connections between centers, but river valleys increasingly defined social differentiation. Settlements were isolated one from the next, north to south, and increasingly grew connected east to west, following the vertical rise from the arid shore to the highlands. Exchange networks linked coastal habitations to highland sites via these valleys, creating independent vertically oriented lifeways. Since shoreline environments exploit different resources and have different growing capabilities than valley and highland habitats, and vice versa, commodity exchange between them augmented the daily life of individuals and brought valley communities into increasingly dependent relationships with one another. Some scholars have seen the various valley centers as independent minor polities linked by kinship, shared ideology and ceremony, and technology and exchange networks. Despite numerous links, they appear to have remained fairly autonomous.

Huaca La Florida (ca. 1800 B.C.E.)

La Florida, in the Rímac Valley, is a huge mud and fieldstone structure still standing in a residential Lima neighborhood. Settlement began sometime during the transition from the Cotton Pre-Ceramic to the Initial Period, with ceramic-period occupation radiocarbon-dated to around 1610 B.C.E. It is a U-shaped complex with a primary pyramid structure built rapidly in superimposed stages. The primary pyramid rises 17 meters (55 ft.) and is flanked by two parallel arms that extend some 500 meters (1,640 ft.) outward, facing northeast toward the foothills. Ceramics at La Florida are the earliest recorded on the central coast. Domestic middens and a central mound and several smaller mounds suggest a small resident population lived in and around the center. The site was built, used, and abandoned within a few centuries.

Alto Sechín Complex (begun ca. 1650 B.C.E.)

The principal pyramid at Alto Sechín in the lower Casma Valley north of Lima is described by Julio Tello, one of the great Andean archaeologists, as the largest monument of its kind surviving in Peru. The principal pyramid is faced with granite, is U-shaped, measures 300 meters by 250 meters (984 × 820 ft.) and rises 44 meters (144 ft.) above the valley floor. Five large plazas or courts extend outward in front of the main pyramid, covering an area roughly 400 meters by 1,400 meters (1,312 × 4,593 ft.). The second and fourth courts contain great circular pits, 50 meters (164 ft.) and 80 meters (262 ft.) in diameter, respectively. Other lesser pyramid structures at the site are of a corridor type, extending primarily along a central axis.

CERRO SECHÍN (CA. 1300–600 B.C.E.)

A smaller center in the Casma Valley, closely related to Alto Sechín, Cerro Sechín's most distinctive feature is a revetment wall faced with more than 300 sculpted stone reliefs fronting a three-tiered temple structure. The large stones depict a procession of macabre figures leading toward a central doorway. Warriors are depicted wearing pillbox hats, and victims are displayed as disarticulated heads, severed torsos, arms, legs, and entrails. Interpretations of the scene vary from the commemoration of a mythical battle or historical event to a symbolic shamanic initiation.

Caballo Muerto (ca. 1700–850 B.C.E.)

The Caballo Muerto complex lies in the Río Seco gorge 50 kilometers (31 mi.) inland from the northern coast in the Moche Valley. The site consists of 17 mounds spread over an area of two square kilometers (0.77 sq. mi.). The best preserved of the mounds is called the Huaca de los Reyes, considered by many to be the epitome of the north coast architectural style. Its plan is U-shaped, and in all, it covers 230 meters by 240 meters (755 × 787 ft.). The facade is decorated with high-relief friezes painted red, yellow, and white. A series of levels continuously isolates and narrows the approach, restricting access to fewer and fewer participants but focusing the vision of observers in lower courts. The summit of the principal mound contains colonnades of rectangular pillars, semi-sunken rectangular courts, and rectangular rooms and towers made of stone and set in mortar. The main facade of the lower mound was ornamented with monumental adobe heads portraying a creature with pendant irises, a wide feline nose, fangs in drawn-back lips, and pronounced facial lines. The ornamental friezes and colonnades made Huaca de los Reyes more elaborate than other sites. Caballo Muerto is linked to the Cupisnique culture in the later Early Horizon.

Cuzco Basin (ca. 1300 B.C.E.)

Two Initial Period cultures, Chanapata and Marcavalle, are known in the Cuzco Basin. The Cuzco Basin later became the center of the Inca Empire. The Chanapata is recognized in the material data

by thick black or red pottery, straight-walled vessels, and neckless jars with flat bottoms. Decoration is by burnishing, painting, or incisions filled with pigment after firing. Common motifs include geometric forms, animal figures, and occasional human representations. Marcavalle is considered to predate Chanapata. Pottery related to Chanapata, albeit with more emphasis on painted decoration, has been found. More typically Marcavalle pottery is distinguished by decoration with metallic pigment. It is noteworthy, too, that pottery associated with the Qaluyu culture, located on the northern shores of Lake Titicaca, has also been found in the Cuzco Basin, attesting to ancient links between the two regions.

Chiripa (ca. 1450–800 B.C.E.)

The shores of Lake Titicaca have long supported human populations. On its southern shore the site of Chiripa was settled for many centuries before a platform mound was erected; this platform subsequently underwent numerous remodeling stages and eventually was used by the later Tiwanaku (Tiahuanaco) culture. It has been argued that Chiripa architectural features—single-entry, small rectangular buildings built of adobe; double walls; nichelike interior windows; and double-frame doorways—mark the onset of Titicaca architectural traditions and may have been a far-distant antecedent of Inca *cancha* (single-room building units) construction.

EARLY HORIZON (CA. 1500–200 B.C.E.)

By the Early Horizon, coastal civic-ceremonial centers had been abandoned, and many highland sites dwindled as a result of protracted drought, a condition the people were unfamiliar with and unable to adapt to. During the Early Horizon the appearance of large centers with religious functions and uniform art styles appeared throughout the north, central, and south coasts and the north and central highlands. The Early Horizon is a time unit most closely associated with the artistic and religious influence of Chavín de Huántar, a north coast ceremonial center that became prominent after the fall of U-shaped centers. Though it varied by region, the period is typified by a mixed reliance on agriculture, animal husbandry, and hunting and collecting. Larger and more dramatically decorated architecture and large quantities of fine pottery are also common. Anthropomorphic images (images with human characteristics) that arose during the Initial Period take on added significance and become an important part of the artistic program. Similar ways of making a living promoted shared technology and ideas. Further consolidation, especially under the influence of Chavín, became the focal point of the horizon.

Chavín (ca. 900–200 B.C.E.)

The Chavín stylistic horizon was centered at Chavín de Huántar, the north coast ceremonial center, which lies at 3,150 meters (10,335 ft.) above sea level in the Callejón de Conchucos, east of the Cordillera Blanca. Early scholarship differed profoundly in its initial interpretation of Chavín's own origins as well as its relation to contemporary and later cultures. For instance, scholars variously attributed Chavín origins to the Olmec of Mesoamerica or as having come out of the Amazon lowlands. They conceptualized it as a pilgrimage center for a proselytizing religion or theorized it as the capital of an empire. Tello, one of the founding fathers of Peruvian archaeology, believed Chavín was a "mother culture" from which advanced culture "irradiated," or spread, to the coast and highlands and was therefore responsible for most, if not all, subsequent Andean cultural development. The first Spaniards to arrive in the area, in the 1550s, recognized that Chavín predated the Inca but decided that it had been built by a race of giants. Overall, Chavín synthesized Initial Period aesthetic systems of both coast and highlands, bringing together the sunken circular courtyard, the U-shaped structure, and imagery of jaguars, snakes,

and other animal-human transformers. Scholarship is still undecided about the exact nature and role of the Chavín cultural expression, though in general it is evident in the archaeology that its art, architecture, and religious influence was widely spread and acted as a unifier between numerous sites.

John Rowe, one of the more methodical scholars of the pre-Columbian and colonial Americas, has termed an important component of Chavín imagery as *visual metaphoric substitution*. In other words, one element—say, the image of a bird, snake, or feline—is used to replace something visually analogous. For example, snake imagery might take the place of hair. As a result, human-animal composite images play an important role in Chavín iconography. Shamans in transformation, staff-bearing deities, raptorial birds, and predatory animals are also common. The great emphasis in Chavín art on portraying two states at once has led scholars to consider it "transformational" in nature and effect. Some of the representational patterns, such as the presence of central images flanked by attendant figures, even provide hints at the nature of Chavín social organization. The primary character in these works suggests paramount rulership, and additional symbolic elements, such as fangs—commonly associated with ancestral, supernatural powers of rulers—probably relate to concepts of divine kingship. By extension, then, the iconographic messages, encoded in portable art, relayed Chavín's symbolic, political, and religious messages far and wide.

CHAVÍN DE HUÁNTAR

Highland people schooled in farming, llama herding, and deer hunting founded Chavín de Huántar. They assembled pottery that was well made and dark colored emphasizing motifs that were either fairly straightforward and representational or supernatural in nature, such as fanged animals. Architecture at Chavín de Huántar is perhaps best described as an eclectic appropriation of familiar foreign elements continuously reemployed throughout its history. Scholars divide Chavín art into two periods corresponding to construction cycles and related sculpture at the Old Temple, ca. 900–500 B.C.E., and the New Temple, ca. 500–200 B.C.E. By 500 B.C.E. Chavín had become a flourishing ceremonial center whose influence extended from the modern city of Cajamarca in the north and Ayacucho in the south.

THE OLD TEMPLE

The Old Temple was large and impressive and faced the rising sun in the east. Its U-shaped plaza and sunken circular court (large enough to hold 500 people) were familiar from the Initial Period. Finely incised relief carvings of an anthropomorphic and transformational nature surround the circular pit in panels that make up its retaining wall. Large, carved-stone tenon heads depicting fanged half-human creatures were embedded in the walls and projected out well above the heads of spectators. The temple's interior was honeycombed with chambers and passageways. The entire structure was built around a central monolithic (single large stone) sculpture referred to as the Lanzón (great lance), which was embedded in the floor deep in the center of the temple. It depicts a fanged being with clawlike fingers and toes. Its placement represented the four directions and established the spot as the *axis mundi*, or the sacred center of the universe, and its cult image of a supernatural being tied it symbolically to successful harvests and human survival.

THE NEW TEMPLE

The New Temple featured extensive development and elaboration of a new ceremonial focus in architecture, while the Old Temple, neither destroyed nor interred, apparently remained symbolically potent. The New Temple centered on a platform construction adjacent to the Old Temple, with a new U-shaped plaza that featured a sunken rectangular courtyard in front of it. The eastern facade of the New Temple was focused on an entryway referred to as the Black and White Portal, so-called because it was constructed of light and dark stone. The portal includes two elaborately carved columns depicting crested eagles and is topped by a carved lintel. The Black and White Portal lead to a square patio, then a monumental stairway, and finally the Main Plaza, which enclosed a sunken court. Altogether the plazas and courts could have held up to 1,500 worshippers. The architecture carefully dictates how people move through the religious core,

growing more and more restrictive in space as one advances.

RAIMONDI STELA

Closely associated with the New Temple and the Black and White Portal is the co-called Raimondi Stela, a two-meter-high (6.5-ft.) granite monolith named after a 19th-century naturalist. It depicts a staff-bearing deity—according to some scholars an evolution of the Lanzón image—as a forward-facing supernatural holding elaborate staffs in each hand. Interestingly, the stela can be "read" when inverted, employing an effect known as "contour rivalry" to allow the same incised lines to create different readings. Like the Lanzón, the Raimondi image is associated with agricultural fertility.

Cupisnique (ca. 900–200 B.C.E.)

The coastal manifestations of the Chavín horizon were dominated by the Cupisnique culture. The close relationship between Cupisnique and Chavín is attested to by great quantities of Cupisnique pottery found at Chavín de Huántar, suggesting that it was within Chavín's sphere of influence. Likewise, material caches have been found on the coast with motifs very similar to those of the stone sculptures at Chavín de Huántar. Cupisnique funerary art in the form of elaborate burial caches gives the earliest evidence of paramount rulership in Peru. For example, in one burial at the site of Chongoyape three gold crowns were found, one of which had an image of a staff god, and corpses wore gold jewelry decorated with snakes and birds. The elaborate burial items suggest that the individual must have been of exceeding importance.

Paracas (ca. 600 B.C.E.–0)

Settled on the Paracas Peninsula, the south coast site of Paracas was a village culture with a high-prestige burial center referred to as the Paracas Necropolis. Fishing was a primary focus; the Humboldt Current, one of the richest marine resources in the world, was just offshore. Fishing was supplemented by long-distance trading and farming operations in the nearby Pisco Valley. Early Horizon influence spread from the north at Chavín, as is evidenced in the early ceramic samples with clear Chavín-style motifs and styles, while later influence, seen in generic similarities in textiles and ceramics, indicate Paracas was more closely aligned with the southern highland traditions of Pukara and Tiwanaku.

PARACAS NECROPOLIS

The seaside necropolis, or cemetery, contained numerous elite individuals interred as seated mummy bundles wrapped in extraordinarily complex textiles. For burial the corpse was placed in a flexed seated position—practically an upright fetal position—with its knees pulled close to the chin and bound with cords to maintain the pose. The body was then wrapped in textiles and placed in a large basket containing other offerings, after which both the body and the basket were wound in many layers of plain textiles and placed in subterranean crypts. Sometimes as many as 60 mantles (long, rectangular textiles) and shrouds were used, the finest of which are estimated to have taken from 5,000 to 29,000 hours to complete.

Paracas underground burial vaults included the *"cavernas"*-type pits of Cerro Colorado and "necropolis"-type pits of the Paracas Necropolis at Wari Kayan. The earlier *cavernas*-type burial pits are beaker-shaped caverns with a circular vertical shaft connecting it to the entrance. The entrance is typically a round hole surrounded by a rough masonry retaining wall, which would have then been covered by desert sand and earth. These pits contained numerous mummies believed to be kin related. Necropolis-type masonry crypts differ in form but not in function. The necropolis-style vault is rectangular and masonry constructed, and it has a rectangular shaft whose base consists of a few steps leading into the vault.

TEXTILES

Paracas textiles, perhaps the finest in the ancient world, are worth a brief mention. The vast majority of Paracas textiles were embroidered and fall into three stylistic groups: linear, broad-line, and block-color. Linear style, as its name implies, consists of narrow bands on the horizontal, vertical, and diagonal and almost always uses the colors red, green, gold, and blue. It is formally, iconographically, and conceptually abstract. The broad-line style is related to the linear in that it favors depictions of ideographs, or picture-symbols, representing an idea over actual objects. The block-color style was used for closer description of the actual world, including the flora and fauna of the Paracas Peninsula and personages whose garments and adornments are represented in actual burials. Characteristic broad-line motifs are abstract images combining felines, birds, snakes, and faces. By contrast, block-color style emphasizes curvilinear figures, uses as many as 19 different colors, and favors clear figural representation of humans in zoomorphic transformational roles, such as a condor impersonator, a falcon impersonator, or a pampas cat impersonator. In general, in the long tradition of Andean weaving, both including and beyond Paracas, many of the important ideas of the society are expressed in the medium of cloth.

Pukara (500 B.C.E.–200 C.E.)

During the last centuries B.C.E., Pukara (Pucará), located in the highlands 75 kilometers (47 mi.) north of Lake Titicaca, assumed prominence as a regional political center. Artistically the center is associated with complex slip-painted ceramics (ceramics made with a mixture of finely divided clay and water and then painted) drawing on stylized and realistic motifs, richly ornamented *keros* (libation vessels), and stone carvings both in the round and in relief. The most common images include birds, felines, llamas, serpents, lizards, fish, and humans, the latter especially among stone sculpture. The few surviving textile fragments similarly emphasize humans accompanied by trophy heads. Though the range of Pukara's political extent was limited to the northern Titicaca basin, its art was widely dispersed, suggesting economic interaction far afield. The primary architecture of Pukara is reminiscent of the Chiripa complex previously mentioned, with a central sunken court surrounded on three sides by a series of one-room structures with inner and outer walls. The central structure at Pukara was made of dressed stone foundations surmounted by adobe walls. In addition to its art and architecture, Pukara's inhabitants invested significant labor in agricultural works including ridged fields and shallow ponds, called *cochas*. During the rainy season *cochas* filled with water; as they dried and the water level dropped, the banks and finally the bottom were planted with crops, effectively extending the rainy season in a region that has an otherwise restricted growing period.

EARLY INTERMEDIATE PERIOD (CA. 400 B.C.E.–540 C.E.)

The Early Intermediate Period reflects a landscape of fragmented regional developments, the growth of sites in size and complexity, and continued elaboration of material and ritual culture. With the waning authority of Chavín de Huántar, some local settlements extended their influence over adjacent valleys. Artistic representation generally turned away from expressions of the metaphysical toward the earthly. Ceremonial centers decreased in relation to residential settlements. The rise of a distinct elite class, called *curacas*, was reflected in governance practice; those who ruled claimed special descent from founding fathers. Overall, due to varied and unique developments by region, the period is difficult to characterize.

Along the north coast there was a general shift away from commemorating identity through ceremonial construction toward defending it through the construction of defensive fortifications, which in itself is a signal of increased competition and hostilities. Despite a rise in the number of fortified hilltop sites, undefended residential settlements were still the norm. Along the central and south coasts the influence of U-shaped centers passed, and

the period is generally marked as one of transition and reorganization. And in the altiplano around Lake Titicaca, Pukara, which had brought a sense of integration to the southern highlands, declined due to the effects of sustained drought. While Pukara was failing, Tiwanaku, adapting better to the changing climate, gradually matured.

Nazca (ca. 150 B.C.E.–650 C.E.)

On the arid coastal desert plain of south-central Peru, inhabiting the Nazca River system south of the Paracas Peninsula, the Nazca people constructed large pyramidal structures with intricate underground canals, worked gold in a manner that is virtually indistinguishable from Paracas, made textiles and vibrant slip-painted ceramics that are among the finest in the world, and, most perplexingly, laid out a series of lines and figures across the desert plain by removing dark stones from atop lighter stones. Politically the Nazca people do not fall neatly into either state or chiefdom categories and appear to have been dispersed farming communities that maintained a level of independence while interacting frequently. By 100 C.E. the site of Cahuachi, on the Nazca River 50 kilometers (31 mi.) inland at a rare spot of year-round water, was an important but irregular settlement. It consisted of 40 mounds and appears not to have had a substantial permanent population; consequently, it appears to have served as a transitory ceremonial or ritual settlement for the entire Nazca population.

NAZCA LINES

These figures, today called geoglyphs, represent animals, fish, birds, geometrical designs, and anthropomorphic figures. They are so monumentally huge—some of the figures are more than 100 meters (328 ft.) long, and some of the lines stretch for miles (one runs perfectly straight for 20 kilometers [12.4 mi.])—that they can only be completely seen from the air. Many of the figures in the desert are also portrayed in the ceramic and textile samples attributed to the Nazca people, thereby eliminating any doubt as to the images' creators.

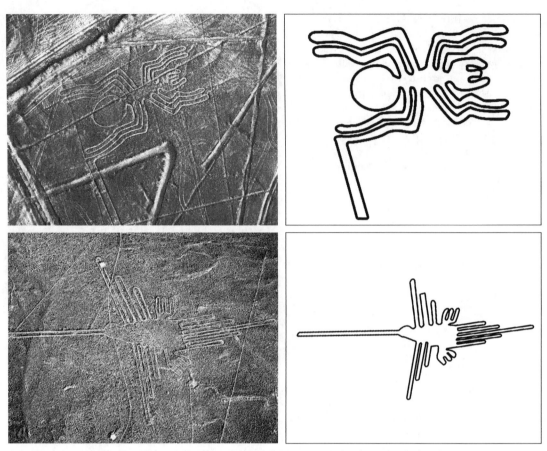

2.2 *Nazca lines in the shape of a spider and hummingbird. These geoglyphs, from the Nazca Plain, date to ca. 150 B.C.E.–650 C.E.* (Drawings by Rafael Aponte)

While it is known who constructed the lines, why they made them remains more elusive. Theories that tie them to celestial observation are inconclusive because the lines correlate with celestial phenomena at no greater incidence than would occur by chance, and the animal figures have not been associated with certainty to any star patterns. Many lines radiate out from hills or high vantage points, called ray centers. Figures such as flowers, trees, and birds (for example, the heron and the condor) suggest water and fertility symbols. Some of the linear and geometric arrangements are associated with processional ceremonies that are again affiliated with water and fertility cults.

Tiwanaku (ca. 3200 B.C.E.–1100 C.E.)

Tiwanaku (Tiahuanco) lies at a breathtaking 3,850 meters (12,631 ft.) above sea level in Bolivia to the south of Lake Titicaca. Its rise followed the cultural florescence of local antecedent sites, Chiripa and Pukara. Construction of the city's carefully planned ceremonial center began by 300 C.E., although major building had started the previous century. By 500, marking the onset of the Middle Horizon, it had become a prosperous urban center and the hub of an expanding empire, which held sway in the highlands for another 500 years. At its peak the ceremonial core covered 400 hectares (990 acres), and the total urban area could have been as large as 600 hectares (1,485 acres), housing anywhere from 20,000 to 40,000 persons. Few other settlements in the Andes had such a long occupation.

The keys to its long prosperity included a hinterland devoted to raised-field agriculture, called *waru-waru*; herding llama and alpaca; and exploiting the natural resources of Lake Titicaca. In the raised-field system, earthen platforms five to 15 meters (16–49 ft.) wide and up to 200 meters (656 ft.) long absorb solar radiation during the day and release conserved energy during the night, thereby mitigating any potential frost damage. Effective resource production based on this system, across a broad hinterland, sustained an estimated rural population of 250,000 persons. In turn, this allowed for the growth of the capital and facilitated Tiwanakan expansion, which, together with the Wari (Huari) culture, defined the Middle Horizon. Attesting to its growth and influence, Tiwanakan goods were found more than 800 kilometers (500 mi.) away.

Around 950 the weather changed for the worse, and the region entered a severe and prolonged drought cycle that initiated the demise of Tiwanaku. Nevertheless, Tiwanaku regained some of its former symbolic grandeur in late pre-Hispanic times because it was identified as a place of origin in Inca creation myths and became a pilgrimage center.

CEREMONIAL CORE

Tiwanaku's ceremonial core, surrounded by a moat in the image of a sacred island, was at once the principal seat of the ruling lineage, the locus of the royal court, and the holiest shrine in the empire. The Akapana Temple at Tiwanaku was the most sacred shrine, thought to conceptually represent the idea of sacred mountain. Roughly cross-shaped in plan, it measures almost 200 meters (656 ft.) on a side and rises nearly 17 meters (56 ft.) high in seven step-fret terraces or platforms. The walls of each level were constructed of fine rectangular ashlar masonry, which many scholars believe was influential much later in Inca masonry construction. The

2.3 *View of the sunken courtyard of the Kalasasaya complex at Tiwanaku, showing masonry, tenon heads, and portal, ca. 200 B.C.E.–1100 C.E.* (Photo courtesy of Pedro Pérez-Cabezas)

summit platform contained a rectangular sunken court, covering 50 square meters (538 sq. ft.) and flanked by rooms that might have been living quarters for priests.

The Pumapunku, a T-shaped mound of three terraces with a sunken court, was a second, smaller ceremonial area. Carved doorways and lintels embellish its eastern entrance, suggesting that it could have been the original site for the Gateway of the Sun—a monolithic carved stone gate with a staff-bearing central figure referred to as the Gateway God, probably Thunupa, a weather deity and sun god. It is important to note that the Gateway God is a resurrection and revitalization of the Chavín Staff God. The Semi-Subterranean Temple (also referred to as the Kalasasaya complex) is a rectangular sunken court lined with sandstone ashlars and stylized human tenon heads fashioned in its walls. The so-called Bennett Stela, the largest carved stela in the Andes at over seven meters (23 ft.) tall, named after its discoverer, Wendell Bennett, was uncovered here, though today it is in La Paz, the Bolivian capital. The last major structure in the ceremonial core is the Kalasasaya, a low-lying rectangular platform, measuring 130 meters by 120 meters (427 × 394 ft.) reached by a stairway set between two large, vertical pillars.

Gallinazo
(ca. 250 B.C.E.–250 C.E.)

By the first century B.C.E., Gallinazo, a north coast precursor to the Moche in the Chicama, Moche, and Virú Valleys, was undergoing substantial population growth coincident with the construction of major irrigation canals that opened the lower valleys to farming and settlement. Elite ceramic production at this time reflects a consolidation within individual valleys; numerous small farmsteads and hamlets gave way to fewer but successively larger secondary settlements that were overshadowed by a primary center or capital. Construction at major Gallinazo centers such as Licapa, Cerro Orejas, Cerro Blanco, Santo Castillo, and Tomoval reflect new notions of the sacred mountain; built in or on the foothills, they represent an evolution from ear-

lier U-shaped centers, which were oriented toward the mountains. Late Gallinazo overlapped and was indistinguishable from early Moche.

Moche/Mochica
(ca. 100–700)

North coast political transformations stemming from the late Gallinazo led to more centralized governance under the Moche, probably as a result of marriage and kin alliances. These alliances adopted the Moche style as their signature, which fostered continuities in settlement patterns, monumental architecture, burial patterns, ceramics, and iconography that merged into the first evidence of nascent state and urban development. Moche burials and iconography suggest Moche leaders blended sacred, military, political, and social roles without developing distinct administrative institutions seen elsewhere in the ancient world. Realistic depictions of warriors and combat painted and modeled on murals and thousands of ceramic vessels constitute evidence for those who claim that the Mochica polity was an aggressive state led by a strong secular king, though some scholars argue the scenes depict ritualized battles instead of real ones. Nevertheless, mass sacrifices have been verified, which probably maintained entrenched social orders or established new ones.

The Moche were divided into a northern and southern sphere. The capital of the northern sphere was Pampa Grande, and the southern sphere's capital was Moche. The political situation between the two fluctuated, as it seems the southern sphere briefly dominated the northern, a situation that later reversed, until finally both collapsed about the time that Wari influence was spreading out of the highlands during the Middle Horizon. Regardless of the political situation, the Moche aesthetic was a highpoint in Andean history at the same time that it fully served the political order. The Moche managed the construction of the largest adobe structure in the Americas, designed elaborate burials that expressed wealth and power, and modeled extremely fine expressions in metalwork, portrait vessels (vessels in the form of strikingly realistic human heads), fine-line narrative vessels (vessels with narrative scenes drawn out in lines), and murals grounded in a selective naturalism that make them both accessible and beautiful, even though they might be simultaneously operating on a symbolic level that is not yet fully understood.

Severe climatic events—a 32-year drought followed by a 30-year rainy period—led to the abandonment of the Moche capital in the first half of the seventh century. The late Moche sites of Galindo and Pampa Grande flourished for a while longer. Mountainlike *huacas*, similar to those at Moche, dominated these sites. One such mound at Galindo lay within an enclosure, which foretells the *ciudadelas* (citadels, or little cities) of the Chimú capital of Chan Chan in the same valley centuries later. Around 700 Pampa Grande came to a sudden and violent end, which some scholars attribute to unrest exacerbated by wetter than usual El Niño conditions followed by drought, while other scholars attribute it to the rise of the Wari Empire in the highlands.

HUACA DEL SOL AND HUACA DE LA LUNA

The Moche state constructed buildings in nearly every valley on the north coast. The buildings were recognizable by their adobe brick constructions, graduated levels, ramps, and small slant-roofed structures on top. The two largest were the Huaca del Sol (Pyramid of the Sun) and Huaca de la Luna (Pyramid of the Moon) at the Moche site. Huaca del Sol, the larger of the two, was made from roughly 143 million adobe bricks. Its scale is meant to mimic that of the mountains, thereby completing the progression from the early U-shaped centers to building on the foothills, to building mountains in and of themselves. Its original contour is thought to have been roughly in the shape of a cross; about two-thirds of the structure has been washed away due to the conquest-era search for gold, when the Spanish diverted the adjacent river into the structure to wash it away. It covers 340 meters by 160 meters (1,115 × 525 ft.) and rises at least 40 meters (131 ft.) above the ground. As the Moche theocracy evolved, successive rulers enlarged the structure, contributing to its already undeniable evocation of power.

The Huaca de la Luna was originally a complex of three platforms enclosed by an adobe wall. The Huaca de la Luna was smaller than the Huaca del Sol, constructed of some 40 million adobe bricks, but was richly ornamented with painted murals. Mural motifs included the figure of a large supernatural being with canine teeth, spiderlike creatures, anthropomorphic beings, and the parading of captive warriors. Some scholars believe the Huaca de la Luna was the setting for ceremonies of human sacrifice.

SIPÁN

Excavations at the Moche site of Sipán, in the Lambayeque Valley, uncovered 12 tombs of leaders, priests, retainers (royal attendants), and assistants, including Tomb 1, that of a middle-aged man known as the Lord of Sipán who corresponds with a figure known from painted vessel images referred to as the "sacrifice ceremony." The Lord of Sipán was buried beside two retainers. His body was lavishly covered in belt bells, his right hand held a scepter, his ears were covered in three spectacular pairs of gold and turquoise earspools, and he wore a stunning gold and silver peanut-shell necklace around his neck. In all, 451 items were interred with him in Tomb 1. Tomb 3, perhaps five generations previous to the Lord of Sipán, held a high-ranking individual referred to as the Old Lord, whose burial was strikingly similar to that of Tomb 1. His burial included gold and silver scepters and six necklaces, one of which was a 10-bead spider necklace of superb craftsmanship. Many of the remaining tombs contain only copper items and allow a view of the levels of the Moche political/spiritual hierarchy. Recent excavations dating to the first century suggest that the Sipán dynasty existed from the beginning of the Mochica.

MIDDLE HORIZON (CA. 540–900)

The Middle Horizon was defined by the withering of old states amid environmental stresses and the replacement of the old by the rise of the new. The demise of Moche in the north, the continued influence of Tiwanaku (the Middle Horizon corresponds with what is called Phase V Tiwanaku) in the southern highlands, and the rise of Wari in the south-central highlands distinguished the period. For Tiwanaku, integration of the southern highlands continued. Following a major drought period that lasted from 562 to 594, Tiwanaku tightened control both in the heartland and in distant colonies, reflecting a period of general prosperity. Drought returned to the southern highlands around 1100, and Tiwanaku collapsed soon thereafter.

Developments during the Middle Horizon were fundamental to and, in many ways, defined the eventual florescence of the Inca Empire. Not only did the Incas adopt Tiwanaku as a mythical homeland, but they also claimed the area's vast llama and alpaca herds as a major source of wealth. And, from the Wari culture the Incas borrowed labor relocation strategies as well as strategies of political control, including the adaptation of a Wari road-and-settlement system into their own system of provincial control. The Incas also borrowed the Wari quipu, a knotted-string recording device that was essential to Inca administration. Both Wari and Tiwanaku were fundamental precedents to later Inca institutions.

Wari (ca. 500–1000)

The ancient city of Wari (Huari) lies in the south-central highlands of Peru, roughly 700 kilometers (435 mi.) northwest of Tiwanaku and 25 kilometers (15.5 mi.) north of modern Ayacucho. Wari was preceded in the region by the Huarpa culture, which was distinguished by scattered village communities and by ceramics that show an influence from Nazca. The Wari culture's hallmark became its high-walled enclosures, climbing as high as 12 meters (39 ft.), which were found both in the empire's heartland and at its far-flung satellites. The nature of Wari is still debated. Some scholars favor a picture of Wari as a religion practiced among confederated states; others view it as a militaristic entity spreading rule by force, while still others, such as the Andean archaeologist Michael Moseley, favor the middle

ground, stating that Wari offered economic innovations in combination with religious fundamentalism in order to spread state institutions further afield.

By 600 the capital of Wari had become a ceremonial and elite residential center with an estimated population range of between 10,000 and 70,000. Its signature high walls, most of which were quarried stone set in mud mortar, segregated the city into numerous rectangular sections that were further subdivided by walls into two- to three-story compounds, many of which were associated with specialized craft production. Some of the compounds contained burials with imported items that indicated long-distance contacts. Interestingly, a rectangular sunken court dated to around 580 that remained in ceremonial use for as long as 200 years was probably borrowed from Tiwanaku. Along with the court's ritual, ideological, and iconographic patterns, the Wari adopted the image of a staff-bearing god related to agriculture that traces, though perhaps indirectly, all the way back to Chavín times. Wari appropriation of Tiwanakan forms is thus also a resurrection of ancient Andean traditions.

A key element in Wari's success was the use of innovative agrarian adaptations throughout the highlands that opened up new land to production at a time when other cultures, most notably at Moche, were suffering through extended drought. Through extensive terracing and irrigation the Wari solidified control at the center and then adapted their system at other locations, thereby increasing the reliability of resources in otherwise unpredictable environments. Azángaro, near the center; Jinca-mocco, halfway to Nazca; Viracochapampa, 700 kilometers to the north; Pikillacta, near Cuzco; and Cerro Baúl, in the Tiwanaku heartland, were all major Wari highland provincial settlements that expressed Wari architectural, political, religious, and administrative programs. However, because a large amount of Wari imperial success was based on irrigation adaptation and land reclamation, they found less success on the desert coasts; consequently, Wari colonial expression looked different on the arid coastal range, persisting in modified forms meant to enrich local development. It is important to note that the Wari administrative center at Pikillacta was very near Cuzco, the Inca capital. By the time of the Incas, Pikillacta had been long abandoned but nevertheless influenced aspects of Inca development.

Wari political and economic success was facilitated by the movement of art and textiles that some scholars argue contained state propagandistic messages. They claim that Wari textiles represented the corporate Wari message; in a sense, the visual forms addressed in textiles are analogous to the principles of Wari imperial urban forms—that is, rectilinear structures internally subdivided and separated. Furthermore, Wari metalwork and ceramics often reflected textile imagery and style; metalwork favored geometric abstraction and ceramics tended toward realistic images of the natural and supernatural world.

LATE INTERMEDIATE PERIOD (CA. 900–1438)

Developments leading to the Late Intermediate Period began many centuries earlier when civilizations were reorganizing due to rainfall fluctuations. Following the decline of Wari in the south-central highlands and the abandonment of Tiwanaku in the southern altiplano, the cultural initiative shifted again to the coast. The legacy of Moche on the north coast of Peru spawned two prominent successor civilizations: Lambayeque, or Sicán, in La Leche and Reque Valleys, and Chimú, or Chimor, based in the Moche Valley. The Chancay and Chincha cultures rose on the central and south-central coast, and the coastal oracle site of Pachacamac, established earlier, continued to flourish.

In the Lake Titicaca region increased pastoralism, or devotion to livestock raising—in this case, alpaca—was an important response to drought. Drought also meant increased competition for scarce resources; consequently, there was a general population shift to higher elevations where rain was somewhat more consistent, allowing for continued agriculture despite the need for intensive terracing, a practice the Incas adapted in full. Drought-induced resource competition also contributed to

defensive construction, with walls and fortified hilltop sites more prominently featured and the corralling of livestock necessary. Population movements upward, again spurred by drought, also occurred in the central and northern sierra; in essence, mountain people in these areas moved higher.

Along the central and southern coasts, prior to the rise of Chimú, a corporate style known as the Chancay achieved a degree of political integration. Farther to the south the site of Cerro Azul rose to prominence as a maritime center. The coastal Chincha people maintained trade networks to Ecuador for the valuable spondylus shell, which was later of elemental importance to the Incas. And further south still, the people of the Nazca and Ica Valleys, under the fading influence of Wari iconography and styles, maintained their textile and ceramic traditions. In general, the Late Intermediate Period was a time of reorganization, and as the immediate precursor to the Inca horizon it set in place many of the more immediate social precedents that the Incas manipulated into a more-or-less unified state.

Lambayeque (ca. 900–1250)

Descendants of the Moche culture established a new center of Lambayeque culture at Batán Grande. The earliest reorganization appears to have taken place between 700 and 900 and was limited to local growth even though outside influences are apparent. Between 900 and 1100 several monumental adobe compounds were built at Batán Grande, although it remained in principle a ceremonial site with minimal residential occupation. The largest irrigation complex built in the past connected numerous settlements across the Leche, Lambayeque, and Zaña Valleys. The people of Batán Grande were exceptional metalworkers, reminiscent of the craftsmen of Moche, and tombs that have since been ransacked were said to contain spectacular amounts of objects such as gold *keros* (libation vessels), gold beads, mummy masks, ceramics, emeralds, necklaces, *naipes* (small, flat I-shaped objects possibly used as currency), and *tumi* (curved ceremonial knives). The vast quantities of *naipes* found at Batán Grande has led some scholars to believe the site was used for the production and distribution of *naipes*. The central design element on many objects was a figure called the Sicán Lord, a culture hero/supernatural who is richly attired, beak-nosed, and occasionally shown with talon feet and wearing a crescent headdress. Around 1100 Batán Grande was abandoned, and its monuments set fire; furthermore, long-term meteorological data indicates a major El Niño event devastated the region with severe flooding. Lambayeque peoples then moved the center to Túcume, where they again built numerous monumental adobe mounds. Túcume flourished until the Chimú conquered it around 1350.

Chimú (ca. 1000–1470)

The Chimú Empire, with its capital city at Chan Chan, stretched more than 1,500 kilometers (932 mi.) along the north coast of Peru, encompassing two-thirds of all irrigated land and, by inference, two-thirds of the population. *Chimú* is the name used to refer to the general style of the empire. The coastal nation-state was defeated by the Incas around 1470, after which the last emperor, Minchancaman, was taken to Cuzco along with numerous metalworkers, whom the Incas valued for their skills. Following their victory, the Incas dismembered the Chimú state, exiled hostile groups to distant colonies, and carved up the nation into local administrative units loyal to the Incas. Chimú history is slightly more secure because of the corre-spondence between archaeology and ethnohistory; colonial-period documents record remembrances of events and conditions of life in Chimú prior to the arrival of the Incas.

Initial Chimú development was based on adapting and expanding the extensive north coast irrigation systems. Later, probably as a result of a major El Niño event that made this already labor-intensive enterprise too difficult, major irrigation efforts were dropped in favor of militaristic initiatives that saw the empire conquer settlements in order to extract tribute.

Art production apparently became a primary focus during the expansion of Chimú. Great care and dedication went toward amassing, storing, displaying, and preserving objects, especially luxury works. To a certain extent quantity was valued over quality; a lack of attention to finishing often undercut the preciousness of the material. The haste may have been a by-product of the demand and use of material items as political propaganda tools or power symbols. It was also common for the same item to be made in clay for the commoner and metal for a member of the elite, thereby reinforcing social hierarchies and stratification. The compounds themselves were works of art, with walls covered in adobe reliefs in geometric and animal-figure motifs.

CHAN CHAN

In its final form Chan Chan was a vast noncentralized metropolis comprising nine to 11 walled compounds whose core was spread over an area of about six square kilometers (2.3 sq. mi.) within a greater settled area of more than 20 square kilometers (8 sq. mi.). These compounds, called *ciudadelas*, functioned as palaces, mausoleums, storage spaces, and offices (called *audiencias*), while some scholars have referred to them as museums due to the vast quantities of objects found there. The *ciudadelas* enclosed space equal to that of several soccer fields. The largest compound, referred to as Gran Chimú and thought to be the palace of a ruler name Qancinpinco, measured roughly 400 meters by 600 meters (1,312 × 1,968 ft.).

Dynastic histories indicate a ruler list of at least nine to 11 kings, leading scholars to interpret the compounds as palaces associated with kingly rule. Each of the compounds was rigorously ordered on

2.4 View of latticework walls at Chan Chan, the capital of the Chimú Empire, ca. 900–1470 (Photo courtesy of Eloise Quiñones Keber)

the inside, though altogether they do not provide much coherence for the overall picture of a unified imperial or capital "city." The lack of coherence may reflect a system of split inheritance governing royal succession. Split inheritance dictates that the heir to the throne receives the right to rule but does not receive his predecessor's land or wealth. Furthermore, while the interior constructions of the compounds retain some formal congruity with earlier U-shaped ceremonial centers, their most dominant features are a single entrance, a burial platform, and massive peripheral walls, whose height and thickness far exceed any conceivable security threat.

The compounds may have been built in pairs, suggesting an affinity with pan-Andean moiety traditions (a moiety is a form of social division based on equal halves). The architecture itself was used to distinguish class and occupation of residents. For example, the majority of craftsmen and technical personnel lived and worked in small rooms and courts constructed of cane walls. Evidence of woodworking, metalworking, and weaving activities has been found in domestic residences. By contrast, the minority elite, comprising lords and the rulers, lived and worked in detached mud-brick enclosures. As time progressed the compounds increasingly developed according to a standardized plan, though at the same time they increased in their mazelike nature, suggesting a high level of exclusivity.

Chancay (ca. 1000–1450)

While the Chimú prospered in the north, Chancay emerged farther south, based in the Chancay Valley, though it also held sway in the Chillón, Huaura, and Rímac Valleys. Evidence suggests that Chancay achieved a degree of political integration with Chimú. Chancay is a vibrant style characterized by black painted pottery on a whitish slip with a matte finish; vessel motifs that favor geometric patterning, although plants, animals, and humans are occasionally represented; tombs containing seated figures and textiles; and corporate architecture employing *tapia*, a clay mixture poured like concrete into wooden molds.

Chanca (ca. 1100–1438)

The defeat of the Chanca and the conquest of their territory by the Incas was the initial step in the expansion of the Inca Empire. The war between the Chancas and the Incas resonates most profoundly in the myths, while the archaeology is somewhat less conclusive. Nevertheless, there is some provisional correlation between the archaeology and the groups that lived in the region and fought against the Incas. The Chancas lived on the other side of the Río Apurímac from the Incas, in diffuse settlements that indicate a large but scattered population. One subsequent theory of organization is that the Chanca were comprised of confederated sites with a more or less homogenous cultural footprint. Chanca settlements were typically unsystematic arrangements of rectangular and circular structures on hillsides. Associated pottery is typically plain with simple patterns of dark brown lines on a cream slip. Significantly, higher elevation settlements displayed architecture with inclined walls, which perhaps contributed to what became a key Inca architectural trait.

Killke and Lucre/Early Inca (ca. 1200–1438)

The ethnic beginnings of the Incas have traditionally been associated with the Killke ceramic style found in the immediate vicinity of Cuzco, the eventual capital of the Incas, and to the northwest of Cuzco. Killke settlements tend to be unfortified, occupying low, open settings near water sources and arable land. By about 1200, Killke was associated with Chokepukio, a Lucre site, indicating the gradual expansion of pre-Inca control. Prior to the Inca occupation of Chokepukio, *cancha*-style enclosures—the single-room stone structures that would become the basic unit of Inca architecture—were built. The spread of Killke ceramics through the area of the Urubamba drainage coincided with a gradual downward shift of populations from hilltop settlements to the valley floor. Occupation of these lower valleys continued uninterrupted into imperial Inca times, after which they constituted the social core of the area around Cuzco that became the heart of the empire.

The village of Acamama was located on the future site of Cuzco. The Spanish chronicles relate that it was a small primitive village that contained both dual and quadripartite divisions. Dual division, adopted into Inca social and spatial division as *hanan* and *hurin*, is associated with dual opposites, notably upper/lower and masculine/feminine distinctions. Quadripartite division is associated with directionality. Inca Cuzco later adopted both of these notions of spatial division. It should be noted that these divisions encapsulated ideas of both opposition and complementarity. Also, this period is associated with the reigns of the first eight rulers of the Inca dynasty.

LATE HORIZON (1438–1534)

In what seems like an extremely brief amount of time, the Incas went from provincial villagers to imperial unifiers. Archaeological evidence indicates a local or regional kingdom existed in the Cuzco area until the reign of Inca Viracocha, the eighth king according to traditional king lists. At this time a number of small villages existed with what is

2.5 View of the Sacred Valley, the location of Inca royal estates (J. J. George)

thought to be a loosely confederated military between them. The nearby Wari center of Pikillacta was abandoned, and the inhabitants resettled at a higher elevation at Lucre. Together with the Killke ceramic style, these elements constitute the pre-Inca foundation.

Following the ebb and flow of pre-Inca history and the rise and fall of Andean empires and regional states, the Incas managed to unify territory on a scale previously unknown, yet when the Spanish took Cuzco in 1534, the Inca Empire was already effectively dissolving. It was already transforming from an imperial enterprise to a fractured state in the middle of a civil war of succession. Soon enough the Incas and their imperial subjects were themselves the subjects of a foreign empire, and a long period of conquest and colonial control ensued. Prior to the Spanish arrival, during Inca administration, local styles and cultures remained somewhat intact, especially as one traveled farther away from the center to the periphery and frontier regions where the tight reins of imperial control slackened and local styles and systems retained some of their own authority. This was true under Spanish rule as well, where local systems of expressions never fully disappeared, which is why an incredibly vibrant indigenous culture still exists in Peru until this day.

READING

Major Pre-Inca Periods

G. L. Bawden, "Galindo and the Nature of the Middle Horizon in Northern Coastal Peru." Ph.D. diss., Harvard University, 1977.

———, "Galindo: A Study in Cultural Transition during the Middle Horizon." In *Chan Chan, Andean Desert City*, edited by Michael Moseley and K. C. Day, 285–320 (Albuquerque: University of New Mexico Press, 1982).

Wendell Bennett, "The Archaeology of the Central Andes." In *Handbook of South American Indians*. Vol. 2, edited by Julian Steward, 61–148

(Washington, D.C.: Smithsonian Institution, 1946).

———, "Excavations at Tihuanaco," *Anthropological Papers of the American Museum of Natural History* 34, no. 3 (1934): 359–493.

———, "Excavations in Bolivia," *Anthropological Papers of the American Museum of Natural History* 35 (1936): 331–505.

———, *A Reappraisal of Peruvian Archaeology*, no. 4 (Menasha, Wis.: Society for American Archaeology, 1948).

Wendell Bennett and Junius Bird, *Andean Cultural History*. 2nd revised edition, Handbook Series, no. 15 (New York: American Museum of Natural History, 1960).

Kathleen Berrin, ed., *The Spirit of Ancient Peru* (London: Thames & Hudson, 1998).

Elizabeth Hill Boone, ed., *Andean Art at Dumbarton Oaks*. Vols. 1 and 2 (Washington, D.C.: Dumbarton Oaks, 1996).

Steve Bourget, *Sex, Death, and Sacrifice in Moche Religion* (Austin: University of Texas Press, 2006).

David L. Browman, "Tiwanaku Expansion and Altiplano Economic Patterns," *Estudios Arqueológicos* 5 (1980): 107–120.

———, "Toward the Development of the Tiahuanaco (Tiwanaku) State." In *Advances in Andean Archaeology*, edited by D. L. Browman, 327–349 (The Hague, Netherlands: Mouton, 1978).

Richard L. Burger, *Chavín and the Origins of Andean Civilization* (London: Thames & Hudson, 1992).

———, "The Occupation of Chavin, Ancash, in the Initial Period and Early Horizon." Ph.D. diss., Department of Anthropology, University of California, Berkeley, 1978.

———, "An Overview of Peruvian Archaeology (1976–1986)," *Annual Review of Anthropology* 18 (1989): 37–46.

———. "The Radiocarbon Evidence for the Temporal Priority of Chavín de Huantar," *American Antiquity* 46 (1981): 592–602.

———, "The Sacred Center of Chavín de Huantar." In *The Ancient Americas: Art from the Sacred Landscape*, edited by Richard F. Townsend, 265–277 (Chicago: Art Institute of Chicago, 1992).

———, "Unity and Heterogeneity within the Chavín Horizon." In *Peruvian Prehistory: An Overview of Pre-Inca and Inca Society*, edited by

Richard W. Keatinge, 99–144 (Cambridge: Cambridge University Press, 1988).

Claude Chauchat, "Early Hunter-Gatherers on the Peruvian Coast." In *Peruvian Prehistory: An Overview of Pre-Inca Society*, ed. Richard W. Keatinge, 41–66 (Cambridge: Cambridge University Press, 1988).

Pedro Cieza de León, *The Discovery and Conquest of Peru*. Translated by Alexandra Parma Cook and David Noble Cook (Durham, N.C.: Duke University Press, 1998).

William Conklin, "The Information System of Middle Horizon Quipus." In *Ethnoastronomy and Archaeoastronomy in the American Tropics*, edited by Anthony Aveni and Gary Urton, 261–282, *Annals of the New York Academy of Sciences* 385 (1982).

Geoffrey W. Conrad, "Cultural Materialism, Split Inheritance, and the Expansion of Ancient Peruvian Empires," *American Antiquity* 46 (1981): 3–26.

R. Alan Covey, *How the Incas Built Their Heartland* (Ann Arbor: University of Michigan Press, 2005).

Terence D'Altroy, *The Incas* (London: Blackwell, 2002).

Christopher B. Donnan, ed., *Ceramics of Ancient Peru* (Los Angeles: Fowler Museum, UCLA, 1992).

———, *Early Ceremonial Architecture in the Andes* (Washington, D.C.: Dumbarton Oaks, 1985).

———, *Moche Fineline Painting: Its Evolution and Its Artists* (Los Angeles: UCLA Fowler Museum of Cultural History, 1999).

Robert V. Dover, Katherine E. Seibold, and John H. McDowell, eds., *Andean Cosmologies through Time* (Bloomington: Indiana University Press, 1992).

Ian S. Farrington, "Prehistoric Intensive Agriculture: Preliminary Notes on River Canalization in the Sacred Valley of the Incas." In *Drained Field Agriculture in Central and South America*, International Series, no. 189, edited by John Darch, 221–235 (Oxford: British Archaeological Reports, 1983).

———. "Ritual Geography, Settlement Patterns and the Characterization of the Provinces of the Inka Heartland," *World Archaeology* 23 (1992): 368–385.

John Hyslop, *An Archaeological Investigation of the Lupaca Kingdom and Its Origins*. Ph.D. diss., Columbia University, 1976.

Richard W. Keatinge, ed., *Peruvian Prehistory* (Cambridge: Cambridge University Press, 1998).

Paul Kirchoff, "The Social and Political Organization of the Andean Peoples." In *Handbook of South American Indians*. Vol. 5, *The Comparative Ethnology of South American Indians*, edited by Julian H. Steward, Bureau of American Ethnology, Bulletin, no. 143, 293–311 (Washington, D.C.: Smithsonian Institution, 1946).

Alan L. Kolata, *The Tiwanaku: Portrait of an Andean Civilization* (London: Blackwell, 1993).

Luis G. Lumbreras, *The Peoples and Cultures of Ancient Peru*. Translated by Betty J. Meggers (Washington, D.C.: Smithsonian Institution Press, 1989).

Thomas F. Lynch, "The Paleoindians." In *Ancient South Americans*, edited by Jesse D. Jennings, 87–137 (San Francisco: Freeman, 1983).

———. "Quaternary Climate, Environment, and the Human Occupation of the South-Central Andes," *Geoarchaeology* 5 (1990): 199–228.

Gordon F. McEwan, "Investigations at the Pikillacta Site: A Provincial Huari Center in the Valley of Cuzco." In *Huari Administrative Structure: Prehistoric Monumental Architecture and State Government*, edited by William H. Isbell and Gordon McEwan, 93–119 (Washington, D.C.: Dumbarton Oaks, 1991).

———. *The Middle Horizon in the Valley of Cuzco, Peru: The Impact of the Wari Occupation of Pikillacta in the Lucre Basin*, International Series, S-372 (Oxford: British Archaeological Reports, 1987).

Fernando de Montesinos, *Memorias antiguas historiales del Perú*. Translated and edited by Philip Ainsworth Means, with an Introduction by Clements R. Markham (London: Hakluyt Society, 1920).

Jerry Moore, *Architecture and Power in the Ancient Andes* (Cambridge: Cambridge University Press, 2005).

———. *Cultural Landscapes in the Ancient Andes* (Gainesville: University Press of Florida, 2005).

Craig Morris, "The Archaeological Study of Andean Exchange Systems." In *Social Archaeology: Beyond Subsistence and Dating*, edited by C. Redman et al., 135–327 (New York: Academic Press, 1978).

———, "Chan Chan: Andean Alternative to the Pre-Industrial City," *Science* 187 (1975): 219–225.

———, "The Evolution of Andean Society." In *Ancient Native Americans*, edited by J. D. Jennings, 491–541 (San Francisco: W. H. Freeman, 1978).

———, *The Incas and Their Ancestors*. Rev. ed. (New York: Thames & Hudson, 2001).

———, *The Maritime Foundations of Andean Civilization* (Menlo Park, Calif.: Cummings, 1975).

———, "Master Design of the Inca," *Natural History* 85, no. 10 (1976): 58–66.

———, *Peru's Golden Treasure* (Chicago: Field Museum of Natural History, 1979).

———, "Subsistence and Demography: An Example of Interaction from Prehistoric Peru," *Southwestern Journal of Anthropology* 28 (1972): 25–49.

Craig Morris and Adriana von Hagen, *The Inka Empire and Its Andean Origins* (New York: Abbeville Press, 1993).

Michael Moseley and K. C. Day, eds., *Chan Chan: Andean Desert City* (Albuquerque: University of New Mexico Press, 1982).

Martin de Murúa, *Historia del origen y genealogía real de los reyes incas del Perú*. Vol. 2, Introduction and notes by Constantino Bayle, Biblioteca "Missionalis Hispánica" (Madrid: Instituto Santo Toribio de Mogrovego, 1946).

Esther Pasztory, "Andean Aesthetics." In *The Spirit of Ancient Peru: Treasures from the Museo Arqueológico Rafael Larco Herrera*, edited by Kathleen Berrin, 61–69 (London: Thames & Hudson, 1997).

César Paternosto, *The Stone and the Thread: Andean Roots of Abstract Art* (Austin: University of Texas Press, 1989).

Thomas C. Patterson, "The Huaca La Florida, Rimac Valley, Peru." In *Early Ceremonial Architecture in the Andes*, edited by Christopher B. Donnan, 59–70 (Washington, D.C.: Dumbarton Oaks, 1985).

Anne Paul, *Paracas Art and Architecture* (Iowa City: Iowa University Press, 1991).

———. *Paracas Ritual Attire* (Oklahoma City: Oklahoma University Press, 1990).

Joanne Pillsbury, ed., *Moche Art and Archaeology in Ancient Peru* (New Haven, Conn.: Yale University Press, 2001).

Rosa Fung Pineda, "The Late Preceramic and Initial Periods." In *Peruvian Prehistory: An Overview of Pre-Inca Society*, edited by Richard W. Keatinge, 67–98 (Cambridge: Cambridge University Press, 1988).

William Hickling Prescott, *History of the Conquest of Peru*. 2 vols. (New York: Harper & Bros. Publishers, 1847).

Jeffrey Quilter, *Treasures of the Andes* (London: Duncan Baird Publishers, 2005).

Anna C. Roosevelt, "Maritime, Highland, Forest Dynamics." In *The Cambridge History of the Native Peoples of the Americas*. Vol. 3, *South America*, edited by Frank Salomon and Stuart B. Schwartz, 264–349 (Cambridge: Cambridge University Press, 1999).

John H. Rowe, "Absolute Chronology in the Andean Area," *American Antiquity* 10, no. 3 (1945): 265–284.

———. *An Introduction to the Archaeology of Cuzco.* Cambridge: Peabody Museum of American Archaeology and Ethnology 27, no. 2 (1944).

———. "The Kingdom of Chimor," *Acta Americana* 6, nos. 1–2 (Mexico) (January–February 1948): 26–59.

Frank Salomon and Stuart B. Schwartz, eds., *The Cambridge History of the Native Peoples of the Americas*. Vol. 3 (Cambridge: Cambridge University Press, 1999).

Katharina J. Schreiber, *Wari Imperialism in Middle Horizon Peru*, Anthropological Papers 87 (Ann Arbor: University of Michigan Museum of Anthropology, 1992).

Izumi Shimada, "Evolution of Andean Diversity (500 B.C.E.–C.E. 600)." In *The Cambridge History of the Native Peoples of the Americas*. Vol. 3, *South America*, edited by Frank Salomon and Stuart B. Schwartz, 350–517 (Cambridge: Cambridge University Press, 1999).

Helaine Silverman, "The Archaeological Identification of an Ancient Peruvian Pilgrimage Center," *World Archaeology* 26, no. 1 (1994): 1–18.

Helaine Silverman and Donald Proulx, *The Nasca* (London: Blackwell, 2002).

Karen Spalding, "Invaded Societies: Andean Area (1500–1580)." In *Cambridge History of the Native Peoples of the Americas*. Vol. 3, *South America*, edited by Frank Salomon and Stuart B. Schwartz, 904–972 (Cambridge: Cambridge University Press, 1999).

Rebecca Stone-Miller, *Art of the Andes*. 2nd ed (London: Thames & Hudson, 2002).

Max Uhle, *Inca Myths*. Reprint (Austin: University of Texas Press, 1999).

———, "Explorations at Chincha," *University of California Publications in Archaeology and Ethnology* 21, no. 2 (1924): 55–94.

———, *Pachacamac. Report of the William Pepper, M.D., LL.D. Peruvian Expedition of 1896* (Philadelphia: Department of Archaeology, University of Pennsylvania, 1903).

Adriana Von Hagen and Craig Morris, *The Cities of the Ancient Andes* (London: Thames & Hudson, 1998).

Gordon Willey, "Functional Analysis of 'Horizon Styles' in Peruvian Archaeology." In *A Reappraisal of Peruvian Archaeology*. Vol. 4, edited by Wendell C. Bennett, 8–15 (Menasha, Wis.: Society for American Archaeology Memoir, 1948).

Margaret Young-Sanchez et al., *Tiwanaku: Ancestors of the Inca* (Denver, Colo.: Denver Art Museum, 2004).

3

BUILDING THE INCA WORLD

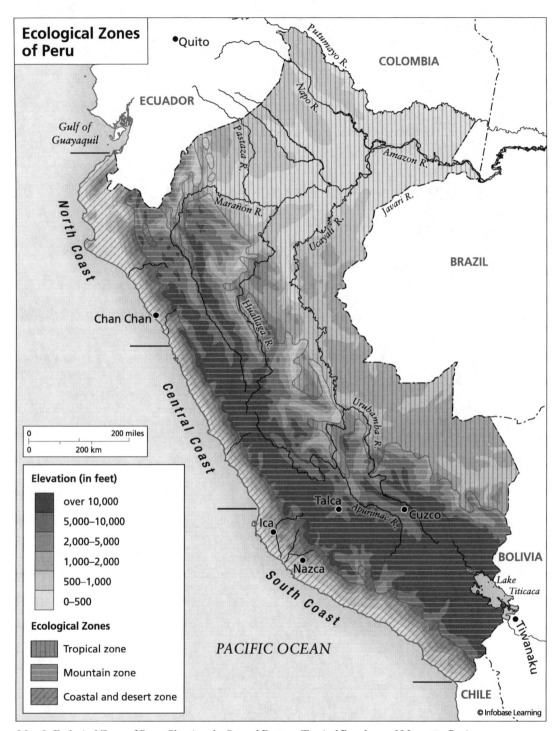

Ecological Zones of Peru

•Quito

COLOMBIA

ECUADOR

Gulf of Guayaquil

Putumayo R.

Napo R.

Pastaza R.

Amazon R.

Marañon R.

Javari R.

Ucayali R.

BRAZIL

North Coast

Huallaga R.

Chan Chan•

Central Coast

Urubamba R.

0   200 miles
0   200 km

Elevation (in feet)

over 10,000

5,000–10,000

2,000–5,000

1,000–2,000

500–1,000

0–500

Ecological Zones

Tropical zone

Mountain zone

Coastal and desert zone

Talca•

Apurimac. R.

•Cuzco

•Ica

Nazca•

BOLIVIA

Lake Titicaca

South Coast

PACIFIC OCEAN

•Tiwanaku

CHILE

© Infobase Learning

Map 2 Ecological Zones of Peru, Showing the Coastal Deserts, Tropical Jungles, and Montaña *Regions*

The Inca Empire encompassed an enormous expanse of territory, stretching north to south from modern-day Colombia to Chile, and east to west from parts of modern-day Brazil, Bolivia, and Argentina to almost the entire stretch of South America's Pacific coast. It contained within its borders the most ecologically and biologically diverse territory of any other pre-Columbian civilization, a land of extreme contrasts. One can encounter every environmental extreme imaginable, from the intensely vertical terrain of the Andes, soaring up to altitudes of 5,000 meters (16,404 ft.) above sea level, to dry, low-lying lands along the western coast of South America. The climatic zones are equally diverse, with some areas that are constantly hot and humid to others with subfreezing temperatures year round. Also within its boundaries are some of the driest places on earth—Chile's Atacama Desert—to some of the most lush—the Amazonian rain forest to the east of the Andes—with a rainy season lasting 11 months of the year.

Within this extreme environmental variation, however, the geography of Inca territory can be divided into three categories: the coast (*costa*), the mountainous region (*sierra*), and the eastern tropical region (*selva*). Covering a staggering 4,000 kilometers (2,485 mi.) of land, the empire flourished through interregional trade networks that enabled the consumption of goods from a variety of ecological zones. Although the Incas controlled many geographical regions, local systems of agriculture and other types of land modification were often maintained, which had developed independently over the course of thousands of years.

PHYSICAL CLIMATE AND GEOGRAPHY

The geography of the Inca Empire is extremely diverse, with the mountainous Andean region, high plains, dry coastal zones, tropical lowlands, and temperate mountain valleys. Each of these areas yields different types of flora and fauna, which thrive at specific temperatures and altitudes. One of the most distinctive elements of the empire's physical geography is the close proximity of radically different ecological zones to one another. The steep nature of the Andean terrain produces a phenomenon in which several biomes are in effect "stacked" upon one another. For example, only a mere 60 kilometers (37 mi.) stretch of coastal desert land separates the Pacific Ocean from the northern highlands. The dramatic variation in altitude across short latitudinal distances results in a diversity of ecological zones that Inca farmers and herders obtained through systems of intermontane exchange, a bartering system the Incas established among their various mountain communities. People began to modify the physical environment since human populations first arrived to South America about 15,000 years ago. The advent of agriculture by 3000 B.C.E. transformed the landscape into farming plots and terraced slopes for the cultivation of crops. Irrigation systems and drainage canals also impacted the physical terrain of the empire, creating lush regions suitable for agriculture in previously uninhabitable lands. Despite these modifications, there are still signs of the wide-ranging variation in the natural geography of this vast area. Each zone has a distinct climate and ecology with a unique set of natural resources, to which its human populations had to adapt for survival.

Coastal Zone

The coastal zone stretches more than 2,000 kilometers (1,243 mi.) from Ecuador to Chile, where dry, desert land meets the waters of the Pacific Ocean. The salinated coastal lands are crosscut by 57 rivers and streams that create small strips of productive farmland. These fertile river valleys, which produced maize, cotton, squash, and cucumber, were maintained through extensive irrigation networks. Fish, mollusks, sea mammals, and marine birds constitute the region's most abundant resources, and indeed, coastal society was governed by powerful families that inherited fishing rights to different parts of the coast. The *algarrobo*, or carob tree, was exploited for its pods, which yielded sweet syrup used in north coast cuisine.

Nearly the entire stretch of the Peruvian and Chilean coast is desert, with low-lying scrub brush, dry grasses, and desert rodents punctuating the landscape. It can be roughly divided into the north coast, corresponding to southern Ecuador and northern Peru; the central coast, corresponding to the land spanning the Chancay River valley in the north to the Cañete River valley to the south. Lima, the present-day capital of Peru, is situated in the central coast region. The southern coast corresponds to southern Peru and northern Chile.

The northern coast runs from Ecuador to the Lambayeque Valley, situated in a semitropical climatic zone. The central coast runs from the Lambayeque to the Cañete River. It is a very dry subtropical zone, with only seven valleys that have a year-round water supply. The noncorrosive desert sands of the central coast provide ideal preservation conditions for mummies, textiles, and other perishable objects. In fact, many elite Incas buried their mummies on the central coast so that they would remain in good condition for the centuries to come. The southern coast, running from the Cañete down through northern Chile, is dominated by extremely arid, inhospitable desert land. The coast becomes increasingly barren as one moves southward, encountering the expansive Atacama Desert. The Atacama Desert, which spans almost 1,000 km (621 mi.) along coastal Chile, is one of the driest places on earth, averaging about one millimeter per year of rainfall. In fact, it is believed that not one drop of rain touched the Atacama Desert for a span of about 300 years. The desert supports little plant life other than at a few scattered oases fed by underground water sources. The lower slopes of the Andes remain barren up to 2,500 meters (8,202 ft.) in this region. However, the area was rich in copper and nitrate, which the Incas exploited for imperial use.

LOMAS

In certain areas of the coast, particularly along hills and knolls, patches of low-lying vegetation manage to survive within an otherwise barren landscape. Known as *lomas*, these patches thrive between the months of June and October, when the coastal climate is slightly cooler and receives more moisture than during the dry season. They are composed of grasses and xerophytic plants such as *Tilandsia*, only requiring the moisture contained within the thick fogs (*garúas*) that move along the coast as a source of water. They also support small edible animals such as mollusks. The *lomas* absorb the humidity released into the air. During the remainder of the year, the *lomas* appear to be dried out and dead but resume their lush appearance when the season changes.

El Niño

The El Niño phenomenon occurs about every four to five years along the north coast of Peru, in which the coastal waters swell up and flood the land, with often immensely destructive and devastating effects. Strong winds that originate in the south help to move Pacific Ocean currents northward. The Humboldt Current is the name given to the cold water current that moves north along the coasts of Chile, Peru, and Ecuador, at which point it travels in a westerly route along the equator. When the Humboldt Current collides with the Equatorial Countercurrent, the waters along the coast of South America become nourished with the biotic material brought up from the ocean floor, which helps to feed marine life closer to the surface of the sea. When moist, warm winds enter the established complex of wind and current patterns that occur along the coast, it causes the tropical waters from the equatorial region to move southward. This results in heavy rains and torrential flooding that can destroy houses and leave settlements in a state of complete disrepair. In the past, the unpredictability of El Niño meant that coastal communities had to continually rebuild themselves, often from complete destruction. The floods could lead to great famines, since they had the potential to destroy agricultural fields for several years until the soils regenerated. Believed to be a great force of cataclysmic proportions, this environmental phenomenon was incorporated into the religious belief systems of coastal civilizations up through the period of Inca domination.

The Andes

The Andes, the longest mountain chain in the world, were the geographical focal point of the Inca Empire. They run almost 6,000 kilometers (3,728 mi.) north to south across the entire western edge of South America, from the Caribbean region of modern-day Venezuela in the north to Tierra del Fuego at the southernmost tip of the continent. There are 57 peaks with altitudes more than 5,300 meters (17,388 ft.) above sea level. The various mountain chains that make up the Andes are known as cordilleras. The two major chains are known as the Cordillera Oriental (also known as Cordillera Blanca) to the east and the Cordillera Occidental (or Cordillera Negra) to the west. The Cordillera Occidental runs parallel to the Pacific coast from southern Ecuador to northern Chile. It is the youngest of the major Andean mountain chains. The Cordillera Oriental is higher in altitude than the Cordillera Occidental, containing 50 of the highest peaks in all of South America. Mount Aconcagua, located at the border of present-day Argentina and Chile, is the highest peak in the Andes, measuring nearly 7,000 meters (22,966 ft.) in altitude. The Cordilleras Occidental and Oriental are connected by a series of mountain passes, known as *nudos*, which run perpendicular to these major mountain chains to form an H shape. Mount Vilcanota, the northernmost *nudo*, serves as the point from which the Andes split into the two major cordilleras. Mount Vilcanota, Mount Pasco, and Mount Loja, the largest *nudos*, divide the Andes into three sections: the Northern Andes, the Central Andes, and the Southern Andes.

NORTHERN ANDES

The Northern Andes roughly correspond to the cordilleras of Colombia, Venezuela, and Ecuador and are delimited by Mount Vilcanota to the south. The Northern Andes consist of narrow parallel ranges that are intersected by short mountain chains. The Andes decrease in altitude as one moves northward and finally descend into tropical lowlands.

CENTRAL ANDES

The Central Andes are of particular significance, serving as the geographical backdrop of the Inca heartland. The Central Andes correspond to the modern boundaries of Peru and stretch between Mount Vilcanota to the second major *nudo* south,

Mount Pasco. An important area within the Central Andes is known as the Callejón de Huaylas, a lush highland valley fed by the Santa River. The upper Mantaro River basin was another important center for agriculture in the Central Andes; an area where cultivatable land is at a premium. The Cuzco Valley, the area surrounding the Inca capital, was another major culture area of highland Peru, supporting the largest population concentration in the Andes under the Incas.

SOUTHERN ANDES

The Southern Andes are associated with the cordilleras of north and central Chile and northwest Argentina and are delimited by Mount Pasco to the north and the third major *nudo*, Mount Loja, to the south. The dominant mountain range of the Southern Andes is the Cordillera Oriental. The environment of the Southern Andes is very dry and largely unforested.

Altitudinal Zones of the Andes

The Andes were far from uniform. Climate, ecology, and plant and wildlife shifted considerably as one ascended to higher-altitude regions. Javier Pulgar Vidal, a Peruvian geographer, was the first to classify the different altitudinal zones of the Andes according to Quechua terminology, and his model has since provided a basis for archaeologists, environmentalists, and ecologists who study the Andes.

YUNGAS ZONE

The *yungas* zone corresponds to the southernmost slopes of the Andes on both its western and eastern sides. It ranges from about 300 to 2,000 meters (984–6,562 ft.) above sea level. This warmer climatic region yields coca, one of the Incas' most treasured plants. The warm temperatures and frequent rains of the *yungas* zone also provide optimal conditions for the cultivation of chilies, sweet potatoes, manioc (cassava), avocados, the maguey cactus (a type of agave), and the abundantly sweet cherimoya and *lúcuma* fruits.

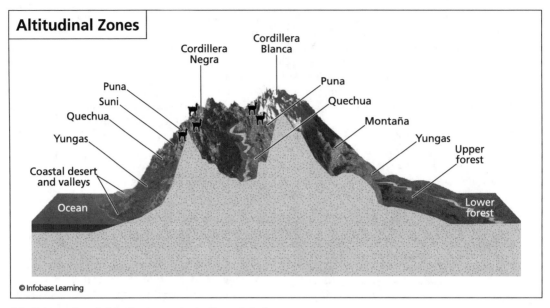

3.1 *Cross section of altitudinal zones in the Central Andes*

QUECHUA ZONE

The *quechua* zone—located slightly north of the *yungas,* from about 2,000 to 3,500 meters (6,562–11,483 ft.) above sea level along the slopes of the Andes—is where the Incas achieved their highest agricultural productivity, including maize, beans, and potatoes. The Incas also cultivated lesser-known crops in this region, such as the tubers *ulluco,* oca, and *mashua;* the grains quinoa and *cañihua;* and the legume *tarwi,* which all only grow in the Andean region. These crops are most easily cultivated in the valley bottoms of the mountains located in this zone.

SUNI ZONE

The *suni* zone, located at an altitude of about 4,000 meters (13,123 ft.) has significantly less agricultural diversity than the *yungas* and *quechua* zones but provided critical resources for the survival of the empire's subjects. Although there is more land suitable for cultivation in this area than in the previous zones, the high altitudes prohibit most crop growth, with the notable exception of the most prized source

of carbohydrates in the Inca Empire: the potato. The *suni* zone also provided hunting grounds for the meat of the guanaco and white-tailed deer.

ALTIPLANO

The Andean altiplano (from the Spanish for "high plain") is a flat, tundralike environment that extends across much of southeastern Peru and western Bolivia. It ranges from about 3,500 to 4,500 meters (11,483–14,764 ft.) above sea level. It is made up of a series of large, flat expanses of land nestled in between mountain passes that measure a total of about 800 kilometers (497 mi.) in length. The Peruvian-Bolivian altiplano is frequently plagued by rain, snowstorms, and freezing winds. Its ice-covered terrain supports little agriculture other than the potato. Despite its extreme temperatures and high altitude, the Altiplano provides the ideal breeding and herding ground for llamas and alpacas. The treeless terrain allows for herds to roam free, unobstructed. Moreover, the vegetation that grows in extremely high-altitude regions, such as short grasses and straw plants, are easily digestible by camelids. *Ichu* and *chilliwa*, both dry, straw plants, are the favored culinary fare of llamas, while alpacas tend to feed on wetter grasses such as *champa pasto* and *rama pasto*. Llamas and alpacas were essential for the economic survival of the Inca Empire, primarily used as sources of wool and meat, and deer, guanacos, and vicuña were also popular for hunting.

The southern half of the altiplano is very dry, producing a desertlike expanse of land with little agriculture or wildlife. It is rich in mineral resources, however, with significant deposits of copper, tin, and silver. The areas to the north and southwest of Lake Titicaca are much wetter, receiving enough rainfall to support some agriculture without irrigation, including maize and potatoes.

PUNA

The puna is a high intermontane plateau, one of which spans from southern Peru to Bolivia. It consists of rolling hills covered in short grasses. Located 4,000–5,000 meters (13,123–16,404 ft.) above sea level, it marks the altitude level at which agriculture no longer grows, with the exception of potatoes. The short grasses of the puna also provide optimal conditions for the herding and grazing of camelids, such as llamas and alpacas.

JANCA ZONE

The *janca* consists of the highest peaks of the Andean mountain range, from 4,500 meters (14,764 ft.) and higher. The terrain is characterized by glaciers and permanent ice caps. Land above 4,800 meters in the Southern Andes and above 5,000 meters in the Northern Andes is covered in snow year round. This zone did not support livestock or agriculture and was typically not settled by human populations. Mountaintops within the *janca* zone typically provided the sites at which Cápac Hucha ceremonies—state-mandated child sacrifices—were conducted and deposited.

Tropical Region

The tropical region can be divided into two major areas: the *ceja de selva*, or "eyebrow of the jungle,"
and the tropical rain forest. The *ceja de selva* corresponds to the eastern slopes of the Andes, which descend into the Amazonian rain forest that occupies much of northeastern Peru and western Brazil.

CEJA DE SELVA AND *MONTAÑA* REGION

The *ceja de selva* and the *montaña* regions correspond to the land below 3,000 meters (9,843 ft.) along the eastern slopes of the Andes. The regions cover 15,000 square kilometers (5,792 sq. mi.) of land. Alternatively known as *chaupiyunga* and *rupa-rupa* by local populations, the *ceja de selva* is roughly equivalent to the *yungas* zone on the western slopes of the Andes in terms of climate and ecology. Unlike the *yungas* zone, however, the *ceja* is wetter because it receives ample mountain runoff of rainwater, approximately 2,000–4,000 millimeters (79–157 in.) of rain per year, en route to the Atlantic Ocean. Moreover, instead of descending into the arid desert coast like the *yungas* zone, the *ceja de selva* descends into the lush, fertile Amazonian basin. Much of this area is covered by thick cloud forest with dense vegetation. Despite the high level of natural vegetation that the *ceja de selva* supports, it is a poor region for agriculture because of the steep, uneven terrain and thin soils. Nevertheless, during the Inca Empire, the prized coca leaf thrived in this region, along with maize, peanuts, and fruits.

AMAZONIAN RAIN FOREST

As one descends into the eastern slopes of the Andes, the mountain environment transforms into a hot, humid biome that supports flora and fauna entirely unique from the rest of the Andean region. This eastern tropical region constituted Antisuyu, the eastern quarter of Tawantinsuyu (the Inca Empire). The inhabitants of this region were seminomadic and were only partially incorporated into the empire, at best. Ethnically and culturally distinct from the Incas, these groups worshipped an entirely different pantheon of gods and followed different cultural and social customs from their highland counterparts. The average rainfall along the eastern slopes of the Andes was about 2,000–4,000 millimeters (79–157 in.) per year. Despite the wetness of the terrain, agriculture did not thrive in this area; the thin, easily eroded soils prevented the same kind of productivity that one would find along the southern slopes of the Andes. The inhabitants of the tropical region therefore practiced a different type of agriculture known as the slash-and-burn, or swidden, technique. After a few planting and harvesting cycles, farmers would burn their plots and leave them to lie fallow for several years. The ashes would eventually replenish the nutrient-depleted soil, and the farmers would move their plots and plant elsewhere while the previous fields regenerated. This agricultural practice was supplemented by hunting and gathering wild plants, which were essential for survival in the tropical rain forest and its immediate environs. The major resources of the tropical region include honey, wax, gold, various dyes, and feathers, which were submitted to the Inca Empire as tribute payment.

Northern Region

The region encompassing the northernmost end of the Northern Andes, including modern-day Ecuador and Colombia, is ecologically distinct from the rest of the Andean region. Dry grasslands known as *páramos*, located above the treeline at 3,000 meters (9,843 ft.) above sea level, occupy the areas between intersecting mountain ranges. The coastal region of Ecuador is dominated by swamps.

Flora and Fauna

The Andes support an incredible diversity of flora and fauna, some of which cannot be found in any other part of the world. Unlike the prehistoric civilizations of Africa, Asia, or Europe, which domesticated large load-bearing animals such as the horse, camel, or oxen, the Americas only had a few domesticates. In the Andean region, preconquest domesticated animals included the dog, llama, alpaca, guinea pig, and muscovy duck.

CAMELIDS

Camelids of the Andes include the llama *(Lama glama)*, alpaca *(Lama pacos)*, guanaco *(Lama guanicoe)*, and vicuña *(Vicugna vicugna)*. Only llamas and alpacas were successfully domesticated. The first archaeological evidence of llama domestication dates to around 4500–3100 B.C.E. in the highlands. Llamas could bear loads of up to 45 kilograms (100 lbs.) and were used to carry cargo across long distances. Members of the camelid family were also used for their meat, which was often dried to make *charqui*, or jerky. They were also used for their wool and their hides, as well as for ceremonial purposes. Llamas frequently served as sacrificial offerings to the deceased or had their intestines examined by specialized priests to help predict the future.

VISCACHA

The viscacha *(Lagidium peruanum)* is a small mammal indigenous to the Andes. It was hunted for its meat, and its soft fur was highly prized and woven into fine mantles for the nobility.

OTHER ANIMALS

The great mountain range also served as the breeding ground for domesticated animals such as the guinea pig (called *cuy* in Quechua), dog, and the muscovy duck. Important undomesticated mammals, used primarily for food and/or hide, included deer, armadillos, monkeys, rabbits, opossums, raccoons, bats, tapirs, partridge, waterfowl, and the bristle rat. The ferocious "power animals" of the Americas, the puma and jaguar, were hunted primarily for ceremonial purposes. Reptiles and amphibians indigenous to South America include the turtle and iguana. Aquatic life such as the seal, otter, sea lion, dolphin, manatee, lobster, clam, and shrimp have inhabited the coastal waters of South America for millennia. The Andean condor, a member of the vulture family, is one of the most important birds of the Andes. For many Andeans, the condor is a significant symbol. They see it as a mediator between the real world and the upper world and as a symbol of the mountains, which are in and of themselves highly sacred spaces.

Cultivation of Crops

Growing crops in the Andes required considerable modification of the landscape in addition to an intimate knowledge of the altitudinal and environmental requirements for different cultigens. Paradoxically, while more land suitable for cultivation is located in the higher altitudes, the majority of crops survive at lower altitudes, where there is less arable land. Terracing, or the practice of carving a series of "steps" into a mountain slope, allowed for intensive cultivation in otherwise agriculturally unproductive zones. Water shortages in the highlands presented another obstacle to crop cultivation, requiring the transportation of water via canals and irrigation systems.

The cultivation of domesticated crops in the Andes occurred around 1800 B.C.E. Many of the staple crops of the South American continent actually traveled southward from Mesoamerica through diffusion. What have come to be called "New World crops" that were cultivated by indigenous inhabitants throughout the Americas include maize, beans, cucurbits (a plant family that includes squash, cucumbers, and melons), chili peppers (*Capsicum*), tomatoes, and avocados. In addition to these pan–New World crops, crops cultivated exclusively in the Andes include quinoa and *cañihua*, both high-protein grains; *ulluco*, oca, and *mashua*, all tubers; and the now-universal potato.

MAIZE

Known more commonly as corn, maize (*Zea mays*) was one of the major agricultural staples of the peoples of the Andes. Under the Incas, intensive agriculture in the Cuzco Valley caused maize yields to reach unprecedented levels. Maize supplanted quinoa as the principal highland crop under the Incas, making up a substantial portion of the Inca diet. It only survives at relatively low altitudes, but this varies slightly depending on location. In the Andean highlands, maize can be grown at altitudes up to 3,900 meters (12,795 ft.) above sea level. To the north of the equator, however, maize can typically be grown only at altitudes below 3,000 meters (9,843 ft.). The growing season for maize in the highlands was from October to May, with harvest occurring in August.

COCA

The coca leaf was grown in the low-altitude *yungas* zone along the western slopes of the Andes as well as the *ceja de selva* along the eastern slopes that descended into the Amazonian basin. It was used for a variety of medicinal purposes; it was most frequently chewed in combination with lime to produce a chemical reaction that combated the negative effects of high altitudes on the body. Coca was also used in teas for similar effects. It played an important ceremonial role, used as an offering in funerary rituals and *huaca* veneration.

CHILI PEPPERS

Chili peppers are warm weather crops that were cultivated in the *yungas* and *ceja de selva* zones of the Andes. They were an important element to the Inca diet as a flavor additive and for their perceived medicinal properties.

CUCURBITS

Cucurbits include squash, cucumbers, and melons. Cucumbers (*Solanum muricatum*) were grown in the coastal valleys of Peru. They came in a variety of shapes, colors, and sizes.

Some members of the cucurbit family were used not only for their food but also for their outer skins, known as gourds. In fact, throughout coastal Peru gourds served as the primary eating and drinking vessels until they were supplanted by the advent of pottery. Despite the advantages of durability and flexibility in size provided by ceramic vessels, gourds, also known as *mates*, have been in continual use from prehistory through the present day.

COTTON

Cotton was produced in the low-altitude zones, both in the *yungas* descending into the Pacific coast and in the *ceja de selva* descending into the Amazonian basin.

QUINOA

In the Andean highlands past the limits of maize cultivation, quinoa (*Chenopodium quinoa*) dominates as the agricultural staple. It is a much hardier crop than maize, for it can survive frosts, short growing seasons, and the colder climates of the upper Andes up to 4,000 meters (13,123 ft.) above sea level. It varies in color, yielding yellow, red, white, or multicolored seeds.

CAÑIHUA

Cañihua (Chenopodium pallidicaula) is a grain grown in the Andes, particularly in the Altiplano region surrounding Lake Titicaca. It is a hardy cultigen and can survive even higher altitudes than its sister grain, quinoa.

TUBERS

The high Andes were the birthplace of several varieties of tubers, including oca (Oxalis tuberosa), mashua (Tropaeolum tuberosum), ulluco (Ullucus tuberosus), and the famous potato (Solanum tuberosum). Oca is a highland tuber, or root vegetable. It thrives in high-altitude, colder regions. There are two varieties of oca: One is sweet and can be eaten raw or cooked; the other is bitter and was typically freeze-dried and stored for times of low agricultural productivity. Freeze-dried oca is known as ckaya. Mashua, also known as añu, is another highland tuber. Mashua, along with a similar root crop known as ulluco, are hardy cultigens resistant to both draught and frost, which are both common occurrences in the high-altitude areas of the Andes.

The Andes are the sole birthplace of the potato, one of the world's most important crops. It was domesticated in the highlands as far back as 6000 B.C.E. in the altiplano near Lake Titicaca. Andean peoples cultivated more than eight species and 3,000 varieties of potatoes, of nearly every conceivable color, shape, and size: from purple to orange to white; from the size of a pinky to the size of a football. Potatoes were grown in the quechua, suni, and puna zones. Surplus potatoes underwent a process of sun- and freeze-drying to create a specialty called chuño, which could last in storage for several years.

Natural Resources

The Andes also yield deposits of minerals and precious metals such as tin, copper, silver, gold, lead, and zinc. Tin ores are primarily found in the altiplano region surrounding Lake Titicaca, western Bolivia, northern Chile, and northwestern Argentina. Tin was alloyed with copper to create tin bronze, used for tools, weapons, and other utilitarian objects. Gold could be found throughout the highlands. Copper abounded in Chile and northwest Argentina, and silver was concentrated primarily in Bolivia.

Guano, animal dung (specifically bird, bat, and llama droppings) used for fertilizing crops, was collected and submitted as tribute payment. It enriched soils with essential nutrients such as phosphorus and nitrogen in order to improve crop yields. A major source of guano was from along the rocky shores and islands off of the southern coast of Peru near modern-day Arequipa, where seabirds would congregate to hide from predators. Bird guano was collected from this area for use in maize and potato cultivation. Special lightweight floats were constructed to transport guano from nearby islands back to the mainland.

Climate

The climate of the many areas of the Inca Empire varied dramatically, including some of the driest places on earth to some of the most humid and lush, from bone-chilling arctic to inconsolably hot temperatures, and all of the gradations that fall in between these extremes. Generally speaking, the northern territories of the empire, particularly those located in modern-day Ecuador and northern Peru, tend to have the hottest climates, with relative temperatures descending as one moves south toward central and southern Peru, Bolivia, Chile, and Argentina. However, altitude plays an important role in the climate of a given region; generally speaking, the higher the altitude, the colder the temperatures. Climates tend to be tropical in regions up to 1,500 meters (4,921 ft.) above sea level. Temperate climates abound in areas between about 1,500 and 3,500 meters (4,921 and 11,483 ft.) in altitude. The colder mountain temperatures with the greatest disparity between cool daytime temperatures and freezing nighttime temperatures are found in areas 3,500–4,500 meters (11,483–14,764 ft.) in altitude. Exceedingly cold temperatures that remain consistently below freezing level dominate in regions of 4,500 meters and above. Although in most cases altitude and temperature are inversely correlated, various microclimates exist in the Andes that defy this generalization. In some cases, special combinations of latitude, altitude, and wind currents create special environments that are much warmer than those of their surrounding area. Warmer microclimates in the Andes were exploited by farmers for their potential to yield crops more typical of lower-altitude regions such as maize, beans, and chili peppers.

Rainfall varied according to region. The Cordillera Oriental is higher in altitude than the Cordillera Occidental, so it prevents rain clouds originating at the Atlantic Ocean from moving farther west. For this reason 90 percent of the precipitation in the Andean region runs east toward the Atlantic, while the remaining 10 percent runs west toward the Pacific Ocean. The western side of the Andes is therefore dramatically drier than the eastern side. The lands along the Pacific coast receive little to no annual rainfall, and inhabitants there depended heavily on irrigation systems that brought rainfall from the highlands down to the western lowlands. The western highlands fared somewhat better; rain generally reached most lands 1,500 meters (4,921 ft.) and above. The lands along the Cordillera Oriental experienced much greater seasonality, with distinct dry and rainy seasons. As one descends into the tropical rain forest, humidity and rainfall increases dramatically; there, the dry season lasts for only one month, and the remaining 11 months receive frequent rains.

Lakes

Located in the altiplano along the Peruvian and Bolivian border, Lake Titicaca is the second-largest lake in South America. It measures about 165 kilometers (103 mi.) wide and 60 kilometers (37 mi.) long and covers a staggering 8,500 square kilometers (3,282 sq. mi.) of land. It also ranks as one of the world's highest-altitude lakes, at nearly 4,000 meters (13,123 ft.) above sea level. The lake drains into Lake Poopó to the south. Titicaca was an important marine resource for highland peoples, who lived a great distance from the Pacific coast. The area

3.2 View of Lake Titicaca, located in the Altiplano on the Bolivian-Peruvian border. It was relevant to Inca origin stories, served as a pilgrimage site, and was exploited for its marine resources. (Eloise Quiñones Keber)

within which the lake is located was inhabited by Aymara-speaking peoples, the progenitors of the great Tiwanaku civilization, who were forcibly incorporated into the Inca Empire. Lake Titicaca yielded bountiful fish harvests, which were distributed by local fishermen throughout the empire as tribute payment. *Totora* reeds float throughout the lake, providing the raw material for the straw boats used for fishing and navigation by inhabitants of the area. The lake forms part of the fertile Titicaca basin, in which a range of agricultural products were grown to support the burgeoning empire. Despite the high altitudes of the Altiplano, the waters of Lake Titicaca prevented the surrounding agricultural lands from freezing over, which permitted the growing of crops. Moreover, the region's inhabitants developed an ingenious system of agriculture that involved the use of *cochas*, or sunken gardens. In times of drought, farmers would dig holes all the way down to the water table and grow crops within these depressions. *Cochas* ensured survival and stability in the face of unpredictable and potentially devastating environmental fluctuations.

LAKE JUNÍN

During the Inca period, Lake Junín was referred to by the Quechua name Chinchaycocha. It is located in the Central Andes in the puna, or high-altitude, arid mountain plateaus, at about 4,000 meters (13,123 ft.) above sea level. The lake was exploited for its marine resources such as fish and algae as well as its surrounding native vegetation.

Rivers

COASTAL AND HIGHLAND RIVERS

The most important rivers of the coast, from north to south, include the following: the Tumbes, Piura, La Leche, Lambayeque, Jequetepeque, Chicama, and Moche Rivers of the north coast; the Chancay, Rímac, Cañete, Chincha, Pisco, and Ica Rivers of the central coast; and the Acarí, Ocoña, and Sama Rivers of the southern coast. In the highlands, the Apurímac, Mantaro, Urubamba, Ucayali, and Marañon Rivers run through some of the most important territories of the Inca Empire. The Apurímac River originates in Lake Vilafro, which is located near the *nudo* of Vilcanota, and runs southeast. Running parallel to the Apurímac is the Urubamba, serving as the major water source for Cuzco, the capital of the Inca Empire.

AMAZON RIVER

The Amazon is the longest river in the world, covering more than 6 million square kilometers (2.3 million sq. mi.) of land. It is by far the most important river in South America, whose more than 1,000 tributaries feed into Brazil, Guyana, Venezuela, Colombia, Ecuador, Peru, and Bolivia. It is the major water source from which the rivers contained within the Inca Empire originate. The Apurímac River, which flows past Cuzco, merges into the Urubamba, which eventually becomes the Ucayali River. The Ucayali merges with the northeastern-flowing Marañón River to become the Amazon.

Earthquakes

Earthquakes are frequent in the areas that once made up the Inca Empire, occurring at intervals of about a decade. The plate tectonics that underlie the massive Andes Mountains are constantly moving, causing the earth to shake. Earthquakes were so common to Andean existence that the phenomenon was incorporated into religious and imperial worldviews; Pachacamac, the great oracle located near modern-day Lima, was considered the "Lord of the Earthquakes," and the Inca ruler Pachacuti was known as the "Earth Shaker."

SETTLEMENTS AND BEGINNINGS

Inca civilization did not emerge from a vacuum; contrary to origin myths that credit powerful gods and mythical kings as the sole architects of Inca cities and settlements, much of the area was already occupied and developed by the cultures that preceded the

Incas. These earlier cultures provided the prototypes for much of Inca settlement planning, architecture, and artistic styles—all of the ingredients of a powerful empire. Around 1400, the period immediately before the Incas ascended to power, the following groups dominated the different regions of western South America: the Chimú in the north coast; the Chancay in the central coast; the Ica and Chincha cultures of the south coast; various competing ethnic groups in the central highlands, including the Chanca, Wanka, Tarma, Xauxa, and Chinchaycocha groups; the Campa (also known as Amuesha) groups along the eastern slopes of the Andes toward the Amazon; and the Aymara kingdoms of the Lake Titicaca region. During the period of Inca conquest and expansion, throughout the 15th century, these regions became subjugated by the Incas, but many still retained much of their original cultural traditions despite their tributary status.

The Cuzco Valley encompassed the heartland of the Inca Empire, which would later come to be known by archaeologists as the Sacred Valley for its profusion of important ritual sites. It is located in the central highlands and is divided into three basins: the Cuzco basin located in the northwestern part of the valley, the Oropesa basin in the center, and the Lucre basin in the southeast. The basins stretch across the 40-kilometer (25-mi.) expanse of the valley. They are fed by the Huatanay River, which runs from Cuzco all the way to the Lucre basin, at which point it merges with the Vilcanota River. The Vilcanota mountain range runs along the northern and western parts of the Cuzco region. The Cuzco Valley ranges in altitude from about 3,000 to 4,800 meters (9,843–15,748 ft.) above sea level. The lower altitude regions support diverse agriculture, including Andean tubers such as *añu*, *ulluco*, and oca as well as grains such as quinoa and *tarwi*. Potatoes were grown in the colder, higher-altitude regions where they were freeze-dried to create *chuño*, a staple of the highland Inca diet.

Pre-Inca Settlement in the Cuzco Region

The Cuzco Valley and its immediate environs have been continuously occupied by human populations since 9500 B.C.E. Their archaeological phases roughly correspond to those of the rest of the Andean region with some local variations. Each phase brought a number of social, political, and cultural transformations to the Cuzco region that would ultimately have an impact on the development of Cuzco and of the Inca Empire as a whole. The chronology of the Cuzco region was made possible by the Cuzco Valley Archaeological Project, headed by archaeologist Brian Bauer and his colleagues.

ARCHAIC PERIOD (9500–2200 B.C.E.)

The Cuzco Archaic Period marks a time at which the last great glacial period of the Andes ended and the earliest human settlers began to populate the Cuzco area. They were hunter-gatherers who lived a nomadic existence and did not practice agriculture. They hunted deer, guinea pigs, foxes, and other mammals and foraged for wild plants as a means for survival. Over time the populations began to adopt a more sedentary existence with increased social complexity. The peoples of the Archaic Period initiated some important pan-Andean cultural practices, such as child sacrifice, that would endure for the next 10,000 years and become incorporated into Inca traditions.

FORMATIVE PERIOD (2200 B.C.E.–200 C.E.)

The Formative Period of the Cuzco region ushered the beginnings of sedentary, stratified agricultural societies. It also marks the period of the development of ceramics, which facilitated the transport and storage of food and water. Some of the earliest domesticates include quinoa, which was developed around 2200 B.C.E., camelids (llamas, alpacas, and vicuñas), and maize and beans, with evidence of cultivation around 200 B.C.E. Nucleated villages and considerable population density proliferated throughout the Formative Period, as well as the political development of chiefdoms. Mortuary evidence suggests that the Formative Period witnessed the emergence of social hierarchies, with a strong distinction between commoner and elite classes.

Wimpillay The site of Wimpillay, located south of where Cuzco would later stand, is the largest settlement of the Formative Period. It was situated northwest of its sister site, Muyu Orco, which may have served as Wimpillay's ritual precinct. Archaeologists believe that it was the locale of a major chiefdom that dominated more than 80 smaller villages in the Cuzco Valley during the Late Formative Period (500 B.C.E.–200 C.E.). Archaeologists have excavated an abundance of finely crafted pottery from the site, which indicates the rise of craft specialization and the existence of elite classes, who would have used these fine wares.

QOTAKALLI PERIOD (200–600)

During the Qotakalli Period the Cuzco Valley was dominated by a series of chiefdoms. Maize agriculture was practiced widely. Wimpillay began to decline in power after the Formative Period and was eclipsed by a number of villages that developed on the western end of the valley. Ample evidence suggests that the site of Pukara, located in the altiplano region, exerted considerable political and cultural influence over the Cuzco region. Unfortunately, little archaeological investigation has been conducted on this period of Andean prehistory, providing an incomplete understanding of it.

WARI PERIOD/MIDDLE HORIZON (540–1000)

After the Qotakalli Period, the Cuzco Valley fell under the sway of the rapidly growing Wari Empire, which reached its apogee around 700. The Wari Empire originated in the region of Ayacucho, located to the northwest of the Cuzco Valley. It was the first true empire in the Andean region, with a codified architectural and ceramic style and a series of administrative centers located throughout the central highlands. Imported and locally imitated Wari ceramics have been excavated at many sites in the Cuzco region, indicating the great spread and power of the Wari state, even outside its heartland. The spread of Wari cultural influence into the Cuzco Valley was certainly facilitated by nearby Pikillacta, which served as the second capital of the Wari. Located 30 kilometers (19 mi.) southeast of Cuzco and strategically situated between the Huatanay and Vilcanota Rivers, Pikillacta functioned as a major administrative center. It was a gridded, square-shaped precinct with administrative, ceremonial, and residential compounds. Pikillacta's construction was carried out by local residents through a rotational labor system. Although the material influence of the Wari on the Cuzco Valley is undeniable, some areas maintained the same settlement patterns throughout the period of Wari domination, suggesting that the empire's political impact was not felt equally by all of the region's inhabitants. Archaeological evidence demonstrates that the Lucre basin, to the southeast of the Cuzco Valley, where Pikillacta was located, underwent greater transformation than did the Cuzco basin.

KILLKE PERIOD/LATE INTERMEDIATE PERIOD (1000–1400)

After the fall of the Wari by 1000, a series of different ethnic groups dominated the Cuzco Valley, which often rivaled one another in the quest for power over the region. These included the Masca, Chillque, Tambo, Anta, Limatambo, Quilliscachi, Yucay, Lupaca, Colla, Chanca, Inca, and Ayarmaca peoples, who populated different parts of the Cuzco basin. The widespread political transformations that occurred between 1000 and 1400 are grouped under the Killke Period because of a particular type of ceramic known as Killke pottery that proliferated throughout the Cuzco Valley during this time. Archaeologists have been able to retrace many of the initial steps toward the development of the Inca state through an analysis of the changes in distribution of this pottery type at different settlements over time.

Several large-scale changes occurred during the Killke Period that set the stage for later Inca expansion. Increases in agricultural productivity went hand in hand with rising population density. Some of the settlements in the Cuzco Valley began to undergo urbanization in order to accommodate growing human populations. The development of defensive architecture and the strategic placement of settlements further confirm the competition among the dominant ethnic groups of the region.

Archaeological and ethnohistorical evidence also tells us that despite the frequent military conflict between the numerous ethnic groups of the Cuzco Valley, many also formed political alliances through trade and strategic marriages among elites and rulers. These political partnerships resulted in the consolidation of the Cuzco Valley's dozens of distinct ethnic groups into a handful of chiefdoms by the end of the Killke Period: the Huayllacan, the Anta, the Ayarmaca, and the Pinahua. These warring chiefdoms later became subsumed by the Inca conquerors in the late 14th and early 15th centuries.

Acamama According to the chronicler Guamán Poma de Ayala, the village of Acamama, founded by the Ayarmaca, served as the early foundation for the great Inca capital of Cuzco. It was situated at the confluence of two rivers, the Huatanay and the Tullumayo, which reflected a pan-Andean belief of complementarity, known as *tinkuy*. Acamama was divided into four parts: Quinti Cancha, known as the hummingbird sector; Chumbi Cancha, the weaver's sector; Sairi Cancha, the tobacco sector; and Yarambuy Cancha, a mixed sector. This division most likely inspired the decision to divide the Inca Empire, Tawantinsuyu (which means "the four parts together"), into four *suyus*. Furthermore, the empire was divided into a *hanan* (upper) and *hurin* (lower) sector, which also manifested itself in the site planning at Cuzco and other Inca cities. Acamama may have laid the foundations for what was later to become Cuzco, but its status as myth or reality remains in question.

Inca Cuzco

Following the legend of the founding of Cuzco, chroniclers recounted that the settlement of Acamama was renamed Cuzco, which literally means "dried-up lakebed." Cuzco is situated at 3,450 meters (11,319 ft.) above sea level, making it one of the highest-altitude cities in the Americas. It is located in the Huatanay River valley, bounded by the Saphi and Tullumayo Rivers. These merge at the southeast sector of Cuzco into the Huatanay River and flow into a gorge 20 kilometers (12.5 mi.) to the east of the city, where the Huatanay becomes the Urubamba River. The city itself was situated on an alluvial fan, which is a deposit of soil and rock left by a stream. The Pampa de Anta, a marshy region, lies to the west of Cuzco. To the north and northwest of Cuzco is a limestone plateau; the lands to the south of the

city were reserved for agriculture. Surrounding Cuzco's immediate environs were a series of agricultural terraces, fed by extensive irrigation canals. The area was also dominated by natural springs, carved and sculpted rocks, natural and human-made fountains, and reservoirs, which were imbued with sacred significance by the Incas.

Constructing an Empire

Although modern terminology guides the categories that describe the physical landscape of the Incas, the empire's rulers and subjects thought of their environment under different terms. The vast territory under Inca rule was divided and subdivided in many ways, each of which corresponded to culturally defined notions of space and the landscape. The Incas often compared the layout of their empire to the human body: Quito, the second Inca capital, located in the north and the present-day capital of Ecuador, constituted the symbolic head of the universe; Cuzco, the main capital, was the navel. The Incas saw their empire as encompassing nearly all of the land and sea of the known universe.

Suyus

The four *suyus*, or quarters, were the largest territorial units of the Inca Empire. Indeed, reference to this division of land is inherent to the very meaning of Tawantinsuyu, the Quechua term for the Inca Empire, which translates into "land of the four quarters," or "the four parts together." These quarters were known as Chinchaysuyu (northern), Cuntisuyu (western), Antisuyu (eastern), and Collasuyu (southern). Each of the *suyus* were named after either the dominant ethnic group that inhabited the territory or an important settlement: Chinchaysuyu was named after the Chinchas; Collasuyu was named after the Colla culture, Cuntisuyu was named after the province of Cunti, and Antisuyu was named

The Four Suyus

Caribbean Sea

ATLANTIC
OCEAN

Chinchaysuyu

Antisuyu

Cuzco

Lake Titicaca

Cuntisuyu

Collasuyu

PACIFIC
OCEAN

N

| 0 | 500 miles |
| 0 | 500 km |

Map 3 The Four Suyus: *Chinchaysuyu, Cuntisuyu, Antisuyu, and Collasuyu*

after the eastern slopes of the continent's famous mountain chain, which in Quechua was called *Anti* and later became hispanicized into *Andes.* This division of land into four *suyus* became integrated into the identity of its inhabitants and served as important boundary markers for demarcating the empire. It also had bureaucratic utility; the dividing up of territory into four manageable entities facilitated the collection of tribute and census taking. Although the most common visual emblem to refer to the four *suyus* was four squares arranged to create one large square, the *suyus* were far from uniform in size, shape, or political importance.

CHINCHAYSUYU

Chinchaysuyu corresponds to the north coast of Peru, Ecuador, the northern highlands, and part of the central highlands. Chinchaysuyu was the most heavily populated *suyu* and was also the most esteemed, as it emanates from the *hanan* region of Cuzco.

CUNTISUYU

Cuntisuyu encompasses a small expanse of land triangulated by the Nazca region of the south coast, Arequipa, and Cuzco. It begins at the area demarcating the *hurin* sector of Cuzco, stretching to the south and southwest quarters of the Inca Empire.

ANTISUYU

Antisuyu includes the eastern territories of Peru and Bolivia. The Huatanay River served as the boundary line between Antisuyu and its southern counterpart, Collasuyu.

COLLASUYU

Collasuyu covers southern Peru, part of Bolivia, Chile, and Argentina. It encompassed the largest amount of land, followed by Chinchaysuyu, Antisuyu, and Cuntisuyu.

Huamani

A *huamani* was the next largest territorial unit after *suyus*, corresponding to an Inca province. It was a conglomerate of different provincial centers and could contain members of different ethnic groups subsumed by the Incas.

Cuzco

Cuzco, considered by the Incas the navel of the universe, was the political, administrative, and sacred center of gravity of the empire. Even though it was a planned city with an extraordinary sense of order, it yielded to the irregular topography and shape of the land to create a dynamic union between the natural and human-made world. Cuzco served as an expression of Inca power through its manipulation of the environment.

The city itself supposedly took the shape of a puma, with the "head" at the fortress of Sacsayhuamán and the "tail" at the lower extreme of the city, although archaeologists continue to debate whether this element of city planning, mentioned in the chronicles, was intended to be taken literally or figuratively. It was divided into an upper section (hanan) and a lower section (hurin). Hanan and hurin were complementary forces, each with a series of distinct associations. Hanan was associated with strength, masculinity, and dominance, while hurin was seen as its feminine counterpart, a weaker and subordinate force. This upper and lower division of Cuzco geographically separated royal descendants of the Inca kings into two locations. The descendants of the first five Inca rulers, from Manco Cápac to Cápac Yupanqui, were distributed throughout the hurin region of Cuzco. The descendants of the last five Inca rulers, from Inca Roca to Topa Inca Yupanqui, lived in the hanan section of the city. Although the hurin part of Cuzco was considered the "weaker" half of its hanan counterpart, the placement of the Coricancha, the most sacred building of the Inca Empire, in hurin territory demonstrates an effort to balance out these unequal components. The hanan section was dominated by aesthetically carved boulders and agricultural terraces, while hurin contained a large number of hilltop shrines.

In addition to the internal divisions within Cuzco that emphasized political and social hierarchies, Cuzco also served as the source from which geographical divisions of the empire emanated. The territorial lines that demarcated the boundaries of the four suyus originated at the Coricancha. The ceques, or imaginary lines punctuated by huacas (sacred location) along which the Incas conducted ritual pilgrimages, radiated out from Cuzco. The ceque system, which was composed of 42 lines and 328 huacas, symbolically connected Cuzco to its outlying provinces. This had the power not only to establish dominance over peripheral regions through state-mandated impositions of pathways and huacas but also to incorporate them into Cuzco's political and religious orbit.

Shrines intended to glorify past rulers formed an important part of the imperial landscape of Cuzco and its environs. The widespread construction of royal shrines began under the reign of Pachacuti, who was considered the great unifier of the Inca Empire. These shrines took the form of houses, fountains, multipurpose buildings, terraces, and thrones. All royal shrines incorporated aspects of the natural environment into their conception, whether through the use of natural bedrock as the foundation or the creation of a fountain to provide a conduit for the flow of natural mountain springs. Shrines served as physical reminders to the populace of Inca domination over the land. Pumamarca, located in the modern-day town of San Sebastián, near Cuzco, is one of dozens of examples of Inca royal shrines. It is a house constructed of finely cut masonry that contained the mummy of Pachacuti's wife. Cusicancha, the birthplace of Pachacuti, and Patallacta, the house in which he died, were also considered important shrines associated with the great Inca ruler. Some of these huacas were located along the ceque lines, thus creating a salient connection between the natural environment and the realm of politics.

Tumbes

Tumbes served as the northernmost settlement of the Inca Empire. It was the last stopping point on the coastal Inca highway, located at the fringes of so-called civilization. Tumbes marked the territorial point at which the Incas could no longer penetrate, having been repeatedly attacked by tribes in the north. Moreover, the tropical forest provided a natural barrier for further development. Tumbes was built as a fortress to prevent from outside attack. It also housed a temple to the Sun God and an acllahuasi, or house of the chosen women, where acllacuna, specialized weavers and chicha brewers who worked in the service of the Inca king, performed their duties.

Caranqui

The settlement of Caranqui is located in the present-day province of Imbabura, Ecuador, just to the north of Quito, the second capital of the Incas. According to Spanish accounts, the Caranqui allied memorate the slaughter of all of the men of Caranqui by Huayna Cápac's army who were subsequently dumped into the lake. Caranqui was located along the Inca highway, and, like Tumbes, was equipped with palaces of finely cut stone, a temple dedicated to the Sun, and an *acllahuasi* with more than 200 *acllacuna*. Two different accounts explain its significance as an Inca site. According to Juan de Betanzos, Atahualpa commissioned the construction of buildings at the site to commemorate the death of his father, Huayna Cápac. According to Fernando Montesinos, however, Huayna Cápac ordered construction to house his court and left his then two-year-old son, Atahualpa, there to be cared for by the locals as a means of establishing his legitimacy in the north. Its inhabitants practiced Inca customs, such as imitating Inca dress and agricultural techniques.

Quito

Quito, the modern-day capital of Ecuador and the second capital of the Incas, was located at the northern fringes of the empire. It officially became incorporated into the empire as the second capital under Huayna Cápac, the penultimate Inca ruler before the Spanish conquest. The original inhabitants of the region, including the Palta and Cañari tribes, had continually resisted Inca domination and posed a constant threat to Inca success. They were ultimately supplanted by new groups of assimilated Incas mandated to settle new territories known as *mitmaqkuna*. Although not as well preserved as Cuzco, remnants of Inca architecture still exist in Quito, and Inca-style pottery fragments have been found, serving as testament to the extent of Inca domination in the area.

Tumipampa

Tumipampa was Ecuador's other important Inca settlement, established in the final decades of Inca rule. It was located in the province inhabited by the ethnic Cañari group, who actively resisted Inca rule through the conquest and even assisted the Spaniards in their destruction of the empire. Like

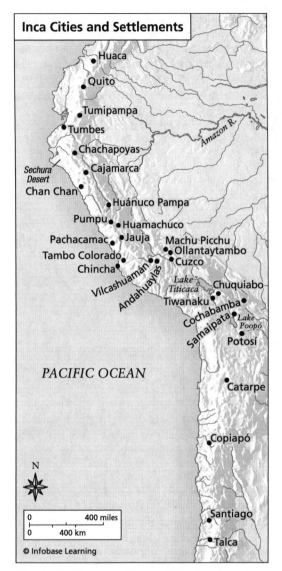

Map 4 *Significant Inca Cities and Settlements*

with the nearby Otovalos, Cochasquis, and Cayambes groups to resist Inca incursions for a total of 17 years. Caranqui was finally converted into an Inca settlement during the famous conquests of Ecuador by Huayna Cápac. The conquest was not a peaceful one, and, indeed, the nearby Lake Yaguarcocha (Lake of Blood) was named as such to com-

Cuzco, Tumipampa (modern-day Cuenca, Ecuador) was positioned at the confluence of two rivers. It contained many sumptuous royal lodgings decorated with objects of precious metals and stones. It also contained an *acllahuasi*, which the chronicler Pedro de Cieza de León noted housed more than 200 chosen women (*acllacuna*). Storage units, known as *colcas*, were situated across the terrain, containing surplus textiles of fine quality along with other luxury goods. Immediately preceding the Spanish conquest, it was the site of military strife between the two half brothers vying for the throne, Atahualpa and Huáscar. The Cañari aided Huáscar in capturing Atahualpa here, but after Atahualpa managed to escape, he staged a violent retaliation, killing many Cañaris in the process. Tumipampa and Quito were connected by the same mountain road that led to Cuzco in the central highlands.

Chachapoyas

Chachapoyas is located to the west of the Marañón River in the northern highlands. It was populated by the Huanca, Chillao, Cascayunca, Paclla, and Chacha ethnic groups, who were all incorporated under the jurisdiction of the Chachapoyas kingdom before their conquest by the Incas. Their dominion, which exerted control over much of the Northern Andes, flourished from about 800 until the late 15th century. The territory encompasses a range of ecological niches, including *páramos*, or grasslands, as well as the *quechua* and *ceja de selva* zones along the eastern slopes of the Andes. These areas supported the cultivation of chili peppers, cotton, coca, maize, squash, and beans, particularly in the fertile Utcubamba Valley. At higher elevation areas, they cultivated potatoes, tubers such as oca, *ulluco*, and *mashua*, as well as quinoa. Other specialty goods at Chachapoyas that were submitted to the Incas as tribute include honey, beeswax (used in metallurgy), dyes, herbs used by shamans (medicine men and women), and feathers. According to Spanish chroniclers, the Chachapoyas were famed as shamans and warriors. They violently resisted Inca expansion, successfully driving out the armies of Huayna Cápac twice before meeting their eventual defeat in the 1470s. Chachapoyas served as an important garrison to prevent incursions from neighboring ethnic groups that had not been successfully integrated into the Inca Empire. After the Inca conquest the Chachapoyas were divided into tribute-paying units. The population was also considerably reshuffled; some were sent to nearby Cajamarca, others were resettled in a Chachapoyas neighborhood in Cuzco, while other groups were sent as far away as Lake Titicaca. In addition to the resettlement of local populations to distant lands, *mitmaqkunas*, or colonists appointed by the Incas to establish order in newly acquired territories, were dispatched to Chachapoyas to spread Inca customs and the Quechua language and to quell potential rebellions.

Cajamarca

Located in the northern highlands between the upper Jequetepeque and Chicama drainage, Cajamarca was an important kingdom prior to the Inca conquest. It was populated by the Cusimancu ethnic group. According to colonial documents, the Cusimancu and the Chimú formed alliances in an effort to defend themselves from Inca domination over the area but eventually succumbed to defeat in the late 15th century. Under the Incas, Cajamarca was transformed into a regal city, with storehouses, royal lodgings, and temples. It also had thermal baths for the nobility, which still survive to the present day. The fertile lands adjacent to the city were used for agricultural cultivation. In terms of administration, the Incas brought in *mitmaqkuna* to manage the tribute payers of Cajamarca and its neighboring settlements. Cajamarca is best known for its significance in the Spanish conquest, as the site where Atahualpa was captured by Francisco Pizarro.

Huamachuco

Located to the south of Cajamarca in a large valley in the northern highlands of Peru, Huamachuco was one of the many provincial capitals of the Incas. Archaeological fieldwork and ethnohistorical documents have revealed that the site was a *tambo*, or an Inca way station for travelers and royalty. It was equipped with many characteristically Inca urban structures: a large trapezoidal plaza; *kallankas*, or long rectangular halls; and *colcas*, or storehouses. It was of particular importance for its proximity to the Inca road system. One road ran southwest from Huamachuco to the highlands, and another ran west all the way to the coast. Colonial-period documents suggest that Huamachuco contained a great number of *mitmaqkunas* relocated from their home communities to work in foreign lands. The homelands of these various groups of *mitmaqkuna* remains unknown, but they likely came from nearby coastal and highland regions.

Huánuco Pampa

Huánuco Pampa was one of the most important provincial capitals of the Incas, located 600 kilometers (373 mi.) northwest of Cuzco near the Marañón River on a high plain. It was a planned settlement covering two square kilometers (0.77 sq. mi.) of land with a large plaza at the center of the site. The plaza served as the locus of public ceremonial activity such as feasting and religious festivities. The site was subdivided into a *hanan* and *hurin* section, and roads leading out from the plaza created 12 equally sized divisions of the territory (which could be further subdivided into four sections), corresponding to the symbolic division of Cuzco. Over the course of Inca rule, Huánuco Pampa witnessed the construction of 4,000 buildings, many of which were used for administrative and economic functions. Archaeological evidence demonstrates the presence of an *acllahuasi*, for chosen women who brewed *chicha* (corn beer) and wove fine textiles for the Inca ruler. The site was also equipped with 500 storehouses along its periphery, containing a wealth of surplus goods such as food, clothing, and military supplies.

Chincha

Chincha was a settlement located in the Chincha Valley off the southern coast of Peru. It was peacefully integrated into the Inca Empire during the latter's period of expansion. Chincha was populated by fishermen, farmers, and merchants who managed the long-distance sea trade. The merchants of Chincha facilitated the exchange of *Spondylus* shells from Ecuador, known as *mullu* in Quechua, which had great ceremonial significance for the Incas. The settlements dispersed throughout the Chincha Valley were originally incorporated into the regional kingdom established there in the Late Intermediate Period. Under the Inca Empire, however, the lord of Chincha was not removed from power like those of other polities forcefully incorporated into the expanding state but was instead accorded with a new title as subsidiary lord. In fact, the lord of Chincha was accompanying Atahualpa when the Inca king met the Spanish conquistador Francisco Pizarro at Cajamarca. The Chincha capital, whose original name is unknown but is referred to as La Centinela by archaeologists, contains several specifically Inca architectural features integrated with preexisting architectural and site-planning traditions of the south coast. These included the Sun Temple, compounds for the production of specialized crafts, and palaces that housed residential and administrative functions. There was also an oracle shrine to the supreme deity of the Chinchas, Chinchaycamac, who was believed to be their creator god, although its location at La Centinela remains unconfirmed by archaeologists. The Incas allowed the continued worship of the oracle, but similar to the oracle of Pachacamac, near modern-day Lima, it was integrated into an Inca architectural backdrop and worshipped in conjunction with other Inca deities.

Vilcashuamán

Vilcashuamán was an important province for the Incas, serving numerous imperial functions. It was located in the Chanca territory, which belonged to the first ethnic group conquered by the Incas. Vilcashuamán was strategically located along the main highland road, making it an important node within the Inca political and ceremonial circuit: It was a site for military training; it had 700 storehouses (*colcas*) that contained surplus maize; and it served as an important ritual center. It was located at the literal center of the Inca Empire, midpoint between

Ecuador and Chile. It had a large plaza that could hold up to 20,000 people as well as an *usnu*, or a stone platform used in Inca ceremony. The *usnu* at Vilcashuamán, located on the eastern end of the plaza, was especially elaborate, with two seats cut into the single stone slab and originally covered with precious stones and metals. Chroniclers mention that at the center of the plaza was another stone slab upon which child and llama sacrifices were conducted.

Cochabamba

Cochabamba, located in present-day eastern Bolivia, contained many of the mainstays of imperial Inca architecture and site planning, such as an *acllahuasi*, an *usnu*, *kallankas*, and *cancha* compounds. It also contained extensive agricultural tracts that were cultivated in the service of the state; according to Spanish chroniclers, 14,000 farmers were employed to work the fields.

Pumpu

Pumpu was a settlement built by the Incas in the central highlands, located in modern-day Junín, Peru. It was chosen as a site for an administrative center for its location at the confluence of three rivers—of propitious significance—as well as its proximity to the Inca road system and easy access to the Pacific coast. It contained the hallmarks of Inca urban planning, including an *usnu*, *acllahuasi*, two *kallankas*, *colcas*, and baths. However, the use of local construction materials and techniques suggest that the actual building of the site was conducted by the region's inhabitants. Pumpu allowed for Inca bureaucrats to oversee economic activities in the area, which centered on the herding of camelids and weaving.

Samaipata

Samaipata is located in the modern-day province of Santa Cruz in eastern Bolivia. According to historical sources, it was an administrative center from which a local leader appointed by the Incas oversaw the eastern region of the empire, known as Collasuyu. It is located at the easternmost limits of the Inca Empire, flanking the tropical lowlands occupied by ethnic groups that had resisted Inca domination. Its exact function and significance remains up for debate; although some documents claim that it also served as a fortress, archaeological evidence suggests that it served primarily as an administrative and ritual site.

Samaipata features three large platforms that each contains a series of buildings. On the lowest platform is a large plaza, measuring 100 meters (328 ft.) in length, facing a *kallanka*, or a long rectangular hall, with eight entryways. Its ritual dimension is embodied in the site's massive stone outcrop, a densely carved and sculpted sandstone ridge. Stone outcrops were the physical markers of Inca presence; it was the way that the Incas made their instantly recognizable mark on the land to demonstrate their domination over land and peoples incorporated into the empire. The stone outcrops at Samaipata rank the largest ever created under the Incas, measuring 250 meters by 50 meters (820 × 164 ft.). They consist of canals to allow for the movement of water, large and small niches, zigzag channels, geometric shapes, and depressions, all deeply carved into the bedrock. There are also carved representations of animals such as serpents and felines. The carvings and depressions in the outcrop facilitated the practice of libations (ritual pouring of liquids as offerings) and other ceremonies conducted on the rock itself.

Catarpe

Located at the southern edge of the Inca Empire in northeastern Chile, Catarpe served as an administrative center and as a *tambo*. It had great significance to the Incas not only for the bureaucratic functions it achieved but for providing a site from which to mobilize the Inca army for their conquests farther south over the rest of modern-day Chile. It was strategically situated along the Inca coastal road and probably served as a stopping point for travelers en route to the Altiplano to the northeast.

Tucumán

Tucumán was located in northwestern Argentina. It was incorporated into the Inca Empire under Huayna Cápac. He developed an alliance with the Diaguita and Calchaquí peoples indigenous to the area, who served as allies to Inca military forces attempting to expand the empire toward the southern and southeastern regions of South America.

Reading

Physical Climate and Geography

Duccio Bonavia, "The Role of the Ceja de Selva in the Cultural Development of Pre-Columbian Peru." In *The Inca World: The Development of Pre-Columbian Peru, A.D. 1000–1534*, edited by Laura Laurencich Minelli, 121–131 (Norman: University of Oklahoma Press, 2000).

Sophie D. Coe, *America's First Cuisines* (Austin: University of Texas Press, 1994).

Hideo Kimura, "Andean Exchange: A View from Amazonia." In *Andean Ecology and Civilization: An Interdisciplinary Perspective on Andean Ecological Complementarity*, edited by Shozo Masuda, Izumi Shimada, and Craig Morris, 491–504 (Tokyo, Japan: University of Tokyo Press, 1985).

Shozo Masuda, "Algae Collectors and *Lomas*." In *Andean Ecology and Civilization: An Interdisciplinary Perspective on Andean Ecological Complementarity*, edited by Shozo Masuda, Izumi Shimada, and Craig Morris, 233–250 (Tokyo, Japan: University of Tokyo Press, 1985).

Craig Morris, "From Principles of Ecological Complementarity to the Organization and Administration of *Tawantinsuyu*." In *Andean Ecology and Civilization: An Interdisciplinary Perspective on Andean Ecological Complementarity*, edited by Shozo Masuda, Izumi Shimada, and Craig Morris, 477–490 (Tokyo, Japan: University of Tokyo Press, 1985).

Michael E. Moseley, *The Incas and Their Ancestors: The Archaeology of Peru.* 2nd ed. (London: Thames & Hudson, 2001).

John V. Murra, "Herds and Herders in the Inca State." In *Man, Culture, and Animals: The Role of Animals in Human and Ecological Adjustments*, edited by A. Leeds and A. Vayda, 185–215 (Washington, D.C.: American Association for the Advancement of Science, 1965).

———, "The Limits and Limitations of the 'Vertical Archipelago' in the Andes." In *Andean Ecology and Civilization: An Interdisciplinary Perspective on Andean Ecological Complementarity*, edited by Shozo Masuda, Izumi Shimada, and Craig Morris, 15–20 (Tokyo, Japan: University of Tokyo Press, 1985).

Javier Pulgar Vidal, *Geografía del Perú: Las ocho regiones naturales del Perú* (Lima: Editorial Universo, 1963).

John H. Rowe, "The Sunken Gardens of the Peruvian Coast," *American Antiquity* 34, no. 3 (1969): 320–325.

Carl O. Sauer, "Geography of South America." In *Handbook of South American Indians.* Vol. 6, edited by Julian H. Steward, 319–340 (New York: Cooper Square Publishers, 1963).

Settlements and Beginnings

Brian S. Bauer, *Ancient Cuzco: Heartland of the Inca* (Austin: University of Texas Press, 2004).

———, *The Development of the Inca State* (Austin: University of Texas Press, 1992).

Brian S. Bauer and R. Alan Covey, "Processes of State Formation in the Inca Heartland (Cuzco, Peru)," *American Anthropologist* 104, no. 3 (2002): 846–864.

Wendell C. Bennet, "The Archaeology of the Central Andes." In *Handbook of South American Indians*, Bureau of American Ethnology, Bulletin 143. Vol. 2, edited by Julian Steward, 61–147 (Washington, D.C.: Smithsonian Institution Press, 1946).

R. Alan Covey, *How the Incas Built Their Heartland: State Formation and the Innovation of Imperial Strategies in the Sacred Valley, Peru* (Ann Arbor: University of Michigan Press, 2006).

———, "A Processual Study of Inca State Formation," *Journal of Anthropological Archaeology* 22 (2003): 333–357.

Richard P. Schnaedel, "Early State of the Incas." In *The Early State*, edited by Henri Claessen and Peter Skalnik, 289–320 (The Hague, Netherlands: Mouton, 1978).

Luis E. Valcárcel, "Cuzco Archaeology." In *Handbook of South American Indians*. Vol. 2, edited by Julian H. Steward, 177–182 (Washington, D.C.: Smithsonian Institution, 1946).

Constructing an Empire

Brian S. Bauer, *The Sacred Landscape of the Incas: The Cuzco Ceque System* (Austin: University of Texas Press, 1998).

Tamara Bray, "Archaeological Survey in Northern Highland Ecuador: Inca Imperialism and the Pais Caranqui," *World Archaeology* 24, no. 2 (1992): 218–233.

Terence D'Altroy, *Provincial Power in the Inka Empire* (Washington, D.C.: Smithsonian Institution Press, 1992).

———, "Transitions in Power: Centralization of Wanka Political Organization under Inka Rule," *Ethnohistory* 34, no. 1 (1987): 78–102.

Timothy Earle et al., *Archaeological Field Research in the Upper Mantaro, Peru, 1982–83: Investigations of Inka Expansion and Exchange*, Monograph 28, Institute of Archaeology (Los Angeles: University of California Press, 1987).

Ian S. Farrington, "Ritual Geography, Settlement Patterns and the Characterization of the Provinces of the Inka Heartland," *World Archaeology* 23 (1992): 368–385.

John Hyslop, *Inka Settlement Planning* (Austin: University of Texas Press, 1990).

Catherine J. Julien, "Guano and Resource Control in Sixteenth-Century Arequipa." In *Andean Ecology and Civilization: An Interdisciplinary Perspective on Andean Ecological Complementarity*, edited by Shozo Masuda, Izumi Shimada, and Craig Morris, 185–232 (Tokyo, Japan: University of Tokyo Press, 1985).

Daniel G. Julien, "Late Pre-Inkaic Ethnic Groups in Highland Peru: An Archaeological-Ethnohistorical Model of the Political Geography of the Cajamarca Region," *Latin American Antiquity* 4, no. 3 (September 1993): 246–273.

Mary B. La Lone and Darrell E. La Lone, "The Inka State in the Southern Highlands: State Administrative and Production Enclaves," *Ethnohistory* 34 (1987): 47–62.

Michael Malpass, *Provincial Inca: Archaeological and Ethnohistorical Assessment of the Impact of the Inca State* (Iowa City: University of Iowa Press, 1993).

Dorothy Menzel, "The Inca Conquest of the South Coast of Peru," *Southwestern Journal of Anthropology* 15 (1959): 125–142.

Craig Morris and Donald E. Thompson, *Huánuco Pampa: An Inca City and Its Hinterland* (London: Thames & Hudson, 1985).

Alberto Rex González, "Inca Settlement Patterns in a Marginal Province of the Empire." In *Prehistoric Settlement Patterns: Essays in Honor of Gordon R. Willey*, edited by Evon Z. Vogt and Richard M. Leventhal, 337–360 (Cambridge, Mass.: Harvard University Press, 1983).

4

SOCIETY AND GOVERNMENT

The Incas first appeared in Andean South America sometime in the 12th–13th centuries, rising in the context of a power vacuum after the collapse of the earlier Tiwanaku (Tiahuanaco) and Wari (Huari) civilizations, centered in the Titicaca basin and central Andean highlands, respectively. The fall of these civilizations created an environment of ministates and chiefdoms acting more or less independently and competing among one another for political and military superiority. By the 14th century the Incas were simply one among many autonomous ethnic and political entities, not yet an empire, not even the most powerful group in the Cuzco Valley—where they would eventually establish their capital. It is somewhat curious why the Inca, and not another group, organized efficiently enough to dominate not only the region around Cuzco but all of Andean South America from northern Ecuador to modern-day Santiago, Chile, and from the coast to the cordillera. There is no single reason why this happened, nor is there any single reason why the Incas grew rapidly and suddenly into a major imperial power, although modern scholarship has proposed numerous tantalizing possibilities regarding how it happened, why so suddenly, and how it was managed. In the broadest strokes the reasons break down into categories of conflict and competition, internal and external transformations, demographics, environmental factors, the quest for wealth, and ideological motives, all of which, at one point or another, were in the Incas' favor. This chapter attempts to put these issues in perspective according to what is known and understood of how Inca society and government were organized. It then discusses factors of empire including growth, development, maintenance, imperial myth, and collapse.

Social Structure and Class Hierarchy

At the onset of Inca expansion the Andean region was divided among ethnic groups of varying power ruled by chiefs called *hatun kuraka*, or great lords. In turn, these great lords ruled over subordinate chiefdoms of lower rank. As Inca hegemony spread, the *hatun kuraka* recognized their own subordination to the Sapa Inca, or "unique Inca," that is, the Inca king. The Sapa Inca was surrounded by the Cuzco aristocracy, which at the time of the Spanish conquest consisted of 10 *panaqas* (*panacas*) or kinship groups of deceased kings, and the royal *ayllu* (plural, *ayllus*), or royal extended family. An *ayllu*, at its most basic, is an extension of the nuclear family unit to include relatives who exchange labor, own land in common, and act as a kind of collective. *Ayllus* were further subdivided into the Incas of royal blood, then Incas of Cuzco (nobles), and lastly, the Incas by privilege, the ethnic groups living within the Cuzco region but outside the capital. Priests and coastal lords deeply enmeshed in trade enjoyed privileged status and could be considered members of an elite social class. Administrators of the Inca imperial bureaucracy similarly assumed positions of confidence and power. Below the elite on the social ladder were artisans, commoners, *mitmaqkuna*, fishermen, and *yanakuna*, each of which will be discussed below.

As the Inca realm spread, new classes of lords and provincial elite emerged. In some instances the Incas adopted local power structures as their own or used preexisting ones to complement the growth of their own institutions of power. Ultimately this meant that despite Inca attempts at a unified social empire, some differences in power structures and class hierarchy remained in place. Beginning around 1470 the Inca conquest of the northern kingdom of Chimú (Chimor), which was centered on the coast of northern Peru and Ecuador, profoundly impacted Inca societal and governmental development. It seems clear that the Incas were highly impressed by the splendor and opulence of the lord of this northern kingdom and in turn tried to emulate the opulence of the nobles and the court. With the conquest of Chimú, the political power of the Sapa Inca was greatly increased.

Social Organization

AYLLU

An *ayllu* was essentially a kin-based community, acting as a collective or corporate entity. In theory the *ayllu* followed the male hereditary line in an endogamous group (meaning marriage only occurs within the group). Common descent from a mythical ancestor tied them all together. The *ayllu* collectively owned territory and water rights and shared reciprocal obligations and labor burdens within the *ayllu*. The *ayllu* provided work groups to the *kuraka*, who was a local chief. Several different *ayllus* could compose a town or community.

Ayllus were further subdivided into two semi-equal halves (moieties) called *hanan* and *hurin* (upper and lower, respectively), and then quarters, called *suyus*. These divisions were geographical (Cuzco as well as other cities were divided into halves and then quarters), social (residents in different quarters pursued different tasks), and administrative. The Inca name for the empire (Tawantinsuyu) derives from this subdivision, as it translates to "land of the four quarters."

HANAN AND *HURIN*

The Inca capital of Cuzco as well as most chiefdoms in the empire were divided into two halves, one upper *(hanan)* and one lower *(hurin)*. In its spatial sense, *hanan* and *hurin* divided the urban plan into complementary upper and lower halves that separated royal kinship groups. Each half was ruled by a chief and was home to a specific part of the population based on kin ranking determined by age—the older lineages were located in the *hanan* designation. Some scholars argue that this relation actually constituted a diarchy, wherein two kings ruled simultaneously. In this sense Inca cities demonstrate the social hierarchy that governed their society. Outside Cuzco, in provincial centers, the Incas reorganized cities and settlements according to the same principles established in Cuzco and thereby replicated the basic tenets of Inca social organization throughout the empire.

Social Classes

Broadly speaking, Inca social classification breaks down into three basic components: 1) elite and nobles, 2) *kurakas*, and 3) commoners. There are a number of other groups that do not fit neatly into these categories or appear to mitigate somewhat the strict hierarchy; these are included below under "Special Classes."

ELITE/NOBLES

The highest ranks of Inca society included the royal family, the descendants *(panaqas)* of deceased kings, nonroyal ethnic Incas, and Incas by privilege. Lower ranking elites included members of society distinguished by lineage, military service, public role, or wealth. These could include priests, provincial lords, and traders, though the lines that delineate these social positions remain unclear. For example, a commoner might achieve elite/noble status of a low rank by gaining wealth or through performance in war. In effect, the categories are fluid. Only the Cuzco aristocracy, or royal kin groups, were allowed to live within the city; the closer one was to the center, the higher one's place in the social hierarchy. As the empire expanded, so too did the social hierarchy, especially among the elite. Whether to assimilate preexisting social patterns into their own model or in an attempt to accommodate the stresses of rapid expansion, the social hierarchy proved flexible and transformational. In one example that illuminates the social complexity of the empire, the Inca scholar Maria Rostworowski Diez Canseco provides a list of Quechua terms that suggests the subtle differences in the hierarchy of lords:

Cápac or Cápac Capa	king or emperor
Cápac Apo	sovereign ruler
Appo	great lord
Appocac	great lord
Yayanc	lord, generic
Curaca [*kuraka*]	lord, principle of subjects
Atipac	powerful
Appocta, Sayani, gui	to be standing before a great lord
Appo Ayllon	lineage of lower nobility
Appoycachani, gui	to outrank
Mussoc Cápac	newly crowned emperor (young)

In this list one can begin to understand the diverse and complex levels of status within the nobility.

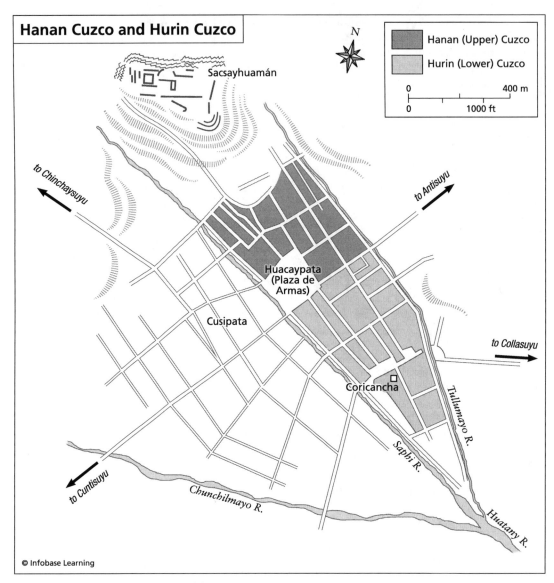

Hanan Cuzco and Hurin Cuzco

Legend:
- Hanan (Upper) Cuzco
- Hurin (Lower) Cuzco

N

0 — 400 m
0 — 1000 ft

Sacsayhuamán

to Chinchaysuyu

to Antisuyu

Huacaypata (Plaza de Armas)

Cusipata

to Collasuyu

Coricancha

Tullumayo R.

Saphi R.

to Cuntisuyu

Chunchilmayo R.

Huatany R.

© Infobase Learning

Map 5 Hanan *and* Hurin *Divisions of Cuzco*

KURAKAS

A *kuraka* (also spelled *curaca*) was a kind of hereditary noble. As a class, the position of *kuraka* had
long been established in the Andes, a tradition of
leadership extending back at least 1,500 years. As a
type of governor or chief, the *kuraka* was responsible for his subjects' well-being, acting, in a sense, as

intermediary between the forces in the cosmos and
the forces on earth.

SPECIAL CLASSES

Incas by Privilege Incas by privilege represented
a class of persons of non-Inca ethnicity that were
selected by the ruler to perform a service or task,

thereby entering into official service to the state. Incas named in this manner formed a special category and led to a new governing class created by the Inca elite. As a result, Incas by privilege held a wide range of administrative positions in the empire. The advantage of this for the Inca elite lay in the creation of a class of loyal supporters of ability, though the position was revocable if the individuals proved incapable. The possibility of revocation therefore practically ensured their loyalty. The indigenous chronicler Guamán Poma, writing in 1615, referred to this class as the "poor Inca" and relates their social position to persons in the Inca origin myth who accompanied the original Inca ancestors, led by Manco Cápac, on the mythical journey to the Cuzco heartland. Like this mythical entourage, the Incas by privilege formed a lower class who paid tribute and supported the ruling elite. According to Guamán Poma these persons were "Inca" by virtue of having ancestral relatives on Manco Cápac's mythical journey and by wearing ear spools, which the Sapa Inca also used as adornment. Ear piercing was a reflection of hierarchical status.

Administrators A rapidly expanding empire necessitates an efficient administrative class, or governing class, to ensure the smooth functioning of the state. For the Incas the responsibilities of this class were vast and included responsibilities ranging from managing state income to judging and the supervision of artisans. These persons formed an administrative class whose special functions were focused on the maintenance of the state. As such, they enjoyed certain privileges above commoners yet were also subject to extraordinary scrutiny and the threat of removal.

Priests If the Inca social hierarchy is envisioned as a pyramid, with the Sapa Inca at the apex and royal descendant kin next, the priestly caste occupied a position in close relation to this latter group. The priestly elite were charged with the maintenance of the ritual and ceremonial aspects of the temples. Furthermore, one can assume that the high priest of the Coricancha, or Temple of the Sun, the most important and sacred temple in the empire, himself occupied a special place of privilege among the elite. Priests attending important oracu-

lar sites, such as Pachacamac on the coast and Apurímac in the highlands, would also have had an elevated social status that reflected their responsibilities at the given site. Similarly, priests were assigned to speak with all *huacas* (shrines or sacred sites), of which there were many. *Huacas* took many forms and were basically religious or ritual idols; the priests who attended them played a special role in society above that of a commoner.

Traders Specialized social classes developed along the coast according to the types of items exchanged. Traders specializing in the Ecuadorean *Spondylus* shell, which had great magical-religious importance in the Andean world even prior to the Incas, apparently achieved a significant class status of their own. Some element of prestige seems to have transferred from the activity to the person, that is, from the trade of a high-value item to the individual's social status.

COMMONERS

The Inca scholar Rostworowski indicates that several categories of commoners existed in Inca society according to their status and the functions they performed. The following is a brief account of several such levels of commoners.

Artisans Craftspeople throughout the Andean region enjoyed special status both before and during the advent of Inca hegemony. This seems to have been the case especially in the northern territory of the Chimú Empire, which the Incas conquered beginning in 1470. Following their annexation to the Inca Empire, Chimú artisans were sent to Cuzco because the Incas admired their skills. The Incas then adopted Chimú styles and techniques into their own artistic, and propagandistic, vocabulary. The state thus became their employer. A great many types of activities existed in the artisan category, many of which would not be considered crafts today, though the ones in greatest demand worked in gold and silver. Pottery specialists and cloth painters were also in great demand and formed specialized groups that were recognized within the state bureaucracy. Conversely, there were numerous specialized artisans who did not form specialized blocks but lived within the context of the majority agriculturalists.

Hatun Runa *Hatun runa*, or adult males, along with their families, who worked as peasant farmers and herders constituted the majority of the Andean population. The population was organized according to the decimal system and divided into units of 10, 50, 100, 500, 1,000, 5,000, and 10,000. Each unit had a representative, with a *kuraka* representing units of 100 and lords representing the larger units. To fulfill the vast labor needs of the empire the state drew on the *hatun runa*. Similarly, the quotas of *mitmaqkuna*, those persons who were resettled by the state in various regions, and the ranks of soldiers were filled by *hatun runa*.

Fishermen Fishermen formed a distinct social class separate from those who cultivated the land. Beaches were not open to everyone but rather allocated to specific *ayllus*, meaning that the rights to fish in specific areas were exclusive to a particular *ayllu*. Fishermen did not own land and lived in settlements on the margins of farming villages. Fishermen appear to have operated, not necessarily by choice, as a fairly closed community. They were endogamous, meaning they married only among other fishing families, and at least in the north, they developed their own dialect.

Mitmaqkuna and **Yanakuna** Several new social groups emerged during the empire's history. Two of the more prevalent groups, each with pre-Inca antecedents, were called the *yanakuna* (*yanaconas*, in Spanish), and the *mitmaqkuna* (*mitimaes*, in Spanish). The *yanakuna* were full-time retainers dedicated to the service of the nobility. They held positions as "servants in waiting." They were exempt from the normal labor taxation, and their primary task was the maintenance of royal estates. The institution may have developed into a self-regenerating entity; that is, the need for dependable labor increased the need for *yanakuna*, and its function as a social institution grew accordingly. Some scholars have suggested that the *yanakuna* made up the majority of the middle and lower echelons of the state administrative bureaucracy and by extension the lower echelons of the social hierarchy.

Mitmaqkuna, on the other hand, were families removed by the state from their place of origin and sent to fulfill specific tasks or missions. Depending on the specific service, the obligation to relocate might be considered a form of deference, a reward, or a punishment. The *mitmaqkuna* were sent under their own local chiefs, and though they were often far from their homeland, they maintained ties of kinship to their homes. Both the *mitmaq* and *yana* classes developed in part as a response to Inca imperial expansion.

Acllas and Mamakuna *Acllas* were young girls between the ages of eight and 10 who were taken from their places of origin and installed in the *acllahuasi*, or "houses of the chosen women," where they enjoyed a privileged status and were occupied in the production of high-quality textiles and preparation of ritual beverages such as *chicha* and sometimes served as wives. They were selected for qualities of beauty, social origin, and aptitudes and maintained something of a special social status. The highest ranked of the *acllas* were the *mamakuna* (dubbed the "virgins of the Sun"), who never married and oversaw the young *acllas* at the *acllahuasi*.

INCA STATESMANSHIP

Predynastic/Early Rule

The earliest rulers, before the Incas were an established political and military force, were likely *sinchis*, war leaders who combined military and political aptitude. Over time the advantage of consistent, successful raids established these warriors as natural leaders within their communities. Similarly, over time it seems likely they instilled in their sons an appreciation for the craft of leadership, which earned them the advantage of firsthand learning from adept practitioners of leadership. Again, as time progressed, local raiding affairs grew into more complex enmities between regional ethnic groups, small groups began to consolidate into larger, aligned entities, and those *sinchis* who had political and military acumen took advantage of the wider scale of competition to become either paramount *sinchi*, acknowledged leader across a fairly wide base population, or even nascent king. To a certain degree, the early dynastic list, unattached to ethnography and only loosely reflected in the archaeology, represents the progression of order along this broadly sketched trajectory. It is also interesting to note that Manco Cápac's son and successor is named *Sinchi*, perhaps reflecting the tendencies described above. It was not until the eighth Sapa Inca of the chronicles Viracocha Inca that the conditions of recognizable kingship and permanent conquest became organized.

Standard Inca Dynastic List

The standard dynastic Inca lists mention between 11 and 13 kings. The history of the first seven, however, is a mixture of history and legend, the exact lines of which remain unclear. Like many peoples who found great power rapidly, the Incas used legend to supplement history and establish a veneer of legitimacy and power. Spanish chroniclers who dedicated portions of their writing to the recording of dynastic history are equivocal and grow less trustworthy the later they wrote, such that some contemporary scholars analyzing 17th-century chroniclers view them, at best, dubiously. This is not to say, however, that those chronicles are useless as anything other than mythology. In many instances those stories seem to reflect a general condition of headmen and chiefs, fractious squabbles and internecine affairs, ethnic disparity and the continuous maneuvering for power among raiding villages. In short, even if the stories do not reflect "truth" and history, they probably attend to a narrative sense of conditions and development, at least according to the perspective of the particular source. The following is the standard list. Beginning with Viracocha Inca (number 8) knowledge of the kings, and consequently of "history," becomes more concrete because of greater accord between ethnohistorical accounts and archaeology.

1. Manco Cápac
2. Sinchi Roca
3. Lloque Yupanqui
4. Mayta Cápac
5. Cápac Yupanqui
6. Inca Roca
7. Yahuar Huacac

8. Viracocha Inca	(r. ?–1438)
9. Pachacuti	(r. 1438–71)
10. Topa Inca	(r. 1471–93)
11. Huayna Cápac	(r. 1493–1527)
12. Huáscar	(r. 1527–32)
13. Atahualpa	(r. 1532–33)

The final two rulers present complications to the list because Huayna Cápac died before naming a successor, and the subsequent disagreement between successors led to the war of succession between Huáscar and Atahualpa. Atahualpa emerged victorious, but it occurred just as the Spanish arrived.

Split Inheritance

A system of split inheritance governed the transition of power in Inca society. Split inheritance was a pan-Andean tradition and found expression in pre-Inca civilizations, most notably during the Chimú Empire (ca. 1000–1470) of the north coast of Peru, which, it should be noted, the Incas eventually conquered around 1470. Split inheritance meant that only the crown and the authority to govern were transferred from the deceased ruler to his successor, while all his material property, palaces, and land were given to the royal *panaqa*, the group of his male descendants, excluding the successor. The institution of split inheritance dictated that the royal *panaqa* received the income from imperial taxes, thereby ensuring that the incoming ruler was effectively privilege-rich but property-poor. In order to live in the royal manner the new ruler had to acquire his own wealth. Toward this goal he had two primary options: He could increase tax revenue by demanding additional periods of service, or labor time, from the citizenry, or he could conquer new territories, annex them to the empire, and impose new taxes on the inhabitants. Some scholars believe that the consequence of split inheritance—whereby the incoming ruler, practically by necessity, had to conquer new territory for its labor wealth and agricultural potential—was a driving force behind the rapid imperial expansion of the Inca state. The stress of split inheritance may have proven unsustainable and, thus, perhaps also led to its quick demise.

DEATH OF THE KING AND CONTINUED VENERATION

Traditions, practices, and beliefs attendant upon the death of the Inca ruler run starkly contrary to contemporary veneration practices. For this reason they are fascinating. Following the death of the Sapa Inca, or "unique Inca," his role in society, though altered, remained poignant and influential. The rights to govern, wage war, and impose taxes were passed to his successor, while his palaces, servants, land, chattel, and other possessions passed to his *panaqa*. Despite being deceased, ownership remained vested in the Sapa Inca, while the *panaqa* served as the dead king's court and continued to treat him as if he were alive, maintaining his mummy and perpetuating his cult and bringing him to state ceremonies. His presence remained a viable state interest, demanding vast expenditures through offerings and sacrifices. In life the Sapa Inca was invested with aspects of divinity through his association with Inti, the sun deity, as one of his sons, while in death his mummy became one of the most sacred objects in the empire, thereby furthering the imperial ancestor cult.

In the early postconquest period the Spanish quickly understood how deep this cult ran through society. They felt, with a great sense of immediacy, that this "pagan" belief must be eradicated; they recognized this well before they had even nominal political control, and they began vigorously hunting down the royal mummies as a means to effect political transition. As a testament to the depth of the Inca piety with regard to the mummies, it took the Spanish 27 years to locate and destroy all the royal mummies, which had all been carefully hidden. The Spanish chronicler Cieza de León commented on this, writing in 1553 that, among the Inca, "they held their memory in such esteem that when one of these mighty lords died, his son took for himself nothing but the crown, for it was a law that among them that the wealth and royal possessions of him who had been the Inca of Cuzco were not to belong to anyone else. . . . [The royal mummies] had their chacaras, which is the name they give their plantations, where they raised corn and other victuals . . . even though they were already dead."

Overview of Inca Dynastic Rulers

The Incas organized themselves into descent groups based on divisions that traced their lineage to a founding father. The Inca dynastic rulers all traced their lineage to Manco Cápac. Lines of succession were clear in theory but often involved trickery, violence, and even war. The history of many of the rulers, especially the early rulers, is unclear because the histories recorded by the chronicles are themselves contradictory and confusing. It is therefore only possible to sketch out a rough trajectory for each. Knowledge of the later kings is on somewhat firmer ground as their reigns coincided with the lives of persons interviewed by some of the chroniclers.

SINCHI ROCA

Sinchi Roca was the son of Manco Cápac and Mama Ocllo and was born on the mythical foundation journey. The name Sinchi is in fact a title for a war chief. Sinchi Roca married Mama Coca and by doing so facilitated a political alliance. For unknown reasons Sinchi Roca did not designate his oldest son, Manco Sapaca, as his heir, highlighting from the beginning the lack of clear and present rights of succession.

LLOQUE YUPANQUI

The younger brother of the overlooked Manco Sapaca, Lloque Yupanqui appears to have been ineffectual as a leader. Conquests and alliances corresponding to his reign are absent. The relationships he established with down-valley neighbors are thus a result of negotiation rather than valor. He had a child, Mayta Cápac, only late in life. Soon thereafter it is said he became senile, and governance transferred to a pair of regents. Cuzco at this time may have been a series of loosely affiliated hamlets.

MAYTA CÁPAC

The legend of Mayta Cápac as being a belligerent, precocious, and powerful infant may well translate as a metaphor for contemporary village consolidation and an emerging sense of Inca authority. During Mayta Cápac's reign the Incas gained control of their neighbors, the Alcaviza, through military force and instituted a policy of strong rule. Mayta Cápac's defeat of them registers, be it myth or fact, as the first significant military victory in Inca history. He is credited, too, with instituting the *mitmaqkuna* system of forced resettlement of loyal Incas in conquered territory as a means of colonization, observation, and control. Lastly, some sources suggest he instituted Sun worship as the official cult. By instituting the worship of Inti, the sun god, he simultaneously reorganized *huaca* worship along Inca lines and set in place the primary symbol of Inca rule.

CÁPAC YUPANQUI

Cápac Yupanqui and all subsequent rulers continued the policy of violent warfare; Cápac Yupanqui is believed to have earned the first victories beyond the Cuzco Valley, most likely in the Yucay Valley. Cápac Yupanqui also had a separate palace built for himself and his family. All previous rulers had lived in the Coricancha (Sun Temple), and each subsequent ruler followed this example and built his own palace compound in the city. Until this time all the rulers had come from *hurin* Cuzco (Lower Cuzco); following Cápac Yupanqui all the rulers came from *hanan* Cuzco (Upper Cuzco). The reason for the change is unclear.

INCA ROCA

The events of Inca Roca's reign (the first ruler to be called "Inca") continue to build on previous consolidations of power against rivals in the Cuzco region. Inca Roca married an already-betrothed woman by the name of Mama Micay. Tocay Cápac, to whom she had been promised, was greatly offended and took his tribe, the Ayarmaca, to war against her tribe, the Guayllacan. While the Ayarmaca and Guayllacan were at war, Inca Roca and Mama Micay had a son (Yahuar Huacac). The boy was supposed to have been kidnapped by the Guayllacan and given to Tocay Cápac and killed as the price for peace, but legend says the boy wept tears

of blood that frightened Tocay Cápac into releasing him. Other significant developments attributed to this reign is the initiation of the class status of "Inca by privilege," whereby nonethnic Incas were inducted into honorary Inca status and all the rights and privileges that come with it. Also, the institutionalization of the *panaqa* system reportedly began at this time.

YAHUAR HUACAC

Not much is recorded pertaining to the reign of Yahuar Huacac. It was supposedly a period marked by turbulence, though to what degree is unclear. He was eventually assassinated at a feast by captains from Cuntisuyu, one of the four quarters of the empire.

VIRACOCHA INCA

The reign of Viracocha Inca marks the beginning of an era generally considered to be historical. Immediately, however, there is some difficulty with this assertion because his son and successor, Pachacuti, rewrote Inca history, effectively promoting his own accomplishments and even attributing many of his father's successes to himself. Thus, disentangling the two histories is problematic. Nevertheless, following the assassination of Yahuar Huacac, the principal lords of Cuzco met and chose, from among many contenders, the next ruler, Hatun Topa Inca. After his installation as monarch he set out on a series of conquests, as opposed to the raids and withdrawals of his predecessors. He is credited with incorporating the Urubamba Valley, the eastern end of the Cuzco Valley, and lands as far as 120 kilometers (75 mi.) south into the empire. When he met the formidable armies of the Colla ethnic group in the Titicaca basin, instead of engaging them militarily, he negotiated peace.

While in the south, he captured the shrine of the creator god Viracocha, received a vision approving his conquest, took the name Viracocha, and began promoting the cult of Viracocha. In 1438 the Chanca group from the north forced Viracocha Inca, along with his chosen successor, to withdraw from Cuzco to a more defensible position. Another son, Inca Cusi Yupanqui—later to become

Pachacuti—remained behind and scored an improbable victory over the Chancas, which ultimately resulted in Viracocha's forced deposal and Pachacuti's taking of the crown. There is some evidence suggesting that the Chanca victory was indeed Viracocha's but that Pachacuti rewrote history claiming it as his own.

PACHACUTI

The word *pachacuti* in Quechua means "cataclysm" or "world upheaval" and signifies a major historical rupture, an overturning of world order. It is an appropriate moniker for the ninth Sapa Inca. As soon as he was in power he began consolidating territory and advancing on new campaigns of conquest, expanding the empire to the west, north, and south. Following his successes, he turned over the military to his son Topa Inca and returned to Cuzco to undertake a major redesign of the capital city, reorganizing it along multiple social and spatial metaphors. In addition to the redesign of Cuzco, Pachacuti also undertook many public works such as canals, aqueducts, storehouses, terraces, highways, and a number of royal estates, such as at Pisac, Ollantaytambo, and Machu Picchu. He is credited with codifying Inca law, institutionalizing the taxation system, formalizing ancestor worship, and inventing the agricultural and religious calendars. As great as his achievements were, there remain questions as to which can be accredited to him.

TOPA INCA

Pachacuti's chosen successor was a son by the name of Amaru Inca, who had served as coregent for six years. It appears, however, that Amaru was not aggressive enough, so Pachacuti's generals engineered Topa Inca's election. Topa Inca (Túpac Yupanqui) had clearly demonstrated his valor in numerous military campaigns during his father's reign, greatly expanding the empire's boundaries—to such an extent, in fact, that he is sometimes referred to as the Incan Alexander the Great. His major conquests included territory in Ecuador, the territory of the Chimú Empire along the north coast of Peru, and territory south along the coast to Nazca. During his reign he quelled rebellion in the Titicaca basin and annexed the territory of modern Bolivia and northern Chile.

HUAYNA CÁPAC

Topa Inca's eldest son, Titu Cusi Hualpa, succeeded his father, took the name Huayna Cápac, and continued to expand the boundaries of the empire. Huayna Cápac spent a great deal of time and energy fighting costly wars at the northern periphery to the extent that Inca society began to fracture during his absence. While a second court grew up around Huayna Cápac in Tumipampa (modern Cuenca, Ecuador), unrest among the nobility in Cuzco started to boil over. The processes of admin-

4.1 *Painting of four Inca kings: Topa Inca (Túpac Yupanqui), Huayna Cápac, Huáscar, and Atahualpa* (Courtesy Brooklyn Museum)

istration had grown so unwieldy that the day-to-day business of the empire flagged. By 1527 two new crises presented themselves that would directly, profoundly, and irrevocably change the Inca Empire. First, by 1527 Huayna Cápac was aware of the European presence. Second, as if a part of an advance guard, European disease had arrived and decimated the Andean population. Exact numbers are speculative, but the toll certainly reached many million, among them most likely Huayna Cápac and his heir apparent, Ninan Cuyochi.

HUÁSCAR AND ATAHUALPA

The period following the death of Huayna Cápac was marked by confusion and division in the empire. Huáscar had been acting as coregent in Cuzco during Huayna Cápac's long absences and perhaps rightfully felt his line of accession to the throne was clear. He was installed according to all the regular customs. However, in the north, the armies backed another of Huayna Cápac's sons, Atahualpa, and soon a civil war broke out between the brothers and their supporters. Atahualpa's forces pushed slowly and steadily southward and eventually captured Cuzco in 1532. Huáscar was defeated, captured, and, partly because of pressure from the Spanish, whom he met at Cajamarca on his way south, eventually killed by Atahualpa. Atahualpa himself was never officially installed, and he was killed by the Spanish in July 1533.

POLITICS THROUGH THE EMPIRE

The Spanish first got hint of a large empire to the south when Bartolomé Ruiz, the main pilot for Francisco Pizarro, encountered a native balsa craft off the coast of Ecuador in 1526. The craft contained ceramics, textiles, gold, silver, and emeralds, which was enough to justify a later return under the promise of vast wealth. After internal struggles, halted adventures, resupply, and reorganization, expeditions returned to the area in 1528 and again

in 1532. At this point Spanish conquistadores led by Francisco Pizarro first encountered the vast Inca Empire at its northernmost extent, in the vicinity of contemporary Quito, Ecuador, in 1532. Both perceptive and calculating, the Spanish quickly ascertained that the empire was vulnerable and fragile as a result of the ensuing dynastic war of succession between the half brothers Atahualpa and Huáscar, sons of the late Inca ruler Huayna Cápac, who had died in 1527, most likely as a result of European disease. Huayna Cápac's apparent successor had also died, thus leading directly to the war that split the empire.

The half brothers drew support from different parts of the empire, each claiming the right to rule based on related though competing lines of power. Atahualpa drew his support in the north, specifically around Quito and Tumipampa (now Cuenca), Ecuador. His line of succession was centered on his mother's family, which descended from the ninth Inca king, Pachacuti. Huáscar's power was based at Cuzco, Peru, the traditional capital of the empire, and was supported by his mother's kin, whose lineage stemmed from the 10th Inca ruler, Topa Inca. Atahualpa's generals captured Huáscar in 1532, bringing the civil war to an end. In November of that year Francisco Pizarro and his soldiers met Atahualpa at Cajamarca in northern Peru and in an ambush captured him. Though the empire was already in a state of fracture and turmoil, Atahualpa's capture was in a sense the initial maneuver in the conquest and end of the Inca Empire as a purely indigenous political entity.

The following sections will briefly examine the development, expansion, policies, and institutions that facilitated the growth and maintenance of the empire. They will also discuss the systems of administration and the physical infrastructure that helped define its shape and function.

Beginnings of Empire

The entity that became the Inca Empire began as a small yet complex polity in the midst of more powerful polities and alliances. Its narrative beginnings are closely intertwined with its own myths and legends. The Spanish chronicler Juan de Betanzos, writing in 1551 about Inca origins, said of the pre-imperial Inca: "In ancient times in the province of Peru on the location that is today Cuzco, before the existence of the lords Orejones, Inkas, and Capaccona, who were called kings, there was a small village of up to thirty small thatched, poor houses. In them were thirty Indians, and the head and chief of this village was called Alcaviza. . . ." As such, Betanzos provides a glimpse, albeit a mixture of fact and legend, into who the Incas were before they were the imperial Incas who forever changed the landscape of the Andes. A brief recounting of two stories, namely the legend of the founding of Cuzco and the legend of the war against the Chancas, will suffice as an introduction to the mythical underpinnings that ground the reality of the Inca Empire.

4.2 *Pacariqtambo, the cave from which Inca mythical ancestors originated* (Felipe Guamán Poma de Ayala)

LEGENDARY FOUNDING OF CUZCO

One of the legends of the founding of Cuzco begins with four brothers and four sisters emerging from a cave at a place called Pacariqtambo. They wandered slowly through the high Andes in search of a place to settle. In the story as related by the chronicler Inca Garcilaso de la Vega, these original Incas emerged from the area of Lake Titicaca, which became an area of great symbolic importance to the Incas and established a theoretical link to the Tiwanaku civilization that had thrived in that area 500 years before. In drawing a connection between themselves and this earlier empire, the Incas were attempting to legitimate their own imperial authority by augmenting their historical depth. Eventually these legendary founders settled in Cuzco and founded the royal line of descent.

The myth is retold in greater detail elsewhere, but for the purposes here it is most important to note that the Incas incorporated elements from the stories as significant elements of imperial strategy and freely rearranged their "history" to justify their authority. Lake Titicaca, caves, dynastic descent, and Tiwanaku, for example, held religious or historical importance that was then applied to the Inca Empire.

QUASI-LEGENDARY WAR AGAINST THE CHANCAS

The beginning of Inca imperial expansion is tied to the narrative of the war against the Chancas. The Chancas were a powerful ethnic group neighboring the Incas with their own expansionistic ideas. The narrative is a mix of fact and myth and serves to explain the Inca imperial existence as well as relate the events that unleashed Inca expansion. The most detailed depiction of the story is found in Betanzos's *Narrative of the Incas.* Betanzos had access to *panaqa* member of the ninth Inca king, Pachacuti, and Betanzos's version is a kind of lineage history. The legend of the war against the Chancas thus serves as a form of validation of Pachacuti's reign.

The basic importance of the legend can be summed up in several points. First, the Incas emerged victorious contrary to all likelihood, thus establishing their superiority. Second, the Incas were aided by the miraculous appearance of *purur-aucas*, stones that came to life as warriors at the critical moment of battle, thereby ensuring Inca victory and ingraining the notion that the Incas were greatly favored by the gods. Third, Pachacuti was the primary agent of victory and assumed leadership after his father fled, establishing himself as the rightful ruler. Fourth, the unexpected victory allowed the Incas to collect a vast amount of booty with which they could establish mutually beneficial relationships with possible allies as well as providing them with a critical early advantage over potential adversaries. And, finally, it became suddenly clear to neighboring tribes or villages that the Incas were very powerful. All of these factors played a part in early Inca expansion.

ARCHAEOLOGICAL SUPPLEMENT TO THE FOUNDATION OF CUZCO

The legendary founding of Cuzco reflects the idea that the serendipitous outcome of a single battle and the influence of a handful of individuals determined the outcome of the Incas. Recent archaeological work, by contrast, is beginning to define the rise of the empire as a consequence of longer historical and developmental processes. This line of thought suggests that the imperial strategies used by the Incas developed between 1000 and 1400 C.E., eventually promoting Cuzco to an urban center that came to dominate its neighbors and extend its control, over the course of a few centuries, either through unification or elimination.

Expansion

There is no single reason why the Incas, as opposed to any other group, expanded so rapidly. Rather, a complex combination of environmental, political, economic, military, and ideological factors, mixed together with luck, skill, and determination, created the conditions of success. The Incas demonstrated a preimperial insistence on leaders who could provide security and opportunities for plunder in an environment where they were constantly under threat from aggressive neighbors. Additionally, ecological concerns such as prolonged drought

intensified their desire for control over more land. The initial victory over the Chancas mentioned above, even though it registers as a mixture of fact and legend, in effect kick-started the quest for expansion and provided considerable booty that some scholars suggest allowed the Incas to substantiate alliances. Following their initial victory, the Incas set their sights upon resource-rich territories, such as the agricultural region around the Titicaca basin to the south of Cuzco, the mineral-rich territories of the southern Andes, the alpaca-friendly lands of the altiplano, the gold and feather wealth of the jungles, and the tropical waters off Ecuador rich with the shells they used as currency. Conquest of these regions ultimately translated into wealth, which in turn allowed for further expansion and thereby created the need for new sources of wealth and land. In a sense the cycle was both unstoppable and unsupportable, yet while it flourished, it provided the basic mechanisms for Inca expansion.

TERRITORIAL ACQUISITION BY RULER

Inca policies that made territorial acquisition necessary, combined with Inca militarism, meant that imperial expansion occurred rapidly over a vast amount of land. Although it was rapid, it was not always conclusive, as remnants of opposition almost always remained in place, especially in distant territories where the imperial infrastructure was less definitively set in place. Nevertheless, despite the expense in labor and booty each successive ruler, beginning with Viracocha Inca (r. ?–1438), made conquest a major policy initiative. A wide array of provincial documents and chronicles detail the chronology of Inca conquests, and the sections that follow are a general synopsis of those campaigns and the territories annexed as a result.

Inca expansionist policy is typically thought to have begun under Viracocha Inca, who established a presence in the highland Titicaca basin, the fertile land to the south of Cuzco surrounding Lake Titicaca. Eventually Viracocha Inca's son, Pachacuti (r. 1438–71), described in numerous sources as the primary instigator of Inca expansion, secured this territory as well as land farther south and throughout modern Bolivia. Pachacuti, with his brother Cápac Yupanqui (different from the fifth ruler of the same name), followed by his successor-son, Topa Inca (r. 1471–93)—regarded by many scholars as the Inca equivalent of the Greek emperor and general Alexander the Great— followed the early southern acquisitions by solidifying territory in what is northern Peru, that is, except for the coast. These conquests successfully annexed and solidified territory from contemporary Lima northward to what is today the central Ecuadorean coast. They succeeded in claiming territory from the coast to the highlands. Topa Inca continued the extraordinary expansion in the southern zones by conquering territory in contemporary Chile, beyond modern-day Santiago, from the coast into northwest Argentina. Similarly, Topa Inca succeeded in conquering territory in the Altiplano to the southwest and northeast of Cuzco that extended to the north and west territory already annexed by his father, including territory surrounding Quito. It needs to be said that Topa Inca's campaigns to annex new territory coexisted with campaigns to quell local rebellions, and one can well imagine the massive costs—in both manpower and booty—necessary for continued successful campaigns on multiple fronts.

Huayna Cápac (r. 1493–1527), the penultimate Inca ruler before the arrival of the Spanish, while spending considerable energy trying to hold the empire together, nevertheless managed to consolidate territory to the west and north of Quito and, much farther south, extended the borders into eastern Bolivia. Finally, following the untimely death of Huayna Cápac and the ensuing dynastic war of succession between his sons Huáscar and Atahualpa, Huáscar (r. 1527–32) managed to consolidate a small parcel of land to the north of Chachapoyas, Peru, extending almost to the Ecuadorean border. Not unexpectedly, however, under the strain of civil war, the empire suffered from a period of natural disintegration, as the energy and resources of the competing factions went toward fighting each other rather than toward imperial maintenance. At this point the Spanish arrived in the northern reaches of the empire, eventually encountering Atahualpa, the victor in the war of succession, at Cajamarca, Peru, in November 1532.

Policies and Institutions that Promoted Unification

Maintaining a unified imperial state is an exceedingly difficult proposition. Throughout history, and regardless of place, managing an empire demands a range of strategies that must be flexible or stringent, as necessary. Inca strategies of unification, which in reality were often designed simply to minimize the likelihood of rebellion, included the manipulation of political, administrative, military, linguistic, economic, and social factors. The following sections detail some of these policies and practices.

RELIGION

The Incas imposed their state religion on all subjects of the empire. Similar to pre-Inca states with pan-Andean territorial ambitions, the Incas used religion as a means of social unification. While there is conflicting evidence regarding the extent to which nature deities were worshipped prior to the rise of the Inca state, the elaborately constructed shrines and temples throughout the empire clearly symbolize deification of the Sun, thunder, the Earth, and the Moon. In some areas the Incas ruthlessly enforced the new religious paradigm while in others, depending on the presence or degree of resistance, the Incas allowed local traditions to remain so long as the Inca pantheon was accepted over and above the local.

Andean religions, including the Incas', were infused with a high degree of superstition. It was typically believed that nearly everything held some kind of supernatural power. The Incas manipulated these conditions through the regular practice of taking hostage principal sacred objects of conquered territories and installing them in the Coricancha, or Temple of the Sun, thereby symbolizing Inca dominion and leveraging the loyalties of the subdued.

Early in the dynastic development of the Inca state, worship of the Sun, whom they named Inti, became paramount. The solar deity was really a cluster of aspects and interrelated parts that allowed for flexibility and broad veneration. Scholars surmise that the rise of the Inti cult was to some extent a conscious manipulation of religion for political purposes, and as the Inca king was increasingly identified with Inti, which grew into a form of divine patronage, it became convenient that the worship of the Sun and the worship of the king became aspects of the same process. The 17th-century Jesuit scholar Bernabé Cobo alluded to this process when he wrote, "The truth is that Inca religion did not remain fixed and unchanging from the birth of the realm onward; they did not cling to the same few beliefs or worship the same few gods. At various times they were adding and discarding many notions. . . . They were induced to make changes in [religious] matters because they began to realize that in this way they could strengthen themselves and keep the kingdom under tighter control." As Cobo indicates, Inca religious belief evolved and adapted to the constantly fluctuating demands of imperial needs. Yet, after the Inca Empire disintegrated, institutions such as these quickly abated in areas beyond Cuzco.

Cápac Hucha (Capacocha)   The Cápac Hucha, which can be translated as "royal obligation," was an elaborate and religiously infused ceremony that ended, in most cases, with the sacrifice and ritual interment of young children of both sexes at mountaintop shrines. These high-altitude ceremonies were especially common in the Southern Andes, even though they took place empire-wide. From the perspective of empire and empire-building, the ceremony served to both initiate and authenticate distant villages within the imperial administrative structure. For instance, though it may seem brutally political, a village leader was awarded incentives akin to power-sharing for the sacrifice of one of the children of his community.

For the ceremony young children chosen for their exceptional beauty, and hence their purity—therein embodying both the essence and substance of the empire itself—were marched to the central plaza of Cuzco (Huacaypata), where priests and the Sapa Inca himself sacrificed selected animals. The children were then paired off and "married," after which they were marched back to their native or other villages, sometimes traversing many hundreds of miles. Upon return they were given *chicha*, a maize beer often used to sanctify a particular event as sacred or simply important, and then interred.

Selection for the ceremony was considered a great honor, for both a family and a village, and came with its own rewards. While unrecorded in the literature, one might expect that there was some resistance to this form of hegemony at the local and familial level. By tying honor and privilege to a ritual practice that to contemporary eyes can only seem foreign and strange, if not barbaric, the Incas were able to blur the distinctions between fear, duty, privilege, and power and create another layer of context wherein the state authority was paramount.

Ancestor Worship   Ancestor worship, or cults of the dead—the belief that spirits of the dead play an active role in the world of the living—was a long-standing pan-Andean tradition adopted by the Incas. It formed part of the essential core of Inca religion. The periodic celebration of funeral rites, the renewal of grave offerings, and the veneration of corpses was both adopted by and transmitted through the Inca Empire as a means of transposing religious belief into political affiliation.

LANGUAGE

By the 1520s, when the Inca Empire had practically reached its maximum extent, hundreds of languages and dialects were spoken within its borders. The administrative complications extending from this are substantial. In order to ease the burdens of communication the Inca dictated that their native language, Quechua, serve as a lingua franca. The name Quechua itself is probably a colonial misinterpretation; its speakers knew it as *runasimi*, or "human speech."

One tangible extension of Inca language policy is that provincial nobles were required to maintain a residence in Cuzco. Their sons were required to attend court schools in order to learn Quechua, making implicit that second-generation nobles would speak the imperial language and thereby, presumably, would be better equipped to facilitate Inca rule. Elsewhere it was stated that all Inca subjects were required to learn Quechua.

RECIPROCITY

According to the Peruvian ethnohistorian Rostworowski, reciprocity was a means of establishing order in a system that did not use money. It organized and accounted for the provision of services at various levels and interlocked the production and distribution of goods. It was a strategy used by the Incas to establish and maintain socioeconomic ties to territories, regulating relationships among lords in proximity to others. It was also a conquest strategy that, when effective, avoided military aggression: In such instances the Incas would offer lavish gifts to a local chief whose territory they wished to annex. If accepted, the transition to Inca sovereignty occurred more or less harmlessly. If denied, the Incas went to war. In instances where the offer of reciprocity was accepted administration facilities were built, Inca religion was imposed on top of the local religion, female workers were dedicated to the production of textiles and ritual beverages, and additional persons were drafted into the Inca labor force. In this way, reciprocal obligations between the state and the affected territory enhanced the bonds between the two. By drafting local production and distribution into the Inca system, Inca administrators created a condition of necessary coexistence, meaning the territory in question became reliant on the state bureaucracy for its own subsistence and existence. In doing so the Inca state managed to create conditions that established at least the appearance of necessary bonds that made order, or a higher level of order, possible.

YANAKUNA AS IMPERIAL STRATEGY

The term *yana* basically means "servant" and is used to refer to a special kind of civic status for males. (In this sense *yanakuna* is related to *camayos* and *mitmaqkuna*; see below.) Although records cannot confirm precisely what exactly *yanakuna* means, it appears that it is a term to describe men recruited by authorities, sometimes the Sapa Inca himself, to serve as personal retainers to the Inca ruler. These duties might include administrative tasks, field cultivation, domestic service, or service as a provincial governor. When performed for the Sapa Inca, any of these might conform to a kind of honorable service. Those who served as *yanakuna* were competent and qualified individuals and worked in service to the Inca ruler. *Yanakuna* was one of the means by which individuals were conscripted by the Inca

state to serve and administer to state needs. As with the *camayos* and *mitmaqkuna*, imposing *yanakuna* service was a major way the Inca state interfered with men's traditional loyalties and created bonds of necessity (and sometimes privilege) to the state.

CAMAYOS AS IMPERIAL STRATEGY

Like the *yanakuna*, *camayos* were expected to work full time for the ruler or the royal governor, typically carrying out specialized activities such as building walls, pottery making, engaging in the specialized production of coca leaves, or maintaining causeways, bridges, or river channels. The term itself broadly refers to a male official who sees that jobs get done, often in charge of fields, craftsmen, or other workers. An individual could be both a *yanakuna* and a *camayoc*. *Camayos* were often resettled in large numbers away from their home territory according to where the Sapa Inca decided they should be placed. One of the effects of the *camayo* program would have been to weaken local loyalties of some *camayos* and create bonds to the Inca state.

MITMAQKUNA AS IMPERIAL STRATEGY

Some *mitmaqkuna* were *camayos*, *yanakuna*, or both, though there were other kinds of *mitmaqkuna*. In general terms a *mitmaqkuna* is a person sent by the state to a distant location to serve a specific function. One kind of *mitmaqkuna* was incorporated into the administrative organization of the provinces, either serving the Inca government directly or as subjects of the local administration. These were individuals sent by the state to populate unstable or hostile territories as a policy relating to unification. In practice, they were blocks of persons, always ethnically homogenous, numbering perhaps 100, 200, or 1,000 married men, who with their families resettled in a foreign territory in order to help ensure that loyalties to the Inca state remained intact. Perhaps understandably, the local population apparently often viewed *mitmaqkuna* settlements with great suspicion and considered them as spies for the government. Rather than instilling unity, however, this practice often created points of tension that perhaps deflected animosity away from the government onto newly created ethnic conflict.

In order to ensure a visible register of ethnic identity the Incas insisted that all subjects maintain their traditional costumes.

ACLLAS

Just as young men were selected for various types of service, young women were selected to serve as *acllas*, or "chosen women." They were chosen for their beauty and were often the daughters of the highest nobility. The Sapa Inca often gave these women as brides to men whom he wished to honor or show favor. The women were often given to men from provinces foreign to the women in order to create a cosmopolitan diversity, at least amongst the ruling elite. A hoped-for sociopolitical by-product of this type of gift-giving was the creation of fealties between provincial rulers, their populations, and the Inca state.

CHICHA AND DRINKING

Political authorities used ceremonies involving *chicha*, a fermented, alcoholic maize drink, to substantiate the division between the rulers and the ruled. Research in the north coast of Peru by the ethnohistorian Rostworowski has shown that local chiefs operated what appeared to the Spanish as "taverns" and that when the chiefs traveled they were always accompanied by great quantities of *chicha* carried in containers by porters. When the chief rested, people from the area came to drink with him at his expense, demonstrating that political power and economic right were tied to the ceremony involving drink. These transactions between local chiefs, as representatives of Inca authority, and the people served as subtle reminders of the power structures of empire.

Similarly, excavations at Huánuco Pampa, a major provincial center in the north-central highlands of Peru, show that a major investment by the Inca state was in the production and storage of *chicha*; literally tons of jars and fragments of jars were found there and thought to be associated primarily with *chicha*. If the system was redistributive, meaning that the *chicha* was there to be distributed in order to further the ritually established bonds of leaders and the led, and the population had become in a sense dependent on the gifts, then it is strongly possible that the state was using *chicha* and chicha-

drinking rituals to enhance its indirect control at the local level.

INCA TRIBUTE SYSTEM

According to the Inca scholar Catherine Julien, the Inca government extracted goods and services from provinces organized in the form of tribute payments. While land and transportable property were extracted at the time of annexation, the province's principal contribution over time was in labor service. Individuals could be designated to either permanent or temporary assignments, though only one type of service was performed at any time. Permanent assignment typically meant being relocated by the state in a province foreign to one's home province. Tributaries on permanent assignment passed their assignments on to their descendants, indicating a kind of social rigidity common to the imperial social fabric. Individuals on both permanent and temporary assignments were organized according to a system known as the Inca decimal system.

Administering the Empire

A triad of institutional initiatives can be broken down broadly into civil administration, religious hierarchy, and state military apparatus supported by the Sapa Inca.

CIVIL (INCA DECIMAL) ADMINISTRATION

Inca decimal administration functioned primarily as a means of organizing and distributing the labor obligation (*mita*) the state government requested from its provinces. In practice the labor obligation looked like a form of tax paid through labor. The labor assignment took two forms, either temporary or permanent. Permanent service often meant laborers were relocated outside their home province, where they were required to produce goods or provide service on a regular basis. Labor assignments varied greatly and included, but were not limited to, service as gold and silver miners, masons, guards, honey gatherers, dye makers, cultivators of coca, hunters for royal deer hunts, guards for corn fields, herders, and soldiers. Though labor was the primary form of extraction, the Incas also appropriated land and transportable goods.

All persons in the labor pool were organized into decimal units, with *chunka* being the smallest named unit, equivalent to 10. Each unit was composed of a tributary household, which usually included a married couple. From *chunka* the units increased incrementally and included *piska chunka* (50), *pachaka* (100), *piska pachaka* (500), *waranqa* (1,000), *piska waranqa* (5,000), and *hunu* (10,000). At each level one individual (*akuraka*) acted as a division head and was in charge of administering the rest of that unit. One by-product of this type of organization was the recognition of a social hierarchy based on increasing levels of authority corresponding to the number of persons in one's charge.

Information on the Inca decimal system is known through existing *visitas*, which were royal inspections carried out by the Spanish during the 16th-century transition to colonial rule. Their accuracy is largely attributed to the maintenance of the quipu, an indigenous notational device consisting of knotted string, which were "read" by native specialists (*quipucamayos*) and translated directly into *visitas* recorded by the Spanish for administrative purposes.

Kurakas, defined as a type of chief, principal lord, or native elite, were in charge of administering each decimal unit. Scholars disagree over the application of the term *kuraka*, given some disparity in the chronicles as to whom exactly the naming applies. In brief, some scholars believe the term applied only to those individuals heading the upper ranks of the decimal system, while others extend the term downward into the lower ranks. Nevertheless, there was a difference in status between ranks that corresponded to the number of individuals for which one was responsible. One consequence of this was that during agricultural projects in which everyone participated, even the Sapa Inca himself, those members of higher rank tended to work less over time. During the colonial transition, when Inca provincial rule disappeared and Spanish rule was being introduced, the *kurakas*, almost by default, and perhaps sensing a shifting world, navigated themselves into positions of local representation and established themselves in positions of authority over the entire tributary population.

RELIGIOUS HIERARCHY

The Inca religious hierarchy functioned distinctly and separately from the civil administration, though it was organized in grades roughly corresponding to the governmental structure. It should be noted that some of the terms used here reflect the Western Christian tradition familiar to the Spanish chroniclers and can be understood as roughly analogous to positions in the Inca hierarchy. At the apex of the religious hierarchy was the high priest in Cuzco, usually a close relative of the Sapa Inca, who presided over the Coricancha, or Temple of the Sun, the primary temple in the Inca Empire. The high priest was one of the most important officials of the government. Beneath the high priest, 10 "bishops" supervised the multitudes of religious specialists, or priests in charge, in attendance at *huacas* (shrines) throughout the empire. The lowest rank, then, consisted of assistants at these shrines, with various responsibilities according to the size and importance of the site.

These religious specialists were subdivided into categories according to function. The literature uses different terminology to describe the priests, and their functions were probably not rigidly departmentalized. John H. Rowe, perhaps the preeminent Inca scholar, mentions the categories of "diviner," "confessor," "consultant of the dead," "interpreter of oracles," "diviner from the lungs of sacrificed animals," and "curers." Elsewhere the categories are described using the terms *ritualist, confessor, diviner,* and *inspector*. In general, ritualists instructed communities with regard to agriculture as it corresponded with the calendar, advising on the proper times to sow, plant, and harvest. They also led any rituals that accompanied the agricultural process. Confessors were usually priests of either sex consulted by "sinners" under the expectation of total truth. The confessor would hear the confession and then consult small stones or the entrails of an animal to determine if the whole truth had been told. Penance assigned by the confessor might include fasting or a night spent in prayer at the shrine.

MILITARY APPARATUS

For much of its history the Inca Empire did not maintain a standing army but fielded its soldiers from among conscripted peasant farmers paying their state labor obligation *(mita)* and following their local lords. Like the civil administration, the military was organized on a decimal basis. The units were organized into commands of 10, 100, 1,000, and 10,000 heads of households, or *hatun runa* (adult male commoners between the ages of 25 and 50). The Sapa Inca was the commander-in-chief and theoretically the lead field general, though in practice, as the empire developed, he spent less and less time in the field and eventually gave over command to generals/officers, usually close relatives. A hierarchy of officers ranged downward from the generals/officers to ethnic leaders of the fighting units.

The Sapa Inca had a personal guard called the *orejones*, meaning "big ears" in Spanish, drawn, at least initially, from the Cuzco aristocracy. They were trained since youth as warriors and formed an elite corps and thus held an esteemed position within society. Some evidence suggests that later emperors recruited their own personal guard from various ethnic groups throughout the empire, especially those known for their loyalty. For the greater part of the empire's history the *orejones* were the only standing army regularly employed by the Inca.

Imperial Infrastructure

Much of the current scholarship dealing with the Inca imperial infrastructure—that is, the literature that examines the built or constructed environment—assumes that the infrastructure was created to support armies of soldiers and of bureaucrats traversing the long miles between the capital at Cuzco, hinterland centers, and military outposts. This scenario is indeed a primary element in the maintenance of the Inca roads and the construction of communication centers, storehouses, and other facilities along the roads, but it is not necessarily the whole picture. Research in the north-central highlands of Peru by the anthropologist Craig Morris indicates that activities at these remote centers suggest its infrastructure was geared toward supporting rituals and ceremonies useful to Inca provincial administration at least as much as they were geared toward the logistics of

mobile army and bureaucratic units. The following sections provide a brief overview of Inca constructions as they reflect and facilitate imperial prerogatives.

COMMUNICATIONS AND SUPPLY

Collection, dissemination, and action upon information is fundamental to the maintenance of a functional state. Given the absence of rapid communication technology, the Incas relied on a system of transportation and human relay networks to get the information to the people making decisions and, conversely, to get those messages back to the persons whose job it was to implement those decisions. The Inca "highway" system *(capac ñan)*, rightfully legendary, consisted of road networks that predated the Incas but that the Incas maintained and augmented with new roads built to expand the existing system. These roads altogether, totaling approximately 30,000 kilometers (18,641 mi.), constituted the backbone of the Inca communication, transport, and supply network. The efficient transport of goods and people along the roads, over the vast distances of the empire, was as fundamental as it was complicated with respect to the overall functioning of the state. Moving people with messages was made more reliable through the use of the quipu as a notational device.

An overlay of way stations, called *tambos (tampus)*, and "administrative" centers provided the infrastructure to support, monitor, and supervise the flow of goods, services, and information to and from the capital at Cuzco and into the hinterlands. Characteristic architecture at the smaller sites included storage facilities *(colcas)*; the so-called *kallankas*, or large buildings with unbroken interior spaces thought to have been used as temporary shelters for travelers; and other shelters that displayed less use and were perhaps official residences. Larger centers, such as that of Huánuco Pampa in the central Peruvian highlands, display a much greater complexity and are believed to have supported activities far more complex than that of a simple supply depot. The overriding functional similarity between larger and smaller centers or sites is in accordance with their service to facilitate state enterprises.

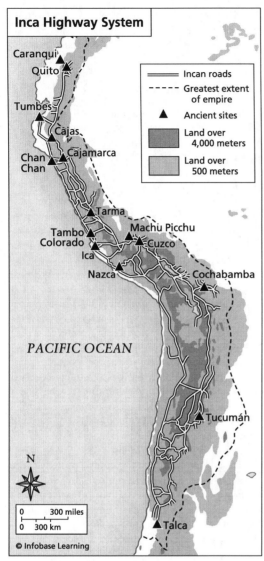

Inca Highway System

Caranqui
Quito
Tumbes
Cajas
Chan Chan
Cajamarca
Tarma
Machu Picchu
Tambo Colorado
Ica
Cuzco
Nazca
Cochabamba

PACIFIC OCEAN

Tucumán

N

0   300 miles
0   300 km

Talca

© Infobase Learning

━━━━ Incan roads
- - - - Greatest extent of empire
▲ Ancient sites
⬛ Land over 4,000 meters
⬜ Land over 500 meters

Map 6 The Inca Highway System

BUILDING CAMPAIGNS

The impact and presence of the Inca Empire is perhaps most identifiable in its architectural remains. The Incas worked in a distinctive masonry style that was easily identifiable and easily repeated, albeit at the generous expense of labor. Inca stone masonry resulted from the rigorous cutting, shaping, and smoothing of stone that, generally speaking, corresponded with levels of political or religious importance invested in the particular structure. For example, important shrines and temples often displayed smooth, regularly coursed ashlar masonry, whereas structures of little ritual or political significance, such as canals, were generally built using the roughest type of masonry. Using a few basic types of masonry style, the Incas enacted a building campaign that coincided with the state's imperial expansion, in effect dotting the landscape with structures whose impressiveness were equated with power and authority and therefore were read as instruments of empire.

Fortifications Fortifications and other military structures are perhaps the type of architecture most clearly equated with the expansionistic principles of empire. In some cases the Incas built their own fortresses, whereas in other cases they coopted previously existing structures for their own ends. Defensive terracing, concentric walls, zigzagging fortifications, moats, and observation posts were typical elements associated with fortress construction. Due to dramatic and varied topography, Inca engineers adapted each structure to its site, often creating units that display a surprisingly harmonious landscape aesthetic that belies the nature of their function. Their position in relation to cities varied by region and situation, with some fortresses placed nearby but outside cities, while in other regions, depending on necessity, they were placed in remote locations to monitor key traffic points through the mountains.

Colca In order to supply an empire that placed monumental demands on conditions of mobility, such as the efficient and rapid maneuvering of armies or large labor forces, the Incas maintained a network of storehouses, or *colcas*, along the Inca highways and in close proximity to towns and villages. The Inca system borrowed and elaborated on centuries of pan-Andean storage practices. Inca storehouses were typically circular or rectangular and sited outside a settlement in high, cool, windy locations. The extent of the system was immense, and the *colca* facilities stored everything necessary to sustain a large, mobile population, including sandals, blankets, weapons, clothes, and staple foodstuffs such as maize or dried potatoes.

Controversies over Unity

It is arguable to what degree an imperial entity finds it necessary to promote a general ethos that may or may not be called national unity. For the Incas, problems in cultural unity were exacerbated by the tension between rapid Inca expansion, the majority of which happened in 60 to 70 years, and surviving local political-cultural traditions, which remained variously intact. In what may be a fundamental irony, the conditions and factors that coalesced to allow for their meteoric rise to pan-Andean hegemony ultimately compromised the Incas' ability to make it all cohere. Given the technology of the day, this is only too understandable. Also, it is worth questioning to what extent the Incas even promoted the idea of cultural unity. For example, Rowe tends to agree with the Jesuit chronicler Cobo, who wrote in 1653, "the whole foundation of their policy of government rested on means designed to keep their people subject and deprive them of the zeal to revolt against them." Perhaps, then, the imperial objective was unity as a consequence of disunity; keeping the various polities fractious and internally contentious practically precludes the organization needed for large-scale revolt. It is difficult to say which is a more effective policy in terms of cohesive imperial government, and the Incas likely adopted variations of both according to necessity.

By the time Spanish forces under Francisco Pizarro met Atahualpa at Cajamarca, Peru, the Inca governmental structure had already begun to dissolve. The dynastic war between Atahualpa and Huayna Cápac's other son, Huáscar, facilitated what turned out to be the empire's last stand. Of course, neither of the opposing forces could have anticipated the deleterious consequences of the Spanish arrival, even though its more shadowy and equally destructive agent had already arrived in the form of smallpox and European disease.

READING

Social Structure and Class Hierarchy

Brian S. Bauer, *Ancient Cuzco: Heartland of the Inca* (Austin: University of Texas Press, 2004).
———, *The Development of the Inca State* (Austin: University of Texas Press, 1992).
———, *The Sacred Landscape of the Inca: The Cusco Ceque System* (Austin: University of Texas Press, 1998).
Burr Brundage, *Lords of Cuzco: A History and Description of the Inca People in Their Final Days* (Norman: University of Oklahoma Press, 1967).
Pedro de Cieza de León, *The Incas of Pedro de Cieza de León*. Translated by Harriet de Onis and edited by Victor W. von Hagen (Norman: University of Oklahoma Press, 1998).
Bernabé Cobo, *Inca Religion and Customs*. Translated and edited by Roland Hamilton (Austin: University of Texas Press, 1990).
Paul H. Gelles, "Equilibrium and Extraction: Dual Organization in the Andes," *American Ethnologist* 22, no. 4 (1995): 710–742.
Felipe Guamán Poma de Ayala, *Letter to a King: A Picture History of the Inca Civilisation*. Translated and edited by Christopher Dilke (London: George Allen & Unwin, 1978).
———, *El primer nueva corónica y buen gobierno*. 3 vols. Edited by John Murra and Rolena Adorno. (Mexico: Siglo Veintiuno, 1992).
Catherine Julien, *Inca Administration in the Titicaca Basin as Reflected at the Provincial Capital of Hatunqolla*. Ph.D. diss., Department of Anthropology, University of California, Berkeley, 1978.
———, "Inca Decimal Administration in the Lake Titicaca Region." In *The Inca and Aztec States, 1400–1800*, edited by George A. Collier, Renato I. Rosaldo, and John D. Wirth, 119–152 (New York: Academic Press, 1982).
Michael A. Malpass, *Daily Life in the Inca Empire* (Westport, Conn.: Greenwood Press, 1996).

Susan A. Niles, *Callachaca: Style and Status in an Inca Community* (Iowa City: University of Iowa Press, 1987).

María Rostworowski de Diez Canseco, *History of the Inca Realm*. Translated by Harry B. Iceland (Cambridge: Cambridge University Press, 1999).

John Rowe, "Inca Culture at the Time of the Spanish Conquest." In *Handbook of South American Indians*, Bureau of American Ethnology, Bulletin 143. Vol. 2, *The American Civilizations*, edited by Julian H. Steward, 183–330 (Washington, D.C.: Smithsonian Institution, 1946).

Jeanette E. Sherbondy, *The Canal System of Hanan Cuzco*. Ph.D. diss., University of Illinois, Urbana, 1982.

———, "Water Ideology in Inca Ethnogenesis." In *Andean Cosmologies through Time: Persistence and Emergence*, edited by Robert V. H. Dover, Katherine Seibold, and John McDowell, 46–66 (Bloomington: Indiana University Press, 1992).

R. Tom Zuidema, *Inca Civilization in Cuzco*. Translated by Jean-Jacques Decoster (Austin: University of Texas Press, 1990).

———, "The Inca Kinship System: A New Theoretical View." In *Andean Kinship and Marriage*, no. 7, edited by Ralph Bolton and Enrique Mayer, 240–281 (Washington, D.C.: American Anthropological Association Special Publication, 1977).

Inca Statesmanship

Juan de Betanzos, *Narrative of the Incas*. Translated and edited by Roland Hamilton and Dana Buchanan (Austin: University of Texas Press, 1996).

"Discurso de la sucesión y gobierno de los yngas" [ca. 1570]. In *Juicio de límites entre el Perú y Bolivia; Prueba peruana presentada al gobierno de la República Argentina*, vol. 8, edited by Victor M. Martúa, 149–165 (Madrid: Tipografía de los hijos de M. G. Hernandez).

Garcilaso de la Vega, El Inca, *Royal Commentaries of the Inca and General History of Peru* (Austin: University of Texas Press, 1987).

Catherine Julien, *Reading Inca History* (Iowa City: Iowa University Press, 2002).

Paul Kirchoff, "The Social and Political Organization of the Andean Peoples." In *Handbook of South American Indians*, Bureau of American Ethnology, Bulletin, No. 143. Vol. 5, *The Comparative Ethnology of South American Indians*, edited by Julian H. Steward, 292–311 (Washington, D.C.: Smithsonian Institution, 1946).

George Kubler, "The Behavior of Atahualpa, 1531–1533," *Hispanic American Historical Review* 25, no. 4 (November 1945): 413–427.

———, "The Neo-Inca State (1537–1572)," *Hispanic American Review* 27, no. 2 (May 1947): 189–203.

———, "A Peruvian Chief of State: Manco Inca (1515–1545)," *Hispanic American Historical Review* 24, no. 2 (May 1944): 253–276.

Gordon F. McEwan, *The Incas: New Perspectives* (Santa Barbara, Calif.: ABC-CLIO, 2006).

Fernando de Montesinos, *Memorias antiguas historiales del Perú*. Translated and edited by Philip Ainsworth Means, introduction by Clements R. Markham (London: Hakluyt Society, 1920).

John Murra and Craig Morris. "Dynastic Oral Tradition, Administrative Records and Archaeology in the Andes," *World Archaeology* 7, no. 3 (1976): 259–279.

Susan Niles, "The Nature of Inca Royal Estates." In *Machu Picchu: Unveiling the Mystery of the Incas*, edited by Richard L. Burger and Lucy C. Salazar, 49–70 (New Haven, Conn.: Yale University Press, 2004).

———, *The Shape of Inca History* (Iowa City: University of Iowa Press, 1999).

Richard P. Schaedel, "Early State of the Incas." In *The Early State*, edited by Henri Claessen and Peter Skalnick, 289–320 (The Hague, Netherlands: Mouton, 1978).

Nathan Wachtel, "The *Mitimas* of the Cochabamba Valley: The Colonization Policy of Huayna Capac." In *The Inca and Aztec States, 1400–1800*, edited by George A. Collier, Renato I. Rosaldo, and John D. Wirth, 199–235 (New York: Academic Press, 1982).

Politics through the Empire

Brian Bauer, *Ancient Cuzco: Heartland of the Inca* (Austin: University of Texas Press, 2004).

———, "The Legitimization of the Inca State in Myth and Ritual," *American Anthropologist* 98, no. 2 (1996): 327–337.

Ralph Bauer, ed., *An Inca Account of the Conquest of Peru by Titu Cusi Yupanqui* (Boulder: Colorado University Press, 2005).

Joseph Bram, *An Analysis of Inca Militarism*, American Ethnological Society Monographs 4 (1941).

David L. Browman, "Tiwanaku Expansion and Altiplano Economic Patterns." In *Estudios Arqueologicos* 5, 107–120 (Autofagasta: Universidad de Chile, 1980).

———, "Toward the Development of the Tiahuanaco (Tiwanaku) State." In *Advances in Andean Archaeology*, edited by D. L. Browman, 327–349 (The Hague, Netherlands: Mouton, 1978).

Burr C. Brundage, *Empire of the Inca* (Norman: University of Oklahoma Press, 1963).

———, *Lords of Cuzco: A History and Description of the Inca People in Their Final Days* (Norman: University of Oklahoma Press, 1967).

———, *Two Earths, Two Heavens: An Essay Contrasting the Aztecs and the Incas* (Albuquerque: University of New Mexico Press, 1975).

Richard L. Burger and Lucy C. Salazar, *Machu Picchu: Unveiling the Mystery of the Incas* (New Haven, Conn.: Yale University Press, 2004).

Pedro Carrasco, "The Political Economy of the Aztec and Inca States." In *The Inca and Aztec States, 1400–1800: Anthropology and History*, edited by George A. Collier, Renato I. Rosaldo, and John D. Wirth, 23–40 (New York: Academic Press, 1982).

Pedro de Cieza de León, *The Discovery and Conquest of Peru* (Durham, N.C.: Duke University Press, 1998).

Geoffrey W. Conrad, "Cultural Materialism, Split Inheritance, and the Expansion of Ancient Peruvian Empires," *American Antiquity* 46 (1981): 3–26.

David Noble Cook, *Born to Die: Disease and New World Conquest, 1492–1650* (Cambridge: Cambridge University Press, 1998).

———, *Demographic Collapse: Indian Peru, 1520–1620* (Cambridge: Cambridge University Press, 1981).

R. Alan Covey, *How the Incas Built Their Heartland* (Ann Arbor: University of Michigan Press, 2005).

Terence N. D'Altroy, *The Incas* (London: Blackwell, 2002).

———. *Political and Domestic Economy in the Inka Empire*. Columbia-NYU Latin American, Caribbean, and Iberian occasional papers, no. 3 (New York: The Consortium of Columbia University Institute of Latin American and Iberian Studies and New York University Center for Latin American and Caribbean Studies, 1988).

———, *Provincial Power in the Inka Empire* (Washington, D.C.: Smithsonian Institution, 1992).

Terence N. D'Altroy and Christine Ann Hastorf, *Empire and Domestic Economy, Interdisciplinary Contributions to Archaeology* (New York: Kluwer Academic, 2001).

Nigel Davies, *The Incas* (Niwot: University Press of Colorado, 1995).

Timothy K. Earle and Terence N. D'Altroy, "The Political Economy of the Inka Empire: The Archaeology of Power and Finance." In *Archaeological Thought in America*, edited by Carl C. Lamberg-Karlovsky, 183–204 (Cambridge: Cambridge University Press, 1989).

Ian S. Farrington, "Prehistoric Intensive Agriculture: Preliminary Notes on River Canalization in the Sacred Valley of the Incas." In *Drained Field Agriculture in Central and South America*, International Series, No. 189, edited by John Darch, 221–235 (Oxford: British Archaeological Reports, 1983).

———, "Ritual Geography, Settlement Patterns and the Characterization of the Provinces of the Inka Heartland," *World Archaeology* 23 (1992): 368–385.

Graziano Gasparini and Louise Margolies, *Inca Architecture*. Translated by Patricia Lyons (Bloomington: Indiana University Press, 1980).

Adriana von Hagen and Craig Morris, *The Cities of the Ancient Andes* (London: Thames & Hudson, 1998).

Ian Heath, *The Armies of the Aztec and Inca Empires, Other Native Peoples of the Americas, and the Conquistadors, 1450–1608*. Vol. 2, *Armies of the Sixteenth Century* (Guernsey, England: Foundry, 1999).

John Hemming, *The Conquest of the Incas* (London: MacMillan, 1970).

John Hyslop, *The Inka Road System* (Orlando, Fla.: Academic Press, 1984).

———, *Inka Settlement Planning* (Austin: University of Texas Press, 1990).

———, *Inkawasi: The New Cusco, Cañate, Junahuaná, Peru*, BAR International Series 234 (Oxford: British Archaeological Papers, 1985).

Ann Kendall, *Aspects of Inca Architecture: Description, Function, and Chronology*, Bar International Series 242, 2 vols. (Oxford: British Archaeological Papers, 1985).

Sabine MacCormack, *On the Wings of Time: Rome, the Incas, Spain, and Peru* (Princeton, N.J.: Princeton University Press, 2006).

Colin McEwan and Maarten van de Guchte, "Ancestral Time and Sacred Space in Inca State Ritual." In *The Ancient Americas: Art from Sacred Landscapes*, edited by Richard F. Townshend, 359–373 (Chicago: Art Institute of Chicago, 1992).

Jerry D. Moore, "The Archaeology of Plazas and the Proxemics of Ritual: Three Andean Traditions," *American Anthropologist* 98, no. 4 (1996): 789–802.

———, *Architecture and Power in the Ancient Andes* (Cambridge: Cambridge University Press, 2005).

———, *Cultural Landscapes in the Ancient Andes* (Gainesville: University Press of Florida, 2005).

Craig Morris, "The Infrastructure of Inka Control in the Peruvian Central Highlands." In *The Inca and Aztec States, 1400–1800: Anthropology and History*, edited by George A. Collier, Renato I. Rosaldo, and John D. Wirth, 153–171 (New York: Academic Press, 1982).

———, "Inka Strategies of Incorporation and Governance." In *Archaic States*, edited by Gary M. Feinman and Joyce Marcus, 293–309 (Santa Fe, N. Mex.: School of American Research Press, 1998).

———, "Master Design of the Inca," *Natural History* 85, no. 10 (1976): 58–67.

———, "State Settlements in Tawantinsuyu: A Strategy of Compulsory Urbanism." In *Contemporary Archaeology: A Guide to Theory and Contributions*, edited by Mark P. Leone, 393–401 (Carbondale: Southern Illinois University Press).

———. "Symbols to Power: Styles and Media in the Inka State." In *Style, Society, and Person: Archaeological and Ethnological Perspectives*, edited by Christopher Carr and Jill E. Neitzel, 419–433 (New York: Plenum Press, 1995).

Craig Morris and Adriana von Hagen, *The Inka Empire and Its Andean Origins* (New York: Abbeville Press, 1993).

Craig Morris and Donald E. Thompson, *Huanuco Pampa: An Inca City and Its Hinterland* (London: Thames & Hudson, 1985).

Michael Moseley, *The Incas and Their Ancestors*. Rev. ed. (New York: Thames & Hudson, 2001).

John Murra, "Cloth and Its Functions in the Inca State," *American Anthropologist* 64 (1962): 710–728.

———, "The Economic Organization of the Inca State." 1955. Reprint, *Supplement No. 1 to Research in Economic Anthropology* (Greenwich: JAI Press, 1980).

———, "The Mit'a Obligations of Ethnic Groups to the Inka State." In *The Inca and Aztec States, 1400–1800*, edited by George A. Collier, Renato I. Rosaldo, and John D. Wirth, 237–262 (New York: Academic Press, 1982).

Susan A. Niles, "Inca Architecture and the Sacred Landscape." In *The Ancient Americas: Art from the Sacred Landscapes*, edited by Richard Townsend, 347–357 (Chicago: Art Institute of Chicago, 1992).

———, *The Shape of Inca History* (Iowa City: Iowa University Press, 1999).

Franklin G. Y. Pease, "The Formation of Tawantinsuyu: Mechanisms of Colonization and Relationship with Ethnic Groups." In *The Inca and Aztec States, 1400–1800*, edited by George A. Collier, Renato I. Rosaldo, and John D. Wirth, 173–198 (New York: Academic Press, 1982).

Pedro Pizarro, *Relation of the Discovery and Conquest of the Kingdoms of Peru*. Translated and edited by Philip Ainsworth Means (New York: Cortes Society, 1921).

Jean-Pierre Protzen, "Inca Architecture." In *The Inca World: The Development of Pre-Columbian Peru, A.D. 1000–1534*, edited by Laura Laurencich Minelli, 193–217 (Norman: University of Oklahoma Press, 1992).

———, *Inca Architecture and Construction at Ollantaytambo* (London: Oxford University Press, 1993).

John Rowe, "Inca Policies and Institutions Relating to the Cultural Unification of the Empire." In *The Inca and Aztec States, 1400–1800*, edited by George A. Collier, Renato I. Rosaldo, and John D. Wirth, 93–118 (New York: Academic Press, 1982).

———, "What Kind of Settlement Was Inca Cuzco?" *Ñawpa Pacha* 5 (1982): 59–77.

Frank Salomon and Stuart B. Schwartz, eds., *Cambridge History of the Native Peoples of the Americas*, vol. 3 (Cambridge: Cambridge University Press, 1999).

Richard P. Schaedel, "Early State of the Incas." In *The Early State*, edited by Henri Claessen and Peter Skalnick, 289–320 (The Hague, Netherlands: Mouton, 1978).

Katharina J. Schreiber, *Wari Imperialism in Middle Horizon Peru*, Anthropological Papers 87 (Ann Arbor: University of Michigan Museum of Anthropology, 1992).

Mary Van Buren, "Rethinking the Vertical Archipelago: Ethnicity, Exchange, and History in the South Central Andes," *American Anthropologist*, New Series, 98, no. 2 (1996): 338–351.

R. Tom Zuidema, "Guamán Poma and the Art of Empire: Toward an Iconography of Inca Royal Dress." In *Transatlantic Encounters: Europeans and Andeans in the Sixteenth Centuries*, edited by K. J. Andrien and Rolena Adorno, 151–275 (Berkeley: University of California Press, 1991).

5

MILITARY AND WARFARE

The history of Tawantinsuyu (Tahuantinsuyo), or the Inca Empire (1434–1534), begins and ends with military actions. Given extremes of geography and distance—from the empire's center at the capital of Cuzco, stretching to Santiago, Chile; Quito, Ecuador; and from the coast over the Andes Mountains to the Amazon—the success of the military, and to a great extent the success of the empire, was predicated on the Incas' ability to organize effectively on a grand scale. Although Inca imperial strategy combined the use of diplomacy, coercion, ceremonial exchange, marriage, and enculturation, warfare remained essential. To effectively wage war the Incas had to mobilize tens of thousands of soldiers and thousands of auxiliary personnel for campaigns that could last months, if not years. In order to do so efficiently and effectively the Incas established a vast infrastructure of garrisons, frontier forts, depots, communication relay stations, and storage facilities—all tied together via the Inca road network (*capac ñan*), which itself was built on older roads and expanded, totaling some 25,000–30,000 kilometers (15,534–18,641 mi.).

Inca warfare was largely an offensive operation; the Incas took the fight to the enemy, not the other way around. Yet, even after the successful conquest of a region, insurrection was a common and recurring problem. In a broad sense the rapid growth of the empire and its even quicker demise at the hands of the Spanish never allowed conquered regions to settle in and identify themselves as Inca subjects let alone as part of a single political economy. As a result of this instability the goals of military policy eventually shifted from a focus on acquisition toward pacification, quelling rebellion, and securing the frontier. In order to do so Inca infrastructure was upgraded, with each geopolitical theater presenting its own difficulties to which the Incas had to adapt accordingly. As broad policies were ineffective in dealing with the variety of regional problems, the Incas dealt with each according to its own criteria, emphasizing policy changes as the situation dictated. The role of the military, or the effect of a strong military presence, was often a key instrument in negotiating or implementing these policies.

A fair amount of information on Inca warfare exists from the early 16th century, in part because many of the early Spanish chroniclers were themselves soldiers who directly engaged the Incas on the field of battle. Their accounts, however, must be read with caution, owing to their tendency toward self-aggrandizement. They must also be read with an awareness of 16th-century cultural predilections; often their accounts more directly reflect their own European education, religion, and station rather than attempting a critical, unbiased narrative. Similarly, accounts based on the recorded interviews of Incas must also be read with a discerning eye because their accounts, too, tend to glorify their own actions and history. The following chapter examines a broad range of Inca military subjects, including organization, logistics and support, tactics, infrastructure, weaponry, and clothing. It ends with a synopsis of primary Inca military campaigns, both real and quasi-historical, that catapulted the Incas into their imperial trajectory and which ended only with the dynastic war and the arrival of the Spanish.

MILITARY ORGANIZATION

For much of their history the Incas lacked a standing army in the modern sense and relied on the *mita* labor system to supply its military personnel; in the case of military service this system had a similar effect as a draft. The *mita* labor system was essentially a service tax paid to the state through labor, which all Inca subjects were required to pay. As a result, the Inca military consisted of peasant laborers, males 25–50 years old, subject to call-up on a rotational basis. The army chain of command was similar to a pyramidal hierarchy, with the Sapa Inca as the commander-in-chief and an occasional field general, although the Inca ruler's military responsibilities turned toward delegation as the empire expanded and other administrative and governmental concerns required his direct attention.

The officers reporting directly to the king, who would be more or less analogous to an upper echelon of generals, were usually royal kin, although other non-Inca elites could hold elevated positions. It should be mentioned that while choosing relatives for high positions made sense, the practice was fraught with potential intrigue. Increased glory tended to translate into a direct threat to the throne; thus, it was not uncommon for the king to execute successful military commanders, even when they were family. Failed generals appear to have been removed and disgraced but not executed.

Leadership and Command Structure

Probably mimicking Inca social structure, two or four commanders typically led a campaign. The chroniclers who recounted such events referred to these leaders in distinctly European terms, referring to them as field generals or field marshalls and masters of the camp or general administrators of the army. The commander of an Inca field army was referred to as *apusquipay*; he was assisted by a deputy commander called an *apusquipratin*. The units were usually organized in a decimal structure made up of soldiers from particular ethnic groups led by their own lord. The decimal structure used to organize the military mimicked the decimal system used to organize society in general. The smallest unit contained 10 heads of household (*hatun runa*, or adult males) under the command of a *chunka camayoc*. Fifty soldiers were under the command of the *piska camayoc*; 100, under the *pachaka camayoc*; 1,000, the *waranqa camayoc*; 2,500, the *apu*; 5,000, the *hatun apu*; and 10,000 were under the command of the *hunu kuraka*. Each of these divisions contained two halves, each with its own leader, in keeping with the general Inca tendency toward dual organization. Furthermore, Inca military groups were further divided by a practice known as tripartite organization, a condition possibly borrowed from the neighboring Chanca people.

Spanish sources mention two chiefs for each Inca army, a dual command structure that directly reflected the concept of Inca social division into moieties (a form of dual social organization); in turn, this aspect of division by halves further reflected Inca spatial division through its *hanan* and *hurin* (upper and lower) sections. In other words, the dual command structure represented the two parts of Inca society from Upper and Lower Cuzco, which ultimately reflected a condition both of balance and the subdominant privilege of the lower division.

At its source, tripartite division probably reflected religious and social ideology. The Andean scholar Rostworowski suggests the tripartite division corresponds to the pan-Andean kin distinctions referred to as *collana, payan*, and *callao*—each of which corresponds to a familial-social hierarchical place: *Collana* is a term that refers to an elder brother, indicating the most important; *payan* refers to femininity, from *paya*, meaning "noblewoman"; and *callao* is a term referring to younger brother and by extension common people.

Creating an Army

The raising of an army could come at any time and proved a tremendous burden on communities, which sometimes contributed a quarter of their population to any campaign and thus lost that number of able-bodied field hands. Word was sent via the regular administrative structure to local lords who then mobilized the required numbers of men. Traditionally those who stayed behind farmed the fields of those who left. Most, if not all, married males between the ages of 25 and 50 were subject to call-up, and unmarried men aged 18–25 were similarly called to service, though their responsibilities were to bear messages and cargo. Wives and close kin often accompanied the men on their campaigns, thus adding to the burden on the settlement while simultaneously multiplying the logistical difficulties of maintaining a mobile army. In early plunder campaigns the men were called up for a definite and limited period of time; later, however, as the burden of imperial maintenance became more complicated, troops were sometimes called away for years.

As the empire expanded, new subjects, including various ethnic polities, were required to serve in the military. Increased ethnic diversity among the troops, however, increased communication inefficiencies due to language barriers and therefore limited on-the-field strategy changes. It appears that some polities paid in greater numbers than others, depending on the circumstance. In some cases, the added burden was punishment for previous resistance, but in other cases the heaviest contributions were requested according to perceived loyalty. For example, during the reign of Huayna Cápac (according to traditional king lists, Huayna Cápac was the 11th and final Inca monarch; following his death the empire descended into a bloody war of succession, which was followed immediately by the arrival of the Spanish) the Collas, an ethnic group from Collasuyu, the section of the empire to the south of the capital Cuzco, made the heaviest contributions, quite possibly because they had been incorporated into the empire early in its expansion phase and were considered trustworthy. It is also possible that their *mita* burden, or labor tax, was greater because the region was more heavily populated, thus accounting for a greater number of contributing individuals.

TRAINING

Warrior training often began early in youth in the form of ritual battles and training in martial arts. According to the Spanish chronicler Cobo, a Jesuit priest who entered Peru in 1599 and spent many years traveling among the native Andeans, captains and officers were distributed in many precincts throughout the empire to train the youths typically aged 10–18. Similarly, ritual battles, as an aspect of a young male's initiation, were used to distinguish eventual warriors. The army's elite corps was called the *orejones* ("big ears," in Spanish). They were the only standing army the Incas maintained throughout the empire's duration and manned by troops trained from youth as warriors with the specific task of personally defending the person of the Sapa Inca. Recruits for the rank of *orejón* typically came out of Cuzco's aristocracy, though later versions of the corps suggested more ethnic affiliations that extended beyond the city limits and better reflected the diversity of the empire.

TROOP STRENGTH

A major part of the Incas' military strength came from its numbers. Overall troop strength varied by campaign, but Spanish accounts and oral histories indicate the Incas could field armies upward of 100,000 men, not including family members, retainers, porters, and servants who accompanied the army. The ninth Inca king, Pachacuti, fielded an army of 70,000 in his early campaigns and perhaps as many as 200,000 for the war against the Colla. Topa Inca, Pachacuti's successor, was said to have fielded an army of 250,000 for his campaigns in the northern hinterland of the empire. Manco Inca, an Inca king installed by the Spanish following the death of Atahualpa, may have fielded 200,000 men in his failed bid to vanquish the invading Spaniards. The numbers are cause for skepticism, especially in the wars against the Spanish, as both sides were accustomed to inflation.

MITMAQKUNA

A particularly important aspect of Inca military organization was its use of Inca and loyal non-Inca settlers called *mitmaqkuna* (*mitimaes*, in Spanish). The *mitmaqkuna* were essentially colonists following the Inca state strategy of forced resettlement; *mitmaqkuna*, as loyal subjects to the state, were introduced into conquered territory as a means of control and ensuring stability. The military duties of *mitmaqkuna* included manning forts and making weapons. But the concept of *mitmaqkuna* also worked in the reverse: Instead of placing loyal settlers into a newly conquered territory, the Incas also forcibly removed residents from areas of instability, those that were deemed prone to rebellion or insurrection, and resettled people either within their traditional territory or in far-distant provinces. From the Inca standpoint, the *mitmaqkuna* system ensured balance in newly conquered lands, yet from the conquered non-Incas' perspective, resettled *mitmaqkuna* were likely thought of as spies. There is evidence, too, that being a *mitmaqkuna* was a privileged position in the Inca hierarchy, as they were given land and even gifts by the state.

The chronicler Sarmiento de Gamboa, in his 1572 *Historia índica*, wrote that the Inca king himself was responsible for decisions regarding forced resettlement. According to Sarmiento, for example, the ninth king, Pachacuti, instructed his own people to go to the subject provinces and examine them and make models of them, after which the "models and descriptions were placed before the Inca, who examined them and considered the plains and fortresses. He ordered the investigators to watch what he was doing. Then he began to level the fortresses he wished and moved those inhabitants to lower land. And he moved those of the plains to the heights and mountains, each so far from the others and so from their natural land that they could not return to it." Archaeological settlement pattern studies in at least a few areas confirm statements such as this one by Sarmiento, to the effect that fortified settlements were abandoned while new settlements were founded in other areas.

MILITARY INFRASTRUCTURE

Provincial Centers

The Incas built provincial capitals that served governmental, religious, and military purposes. These centers often lay at intersections of natural conduits, adjacent to open valleys or plains where armies could be conveniently bivouacked. Because many regions were never perfectly secure, it has been suggested that these settlements were located in part to reduce the chance of rebellion and to support reprisals when they did occur. As the system of support grew in quantity and quality, so, too, did the army and its ability to wage war. Each major center along the road network had hundreds if not thousands of storehouses (colcas) continuously supplied and resupplied with all military provisions necessary to maintain a standing army.

Provincial centers afforded the Incas numerous military advantages, including but not limited to a center that served simultaneously as a staging ground, a place to advance from or withdraw to, a site for organization and administration according to shifting military needs, a visual signifier of Inca domain, a place from which to keep tabs on insurrection-minded populations, a storage site, a shelter

for ritual or ceremony, and a bivouac location for mobile army units. Given the disadvantages of distance and technology that defined the empire at this time, the subsequent advantages of distant population centers with storage and housing capabilities become apparent.

The *kallanka*, a staple architectural unit in the Inca building vocabulary, was a type of hall that provided barracks for the soldiers. The *kallanka* is essentially a large rectangular open-plan enclosure constructed with both masonry and adobe. Its archaeological footprint has been found both in the heartland and at provincial centers. As the interior had no divisions it was an effective structure for gathering and holding assemblies and certainly could have been used to shelter portions of an army on the march. *Kallankas* were known to be as large as 78 meters by 26 meters (256 × 85 ft.). Excavations at Huánuco Pampa, a major provincial outpost along the Inca highway in the north-central highlands, uncovered a *kallanka* that measured 70 meters by 12 meters (230 × 39 ft.).

Fortifications and Garrisons

Forts and fortifications were most common at the frontier and border regions, as well as in the highlands generally. As the empire annexed new territory beyond the Cuzco basin, new infrastructure was needed to safeguard new conquests. Forts cluster mostly in northern Ecuador and along the perimeter of Collasuyu (the southeastern part of the empire)—in Bolivia, Argentina, and Chile—suggesting greater stresses at the edges. Fortifications are absent in much of the heartland surrounding Cuzco, although there are plenty of sites that appear chosen in part because they are atop hills or at other readily defensible locations. Two important heartland sites that did play a military role—Sacsayhuamán, above Cuzco, and Ollantaytambo, in the Urubamba Valley—were only partially designed as fortifications, though they were effective military structures when needed due to the nature of their architecture and site planning. Sacsayhuamán is often referred to as a fortress temple, though it likely had many functions; Ollantaytambo similarly was referred to as a fortress-garden, in part because Inca forces held up there following the fall of Cuzco to the Spanish in 1534.

Many Inca sites, if not outright military installations, nevertheless presented themselves as defense-minded. At a site such as the famous Machu Picchu, for example, naturally located atop a nearly impenetrable mountaintop, the presence of intensive wall construction has led some scholars to believe they were for defensive purposes. Other scholars argue they are better understood as a means to delimit sacred space. Even when the function of a site is not explicitly understood in the archaeology, it is nevertheless apparent that many sites, Machu Picchu included, could be readily adapted as a defensive position if necessary. Above and beyond their function, fortresses and garrisons reflected Inca authority and indelibly stamped an imperial signature on the landscape.

OLLANTAYTAMBO

Ollantaytambo is a town situated on the Vilcanota-Urubamba River, roughly 60 kilometers (37 mi.) northwest of Cuzco, in what is referred to as the Incas' Sacred Valley. It is one of the longest continually inhabited towns in the Americas, and it is the site of spectacular Inca ruins. The site is associated with the ninth Sapa Inca, Pachacuti, who conquered the territory and then built the town as one of his royal estates. Perhaps the most distinctive features of the site are its extensive waterworks and its 17 agricultural terraces leading steeply up the side of a hill. Spanish chroniclers wrote that the terraces were planted with flowers, which accounts for the site being referred to as a "fortress-garden."

In military terms the location of the site—surrounded by mountains and pitched against a steep mountain wall—affords a natural defensive. The approach to the site from the direction of Cuzco also offered a natural defensive capability, as the route to the city wound back-and-forth across the river, meaning that any invading force would necessarily have to ford the river. This proved to be the case following the Spanish capture of Cuzco, the installation of Manco Inca as regent, and his subsequent rebellion. It was during the early stages of the rebellion that Manco retreated to Ollantaytambo, elaborated its defenses, and fortified the approach

along the river. In 1536 Manco fended off an invading Spanish force, but soon enough his position there became untenable, and he retreated deeper into the heavily forested Vilcabamba region, where a remnant fraction of the empire held out into the 1570s as a neo-Inca state.

SACSAYHUAMÁN

On the hillside above Cuzco lay the fortress temple of Sacsayhuamán. It is an astonishing example of the Incas' ingenuity in using stone as a building material. Its most pervasive features—in fact, the only features that survived the Spanish using the site as a quarry—are its walls, which run for 380 meters (1,247 ft.) along three terraces in zigzag fashion. The three terraces are constructed of gigantic polygonal masonry sometimes referred to as "cyclopean." In polygonal masonry constructions, interlocking blocks are set against each other without mortar in a jigsaw-puzzle fashion, polished to a rusticated smoothness and displaying a slight bulge over its full surface, called an "entasis." Some of the larger blocks at Sacsayhuamán measure as much as five meters by five meters by two and a half meter (16 × 16 × 8 ft.) and are estimated to weigh as much as 126 tons. Access to the interior is gained only through a narrow doorway inset at the deepest portion of the zigzag; there are only a couple doorways along the entire perimeter, thereby emphasizing its defensive capacity. It was designed this way so that an enemy approaching the doorway would face a barrage from above on two sides. The massiveness of the walls alone speaks directly to Sacsayhuamán's virtues as a fortress.

The chroniclers differ on whom to attribute its construction to. Depending on the source, it is attributed to Pachacuti, the ninth Inca, or his son, Topa Inca. Construction lasted more than 50 years, and some scholars estimate that as many as 20,000 laborers worked on it at any single time. It was large enough to contain 5,000 persons. Though it has clear advantages as a fort, its actual function is debated, and it probably served multipurposes, including temple, warehouse, ceremonial complex, and shrine.

Sacsayhuamán and the Spanish Conquest
Cuzco fell to the Spanish in 1534. In 1536 Manco

5.1 Sacsayhuamán was in part an Inca military fortress located above Cuzco. (Photo courtesy Ananda Cohen Suarez)

Inca led a revolt to retake the Inca capital. Manco Inca was one of the former monarch Huayna Cápac's sons and had been installed by the conquistadores as a puppet ruler following the death of Huáscar and after the seizure and eventual garroting of Atahualpa. Huáscar and Atahualpa, also sons of Huayna Cápac, had been fighting a war of succession for the right to rule the empire; Atahualpa had had Huáscar killed, but before his rule was solidified, the Spanish arrived. Manco, then, following the death of his half brothers ruled first as a token figurehead but then fled Cuzco to assemble an Inca army to retake the city. Returning, he took Sacsayhuamán as his base during the siege of Cuzco, in which an estimated 200,000 to 400,000 indigenous soldiers and accessories gathered. Juan Pizarro, head of the Spanish troops in Cuzco and a half brother of chief conquistador Francisco Pizarro, realized the only way to counter-direct

Inca attacks was by taking the citadel at Sacsayhuamán. The Spanish assaulted the fortress, climbed its walls with ladders, and fought the Incas in hand-to-hand combat. Despite a gross advantage in numbers, the Incas succumbed to Spanish steel, and the Spaniards retook Sacsayhuamán. During the rebuilding of Cuzco, which had been burned during Inca revolt, the Spanish scavenged the masonry of Sacsayhuamán for their own houses, to the extent that some chroniclers claimed that masonry from the site was reinstituted in every house in Cuzco. The site in its current form is a direct result of this process.

Sacsayhuamán and St. James There is an apocryphal story regarding the Spanish taking of the fortress that is worth recounting. The story is predicated by overwhelming Inca numeric superiority; by some estimates the Incas held a thousand-to-one advantage over the Spanish. Yet, despite overwhelming odds, and even considering the advantage the Spanish maintained with horse and steel, the Spaniards managed not simply to escape but even to retake the fortress on high ground and scatter the Inca forces. Given the numbers, how was this possible? According to later accounts, Spanish victory was a direct result of the miraculous intervention of St. James. St. James had been a useful figure and patron saint in the Spanish wars against the Moors to retake the Iberian Peninsula (Reconquest), where he was adapted as Santiago Matamoros, or St. James the Moor-Slayer. In the conquest of the Americas St. James the Moor-Slayer became Santiago Mataindios, or St. James the Indian-Slayer. Thus, conveniently enough for the Spanish, all the proposals of conquest were divinely sanctified.

SACRED VALLEY FORTS

The Sacred Valley of the Inca, to the north and east of the Cuzco basin along a stretch of the Vilcanota-Urubamba River, was a key settlement area of the empire. It is well known in both historic documents and archaeological literature because it was the location of royal estates. Inca-style architecture and ceramics further help identify the region as associated with elite, royal settlements. A number of sites in the valley dating from the early expansion period or even earlier strongly suggest a defensive nature.

Raqchi   The fort at Raqchi is associated with a village that predates the earliest dates of Inca imperial expansion and thus probably reflects a pre-Inca site taken over by the Incas. The fort is located on a prominent ridge to take advantage of the natural defenses of the steep slopes. Several large rectangular structures suggest a densely populated area, and walls preserved to a height of three meters (10 ft.) indicate its defensive nature. There is also a dry moat dug around the ridge in order to restrict access. The Incas may have built the fortress after conquering a pre-Inca village.

War'qana and Pumamarca   A similar scenario probably holds true for the Sacred Valley sites of War'qana and Pumamarca. War'qana is located atop a prominence and has rectangular structures

similar to those at Raqchi. Research indicates that fortification walls associated with a defensive ditch restricted access to the ridge. Interpretations suggest that it, too, was a pre-Inca village converted to a fortress after the Inca conquered the area. Pumamarca is located near Ollantaytambo along a route to the lowlands. It has evidence of three forts that suggest the Incas conquered the area and then built the forts in defensible locations in order to monitor traffic along the traveler's route.

REMOTE FORTRESSES

An especially high concentration of fortified sites existed near Quito, Ecuador. The site of Pambamarca, 32 kilometers (20 mi.) northeast of Quito, contained 14 fortified hilltops. Its site appears to have been chosen in order to control a point of transit through a mountain pass. Elsewhere in central and southern Peru and in Bolivia, important fortified sites were located at Incallacta, Batanes, Incawasi, and Pocona. Numerous fortified locations lay south of Lake Titicaca in the frontier region of Argentina, such as at Pucará de Andalgadá, and in Chile at Cerro del Inga, Chena, and Angostura, indicating an intense Inca interest in the security of those regions and, consequently, their instability. Like Pambamarca, Cerro del Inga and Pucará de Andalgadá were located strategically at mountain passes. Many of these structures formed a defensive line well within the eastern border. While there are certainly many others, only a few are mentioned here.

Pambamarca   Pambamarca was a major military site at the Inca's northern frontier. East of Quito, it consists of at least 14 walled installations spread over variable topography. Several hundred meters separate the units from each other, and the total site is spread more than six kilometers (4 mi.). The highest unit, referred to as Unit 1, rests at 4,075 meters (13,369 ft.) above sea level, and the lowest is over 600 meters (1,969 ft.) lower. Early colonial sources describe it as having been occupied by *mitmaqkuna*, and one describes it as having been built by Cañari Indians, who resided in the area prior to the arrival of the Inca, as punishment for rebellious behavior.

Dominant features include concentric walls, elaborate gates for doorways using zigzag approaches, dry moats or ditches, and *kallankas*, the large, open halls. The concentric walls are a pre-Inca invention. The largest unit, Unit 1, has five increasingly higher levels sustained by concentric walls. Another unit, referred to as Quitaloma, has a spiral wall on its north side that encloses a platform, similar to an *usnu* (a ritual complex/platform) four meters (13 ft.) tall. Graves, pottery, and the ruins of more than 80 one-room structures have been found on its premises. Overall, Pambamarca appears to have been a permanent garrison housing Inca military units from which attacks were launched.

Incawasi The fortress-garrison Incawasi (Inca-huasi) is in the Cañete Valley of Peru's central desert coast. Incawasi is noteworthy for its large number of rectangular enclosures used as residential units and storage facilities, a large central plaza with an *usnu* platform, its strategic location, and what is possibly a temple of the sun. Incawasi appears to have been built quickly and crudely, primarily of stone mixed with clay and mud, with no intention of a long occupation. The lack of debris and sealed doorways suggests the site was closed after brief use.

Incallacta The site of Incallacta, in the department of Cochabamba, Bolivia, defended the eastern frontier against Chiriguano Indians, who overran it just before the Spanish conquest. Early colonial sources attribute its construction to Topa Inca, the 10th ruler by standard king lists. Its strategic location and extensive surrounding wall identify it as a military site. An enormous *kallanka* was probably used for ceremonies and is the site's most prominent building. Seven smaller *kallankas* may have served as barracks. Its massive wall is in some places five meters (16 ft.) tall and two meters (6.5 ft.) thick. In some areas it is built in a zigzag design similar to those at Sacsayhuamán. In several places features of the wall increase its military effectiveness. These include small, oblique windows that would have hindered direct passage of arrows or sling stones. A long, low platform is attached to the lower portion of the wall, upon which troops could walk the perimeter and peer over the top. And in a few places smaller wall segments create open spaces from which weapons could be slung. In addition to its

military function it may have served as an administrative center.

ATTACKING FORTRESSES

In the highlands and coastal regions fortresses or fortified sites were a common feature in the landscape. Provinces under attack by the Incas or provinces mounting a rebellion normally withdrew to fortified locations in the face of numerically superior Inca forces. Especially in the highlands fortresses were built at strategic spots such as mountain passes or hilltops. Barricaded behind fortress walls, the defenders would roll large boulders down on the approaching forces and launch a barrage of sling stones, to which the Incas defended themselves with rolls of tough, quilted cotton tented over their heads. The rolls of cotton were sometimes large enough to cover 100 men.

Given the topographic advantage most fortresses provide its defenders, a typical Inca strategy was simply to cut off the enemy from their supplies and wait while their food and water dwindled. This was especially useful along the coast, where a community's water flowed down from the mountains and could be diverted and cut off at its highland source. In other instances the Incas relied on trickery to lure the enemy out of their stronghold. In the war against the Caranquis in Quito, for instance, the Incas divided their force into three divisions, one of which pretended to weaken and flee. When the Caranquis left the fort to pursue the fleeing Inca division, a second division attacked from behind, and a third division entered the undefended fortress.

Types of Conquest

The Inca promulgated at least three different strategies of conquest, not all of which were predicated on war or seizing territory by force, though this certainly occurred. Three primary strategies were plunder, reciprocity, and what we might call retribution. The desired result of all three is effectively the same—a redistribution of power and authority in favor of the Inca.

Plunder

Plunder as a means of conquest was common during the Late Intermediate Period (ca. 900–1438) and at the beginning of the Late Horizon, when Cuzco was just another chiefly village in an Andean world full of small chiefdoms. The objective of wars of plunder was to seize the enemy's goods. Successful plundering had the benefit of instilling fear, thereby abetting the likelihood of immediate reprisal. Raids of this type typically ended with little or no exchange of territory.

Reciprocity

Reciprocity as conquest was carried out by means of ties established through the exchange of women and gifts. Elementally passive by comparison, this type of conquest involved an agreement to accept Inca rule in exchange for lavish gifts and communal feasting in the public plaza. In effect the gifts created a situation of indebtedness that could only be repaid through acquiescence. The "generosity" of the Incas and the passive acceptance of the new subjects were thus means to avert bloodshed. The public nature of the setting was an explicit acknowledgment and constituted a ritualized public contract. The passive nature of reciprocal agreements meant the avoidance of violent conflict, which probably suited all parties. From the Inca standpoint, an army of tested soldiers and a general aura of invincibility helped maintain existing agreements.

Reciprocity is a good example of the Inca ability to annex territory without military conflict. According to the Peruvian ethnohistorian María Rostworowski de Diez Canseco, reciprocity was a means of establishing order in a system that did not use money. By codifying the production and distribution of goods along political lines, and by interlocking various services, the Incas created a means wherein the recipient in effect became dependent on the giver. As a war strategy it has the advantage of avoiding war, though of course the agreement was most effective when backed by the threat of force. Ultimately it served the growth of the Inca state. For example, early in the period of expansion General Cápac Yupanqui, sent by his "brother"

Pachacuti, the ninth Inca king, arrived in lowland Chincha with a large force. According to the chronicles, he said he desired nothing from them but instead came with lavish gifts from Cuzco. Impressed by his offer, the local chiefs accepted the Incas as their rulers. Of course, the mere presence of the Inca forces in the background probably made this an easy decision.

In return, Cápac Yupanqui requested the construction of a house, a *hatuncancha*, which likely served as an administrative facility, and for women dedicated to the production of textiles and the preparation of beverages (*acllas*). Of course, another benefit of the arrangement for the Incas was the granting of an increased labor force of artisans and agriculturalists to work Inca lands, whose products would go to fill Inca storehouses. In a real sense these items—male and female labor and the products of cultivation—constitute the basis of Andean wealth. As time went on, the Inca polity grew stronger, and their demands often became more oppressive. While other processes that had been playing out over time contributed to imperial growth, it seems that similar scenarios of rapid capitulation based on reciprocity agreements, played out time and again, were one reason for the quick expansion of the Inca state. Conversely, however, this scenario of rapid expansion and forced inclusion offered little in the way of solidifying "national" identity, which in turn contributed to endemic rebellion and ultimately to the conquest of the Inca Empire by the Spanish.

Civil Conflict

The third type of conquest might be called retribution and is associated with Huayna Cápac, the 11th and final independent Inca ruler. Following his death a dynastic war of succession broke out between his sons Huáscar and Atahualpa. By this time the empire had reached, by most measures, its maximum in area to both the north and the south. Huayna Cápac's late conquests occurred on the borders of the realm and were marked by a greater belligerence and aggressiveness. Some scholars have ascribed this bellicosity to the lack of a tradition of reciprocity among societies in the frontier regions of the empire. In other words, instead of accepting Inca "generosity," local lords rejected the offer of assimilation and offered resistance, with the Incas typically emerging victorious after battle. Defeated lords were then taken to Cuzco and sacrificed in the plaza, after which the emperor named someone loyal to him to rule the area. In instances where resistance was particularly fierce or prolonged, sanctions fell on the entire male conquered population.

Strategy, Logistics, and Tactics

Following earlier periods of plunder, sometime in the mid-15th century, as the Inca imperial period began, strategy shifted to annexing land. Combinations of alliances, diplomacy, ceremony, and gift exchange, together with military action, became the linchpins of expansion. Inca warfare began with ritual preparations meant to ensure that all obligations to the gods were fulfilled and a favorable outcome was granted in return. It was facilitated through the Incas' extraordinary administrative and organizational capabilities and through infrastructure such as roads and storehouses. Although the preference was to avoid direct combat, it was perhaps inevitable that warfare ensued. When diplomacy failed and battle became unavoidable, the Incas planned accordingly, surveyed the terrain and their opposition, and relied on overwhelming force and a few favored tactical maneuvers to overwhelm their enemy. These issues are discussed in greater detail in the following sections.

Ritual Preparation

Religion was inseparable from Inca warfare. The Andean archaeologist Rowe wrote that religion was used to justify Inca conquest on the pretext that Inca religion was the highest and purest form of worship and that it was the Incas' duty to spread

this religion throughout the world. This is probably not dissimilar to earlier Andean forms of empire, such as the Early Horizon (ca. 1500–200 B.C.E.) religious cult centered in the north at Chavín de Huantar and the Middle Horizon (ca. 540–900 C.E.) empire centered at Wari in the central highlands. As was seen with the Wari Empire, for which religion was a primary motivation for warfare, the expansion of the Inca Empire was in part a result of the Incas' desire to spread what they considered the true religion.

The highly ritualized nature of Inca society was directly reflected in preparation for battle. Believing that they were driven by a divine mandate to spread the religion of the creator god Viracocha, the sun god Inti, and other deities, the Incas incorporated numerous rituals as preparation to ensure victory. For instance, they carried into battle stones painted or carved with images of snakes, birds, toads, pumas, and jaguars, presumably to extract some practical essence from the idol. In one ceremony a black llama was starved and then sacrificed, its weakening thought to correspond to the weakening of the enemy. Another ceremony, called the *itu*, was performed when the emperor went to war, and everyone in Cuzco refrained from sex and fasted for two days. Following that, women with dogs and all other animals left the city, and images of the gods were brought into the main plaza, Huacaypata, where two llamas and sometimes children were sacrificed.

BATTLE PREPARATION AND DIVINATION

Divinations were conducted to ascertain the outcome of battle. When the armies were ready to depart Cuzco they carried with them sacred idols, or *huacas*, usually stones representing mythical ancestors. These *huacas* were not simply symbols but embodied potent spirits. Similarly, seizing an enemy's idols was the same as seizing his power, and captured idols were taken to and stored in Cuzco as a symbol of imperial control. In the event that a subject group rose in insurrection or rebellion, their captured idols were often brought into the public square and flogged, intending to humiliate the group and cause them come into line.

Ritual preparation had a negative component in that its predictability could be taken advantage of, especially when the opponent does not adhere to the same rules of engagement. Such was the case during Inca incursions with the Spanish. For example, the Incas reserved the night of the full moon for ceremonies, even in the midst of a campaign. During Manco Inca's siege of Cuzco in 1536, in which Inca forces surrounded the city in an attempt to dislodge the Spanish soldiers there, the Spanish took the advantage of Inca full-moon ceremonies and staged a last-ditch charge up the hillside, eventually capturing the fortress temple Sacsayhuamán, which Manco Inca and his forces had held. Taking Sacsayhuamán ensured Spanish survival and proved to be a key moment in the diminishing hopes of Inca restoration.

Logistics

The road system was designed to facilitate the movement of large forces. Along the road *tambos* (*tampu*), or way stations, assisted operations by serving as places of refuge. *Tambos* were for royal or official parties only, so it is reasonable to think that during marches only the commanders made use of them. Aside from the road itself the most impressive facet of Inca logistical operations was the vast supply system of state storehouses (*colcas*), which stockpiled enormous amounts of food, arms, clothing, and other supplies. Before the army embarked, an advance mission was sent forward to request all local societies to ready supplies in order to ensure the storehouses were complete, which increased the preparedness of the army in its day-to-day maneuvers.

Llama caravans and human porters transported the bulk of goods when the army was on the march. The use of llamas and humans to carry matériel limited the daily range to about 20 kilometers (12 mi.) per day, which, not coincidentally, was the distance between *tambos* along the highway. The great number of porters and support, needing to resupply their own foodstuffs every few days, was a drain on the overall supply system. The most efficient means of resupply for the army and accompanying personnel was therefore a system of local and regional supply depots.

Strategy

Inca military strategy was initially concerned with extending borders, annexing territory, and asserting control over new populations. The primary plan in any given engagement was to avoid conflict and use the army as a means of intimidation, coercing the enemy to surrender. Diplomacy in this fashion often worked. The Sapa Inca, or Inca king, sent emissaries to explain the advantages of voluntary submission and what benefits would come from joining the empire peacefully. Simultaneous to these negotiations the Sapa Inca also sent emissaries to potential allies of the enemy in order to cut off any possible help.

It is generally believed that the ninth Sapa Inca, Pachacuti, and his son and successor, Topa Inca, established the majority of the empire. Their successes came through a combination of diplomacy, reciprocity, and force. Following the annexation of territory and the new rule on imposition of foreign ethnic polities, the Incas turned to securing borders, which meant a greater investment in building garrisons and forts and the resettlement of populations through internal colonization

Tactics

Inca tactics, or battle plans, were based on information gathering, planning ahead, and overwhelming numbers at the time and point of attack. The Sapa Inca sent out reconnaissance missions in advance of engagement in order to survey the battlefield. Following this survey, clay models of the terrain were made, probably in order to decide the most effective means of deploying troops. And when it came to the battle itself, the Sapa Inca or his generals typically relied on overwhelming numbers to diminish any tactical advantage the enemy might have gained. As a further Inca advantage, the Incas favored feigned retreat countered by flanking maneuvers and pincer counterattacks, which is an attack by two coordinated forces from different directions. They also made use of grass fires, flooding, ambushes, and dawn attacks, all to maneuver the foe toward territory that favored the Incas.

Battle formation was organized by ethnic group, with each group forming a squadron specializing in its own weapons. Horses were not introduced to South America until the arrival of the conquistadores, so there were no calvaries; all combat was on foot. Each formation was led by the commander. The formations closest to the Sapa Inca tended to be those that had been in the empire longest. Arrows, sling stones, and javelins typically initiated engagements in the hopes of softening the enemy's defenses from a distance. Following the initial volley, hand-to-hand combat ensued between warriors handling maces, clubs, and spears. The Incas' preferred weapon was a stone or bronze star mace mounted on a wooden handle about one meter (3 ft.) long. Troops defending fortified sites would have a similar array of weaponry plus large boulders to be rolled onto advancing troops.

Once the troops were engaged in hand-to-hand combat, both discipline and the superiority of Inca numbers broke down amid the chaos, and warriors tended then to fight one-on-one for personal victory. Demoralization of the enemy was a key to victory, and this was most readily accomplished by capturing the leader or the idol of the enemy. The significance of the loss of a warrior's idol, usually a stone, speaks to the profound presence of the supernatural in Andean warfare.

Victory

Unlike in the Aztec Empire, the Incas' Mesoamerican contemporary, where the practice of capturing prisoners for sacrifice was valued, there was no incentive for the Incas to take prisoners of war at random. If an important personage was captured, however, he would be killed and his skull, lined with gold, was fashioned into a ceremonial drinking cup. Following defeat, some prisoners were taken to Cuzco, sometimes as many as several thousand, for triumphal display, but most people were simply left to return to their daily lives, although they were now subject to Inca policy and administration.

After a successful conquest, elaborate ceremonies were carefully organized for the return of the army. The most impressive war booty, prisoners, and trophies were displayed before the people. Prisoners were made to lie prostrate in the Coricancha (Temple of the Sun), the main temple in Cuzco,

while the emperor symbolically trod on their backs and necks in a ritual expression of conquest. Very important or especially troublesome captives might be sacrificed. Following the ceremonies, gifts of clothing, gold, and pendants were awarded to soldiers who had performed especially well. Favorites of the Sapa Inca might receive an administrative post, a gift of land, or even a wife. Following the awards, the army was disbanded.

UNIFORMS AND WEAPONS

The army on the march and in the field would have been a spectacular display of pomp and color. Captains and generals wore splendidly arrayed tunics as uniforms and wore plumed helmets in battle. Furthermore, soldiers from each ethnic group wore distinctive regional gear. The chronicler Cobo described the warriors and their dress: "Over this defensive gear, they would usually wear their most attractive and rich adornments of jewels; this included wearing fine plumes of many colors on their heads and large gold and silver plates on their chests and backs; however, the plates worn by poorer soldiers were copper." The plates that Cobo refers to are probably round metal disks draped on the chest and back that were awards and indicated rank, with gold signifying the highest rank and accomplishment. Many soldiers wore woolen fringes below their knees and ankles. Soldiers also protected themselves with wood-slat armor made of hard chonta palm and cotton. They protected their arms with square or round shields made of wooden boards. The shields were typically covered with deerskin or metal and decorated with a hanging cloth painted with an emblem. In addition, soldiers wore a long cloth or shawl that had some minimal defensive function.

The Inca and enemy arsenals included arrows, sling stones, bolas, javelins, maces, clubs, and spears. A favorite weapon was a club with a circular stone, copper, gold, or silver head with six projections, commonly referred to as the star-headed mace. Protective gear consisted of quilted cloth armor, shields, plates of metal to protect chest and back, and cane helmets, often decorated. The use of certain weaponry was a specialized ability based largely on geography; just as each ethnic group wore its own regional costume, each also specialized in its own traditional weaponry, which the Incas incorporated into overall strategy. For example, the Collas were specialists in the use of the bola, which is made of three stones tied to cords united into one long cord; when thrown, the bola could easily entangle the legs of men and animals. Forest Indians from Antisuyu, the region to the northeast of Cuzco, were expert in the use of the bow and arrow, though they were relative latecomers into the empire. And spear-throwers and darts with fire-hardened points were the principal weapon of coastal tribes and Ecuadorean ethnic groups.

Visual Representations of Weapons and Uniforms in Guamán Poma

Felipe Guamán Poma de Ayala's *El primer nueva corónica y buen gobierno* (1615) is an unparalleled primary source on the Incas, including, but not limited to, issues specific to military and warfare. Guamán Poma's 1,100-plus-page letter addresses the king of Spain and includes almost 400 line drawings; while the text catalogs in great detail the abuses foisted upon native Andeans by the Spaniards, the drawings constitute an essential compendium of visual information that scholars use to investigate various fields of Inca life. For example, in one drawing Guamán Poma illustrates Inca forces storming an Andean fortress *(pucará)*. The defenders are shown standing atop a masonry wall rendered in stylized fashion and dressed in standard but unadorned tunics. Each of the visible figures holds a round stone with both hands raised to eye level in the moment before launching the stones upon the attacking forces.

On the opposing side the figure of the seventh Sapa Inca, Mayta Cápac, is prominently displayed

at the attacking vanguard. He wears a tunic that is plain at the top but decorated on the bottom half with squares, not unlike a checkerboard, which are further broken down into rectangular segments. He wears sandals as well as fringed bands at both his ankles and knees. In his left hand he holds a rectangular shield decorated with squares inset within squares; another fringed element hangs down from this decorative element. In his right hand, though partially obscured by the shield, he holds a lance or spear that ends in a crescent tipped by a sharp point. A type of helmet with feathers covers his head. Another figure beside him holds a common spear, and yet another figure, interestingly enough, extends with both hands a small

5.2 Drawing of the seventh Sapa Inca and military leader, Mayta Cápac (bottom right), *featuring military regalia and fortress* (Felipe Guamán Poma de Ayala)

figurine that is probably a *huaca* (religious or symbolic object).

PRINCIPAL INCA MILITARY CONQUESTS

While there remains significant disagreement over the exact nature of Inca expansion, it is beyond doubt that the military played a significant role. Each successive ruler was forced to take on an expansionist policy due to the Inca system of split inheritance, under which the incoming Sapa Inca inherited the title and the crown but none of the land or wealth of his predecessor, the latter going instead to the ruler's *panaqa* (kin group or lineage corporation), which managed the predecessor's affairs despite his death. As a result, the new Sapa Inca had no choice but to take on an expansionist policy in order to secure his own land and wealth, which in turn ensured his own veneration by his *panaqa* once he died. The following sections provide a brief overview of the principal military engagements of the last three independent rulers and the dynastic war of succession. The overview provided is more or less chronological, though it should be noted that the temporal nature of the wars is debated, as is the effect of chronology on a society that thinks of time in a very different manner.

The Chanca War and the Role of the Supernatural

The narrative of the Inca war against the Chancas is an amalgam of myth and factual history. The legend of the war relates to the Incas' need to explain themselves and to define the events that unleashed their expansion. As such it is impossible to tell exactly when it took place, but it is likely that it represents the climax of a history of confrontation between the two ethnic groups. The Chancas, a more powerful highland neighbor of the Incas, had imperial ideas of their own, had had recent expansionistic successes, and quite possibly were primary actors in the disintegration of the Wari, the central highland empire that preceded the Incas during the Middle Horizon Period (540–1000). According to the legend, the Chancas sent emissaries to the Incas expressing their intention of conquering the Incas, leading to the Inca ruler (most often listed as the eighth ruler in the traditional king lists, named Viracocha, after the major Inca deity) abandoning the city along with two sons, Urco and Socso. Only Cusi Yupanqui, later to be named Pachacuti, and several generals remained behind to defend the city; among the generals was Cusi Yupanqui's "brother" Cápac Yupanqui, who would later lead the Inca imperial advance northward.

Local lords were reluctant to aid the Incas because they feared the Chancas. When the Chancas advanced on the city, legend says that the miraculous intervention of the *pururaucas*, or stones that become mythical warriors, aided the Incas in repelling the Chanca advance. Cusi Yupanqui took the opportunity to seize the enemy banner and the mummy of an important Chanca ruler, Uscovilca, at which point the Chancas turned and fled. Watching from a hill above the valley, the local lords joined in the Inca pursuit of the Chancas, which ended at either Ichopampa or Xaquixaguanas with the routing of the Chancas. By defeating the Chancas, the Incas were able to acquire great hordes of booty, allowing them to generously oil the gears of reciprocity, by which the Sapa Inca could convince neighboring lords to provide the labor without which the Inca state machine would have stalled or faltered. Thus, the initial coup of an unlikely victory, aided by the mythology of warrior stones, catapulted the Incas into a position from which conditions were favorable for rapid expansion.

Juan de Santacruz Pachacuti Yamqui, a native Andean chronicler writing in the early 1600s, relates the myth of the legendary *pururaucas*, the stones that transformed themselves into warriors during the Chanca attack on Cuzco. Pachacuti Yamqui writes that an old priest at the Temple of the Sun named Topauanchire placed some stones near the sanctuary and added helmets and weapons to simulate soldiers at war. During the battle, as the

Chancas pressed their initial advantage and it looked like the Inca defense might fail, the *pururaucas* transformed into soldiers, turned the tide of the battle, and contributed to an unlikely Inca victory. In Andean ideology gods and mythical beings were transformed into stones, but here the reverse occurred. Subsequently, the supernatural power that emanated from them produced terror and caused many native peoples to fear the Incas.

Pachacuti's Conquests

According to traditional accounts, following the successful campaign against the Chancas, Pachacuti—newly strengthened and emboldened, with his power consolidated in the Cuzco region—initiated campaigns in the lower Urubamba Valley and in Vilcabamba regions of central highland Peru. At this point he sent Cápac Yupanqui to the north to extend Inca dominion, while he himself marched south to the Lake Titicaca region because of unrest among the Ayaviri and Lupaca peoples, who were supposed to be allies but probably were becoming increasingly paranoid about growing Inca power. Pachacuti ruthlessly crushed their revolt and continued south to subjugate the southern and eastern shores of the lake region. Following his excursions in the south, Pachacuti turned his energies toward rebuilding Cuzco, though he undertook one final campaign to the southwest, where he carried out an expedition to the Chumpivilca. Pachacuti then delegated many military matters to his son, Topa Inca. Pachacuti died in about 1471, after a reign of 33 years.

The Chimú War

The Chimú Empire (called Chimor by the Spanish) stretched along the north coast of Peru for more than 1,000 miles. The first contact between Chimú and Inca forces took place under the command of General Cápac Yupanqui, even though he was under strict orders from Pachacuti not to go beyond a certain point that should have precluded his engagement with Chimú. However, Cápac Yupanqui had with him a contingent of Chanca warriors,

who got along badly with the rest of the army and eventually deserted. Using their desertion as cause, he followed them north, ultimately engaging the Chimú. Cápac Yupanqui advanced on the town of Cajamarca, which was then ruled over by a lord named Guzmango. The Chimú ruler, Minchacaman, rushed to aid Guzmango, who was killed; Minchacaman quickly returned to the coast. Despite his success in the field, Cápac Yupanqui was executed upon his return because he had disobeyed orders and because he had let the Chancas escape. It is also likely he was killed because he had achieved too much power, which threatened Pachacuti's rule.

The young Topa Inca, who later became emperor around 1471, was sent to the north. Known as a great conqueror, he overcame many instances of local resistance and then descended the Moche River, which fed the heartland of the Chimú Empire. The Chimú could not resist the Inca advance and were defeated, with Minchacaman taken as a prisoner to Cuzco. Topa Inca also brought back enormous amounts of treasure and many craftsmen skilled in weaving, metallurgy, ceramics, and featherwork. The Incas apparently adopted the magnificence of the Chimú aesthetic, which later impressed the Spanish.

Subsequent Conquests by Topa Inca

After defeating the Chimú, Topa Inca returned to Cuzco for a few years before advancing north along the trunk road of the royal highway (*capac ñan*), seeing to it along the way that Inca administration was in order. Reaching what is today Ecuador, he defeated the Cañaris and their allies, the Quito. He ordered *mitmaqkuna* (colonists) sent north in order to build a city. After a rest in Quito, he headed for the coast, near the modern border of Peru and Ecuador, where he engaged the Huancavilcas in war. Following typical Inca strategy he divided his army into three parts, with himself leading a division into the mountains so he could attack from the east. Of the other two divisions one attacked from the land and one from the sea. Following this engagement and following a nine-month sojourn at

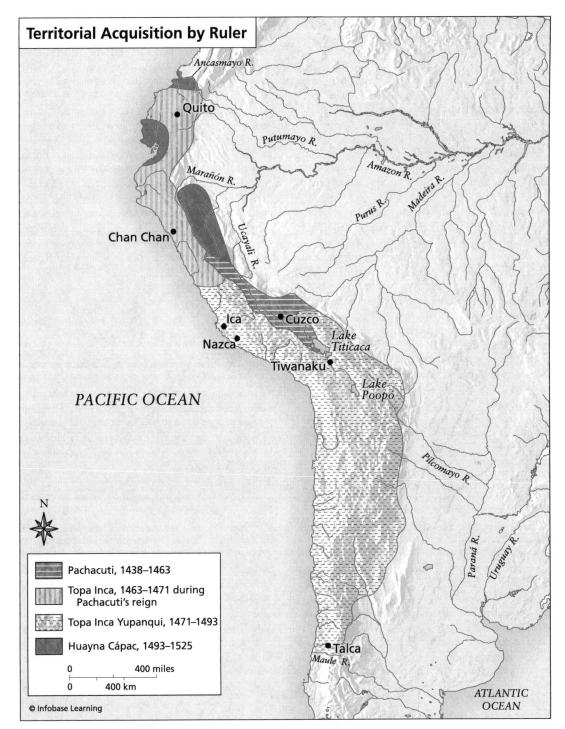

Territorial Acquisition by Ruler

Ancasmayo R.

Quito

Putumayo R.

Amazon R.

Marañón R.

Madeira R.

Purus R.

Chan Chan

Ucayali R.

Ica

Cuzco

Lake Titicaca

Nazca

Tiwanaku

Lake Poopó

PACIFIC OCEAN

Pilcomayo R.

N

Paraná R.

Uruguay R.

Pachacuti, 1438–1463

Topa Inca, 1463–1471 during
   Pachacuti's reign

Topa Inca Yupanqui, 1471–1493

Huayna Cápac, 1493–1525

| 0 | 400 miles |
| 0 | 400 km |

Talca

Maule R.

ATLANTIC
OCEAN

© Infobase Learning

Map 7 Territorial Acquisition by Ruler

sea, which the chronicler Sarmiento de Gamboa describes, Topa Inca headed back to Cuzco along the coastal route of the Inca highway network, subduing the coastal valleys as far south as Nazca and Mala. Simultaneously, another division traversed the highland route. On their journeys both divisions monitored the administration of the state. It is believed that at this time Pachacuti died and Topa Inca assumed absolute power as Sapa Inca.

Following the assumption of power and a long rest in Cuzco, Topa Inca led his troops into the jungle region of Antisuyu, to the northeast of Cuzco. On this occasion the Incas conquered the Optaris, the Manosuyus, the Mañaris, and the Chunchos. While the Sapa Inca was in the jungle, rumor of his death, spread by a deserter, led to rebellion in the Lake Titicaca region, forcing Topa Inca to leave the jungle and deal with the insurrection. He pacified the Callao and Charcas territory and then turned toward modern Bolivia, conquering the whole of highland Bolivia, and from there entered Chile as far south as the Maule River at the modern town of Constitución, where he set up the boundary markers of his empire. (Beyond that border the Araucanian Indians were too fierce and too far from the heartland to be an attractive conquest to the Incas.) Tucumán and most of highland northwest Argentina also submitted to Topa Inca. After his final campaign into the eastern forests he turned his attention to the organization of the state. He died in about 1493, after a reign of 22 years, and was succeeded by his son Huayna Cápac.

Conquests by Huayna Cápac

Huayna Cápac succeeded Topa Inca as emperor. There are discrepancies in the chronology of his operations as recorded by the chroniclers, but the general outline is as follows. His initial obligation was an inspection of the southern regions of the state. While he was in the south insurrection in the north at Quito, Pasto, and Huancavilca forced him to return to Cuzco, raise another army, and begin a campaign in the north. Heading north, he passed through Cajamarca and Jauja and then set out for Chachapoyas, where local lords had rebelled. After settling the situation there, Huayna Cápac contin-

ued north, where reciprocity was apparently not tradition. As a result, Huayna Cápac met fierce resistance all along the way, and his victories came at great expense. At Tumipampa he reorganized his army into three parts, each commanded by two chiefs, and then set out to retake Pasto, in the far north, first. Huayna Cápac spent many years in the north based at Tumipampa, gradually incorporating new ethnic realms into the state. In 1526 Francisco Pizarro and his men made preliminary contact with northern coastal peoples at Tumbes, and word soon reached the Incas. But, before Huayna Cápac himself could meet these strange bearded persons, a tremendous epidemic of smallpox and measles ravaged the northern provinces. In 1527 Huayna Cápac died in Quito, possibly as a result of the foreign disease. In the meantime, the Spanish were unable to penetrate the interior or take hold at their initial landing and had returned to Panama.

The Dynastic War

In the five years between Huayna Cápac's death and the Spanish invasion, the Inca Empire was internally besieged by civil war. Upon his death Huayna Cápac had failed to name a successor. The high priest in Cuzco named one of Huayna Cápac's sons, Huáscar, as the Sapa Inca. Meanwhile, Huáscar's brother, Atahualpa, assumed power in Quito. The dispute was settled violently, with Atahualpa the decisive victor.

When the civil war began, Huáscar, based in Cuzco, controlled the most territory, up to the province of the Cañari, where he was in command of a small force led by a general named Atoq. By contrast, Atahualpa controlled only the northern half of modern Ecuador but had the presence and support most of Huayna Cápac's army, which had remained in Quito, and two of his best generals, Quisquis and Challcuchima. A series of battles ensued beginning in Quito, continuing south, and ending with a great encounter near the Apurímac River on the approach to Cuzco. Atahualpa's generals were consistently successful in their southward march and gained confidence with each encounter. In the final battle Quisquis and Challcuchima crushed Huáscar's forces, captured him, and killed

EL DECIMO CAPITAN
CHALLCOCHIMA

5.3 Drawing of Challcuchima, a general in Atahualpa's army who was instrumental in defeating Huáscar's forces (Felipe Guamán Poma de Ayala)

all the leaders of his ranks that they could find. News of the victory reached Atahualpa in Cajamarca at about the same time that the Spanish, led by Francisco Pizarro, arrived.

THE SPANISH CONQUEST

When the Spanish returned in 1531 to the Ecuadorean coast, they had already been pushing slowly south for more than 15 years. At that time the Inca Empire had been in existence for only 50–60

years—certainly not enough time for any substantial or meaningful identity as "Incas" to have developed among more recently conquered peoples, let alone Inca subjects. Inca hegemony, in other words, was still a thing to resist as opposed to an accepted reality. The Spanish commander, Francisco Pizarro, likely recognized this situation and used this fledgling desire for liberty to his tactical advantage, taking the opportunity to offer support to the cause of local lords who wished to rid themselves of the Incas. What the local lords did not realize, of course, is that they were trading one form of submission for another.

Pizarro and his men met Atahualpa in Cajamarca on November 15, 1532. Having arranged the day before to meet the Inca ruler in the plaza, Pizarro planned an ambush. With only 168 men in comparison to the Inca retinue of several thousand, Pizarro and his men nonetheless inflicted monumental carnage upon the Incas, killing an estimated 7,000 and capturing Atahualpa. The Spanish desire for material wealth, specifically gold and silver, was clear, so Atahualpa offered, in return for his freedom, enough gold ransom to fill a room 6.7 meters by 5.17 meters (22 × 17 ft.) up to a white line 2.45 meters (8 ft.) above the floor. Over the next eight months numerous events played out that defined the motives of the Spanish and provided the Spanish with a clearer picture of the continental situation. As the ransom arrived and the Spanish waited for reinforcements, Atahualpa ran the empire from captivity, Spanish expeditions were sent to Cuzco and the coastal oracle site of Pachacamac; and Pizarro gleaned much information from Atahualpa regarding the politics of the state, from which he learned of the numerous disgruntled subject polities he might exploit. These events in effect helped solidify the Spanish position regarding military possibilities and strategies.

Spanish Conquest: 1533

On Saturday, July 26, 1533, Atahualpa was ceremoniously, if not hastily, convicted of treason and garroted, leaving the Inca Empire without a ruler or military commander and the Spanish without a figurehead to rule through. While Atahualpa's death was a terrible loss for many, it was received with equal joy by the forces that had supported Huáscar in the dynastic war of succession as well as many of the polities who wanted to be rid of Inca rule. It also meant that Atahualpa's generals, who had been unable to do anything while Atahualpa was alive, for fear of risking his life, were now free to attack the Spanish.

Pizarro installed Topa Hualpa, another of Huayna Cápac's sons—Huáscar's younger brother—as a puppet ruler and set out for Cuzco to make it official in the customary Inca manner. Pizarro met and overcame resistance near Hatun Jauja in the Mantaro Valley by forces loyal to Atahualpa, while the local people, allying themselves with the Spanish, celebrated in the streets. Unfortunately for the Spanish, Topa Hualpa succumbed to illness while in Hatun Jauja. The Spaniards continued south and defeated an Inca force at Vilcashuamán but then suffered their first real defeat on the initial approach to Cuzco. The Spaniards regrouped and, joined by reinforcements, met General Quisquis's forces at a pass outside Cuzco. The Inca forces held the pass for a while but soon abandoned the city's defenses. The Spanish entered the city on November 15, 1533.

Spanish Conquest: 1534

The situation in Peru for both the Incas and the Spaniards churned with chaos. In December 1533 Pizarro installed Manco Inca, yet another son of Huayna Cápac, as Inca ruler and Spanish puppet. Manco Inca was aligned with the Huáscar faction and as such perpetuated the Huáscar-Atahualpa factionalism still resonant from the dynastic war. On the Spanish side resentment grew against Pizarro as more and more Spanish arrived in Peru in search of gold and glory. An intense, and eventually deadly, rivalry grew between Spaniards loyal to Pizarro and those loyal to Diego de Almagro, a fellow conquistador who had split with Pizarro over the administration and distribution of war spoils. The ensuing factionalism effectively split the Spanish and contributed to the chaos. As a puppet of the Spanish, Manco was invested with defeating Quisquis's forces, which had been staging a prolonged series of campaigns against the Spanish, especially in the north. This was well in line with his own ambition to destroy the Quito forces previously loyal to Atahualpa. Yet, after about a year of increasing restlessness, Manco began to see that Quisquis was not the real problem and secretly began setting the conditions for a wide Inca rebellion against the Spanish.

Spanish Conquest: 1535–1537

Manco Inca's revolt came to fruition in 1536 when coordinated armies were assembled to lay siege to Cuzco and the new Spanish city, Ciudad de los Reyes (Lima); simultaneous actions were planned elsewhere with the intent of countering Spanish reinforcements. A few hundred Spanish held Cuzco, while numerous Spanish war parties had been drawn outside the city to deal with rebellions in other parts of the province, many of which had been organized by Manco. The siege of Cuzco began on April 18, 1536, when an Inca army estimated between 200,000 and 400,000 converged upon the four roads leading to Cuzco and set fire to outlying buildings; the fires continued inward and forced the Spanish to shift from house to house toward the center. The Spanish situation looked hopeless, but Juan Pizarro, Francisco's half brother, led a bold attack up the slopes of Sacsayhuamán, which was then defended by only 1,500 men, and drove the Incas from the citadel. Slowly, yet inexorably the Inca soldier-farmers disbanded into the surrounding hills.

In Lima the Inca general Quizo Yupanqui amassed a huge army in the hills in hopes of surrounding and destroying the Spaniards entrenched within the city. The army advanced from the north, east, and south, with the Inca general carried in a litter at the head of the troops. The three-pronged attack probably reflected tripartite divisions within the army. Spanish cavalry attacked once the Inca forces were within the city, targeting the general, who was killed in the advance. Inca forces, lacking their leader, quickly fell into disarray and melted into the hills in the night. Inca forces did meet with some success outside the cities, inflicting numerous casualties at Cuesta de Parcos and Jauja, but it was not enough to turn the momentum of the conquest backward. By February 1537 the siege of Cuzco ended, and Manco Inca retreated up the Urubamba Valley.

The Neo-Inca State

Following the losses at Cuzco and Lima, Manco Inca retreated first to Ollantaytambo and eventually Vilcabamba, some 200 kilometers—down the Urubamba river from Cuzco. Switching to guerrilla tactics, Manco and his successors, Sayri Túpac, Titu Cusi, and Túpac Amaru—harassed the Spanish through hit-and-run raids and punished Andean collaborators. Hernando Pizarro, another of Francisco's brothers, advanced on Ollantaytambo, initially with little success; the Incas were too elaborately dug in and the geography too difficult to allow the Spanish to gain any advantages. By 1537, however, the situation in greater Peru had changed. Spanish reinforcements had arrived and were rapidly gaining control of all of Peru to the extent that Manco Inca felt insecure at Ollantaytambo and retreated even farther into the vastness of the high Andean cordillera at Vilcabamba. At this final redoubt the Incas held out until 1572, when forces sent by Viceroy Toledo, the Spanish authority in the colony, captured the last Inca ruler, Túpac Amaru. On September 24, 1572, Túpac Amaru was led to Huacaypata plaza in Cuzco, the plaza of his ancestor rulers, and beheaded.

READING

Military Organization

Joseph Bram, *An Analysis of Inca Militarism* (Seattle: University of Washington Press, 1944).

Terence D'Altroy, *The Incas* (London: Blackwell, 2002).

Michael A. Malpass, *Daily Life in the Inca Empire* (Westport, Conn.: Greenwood Press, 1996).

———, "The Expansion of the Inka State: Armies, War, and Rebellions." In *Anthropological History of Andean Polities*, edited by John V. Murra et al., 49–59 (Cambridge: Cambridge University Press, 1986).

———, "La guerre et les rebellions dans l'expansion de l'État Inca in Anthropologie historique des sociétés andines," *Annales Economies, Sociétés, Civilisations* 34, nos. 5–6 (1978): 927–935.

Military Infrastructure

Graziano Gasparini and Louise Margolies, *Inca Architecture*. Translated by Patricia Lyons (Bloomington: Indiana University Press, 1980).

John Hemming and Edward Ranney, *Monuments of the Inca* (Albuquerque: University of New Mexico Press, 1992).

Ann Kendall, *Aspects of Inca Architecture: Description, Function, and Chronology*. 2 vols., Bar International Series 242 (Oxford: British Archaeological Papers, 1985).

Jerry D. Moore, "The Archaeology of Plazas and the Proxemics of Ritual: Three Andean Traditions," *American Anthropologist* 98, no. 4 (1996): 789–802.

———, *Architecture and Power in the Ancient Andes* (Cambridge: Cambridge University Press, 2005).

Craig Morris, "The Infrastructure of Inka Control in the Peruvian Central Highlands." In *The Inca and Aztec States, 1400–1800: Anthropology and History*, edited by George A. Collier, Renato I. Rosaldo, and John D. Wirth, 153–171 (New York: Academic Press, 1982).

———, "State Settlements in Tawantinsuyu: A Strategy of Compulsory Urbanism." In *Contemporary Archaeology: A Guide to Theory and Contributions*, edited by Mark P. Leone, 393–401 (Carbondale: Southern Illinois University Press, 1972).

Susan A. Niles, "The Nature of Inca Royal Estates." In *Machu Picchu: Unveiling the Mystery of the Incas*, edited by Richard L. Burger and Lucy C. Salazar, 49–70 (New Haven, Conn.: Yale University Press, 2004).

———, *The Shape of Inca History* (Iowa City: Iowa University Press, 1999).

Jean-Pierre Protzen, "Inca Architecture." In *The Inca World: The Development of Pre-Columbian Peru, A.D. 1000–1534*, edited by Laura Laurencich Minelli, 193–217 (Norman: University of Oklahoma Press, 1992).

———, *Inca Architecture and Construction at Ollantaytambo* (London: Oxford University Press, 1993).

Types of Conquest

Pedro de Cieza de León, *The Discovery and Conquest of Peru* (Durham, N.C.: Duke University Press, 1998).

Bernabé Cobo, *History of the Inca Empire (1582–1657)*. Translated and edited by Roland Hamilton (Austin: University of Texas Press, 1990).

———, *Provincial Power in the Inka Empire* (Washington, D.C.: Smithsonian Institution, 1992).

———, "Transitions in Power: Centralization of Wanka Political Organization Under Inka Rule," *Ethnohistory* 34, no. 1 (1987): 78–102.

Timothy K. Earle and Terence N. D'Altroy, "The Political Economy of the Inka Empire: The Archaeology of Power and Finance." In *Archaeological Thought in America*, edited by Carl C. Lamberg-Karlovsky, 183–204 (Cambridge: Cambridge University Press, 1989).

Garcilaso de la Vega, El Inca, *Royal Commentaries of the Inca and General History of Peru*. Translated by Harold V. Livermore. 2 vols. (Austin: University of Texas Press, 1966).

Jonathan Haas et al., eds., *The Origins and Development of the Andean State* (Cambridge: Cambridge University Press, 1987).

Henri S. Lewis, "Warfare and the Origin of the State: Another Formulation." In *The Study of the State*, edited by Henri J. M. Classen and Peter Skalnik, 201–221 (The Hague, Netherlands: Mouton, 1981).

Sabine MacCormack, *On the Wings of Time: Rome, the Incas, Spain, and Peru* (Princeton, N.J.: Princeton University Press, 2006).

Craig Morris and Adriana von Hagen, *The Inka Empire and Its Andean Origins* (New York: Abbeville Press, 1993).

Michael Moseley, *The Incas and Their Ancestors*. Rev. ed. (New York: Thames & Hudson, 2001).

Kurt A. Raaflaub, *War and Peace in the Ancient World*, The Ancient World—Comparative Histories (Malden, Mass: Blackwell Publication, 2007).

Strategy, Logistics, and Tactics

Brian S. Bauer, *Ancient Cuzco: Heartland of the Inca* (Austin: University of Texas Press, 2004).

———, *The Development of the Inca State* (Austin: University of Texas Press, 1992).

———, "The Legitimization of the Inca State in Myth and Ritual," *American Anthropologist* 98, no. 2 (1996): 327–337.

———, *The Sacred Landscape of the Inca: The Cusco Ceque System* (Austin: University of Texas Press, 1998).

Geoffrey W. Conrad, "Cultural Materialism, Split Inheritance, and the Expansion of Ancient Peruvian Empires," *American Antiquity* 46 (1981): 3–26.

R. Alan Covey, *How the Incas Built Their Heartland* (Ann Arbor: University of Michigan Press, 2005).

Ian S. Farrington, "Ritual Geography, Settlement Patterns and the Characterization of the Provinces of the Inka Heartland," *World Archaeology* 23 (1992): 368–385.

Craig Morris, "Inka Strategies of Incorporation and Governance." In *Archaic States*, edited by Gary M. Feinman and Joyce Marcus, 293–309 (Santa Fe, N.Mex.: School of American Research Press, 1998).

Richard P. Schaedel, "Early State of the Incas." In *The Early State*, edited by Henri Claessen and Peter Skalnick, 289–320 (The Hague, Netherlands: Mouton, 1978).

Uniforms and Weapons

Felipe Guamán Poma de Ayala, *El primer nueva corónica y buen gobierno*. Edited by John Murra and Rolena Adorno. 3 vols. (Mexico: Siglo Veintiuno, 1992).

———, *Letter to a King: A Picture History of the Inca Civilisation*. Translated and edited by Christopher Dilke (London: George Allen & Unwin, 1978).

John Murra, "Cloth and Its Functions in the Inca State," *American Anthropologist* 64 (1962): 710–728.

Martin de Murúa, *Historia del origen y genealogía real de los reyes incas del Perú.* Introduction and notes by Constantino Bayle. Biblioteca "Missionalis Hispánica," vol. 2 (Madrid: Instituto Santo Toribio de Mogrovego, 1946).

Principal Inca Military Conquests

Nigel Davies, *The Incas* (Niwot: University Press of Colorado, 1995).

John F. Guilmartin, Jr., "The Cutting Edge: An Analysis of the Spanish Invasion and Overthrow of the Inca Empire, 1532–1539." In *Transatlantic Encounters: Europeans and Andeans in the Sixteenth Century*, edited by Kenneth J. Andrien and Rolena Adorno, 40–69 (Berkeley: University of California Press, 1991).

Alistair Hennesey, "The Nature and Conquest of the Conquistadores." In *The Meeting of Two Worlds: Europe and the Americas, 1492–1650*, edited by Warwick Bray, 5–36 (Oxford: Oxford University Press, 1993).

George Kubler, "The Behavior of Atahuallpa, 1531–1533," *Hispanic American Historical Review* 25, no. 4 (November 1945): 413–427.

———, "The Neo-Inca State (1537–1572)," *Hispanic American Review*, 27, no. 2 (May 1947): 189–203.

———, "A Peruvian Chief of State: Manco Inca (1515–1545)," *Hispanic American Historical Review*, 24, no. 2 (May 1944): 253–276.

Thomas C. Patterson, *The Inca Empire: The Formation and Disintegration of a Pre-Capitalist State* (New York: St. Martin's Press, 1991).

Franklin G. Y. Pease, "The Formation of Tawantinsuyu: Mechanisms of Colonization and Relationship with Ethnic Groups." In *The Inca and Aztec States, 1400–1800*, edited by George A. Collier, Renato I. Rosaldo, and John D. Wirth, 173–198 (New York: Academic Press, 1982).

William Hickling Prescott, *History of the Conquest of Peru.* 2 vols. (New York: Harper & Brothers Publishers, 1847).

María Rostworowski de Diez Canseco, *History of the Inca Realm.* Translated by Harry B. Iceland (Cambridge: Cambridge University Press, 1999).

John Rowe, "Inca Culture at the Time of the Spanish Conquest." In *Handbook of South American Indians*, edited by Julian H. Steward. Smithsonian Institution, Bureau of American Ethnology, Bulletin no. 143, vol. 2 (1946).

———, "Inca Policies and Institutions Relating to the Cultural Unification of the Empire." In *The Inca and Aztec States, 1400–1800*, edited by George A. Collier, Renato I. Rosaldo, and John D. Wirth, 93–118 (New York: Academic Press, 1982).

———, "The Incas under Spanish Colonial Institutions," *Hispanic American Review* 37, no. 2 (May 1957): 155–199.

Patricia Seed, "Conquest of the Americas, 1500–1650." In *Cambridge Illustrated History of Warfare: The Triumph of the West*, edited by Geoffrey Parker, 132–154 (Cambridge: Cambridge University Press, 1995).

S. J. Stern, *Peru's Indian Peoples and the Challenge of the Spanish Conquest: Huamanga to 1640.* 2nd ed. (Madison: University of Wisconsin Press, 1993).

6

RELIGION, COSMOLOGY, AND MYTHOLOGY

The stories written by Spanish chroniclers about the Inca Empire, an empire that existed for less than a century before the Spanish conquistadores reached the Inca capital at Cuzco, Peru, in 1533, are sometimes referred to as fables. Even though some of them record events in the lives of real persons, the reliability of the informants and their material was often questionable because most of them had not been witness to the events they describe. Both Spanish and Andean authors (after the conquest and following European educational traditions) were acquainted with European classical texts, and the history of the Roman Empire was the paradigm by which many of them explained the Incas. In these narratives the actions of gods and heroes had been interwoven, and the incorporation of fabulous events with reliable historical events was a recognized tradition and did not provide an obstacle to accepting them as history. Similarly, Inca origin stories, myths, cosmological stories, and stories of religion bear witness to a mixture of the fabulous and the real.

Complicating the disentanglement of myth from history is the fact that the native Andeans did not have a recognizable form of written history. The content of records left behind by the Incas, in the form of visual art, song, oral epic poetry, painted wooden tablets (which no longer exist), and quipus (a series of knotted cords suspended from a central cord that, through color, technique, or position, records information) is greatly debated. Thus, the exact context and content of Inca religion, mythology, and cosmology—of what is truly Andean and what is a product of Spanish cultural biases, given the filters of language, religion, and culture—while growing clearer, remains open to debate.

It is believed by many scholars, furthermore, that the Inca relationship to "the world beyond" is grounded in political and social organization; patterns that seem to explain the universe beyond the human realm almost invariably reflect analogous systems as diverse as kin relations, social hierarchy, and water rights. In this sense Inca cosmology is about people and their relationship to the immediate world, to their geographical and political environment, as expressed in stories and rituals that bring them into dialogue with the world beyond them. Unlike the Aztecs and Mayas, who recognized no less than 13 heavens and nine underworlds, the Incas had no such concept. Their world and their place in the universe were thus worked out in stories that integrated social, political, calendrical, and dynastic imperatives. This chapter examines the construction and content of Inca religion, mythology, and cosmology to gain an understanding of how the Incas viewed themselves in relation to both the earthly and heavenly realms.

STATE RELIGION

Despite Spanish attempts to eradicate all traces of Inca religious practice, the native Andeans displayed such great ingenuity in retaining their rites and rituals that some aspects of their original religion survived with little or no change while other aspects survived in hybrid form. Inca religion emphasized rituals focused on natural phenomena, agriculture, curing, and prognostication. In a sense, it was less spiritual than it was practical. Knowledge of the heavens and the intimate workings of gods dictated the day-to-day life of royalty and commoner alike.

Religious practice among the general population remained largely local in nature, informed by traditions that predated Inca hegemony, even while the centrifugal forces of empire attempted to realign many of those practices to the religious leanings of Cuzco. In some cases, especially in areas outside the heartland, long-standing pre-Inca rituals were either adopted into the Inca system or the Inca system was adopted in theory and then subtly subverted, not unlike what happened under Spanish authority. To their credit, the Incas realized the value of flexibility. It was Inca policy to permit conquered polities considerable religious freedom and continued worship of their own gods so long as they accepted the Inca gods above their own deities and any other demands levied by the state. In many cases, anyway, the conquered peoples worshipped similar gods by a different name. Furthermore, it was not uncommon for the Incas to show a certain amount of respect for local oracles or shrines and even worship or consult them themselves.

Inca political rulers were divine or semidivine descendants of the Sun, and the mummies of deceased rulers were worshipped as deities. The Incas worshipped stone, water, rivers, caves, and springs because they were essential ingredients in their origin stories and myths. They planned their calendar, measured time, and planted crops according to knowledge of the heavens. Many of these ideas were tied together in the concept of *huaca* worship (a *huaca* was any thing or place that had transcendent power). Sacrifice and pilgrimage were vital components of many important ceremonies. Overall, the Inca felt it was their right and their obligation to spread this religion; subsequently, religion was a primary motive and justification for imperial expansion.

Huacas

The Incas worshipped places, objects, and natural features of the landscape imbued with perceived supernatural forces. Anything unusual and out of the ordinary could be a *huaca*, even an oddly shaped ear of corn. The Incas saw no contradiction between *huaca* worship and worship of the formal pantheon of gods. In the Cuzco region these *huacas* were organized in a pattern referred to as the Cuzco *ceque* system. A *ceque* is generally understood as a line along which the *huacas* were built and connected. It must be noted that *ceque* lines were imaginary and not physically present in the landscape. The Jesuit scholar Bernabe Cobo's 1563 *Historia del nuevo mundo* is dedicated to recording this system; he notes at least 328 *huacas* and 42 *ceque* lines, although other sources suggest there are more *huacas*. In addition, he records the objects offered to the *huacas*, the *huacas*' relative order along the *ceques*, and how they were maintained and worshipped. Contemporary scholarship has sought to clarify the understanding of the system, though with little agreement.

All *huacas*, no matter how large or small, facilitated communication with the supernatural world. Common *huacas* listed for Cuzco included temples, cult objects, tombs of ancestors, stones, fountains, springs, calendar markers, hills, bridges, houses, quarries, caves, and, in general, places associated with mythology or previous rulers. *Huacas* were worshipped to guard against sudden death, to pre-

vent children from dying, for the preservation of corn after harvest, for victory in war, to prevent springs from drying up, and for safe journeys. The major deities—Viracocha, Inti (the Sun), and Inti Illapa (thunder)—received offerings at numerous shrines. The two most important *huacas* were the mountain Huanacauri and the Coricancha in Cuzco. Huanacauri was worshipped because it was believed that a stone on its summit was the transformed brother of the mythical first Inca, Manco Cápac. The *ceque* system itself originated at the Coricancha (Temple of the Sun) in Cuzco; some sources list the Coricancha as a single *huaca*, while others list parts within the Coricancha as *huacas*. After the Spanish conquered the area, they went to extraordinary lengths to eradicate the *huaca* system because to them it exemplified pagan worship. *Huaca* reverence survived, however, often in transformed ways and in some cases still survives today.

6.1 *Inca* huaca *worship* (Felipe Guamán Poma de Ayala)

Religious Practitioners

PRIESTS AND PRIESTESSES

The state religion was organized hierarchically in a manner similar to the state's political organization. The Sapa Inca (Inca king) was the ultimate religious authority. Next, the high priest, called the Uillac Uma in Cuzco, was the head of a hierarchy of priests throughout the empire. As the Incas justified their imperial ambition as a form of religious proselytization—that, in effect, they were obligated to spread their religion—priests took on a very important role. Beneath the high priest was the Hatun Uillca, who functioned like a bishop and was the head of one of 10 dioceses. Beneath him was the Yana Uillca, or ordinary priest.

The Uillac Uma was apparently so revered that he competed in authority with the Sapa Inca. He had power over all shrines and temples and appointed priests. His duties included divining, interpreting oracles, prescribing penance, praying, interceding for the dead, performing sacrifices, diagnosing and treating illness, and presiding over various rituals. Similarly, priestesses were sometimes given positions of high authority. They were generally associated with serving the shrines of the Moon and carrying her silver image. A group of "chosen women," the *acllas*, served in the Coricancha. They formed an order under a high priestess.

HEALERS

Inca men and women who practiced a type of shamanistic medicine were called either *camasca* or *soncoyoc*. Curing depended on a combination of medicinal and herbal remedies and spiritual intervention. Healers were well paid for their interventions with silver, cloth, and food.

DIVINERS

Communication with the spirits or deities was achieved through various means. The most solemn came through divination by fire in which the diviner summoned spirits through a banquet around fires built in metal or pottery braziers. When the spirits accepted the offering, the diviner would ask questions of them; flames emitted through openings in the brazier represented their statements. Assistants manipulated the fire by blowing through tubes. Simpler methods of communication with the spirits included counting objects such as maize kernels, beans, pellets of llama dung, and pebbles. The objects were supposedly charged with something magical. Some diviners chewed coca and spat the juice in their hands; if it flowed evenly over two fingers, the omen was good; if uneven, the omen was bad. Burning llama fat and coca leaves, watching the way animals move, reading dreams, and celestial occurrences such as comets, shooting stars, and eclipses were other forms of augury.

The Incas believed in the necessity of consulting their deities before making important decisions or taking authoritative action. According to the Andean archaeologist Rowe, divination was practiced to diagnose disease, determine the truth of a confession, locate lost property, identify hostile sorcerers, choose between possible heirs, determine the most acceptable sacrifice to a deity being worshipped, and in warfare to determine timing, strategy, and the likelihood of the success of an attack.

The oracle was the most direct type of divination. Each *huaca*, with its attending priest, might be able to answer questions, but only a few oracles had empire-wide prestige and were consulted by distant peoples. In some cases, such as the oracle at Pachacamac on the central coast, the oracle long predated the Incas, and the Incas, in their empire building, recognized the oracles' essentialness and adopted them into their own system. The most famous oracles were the aforementioned Pachacamac, on the central coast; Apurímac, or "lord oracle," on the banks of the Apurímac River near Cuzco; Rímac, or "oracle," near Lima; and the oracle at Wari in the valley of Jauja. In most cases the oracle had to be interpreted by the attendant priest.

Acts of Devotion

GESTURES

Religious devotion permeated nearly every element of Inca life. Appropriate gestures were mandated upon approaching a shrine or *huaca*, when drinking *chicha*, when addressing the gods or the emperor, or when approaching an idol. The appropriate gestures might include tossing chewed coca or maize at a sacred object, flicking a small portion of *chicha* on the earth, removing shoes or earplugs, or when addressing gods or the emperor, bowing solemnly, hands out and palms down, while making smacking sounds with one's lips.

PRAYER

Inca prayers could be said silently or aloud and could be quite elaborate, following tradition or tailored to the specific occasion. They were addressed to both the pantheon of gods as well as to *huacas*.

RITES

Confession, penance, and fasting were commonly observed rites. Confessions were pronounced out loud to priests, penance was assigned by the confessor and might include fasting or prayer at a shrine or even flagellation, and fasting depended on the occasion and usually included abstentions from salt and chili and, under more serious circumstances, from meat, *chicha*, and sexual relations.

SACRIFICE

Sacrifice was a common element of Inca religious practice, often forming as integral part of seasonal festivals or ceremonies. The usual sacrifices were of llamas and guinea pigs. Llamas were taken from flocks specifically tended for religious purposes, with part of each flock reserved for a particular *huaca*. The priest determined the appropriate offering according to the god being ritualized, with color, amount of wool, and markings taken into consideration. Brown llamas were offered to the creator Viracocha; white llamas and alpacas, to Inti, the Sun; and multicolored llamas, to Inti-Illapa, the thunder god. The most valuable sacrifice, however, was of human beings. In comparison to the Aztec and Maya civilizations of North and Central America, human sacrifice among the Incas was rare. In times of great importance or stress, such as war, pestilence, or famine, the coronation of a new emperor or when the emperor was sick, or when a new province was conquered, the appropriate offering was of a human life.

The Cápac Hucha ceremony, which can be translated as "royal obligation," though fundamentally foreign and strange to modern eyes, was an elaborate ceremony that ended in the sacrifice and interment of children accompanied by votive figurines of precious metals. The children were chosen for their exceptional beauty and perceived perfection. Children were sent from every part of the empire to Cuzco and, once there, were assembled in the main square in front of statues of the main gods. Inca priests and the ruler himself then sacrificed selected animals, after which the children were paired off and ceremonially married. At the culmination of the ceremonies in Cuzco the children were marched home, in as straight a line as possible, in some cases over many hundreds of miles. Upon arrival at the chosen location in their home territory, the children were given *chicha*, a maize beer, and ceremonially interred, buried in specially constructed shrines alongside metal figurines.

In effect, the extraordinariness of the Cápac Hucha ceremony served to authenticate the role of the village in the empire. In return for the sacrifice of one of their children the village leader rose in the state hierarchy. In terms of Inca cosmology the children did not "die" but transcended to the realm of the ancestors, who watched over villages from high mountain perches. Their death was viewed as an essential restoration of balance after a great upheaval.

Mummies and Ancestor Worship

The worship and care of mummies was central to Andean and Inca religious practice. Mummies, or *mallquis*, of Inca kings and the ancestors of *ayllus* (kinship groups) were revered and cared for as if they were living, functioning beings. The practice of embalmment was not unique to the Incas, but their intention to maintain the deceased as a functioning member of society marked the practice as unique. The lives and deeds of the dead became mythologized within the broader social fabric and, in a sense, became a form of history for the kin and the empire itself. In the case of the Inca kings' mummies their remains were publicly displayed and even consulted. In other cases, mummies were stored in caves and cared for by descendants. Their placement in caves was specifically related to Inca myths that tied origin to caves; thus, caves themselves were highly charged spiritual places.

It was believed that caring for and offering food and drink to the ancestral mummies was required to maintain cosmic order, ensure the fertility of crops, and sustain the health of herd animals such as llama. The relationship between the living and the dead reflected a reciprocal contract: The living looked after the dead, and the dead in return ensured sustainability for the living. This relationship was deeply ingrained into the Inca way of thinking. In the Inca sociopolitical system power, prestige, and land and water rights were determined by one's descent from a founding father. The embodiment of that lineage—the titleholder to all the land and wealth, and, thus, power—was the *mallqui*. Loss or harm to the corpse was a very serious matter; therefore, everything possible was done to ensure its survival.

The Spanish considered these indigenous practices idolatrous, and great effort was expended in finding and disposing of mummified remains. So highly valued, however, were these remains that even after the Spanish found and cremated mummies, reports state that *ayllu* members collected the ashes and worshipped these instead. In at least one instance, the Spanish, after witnessing this practice, resorted to pouring the ashes over the side of a bridge into a river, to no avail. It was reported afterward that native peoples returned and gathered at this spot because it had taken on the religious significance of the mummy.

Inca Pantheon

The Inca pantheon of deities reflects a societal concern for hierarchical organization and ritual practice. The gods had power over food production; the health of humans, animals, and plants; fertility, and water—all of which reflect the acute attention this agropastoral community paid to the intricacies of the physical world upon which they relied. The principal gods of the Inca pantheon follow.

VIRACOCHA

Viracocha was the creator god and the greatest god in the Inca pantheon, a being without beginning or end. Viracocha had both male and female aspects and was associated with the puma. The Spanish reported seeing representations of the creator god as a golden statue. Viracocha created other deities, humans, animals, and the heavens and the Earth. The name Viraocha is actually a Hispanicization taken from a series of titles by which the creator god was referred. His usual title translated as "Ancient foundation, lord, instructor of the world." The Andeans believed Viracocha lived in the heavens and was the source of all divine power but had delegated authority to a series of lesser, though powerful, supernatural beings. Despite his importance the Incas devoted relatively little energy to his worship, especially when compared to the god Inti, and few temples were built in Viracocha's honor. This is owing in part to his nature as an invisible, elusive, and essential being. The chroniclers often portrayed him as part of a triad of Inca gods, along with Inti (the Sun) and Inti Illapa (thunder), and the rest of the pantheon became servants of the creator god.

Viracocha was responsible for creating humanity at the site of Tiwanaku in Bolivia or on the Island of the Sun in Lake Titicaca, which straddles the border between Peru and Bolivia. Both of these sites became very important pilgrimage sites for the Incas. After creating humanity he traveled throughout the land in the disguise of an old man with a long beard; those who were kind to him were rewarded, and those who were not, he punished. After traveling the length of the Andes he set off across the Pacific Ocean from a point in Ecuador, walking on water. Interestingly, Topa Inca, the 10th Sapa Inca, reportedly went to sea for nine months after defeating the Chimú Empire in the vicinity of where Viracocha had left the mainland—perhaps reenacting this myth. The Incas constructed shrines to Viracocha in all the places where he had stopped on his journey through the Andes.

Some scholars suggest that Viracocha was simply a theoretical construct rather than a deity. This is partly derived from the Spanish chronicler Murúa, whose 1613 *Historia general del Perú* reported that the fifth Inca king, Cápac Yupanqui, asked his advisers whether Viracocha was more important than Inti, and after long debate Cápac Yupanqui revealed that because the Sun was sometimes obscured by the smallest clouds, it must necessarily be under orders from the greater god. Thus, the argument goes, Viracocha as supreme deity became an intellectual necessity.

INTI

Inti was the sun god. Sun worship was central to Inca life, and the Sun was believed to be the divine ancestor-father of the Inca dynastic line and the patron of the empire. As a consequence, Inca rulers believed themselves to be the "son of the Sun," an idea that was used to social and political advantage. Inti was thought of as a male, and a golden statue of a young boy often represented the Sun. Similarly, he was represented by a golden disk with rays and a human face; many such disks were reportedly kept in the capital at Cuzco as well as in shrines throughout the empire. The most significant image was found at the Coricancha, the most important temple in the empire, itself referred to as the "Temple of the Sun." This image was called *punchao*, meaning "day"; it was adorned with earspools, a pectoral, and a royal headband; and reportedly had lions and serpents projecting from its body—all of which was in accord with a quasi-mythical dream by the ninth Inca ruler, Pachacuti. Some chroniclers list Pachacuti as the founder of the Sun cult, while others mention Viracocha Inca, Pachacuti's father and the eighth ruler, as the one who established Sun worship.

The worship of and cult of the Sun reflected the importance of the Sun to an agricultural economy. The relation of the Sun to the study of astronomy and calendrics, both of which are means of organizing and understanding the world, was fundamental to determining proper agricultural practice, which in turn ensured the health and livelihood of the people of the empire. As such, the worship of the Sun took on paramount significance, and the Incas went to great lengths to ensure Sun worship remained center stage. One way they accomplished this was through the construction of numerous sun temples in provincial centers far from the center at Cuzco. As government constructions, the temples bore the

stamp of Inca authority and therefore served to promote religion and remind people, via architecture, of Inca power. Each temple had priests whose obligation was to serve the Sun. The head priest of the Sun was, of course, in Cuzco. All the various sun priests were chosen from a single *ayllu*, or kin group.

As the patron deity of the empire, numerous rituals and ceremonies were held in Inti's honor to ensure the welfare of the state, the welfare of the ruler, and the harvest. Sun worship was such an elaborate institution that lands were given over to it, temples were built in its honor, and expansive resources set aside (every province was supposed to set aside land explicitly for the cult of the Sun) in order to maintain the appropriate level of worship. Perhaps inevitably, the land burden on already-disenfranchised subject communities led to discontent and in some instances revolt. Nevertheless, the great expenditure on Sun worship was considered essential within the system of reciprocal balance and was therefore thought to ensure viability, continuity, and power.

PACHACAMAC

Pachacamac was a creator deity in the Andean pantheon. The word *pacha* means "time/space, universe/earth, state of being," and the word *camac* means "one who creates, animator." Pachacamac is also the name of a major oracle site at the mouth of the Lurín River, just to the south of modern Lima. This shrine was the seat of a cult of Pachacamac that long predated the Incas, dating at least to the Middle Horizon (ca. 540–1000). It was one of the most sacred places in all of the Andes; as a result, it was a major pilgrimage destination for people from throughout the Andes seeking the guidance of its oracle. Eventually, the Incas coopted the Pachacamac cult and, despite its apparent conflict with Viracocha, allowed it to flourish. The Incas even enlarged the original adobe platform and pyramid architecture, which is what the Spaniards saw when they arrived at the site in 1533, constructing an *acllahuasi* (house of the chosen women) and a temple of the Sun.

The object of veneration at the site was a powerful, carved wooden idol attended to by priests. Pilgrims intending to consult the oracle had first to pass through three successive gates; supplicants never interacted with the idol itself, and a priest was there to act as intercessory. Pachacamac idols in museum collections today most likely bear a resemblance to the original idol, which was reported as a staff topped with a rectilinear human figure with two faces, one on each side. Lightly incised relief decorations favoring geometric and/or zoomorphic patterning further characterize idols known today.

MAMA QUILLA

The female moon deity, Mama Quilla, complemented and was married to the masculine sun deity in the Inca pantheon. As the Inca ruler was associated with the Sun, so his wife was associated with the Moon. And, just as gold was believed to be the sweat of the Sun, silver was regarded as the tears of the Moon. The Moon was especially important to the Incas in calculating time and regulating the festival calendar, as many rituals were based on lunar cycles. The Moon had its own temple in Cuzco and was attended to by its own priestesses.

INTI ILLAPA

After the Sun, the thunder god, Inti Illapa, also the god of weather and meteorological phenomena such as lightning and rainbows, ranked most powerful. He was a messenger and servant of the Sun. He was often represented as a male wielding a sling or war club, or one in each hand, and wore shining clothes. The crack of the sling represented thunder, lightning bolts were sling stones, and a lightning flash was the shimmer of his garments as he moved. Inti Illapa was associated with the puma; in the highlands he was associated with Venus, the Morning Star. When rain was wanted, the people prayed to this deity; when it rained, it was believed that he broke a rain jug held by his sister. His importance was in direct relation to the absolute necessity of rain in an agricultural environment.

PACHAMAMA AND MAMACOCHA

Pachamama, or Mother Earth, was associated with the earth and agriculture and was supposed to make the fields fertile. She played a particularly important role in the highlands, where agriculture was especially important. The Incas made sacrifices to Pachamama for successful crops, and farmers reportedly worshipped Pachamama in the form of a stone in the middle of their fields. It is still common today to make an offering of *chicha*, a maize beer favored since Inca times, to Pachamama by pouring a small amount on the earth. By comparison, Mamacocha was a female sea deity especially important among coastal communities, whose livelihood depended on bountiful waters. Not only did the Incas worship the Pacific Ocean as a goddess, but springs and streams through Inca territory were venerated as daughters of the sea.

STARS AND PLANETS

The Incas were the last in a long line of Andean communities to devise a complicated mythology around stars, constellations, and planets. Stars were thought of as the children of the Sun and Moon. The Incas made no linguistic distinction between stars and planets, which is perhaps the reason that the planet Venus was their chief representative. The Spanish chronicler Polo de Ondegardo's 1585 manuscript *De los errores y supersticiones de los indios* is the source most commonly cited on Inca stargazing. In it he writes, "Among the stars, as a rule, all of them worshipped one they call Qolqa, which we call the Pleiades. And the other stars were venerated especially by those who believed that they were in need of their assistance. For they attributed various offices to various stars. Thus, the shepherds worshipped and sacrificed to a star they call Urcuchillay, which they say is a sheep [llama] of many colors, which is concerned with the conservation of livestock, and it is understood to be the one the Astrologers call Lyra." Ondegardo goes on to describe other stars that were worshipped for various reasons. In general, the Incas believed that each animal and bird on earth had its equal in the sky. The stars were thought of as doppelgangers and were responsible for their earthly counterparts' preservation and growth in numbers.

Rituals and Religious Ceremonies

The Incas celebrated regular and numerous ceremonies that correlated with the agricultural cycle, the solar and lunar cycles, and the calendar. Other festivals were reserved for extraordinary times such as drought or disaster or for the coronation or the burial of a king. Many of the ceremonies took place in Cuzco, which was the empire's religious and ceremonial center. In Cuzco major public ceremonies usually took place in the main plaza, called Huacaypata. Each of the primary festivals had its own month, and they were held in order and according to specific rites and sacrifices. Among the most important ceremonies were Cápac Raymi, which occurred in December and was tied to the summer solstice; Ayriwa, which took place in April and was associated with the maize harvest; Inti Raymi, or the "sun festival," which occurred in June and was associated with the winter solstice; and Ayamarka, which was a time of great preparations for Cápac Raymi. Other ceremonies, to name a few, included Camay, in February, which was intended for the disposal of the previous year's sacrificial remains; Chahua Huarquis, in July, during which sacrifices were made to important water sources; and K'antaray, which was held during October and was associated with rain ceremonies. Many small ceremonies took place every day to ensure good relations with or to seek the aid of the gods; these might include burning wood, food, or cloth to Inti. The following is a brief account of the entire ceremonial cycle. It should be noted that the name of the month and the particular ceremony represent inexact correspondences. The modern calendar months given below provide a general framework for the cycle.

THE CEREMONIAL CYCLE (RITUAL CALENDAR OF THE STATE RELIGION)

Cápac Raymi The Cápac Raymi, or "magnificent festival," was one of the most important for the Incas. It is part of a set of rituals that were celebrated in Cuzco around the first full moon following the December (summer) solstice and lasted up to three weeks of January. During this festival all non-Inca residents of the city—that is, all persons who were born outside the city and not "true" ethnic Incas—had to leave the city. Members of the 10 Cuzco *panaqas* (lineage or descent groups of rulers) gathered in Cuzco's Huacaypata plaza and sacri-

ficed 10 llamas for the health of the king. Later that night each *panaqa* burned a tunic to a particular deity, two each to the Sun, Moon, thunder, Viracocha, and Earth. Tunics were highly valued possessions, the products of hundreds and sometimes thousands of hours of labor; the ruler himself was said to have worn a new tunic each day, ritually burning it when done.

These rituals were part of a more elaborate routine, including the festival of Camay. In the first stage 100 brown llamas from the four quarters (*suyus*) of the empire were sacrificed by the priests of the Sun, who offered them in the Sun's name to Viracocha. In the second stage newly initiated boys, provided with breechcloths and earplugs—status symbols and symbols of male adulthood—engaged in a ritual battle, and in turn they offered a young llama, which was sacrificed by the priests. In the third stage, held after the day and night of the full moon, llamas were sacrificed for the health of the people in town. At a certain point after the sacrifices, all the ashes from sacrifices made during the previous year were tossed in the Huatanay River in order that they be washed to the ocean, which the Incas viewed as both surrounding and supporting the Earth.

After three weeks the non-Inca citizens were allowed to return to the city, and several days of dancing and drinking ensued. They were fed with a mixture of corn flour and llama blood and told it was a gift of the Sun and that it would stay in their bodies and would inform the deity if they spoke ill of the Sun or the king. Altogether the sacrifices and the rituals, as obligations to the gods, ensured social health, the health of the king, and acted as repayment and tribute to the gods. As the rituals occur during the period when the Sun is at its zenith (the period when the Sun reaches its highest point above the horizon), they are also concerned with the continued cycles of the solar year.

Hatun Puquy At the height of the rainy season in February, 100 chestnut-colored llamas were sacrificed. Many people gathered in fields that were to be cultivated and an offering of 20 guinea pigs was made to the Sun along with 20 bundles of firewood. After the sacrifice they implored the Sun to help them with their fields. The *mamakuna* of the Sun—

women dedicated to the service of the Inca gods—were present, and they were supplicated with food. Once finished, the people began working in the fields.

Paucar Huaray   According to John Rowe, *paucar huaray* means "earth ripening," and the ceremony corresponds with March. Little else is know about the activities of this festival month.

Ayriwa (Ariguaquiz)   On the first day of the month of April, 100 spotted llamas were sacrificed, and symbols of royal insignia were honored. An old llama that had been previously selected was put in the middle of the square and watched over for the whole month. Unlike the other llamas, it was never killed but was a spectacle in the middle of the plaza. It was given coca and *chicha*, an alcoholic beverage made from fermented maize or fruit. Jars of *chicha* were intentionally placed near the llama so that it might kick one over, thereby making an offering in its own name in the cause of agriculture and fertility. In addition, 15 llama were burned there so that the maize seeds would develop. The festival culminated with the burning of a large number of guinea pigs and chilis.

Aymoray (Hatun Cuzqui)   The festival of Aymoray, meaning "great cultivation," took place during May. During this festival a ritual harvest of sacred maize fields occurred, accompanied by dancing and singing songs whose message asked that the grain not run out before the next harvest. One hundred more llamas of all colors were sacrificed, and the meat was distributed to all the Incas. Later, 30 more llamas were burned and sacrificed for *huaca* maintenance; a little meat was burned at each *huaca*, the amount of which varied by its importance. On the 15th day, five old llamas were sacrificed and their meat again distributed. The young men initiated that year ritually harvested the maize and brought it into the city, and later all the people of the city went out into the fields to plow them as a symbol of the importance of the maize harvest. During this month another ceremony, Mamasara, was simultaneously enacted in each family's home. In this ceremony unusually shaped ears of corn were wrapped

in fine textile. Afterward they were considered *huacas* of the corn deity and were asked to predict a good harvest in the coming year.

Inti Raymi (Aucay Cuzqui)   Celebrated in June, this festival included the June (winter) solstice and a great festival in honor of the sun god, Inti. The festival took place on a hill outside Cuzco called Manturcalla. Only Inca males of royal blood were allowed to participate. On the first day an offering of 100 brown llamas was made to the Sun. On the following day 30 more llamas were sacrificed, this time not only to the Sun but also to Viracocha and the thunder god. The participants made a large number of wooden statues and dressed them in fine cloth; at the end of the festival these were burned. A special dance called the *cayo* was performed four times a day. After the sacrifices were made on Manturcalla, the group divided into halves, with half remaining behind to continue dancing and drinking, while the other half divided once again with one group ascending the hill called Chuquichanca and the other ascending another hill, called Paurcacancha, where six more llamas were sacrificed. After the sacrifices, effigy figurines made of gold, sent by the Sun, were buried on three nearby hills. The climax of the festival involved the sacrifice of special young llamas to Viracocha, whose image had been carried in on a litter on the shoulders of important individuals. At the very end of the ceremony all the charcoal and ashes were gathered up and thrown on a flat space near the hill. The celebrants then returned to Cuzco, scattering coca, flowers, and feathers along the way, and gathered in the main square, where they drank and sang for the rest of the day.

Chahua Huarquis   During this July festival 100 brown llamas were sacrificed. Additional sacrifices were made to the *huaca* of Tocori, which presided over the irrigation system of Cuzco. One llama was taken to where the valley irrigation began, and one, to where it ended in order to preserve the water in the hopes of ensuring its abundance. This was done because the Incas believed that Inca Roca, the sixth king, had magically increased the water supply from this source.

Yapaquis Associated with August, this festival saw the sacrifice of 100 brown llamas to all the *huacas* of Cuzco. One thousand *cuy*, or guinea pigs, were provided by the provinces for sacrifice in the same field that had been sown in May. The *cuy* were sacrificed to ensure protection from inclement weather and to ensure a plentitude of water and sun. This field was then ritually planted.

Coya Raymi (Citua) The ninth month of the Inca calendar saw the "queen's festival" take place. During this festival, celebrated at the beginning of the rainy season, 100 white llamas were sacrificed in order to prevent sickness caused by the changing weather. All provincials, the sick, anyone with a physical defect, and dogs (because their howling at the Moon was considered an ill omen) were sent out of Cuzco. The people remaining in the city gathered at the Coricancha and waited for the appearance of the new moon. When it appeared they began to run and shout and playfully struck at each other with lit torches. Then everyone returned to their homes and shook out their clothes and blankets, symbolically throwing out evil, sickness, disaster, and misfortune. Simultaneously, a group of 100 warriors-runners took up the cry of the people and the priests and set out along the four main highways leading out of Cuzco. Each runner passed the message of "Go away, evil, from the land" to a subsequent runner, the last of whom ritually bathed in a river so that the evil would be carried away in the running water. While the message was being relayed along, the people remaining in the city ritually bathed themselves and then took a maize porridge and smeared it on their faces and on the lintels of their doors as a symbol of purification. Dancing and feasting marked the following days, more llama sacrifices occurred, and finally the provincials were allowed to reenter. Divination ceremonies were undertaken to see if the coming year would be bountiful. The ceremonies concluded with all the peoples of the empire bringing their own *huacas* to the central plaza where they would pay tribute to and show allegiance to the Sapa Inca.

K'antaray (Homa Raymi Puchayquiz) Activities during this festival month, coinciding with October, focused on ensuring sufficient water for a healthy crop. One hundred llamas were sacrificed, and if the amount of rain was insufficient additional sacrifices were undertaken to induce the gods to bring rain.

Ayarmarka This last festival, held in November, was the precursor to and set the preparation for the Cápac Raymi. On the first day 100 llamas were sacrificed. On the following day all the boys who were to be initiated the following month went to Huanacauri hill and offered a sacrifice to the *huaca* there, one of the most important in the entire *ceque* system. The boys asked permission to be initiated and then slept the night there in imitation of the journey of their mythical ancestors. Each boy drew blood from the ear of a llama they had towed up the hill, drew lines on their faces with the blood, and later sacrificed the animal. The next day the boys returned to the city and fasted. They spent the whole month preparing for the initiation ceremonies that would happen the following month.

Other Ceremonies The Incas held certain ceremonies without regard to the calendar. While these ceremonies were not held at a specific time, only specific people were permitted to perform them. The most important of these ceremonies was the Itu, which might be held whenever the Incas wanted the gods' help: for example, in time of drought, pestilence, natural disasters, or when the emperor went to war. Leading up to the ceremony all the men fasted, ate nothing with salt or chili, refrained from sexual contact, and did not drink *chicha*. All the women who had dogs or other animals were sent out of the city. Anyone from the provinces was also forced to leave.

Once these preparations had been settled, llamas were sacrificed, their number and color depending on the petition to the gods. If it was especially serious, children might also be sacrificed. Young men up to 20 years old wore special costumes of red tunics with long fringes and ornaments, shell necklaces, and large crowns made of feathers. They carried small dried green birds and drums. Everyone else covered their heads with mantles or capes, and a strict silence was observed for the whole day.

The young men in costume walked slowly in a procession around the square beating their white drums and then sat down in silence. A noble then repeated the act, circling the square while spreading coca on the ground. After a short interval the boys got up and followed their procession, and more coca was spread on the ground. This ritual was performed eight times. That night they prayed to the Sun as intercessor, directing their prayers toward whatever they needed. When morning arrived, they removed and stored their clothing and began drinking and singing and dancing, which continued for the next two days.

MYTHS: CREATION AND ORIGIN STORIES

Numerous myths explain the Inca universe and ultimately help shape an understanding of the Incas that is often as complex as it is convoluted. The myths are one part of an interrelated system of thoughts and ideas. Though neither "fact" nor "history," they do tell us something about how the Incas perceived themselves, a situation that is greatly complicated by the lack of a written language. As a consequence, this means that Inca myths (and history, culture, etc.) come to us filtered through the eyes and words of Spanish chroniclers, most of whom were untrained observers, faithful to their own literary and intellectual traditions, and biased in one way or another. The following section provides a brief discussion of the primary resources related to myths, after which a number of fundamental Inca myths are summarized.

Sources for the Study of Inca Myths

Because the Incas did not have a recognizable written language, or at least a written language

that is currently understood by scholars, the work of a couple dozen Spanish chroniclers writing during the 150 years following the conquest of the Incas provides the material for the study of myth. The following list, by no means inclusive, nevertheless highlights the most significant sources for Inca myths. The list here is based on the work of the Andean scholar Gary Urton, who has researched widely and written eloquently on the nature of Inca myths. The sources mentioned below were written during the colonial period and reflect a process of mixing and blending the two cultures, referred to as syncretism, which was indicative of the period. Syncretism suggests that it is difficult to distinguish what is purely Inca from what has been recorded with the cultural inflections of the Spanish authors themselves. It is important to remember that the further one gets from the date of the conquest, the less reliable the chronicles tend to be.

Pedro de Cieza de León, a Spanish soldier who traveled widely and talked to numerous informants, published *The Chronicle of Peru* in two parts in 1553 and 1554. The second part, *El señorío de los incas*, is one of the earliest sources on the history and mythology of the Inca Empire. Juan de Betanzos, considered one of the foremost translators of his day, married an Inca princess, niece of the last Inca king, Huayna Cápac. Betanzos became fluent in Quechua, the empire's lingua franca, and was ordered in 1551 by the viceroy of Peru to write a history of the Incas. Completed in 1557, his *Narrative of the Incas* is one of the best sources on Inca myths from the perspective of Inca nobility. Juan Polo de Ondegardo was a top colonial administrator of Cuzco with a deep interest in native customs and "superstitions." He produced a number of reports, published in the late 1560s, that later served as source material for other chronicles.

Ideological and political underpinnings inform many of the Spanish chronicles, and they thus must be read critically in order to disassociate Spanish motivations from the narrative. Many chronicles were published in relation to the reorganization of the colonial state under Spanish authority and were thus undertaken as a basis for instituting reforms. Among the chronicles inflected with this context are Pedro Sarmiento de Gamboa's 1572 *Historia índica*, Cristobal de Molina's 1575 *Account of the Fables and Rites of the Incas*, and Jose de Acosta's 1590 *Natural and Moral History of the Indies.*

Appearing in the 17th century, and written by Quechua-speaking authors, were two of the most important sources recording myths. The first is Felipe Guamán Poma de Ayala's 1614–15 *First New Chronicle and Good Government*, a monumental narrative written in the form of a letter to the Spanish king documenting abuses against native Peruvians. While the text is partially suspect, Guamán Poma's manuscript included almost 400 ink drawings illustrating various aspects of Inca life. They are of invaluable worth and constitute one of the best visual sources on daily life, ritual, worship, and dress, among other things. The other text is Juan de Santacruz Pachacuti Yamqui Salcamaygua's 1613 *Relación de antigüedades deste reyno del Perú*, which recounts myths as well as quasi-historical data that can be linked to myths recounted in other authors' works.

Finally, one of the most reliable sources on Inca myths, ceremonies, and religious beliefs and practices comes from Bernabé Cobo, a Jesuit priest who entered Peru in 1599 and spent many years traveling among the native Andeans. Cobo drew extensively on previous chroniclers and synthesized a comprehensive and balanced chronicle of life in the Inca Empire.

Cosmic Origin Myth

Inca cosmic origin myths center on the Lake Titicaca region in the south-central region of the empire, an area that today straddles the Peru-Bolivia border. It is also, significantly, the region of the pre-Inca imperial culture centered at Tiwanaku, south of the shores of the lake, which existed ca. 200 B.C.E.–1100 C.E. Though versions of the origin story vary, most begin by stating that at the beginning of time the world was in darkness because the Sun, Moon, and stars did not yet exist. The creator god, Viracocha, who appears in vari-

ous versions as Con Ticci Viracocha, Thunupu Viracocha, and Viracocha Pachayachachic, emerged from Lake Titicaca in the period of darkness and created the first race of beings to populate the landscape. Most of the chronicles refer to these first beings as giants. For unspecified reasons this first race angered Viracocha, who sent a great flood over the land and transformed the original inhabitants into stone.

Viracocha then set about creating the second wave of humanity. First, however, he created the Sun, Moon, and stars, calling them forth from the Island of the Sun in Lake Titicaca. (This island subsequently became a major pilgrimage destination during the Inca period.) Having created the Sun, Moon, and stars, Viracocha then created the second race of beings, in some accounts from lakeshore stones and in other accounts from clay. He sent them underground so that later they could emerge from springs, caves, mountaintops, and other places, in effect "seeding" the nations that would later constitute the empire. These landscape points were subsequently recognized as origin places and became sacred shrines, or *huacas*. With his creations in place throughout the territory that would eventually constitute Tawantinsuyu, Viracocha himself, along with two "sons" he had created earlier and kept, set out over the land, each following a different route, and called on the ancestors to emerge, thereby populating the land. Viracocha and his sons continued to the northwestern edge of the empire in Ecuador and there passed over the sea, continuing until they disappeared over the horizon.

Guamán Poma's Four Ages of the Indians

Guamán Poma's version of the world, *First New Chronicle and Good Government*, recorded in his monumental letter to King Phillip III of Spain, depicts a succession of ages, each a regular episode that ends in a great cataclysm referred to as *pachacuti*, meaning "revolution or turning over/around"; "world reversal." These mythic ages of

6.2 *The first age of the Indians, according to Felipe Guamán Poma de Ayala: a period of darkness and rudimentary technology* (Felipe Guamán Poma de Ayala)

6.3 *The second age of the Indians: primitive people* (Felipe Guamán Poma de Ayala)

destruction and replacement overlap with the notion of cosmic origin discussed above and introduce other cosmological themes.

In Guamán Poma's version, which also overlaps significantly with Christian theology, each age is referred to as a "sun" and endures for 1,000 years. The first age, an age of darkness, was the period of the Wari Wiracocharuna, a people Guamán Poma believed descended from Spaniards from the time of Noah's Ark. They had only rudimentary technology, wore clothes made of leaves, and worshipped the Christian God. They lost faith, however, and began worshipping the Andean creator deities Viracocha and Pachacamac. The first world came to an end in an unspecified manner.

The second age was the period of the Wari Runa, a people who wore animal skin clothing, practiced basic agriculture, and lived without warfare. This age ended in a deluge. In the third age, that of the Purun Runa, or "wild men," civilization was growing increasingly complex. People wore spun and dyed wool clothing, made jewelry, practiced agriculture, migrated outward, but also engaged in greater conflicts and warfare. The fourth age was that of the Aucun Runa, or the "warlike people." During this age the world was divided into four parts, warfare increased, people lived in stone houses, and, in general, technology grew more advanced. He does not state how this age ended.

6.4 The third age of the Indians: wandering people
(Felipe Guamán Poma de Ayala)

6.5 The fourth age of the Indians: warlike people
(Felipe Guamán Poma de Ayala)

Inca Origin Myth: Pacariqtambo Version

Sarmiento de Gamboa's 1572 *Historia índica* provides the most detailed account of Inca origin. Though he refers to his narrative as history, much of it clearly falls in the realm of mythology. According to Sarmiento, the origin of the Incas was at a mountain called Pacariqtambo ("inn, or house, of dawn"; "place of origin"), about 30 kilometers (19 mi.) south of Cuzco, in which there were three caves. At the behest of Viracocha, the ancestors of the Incas emerged from the central cave, called Cápac Tocco. Two other indigenous groups, the

Maras and the Tambos, emerged from the flanking caves, which were called Maras Tocco and Sutic Tocco. (According to the legend, the Tambos were later divided into 10 *ayllus*, or ancestor groups, with five assigned to Hanan Cuzco and five assigned to Hurin Cuzco.) The founders of the Inca dynasty emerged from Cápac Tocco; those who accompanied them on their eventual journey, who would come to make up the other tribes of the Andes, emerged from the other caves. The Incas were eight brothers and sisters who emerged in pairs as married couples; Sarmiento refers to them as spouses. These pairs of brothers-sisters/husbands-wives are as follows, listed in order of emergence: Ayar Manco (later, Manco Cápac) emerged with Mama Ocllo;

Ayar Auca with Mama Huaco; Ayar Cachi with Mama Ipacaura/Cura; and Ayar Ucho with Mama Raua. It should be noted that *Ayar* comes from the word for "corpse," thus establishing a link between mythical ancestors and the worship of the mummified remains of kings. It should also be noted that in the chronicles of Guamán Poma and Murúa these ancestors originally passed underground from Lake Titicaca, a version of which is discussed below.

Ayar Manco led the ancestors to the north in search of land to settle. They carried with them a golden bar, which would be plunged into the earth and would signify home. They stopped in numerous places along the way. Ayar Manco and Mama Ocllo conceived and gave birth to a son who was called Sinchi Roca and would succeed his father as the second king of Cuzco. One of the brothers, Ayar Cachi, reputedly a great burden on the others, was tricked into returning to Pacariqtambo, where he was closed in forever by a great boulder blocking the entrance. Moving on, the ancestors arrived at the foot of the mountain Huanacauri, which they ascended and then saw for the first time the valley of Cuzco. The gold bar was lofted into the air toward the valley. When it hit the ground, it sank all the way into the earth, thereby indicating to the ancestors that they had found their homeland.

The youngest ancestor-brother, Ayar Ucho, was then transformed into stone at the hill of Huanacauri. In other versions he first takes flight, flies into the heavens, and speaks to the Sun, who tells him that the entourage should proceed to Cuzco and that Ayar Manco should hereafter be called Manco Cápac ("supreme rich one," in other words, king), at which point Ayar Ucho returns to the group, repeats what he was told, and then is transformed into stone. Huanacauri was thereafter worshipped as one of the principal *huacas*, and idols of it were even carried into battle. The ancestor group continued on to Cuzco. When they arrived either Manco Cápac or Mama Huaco planted maize. When they reached the center of what would become the city, what was to become the plaza of Huacaypata, Ayar Cápac, the last remaining brother-ancestor of Manco Cápac, transformed into a stone pillar. The remaining members, led by Manco Cápac and the boy Sinchi Roca, founded and built the city that would become the capital of the empire.

Inca Origin Myth: Lake Titicaca Version

A second version of the Inca origin story is set on the Island of the Sun in Lake Titicaca. Manco Cápac and Mama Ocllo, rendered in this version as children of the sun god Inti, were given the mission of civilizing the peoples of the world. Manco Cápac and a number of followers set out to do so, bringing along, of course, the familiar golden bar; when they arrived in Cuzco, they tested the soil with the bar and found it suitable. Upon the bar's sinking they knew they had arrived at their chosen land and set about building the royal residence and the Temple of the Sun. Recognizing Manco Cápac as their divine ruler, the inhabitants of the land accepted him and chose to follow his authority.

Other Origin Myths

A less familiar origin story is recounted in a text written around 1642 by the Spanish chronicler Fernando de Montesinos. While the myth overlaps with the Pacariqtambo myth, it significantly extends the narrative back in time by relating a history of four dynasties and a dynastic list of 108 kings. In this story the powerful Amauta dynasty had ruled for a long time but were defeated in a battle south of Cuzco. The survivors fled, resettled near Cuzco, and founded a new dynasty. After a succession of usurpers overtook the throne, a legitimate heir of the original dynasty took the throne and founded the Inca dynasty. If the dynastic list is accurate, it would extend the Inca lineage back to the Middle Horizon (ca. 540–900 C.E.), when the Wari and Tiwanacu dynasties ruled. Recent archaeological work has been interested in this account, as it better correlates to what some scholars feel is the gradual emergence of what became the Inca Empire, as opposed to the epic florescence traditionally detailed in most chronicles.

Inca Myth of State Expansion

The story of the Inca war against the Chancas, a powerful nation-state to the west of Cuzco, is of great importance to the overall narrative of the empire. While the story cannot properly be called history because many of its details are clearly mythical in nature, it nonetheless reflects a critical moment in the evolution of the Inca state from provincial valley dwellers to imperial conquerors.

As the Chanca armies advanced on Cuzco, everyone in the town fled, including the king. The defense of the city was left to a young prince and a few companions, who stayed behind despite the overwhelming odds against success. Some sources say this was Viracocha Inca, the eighth king, while others say it was his son Pachacuti. The defenders held on desperately during the first two waves of the Chanca assault. During the final assault the prince received the aid of rocks and stones in the valley, which were miraculously transformed into warriors. The rocks, called *pururaucas*, assured the Incas of victory, and after the battle they transformed back into stones and were venerated thereafter as important *huacas*. The victory over the Chancas catapulted the Inca toward imperial hegemony.

Provincial Myths

Not all myths that existed during the Inca period originated with the Incas; some were pre-Inca at their roots, and some were adopted into the Inca mythology. The *Huarochirí Manuscript*, an important early 17th-century document written in Quechua distinctive to the province of Huarochirí, to the east of Lima, records many such myths. One important myth attempts to explain the distinctions and links between the two worlds of the Andean coast and mountains. In doing so it discusses two creator gods, Viracocha and Pachacamac. In highland provincial centers the adopted belief was that Viracocha had made them Inca, while along the coast they believed Pachacamac had made them Inca. In one sense these are simply two different names for the creator deity reflecting the differences between coast and highlands.

Pacahacamac, however, was an important oracle site on the central coast that had a very long history of its own, one which the Incas recognized and adapted. Inca-period architecture at the site signals a colonial history of its own; the Incas conquered the region and took possession of the site but allowed it to retain its privilege as a pilgrimage site. The site, and quite possibly myths tied to the site, was reordered to fit the Inca conceptual model. The conquerors built an Inca-style masonry temple and installed a priest dedicated to the Inca cult of the Sun. In a myth recorded by Antonio de la Calancha, Pachacamac and the Sun are in very close association. According to this myth, Pachacamac created the first man and woman. The man died because there was no food, leaving the desperate woman to plead to the Sun for help. The Sun impregnated her with his rays, and she bore a son after only four days, which greatly angered Pachacamac, who tore the boy to pieces. To solve the problem of the lack of food, he sowed the boy's teeth in the earth and from them grew maize. He planted ribs and bones and grew yucca, and from planted flesh came vegetables and fruit trees.

The Sun then created another son from the remains of the corpse and named him Vichama or Villama. Like his father, he wanted to travel. When Vichama left on a journey, Pachacamac killed the woman, Vichama's mother. Pachacamac then created a new human couple, who began to repopulate the land. When Vichama returned, he reassembled his mother and brought her back to life. Fearing reprisal, Pachacamac fled into the ocean. Vichama then turned the newly created people into stone; his anger later softened, and he transformed some of these into *huacas*. Finally, Vichama asked his father, the Sun, to create a new race of people. Some sources say the Sun sent eggs, and others say he sent stars. Either way, a new race of people then began.

Cosmology/ Worldview (Structure of the Universe)

The Andean worldview was based on the principles of duality, the balance between opposing forces, and reciprocity, the exchange between active elements. The opposing forces in the Andean worldview emphasized fundamental binary relations such as light and dark, male and female, upper and lower, Sun and Moon, and other similar binary oppositions. Keeping these relations balanced was crucial, and proper balance ensured a worldly equilibrium that signified the ideal physical and metaphysical state. Reciprocal exchange ensured balance between these elements. Disequilibrium, however, resulted from real world changes that somehow shifted the sense of equilibrium. A state of disequilibrium could only be restored to a state of equilibrium through the mediating effects of reciprocity. In effect, both positive and negative changes could be made through the appropriate exchange with the supernatural world: Humans made offerings to deities and deities exercised their power in the manner that would restore balance for the affected party. This, then, was the intention behind Andean cosmology—to seek and keep harmony in the form of balanced dualities mediated by reciprocity. These principles were given visual representation in an important native manuscript written in the early 17th century.

Worldview Model: Santacruz Pachacuti Yamqui Salcamaygua

The native author Juan de Santacruz Pachacuti Yamqui Salcamaygua published the *Relación de antigüedades deste reyno del Perú* in 1615. In it was included a famous drawing that is generally agreed to be both a conceptual model of the Coricancha, the main Inca temple in Cuzco, and a conceptual model of the Inca universe. In the Inca religious model the Coricancha is the sacred center; Pachacuti Yamqui held his drawing to be a model of the Inca world system and a depiction of the creation of space/time and life, the reproduction of life, and the dynamic conjunction of masculine and feminine forces. Ultimately, it is a depiction of the structure of the universe.

6.6 *View of the Coricancha, the most sacred temple in the Inca Empire* (Ananda Cohen Suarez)

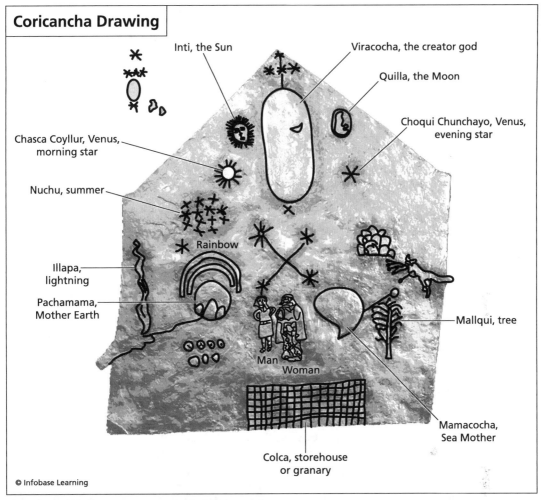

Coricancha Drawing

Inti, the Sun

Viracocha, the creator god

Quilla, the Moon

Choqui Chunchayo, Venus, evening star

Chasca Coyllur, Venus, morning star

Nuchu, summer

Rainbow

Illapa, lightning

Pachamama, Mother Earth

Man

Woman

Mallqui, tree

Mamacocha, Sea Mother

Colca, storehouse or granary

© Infobase Learning

6.7 *This diagram depicts both the symbolism of the Coricancha itself and the duality that exists in the Inca universe. The god Viracocha is represented at the top by the oval and divides the image in half. The signs for masculinity are on the left and those for femininity are on the right. The left depicts Venus as morning star, a group of stars that indicate summer, a rainbow covering the earth, lightning, the river of origin, and a man. The right side represents Venus as evening star, winter, hail, a feline, the sea (Mamacocha), a tree, and a woman.* (Juan de Santacruz Pachacuti Yamqui Salcamaygua)

The image is read from a perspective internal to the visual space. This means that the left as it is viewed is actually the right in its relation to the cosmological system. Centered at the top is an image of the Inca creator god, Viracocha, rendered as an oval. The oval represents Viracocha's ability to transcend duality. This image serves as an axis dividing the drawing into two sides. To the left of the image of Viracocha is a sun, which the Incas thought represented masculinity. On the right is the idea of femininity, which is drawn as a moon. Beneath the sun there is the image of Venus as morning star, a grouping of starlike images meant to depict summer, an image of a rainbow covering the earth with the word *pachamama* (meaning "earth") inscribed inside it, and finally images of lightning, the river of origin, and man. On the right side, to establish the principles of necessary balance, the images beneath the moon are Venus as evening star, winter, hail, a feline, the sea (Mamacocha), a tree, and woman. The right side symbolizes state functions, and the left, family functions.

The symmetry between the two sides of Pachacuti Yamqui's image encodes a hierarchical relation of domination and subordination that corresponds to *hanan*, or "right"—the Andean notion for what is spatially above and dominant—and *hurin*, or "left"—the lower, subordinate side. The principles of *hanan* and *hurin* or, rather, the fusion of the two are exactly the symbolic construction of space that organized the Inca city of Cuzco into two halves, an upper and a lower, a pattern that was extended over the whole empire. *Hanan* and *hurin* also define Inca social division into complementary moieties. Overall, the system is simplified in the following equivalencies:

hanan = upper = masculine = right = Sun = domination
hurin = lower = feminine = left = Moon = subordination

Yet, the image also contains symbols of unification that draw the two sides together. An image of a man and a woman, the oval representation of Viracocha, and the stellar cross all suggest unification. As such, the image of the man and woman constitute a central focal point of the diagram, thereby illustrating the centrality of humans to the cosmos. At the very

bottom is a gridlike image that is labeled (in translation) on the masculine side as a "storehouse" and on the feminine side as a "terrace," in both instances indicating the Earth.

In short, Pachacuti Yamqui's conceptual image breaks down the conceived universe into dual symmetrical principles, on the one side dominated by the Sun and the masculine and on the other by the Moon and the feminine. It seems to reinforce the idea that one of the Incas' principal concerns was to maintain a state of equilibrium in a universe where dual forces were constantly threatening to come unbalanced. Situated, then, at the conjunction of the two halves are humans, who mediate the various forces of the universes.

Three-Part Cosmos

According to the Inca worldview at the time of the conquest, the universe was constructed of three interrelated divisions: *hanaq pacha* (the world above), *kay pacha* (this world), and *ukhu pacha* (the world below). While this structure may seem connected to Christian concepts of heaven, Earth, and hell, the Incas did not apparently think of them this way. Nevertheless, much of the information recorded by the Spanish chroniclers placed these three parts in that context, thereby confusing their meaning and function. It was an easy mistake for them to make, seeing that the idea of the tripartite universe was so thoroughly ingrained in their way of thinking.

The confusion with heaven and hell is obvious in the translations of the words themselves. In general it seems that the majority of the lay population was said to travel to *ukhu pacha* at death, while only nobles and the elite went to *hanaq pacha*; in other words, the Inca noble class consciousness even distinguished their resting place from that of the peasantry, in effect allowing the elite to reside "above" with their gods. Further interpretive confusions arise in the notion that "above" and "below" are typically understood in directional terms, with above commonly referenced as north and below commonly understood as south.

At specific times of the year it seems that the Inca ceremonial calendar allowed for rituals that precipitated a bridging between these levels and spaces, such that the dead could return to Earth reanimated and commune with the living. This, too, reinstalled a sense of equilibrium in the Inca cosmological formula.

Cuzco as Sacred City and Axis Mundi

Cuzco was the seat of the royal dynasty, the political core of the Inca polity, and the spiritual and geographic center of the empire. Its reconstruction, following a plan most accounts attribute to the ninth Inca king, Pachacuti, helped define its transition from a small village of minor local interest into an imperial capital. In this role it balanced administrative and bureaucratic functions with its symbolic, cosmological, and religious significance. In effect, Cuzco was a sacred object. Sacredness within the city found expression in function as well as in its physical form, where such things as urban design and masonry construction techniques were deeply ingrained with ritual, mythical, and sacred principles. Furthermore, the city was at the center of a sacred shrine system, the Cuzco *ceque* system, which helped ritualize local religious practice.

The Spanish chronicler Ondegardo wrote in 1571 that "the city of Cuzco was the house and dwelling place of the gods, and thus there was not in all of it, a fountain, or road, or wall that they did not say contained a mystery." Further echoing this sentiment, contemporary scholars have suggested that even beyond Cuzco the Andean landscape itself is imbued with sacredness and that there is a deep and profound connection between human centeredness and the spirits of mountains, rocks, springs, rivers, and other topographic features. The native peoples worshipped cosmological powers in the physical topography, most typically in the form of *huacas*, and the structure of the sacred system meant Cuzco was at the center of everything.

According to some theories, urban construction in the imperial hinterlands reflected these sacred and social systems associated with the urban model initially established in Cuzco, creating a kind of recognizable, organized matrix that ultimately reflected imperial might and control. Cuzco, then,

in its role as the center of religious universe, as the anchor of centripetal religious forces, acted as an axis mundi—the conceptualized center of the world around which the Inca physical and metaphysical universe revolved. The city was, for the Inca, the center of the Andean cosmological order.

CUZCO *CEQUE* SYSTEM

Perhaps the most significant reflection of Cuzco as axis mundi is its centrality in the Cuzco *ceque* system. The *ceque* system is a ritual system defining the sacred landscape of Cuzco and its environs and is composed of several hundred shrines (*huacas*) connected by a system of ritual lines (*ceques*). Cobo's 1653 *Historia del nuevo mundo* provides the most detailed account of the system. Brian Bauer and R. Tom Zuidema, two preeminent contemporary Andean scholars, have done much work advancing knowledge of the *ceque* system.

To understand how the *ceque* system is organized it is first necessary to understand the basic principles by which the city, and thus the empire, was divided. The city was divided into four quadrants that converged at the Huacaypata plaza and followed the four main roads out of Cuzco. These roads then divided the Cuzco Valley into four regions, or *suyus*, from which the name for the empire itself derives—Tawantinsuyu, meaning "land of the four parts." The point within the city where the four parts conjoin is a fundamental reflection of its role as axis mundi. The city was further divided into moieties, or halves, which established social divisions based on the urban plan. The upper half was called Hanansuyu, and the lower half was Hurinsuyu. Each of these halves contained two quarters. In Hanansuyu the northwest quarter was referred to as Chinchaysuyu, and the northeast quarter was called Antisuyu. Hurinsuyu was similarly divided, with Collasuyu located to the southeast and Cuntisuyu to southwest. Following and extending the quadripartite division of the city and the valley, the empire itself was divided into analogous divisions.

The *ceque* system, then, is an even more complex, symbolically infused overlay on this system of partitioning. It is ultimately based on the location of sacred *huacas*, or idols or shrines, throughout the

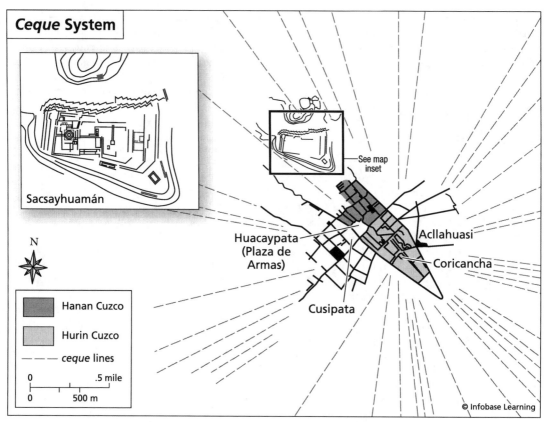

Map 8 *The* Ceque *System, Showing the Theoretical Lines That Emanate from the Coricancha and Connect the* Huacas

landscape. The shrines themselves were considered sacred because they were associated with legendary, mythical, or cosmological events or were simply a strange and perhaps powerful aberration in the landscape. In addition to the moieties and the quarters, the *ceque* system partitioned the landscape with 42 abstract lines *(ceques)* whose orientations were determined by the location of no less than 328 *huacas* located in and around Cuzco. According to Cobo, Chinchaysuyu, Antisuyu, and Collasuyu each contained nine *ceques*. The fourth, Cuntisuyu was more complex and had 15 *ceques*. The number of *huacas* associated with any particular *ceque* varied greatly.

***Ceque* and *Huaca* Maintenance** Inca kin groups were responsible for the proper maintenance of

each *huaca*. According to Cobo, "Each *ceque* was the responsibility of the partialities and families of the city of Cuzco, from within which came the attendants and servants who cared for the guacas [*sic*] of their ceque and saw to offering the established sacrifices at the proper times." In this sense the *ceque* system was linked to the social organization of the city and imposed ritual obligations. Encountering a *huaca* required a prayer or an offering, and the number of persons responsible for its maintenance varied from *huaca* to *huaca*. Some of the most important *huacas* had lands designated especially to their maintenance, from which would be drawn all the required kinds and amounts of sacrificial or offertory items.

The offerings presented to a *huaca* varied according to its importance. The most significant *huacas* received offerings in the form of human sacrifice, generally in tandem with the major ceremonial festival the Cápac Hucha (also, Capacocha), during which all the major *huacas* of the empire were visited. Less significant *huacas* might receive an offering of a sacrificed llama, guinea pigs *(cuy)*, sheep, a few coca leaves, bundles of carved firewood, buried gold or silver figurines, seashells, or miniature textiles.

Coricancha All the lines in the Cuzco *ceque* system converged in or near Cuzco's primary sacred temple, the Coricancha. Its fine ashlar masonry walls signaled the Coricancha's significance architecturally. Its most prominent wall was a curved wall, one of only a few in the entire empire. Many chronicles relate that the temple housed enormous amounts of gold and silver, ultimately reflecting its affiliation with both the Sun and Moon, respectively. Its walls were reportedly sheathed in gold plates. A golden maize effigy garden graced the interior. Yet, of all the golden items the temple was said to contain the most significant was a golden sun disk, referred to as *punchao*, representing the sun god, Inti, whom the Inca worshipped above all other gods. The Sapa Inca was referred to as the "son of the Sun," and the Coricancha thus became, to a certain extent, his sacred house. The Coricancha was therefore the geographical, religious, and administrative axis point around which the empire revolved. And, as the axis point of the *ceque* system, and to some extent the axis of the empire itself, the structure was invested with extraordinary symbolic power.

READING

State Religion

Pablo Joseph de Arriaga, *The Extirpation of Idolatry in Peru*. Translated and edited by L. Clark Keating (Lexington: University of Kentucky Press, 1968).

Brian S. Bauer, *Ancient Cuzco: Heartland of the Inca* (Austin: University of Texas Press, 2004).

———, *The Development of the Inca State* (Austin: University of Texas Press, 1992).

———, "The Legitimization of the Inca State in Myth and Ritual," *American Anthropologist* 98, no. 2 (1996): 327–337.

———, *The Sacred Landscape of the Inca: The Cusco Ceque System* (Austin: University of Texas Press, 1998).

Brian S. Bauer and David S. P. Dearborn, *Astronomy and Empire in the Ancient Andes* (Austin: University of Texas Press, 1995).

Brian S. Bauer and Charles Stanish, *Ritual and Pilgrimage in the Andes* (Austin: University of Texas Press, 2001).

Pedro Cieza de León, *The Discovery and Conquest of Peru* (Durham, N.C.: Duke University Press, 1998).

Bernabé Cobo, *History of the Inca Empire*. Translated and edited by Roland Hamilton (Austin: University of Texas Press, 1979).

———, *Inca Religions and Customs*. Translated and edited by Roland Hamilton (Austin: University of Texas Press, 1990).

———, "Relación de las guacas del Cuzco." In "An Account of the Shrines of Ancient Cuzco," translated and edited by John H. Rowe, *Ñawpa Pacha* 17 (1979): 2–80.

Terence D'Altroy, *The Incas* (London: Blackwell, 2002).

Nigel Davies, *The Incas* (Niwot: University Press of Colorado, 1995).

Arthur Andrew Demarest, *Viracocha: The Nature and Antiquity of the Andean High God*, Peabody Museum Monographs 6 (Cambridge, Mass.: Harvard University, Peabody Museum of Archaeology and Ethnology, 1984).

Garcilaso de la Vega, El Inca, *Royal Commentaries of the Inca and General History of Peru*. Translated by Harold V. Livermore. 2 vols. (Austin: University of Texas Press, 1966).

Graziano Gasparini and Louise Margolies, *Inca Architecture*. Translated by Patricia Lyons (Bloomington: Indiana University Press, 1980).

Jonathan Haas et al. eds., *The Origins and Development of the Andean State* (Cambridge: Cambridge University Press, 1987).

John Hemming, *The Conquest of the Incas* (London: MacMillan, 1970).

————, "Pachacuti: Miracles, Punishments, and Last Judgment: Visionary Past and Prophetic Future in Early Colonial Peru," *American Historical Review* 93, no. 4 (October 1988): 960–1,006.

————, *Religion in the Andes: Vision and Imagination in Early Colonial Peru* (Princeton, N.J.: Princeton University Press, 1991).

Colin McEwan and Maarten van de Guchte, "Ancestral Time and Sacred Space in Inca State Ritual." In *The Ancient Americas: Art from Sacred Landscapes,* edited by Richard F. Townshend, 359–373 (Chicago: Art Institute of Chicago, 1992).

Kenneth Mills, *Idolatry and Its Enemies: Colonial Andean Religion and Extirpation, 1640–1750* (Princeton, N.J.: Princeton University Press, 1992).

Susan Niles, "Inca Architecture and the Sacred Landscape." In *The Ancient Americas: Art from the Sacred Landscapes,* edited by Richard Townsend, 347–357 (Chicago: Art Institute of Chicago, 1992).

Johan Reinhard, *Machu Picchu: The Sacred Center* (Lima, Peru: Nuevas Imágenes, 1991).

Veronica Salles-Reese, *From Viracocha to the Virgin of Copacabana: Representations of the Sacred at Lake Titicaca* (Austin: University of Texas Press, 1997).

Robert J. Sallnow, *Pilgrims of the Andes: Regional Cults in Cuzco* (Washington, D.C.: Smithsonian Institution Press, 1987).

Max Uhle, *Pachacamac. Report of the William Pepper, M. D., LL. D. Peruvian Expedition of 1896* (Philadelphia: Department of Archaeology, University of Pennsylvania, 1903).

Myths: Creation and Origin Stories

Catherine Allen, "Patterned Time: The Mythic History of a Peruvian Community," *Journal of Latin American Lore* 10, no. 2 (1984): 151–173.

————, "Time, Place, and Narrative in an Andean Community," *Bulletin de la Société Suisse sus Américanistes* 57–58 (1993–94): 89–95.

————, "When Utensils Revolt: Mind, Matter, and Models of Being in the Pre-Columbian Andes," *RES: Anthropology and Aesthetics* 33 (Spring 1998): 19–27.

Juan de Betanzos, *Narrative of the Incas.* Translated and edited by Roland Hamilton and Dana Buchanan (Austin: University of Texas Press, 1996).

Felipe Guamán Poma de Ayala, *El primer nueva corónica y buen gobierno.* 3 vols. Edited by John Murra and Rolena Adorno. (Mexico: Siglo Veintiuno, 1992).

————, *Letter to a King: A Picture History of the Inca Civilisation.* Translated and edited by Christopher Dilke (London: George Allen & Unwin, 1978).

Catherine Julien, *Reading Inca History* (Iowa City: Iowa University Press, 2002).

Sabine MacCormack, "Children of the Sun and Reason of State Myths, Ceremonies and Conflicts in Inca Peru." *Discovering the Americas: 1992 Lecture Series,* Working Papers No. 6, Department of Spanish and Portuguese, University of Maryland, College Park, 1990.

Michael A. Malpass, *Daily Life in the Inca Empire* (Westport, Conn.: Greenwood Press, 1996).

César Paternosto, *The Stone and the Thread: Andean Roots of Abstract Art* (Austin: University of Texas Press, 1989).

María Rostworowski de Diez Canseco, *History of the Inca Realm.* Translated by Harry B. Iceland (Cambridge: Cambridge University Press, 1999).

Paul Steele, *Handbook of Inca Mythology* (Santa Barbara, Calif.: ABC-CLIO, 2004).

Gary Urton, *The History of a Myth: Pacariqtambo and the Origin of the Inkas* (Austin: University of Texas Press, 1990).

————, *Inca Myths* (Austin: University of Texas Press, 1999).

R. Tom Zuidema, "Myth and History in Ancient Peru." In *The Logic of Culture,* edited by I. Rossi, 150–175 (South Hadley, Mass.: Bergin, 1982).

Cosmology/Worldview (Structure of the Universe)

Rolena Adorno, *Guamán Poma: Writing and Resistance in Colonial Peru* (Austin: University of Texas Press, 1986).

Catherine Allen, "Body and Soul in Quechua Thought," *Journal of Latin American Lore* 8, no. 2 (1982): 179–186.

————, "Enfolding Oppositions: Structure and Practice in a Quechua Story," *Journal of the Steward Anthropological Society* 25, nos. 1–2 (1997): 9–27.

————, "The Incas Have Gone Inside: Pattern and Persistence in Andean Iconography," *RES: Anthropology and Aesthetics* 42 (2002): 180–203.

Kathleen Berrin, ed., *The Spirit of Ancient Peru* (London: Thames & Hudson, 1998).

Constance Classen, *Inca Cosmology and the Human Body* (Salt Lake City: Utah University Press, 1993).

Robert V. Dover, Katherine E. Seibold, and John H. McDowell, eds., *Andean Cosmologies through Time* (Bloomington: Indiana University Press, 1992).

Daniel W. Gade, "Lightning in the Folklife and Religion of the Central Andes," *International Review of Ethnology and Linguistics* 78 (1980): 770–788.

————, *The Shape of Inca History* (Iowa City: University of Iowa Press, 1999).

Frank Salomon, "'The Beautiful Grandparents': Andean Ancestor Shrines and Mortuary Ritual as Seen through Colonial Records." In *Tombs for the Living: Andean Mortuary Practices*, edited by Tom D. Dillehay, 315–353 (Washington, D.C.: Dumbarton Oaks Research Library and Collection, 1995).

Juan de Santacruz Pachacuti Yamqui Salcamaygua, *Relación de antigüedades deste reyno del Peru*, Biblioteca de Autores Españoles, vol. 209 (Madrid: Ediciones Atlas, 1968).

Irene Silverblatt, *Moon, Sun, and Witches: Gender Ideologies and Class in Inca and Colonial Peru* (Princeton, N.J.: Princeton University Press, 1987).

Helaine Silverman, "The Archaeological Identification of an Ancient Peruvian Pilgrimage Center," *World Archaeology* 26, no. 1 (1994): 1–18.

Rebecca Stone-Miller. *Art of the Andes*. 2nd ed. (London: Thames & Hudson, 2002).

Gary Urton, *At the Crossroads of the Earth and the Sky: An Andean Cosmology* (Austin: University of Texas Press, 1981).

7

FUNERARY BELIEFS
AND CUSTOMS

Among the Incas, and indeed for all of the Andean cultures that preceded them, death marked the passage into a new state of being. It was not conceived of as the end of life but rather its continuity in another realm. Mummies of dead ancestors, both royal and common, were treated with great care and even fed and consulted by their descendants. Beliefs and practices relating to the deceased permeated many aspects of Inca life, from ancestor worship practiced by his or her *ayllu* (members of a descent group) to full-scale public processionals honoring a dead Inca ruler. Human sacrifice, believed to release the energy or spirit of the victim unto another person or deity, was practiced for the most somber of rituals in the service of the Inca king and to honor the gods.

DEATH AND THE AFTERLIFE

Death involved the passage through several different bodily states; there was no simple dichotomy established among the Incas between an alive and a dead body. The first stage of death was known as *wañuq*, in which the individual entered the realm of the newly dead. During this period the deceased transitioned from the world of the living, in which his or her body was a live material presence, into the world of the dead, in which the spiritual body dominates. After *wañuq*, the body became an *aya*, which simply means a dead body. At this point the spiritual body has separated itself from the physical body, and the person has transitioned into his or her eternal state as an ancestor. However, this separation was not absolute. For example, physical sensation was thought to occur in the bones, which remained with the body for eternity, even after the flesh had deteriorated. Thus, the *aya* could still feel physical pleasure and pain even though it was no longer living.

According to the anthropologist Constance Classen, modern-day Andeans living in the Cuzco area believe that humans are endowed with three souls: the great soul (*kuraq*), the middle soul (*chaupi*),

and the little soul (*sull'qa*). Upon death the *chaupi* was the only soul that remains with the body, while the *kuraq* travels to mountain peaks, and the *sull'qa* enters the body of a living being. Although there is no hard evidence to confirm this belief existed in preconquest Cuzco, it is likely that the highland Incas shared some variation of the concept.

The Underworld

For an entire year after death the deceased undertook a journey through the afterlife. This journey took place both in the world of the living, known as Cay Pacha, and in the underworld, known as Ucu Pacha. The Inca underworld, like that of most pre-Columbian civilizations, was thought of as a wet, murky place below ground. As a test of perseverance and strength the deceased was put through a series of physical obstacles. For example, the dead were required to cross a treacherous bridge made from human hair, and many mummy bundles are given offerings of human hair to help complete this task. Other colonial-period accounts describe ferocious packs of dogs that menaced the newly dead on their journey. If the deceased did not pass this series of tests, he or she would remain in Ucu Pacha for eternity. If successfully completed, the dead would finally reach his or her ancestral home among the *huacas* (sacred shrines). This place of origin, from which all humans came, was known as *pacarina*. While humans resided in human-made settlements, constructed from adobe or stone, the souls of the dead returned to the original source that gave rise to human life and culture—the natural world.

The Afterlife

The souls of the dead frequently interacted with the world of the living. They could cause both harm and good, depending on the circumstance. Indeed, the great pains taken to revere ancestors through offerings of food, goods, and sacrificed animals were motivated as much by respect as by fear. The ancestors had the capacity to intervene directly in the life of the living, whether by bringing good luck and prosperity or by inflicting illness and hardship.

Moreover, contact with a contaminated or untreated corpse resulted in a deathly physical illness, referred to by the Incas as *ayapcha oncoyna*.

If the deceased passed the test of strength in Ucu Pacha, he or she had the ability to move freely between the different cosmological realms. In addition to a distinction between the world of the living and the underworld, the Incas also distinguished additional "worlds" in their conception of the Inca universe. Hanan Pacha referred to the sky and the heavens, Cay Pacha was the realm of the living, and Hurin Pacha, literally meaning "lower earth," referred to the physical Earth.

PREPARING THE BODY

Embalming

The bodies of former rulers were drained of all fluids and thoroughly embalmed. This ensured optimal preservation, which was especially important for royalty as their mummies were handled so frequently and had to endure an eternity. Embalming the body also significantly lightened the mummy bundle, making it easier to transport. The 17th-century chronicler El Inca Garcilaso de la Vega marvels that, "The bodies weighed so little that any Indian could carry them in his arms or his back from house to house, wherever gentlemen asked to see them." The bodies of common folk were not typically embalmed, presumably because the process was too time consuming and complicated to be performed by nonspecialists.

Mummification

Mummification of the deceased had been practiced in the Andes for thousands of years prior to the Incas. Deceased rulers and elites were always mummified, but common folk were typically buried in their natural state. The body was mummified to produce the most lifelike effect; this coincided with the Inca belief that the dead continued to partici-

pate in the world of the living, albeit in a new form. Deceased royalty and elites were placed in a seated position, with their legs crossed, their arms crossed over the chest, and the head pointing slightly downward. Cobo, a Spanish Jesuit priest, marveled at the royal mummy he saw:

> This body was so well preserved and adorned that it looked as if it was alive. The face was so full, with such a natural skin complexion that it did not seem to be dead, though it had been for many years. The face was preserved in that way because there was a calabash rind placed under the skin of each cheek. As the flesh dried out, the skin had remained tight and had taken on a nice gloss. The artificial eyes were open, and this gave the impression that it was looking at those who were present.

The process of mummification among the Incas remains relatively unknown. The bodies may have been treated with a chemical substance to induce mummification. Another alternative was that they were taken to high-altitude areas with consistent subfreezing temperatures until the skin had fully dried, at which point they would be brought back to Cuzco to finish the preparation of the mummy bundle. For children and young adults that were sacrificed during the Cápac Hucha ceremony, mummification occurred naturally because of the extremely cold, dry conditions that the high mountain peaks at which they were deposited provided. Not all instances of this ceremony took place at mountaintop sites, but for those that did mummification was a natural consequence.

BURIAL AND FUNERARY PRACTICES

Tombs

Pucullos, also known as *chullpas*, were burial vaults that stored bodies of the deceased. The detailed drawings and descriptions of the native 17th-century

7.1 *A burial in Chinchaysuyu* (Felipe Guamán Poma de Ayala)

7.2 *A burial in Antisuyu* (Felipe Guamán Poma de Ayala)

chronicler Guamán Poma de Ayala provide us with the most information on Inca burial practice and, specifically, on the types of burial architecture used by the empire's inhabitants. *Pucullos* were generally located near residences for easy access to the mummies, which would be removed a couple of times a year for rituals. In Chinchaysuyu (the northern quarter) the body remained in the open for a period of five days, during which festivities and llama sacrifices occurred. It was then carried to the *pucullo* during a procession that involved the entire community. In Antisuyu (the eastern quarter) the Indians of the tropical rain forest, who were only partially conquered by the Incas, maintained their own burial customs, which did not include the use of *pucullos*. Instead, the bones of the dead were placed and sealed inside the cavity of a tree. However, in Collasuyu (the southern quarter of the empire), *pucullos* were located far from the town and made up a "vil-

lage of the dead" that would be visited periodically by the local community. In Cuntisuyu (the southwestern quarter), where the dry, mountainous environment provided natural nooks and niches, mummies were kept in caves and cliffs called *machay*. These, too, were considered villages of the dead, providing the sacred site for rituals honoring the deceased.

Pucullos varied in size, shape, and construction among cultures. Some *pucullos* were constructed from ashlar masonry (stones fit tightly together without the use of mortar), while others were made from rough fieldstones and mortar or from adobe bricks. The *pucullos* of the coastal areas were large, rectangular multichambered structures made from adobe bricks. *Pucullos* could be rectangular, circular, or square, depending on the region, with vaulted or flat roofs. Those of the highlands often took the form of towers, reaching heights of up to 30 feet.

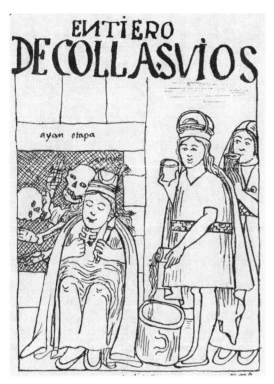

7.3 *A burial in Collasuyu* (Felipe Guamán Poma de Ayala)

7.4 *A burial in Cuntisuyu* (Felipe Guamán Poma de Ayala)

Traces of pigment found on archaeological remains suggest that many were originally painted red. Most *pucullos* had a narrow open doorway in which a skull and a bone were displayed, perhaps to signal the building's function. *Pucullos* generally only held the remains of a small group of individuals. Niches on the interiors contained *conopas*, or small funerary idols. *Pucullos* were arranged in groups, in a fashion similar to *colcas* (granaries), prominently positioned on a hill on the outskirts of town.

Commoner Funerals

Lack of clarity in the sources makes it difficult to determine whether or not funerary practices for women were as elaborate as those for men. The information that follows is based on sources that speak more specifically about funeral practices for

men. They were solemn affairs that lasted about five days, involving the entire community to which the deceased belonged. Despite their solemnity, however, they were far from stoic; performances, speeches, song, and interactions with the dead were all integral to the Inca mourning process. Singers and dancers performed hymns that extolled the virtues of the individual throughout his or her lifetime. Processions occurred throughout the town in the person's honor. The widow and other relatives wore all-black mourning clothes for weeks, and sometimes months, after the person's death. Animal sacrifices were made a few days after the initial mourning period. A llama or other type of large mammal was specially sacrificed for the occasion. A special priest would extract the lung and blow into it so that it swelled up like a balloon. Depending on the appearance of the lung and the esoteric clues it provided, priests were able to offer important predictions for the future. Its head was served as a food offering to the deceased, and the rest of its body was served to the mourners and ancestor mummies of the community. Blood collected from the sacrifice was sprinkled in the streets as the town's inhabitants embarked on a funerary procession.

The tomb contained many grave goods intended to provide materially for the person in the afterlife. Sacrificed animals, food, coca leaves, pottery, and objects related to the profession and social position of the deceased were deposited into the tomb. Grave goods varied in quality and quantity depending on the social status of the deceased. Some of the individual's possessions were burned upon death, including a small tract of farmland that had been cultivated by the deceased during his lifetime.

The body was treated with great care; it was first sprinkled with cornmeal and the blood of the sacrificed llama, and on the fifth day it was ritually washed by the widow and other relatives at the meeting point of two rivers. The places where two rivers met were considered sacred sites by all post-Chavín Andean cultures. Washing not only spiritually purified the cadaver but also cut down on the amount of toxins released, making it safer for the living to handle the mummy for ancestor worship rituals. Mourners typically placed a lump of silver, gold, or precious stone in the mouth, hands, and chest of the deceased. The body was placed in a seated position with the head facing down and dressed with great finery, often wearing clothing and accessories that exaggerated the individual's social and economic position.

Kuraka Funerals

Regional rulers, known as *kurakas*, were venerated in much the same way as their royal counterparts. The *kuraka* was mummified and placed in a special *pucullo* filled with various grave goods to prepare him for the afterlife. Local communities would perform ritual sacrifice of llamas and *cuy* and offer fine textiles, ceramics, and *chicha* at the gravesite. In the same way that Cuzco's inhabitants traveled to the different sites associated with the king's military victories or political campaigns, local communities embarked on pilgrimages throughout the province

to honor the good deeds of their *kuraka*. Public displays of crying and musical performances honored the deceased with the utmost respect. The body of the deceased was placed in a seated position typical of all Inca burials but in this case on a special chair or platform as a symbol of his higher status.

Royal Funerals

Death rituals associated with the Inca ruler loosely conformed to commoner burials but with far greater pomp and circumstance. The death of the ruler was kept secret by the royal family until a successor had been named. Once a successor had been safely installed, the populace was informed about the previous ruler's death. He was then embalmed, mummified, and placed in the Coricancha (Temple of the Sun), the most sacred religious building in the Inca Empire, with the other mummies of past rulers. Offerings included *chicha*, food, extra garments and shoes, gold and silver serving vessels, and sacrificed llamas. One thousand children were ritually sacrificed in male-female pairs at mountain shrines located throughout the empire. Many of the king's secondary wives were served large quantities of *chicha* until drunk and then strangled and deposited in his grave as sacrificial offerings to accompany him in the afterlife. All of the silver, gold, and other wealth that the king had accumulated over the course of his life went to his *panaqa*, who retained his royal estates and maintained and honored his mummy as if it were alive.

The city's inhabitants participated in public rituals held at Cuzco's Haucaypata (main plaza), proclaiming his major deeds and accomplishments in life. Mourners paid their respects through song and dance as well as through various codes of conduct that demonstrated their devotion to the king. Some women even reportedly pulled out their eyelashes. These initial Cuzco-centered mourning rituals lasted for 10 days. The subsequent 15 days were spent traveling to all of the significant monuments, battlegrounds, agricultural fields, and *huacas* associated with the former ruler. Carrying items of his clothing, weapons, and tools he once used, mourners would speak about his important victories and conquests as they passed these sites.

After this the mourners participated in the *puru-caya* festival that commemorated the ruler's entry into the realm of Inti, the sun god, who was believed to be his father. In celebration mourners dressed in feathers and finery and performed dances choreographed to reenact the ruler's military victories. All of Cuzco's inhabitants wore black for a month after the Sapa Inca's death, and his principal wife cut her hair short and wore black mourning clothes for a year. After the first month these same mourning rituals were repeated at each full moon for an entire year.

Cobo, a Spanish Jesuit who wrote extensively about Inca religious customs, describes royal funerals in great detail:

> At death, his family unit took charge of him, and before all else they took out his entrails and put them in a safe place with great solemnity and public lamentations, which lasted many days. At this time they had great drinking bouts with dances and mournful songs. They visited the places where the deceased usually went for his recreation; his relatives would carry in their hands his garments and weapons, telling in the dirges and sad songs of the heroic deeds that he had done with his weapons, and the victories and trophies that he had achieved, recounting his laudable customs, his virtues and his generosity with everyone. They killed the wives whom he liked the most and the servants whom he seemed to need here in this world as well as different officials and servants from each occupation. Their love for the king was so sincere that they willingly offered their lives, considering themselves fortunate to accompany their king.

ROYAL MUMMIES

The ruler's mummified body was dressed in a fine *uncu* (tunic), sandals, headgear, jewelry, and earspools, the same type of adornment he would wear in his lifetime. He was then wrapped in five to six layers of the most precious *cumbi* textiles (the highest-quality cloth, woven from vicuña fur and often interlaced with silver, gold, feathers, and *Spondylus* shells). A coca leaf or piece of silver or gold was placed in his mouth. The king's grave was also supplied with extra changes of clothing, shoes, jewels, food, and weaponry for the afterlife.

The *panaqa*, or group of relatives that claimed direct descent from the Sapa Inca, cared for the sacred mummy. Although the Spanish chronicles provide conflicting accounts of where the royal mummies were stored, they were most likely kept in separate temples within the Coricancha, each with its own niche and altar. Different members of the *panaqa* periodically cleansed, fed, and consulted with the mummies as if they were living beings. In fact, it was believed that royal mummies continued to rule in death as they had in life.

HUAQUE

An artificial mummy bundle known as a "brother" mummy, or *huaque* (also spelled *guague*), accompanied the Sapa Inca through both life and death. The "brother" was a statue of the ruler made from wood, gold, or silver and wrapped in sumptuous textiles. To add another dimension of authenticity, it also contained the king's afterbirth. The *huaque* was treated with great respect and was considered the king's equal. In fact, it even owned a house and was attended to by servants. Over the course of the Sapa Inca's life, the *huaque* was brought to battles, official ceremonies, and other public activities. At times he served as a stand-in—almost like a body double—for the king when he was unavailable to make a personal appearance. Upon the ruler's death all of his hair and nail clippings, collected since birth, were integrated into the *huaque*'s bundle. The king's body was considered so sacred, that even his outer growths were saved and venerated. Although the "brother" mummy bundle did not house the actual royal body, its containment of the king's essences rendered it authentic, representative of the king's "second self." The mummies of the Sapa Inca and the *huaque* were housed together in the Coricancha and carefully preserved by descendants. During special ceremonies that venerated past rulers the royal mummies were brought out for public viewing. Given the great pains taken to preserve the fragile royal mummy bundle, the "brother" mummies were brought out only during more minor ceremonies.

ANCESTOR WORSHIP

The ancestors of the Incas, both real and mythical, were venerated by the living through ritual and ceremonial acts. Deceased Incas were worshipped by their direct descendants for two generations. This entailed periodically visiting the ancestral mummy; providing him or her with food, *chicha*, and other sacred offerings; and incorporating the mummy into public ceremonies that commemorated the dead. On the outskirts of most villages, where the *pucullos* were located, were also ceremonial platforms known as *cayan*, intended for the performances of such ceremonies.

Families also consulted with ancestors to aid in decision making and to provide favors and predictions for the future. Prior to marriage the bride and groom were presented to the ancestors for approval. Whenever something was asked of an ancestor, family members provided material compensation in the form of food, coca leaves, and *chicha*. After two generations had passed—once the grandchildren of the deceased had passed away—the mummy fell into disuse.

Mallquis

The founding member of an *ayllu* was venerated similarly to family ancestors. The *ayllu* was the basic kin structure that undergirded Inca social organization, made up of two principal lineages known as moieties. The mummy of the founding ancestor was known as a *mallqui*, or as a *munao* in the lowland areas. Considered the most sacred of Inca ancestors, *mallquis* were treated with utmost care and respect throughout the entire course of Inca history. Specialists entrusted with the maintenance of these mummies were known as *mallquipavillac*. *Mallquis* were thought of as the offspring of *huacas*. They were located in caves or mountain shrines known as *machay*. Classen notes that the word *mallqui* actually means "young plant" in Quechua, which is appropriate to their function. In the same way that plants both reach down into the earth and up into the atmosphere, *mallquis* mediate

between two realms: the world of the living and the world of the dead. The royal equivalent to the *ayllu*, the *panaqa*, also venerated *mallquis*, which were the mummified remains of past rulers, both real and mythical. *Ayllu* members frequently visited *mallquis* at their burial sites and left offerings, changed their clothes, and tended to the general upkeep of the mummy and its surroundings.

Chacrayoc, Huancas, and *Marcayoc*

Alternately referred to as *chacrayoc*, *huancas*, and *marcayoc*, these ancestors are considered the oldest of the realm, having already transformed from bodily form into petrified stone. Although not connected to any particular *ayllu*, their veneration was incorporated into Inca mountain worship. They were regarded as *huacas* and received frequent offerings of *chicha*, sacrificed llamas, and food by members of the surrounding community.

Royal Ancestor Worship

The lives of royal mummies were almost as active as those of their living counterparts. Members of different *panaqas* clothed, cleansed, and tended to their respective royal mummies. During special political religious ceremonies in Cuzco that involved the living ruler, all of his deceased predecessors were also brought out to the plaza to participate. Described by several Spanish chroniclers in breathtaking detail, they were brought to the main plaza and arranged hierarchically, from the oldest former ruler to the most recently deceased. They feasted alongside the living *panaqa* members, eating out of gold and silver servingware and drinking *chicha* out of gold and silver pitchers called *vilques*. After performing a series of toasts to the *mallquis*, the *panaqa* members poured the *chicha* for the dead onto a circular stone set in the center of the plaza, which was channeled through a system of drains constructed below the monument. Dancers and musicians bedecked in special uniforms and feather headdresses provided entertainment for the feasters.

Royal mummies actively participated in the political process, serving as advisers to the Sapa Inca and providing prognostications for future events. Royal *mallquis* were considered integral to the success of the empire, evidenced by their revered status. They were lavished with such great attention and luxury offerings that Huáscar, one of the last Inca rulers before the Spanish invasion, tried to eradicate ancestor worship altogether, claiming that the dead of the Inca Empire had more power than the living. In addition to pleasing the royal ancestors and soliciting their wisdom, there were also material incentives for venerating these mummies. Members of the *panaqa* that cared for the royal mummies received tracts of land for their service.

Festivals Honoring the Dead

Aside from ancestor veneration among families, community-wide festivals took place throughout the year that incorporated the *mallquis* and mummies of many different lineages. They were often called upon to help improve crop or herd fertility, a constant preoccupation among inhabitants of the highlands.

Ayamarka Killa, or the "month for carrying the dead," which roughly coincided with November of the modern calendar, celebrated the deceased over a period of about 30 days. During this time the dead were brought out from their *pucullos* and carried on litters throughout the city or town. They were dressed in fine feather headdresses and other ceremonial gear and paraded with great festivity. Songs, feasts, and dances occurred throughout this period, at the end of which the mummies were brought back to their *pucullos*. Family members deposited new offerings with the dead, including serving dishes and food.

In an unnamed festival described by the 16th-century Spanish chronicler Cieza de León, all of the royal mummies as well as portable *huacas* were brought out to the central plaza in Cuzco once a year. They would consult each member of the gathering individually, asking questions about the future of the empire and other predictions.

7.5 *During Ayamarka Killa, the month of carrying the dead, the Incas performed elaborate ceremonies to honor the deceased.* (Felipe Guamán Poma de Ayala)

HUMAN SACRIFICE

Cápac Hucha

The Cápac Hucha (Capacocha) ceremony involved the sacrifice of young children. The "purest" and most beautiful boys and girls were handpicked from each of the four quarters (*suyus*) of the Inca Empire. They were sent to Cuzco to be sanctified by a priest and prepared for sacrifice. The young sacrificial victims also participated in days of festivity and feasting held in their honor. Upon sanctification the young children, accompanied by several priests and other official personnel, would embark on a pilgrimage homeward. Though the ritual took place empire-wide, the most dramatic ceremonies occurred in the southern Andes, where nearly all of the known sacrifices took place at mountaintop shrines. The child would first receive a blow to the head or be strangled or asphyxiated. Still wearing the same clothes and ornaments, the boy or girl was arranged in a flexed, seated position, tightly wrapped in additional cloths to create the mummy bundle, and buried alive. Priests and other worshippers left offerings near the body that were intended to prepare the individual for the afterlife. Extra articles of clothing, food, ceramic serving vessels, jewelry, and figurines accompanied Cápac Hucha burials. Gender-specific implements were also buried with the mummy bundle; girls were often given weaving implements, whereas boys were given llama effigies (associated with herding) and hunting weapons.

The archaeologist Constanza Ceruti notes that miniature human and llama figurines crafted from gold and silver were often deposited close to the body of the Cápac Hucha victim, signifying either

7.6 Silver alpaca figurine. Finely crafted miniatures such as this one accompanied Cápac Hucha burials as sacred offerings. (John Bigelow Taylor/The Library/ American Museum of Natural History)

an aspect of the individual's identity or serving as a stand-in for a real being. Llama figurines in particular may have served as Cápac Hucha offerings to ensure the health and bounty of the herds.

The Cápac Hucha ceremony was performed foremost to honor the Inca ruler during pivotal moments in his life, such as upon ascension to the throne and during times of illness. Upon coronation 200 children were sacrificed. After his death 1,000 young boys and girls were paired together and "married" before becoming sacrificed at mountaintop shrines and other locations throughout the realm. The Incas believed that the vital energy of the child was released upon sacrifice and transferred back to the Sapa Inca as a form of spiritual sustenance. It was also conducted to ensure agricultural success as well as ward off natural disasters. At a cosmological level Cápac Hucha was important for maintaining balance among the different forces of nature. While the child sacrifices served as sacred offerings to the Inca king, they were also offerings to the *huacas* in which they were placed. Communities throughout the empire would sacrifice llamas and pour *chicha* on local *huacas* as offerings. The sacrifice of a sanctified human was the highest form of veneration to the natural world. Aside from its religious and cosmological associations this rite required the mobilization of people and the allocation of immense wealth (in the form of grave goods)—something that could only be accomplished through organized administration and a powerful state with loyal subjects.

The Ice Maiden Discovered at the peak of Mount Ampato near modern-day Arequipa, Peru, the young female mummy who became known worldwide as the "Ice Maiden" revolutionized modern understanding of Inca child sacrifice. Although the Spanish chroniclers had described these ceremonies in great detail, early archaeologists found little material evidence to corroborate their claims. The inaccessibility and frigid temperatures of high-altitude mountain shrines where Cápac Hucha sacrificial victims were buried prevented their discovery for more than 400 years. The so-called Ice Maiden, a 15-year-old girl, was discovered intact, almost perfectly preserved, and in situ (in her original location)—a phenomenal combination of circumstances. She was buried in a seated position, wrapped in layers of finely patterned textiles, and clad in leather moccasins, silver bracelets, and an elaborate feathered headdress. Her grave contained a bag filled with hair and nail clippings, presumably saved from her first haircut and naming ceremony, a rite of passage for all Inca children known as *rutuchicoy*.

This site was significant for a number of reasons. As a pristine, unlooted archaeological site, it provided crucial data on the ceremonial structures associated with Cápac Hucha burials as well as the various types of grave goods deposited at these sites. The first female Inca mummy excavated revealed how women dressed and adorned themselves—something that was described in the chronicles through written descriptions and drawings but never seen in the flesh. Bodily evidence revealed that the Ice Maiden was killed by a strong blow to the head. This confirmed claims that Cápac Hucha sacrifices involved violent means of execution.

Mount Llullaillaco Ceremonial Complex The sacrificial remains discovered at Mount Llullaillaco by the archaeologist Johan Reinhard and his colleagues in 1999 are considered some of the most impressive Inca mummy burials found yet. The Mount Llullaillaco ceremonial complex, located in northwestern Argentina at 6,715 meters (22,031 ft.) above sea level, also ranks as the highest-altitude archaeological site in the world. Its major architectural feature is a burial platform inside which the beautifully preserved mummies were located. The remains include a six-year-old girl, a seven-year-old boy, and a 15-year-old young woman. The girl was found in a seated position, adorned with a dress, shawl, moccasins, and a metal headdress. The archaeologists discovered several burn marks and depressions on her body, leading them to conclude that the mummy was struck by lightning after she had been buried. She was surrounded by a series of burial offerings, including food, two pairs of shoes, Inca-style pottery, and four female figurines made from silver, gold, and *Spondylus* shell. The boy was discovered wearing a red tunic, moccasins, and a silver bracelet. His head was wrapped in a sling, and his forehead, covered with white feathers. Like the girl, he was also in a seated posi-

tion, surrounded by offerings. Slings, extra pairs of shoes, a bag containing coca leaves, Inca-style ceramics, and a llama and male figurine were all associated with his burial. The young woman, meanwhile, was buried wearing a dress and shawl fastened with *tupus* (metal garment pins), moccasins, and a feather headdress. Her burial was accompanied by bags containing food, various ceramic serving vessels, belts woven from camelid fur, two *qeros* (wooden flared drinking vessels), and three female figurines made from silver, gold, and *Spondylus* shell. All of the burials were accompanied by a small bag containing a sample of the sacrificial victim's hair. The Cápac Hucha victims at the Mount Llullaillaco ceremonial complex are illustrative of Inca ritual sacrifice, and their remarkable preservation has further validated claims made by Spanish chroniclers of their appearance and the grave goods associated with the burials.

READING

Death and the Afterlife

Catherine Allen, "Body and Soul in Quechua Thought," *Journal of Latin American Lore* 8, no. 2 (1982): 179–196.

James A. Brown, "Andean Mortuary Practices in Perspective." In *Tombs for the Living: Andean Mortuary Practices*, edited by Tom D. Dillehay, 391–406 (Washington, D.C.: Dumbarton Oaks, 1995).

Constance Classen, *Inca Cosmology and the Human Body* (Salt Lake City: University of Utah Press, 1993).

Glynn Custred, "Inca Concepts of Soul and Spirit." In *Essays in Humanistic Anthropology: A Festschrift in Honor of David Birney*, edited by B. T. Grindal and D. M. Warren, 277–302 (Washington, D.C.: University Press of America, 1979).

Patricia J. Lyon, "Death in the Andes." In *Tombs for the Living: Andean Mortuary Practices*, edited by Tom D. Dillehay, 379–389 (Washington, D.C.: Dumbarton Oaks, 1995).

Paul R. Steele and Catherine J. Allen, *Handbook of Inca Mythology* (Santa Barbara, Calif.: ABC-CLIO, 2004).

George Urioste, "Sickness and Death in PreConquest Andean Cosmology." In *Health in the Andes*, edited by J. Bastien and J. Donahue, 9–18 (Washington, D.C.: American Anthropological Association, 1981).

Gary Urton, *At the Crossroads of the Earth and the Sky: An Andean Cosmology* (Austin: University of Texas Press, 1981).

Preparing the Body

Constance Classen, *Inca Cosmology and the Human Body* (Salt Lake City: University of Utah Press, 1993).

Garcilaso de la Vega, El Inca, *Royal Commentaries of the Incas and General History of Peru, Parts 1 and 2*. Translated by H. V. Livermore (Austin: University of Texas Press, 1966).

Michael E. Moseley, *The Incas and Their Ancestors: The Archaeology of Peru*. 2nd ed. (London: Thames & Hudson, 2001).

Burial and Funerary Practices

Adolph F. Bandelier, "On the Relative Antiquity of Ancient Peruvian Burials," *Bulletin of the American Museum of Natural History* 20 (1904): 217–226.

Bernabé Cobo, *Inca Religion and Customs*. Translated by Roland Hamilton (Austin: University of Texas Press, 1990).

Felipe Guamán Poma de Ayala, *Letter to a King: A Picture-History of the Inca Civilisation by Huamán Poma (Don Felipe Huamán Poma de Ayala)*. Translated by Christopher Dilke (London: George Allen & Unwin, 1978).

———, *El primer nueva corónica y buen gobierno*. 1615. Reprint, Mexico City: Siglo Veintiuno, 1980.

William Isbell, *Mummies and Mortuary Monuments: A Postprocessual Prehistory of Central Andean Social Organization* (Austin: University of Texas Press, 1997).

Sabine MacCormack, *Religion in the Andes: Vision and Imagination in Early Colonial Peru* (Princeton, N.J.: Princeton University Press, 1991).

Michael J. Sallnow, *Pilgrims of the Andes: Regional Cults in Cuzco* (Washington, D.C.: Smithsonian Institution Press, 1987).

Frank Salomon, "'The Beautiful Grandparents': Andean Ancestor Shrines and Mortuary Ritual as Seen through Colonial Records." In *Tombs for the Living: Andean Mortuary Practices*, edited by Tom D. Dillehay, 315–354 (Washington, D.C.: Dumbarton Oaks, 1995).

Tom Zuidema, "Shafttombs and the Inca Empire," *Journal of the Steward Anthropological Society* 9 (1978): 133–178.

Ancestor Worship

Pablo Joseph de Arriaga, *The Extirpation of Idolatry in Peru*. Translated by L. Clark Keating (Lexington: University of Kentucky Press, 1968).

Bernabé Cobo, *Inca Religion and Customs*. Translated by Roland Hamilton (Austin: University of Texas Press, 1990).

Tom Zuidema, "Hierarchy and Space in Incaic Social Organization," *Ethnohistory* 30, no. 2 (Spring 1983): 49–75.

Human Sacrifice

Constanza Ceruti, "Human Bodies as Objects of Dedication at Inca Mountain Shrines (North-Western Argentina)," *World Archaeology* 36, no. 1 (2004): 103–122.

Johan Reinhard, "High Altitude Archaeology and Mountain Worship in the Andes," *American Alpine Journal* 25 (1983): 54–67.

———, *The Ice Maiden: Inca Mummies, Mountain Gods, and Sacred Sites in the Andes* (Washington, D.C.: National Geographic, 2005).

———, "Llullaillaco: An Investigation of the World's Highest Archaeological Site," *Latin American Indian Languages Journal* (1993): 31–54.

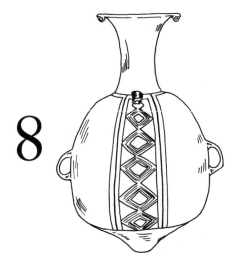

8

INCA ART

Inca Art in Perspective

Within the span of only a few generations the Incas managed to produce and disseminate a distinctive artistic style that communicated a wide range of imperial values through the visual language of stone, precious metal, ceramic, cloth, and other media. The visual arts were closely associated with performances and rituals of all kinds, religious, symbolic, or otherwise. It is therefore important always to consider the social setting within which artistic objects were used and, in a sense, brought to life. The European notion of "fine art" produced solely for elite consumption and visual fancy does not easily fit into the context of Inca history or culture. Like many pre-Columbian civilizations, for the Incas the portable arts, such as pottery, small-scale sculpture, and textiles, often doubled as utilitarian items, talismans, or ceremonial objects. Often, such works of art acquired significance and beauty from their movement through space, as the result of exchange or gift giving, ritual deposit as an offering to higher powers, or even destruction in the form of material sacrifice. Monumental works of art such as stonework were engaged in intimate dialogue with their surroundings and thus must be understood in light of both the built and natural environments of the Andes. In other words, an interpretation of Inca art without an acknowledgment of these external forces would do a great disservice to a subtle yet enormously complex and sophisticated visual tradition.

Inca art did not emerge from a vacuum. Previous artistic traditions initiated by the Moche, Paracas, Nazca, Tiwanaku, Wari, and Chimú cultures intermingled with new Inca styles developed by the state. This occurred in a variety of ways. The importation of artisans trained in their respective regional traditions to Cuzco significantly impacted Inca aesthetics, particularly its fiber arts and ceramics. The Incas drew much of their artistic inheritance from the Chimú, who had attained considerable influence over a vast stretch of the Peruvian coast. Artists relocated from their capital city of Chan Chan on the north coast were particularly admired for their technical skills and stylistic virtuosity. The Incas also consciously revived the arts of Tiwanaku, their supposed predecessors according to origin myths. Although many techniques and artistic forms were directly borrowed from other cultures, an entirely new decorative vocabulary emerged that embellished the surfaces of objects and wove its way into textiles, imbuing familiar forms with a sense of vitality and newness.

Unlike many of the artistic traditions that preceded it, Inca art lacked a figural tradition. Although there are some examples of stonework and ceramic decorations that feature schematic representations of humans, references to the human body are almost entirely absent in Inca art. Instead, geometric designs and alternating *tocapus* (squares inscribed with a particular symbolic pattern) arranged into bipartite (two-part) and quadripartite (four-part) design schemes dominated the visual arts; this has been referred to by some as a "corporate style." Scholars speculate that this tendency toward abstraction stems largely from Inca desires to transmit an imperial message of inclusiveness that was immediately recognizable and coherent to a wildly diverse and enormous subject population that reached 10 million at the height of empire.

Stonework

Monumental Stonework

The Incas made great use of stone and rock in the form of masonry, stone architecture, sculpted rock and stone outcroppings, terraces, towns, and walls, the sum of which tells us something about the sense the Incas had of themselves in relation to the natural world. The modeling of stone following abstract patterns, typically on a monumental scale, reflected the Inca imperial project and makes up its most substantial visual component. The presence of sculpted stone in the landscape served as a material reminder of Inca political aspiration by projecting ideas of permanence, sustainability, and power. The mark that Inca rulers left on the natural world was, for their subjects, a physical encounter with empire. The range of motifs sculpted on stone adhered to geometric and organic forms, and the line between altered and untouched rock forms was sometimes seamless. Steps and step forms, rectangular shelves and niches, zigzag channels, and the occasional semicircle were the preferred abstract forms. Figural representation was less common in stonework though animal and human images are known in a few instances.

The art historian Rebecca Stone-Miller says understanding the organizational and religious aspects of imperial vision form the necessary background to an appreciation of Inca stonework. Understanding that the Incas deified natural forces and made their greatest political and religious statements by sculpting nature helps one appreciate the Inca investment in stone. Each individual unit, be it on the scale of a settlement or that of a sculpted rock, is like a small essay on harmony between the constructed and the natural environment. Time and again Inca stonework synthesizes and reflects a clear appreciation of the broader physical environment. It was a conscious principle to take advantage of the extreme physicality of the landscape, often framing it through views in windows in architecture. Stonework reflected and united the disparate social elements of the imperial program through its religious, mythical, and symbolic connotation. Inca stonework worked as a permanent and poignant reminder not only of state authority but also of greater Inca cultural history.

The Incas were equally invested in the aesthetics of both the visual and physical experience of stone; sight and movement were directed over, into, through, around, and between different parts of the landscape. Further enhancing the visual experience, the sharp, clear light of the high Andes creates an intense interplay of bright light and distinct shadows that emphasize the edges, planes, and mottled surfaces of the rock face. Individual units stand as singular aesthetic achievements within the broader imperial project. In Inca stonework the material inherits the responsibility of expression. The following sections describe important myths that serve to underscore the place of stone in the Inca Empire.

Stone and Inca Creation Myth

The Quechua linguist Susan Malverde-Howard notes that words for rocks are not only nouns but also verbs; for instance, the Quechua word for *boulder* also signifies "to begin." Although Inca subjects spoke a variety of regional languages, Quechua became the official language of the empire. Appropriately enough, then, the Inca relationship with stone begins with and is grounded in creation myths, origin stories, and the mytho-historical beginning of their imperial ascendance. Some 40 cycles of origin myths are found in early sources, and despite various and even contradictory lines of evidence, themes and motifs emerge from the stories' commonalities that allow for a general outline.

Most universal Andean creation myths begin at Lake Titicaca where the creator god Contiti Viracocha, "creator of the world" (elsewhere Wiraqocha Pachayachachic, "creator of all things," and Ilya-Tiqsi Wiraqocha Pacayaciq, "ancient foundation, lord, instructor of the world"), fashioned a race of giants as a trial. Finding them too large he made them instead in his own image. According to the version recounted by the Spanish chronicler Betanzos in his *Narrative of the Incas*, which was finished around 1557 and drew on testimony of Inca kings, these mythical first people, filled with hubris and greed, did some disservice to the creator god Viracocha, and in his anger he turned them to stone.

Following this initial disappointment, Viracocha destroyed the world and then crossed Lake Titicaca to land at Tiwanaku with two servants he had spared. There, again according to Betanzos, he made some people from stone as a kind of model. Betanzos says that when Viracocha was done, he set them aside and then made more people for another province. Viracocha made all the peoples of Peru this way, beginning in Tiwanaku. These people, made from stone, became not just the Incas but all Andean peoples.

Stone and Inca Origin Stories

Like many ancient Andean peoples, Inca origin stories, reflecting local history, are associated with emergence from natural features in the landscape.

The most universally repeated story describes the emergence of four brothers and four sisters, two of whom became the progenitors of the Inca dynastic group, from the central of three windows in a cave at a place called Tambotoco (house of windows) or Pacariqtambo (inn of dawn). In Betanzos's version the primordial ancestors emerged from the cave as couples, with the women following the men and everyone finely dressed. They left that place and eventually settled in the high mountain basin that is today Cuzco, even though it was already occupied by the Cancha people. On the way one of the brothers was transformed into a stone, which is now a shrine called Huanacauri. And in Sarmiento de Gamboa's version Cuzco was chosen when one of the brothers saw a rock, flew to it, and when sitting down on it transformed himself into a stone pillar, thereby marking the seat and occupying the land. Other versions of the Inca origin story begin in Lake Titicaca, though still with a prevalent role for stone.

Stone and the Myth Regarding the Beginning of Empire

Although there is some disparity in the chronicles, Inca imperial ascendance is typically described as beginning with the reign of the eighth Inca ruler, Viracocha Inca, by the standard king list, and his successors—his son Inca Yupanqui, later called Pachacuti ("earthquake," or "reverser of the world"), and his grandson, Topa Inca. One of the key moments came during a war with the rival Chanca people. Viracocha Inca fled Cuzco in the face of attack, leaving Pachacuti to attend to the city. Instead of retreating, Pachacuti rallied local lords to hold their territory, and at a critical moment in the initial battle, warriors appeared from nowhere to ensure Pachacuti's victory. Several chroniclers relate that stones in the fields had transformed into these warriors; then, following victory, they metamorphosed back into stone and were subsequently venerated as the sacred *pururaucas*, meaning "hidden thieves." Variations in the narratives suggest that the Incas found it necessary to amend or adopt

their myths to fit their expanding world, and stone's primacy in the various narratives indicates its centrality in Inca culture and its fundamental importance in the shaping of the empire.

Masonry

The use of dressed stone in architectural construction developed out of a long history of stone construction in pre-Columbian South America. Early manifestations occur at Cerro Sechín sometime before 1000 B.C.E., at Chavín de Huántar in northern Peru ca. 900 to 200 B.C.E., in the south at Pukara, and, most notably, at Tiwanaku between ca. 200 B.C.E. and 1100 C.E. Spanish chroniclers and many subsequent researchers generally believed Inca masonry was directly linked to Tiwanakan techniques. Diagnostic Tiwanakan masonry techniques are exemplified by carefully fitted coursed ashlar masonry (rectangular masonry bricks with smooth, flat surfaces laid to appear as if in straight rows). Having conquered the region and seen the ruins of Tiwanaku, the Incas would have been intimately familiar with the masonry style. The Incas later imported laborers from that area to work on their own construction projects. However, close study of the material remains of both cultures suggests that Inca stonemasonry and architecture were, in the final analysis, authentic inventions.

Inca masons were skilled craftsmen who turned the mundane functionality of walls and the ordinariness of rock into works of art. The artistic appeal of Inca masonry derives from the play of light and shadow over surface and edges, the regularity of shape and form, and an appreciation of the technical skill and labor involved. Similar appreciation extends to the ideas of interchangeability and transformation borrowed from myth and religion that are invested in stone and play a prominent role in understanding the symbolic role of Inca masonry. As illustrated in the Chanca war story, where rocks transformed into living warriors, stone embodied an active, transformational quality that literally brought them to life. As an imperial cultural statement Inca masonry was meant to impress upon their subjects the Incas' ability to manage the Earth itself. The Incas capitalized on

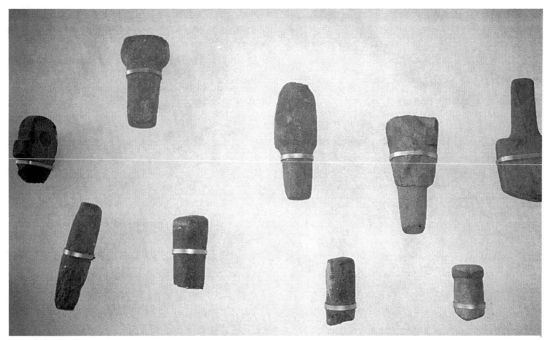

8.1 Hammerstones were used to cut and dress masonry. (J. J. George)

these associations to reconstruct, enhance, and frame the Earth's natural forms.

To cut and dress stones the Incas used simple river cobbles as hammerstones. The hammers come in different sizes, some as small as an egg and others as much as three times the size of a football. The largest hammerstones were used to break up and roughly shape the building blocks, some of which weighed more than 100 tons, and the smallest were used to cut and shape the edges and corners. The impact of the hammer left small pitmarks on the surface of the stone. At the edges glancing blows left beveled joints (joints that did not meet flush or at right angles) that account for the particular chiaroscuro effect.

Walls

The functionality and artistry of Inca wall construction is perhaps unsurpassed in history. There is, however, no agreed-upon nomenclature with which to describe Inca masonry. The various ter-

minologies all reflect a restricted range of forms, and in describing walls they describe the look and fit of the stone. The basic vocabulary of walls includes the *pirca*, a wall made of roughly shaped fieldstones or sundried adobe; polygonal walls made of blocks of stone cut with precision interlocking in an irregular manner, like a jigsaw puzzle; and coursed, walls for which rectangular ashlars with smooth faces were laid in horizontal or near-horizontal rows (courses).

Surface appearance of walls ranged from extremely rough, with pitmarks and a slight bulge, to regularly smooth planes. The slight bulge is referred to as *entasis*, which lends an essence of gravity to a wall and makes it appear as if the weight of the wall itself is forcing the stone to pillow outward. So well crafted are Inca walls that many have survived catastrophic earthquakes, while the superstructures built by Spanish colonists atop the walls have crumbled. Furthermore, a direct correlation exists between the quality of stonework and its use in particular structures, with the roughest work used for structures such as canals and terraces and the finest work reserved for the most sacred buildings, such as the Coricancha.

Sculpted Stone and Rock Outcroppings

Sculpted rocks range in size from small boulders to massive outcrops. The Cuzco Valley and the nearby Sacred Valley contain the greatest concentration of manipulated rock and stone, some sculpted minimally and some elaborately. Large stones are often felt to be the residences of spirits, and in some cases these spirits are those of ancestors. When found next to fields or villages, they frequently are perceived as protector spirits. They are also conceived of as representing mountain gods and are often worshipped because of their association with major mountains. The 17th-century Spanish chronicler Cobo made the most complete accounting of what is called the Cuzco *ceque* system, a network of sacred shrines *(huacas)*. Cobo lists at least 328 *huacas*, of which 95 *huacas* are rocks, boulders, or stones. The examples that follow include some that are part of the system and some that are not. Machu Picchu, perhaps the most famous of all Andean sites and itself part of the sacred geography of the Incas, similarly provides many examples of Inca stonework. Taken together, the examples described below represent a small portion of the total. While their religious and cosmological significance is only partially understood, they are nonetheless extraordinary examples of the Inca aesthetic in stone.

KENKO

The site of Kenko, to the north of Cuzco, is thought to have been the death house of Pachacuti. It was also referred to as Patallaqta. The site boasts a large

8.2 *View of Kenko, a sacred Inca site* (Eloise Quiñones Keber)

unworked pseudo-triangular monolith often referred to as the "seated puma" and a massive outcrop whose surface has been heavily modified with numerous sculpted steps, shelves, zigzag channels that branch and rejoin, indentations, and gnomons (objects that by the position of their shadow tells the time of day). A semicircular courtyard creates a small amphitheater framing the "seated puma" monolith and emphasizing its ritual space. A cleft in the outcrop has been worked into a passageway leading to a small cavelike room probably used for ritual purposes. The room contains a finely carved stone altar that may have been a tomb.

TAMBO MACHAY

Built directly into a hillside above Cuzco, Tambo Machay is a *huaca* associated with Pachacuti's son Topa Inca. *Tambo* is a Quechua word denoting "way station or inn," or any small rest stop along the Inca highway system. It is thought that royal pilgrims along routes to *huacas* or on royal business used *tambos* as places of respite along their journey. Tambo Machay, however, appears to have been a more specialized *tambo* with ritual and royal significance. It has three shallow terraces, fine dressed-stone masonry, and a natural spring that emerges from below a plain wall in the second terrace. The spring water emerges, falls to the next lower level, then disappears below ground, and finally reemerges in two streams cascading down the last terrace. The site itself is more of a frame calling attention to the expression of water than an example of architecture. Stone and water interact as complementary material, subtly and expressively creating an aural, tactile, and visual experience that highlights Andean principles of emergence, transformation, and essence.

HUANACAURI

Both a hill and an uncarved stone on the hill, Huanacauri was a potent symbol of Inca mytho-history and was generally regarded as the second most important shrine after the Coricancha in Cuzco. Believed to be the petrified remains of Manco Cápac's brother, one of the four original brothers who emerged from the primordial origin cave at Pacariqtambo, it is also regarded as the second oldest *huaca*. Father Cobo describes it as being "of moderate size, without representational forms, and somewhat tapering." It found expression in solstice festivals and ritual pilgrimages, and an idol of the stone even accompanied the Incas in warfare as a patron of noble warriors. Huanacauri was a key *huaca* in the Cuzco *ceque* system.

INCA "THRONES" AT SACSAYHUAMÁN

Just above modern Cuzco the ruins of Sacsayhuamán, which scholars believe to have combined many functions—including temple, storage facility, shrine, fortress, and monument to the Inca victory over the Chancas—provide many fine examples of sculpted stone. For example, one "throne" may have been a place for the Sapa Inca to review his troops and watch ceremonies in the grassy plaza fronting the site's zigzag cyclopean stone walls. Another "throne"—actually two "thrones" almost directly beside each other—are seats carved directly into the rock itself. They may have been used to review processions, receive attendants, or supervise ceremonies.

8.3 An Inca throne at Sacsayhuamán (J. J. George)

STONE OF SAYHUITE

Part of a larger shrine to the west of Cuzco, the stone of Sayhuite is a highly modified semicircular boulder that looks like half an orange with a dramatically undulating surface. It is 2.6 meters (8.5 ft.) at its highest point, and its diameter ranges from 3 to 4.1 meters (10–13.5 ft.) across. It displays an elaborate symbolic scene of human, natural, and built landscapes. Carved directly into the boulder are high-relief representations of pumas, serpents, lizards, vicuñas, birds, monkeys, humans, maize stalks, and a miniature building illustrating traditional Inca architectural motifs, including trapezoidal niches or doorways, a staircase, and platforms. A network of grooves and channels once carried liquids past all the figures during divination ceremonies. Scholars believe the figurative landscape may represent a map of the Inca cosmos.

INTIHUATANA

Little is known for certain about Machu Picchu's Intihuatana, also known as the "Hitching Post of the Sun," though its privileged location at the highest point in the sacred sector indicates its importance. It may also have been significant in astronomical alignments, perhaps serving in solstice ceremonies, and may have been tied to mountain worship. When viewed at certain angles the shape of the stone and the play of light and shadow on its surface appears to replicate, in abstract form, that of the adjacent peak, Huayna Picchu. Carved from a single boulder at the highest point of the site, the primary feature of the stone is a gnomon-like trapezoidal form thrusting skyward from a broad base. The base is further modeled with forms common to the Inca repertoire including step forms, horizontal shelflike planes, and thronelike impressions. The lower portion of the boulder is largely untouched so that as the eye moves over the stone, it moves from the natural to the constructed as it simultaneously discovers the process of reductive sculpting through which the Incas revealed the "heart" of the boulder.

Another feature typical of the Inca aesthetic used here is the controlled approach that more or

8.4 The Intihuatana at Machu Picchu, also known as the Hitching Post of the Sun. It was used in solstice ceremonies and mountain worship. (J. J. George)

less enforces a processional quality on the experience. The approach emphasizes the methodical care with which the Incas managed the physical and visual experience of the object itself and contextualizes it within the greater natural environment, highlighting views, juxtapositions, and backgrounds that further illuminate the reciprocity of material and environment. A similar *intihuatana* is at Pisac, another royal site associated with the ninth Inca ruler, Pachacuti.

"SACRED ROCK" AT MACHU PICCHU

Although there are many sacred rocks at Machu Picchu, this particular boulder has assumed a privileged aspect in many sources, at least in part because it is in a prominent location at the north end of the site, because of its large size, because of its demarcation by a stone platform, and because of its formal similarity to surrounding mountain peaks. A controlled approach, not unlike that of the Intihuatana, seems to indicate that the stone is meant to be viewed with the peripheral mountains framing it in the background. Two mountains in particular, Yanantin and Pumasillo, seem to be better, though imperfect, matches than others. If the stone is meant to reflect the surrounding mountains, imperfect representation seems to be the strategy employed, thereby grounding the visual experience in the encompassing sacred geography.

8.5 The "Sacred Rock" at Machu Picchu is associated with mountain worship. It was carved to evoke the shape of the mountains behind it in the distance. (Ananda Cohen Suarez)

TORREÓN

Perhaps the most comprehensive expression of Inca stonework is the Torreón at Machu Picchu. Originally named the "Semicircular Temple" by the Yale historian and amateur archaeologist Hiram Bingham, who "rediscovered" Machu Picchu in 1911, the Torreón, or "observatory," is essentially a single rock outcrop with a building framing a boulder atop a cave. Therein lies, however, a spectacular range of Inca expressions in stone. There are essentially three complementary focal points in the Torreón complex: a curved, P-shaped wall made of regular coursed ashlars with alternating windows and interior niches; an irregularly modeled boulder, which in fact is the top of the outcrop itself, framed inside the wall; and beneath the wall an interior space, an elaborate modification of a natural cleft in the outcrop, which has been ornately sculpted into a chamber not altogether dissimilar in kind from the interior room at Kenko.

Taken altogether these elements combine to form a near-complete representation not simply of the skill and vision of Inca masons but also of their unique ability to synthesize material with its symbolic, mythic, and religious connotations. For example, the interior of the upper walled space surrounds a boulder that could have been used as an altar. Trapezoidal niches inset into the wall could have been used for idol display or ritual offerings. Markings carved on the boulder align with the sun coming through the central window and appear to have aided in observing the June solstice. The same window also allows observation of the star cluster Pleiades; Pleiades was closely associated with crop fertility and weather forecasting. One further extrapolation suggests that the curved wall at Machu Picchu is directly linked to the curved wall of the Coricancha, the sacred center of the Inca Empire and its cosmological and religious heart. Their formal congruence and common use of finest-quality masonry, along with their close association to the reign of Pachacuti, are suggestive of a broad aesthetic unity underscoring the shape of the empire.

Finally, the cleft in the lower portion of the outcrop was recarved and set with masonry to create a small room, which Bingham initially referred to as

8.6 The grotto beneath the Torreón at Machu Picchu is one of the finest examples of Inca masonry found in a single structure. (Eloise Quiñones Keber)

the "Royal Mausoleum." It is also referred to as the tomb or grotto. This room readily correlates with the primordial cave in Inca mythology. All levels of intervention with the stone are visible. The far left remains untouched mottled stone that transitions at the left side of the slanting cleft to a smoother but not perfectly straightened edge. The right side of the entrance was carved into a step form, though not altogether perfectly. And immediately to the right of the entrance an interstice, shaped as a distorted hourglass, is filled with stonework that fits, despite its courses, as liquid poured into a mold. The interior of the cave was carved with niches, stone pegs, a gnomon, and steps forms, possibly emphasizing ritual display.

Terraces

Flat agricultural land is at a premium in the rugged, vertical world of the Andes. To counter this problem the Incas built great agricultural terraces, thereby maximizing cultivable land while simultaneously minimizing the possibility of landslide. Examples of sophisticated hillside terracing exist at Arequipa; in the Colca Valley; in some valleys on the eastern slopes of the Andes; at Chinchero, northwest of Cuzco; and at neighboring sites such as Wiñay Wiña, Machu Picchu, Patallaqta, Ollantaytambo, and Pisac. Elaborate

terracing was foremost an attribute of royal estates and was not necessarily practiced as a general agricultural policy by the Inca state. Similar to other Inca constructions, terracing expresses the Incas' ability to manipulate and control the earth.

The craft of building terraces, sometimes transforming entire hillsides and valleys, became the art of landscaping at the grandest scale. A typical terrace, or *pata*, would be from 1.5 to 4 meters (5–13 ft.) high with a roughly shaped fieldstone retainer wall sloping slightly to the back. Effective irrigation was a necessity, and complex and intricate waterworks accompanied the terracing. The terraces create a stunning horizontal linearity that contrasts with the vertical orientation of the mountainside, a clear expression of monumentally scaled transformation and the reciprocal relationship of the constructed and natural world.

OLLANTAYTAMBO

In 1534 Pizarro subdued the Inca capital of Cuzco. Manco Inca, initially installed as a figurehead ruler, soon chafed under Spanish authority and gathered an indigenous army and lay siege to Cuzco in hopes of returning the kingdom to Inca rule. Having failed, Manco Inca and his forces retreated up the Urubamba River to the fortress garden of Ollantaytambo, associated previously with the reign of Pachacuti. From there they staged a guerrilla war against the Spanish. Perhaps the most distinctive feature of the city is its flight of 17 terraces bridging the gap between a lower and higher overlook. Spanish sources relate that the terraces were planted exclusively in colored flowers, which is an extravagant gesture balancing the natural and constructed world. Steps that ascend through the center before veering abruptly left and then right again, calling attention to controlled ritual movement, mimic the geometry of the terraces and highlight their architectural division.

The stairway through the terraces leads to a religious precinct that is surrounded by a wall. Only the foundation of what was probably going to be a sun temple remains; the ruins are now referred to as the Wall of the Six Monoliths. Nearby, partially worked and finished stones lay strewn about; the

Spanish invasion appears to have cut short an ambitious remodeling plan. Work on the Wall of the Six Monoliths appears to have also ceased rather abruptly. Standing upright, the wall consists of six large, unfinished rectangular monoliths with irregular surface fronts. A vertical series of lightly modeled step forms that look like carved diamonds adorns portions of the wall, emerging only when the play of light and shadow is exact and disappearing when the sunlight dims. As a common pan-Andean motif, the step form here reinforces the geometry of the terraces themselves.

PISAC

Pisac lies about 30 kilometers (19 mi.) to the northeast of Cuzco, astride the Vilcanota River in the Sacred Valley, a lush agricultural zone overshadowed by snowy mountain peaks. Pisac was one of Pachacuti's royal estates and was used to provide sustenance and wealth to the monarch and his lineage group. The royal settlement was built around a large carved rock high atop a ridge, with a broad series of splendid terraces cascading down the mountainside. Unlike at Ollantaytambo, whose terraces might have been ornamental, the terraces at Pisac supported a full agricultural operation, most likely supplying staples of maize and potatoes. Yet, similar to Ollantaytambo and other sites, the terracing at Pisac is consistent with the Inca desire to express imperial power through overwhelming projects reflecting the ability to control the earth itself.

MORAY

Unlike the terraces of Ollantaytambo and Pisac, the terracing at Moray, just over 50 kilometers (31 mi.) from Cuzco, is not attached to a settlement. Three large circular depressions with concentric terraces follow, yet regularize, the topography, ultimately calling attention to and complementing its natural variations. The lack of any known canals suggests that the site was constructed for aesthetic purposes, as a shrine, or for special agricultural purposes. (It has been suggested that the site was an agricultural laboratory where each terrace replicated the climatic variation in a different ecological zone of the empire, therein helping Inca officials calculate productive yields.)

Small-Scale, Portable Stone Objects

The Incas produced a wide range of portable stone objects for utilitarian and ceremonial purposes. The vast range of objects, quite often crafted with a high degree of skill and aesthetic detail despite their common, and sometimes brutal, functions, include geometric-shaped pendants, apparently to be hung from a cord or necklace; miniature carvings in the shape of special knives, called *tumis*, which were normally made of bronze; hammerstones; clod breakers used to break apart soil for planting; mace heads attached to the ends of meter-long clubs used in war; waisted or grooved bola stones for use in hunting or combat; polished small bowls; stone mortars and pestles, sometimes carved with animal heads; stone platters with geometric incisions; miniature, highly polished effigies of camelids and other animals, especially birds; zoomorphic ceremonial containers and anthropomorphic stone effigies; stone architectural effigies, possibly used as models for new construction; and decorated stone boxes. Though many of these objects were not very important culturally or economically, their production was nonetheless attended to with discipline and care.

The types of stone varied from local to exotic and were shaped either through grinding and polishing or by flaking. Chloritic schist, basalt, igneous rocks, granite, river cobble, and stones in distinct hues of black, gray, and dark brown were commonly used. A similar attention and appreciation to the vitality of the material is as apparent in small-scale objects as in the monumental. Natural irregularities in shapes and colors as well as deformities or unique patterns in the stone were often highlighted to create a unique and beautiful object. Sculpted motifs or design on the body of the object are less common, thus the textures and details rely on and reflect the material itself. The burial contexts from which many portable objects have been found only further reflect their importance and value.

Ceramics

Techniques

The pottery wheel did not exist in the Americas until the arrival of the Spanish, but Amerindian ceramists were nevertheless able to construct visually stunning and structurally complex vessels with limited technology. Pottery was constructed through modeling or with molds. Modeling simply refers to handling the clay by hand. The most common modeling technique employed by artisans in the pre-Hispanic Andes was coiling. This required rolling out the clay into a snakelike form and coiling it tightly into the desired shape. The vessel would then be smoothed out and ready for firing. Molds, on the other hand, were used for mass production. The clay would be pressed flush against a hardened material to conform to its shape. Mold-made ceramics were usually composed of two or more pieces that would be joined together to produce the finished piece. Despite standardization of iconography and motifs in Inca art as a whole, Inca pottery was primarily handmade. Clays were extracted from sites that yielded the best consistency and mineral composition. They were then mixed with crushed organic material, called temper, to strengthen the clay. Although stone is the most common material used for temper, artisans also use crushed shell, plant materials, or animal bones. More finely ground tempers produced delicate clays for decorative and elaborate vessels, while coarser ones were used to create durable utilitarian wares.

There are no surviving archaeological remains of Inca kilns or ceramic production centers. Fortunately, broken pottery fragments, known as sherds, provide ample clues as to the nature of ceramic production and consumption during the Inca Empire. The location and distribution of sherds can reveal the popularity of a particular vessel type and style over time in a given region. Diagnostic sherds, such as rims and handles, help to reconstruct the original appearance of different vessels and the approximate dimensions and diameter. Surviving motifs and decorations also allow researchers to determine the specific iconography associated with Inca rule that was disseminated throughout the Andes and coastal regions. Archaeologists can also examine their chemical composition to determine the source of the clay, which in turn tells something about the context within which the vessels were created. Generally, if the clay came from a distant source, the item was probably imported, whereas if it was from a nearby source, this would suggest that the ceramics were produced by local artisans.

Ceramics throughout the Andes were slip-painted, incised, sculpted, appliquéd, or embellished with any combination of these techniques. Artisans would create slips by mixing different colored clays with water to produce a paintlike substance. Earth tones tended to dominate the color schemes of Andean ceramics, although rare and highly valued colors were obtained through long-distance trade for more elaborate wares. Once the slip was applied to the slightly wet, unfired piece, the vessel would then be fired. Pottery was fired at low temperatures in either an open-air or a closed oven. Pottery was often buffed, meaning that the vessel was highly polished before firing to produce a reflective sheen.

Uses of Ceramics

Inca ceramics drew from both preexisting pottery traditions prevalent in the Central Andes and characteristically Inca vessel forms and designs. Utilitarian ceramics retained much of their local flavor, while fancier wares conformed more closely to Inca aesthetic canons. Utilitarian vessels included cooking pots; serving dishes such as bowls, drinking cups, jars, and plates; and storage containers for holding foods and beverages. These types of ceramics are classified as "conservative technologies"; that is, they are less prone to innovation and change than other types of objects that are more sensitive to fluctuations in the social, economic, or political fabric of a society. Fancy ceramics for elite consumption are one such type of object. Anthropomorphic and zoomorphic double-spouted vessels and grave goods all fall into this category, along with elaborately decorated serving wares. They can fulfill a variety of often overlapping functions. Like other works of art such as textiles and metalwork, ceramics were often used as tools of diplomacy or as containers for grave offerings. Ceramic pots were offered as gifts to rulers or to honor the deceased.

Inca and Provincial Ceramics

Although the exact chronologies and ceramic phases during the Inca period remain under debate, the generally accepted ceramic sequence of the Central Andes, originally proposed by archaeologist John Rowe, includes the Killke series during the early period of Inca expansion (ca. 1200–1438) and the Cuzco series during its apogee (ca. 1428–1532). Inca ceramics were typically painted or incised with geometric motifs, including bands of repeating triangles, squares, straight and stepped lines, and stylized vegetal forms.

A new ceramic type developed under the Incas that is known by the Quechua term *urpu* (also referred to as *aryballos*, the Latin term for "amphora"). The *urpu* is a long-necked, flare-rimmed vessel with handles on each side and a pointed base. The pointed base allowed users to nestle it into the ground upright for easy use. They were designed for easy transport; traders would string rope through the handles and tie them onto their backs. It was most frequently used to store and transport maize beer, known as *chicha*, throughout the empire. Archaeologists believe that the major center for *urpu* production was located in Cuzco. *Urpus* were decorated with geometric motifs such as painted crosshatched lines, circles, vertical stripes, stylized plant stalks, and, at times, schematized human and animal representations. They were painted in earth tones and usually burnished. Shallow bowls and plates also became ubiquitous during the Inca Empire, often featuring a small rounded handle resembling an animal head. Jars of all sizes became of special importance for distributing water and foodstuffs to the Incas' burgeoning subject population.

Ceramics outside the Inca heartland absorbed and reinterpreted imperial styles to varying degrees across time and space. Some regions, such as Ica on the south coast, integrated certain aspects of Inca corporate symbolism into the local pottery tradition, creating a new hybrid style. Other areas adopted Inca ceramic traditions wholesale because of the prestige associated with state-sponsored goods. In Chincha, for example, imperial ceramic forms and styles almost completely replaced the original ones through both imitation by local artisans and importations of pottery from Cuzco. On the north coast, particularly in the area where the Chimú culture once flourished, local styles endured with little to no stylistic modification. The stirrup-spout vessel fashioned out of burnished black ware, a major staple of north coast material culture since the Moche, continued to be produced throughout the period of Inca rule. As archaeologists continue to take an interest in the provincial areas that were incorporated into the Inca Empire, the relationships between local and centralized pottery styles will become increasingly evident.

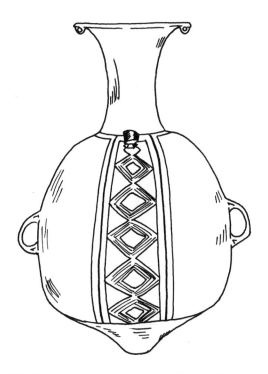

8.7 *An* urpu, *also known as an* aryballos, *is a large ceramic vessel that was used to transport and store liquids, especially* chicha. (Drawing courtesy Michel Besson)

Textiles

Textiles ranked as the most highly valued goods in the Inca Empire. They occupied nearly every sphere of human life, serving as clothing, ritual object, work of art, sociopolitical currency, or tribute. Cloth was so prized among the Incas that during the Spanish conquest individuals would burn it rather than witness its confiscation, which also explains the dearth of extant Inca fiber art. Weaving had been practiced throughout the Andes since 2300 B.C.E., making it one of the oldest artistic traditions in South America. The term *textile* refers to clothing, bags, blankets, and other items made out of woven plant fibers or animal fur. The oldest surviving textile fragments were discovered at the site of Huaca Prieta on the Peruvian north coast by the archaeologist Junius Bird. Due to bad preservation conditions in the highlands, most Inca textiles have not survived. However, some complete pieces and fragments, especially those that were exported to the dry coastal regions or preserved at high-elevation shrines, have withstood the test of time to help reconstruct the appearance and manufacturing techniques of Inca textiles at the height of empire.

Techniques

The process of weaving was a laborious one, involving many steps that required a great deal of human organization and expertise. After the plant fiber or wool was collected, cleaned, and combed, it was ready for dyeing. Cotton, along with llama, alpaca, and vicuña fur (all from the camelid family), was spun into thread for weaving. Camelid fibers required the extra process of mordant treatment, which allowed the pigment to "stick" to the wool. Dyes were primarily extracted from plants, although the use of cochineal and the marine snail present special exceptions. The deep red color found on Andean textiles comes from cochineal, a small insect that lives on the nopal cactus prevalent in arid coastal areas. Marine snails were used to extract a rich purple color. The indigo plant pro-duced the blue found in Inca textiles. After the dyeing process, fiber would be prepared for spinning. Spinning was achieved through use of a drop spindle and distaff. The resultant thread would be twisted clockwise, or "z-spun," and then doubled to ensure durability and twisted in the opposite direction, a technique referred to as "s-plied." Once the thread was spun, it was ready to be tied to the loom, a process known as warping, or dressing. The immobile threads bound to the loom are known as the warp, while the moving threads that are woven into them are called the weft.

The Incas used two different types of looms: the backstrap loom and the vertical loom. The backstrap loom is the oldest type and was used throughout both the Andes and Mesoamerica for millennia. At one end the warp threads are attached to a pole secured to a tree or a post, and at the other end a second pole is stretched tight by a strap that wraps around the weaver's back. This type of loom was most commonly used for small-scale, everyday textiles. The vertical loom is a self-supporting structure with four rods that allow for the production of larger and more elaborate textiles. This form was common in the Andes and was quite large, measuring up to seven feet wide. It was typically reserved for state-sponsored and elite fiber art and could be used by multiple weavers at one time.

There are many different types of weaves, each yielding a distinct appearance and texture in the final product. The most common loom technique was the plain weave, which simply required inserting the weft over and under the warp across the loom at a 90-degree angle. Patterns could easily be created by alternating the warp threads with different colors. A specifically Andean technique, used for more complex patterning, is known as discontinuous warp and weft. Unlike in plain weave, with this method the weft does not reach the end of the loom but instead is woven within an isolated area of the warp to allow for the elaboration of separate interacting design schemes. Tapestry weave was employed for the finest and most elaborate textiles. Several techniques existed that did not even require the use of a loom. These include braiding, knotting, wrapping, and looping. They could be used for creating bags, hats, and appendages to tapestries, such as tassels.

Clothing

Clothing, aside from its utilitarian purposes, indicated the social or political status of its wearer. Men wore an *uncu* (tunic) topped with a mantle, depending on the climate, along with other accoutrements such as waistbands and headbands. Women typically wore simple dresses made of untailored cloth wrapped around the body and held in place with a *chumpi*, or sash. Like men, women would wear a mantle, or *lliclla* on top of their dress but with an added functional accessory known as a *tupu*. *Tupus* were long, sharp decorative pins that could be pierced through layers of clothing to hold it in place. They were made of gold, silver, or copper, depending on the social status of the user. Although men and women tended to wear the same type of clothing, the type of material it was made from and its decorations revealed multitudes about the identity of that person. There existed three different kinds of cloth: *chusi*, which was thick, rough cotton cloth used for blankets and bedding; *ahuasca*, or everyday cloth for clothing and other household items; and *cumbi*, high-quality cloth woven from camelid fur. A fourth and most highly valued type was *cumbi* interlaced with feathers, which was reserved only for members of the royal lineage. There also existed a hierarchy among the camelid furs; llamas had the coarsest furs, alpacas were softer, and woven vicuña thread produced the softest textiles, likened to silk by 16th-century Spanish observers. Clothing hierarchies did not simply exist in theory; there were consequences for wearing fur from a higher class. Individuals could not wear *cumbi* unless they received it as a special gift from the king, and those who wore clothing woven out of vicuña without permission would be severely fined.

Textiles as Cultural Expressions

Textiles were used in a variety of both public and private arenas to mark rites of passage, reinforce social and regional differences, honor and communicate with the supernatural world, and glorify the ruling class. Cloth was often presented as gifts to commemorate births, puberty ceremonies, marriages, and other types of social rituals. At times textiles served as backdrops or props in the performance of such ceremonies.

The historical record is rife with references to social life and textiles among the Incas, although with an elite/royal bias; the activities of commoners generally did not fall under the radar of the major 16th-century chroniclers. The anthropologist John Murra was among the first to glean the conquest narratives for references to cloth and found that during royal marriages elaborate multicolored cloths of feathers and other precious materials were laid out like paths leading to the palace. He also discovered that young men and women would receive gifts of clothes during adulthood initiation ceremonies. As previously noted, individuals of different social rank wore clothing of varying material and decorative quality. Commoners wore clothing out of *ahuasca*, while elites and nobility donned costumes made from *cumbi*.

Moreover, the Inca army wore checkerboard tunics during battle to denote their position as servants to the state. Upon military defeat the winning side would receive gifts of cloth and precious feathers, while the losing army would be forced to don red tunics as a public proclamation of their vanquished status. Aside from marking social differences and military victories clothing also communicated geographical distinctions. Visitors to Cuzco from other regions were required to wear their local dress for quick and easy identification. At the same time, however, when a new territory was conquered by the Incas, the inhabitants would receive gifts of Inca-style clothing as part of the induction process.

Cloth was also burned, or "sacrificed," in the performance of ritual. As previously noted, *cumbi* was sacrificed daily as an offering to the Sun. Sixteenth-century chroniclers noted cloth sacrifices made to Pachamama, or Mother Earth. Moreover, textiles played a role in almost all Inca religious practices, from the burning of elaborately clothed *mallquis*, or royal ancestral mummies, to the ritual burning of cloth during planting and harvesting ceremonies. Cloth figured prominently in mortuary rituals too, in which the deceased would be dressed from head to toe in brand new clothing and left with extra changes of clothes as grave goods.

Design and Color Schemes

Textiles took on a variety of different colors and were interwoven with a range of motifs, depending on the type of textile and the social status of its user. Utilitarian textiles such as blankets and household cloths were generally unadorned and were dyed a single color, if at all.

Tocapus are the most ubiquitous design feature on Inca textiles, consisting of small squares inscribed with geometric motifs. These motifs include zigzags, checkerboard patterns, quadripartite (four-part) motifs, squiggled lines, concentric squares, and diamonds. Some tunics are decorated with a single *tocapu*, others with a band of them encircling the torso, while still others are covered with several rows of *tocapus* or covered entirely. Scholars continue to debate their significance, but a few possibilities include territorial designations and symbols of different social and ethnic groups.

The Dumbarton Oaks Tunic

Although not many Inca textiles have survived, the extant few reveal a great deal about Inca aesthetics in the fiber arts. A famous royal *uncu*, one of the only examples of its kind and part of the Dumbarton Oaks collection, has been the subject of intensive study by art historians and archaeologists for years. It is decorated entirely by various *tocapus*. Although their exact meanings remain unclear, many have argued that each one represents a different community or abstract concept. Some of the *tocapus* have been identified by scholars, such as the one with the diagonal stripe with squares in the opposite corner, which is referred to as the "key motif." This motif reappears in other textiles and other media, including metalwork and wooden cups called *keros*. Another easily identified *tocapu* is the miniature checkerboard tunic, which was the uniform of the Inca army. Despite giving the appearance of uniformity, the distribution of the 211 *tocapus* on this particular *uncu* and others of its kind follows no discernable pattern; they display a strategic haphazardness that actually closely conforms to an Inca aesthetic tendency of unifying dynamism with order.

Scholars have largely been able to identify individual *tocapus* as well as the identities of *uncu* wearers based on drawings from Guamán Poma's magisterial work, *The First New Chronicle and Good Government*, completed in 1615, which documented Inca customs and history before and after the Spanish invasion. As an indigenous Andean, Guamán Poma had ample exposure to the communities about which he writes, providing a distinctively native perspective on pre- and postconquest Peruvian history. Despite his reticence on the topic of textile symbolism, the drawings that illustrate his text help describe visually the complex relationship between textiles and social rank that existed under the Incas. Guamán Poma's drawings of Topa Inca and Huayna Cápac feature the Inca sovereigns wearing *uncus* composed entirely of *tocapus* like the Dumbarton Oaks example. His images of commoners, in contrast, usually feature men wearing plainer *uncus* that may only have one repeated *tocapu* motif, if any. This suggests that wearing a tunic composed of many *tocapus* carried a great amount of privilege and probably signified some sort of domination, whether territorial or ideological. However, one difference between Guamán Poma's drawing and the surviving Dumbarton Oaks tunic is that his *tocapus* are arranged in a discernable order, with the same motif running across the tunic in a diagonal line, whereas the Dumbarton Oaks one is arranged without any sense of strict pattern.

Scholars have labeled some of the recurring *tocapus* that are found on several surviving *uncus* from the pre-Columbian and early colonial periods.

- *casana* motif: four squares inscribed into a larger square
- *collcapata* motif: checkerboard pattern; a miniaturized version of the military tunic
- "key motif": a diagonal line culminating in squares at each corner with squares in the other two corners

Each of these motifs can be found on the Dumbarton Oaks tunic, along with a slew of as-yet undeciphered *tocapus*, some of which are found in other surviving *uncus* and others that were apparently invented for the purposes of this particular tunic.

8.8 Tunic with tocapu *design from the Dumbarton Oaks collection. This tunic would have been worn by an Inca ruler.*
(© Dumbarton Oaks/Pre-Columbian Collection/Washington, D.C.)

8.9 *Viracocha Inca depicted wearing a tunic with a full* tocapu *design* (Felipe Guamán Poma de Ayala)

FEATHERWORK

Featherwork was held in great esteem by the ancient Andean peoples. Its place at the top of the aesthetic hierarchy reflects the difficulty with which feathers were acquired by coastal and mountain people from inhabitants of the Amazonian jungle, where the greatest diversity of iridescent feathers was found. By Inca times feathers had been used in the production of crafts, especially textiles and tunics, for several hundred years. Despite their fragility, several featherwork pieces collected in the extremely dry coastal desert have been preserved in a remarkably pristine condition.

Though little is known for certain regarding specific dates of production and place of manufacture, many of these pieces are certainly pre-Inca and reflect Wari or Wari-related figural iconography, defining a more abstract tradition, and others are clearly Chimú. The feathers have been identified as scarlet macaw or red-and-green macaw for the red feathers, blue-and-yellow macaw for the turquoise and yellow, razor-billed curassow or Salvin's curassow for the dark brown-black, and great egret or snowy egret for the white. Other known examples of featherwork include a Tiwanaku-style hat and a series of large, simple turquoise and yellow checkerboard banners. Feather headdresses adorning miniature gold and silver human effigy figurines associated with the Cápac Hucha ceremony are also known.

METALWORK

In the hierarchy of Inca aesthetics, metalwork ranks below that of stonework, textiles, and featherwork. The Incas drew upon three millennia of metallurgical traditions in the Andes to produce a wide range of objects in three primary metals—gold, silver, and copper—and other metals such as bronze and tin as well as sophisticated alloys. A commonly accepted theory holds that gold work began in the Peruvian highlands in the middle of the second millennium B.C.E. and spread north to Ecuador and Colombia, eventually reaching Panama and Costa Rica by the second century C.E. and Mexico by the ninth or 10th century.

The Incas incorporated non-Inca metalworkers into their workshops, who typically brought with them their own stylistic and technological traditions that the Incas willfully shaped into their overall aesthetic program, which some scholars refer to as a "corporate style." Much Inca metalwork and bronze technology was borrowed from the north coast Chimú Empire, the largest polity of the time, which Topa Inca, the 10th Sapa Inca, conquered around 1460–70. Precious metal production, textile arts, and feather- and shellwork had reached unprecedented levels under the Chimú, and objects made for the elite had become ostentatious displays of wealth and technical virtuosity. Changes in scale and quality of execution indicate the Incas assumed Chimú techniques and styles, then quickly adopted them to fit their overall message. Overall, Inca metalwork was the most mimetic and restricted of the Inca arts.

A comprehensive understanding of Inca metalwork is sadly limited, however, by virtue of the Spanish desire to acquire and melt down precious metals during the conquest. Even though Spanish documentary sources report large-scale sculptures of gods, rulers, and camelids, almost all have been lost. The story of Atahualpa's ransom alone is enough to lament the loss. Atahualpa was the son of Huayna Cápac and fought his half brother Huáscar for the right of succession; emerging victorious, Atahualpa was the ruler when the Spanish arrived. As the story goes, the captured Atahualpa promised Pizarro enough gold to fill a room 6.2 meters by 4.8 meters (20 × 16 ft.) up to a line 2.5 meters (8 ft.) above the floor. Thousands of Indians are said to have arrived with vessels, pitchers, and jars, all made in gold and silver. Yet, the thoroughness with which the Spanish acquired Inca gold and silver was a consequence born not from a collector's appreciation of Inca artistry but from a conquest-driven desire for the economy of precious metals. Melted down and shipped across the Atlantic, much of the metal now gracing European churches had its origin in the Andes.

Gold and Silver

Gold and silver were part of an elaborate symbolic system and had specific associations in the Inca cosmological world. Gold, for the Incas, was the sweat of the Sun and was associated with the masculine world; the Sapa Inca referred to himself as "the son of the Sun." Silver was the tears of the Moon and was associated with the feminine. Together they formed and reflected essential symbolic dualities of Sun and Moon that found further association with other fundamental Inca dualities such as light and dark, day and night, heaven and earth, male and female, right and left, and upper and lower. The mining of gold and silver, symbols of power and prestige, was closely monitored by the state, and possession of any amount of gold or silver objects was highly regulated and would have been available only to the elite. Value for the Incas ultimately derived not in the material itself but when shaped into images. For this reason one might understand reports of confusion in the faces of Inca bystanders witnessing the melting down of gold and silver objects into bars. Erased of shape and function, the simple mineral value was little or nil for the Incas.

Techniques and Metallurgy

Gold occurs in metallic form in nature and is easily worked. It can be obtained from rock by mining or from rivers by panning (placer mining), in which river gravel is washed in a pan, causing the gold flakes, nuggets, and grains to settle at the bottom. Silver, less frequently detailed than gold in the chronicles, has a dendritic, or fibrous, appearance in its natural state and was most commonly mined in its ore form, for example, at the famed mines of Potosí, Bolivia. In underground mining the Incas followed veins of ore in narrow shafts, some allegedly up to 75 meters (246 ft.) long. Later Spanish exploitation of mines limits the archaeological evidence of purely native mining practices.

To separate the metal from the rock the ore was smelted, a chemical process activated by heating the crushed rock in crucibles or furnaces. Three types of furnaces were used. One was a simple pit in the ground used to reduce minerals rich in precious metals. Metalworkers in southern Peru used portable ceramic wind furnaces called *huairas*, which were shaped like flowerpots and had small vents in their walls to create an updraft. The molten metal sank to the bottom of the furnace, where it solidified and was removed for further processing. And the third, known as a *tocochimpu*, was discussed in the chronicles primarily in the context of refining metal.

Sophisticated alloying, almost always employing copper, increased hardness, resistance, ductility, malleability, color, and shine. The earliest working technique was basic hammering of nuggets into sheets over stone anvils, followed by decorative applications employing cutting, chasing, scribing, embossing (hammering the metal over a carved form, usually of wood), and repoussé (working the sheet freehand while it rests on a yielding surface such as pitch or soft wood). Buffing and burnishing the surface with abrasive sand and stone or bone polishers finished the surfaces. In the case of multi-piece objects the items were joined by tabs, staples, nails, and wires, and in some cases soldering, welding, and sweat or pressure welding. The lost-wax method *(cire perdue)* of casting developed a little later.

Male and Female Effigy Figurines

A growing number of male and female effigy figurines are being discovered atop high-altitude peaks that are linked to the child sacrifice ceremony, Cápac Hucha. In the ceremony unblemished boys and girls on average aged six to 10 were symbolically married in Cuzco's central square before returning homeward to be sacrificed and interred. Votive figurines in precious metals usually accompanied their interment. One particular mummy was found at an altitude of 20,000 feet atop Cerro el Plomo in Chile. The child there was layered in elaborate textiles and accompanied by numerous figurines, which were similarly wrapped in exquisite miniature textiles and adorned with feathered headdresses.

Another burial related to the Cápac Hucha ritual was found in 1985 by a group of mountaineers on the southwestern flank of Aconcagua, the tallest mountain in the Western Hemisphere. Like the El Plomo mummy, this child, a male, was accompanied by figurines. Three were male figurines—one of gold, one of a silver-copper alloy, and one of *Spondylus* shell. They averaged about two inches in height and were clothed, had plumed crests, and carried little bags containing fragments of coca leaves. Three other statuettes of llamas, one of gold and two of *Spondylus*, also accompanied the mummy.

The figurines follow the established canon of Inca visual art. Ethnohistorian Colin McEwan and anthropologist Maarten van de Guchte found that virtually identical figurines have shown up in burials thousands of miles apart, suggesting that groups of figurines may have been produced for specific

events and then carried to their different destinations by parties of priests, nobles, and children. Though masterfully made, the details in hairstyle, anatomy, and headdresses are limited. Male figures sport a braided headband, or *llauto*, and boast oversized earspools that identify Inca elite. The females have long hair arranged in braids and tied at the back. The male figurines were sometimes shown with a bulge in the cheek, signifying the chewing of coca. Both male and female figurines, as McEwan and van de Guchte point out, display characteristic gestures found nowhere else in Inca art: Both arms are raised so that the hands, with palms turned inward, touch the chest. Figurines found in other contexts suggest that they were offered to the gods on other occasions as well.

Floral and Faunal Effigies

When the Spanish arrived at the Coricancha, the main temple in Cuzco, they found an extraordinary effigy garden made entirely of gold and silver sculptures. The centrality of maize in Inca ritual and subsistence is well documented, and according to chronicler El Inca, Garcilaso de la Vega, it is similarly well represented. The following is Garcilaso's description of the Golden Garden: ". . . they made fields of maize, with their leaves, cobs, canes, roots and flowers all exactly imitated. The beard of the cob was of gold, and all the rest of silver. . . . They did the same things with other plants, making the flowers, or any part that became yellow, of gold and the rest of silver. In addition to all this, there were all kinds of gold and silver animals in these gardens, such as rabbits, mice, lizards, snakes, butterflies, foxes, and wildcats. . . . Then there were birds set in the trees, as though they were about to sing, and others bent over the flowers, breathing in their nectar." Many such gardens were said to have existed throughout the empire.

While most objects such as those listed by Garcilaso were melted down and shipped to Europe, the few that survive display a masterful propensity for realism that augments the Incas' spiritual affinity with their natural environment. For example, a pair of llama sculptures in the collection of the American Museum of Natural History is arguably the finest examples of Inca silversmithing currently known. Reportedly found near a sacred rock on an island in Lake Titicaca, one figurine has striated, crimped silver sheets representing the hanging fleece of the long-haired llama, and the other wears a red blanket on its back, which is reported in the Spanish chronicles as being associated with royalty. The representations are both lively and imaginative, while the clarity of the forms is carefully realistic.

Drinking Vessels

Gold and silver drinking vessels, or *aguillas*, used to consume *chicha* (maize beer) were emblematic of Inca wealth and power and played a conspicuous role during state and religious ceremony. The general population would have used wooden *keros* and ceramic drinking vessels, whereas precious metal vessels, typically made in pairs for ritual drinking, were distributed and used according to rank. The Inca court and their provincial administrators would have been typical recipients. Precious metal drinking vessels were also associated with the generosity—if not the tactical diplomacy—of the state. Several 16th-century chronicles report that *aguillas* were offered to recalcitrant groups prior to confrontation with Inca military forces, with acceptance of the gift symbolizing capitulation to the Inca order.

Ritual drinking vessels in the shape of human heads, like much artistic or craft production, predate the Incas by at least 500 years. Made by beating flexible gold or silver sheet metal over a solid wooden form, the creations typically offered stylized treatment of mouth, cheeks, eyes, and nose. Stylistic variation by region was common. For example, vessels with prominent beaklike noses, almond-shaped eyes, and simple upturned mouths were produced along the southern and central coast of Peru.

Utilitarian Objects

The range of utilitarian objects made in metal is vast. Many of the following objects were produced for thousands of years in the Andes before their emergence in the Inca Empire. The list includes single-piece hinged tweezers, or depilators, a tradi- tional tool of basic hygiene used to pluck out unwanted hair; bracelets and rings, sometimes with incised geometric designs, made by hammering out a thin metal sheet; silver and bronze shawl pins, or *tupus*, a basic element of female dress used to keep mantles or shawls closed, typically with a large spade-shaped head and a long, thin tapering shaft; lime spoons, which resemble *tupus*, used to remove lime from specialized receptacles as part of the coca-chewing ritual process; hammered disks or bangles, which were especially popular among Chimú metalworkers of Peru's north coast, often sewn into shoes, tunics, mantles, neckpieces, head- pieces, and other items of dress; bells, probably strung around the ankles during festivals and dances; parabolic mirrors, often disk-shaped, used for personal or ceremonial purposes; T-shaped ax heads, sometimes with crescent-shaped edges, either meant to be hafted or used alone as a hand- held tool; chisels, similar to axes but typically with- out the crossbar or T component; and knives known as *tumis*, some with modeled decoration used cere- monially, which were among the most common and widely disseminated objects and were typically made of copper or bronze tin. Many of the above items, such as tweezers, disks, mirrors, *tumis*, and *tupus*, are pierced so that they could be worn with a cord or hung from a peg. Also, many were found in burial contexts.

Precious Metals in the Coricancha

As the primary temple of the Inca Empire, dedi- cated specifically to Inti, the sun god, it should come as no surprise that the Coricancha housed a variety of precious metals in idol form. As men- tioned above, it was home to a golden effigy garden. The Coricancha also housed the golden image of the Sun, named Punchao, which was brought out each day to greet the Sun and returned inside at night. The temple's interior also had been sheathed in gold plates half a meter or more in length, a fact that particularly delighted the Spanish. They removed 700 plates weighing about two kilograms (4 lbs.) each, melted them down into bars, and shipped them to Spain.

OTHER MEDIA

Woodwork

Unfortunately, much woodwork has not survived due to its organic composition and poor preservation conditions in the highlands. The Incas were more renowned for their impressive stonework, although a few examples of wooden sculpture exist. Wood was more commonly used for nonartistic implements such as tools for weaving as well as cooking and serving utensils. The historical record remains relatively mute on the subject of woodworking, perhaps due to its secondary importance to arts of other media or for lack of interest on the part of the chroniclers. One particular art form, however, managed to catch the attention of contemporaries, perhaps for its special ceremonial significance and unique appearance: the *kero*. *Keros* were drinking cups with a flared opening, usually made out of wood (although some ceramic, copper, silver, and gold examples exist). *Keros* existed since the Tiwanaku culture, but they were exploited most extensively by the Incas. Some well-preserved pre-Hispanic examples remain, although the majority of surviving *keros* date to the colonial period. Their survival after the conquest accounts for today's privileged knowledge about *keros*, whose colonial manifestations can provide clues to the appearance and functions of their pre-Hispanic predecessors.

Like *cumbis*, *keros* were exchanged among elites as objects of diplomacy. Lower-status people also used *keros*, usually of plainer design. They were used primarily in the context of feasting, serving as the vessels out of which officials consumed *chicha* and other ceremonial drinks. The work of the art historian Thomas Cummins has afforded us an understanding of the transformations this art form undertook after the rupture of conquest. During the Inca period, *keros* were incised or painted with geometric designs, including circles, lines, stylized vegetation, and highly abstracted human and animal forms. Some *keros* actually take on the shape of a human head, with protuberances for the nose and mouth. Cummins has suggested that, like *tocapu* designs on textiles, the geometric layout of *kero*

decoration may loosely correspond to the division of the empire into four *suyus* or the bipartite division of Cuzco into *hanan* and *hurin*.

Bone Objects

Throughout ancient Andean history common and utilitarian objects with lesser cultural significance were carved out of bone, including tools, ornaments, shawl pins, weaving tools known as *wichuñas*, spindle whorls, musical instruments such as bone flutes, and trowels. As metal objects became more frequent, the use of bone as a raw material declined. Nevertheless, they were sometimes crafted with careful and exacting workmanship. For example, a bone shawl pin found at Machu Picchu is carved with two identical perched birds in profile attached at the beak as if kissing, and diagonal incisions depict the wings. They are perched atop a rectangular form decorated with two rows of circle-dot designs. Among the most common bone objects are the *wichuñas*, pointed tools that weavers used to pack threads together and to separate the warp from the weft.

Murals

Cobo, in the 17th century, wrote of Inca mural painting: ". . . they were not accustomed to whitewash [the houses] as we do, although the principal ones of the chiefs commonly had the walls painted in several colors and figures, all rough and graceless." Elsewhere, Cobo notes that the main houses of the elite were decorated with different colors and figures. Another early traveler in Peru noted that along an Inca road near the coast, in the places with frequent settlements, there were long stretches of road planted on either side with trees that met overhead and shaded the travelers. Where trees were lacking, he noted walls were built on either side that were decorated with paintings of monsters and fish and other animals, which he attributed to a kind of diversion to aid travelers in passing the time. Unfortunately, few of the murals have survived intact, likely due to combinations of weathering, vandalism, and their systematic destruction by the Spanish. The majority of murals that have survived are located along the coast, where dry weather conditions are more optimal for long-term preservation.

Those murals that have survived favor the geometric abstraction typical of the overall Inca aesthetic. For example, murals at Tambo Colorado in the Pisco province along the southern coast were recorded as being painted in red, white, and yellow in horizontal stripes, one color above the next. And murals at Huaca de la Centinela in the Chincha Valley, though badly damaged and faded, form a strip continuing from wall to wall; they are described as resembling designs typical of painted ceramic. In red, black, and green on white, the pattern consists of rhomboid figures cut in triangles bordered by five horizontal line segments in black-red-white-red-black combinations. The green seems to have faded to white by the 1950s, as observers after that time noted different colors. Within each triangle a "meander-like hook" form, sort of like a squared-off spiral, is arranged so that it is oriented in an opposite direction as one above or below it. A few examples of murals with figurative decoration exist (or existed) such as one at Huadca, a site in Lima, but they are badly damaged or now destroyed.

Technical aspects of mural painting are difficult to discuss because the murals were long neglected and those that survive are greatly degraded. It appears, however, they were relatively simple and unsophisticated, and they did not vary greatly over time. Inca cut-stone walls were rarely treated with paint, but adobe walls stuccoed with plaster were perfect canvases. Paints were of either mineral or vegetable origin, ground in stone mortars and made into a paste, which was applied with cotton rags for broad application and fine human- or alpaca-hair brushes for more detailed work. There is evidence, too, of continual renewal of the paintings.

READING

Inca Art in Perspective

Catherine Allen, "The Incas Have Gone Inside: Pattern and Persistence in Andean Iconogra-phy," *RES: Anthropology and Aesthetics* 42 (2002): 9–27.

Cecilia Bákula, "The Art of the Incas." In *The Inca World: The Development of Pre-Columbian Peru, A.D. 1000–1534*, edited by Laura Laurencich Minelli, 219–222 (Norman: University of Oklahoma Press, 2000).

Terence N. D'Altroy, "Artists and Artistry." In *The Incas*, 287–310 (London: Blackwell, 2002).

George Kubler, *The Art and Architecture of Ancient America: The Mexican, Maya, and Andean Peoples* (Harmondsworth, U.K.: Penguin Books, 1975).

Craig Morris, "Signs of Division, Symbols of Unity: Art in the Inka Empire." In *Circa 1492: Art in the Age of Exploration*, edited by Jay A. Levenson, 521–528 (Washington, D.C.: National Gallery of Art, 1991).

———, "Symbols to Power: Styles and Media in the Inka State." In *Style, Society, and Person: Archaeological and Ethnological Perspectives*, edited by Christopher Carr and Jill E. Neitzel, 419–433 (New York: Plenum Press, 1995).

Esther Pasztory, "Andean Aesthetics." In *The Spirit of Ancient Peru: Treasures from the Museo Arqueológico Rafael Larco Herrera*, edited by Kathleen Berrin, 61–69 (London: Thames & Hudson, 1997).

César Paternosto, *The Stone and the Thread: Andean Roots of Abstract Art* (Austin: University of Texas Press, 1989).

Jeffrey Quilter, *Treasures of the Andes* (London: Duncan Baird Publishers, 2005).

Rebecca Stone-Miller, *Art of the Andes*. 2nd ed. (London: Thames & Hudson, 2002).

Stonework

Hiram Bingham, *Inca Land: Explorations in the Highlands of Peru*. 1912. Reprint, New York: Houghton Mifflin Company, 1922.

———, "Preliminary Report of the Yale Peruvian Expedition," *Bulletin of the American Geographical Society* 44, no. 1 (1912): 20–26.

Richard L. Burger and Lucy C. Salazar, *Machu Picchu: Unveiling the Mystery of the Incas* (New Haven, Conn.: Yale University Press, 2004).

Graziano Gasparini and Louise Margolies, *Inca Architecture*. Translated by Patricia Lyons (Bloomington: Indiana University Press, 1980).

John Hemming and Edward Ranney, *Monuments of the Inca* (Albuquerque: University of New Mexico Press, 1992).

Colin McEwan and Maarten van de Guchte, "Ancestral Time and Sacred Space in Inca State Ritual." In *The Ancient Americas: Art from Sacred Landscapes*, edited by Richard F. Townshend, 359–373 (Chicago: Art Institute of Chicago, 1992).

Susan Niles, "Inca Architecture and the Sacred Landscape." In *The Ancient Americas: Art from the Sacred Landscapes*, edited by Richard Townsend, 347–357 (Chicago: Art Institute of Chicago, 1992).

Jean-Pierre Protzen, *Inca Architecture and Construction at Ollantaytambo* (London: Oxford University Press, 1993).

Jean-Pierre Protzen and Stella Nair, "Who Taught the Inca Stonemasons Their Skills? A Comparison of Tihuanaco and Inca Cut-Stone Masonry," *Journal of the Society of Architectural Historians* 56 (1997): 146–167.

Johan Reinhard, *Machu Picchu: The Sacred Center* (Lima, Peru: Nuevas Imagenes, 1991).

Ceramics

Tamara Bray, "Inka Pottery as Culinary Equipment: Food, Feasting, and Gender in Imperial State Design," *American Antiquity* 14, no. 1 (March 2003): 3–28.

Justo Cáceres Macedo, *Cerámicas del Perú prehispánico/ Ceramics of the Prehispanic Peru.* Translated by Carolina Cáceres Enriquez and Ruth Monica Cáceres Enriquez (Lima, Peru: J. Cáceras Macedo, 2005).

Christopher B. Donnan, *Ceramics of Ancient Peru* (Los Angeles: Fowler Museum, UCLA, 1992).

Textiles

William J. Conklin, "Structure as Meaning in Ancient Andean Textiles." In *Andean Art at Dumbarton Oaks*, edited by Elizabeth Boone, 321–328 (Washington, D.C.: Dumbarton Oaks Research Library and Collection, 1996).

John V. Murra, "Cloth and Its Functions in the Inca State," *American Anthropologist* 64, no. 4 (August 1962): 710–728.

Ann Rowe, "Inca Weaving and Costume," *Textile Museum Journal* 34–35 (1997): 5–54.

———, "Technical Features of Inca Tapestry Tunics," *Textile Museum Journal* 17 (1978): 5–28.

John Rowe, "All-T'oqapu Tunic." In *Andean Art at Dumbarton Oaks*. Vol. 2, edited by Elizabeth Boone, 453–465 (Washington, D.C.: Dumbarton Oaks Research Library and Collection, 1996).

John Rowe and Ann Rowe "Inca Tunics." In *Andean Art at Dumbarton Oaks.* Vol. 2, edited by Elizabeth Boone, 453–465 (Washington, D.C.: Dumbarton Oaks Research Library and Collection, 1996).

Rebecca Stone-Miller, "'And All Theirs Different from His': The Dumbarton Oaks Royal Inka Tunic in Context." In *Variations in the Expression of Inka Power: A Symposium at Dumbarton Oaks 18 and 19 October 1997*, edited by Richard L. Burger, Craig Morris, and Ramiro Matos Mendieta, 385–422 (Washington, D.C.: Dumbarton Oaks, 2007).

———, *To Weave for the Sun* (London: Thames & Hudson, 1992).

Tom Zuidema, "Guamán Poma and the Art of Empire: Toward and Iconography of Inca Royal Dress." In *Transatlantic Encounters: Europeans and Andeans in the Sixteenth Centuries*, edited by Kenneth J. Andrien and Rolena Adorno, 151–275 (Berkeley: University of California Press, 1991).

Metalwork

Julie Jones and Heidi King, *Gold of the Americas* (New York: Metropolitan Museum of Art, 2002).

Heidi King et al., *Rain of the Moon: Silver in Ancient Peru* (New Haven, Conn.: Yale University Press, 2001).

Craig Morris and Adriana von Hagen, *The Inka Empire and Its Andean Origins* (New York: Abbeville Press, 1993).

Other Media

Duccio Bonavia, *Mural Painting in Ancient Peru.* Translated by Patricia Lyons (Bloomington: Indiana University Press, 1985).

Thomas Cummins, "Queros, Aquillas, Uncus, and Chulpas: The Composition of Inka Artistic Expression and Power." In *Variations in the Expression of Inka Power: A Symposium at Dumbarton Oaks 18 and 19 October 1997*, edited by Richard L. Burger, Craig Morris, and Ramiro Matos Mendieta, 267–312 (Washington, D.C.: Dumbarton Oaks, 2007).

———, *Toasts with the Inca: Andean Abstraction and Colonial Images on Quero Vessels* (Ann Arbor: University of Michigan Press, 2002).

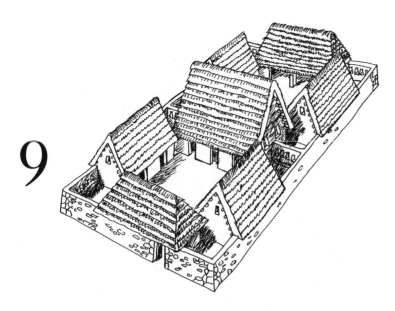

9

INCA ARCHITECTURE AND URBANISM

Almost 200 years ago the German naturalist Alexander von Humboldt marveled at the architecture of the Inca Empire, which spanned South America's Andes mountain range, the coast, and highland valleys. The indigenous empire had flourished from about 1434 to 1532. Humboldt marveled at the architecture's distinctive and unmistakable quality and made note of three characteristics that the style tended to favor: simplicity, symmetry, and solidity. There was a simple beauty in the symmetry of opposed walls and opposed structures mirroring one another, their balanced proportions in a way emblematic of so many Inca objectives. And it was simple enough to be faithfully reproduced throughout the empire and announce Inca presence and solid enough to endure changes within the empire. Yet, in its subtlest moments Inca architecture expresses the range of values of the empire. Simple domestic moments in adobe or stone are quaint, private, and utilitarian, boiled down to a basic unit of walled groupings of single-room enclosures with steeply pitched roofs. Its royal architectural moments are virtuoso stone expressions in unparalleled natural environments, Machu Picchu being the most famous example. And, in aggregate, through a standardized vocabulary of buildings, Inca architecture is a complex expression of power and empire, a means to display the politics of control over diverse and widespread ethnic populations.

The Incas were not great city builders, but they were exceptional site planners. Even Cuzco, high in the Peruvian mountains, despite its singular importance as the capital of the empire, is perhaps better understood as a sacred artifact rather than as a full-scale urban environment. For comparison it is instructive to look at Tenochtitlán, Cuzco's contemporary and the capital city of the Aztec Empire, today buried underneath Mexico City. When compared with Tenochtitlán, Cuzco paled in its overall urban makeup; Cuzco was more sacred shrine than bustling cosmopolis, more axis mundi (symbolic center of the universe) than cityscape. Whereas Tenochtitlán had structures and institutions that were surprisingly modern in their economy—a market, for example, that housed thousands of traders and had additional traders arriving hourly to exchange items from throughout the empire, all while tens of thousands of other individual traded for their daily necessities—Cuzco had nothing of the sort by scale. Its strengths lay elsewhere.

Both within and beyond the limits of the city, a term that is used loosely here, Inca state architecture reflected the demands of empire: barracks to house armies and roaming labor forces, administrative facilities to serve bureaucratic ends, storage facilities for state-acquired tribute, terracing and irrigation projects, royal compounds and palaces serving the minority elite, strongholds, temples, fortresses, provincial centers, rest stops along the royal highways (cápac ñan), and the royal highways themselves linking it all together. It was altogether orderly and uniform and promoted and reinforced its own recognizability; its recognizability ensured the message it was meant to deliver, which fell along the lines of power, control, and authority.

According to the dominant school of thought, once Pachacuti, the ninth Sapa Inca by the traditional ruler lists, acceded to power in or around 1438, the Incas quickly went from provincial villagers to imperial power seekers, eventually governing from Chile to Ecuador and from the coast to the altiplano and parts of the jungle on the eastern side of the Andes. Pachacuti ordered Cuzco rebuilt in stone, and the architectural precedent set there became a massive construction blueprint consistently reapplied throughout the Andes following, and in some cases facilitating, imperial military success. The extent and uniformity impressed the Spanish conquerors such that Rome and the Roman Empire became the standard analogy by which to understand the Inca accomplishment. For example, Pedro Sancho wrote in 1534 of Sacsayhuamán, the Inca fortress temple just above Cuzco, that "neither the bridge of Segovia nor any building that Hercules or the Romans built are so worthy of being seen as this." Most of the architecture that is thought of as Inca probably stems from the reign of the ninth Sapa Inca, Pachacuti, and his successors Topa Inca (1471–93) and Huayna Cápac (1493–1525). Taken altogether the Incas constructed, as

Humboldt suggested, a simple, symmetric, and solid architecture.

STONEMASONRY

The Inca Empire is one built in stonework. In general, based on Spanish chronicles, scholars had long attributed the origin of Inca masonry techniques to the Tiwanaku civilization centered at a site of the same name to the south of Lake Titicaca, just over the modern Peruvian border with Bolivia. Tiwanaku controlled a large region of highland Peru from roughly 200 B.C.E. to 1100 C.E. Masonry found at Tiwanaku comes in a variety of types but is dominated by regular coursed ashlars (cut stones of nearly identical rectangular shape laid in horizontal rows). The similarity between this type of masonry and Inca masonry found in buildings such as Cuzco's Coricancha, the most sacred temple in the capital, led the early chroniclers and later scholars to assume that the Inca borrowed their techniques from Tiwanaku. Recent research, however, has questioned this assertion based on three basic tenets: the hundreds of years between the two civilizations, the lack of major construction at Tiwanaku in the interim, and the unique beddings and joints used by the Inca. While the Incas were familiar with Tiwanakan masonry, and laborers from the Lake Titicaca region were used during the Incas' major imperial construction period, Inca masonry techniques are nonetheless authentic Inca expressions—hybrid forms, perhaps aware of and reflective of the past, but Inca nonetheless.

Inca stonemasonry combines the operations of quarrying, cutting and dressing, fitting and laying, and the handling and transportation of stone. The following sections will consider facets of masonry including what kinds of stone the Incas selected and how it was extracted, what the finished work looked like, the nature of the unique fit between stones, and the typologies of Inca masonry. Graziano Gasparini, Louise Margolies, Jean-Pierre Protzen,

Susan Niles, and Stella Nair are the leading scholars on Inca architecture; much of the following discussion derives from their work.

Quarrying

Quarrying means cutting stone from a rock face or detaching it from bedrock by undercutting. The Incas quarried stone in both manners, as well as foraging rockfall for blocks suitable for their specifications. To pry the stone from bedrock the Incas used bronze pry bars or sticks, as is sometimes done today. Once a block was chosen or cut, it was dressed (shaped) before being sent to the specific construction site. The degree of finishing completed at the quarry varied by site.

Inca quarries were chosen for type and quality of stone with apparently less concern for the logistics of transport. For instance, the quarries of Rumiqolqa, from which most of the andesite used to pave Cuzco's sidewalks comes, are 35 kilometers (22 mi.) southeast of Cuzco, which is a vast distance considering transport logistics and the fact the Incas did not know the wheel as a transport and labor mechanism. The high degree of organization within the layout of quarries further indicates the importance of quarrying operations. The Incas organized a fairly vast infrastructure within each

9.1 View of a quarry from which stones were extracted for use in building projects (Eloise Quiñones Keber)

site to efficiently support quarrying operations, including the construction of access roads, ramps, slides, retaining walls to prevent rockfalls, water canals leading to the site, and, in some cases, organized areas that appear to be specific to stonecutting and storage. In addition to operations-related construction, structural ruins have been found at quarries that appear to be the residences of "supervisors" or "administrators" who may have resided on-site for extended periods of time.

Cutting and Dressing

The Incas used simple river cobbles as hammerstones. They are easily recognized at quarries because they are foreign to the site. Typical hammerstones are quartzite, granite, and olivine basalt and range in weight from a few hundred grams to eight kilograms (almost 18 lbs.). The largest hammers were used to square off blocks by flaking; using the largest hammerstones, the mason worked out the rough shape of the block by knocking at the edge of the boulder, thereby reducing it approximately to the necessary dimensions. The dressing, or the finer work, was done with smaller stones to draft and finish the edges. Directing the hammerstone at an angle of 15 to 20 degrees to the surface being worked increased the efficacy of the strike, shearing away flakes of stone from the surface. Spanish chroniclers witnessed Inca masonry practice, so there is some eyewitness evidence regarding the practice. For example, El Inca, Garcilaso de la Vega, wrote: "They had no other tools to work the stones than some black stones they called *hihuana* with which they dress [the stone] by pounding rather than cutting. To raise and lower the stones they had no machinery at all; they did it all by manpower."

Fitting and Laying

The precise fitting of blocks in Inca stone masonry is achieved on a basis of trial and error. Jean-Pierre Protzen, one of the foremost scholars of Inca construction technology, postulated a general rule regarding the fitting of stones such that both the lateral or rising joint and the bedding joint of every new course is cut in relation to blocks already in place below or beside it. The bedding joint is the horizontal "bed" into which the upper block nestles into the lower block. Unlike modern brick construction where masons lay down a layer of cement mortar between courses, Inca walls were mortarless and needed secure joints to naturally brace the blocks in place. Through trial-and-error hammering Inca masons achieved astonishingly exact results.

Where walls have been dismantled, cuts made into the top face of lower blocks clearly show where the next course is to be laid. Although extremely laborious and time consuming, this technique achieved maximum accuracy. Evidence to this effect is found in the chronicles of José de Acosta, who wrote in 1589, after observing Inca masonry techniques, that though the stones ". . . are not regular but very different among themselves in size and shape, they fit together with incredible precision without mortar. All this work was done with much manpower and much endurance in the work, for to adjust one stone to another until they fit together, it was necessary to try the fit many times, the stones not being even or full."

Since many of the blocks were in excess of many tons, getting them to the site required extraordinary amounts of labor; partially cut and dressed blocks found abandoned at sites display drag markings on their bottom faces, indicating they were most likely lashed with a rope and dragged to the work site from the quarry. Once at the work site, the blocks were most likely rolled or dragged into place using dirt ramps. And what was probably a primitive rope lever system was used to lower stones into bedding joints and raise stones when more shaping was necessary. Small handlelike protrusions remain on many blocks, which may have been used as handholds or as obstructions against which a rope could be fashioned to better facilitate lifting or hoisting. Nevertheless, many questions remain unanswered as far as the exact details of laying and fitting are concerned, especially with regard to the monumental blocks used in the walls of Sacsayhuamán, some of which are in excess of 100 tons and display the same intricate and manifold edging as smaller blocks.

Typologies

When describing Inca walls, scholars are essentially describing the shape of the component stones and the way they fit together—their joints and their "beds." There is, however, some disparity regarding the proper nomenclature with which to describe the types of masonry used in Inca wall construction. The following list combines basic typologies used in several common sources.

PIRKA

Pirkas are roughly shaped fieldstones set in clay mortar. The type of stone varied by region, generally favoring whatever was locally available. It was used in masonry construction throughout Peru long before Inca ascendancy. It was most commonly used in regular houses, terraces, and canals. House walls made with *pirka* sometimes were finished with adobe. A type of masonry closely related to *pirka* is labeled "rustic," a denomination reserved for unworked or only slightly worked stone set in place without mortar.

POLYGONAL

Many of the most famous Inca buildings used polygonal masonry, in which quarried stones were cut, finely dressed, and fitted with absolute (if not baffling) precision. Their uniqueness derives from their irregular interlocking shapes and their "jig-

9.3 Cyclopean-style stonework at Sacsayhuamán. It is described as "cyclopean" owing to its immense size. (Ananda Cohen Suarez)

saw-puzzle" appearance. For example, perhaps the most commonly referenced polygonal stone is the so-called 12-angle stone in Cuzco. The visible face of the stone has 12 corners that fit and bed perfectly against no less than 11 adjacent blocks; horizontal and bedding joints are so perfectly fit that a coin cannot be slipped between any two adjoining stones. Polygonal masonry has deeply beveled, countersunk edges that account for the distinct shadows and the appearance of a dark frame around the face. The favored treatment for the visible faces of the stones was a slight bulge or pillowing effect, called entasis. The entasis accounts for the chiaroscuro effect cast over the stone face as the high-altitude light washes over it.

Similar in style but greater in scale, cyclopean masonry is essentially polygonal masonry. The ruins of the fortress temple Sacsayhuamán provide the most salient examples of cyclopean masonry. Blocks there fit together in the same fashion as in polygonal masonry, but some blocks weigh an

9.2 The famous 12-angle stone: a unique example of Inca polygonal stone masonry found in a wall in Cuzco (J. J. George)

estimated 128 tons and measure as much as five by five by three meters (16 × 16 × 10 ft.). In some sources the term *fitted* has been used instead of *polygonal*, as some authors believe that the latter term misleads readers into visualizing more rectangular or regularly geometric block faces.

COURSED

Coursed is a term that has been used to describe walls constructed with blocks of regular ashlars in horizontal rows. Strictly speaking, an ashlar is a squared building stone, yet its definition is often expanded to include roughly rectangular masonry; thus, coursed ashlar masonry is masonry of squared stones in regular courses where the height of courses may vary one to the next because the ashlars are not all of uniform size. Many of the finest buildings in the empire used this type of construction. For example, the walls of the Cuzco *acllahuasi*, the residence of the so-called chosen women—a kind of cloister for women chosen specifically by the Sapa Inca to specialize in making the finest textiles and *chicha* (ritual maize beer)—and now the convent of Santa Catalina, were constructed of this type of masonry. The superb curved east wall of the Coricancha also uses this type of masonry. And the wall that Bingham, the Yale historian and amateur archaeologist who rediscovered Machu Picchu in 1911, named the "Beautiful Wall" at Machu Picchu is also constructed of coursed ashlars. Elsewhere in the literature *coursed* has been replaced by *sedimentary*, which presumes that the lack of consistent and strict horizontality is better reflected in the natural appearance of sedimentary layers of geological strata, whose horizontality is not always constant.

MASONRY ARCHITECTURE

The most celebrated and best-known Inca sites are those with the finest examples of cut-stone masonry architecture. Both Machu Picchu and Cuzco, whose construction is most often attributed to the ninth

Sapa Inca, Pachacuti, are stone cities with masonry of the finest quality. The finest masonry, in turn, ultimately reflects its exclusive use in royal, noble, religious, or state-imperial buildings. Though Inca architecture never achieved the formal sophistication of Greek or Roman architecture—being largely unadorned or undecorated—it is unquestionably as distinctive. To a certain extent, then, and especially in polygonal masonry, each cut stone is a unique handcrafted entity, while its repertoire of formal elements and design principles remained repeatable. Its effectiveness as an imperial tool was aided by its lack of complexity, which resulted in its rapid deployment across the landscape on the heels of military or diplomatic victory. Its presence served as a tangible reminder of Inca authority, especially to conquered people far from the heartland, where lines of communication and the restraints of direct control often loosen or go slack.

Formal Elements of Inca Architecture

ORNAMENTATION

Architectural ornamentation was kept to a minimum and was reserved for buildings used or occupied by leaders. Fairly simple geometric mural painting was among the most common form of structural decoration. Among the most elaborately decorated structures was the Coricancha, whose walls are known to have had gold and silver plates fastened to them. Buildings along the coast are known to have had decorative moldings. In a few instances low-relief carvings occurred on outside walls, either as small-scale representations of animals on finely fitted blocks or, in a few instances, as carvings in geometric patterns.

BATTERED WALLS

A battered wall is a wall that leans slightly to the inside. For the Incas the typical batter was a slope that ranged minimally, between four and six degrees. Some scholars have argued that the inward lean aids in the stability of the wall, but this is not necessarily the case; its stability is a result of a low, dense profile relative to the ground, with the batter more of an aesthetic detail. For buildings with often-substantial steep-pitched roof structures, a feature that is itself typical of Inca architecture, the inward lean did help to absorb the outward pushing thrust of the roof structure. The interior of some walls had pegs protruding from them, in some cases evidently to secure the roof and in other cases simply to hang things from. In buildings of importance the pegs are carved directly out of the building block, while in lesser structures the pegs are cylinders anchored into pits.

DOORWAYS, WINDOWS, AND NICHES

Trapezoidal doorways, niches, and windows are ubiquitous in the empire's construction program; the trapezoid is, to some extent, an essential mark of the empire. Trapezoidal openings are narrower at the lintel than they are at the sill, and jambs slope inward from the bottom to the top. The structural advantage is obvious (based roughly on the physical soundness of a pyramid), but in Inca building the spans are so small as to render the advantage insignificant. Instead, like the battering evident in walls, the use of the trapezoid is an aesthetic preference of Inca architects. A common variation associated with important buildings, or buildings associated

9.5 Typical Inca windows (Ananda Cohen Suarez)

with important persons, was the trapezoid with double-frame widows and niches. Double-frame doorways are usually found as gateways or portals into complexes as opposed to entranceways into domestic architectural settings. As such, the double-frame is an architectural signifier of the elevated importance of the structure they adorn.

ROOFS

Inca carpenters built hip, gable, and shed roofs with a steep slope of about 60 degrees, resulting in massive roofs that overwhelmed the buildings they covered. The hip roof was used for one-story structures and consisted of a timber frame resting on top of the walls that supported the roof. The gabled roof was used mainly in two-story structures. It was not

9.4 An example of an Inca doorway (drawing courtesy Michel Besson)

9.6 An example of Inca niches (Drawing courtesy Michel Besson)

unusual for a roof to be three or four times as high as a wall. A thick layer of thatch, made from *ichu* grass, covered the roofs, and there is evidence in the chronicles that on significant religious occasions textiles were used to cover the thatch in what must have been a dramatic visual scene.

Design Principles
INDIVIDUAL BUILDINGS

The vast majority of Inca buildings are rectangular, one-story, single-room enclosures. The longer the room, the more entranceways it has. Windows and niches frequently decorate the interior walls and are aligned relative to each other in various patterns.

The layout of the building and its elements is symmetrical, and windows, niches, and doors generally mirror themselves across the short axis of the floorplan. Activities carried out in interior spaces is difficult to discern, thus for many buildings their exact function remains open to debate. Typically, however, there is a direct correlation between the use of highest-quality cut stone—the extremely well-fitted masonry of coursed or polygonal blocks—and the importance of the building relative to its religious, administrative, or royal function. Variations in the size of Inca buildings more often indicated differences in function than in prestige.

A few notable buildings and types of structures do not follow a rectangular floorplan. Two of the most famous such buildings are described by curved

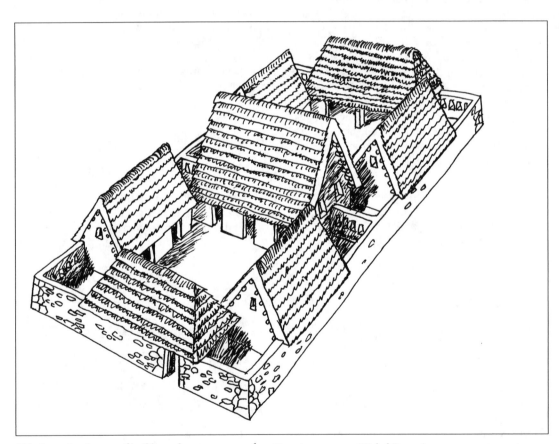

9.7 An enclosed group of buildings, known as a cancha (Drawing courtesy Michel Besson)

walls: the Coricancha in Cuzco and the Torreón at Machu Picchu. Similarly, the circular foundation of a round tower called Muyuc Marca at Sacsayhuamán is known, and conical funerary towers called *chullpas* and circular storehouses, or *colcas*, are also known. Many ethnic groups used buildings with circular plans before being conquered by the Incas, though once under Inca supervision constructions in those areas typically shifted to follow the Inca vocabulary.

GROUPINGS OF BUILDINGS

Inca architects were known to make ceramic and stone architectural models as blueprints prior to construction. There is, for instance, a ceramic model in the Archaeological Museum of Cuzco that represents a *cancha*, a word that means "enclosure" and refers to a basic unit of Inca architecture. A *cancha* consists of a grouping of two, three, or four buildings facing a courtyard. The grouping may or may not be surrounded by a wall. The museum model, for instance, shows a grouping of four individual units, each a single-room enclosure, open to a courtyard and surrounded by a wall. The layout reflects principles of opposition and symmetry where the individual building units face each other across the courtyard as if in a mirror image. In groupings of four units enclosed by a wall, a doorway to the exterior is typically included on the outer wall of a street-facing unit, as opposed to an interstitial space at the corner. In groupings of three units enclosed by a wall the exterior doorway opens directly onto the courtyard. The most famous *cancha* is of course the Coricancha temple, but the style is not reserved for religious structures and can be found as common domestic compounds as well as the model for town blocks. Modern Peruvian herders still live in *canchas*.

Canchas can be exceptionally large and complicated, well beyond the standard three and four structure enclosures. For example, at Huánuco Pampa, a major provincial center in the central highlands of Peru, one compound there includes 19 structures surrounded by a wall. Excavations within the compound revealed hearths and domestic ceramics that together indicate typical residential or domestic activities took place there. The overall layout of the compound lacks the rigid geometric organization of compounds at Cuzco, yet the stonework at Huánuco Pampa in general, including the compound under discussion, is typical cut-stone Inca masonry, even though it tends to lack the fineness found in Cuzco. While the planners at Huánuco Pampa were clearly following a plan in the layout and design of the city and its individual compounds, the majority of the buildings were simply not important enough to receive the strict oversight of Inca administrators. As a result, some departures from Inca style occurred as the influence of local style leaked in. Diminishing levels of oversight in the hinterlands is not uncommon and often extended beyond architecture into social and political realms as well.

BUILDING FUNCTIONS

Great Halls

Many authors refer to the Incas' great halls—larger, rectangular structures often with gabled roofs, numerous doorways, and niched interior walls—as *kallankas*. John Rowe, a preeminent Inca archaeologist, indicates the Incas would not have used this word. For simplicity's sake *great hall* is used here. Great halls are visible in Cuzco, as well as in most provincial centers throughout the empire, where they would have been used as temporary shelter for Inca armies or *mita* labor forces completing their labor tax; the *mita* was essentially an obligatory state tax on individuals to be paid through labor. (Typical labor assignments might include military service or construction work.) Great halls could also have been used as covered festival grounds during inclement weather or as a space to celebrate some religious ceremony or the visit of an important administrative official. As their interior was undivided, they were effective structures for assembly and, when necessary, for storage. Doorways open to the plaza broke up the facade at regular or alternating intervals.

The Andean chronicler Garcilaso de Vega, having seen great halls as a boy in Cuzco, described

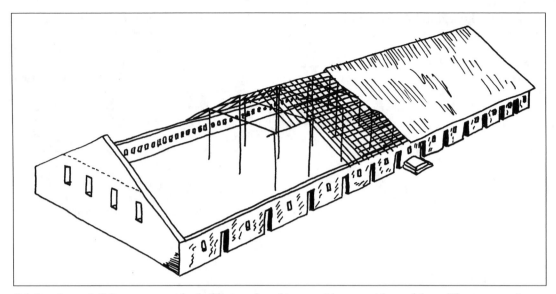

9.8 Inca "great halls" were rectangular buildings such as this one, with many niches and doors. They are sometimes called kallankas. (Drawing courtesy Michel Besson)

them as follows: "In many of the Inca's palaces there were large halls some two hundred paces long and fifty to sixty wide. They were unpartitioned and served as places of assembly for festivals and dances and when the weather was too rainy to permit them to hold these in the open air. In the city of Cuzco I saw four of these structures. . . . The largest was that of the Cassana, which was capable of holding up to three thousand persons." Garcilaso's description clearly shows the massive scale of the structures. Similarly, at Huánuco Pampa the ruins of a great hall facing the plaza measure more than 70 meters by 12 meters (230 × 39 ft.). Another great hall at a site called Incallacta, to the southeast of Lake Titicaca, measures 78 meters by 26 meters (256 × 85 ft.) and is thus one of the largest constructions in the Inca Empire.

At Huánuco Pampa excavations that revealed circular pits running down the long central axis suggest vertical timbers were used as roof supports. The span at Incallacta, however, is too great for a single support, leading to speculation that a four-part nave created through doubling the vertical support could have been used. Overall the great halls are easily recognized because of their size and their placement immediately adjacent to one or more sides of the site's main square.

Palaces

Palaces followed the basic lines of the *cancha* and were built as royal lodging, administrative complexes, and royal country and recreational estates. In Cuzco each Sapa Inca built a palace compound to house, in perpetuity, himself, his handlers, and his *panaqa* (royal lineage group, excluding his heir). The palaces were walled enclosures spread over large sites that occupied at least a single block. They contained many single-room apartments for servants and attendants, large reception halls on the great hall model, bathing suites, stone channels for water, a large court or patio, and rooms and living rooms for the Sapa Inca himself. Entrance to the palace was through one or at the most two doorways. As the palaces were associated with royalty, they were inevitably constructed using the highest-quality masonry techniques.

Cuzco's main plaza, called Huacaypata, was bordered on at least three sides by impressive palaces or compounds. The Hatuncancha, or "Great Enclosure," was said to contain the house of the *mamakuna* or *acllas*, the most privileged women's orders. Another compound, the Amarucancha, or "Serpent Enclosure," was associated with a number of early rulers. Huayna Cápac's palace, the Cassana, lay on the northwest edge of the plaza. Huayna Cápac was the eleventh Inca ruler. His sons, Huáscar and Atahualpa, had just fought a dynastic battle when the Spanish arrived. Huayna Cápac's mummy was said to have been in residence in his palace when the Spanish arrived in Cuzco.

Estates

Traditional Inca king lists mention 11 rulers, with two who fought a war of succession. The first seven kings on the standard list are speculative or mythical, although there exists a theory suggesting that the "mythical" kings were actually coregents from the lesser moiety, an idea that reflects the Inca tendency for duality and reciprocity. Further research will bear this out, but for now it seems that every Inca ruler following the eighth, Viracocha Inca, built country estates as resort-type escapes from the city and as means of providing sustenance and wealth for their descendants. (A primary feature of many estates was elaborate agricultural terracing far in excess of what was necessary to maintain the site itself.) The most elegant estates lay in the Vilcanota-Urubamba river drainage near Cuzco, an area referred to as the Sacred Valley. Along a 100-kilometers (62-mi.) stretch of the valley lay the estates of the eighth ruler, Viracocha Inca, at Juchuy Cuzco; the ninth ruler, Pachacuti, at Pisac, Ollantaytambo, Patallacta, and Machu Picchu; the 10th ruler, Topa Inca, at Urquillos and Chinchero; and of the 11th ruler, Huayna Cápac, at Yucay and Quispiguanca. Earlier rulers probably had private manors. Each ruler's dynastic descent group occupied the estates in perpetuity, although they were subject to seizure as a result of dynastic coups, infighting, and general turmoil. These estates, many of which underwent continuous remodeling, account for the finest examples of Inca site planning, terrace building, waterwork construction, and masonry use in the empire.

The estates were designed to provide access to a wide range of resources including cropland, pastures, settlements, forests, parks, ponds and marshes, hunting grounds, and salt fields. They exemplified the Inca ability to modify terrain and adapt their designs to existing landforms. Most are executed according to a basic plan making use of a central plaza, an agricultural zone, a residential zone, storehouses, platform mounds, and enclosing walls that highlight the central ceremonial core. Viracocha Inca's estate at Juchuy Cuzco, for instance, is 600 meters (1,969 ft.) above the river with expansive views up and down the valley. The buildings at Pisac unfold successively upward on a steep hillside and include a Coricancha-style compound, an *intihuatana* stone (a carved stone outcrop sometimes referred to as a "hitching post of the sun" on account of a signature vertical, gnomonlike element), and elaborate hillside terracing. Machu Picchu, for example, was sculpted atop a spectacular mountain site and includes many of the finest examples of Inca construction technology. Huayna Cápac's estate at Quispiguanca was distinguished as a major feat of Inca engineering in that the estate consisted of tracts of land reclaimed from swamp through channelization of the main river and tributaries. Quispiguanca is further distinguished from earlier estates by its use of sundried adobe bricks covered in mud plaster, which was then painted. Although these examples are few in relation to the total, they nonetheless represent significant examples of royal Inca estate architecture.

Shrines

Huacas came in a variety of constructed and natural forms. Defined variously as "idols," "shrines," and "a sacred thing," a *huaca* could be anything out of the ordinary imbued with sacred and religious significance. The Spanish Jesuit chronicler Cobo's definition of *huaca* adds an important dimension. He says, ". . . the Peruvian Indians used the term *guaca* [*huaca*] for all the sacred places designated for prayers and sacrifices, as well as for all of the gods and idols that were worshiped in these places." Thus, *huacas* take natural forms such as rocks, springs, and caves, as well as constructed forms such as fountains, doorways, and other constructions.

The maintenance of the shrines was allocated to different social groups, who were responsible for leading processions to the *huacas* to pray, chant, and leave offerings. The *ceque* lines had a practical as well as symbolic function in that water rights were established based on their location. The *ceque* system also overlapped with the important child sacrifice ceremony known as Cápac Hucha (also Capacocha), in which unblemished boys and girls were brought to Cuzco, feted, ritually married, then marched home following the *ceque* lines. At the completion of the ceremony the children were given *chicha*, a maize beer, and ritually interred with effigy figurines. Information on shrines is somewhat limited because the Spanish began in the 1540s to systematically destroy the *huaca* system in the express hope of ridding the native Andeans of what the Spanish perceived as pagan practice.

Temples

The main temples were constructed on prominent sites or auspicious locations, often following a similar plan to that of the domestic or palace compound. Large and small niches were used as shelves for important cult objects. In some cases the niches housed the mummies of past rulers, who would be taken out on important occasions and displayed. Some temples are akin to the great hall, or *kallanka*, style of building. The most important temple was the Coricancha in Cuzco.

THE CORICANCHA

The most important and best-known temple is Cuzco's Coricancha (golden enclosure), commonly referred to today as the Temple of the Sun. After the Spanish conquered Cuzco, in a gesture typical of imperial transition, they erected their own religious structure, the monastery of Santo Domingo, directly on top of the Coricancha. A major earthquake in 1950 caused significant damage to the colonial structure, and subsequent restoration has resulted in difficult negotiations attempting to reconcile the damaged colonial-era structure with the remains of its Inca predecessor. Nevertheless, its fundamental importance to the Incas cannot be understated. As a signal of its importance, the layout and design of the Coricancha was the prototype for similar structures at provincial centers throughout the empire, although the farther one ventures from Cuzco, the more variation one sees based on local material, climate, and stylistic tendencies.

The Coricancha is basically analogous to other *cancha*-type buildings and is little different from other palace structures within the city. Though the full ground plan of the Coricancha remains obscured by colonial building projects, it is known to have contained between four and eight rectangular enclosures surrounding a courtyard. The enclosures are all built of fine coursed masonry of the "Cuzco-style" variety—that is, of the finest masonry. It appears that in some areas adobe was used to continue the structure above the masonry wall, and thatched roofs over wooden frames provided cover. Doorways, windows, and niches were often double-jambed, indicating their high religious significance. Its western exterior consisted of the six-meter (20-ft.) high curved wall—the most famous wall in the empire—an elegant arc of coursed ashlar masonry.

The rooms in the Coricancha housed a number of effigies, including *punchao*, the golden sun effigy, which was brought out each day and returned at sunset. Other statues reportedly included one of Viracocha (the creator god), Inti-Illapa (thunder god), Mama-Quilla (moon goddess), *cuichu* (rainbow), and other leading idols. Similarly, the mummies of past rulers were housed there and were brought out for ritual display and ceremonially offered food and drink. Perhaps the Coricancha's most audacious display was its golden effigy garden, which was a monumental garden of realistic gold and silver sculptures replicating maize stalks and numerous kinds of animals, all of which were melted down by the Spanish. Similarly pleasing to the Spanish were the Coricancha's interior walls, which, on the side the Sun rose, were covered in 700 gold plates weighing two kilograms (4.5 lbs.) apiece.

Not only was the Coricancha the repository of sacred idols, but it was also the point from which the *ceque* system emanated, demarcating its sacred geography and invisibly subdividing both space and time. According to Cobo's list of *huacas*, the first was a stone called Subaraura located where the balcony of Santo Domingo was built.

OTHER IMPORTANT INCA TEMPLES

Other important temples similarly reflecting the function of the Coricancha, in theory if not in exact design, were known throughout the empire. The Temple of Apurímac, located to the northwest of Cuzco at the Apurímac river gorge, was dedicated to a river spirit. The idol associated with it was of paramount importance and was attended by a female priestess who was probably a sister or close relative of the Sapa Inca. The Temple of Viracocha (dedicated to the Inca creator god of the same name) located at Raqchi is a complex consisting of courtyards, *canchas*, more than 40 circular structures, and a large hall for the temple itself. The temple here was perhaps the largest structure in the entire empire, measuring 92 meters by 25.25 meters (302 × 83 ft.). The Temple of Pachacamac, to the south of modern Lima, may have been the most sacred shrine in Peru. It predates the Incas, but the Incas, recognizing its importance, freely adapted it into their working religious system and even renovated the existing temple and expanded the site using the standard Inca architectural vocabulary. The Temple of Copacabana complex on two islands in Lake Titicaca—the Island of the Sun and the Island of the Moon—was considered the third most important religious structure in the empire. It is typically associated with the reign of Topa Inca, the 10th ruler by the standard lists.

Colcas

The Incas borrowed from and elaborated on several centuries of Andean storage practice. For example, many hundreds of structures that were probably used for storage are known at the Wari site of Pikillacta. Wari was a pre-Inca imperial civilization that existed in the central highlands of Peru from ca. 540–1000 C.E. *Colcas* (storehouses) are generally situated outside settlements, in high, cool, and windy places in order to avoid the damp. They are usually grouped in rows of identical structures two to three meters (6.5–10 ft.) apart in order to reduce the danger of spreading fires. The structures are typically circular or rectangular. At Huánuco Pampa, for example, circular structures were commonly used to store maize, and rectangular structures were commonly used to store potatoes. Storage systems in the Cuzco region and at Ollantaytambo employ another type of *colca* structure. There the structures are about three meters (10 ft.) wide and from 10 meters to 40 meters (33–131 ft.) long with many door-size openings in the opposing, longer walls. Many structures have sophisticated ventilation and drainage systems built in.

Provincial centers all contained hundreds of *colcas* in order to supply military, religious, and administrative personnel; to supply the *mita* labor force working for the state; as a fallback for the general population in times of crisis; and probably to facilitate state diplomacy in instances where ceremonial politics necessitated the consumption of great quantities of food and drink. The Spanish were particularly impressed with the state storage system, which, according to the chronicler Cobo, was still functioning well enough in 1548 to feed a Spanish army at Jauja for seven months.

The *colca* system supporting Cuzco was reportedly immense. Pedro Pizarro, brother of Francisco Pizarro and chronicler-conquistador, reportedly believed the supplies too immense to ever be exhausted. Pedro Sancho de la Hoz, a secretary, provides another eyewitness account of the scale of the Cuzco *colca*. He wrote that one storehouse alone contained 100,000 dried birds, whose feathers were used for clothing. He also noted the storage of shields, tent poles, knives, other tools, sandals, armor, blankets, wool, weapons, metals, and clothes—that is, many of the things necessary to supply a standing army.

Pucarás

More so than most constructions, *pucarás* (fortresses) display the ingenuity of Inca engineers. Each fortress the Incas built was, by necessity, planned for its specific location; because each site presented its own obstacles, fortresses often took on more virtuoso forms. Most *pucarás* were basically citadel fortresses incorporating a variety of facilities. They were built close to but outside a city, as at Cajamarca and Cusicacha and in the case of Sacsayhuamán at Cuzco, and some were built specifically to facilitate conquest, as at fortresses in Chile and Bolivia. *Pucarás* provided minimal accommodation, water supply, and storage. Defensive terracing, concentric walls, zigzagging fortifications, moats, and observation posts were typical elements associated with fortress construction.

Fortified Inca sites were clustered on the far northern frontier near Quito, Ecuador, well inside the eastern frontier south of Cuzco, and in the far south near Santiago, Chile. In some cases the Incas simply commandeered preexisting fortifications and made them their own. Many frontier *pucarás* were designed and positioned to control traffic at key points rather than repel all incursions into Inca territory. Consisting of more than 800 structures, the coastal site of Incawasi was the most elaborate facility built for military purposes.

Royal estates associated with Pachacuti, such as Pisac, Machu Picchu, and Ollantaytambo, contained fortified elements or were built in locales with clear defensive advantages. At Pisac, for example, 17 kilometers (10.5 mi.) northeast of Cuzco and spectacularly positioned high atop a steep ridge, at least two stone gates and stretches of defensive wall attend every approach road. Massive watchtowers with solid bases suitably positioned to repel attacks from below and conical towers with water cisterns further enhance the defensive-mindedness of the site. On the hillside above Cuzco loomed the "fortress" Sacsayhuamán, an astonishing example of Inca architectural ingenuity in orchestrating environmental design, sculptural form, and surface patterning. It was more than just a fortress, however, and probably combined the functions of shrine, Sun temple, warehouse, and ceremonial complex—which altogether reflects the Inca tendency to bundle functional and symbolic layers of meaning into individual constructions. Although there is some discrepancy in the sources, the construction of Sacsayhuamán is credited to Pachacuti, the ninth Sapa Inca, or his son and successor, Topa Inca.

The cyclopean zigzag walls visible today were only part of the original complex. The entire complex, which extended well beyond the remaining walls, included towers, chambers, habitations, terraces, patios, cisterns, aqueducts, plazas, and numerous examples of carved stones, such as the famous "Throne of the Inca," a series of step-form planes carved directly into a massive rock outcrop, and the "Tired Stone," another carved shrine. The chronicler Cieza de León wrote that 20,000 men were called into service for its construction, where "four thousand of them quarried and cut the stones; six thousand hauled these with great cables of leather and hemp; others dug the ditch and laid the foundation; while still others cut poles and beams for timber." Later sources estimate that as many as 20,000–50,000 persons labored at any one time. Furthermore, it was reportedly large enough to contain more than 5,000 persons. Sacsayhuamán is perhaps the grandest expression of the Inca ability to mobilize, organize, and build on a monumental scale.

Chullpas

Burial practices often provide a context for social statements about individuals within a community. In the Andes, however, mortuary evidence is limited in the archaeology due to thorough sacking by the Spanish and later tomb robbers. At Pisac, for example, an entire cliffside of tombs has been looted. A typical tomb is called a *chullpa*, which is aboveground, freestanding, round or square in shape, with a corbel-vaulted roof, and sometimes coated in a layer of mud stucco. *Chullpas* typically had a small doorway that was blocked after the body had been placed inside.

Guamán Poma, a native Andean chronicler, provided one of the most important sources for Inca scholarship. In a long letter to the king of Spain that was later put in manuscript form and called *The First New Chronicle and Good Government*, Guamán Poma both describes Inca burial practices by region and provides invaluable line drawings accordingly: in Chinchaysuyu, the region of the empire to the northwest of Cuzco, persons were buried in a small, domed *chullpa*; in Antisuyu, the region to the northeast of Cuzco, the dead were typically placed in hollowed tree trunks; in Collasuyu, the southern part of the empire, large *chullpas* were used; and in Cuntisuyu, the small area to the southwest of Cuzco, similar practices were followed as those of Collasuyu, except that in coastal regions tombs were underground.

Infrastructure

The vastness of the Inca Empire, stretching more than 4,000 kilometers (2,485 mi.) from northern Ecuador to southern Chile, necessitated an efficient communication infrastructure. The extensive highway network of more than 25,000–30,000 kilometers (15,534–18,641 mi.) of road—two trunk roads, one along the coast and one through the highlands, and numerous roads connecting them—was the primary facilitator of efficient communication. Observation posts, tollgates, and *chasqui* posts were regularly positioned along the roadway. The *chasquis* were runners who carried messages in relay from post to post. Two runners occupied each *chasqui* station, called a *chasquihuasi*, with each individual occupying a small stone hut. *Chasqui* huts varied stylistically by region and were built at intervals between two and nine kilometers (1–5.5 mi.). More elaborate post houses called *tambos*, often reserved for royalty as way stations to and from their estates and when traveling long distances, each roughly 20 kilometers (12 mi.) apart, also punctuated the highway.

Other Structures

USNUS

Usnus were raised platforms with ceremonial or administrative functions, located almost invariably in the center of or at the edge of a settlement's main plaza, atop which the Sapa Inca could review his armies, preside over festivities, make astronomical observations, or offer sacrifices to the gods. The term *usnu* originally referred to a small sugarloaf-shaped stone on top of the platform, though it eventually came to refer to the platform itself. The Spanish chronicler Cristóbal de Molina described *usnus* in the following way: ". . . and in each town there was a large royal plaza, and in the middle of it was a square high platform with a very high staircase; the Inca and three of his lords ascended it to speak to the people and see the army when they made their reviews and assemblages."

The *usnu* at Huánuco Pampa, for instance, is in the center of an enormous open plaza measuring 550 meters by 350 meters (1,804 × 1,148 ft.). The main *usnu* is 32 meters by 48 meters (105 × 157 ft.) at its base. It sits 3.5 meters (11 ft.) above two lower platforms, which were constructed using undressed stone and fill. Only the faces of the stones on the main platform were dressed, creating a facade of elegantly shaped blocks in the imperial masonry style. The lower platform was apparently built to correct the site's slope and create a level surface for the primary structure. The second platform was built after the main structure. Together the lower platforms increase the overall scale and impact of the structure. The southern side of the structure is dominated by a broad stairway and balustrade.

GARDENS

Gardens were a ceremonial decorative element of Sun temples and palaces and were found in courtyards or terraces. The chroniclers Garcilaso and Cieza de León both made note of gardens, with special attention paid to golden effigy gardens. Garcilaso noted, "Here were the finest trees and most beautiful flowers and sweet smelling herbs in the kingdom, while quantities of others were reproduced in gold and silver, at every stage of their growth." Garcilaso then goes on with a long list of flora and fauna made in gold and silver effigy, including cornstalks, rabbits, mice, lizards, snakes, butterflies, foxes, birds, deer, pumas, and jaguars—almost all of which was melted down and shipped to Europe by the Spanish. The garden reflected dual Inca tendencies—on the one hand to sacralize the natural world and on the other to control and manage it in an aestheticized fashion.

PRISONS

Though rare, prisons warranted special attention from Guamán Poma, who lists three types of prisons, the *uatay uaci zancay*, a subterranean prison or dungeon; the *araway* and *uimpillay*, which were places of execution; and an unnnmamed third type of prison for people of rank and privilege, where comfort was sufficient and visitors were allowed. The dungeon was an altogether sinister tool. Guamán Poma notes that it was designed for "extermination," and the worst criminals, guilty of treason, thievery, or insulting behavior toward the Sapa Inca, were condemned to be eaten alive by wild beasts kept in the dungeons. Guamán Poma catalogs toads, lizards, snakes, bears, foxes, dogs, mountain cats, vultures, eagles, and owls, as well as lions and tigers (which do not actually exist in North America), as among animals kept for dungeons.

Use of Adobe

Adobe construction had been used in the ancient Andes for many thousands of years. Adobe was the usual building material along the dry desert coastal plains. One major example is the Huaca del Sol, the main pyramid of the Moche civilization, which dominated the north coast of Peru from roughly 1 to 700 C.E. The Huaca del Sol contained an estimated 143 million adobe bricks. Inca construction in conquered territories along the coast continued this tradition. The Incas also used sundried adobe bricks atop masonry construction, including the major palaces, to reach the desired height and appearance. Adobe bricks contained a high density of straw, were typically long and flat, measuring some 20 centimeters by 80 centimeters (7.8 × 31.5 in.), and were of different shapes. Evidently they were not made in standardized molds. In general, adobes have not survived well where unprotected, especially in the variable and often severe highland climates.

Adobe structures dating to the Incas can be seen at Puruchucu and Pachacamac near Lima, at Incahuasi in the Cañete Valley south of Lima, and at Tambo Colorado in the Pisco Valley south of the Cañete Valley. But, perhaps the most significant adobe structures are those attributed to the 11th royal Inca, Huayna Cápac, and the construction of his estate in the Urubamba Valley. Unlike his royal predecessors—his grandfather Pachacuti and his father, Topa Inca—whose major construction projects emphasized stone masonry, Huayna Cápac used sundried adobe brick on stone foundations in the most important buildings.

URBAN/SITE PLANNING

It is often repeated that the Incas were unexceptional city builders but extraordinary site planners. Their attention to the place of architecture in the natural topography is complementary and functional; in both design and execution it is unmatched. In theory, the replication of the Cuzco urban model throughout the empire could be construed as true, but close archaeological comparison has shown that general planning principles are difficult to discern, partly because the Incas adapted their settlements, often by necessity, to specific features of a site and its topography.

Given the difficulty in establishing a canon of Inca urban design principles, the scholars Graziano Gasparini and Luise Margolies have suggested that instead of searching for similarities in physical form, one should look for them in the meaning and function of form. They argue that if one accounts for the abstraction of physical form, certain constructed and conceived elements are repeated with considerable frequency. Following this line of argument, there are enough commonalities between Cuzco and distant provincial centers to suggest a planning model based on Cuzco. For example, Gasparini and Margolies suggest the following list of shared features: the division of urban space into *hanan* and *hurin* (moiety divisions, or division into "upper" and "lower" halves), the presence of a principal and a secondary plaza, the location of great halls on the plaza, the regular appearance of an *usnu* (usually a platform mound in central plazas), and the regular presence of an *incahuasi* (the house or palace of the Sapa Inca), *acllahuasi* (a compound for the "chosen women," who wove the finest cloth and made *chicha* for ritual occasions), temple of the Sun, and storehouses. The presence of these forms in multiple centers suggests, at the least, a very basic template of structures that defined a center as Inca.

Ultimately, however, given that it is as difficult to read function in particular ruins as it is to establish conceptual social division in settlement patterns, the case for an overarching planning canon remains largely hypothetical. Many factors, however, were taken into consideration when devising a settlement plan. These included the location of sacred shrines, proximity to natural resources such as water and mines, preexisting settlements, astronomical orientation, terracing, and sight lines to ritually important mountains or passes. Overall, regardless of the degree to which Cuzco was or was not the physical model for Inca urban planning, it was the center of the empire, a sacred object in itself, and its design, both physical and conceptual, defined the essential shape of the empire.

Cuzco

According to traditional accounts, the urban core of Cuzco was planned according to the design of the ninth Inca ruler, Pachacuti, who, in his role of architect, devised an imperial scheme based in stone. Working from a clay model, he rebuilt the entire city to serve as the imperial hub of social, political, administrative, religious, and ritual activity. Furthermore, it served as a metaphor for the Inca universe, as the royal seat of the ruling dynasty, as a symbol of power, and as axis mundi (the sacred pivot point around which the universe revolves). In its original design Cuzco covered 40 hectares (almost 100 acres) and consisted mainly of plazas, temples, housing for royalty and their attendants, and housing for captured or subject provincial lords, whom the Incas required to live in Cuzco as a means of control. In another aspect of control Pachacuti demonstrated his own power and by extension the control of the Incas over the natural forces of the world by ordering the Huatanay and Tullumayo Rivers rechanneled. Members of other (conquered) ethnic groups, laborers, and artisans lived outside the ceremonial core. Overall, population estimates range from 15,000 to 20,000 in the central sector and perhaps between 100,000 and 150,000 in greater Cuzco, extending as much as five kilometers (3 mi.) outside the center.

The design and layout of Cuzco was predicated on four complementary and overlapping spatial metaphors. Not all the literature agrees on the application and limits of these systems. The first division reflects the quadripartite division of the empire, called Tawantinsuyu ("land of the four quarters," or "four parts together"), as a direct extension of the division of urban space in Cuzco. Quadripartite divi-

sion begins in the middle of Cuzco and extends outward following the four main roads. The second system reflects the division of social space based on moiety divisions, or division into halves. In Cuzco the moiety system divided social space into *hanan* and *hurin*, which correspond with upper and lower, and people were assigned space depending on which moiety they belonged to. The third system of spatial organization is the Cuzco *ceque* system, which organizes the *huaca* (sacred shrine) system, demarcates sacred geography, and establishes the water rights of the city and its local environs according to the sacred overlay. The last system, perhaps the most controversial, follows the idea that the Incas conceptualized Cuzco as being in the shape of a puma. Each idea is discussed in greater detail below.

Tawantinsuyu

The Incas envisioned their empire as a unified whole, a totality made up of its people, its history, its landscape, and its myths and cosmologies. The shape of the empire was based on a quadripartite division the Incas called Tawantinsuyu (Tahuantinsuyo), meaning the "four parts together." Tawantinsuyu is, then, a system of political and geographic divisions. Each division represents a part of Cuzco and, by extension, the corresponding part of the empire. Each of its four *suyus*, or parts, is run by a ruler called an *apu*, who advised the Sapa Inca in Cuzco of the affairs of his *suyu*. The quarters were subdivided into smaller provinces, some of which corresponded to pre-Inca ethnic boundaries and some of which were adjusted or divided according to Inca administrative needs. The boundaries of the four parts have their beginnings in Cuzco, initially following lines demarcated by the four roads that lead from the city in each respective direction.

Chinchaysuyu, which was named after the Chincha ethnic group, was the most populous of the *suyus* and comprised the territory and peoples of the northern Peruvian coast, the adjacent highlands, and the Northern Andes. Antisuyu lay to the north and northeast of Cuzco and was named after the mountain, which eventually came to be called the Andes in Spanish. It was by far the smallest region. Collasuyu (Kollasuyu), the largest part of the empire, began in Cuzco and ran south-southeast to encompass Peru's southern highlands, the Lake Titicaca region and western Bolivia, and the Altiplano (high plateau or plain). Collasuyu's borders then turned south to encompass central Chile from the coast to adjacent western Argentina. It took its name from the ethnic Colla (Kolla) peoples who lived on the north side of Lake Titicaca. Cuntisuyu, the second smallest region, lay southwest of Cuzco and stretched to the coast. The *suyus* followed the moiety division of *hanan* and *hurin:* Chinchaysuyu and Antisuyu lay in the *hanan*, or upper, division, and Collasuyu and Cuntisuyu lay in the *hurin*, or lower, division.

HANAN *AND* HURIN

Cuzco's civic plan, and subsequently the empire's, was divided according to a dominant upper moiety called *hanan*, and lower subdominant moiety called *hurin*. The division of upper and lower was a symbolic, social, and geographic distinction; the *hanan* division was literally the upper, or higher, of the two. *Hanan* and *hurin* moieties also correspond with one level of social division. While there is an unavoidable hierarchy in the language used to describe the moiety system, the dual subdivision reflects a pan-Andean tradition of two halves viewed as complementary. For example, despite the priority given by those in the upper (*hanan*) portion, the lower (*hurin*) half contained the Coricancha, the most important and perhaps absolute center of the Inca universe. Residency in *hanan* or *hurin* Cuzco depended on one's ancestral line.

The symbolic division of the urban area into two halves passed through the Huacaypata, Cuzco's main plaza, in a northwest-southeast direction along the axis that coincided with the roads that led to Cuntisuyu and Antisuyu. The two halves were associated with an equal number of *panaqas*, or royal kin groups. According to El Inca Garcilaso, the older brothers (groups) resided in Hanan Cuzco and the younger brothers in Hurin Cuzco. The most exalted kin groups formed a kind of aristocracy. This division has led some researchers to speculate on a dual system of kingship, with one ruler in the upper and one in the lower, but at present the argument remains hypothetical. The first five rulers came from Hurin Cuzco, while all subsequent rulers resided in Hanan

Cuzco. Why the dynasty shifted from one to the other remains a mystery.

PUMA

According to one chronicler, Pachacuti named the whole city the "lion's body," calling the city's residents the limbs of the lion. On this basis some researchers have suggested the city was laid out in the form of a puma (lions belong to the African continent), with the fortress temple Sacsayhuamán as the head and its zigzag wall the teeth. The sector where the city's two rechanneled rivers, the Huatanay and Tullamayo, came together form the tail; this part of the city is still referred to as *puma chupan*, or "puma's tail." Others, however, have suggested that the puma shape should be understood metaphorically.

CUZCO *CEQUE* SYSTEM

The Cuzco *ceque* system was an elaborate system of *huacas*, or sacred shrines, that surrounded the city of Cuzco. The Jesuit scholar Cobo, in his 1653 *History of the New World*, provides the most detailed description of the *ceque* (line) system. He describes a system of at least 328 *huacas* and the 41 (42 following later research) *ceques* that organize them. The *ceques*, which can be described as "rays" or "lines," are conceptual in nature, invisible in practice, and emanate outward from the Coricancha. They link *huacas* together, though not necessarily in a straight line. Cobo writes, "From the Temple of the Sun as from the center went out certain lines which the Indians call ceques: they formed four parts corresponding to the four royal roads which went out from Cuzco. On each one of those ceques were arranged in order the guacas [*huacas*] and shrines which there were in Cuzco and its district, like stations of holy places, the veneration of which was common to all." The *ceque* system thus reflects a kind of landscape architecture in that the system shapes the landscape. In other words, the *ceque* system defined how the Incas used, related to, and navigated the physical-religious environment. The *ceque* system defined ritual space within and extending from the urban environment.

Cobo's account indicates the *ceques* were divided among the four *suyus*. Chinchaysuyu, Antisuyu, and Collasuyu contained nine *ceques* each. Cobo indicates that Cuntisuyu was more complex, containing 14 *ceques*, although later research has found that it actually contained 15 *ceques*. Of the 328 *huacas* listed, 96 are springs or sources of water, and 95 are standing stones. Other major shrines include hills, royal palaces, fields, caves, quarries, stone seats, trees, roads, and sunset markers. The majority of the shrines reflect the deep reverence the Incas held for the landscape. It is most easily envisioned as a radial system, although there is disagreement as to whether the *ceque* lines emanated outward in straight lines. In general, they did not affect the architectural plan of Cuzco but defined and complemented social relationships within it. The *ceques* and their *huacas* were maintained by kin groups from Cuzco, who were responsible for prayers, offerings, and sacrifices at the appropriate time. Determining which groups maintained which *huacas* was based on hierarchy and, thus, privilege. Following this model, the division of space in the Cuzco Valley is also a system of social division wherein rights and obligations are determined by hierarchical-based responsibilities delimited by the *ceque* system.

Provincial Site Planning

Inca settlements beyond Cuzco can best be understood as satellites, as a network of centers linked by the Inca highway, or *cápac ñan*, which stretched more than 25,000 kilometers (15,534 mi.) along two trunk roads—one in the highlands and one along the coast—and intermediate branches linking the two. The layouts of these provincial centers were not all similar, although they shared many characteristics with the basic urban plan of Cuzco modified according to local geologic, topographic, and cultural factors. In principle, like Cuzco, they were divided into *hanan* and *hurin*, were sited around a central plaza with an *usnu*, and had a temple to the Sun, an *acllahuasi*, *colcas*, and great halls *(kallankas)*. The most important of these structures were usually built adjacent to the plaza. In some cases the Incas favored open space for new urban constructions, and in other cases the Incas adapted preexisting settlements to their own specifications.

The principal activities of a site influenced its design. Inca forts, for example, were often built in difficult terrain and surrounded by walls, whereas major administrative centers were built on gener-

ally flat terrain. Sanctuaries may have included dispersed constructions along a carefully laid out route, and royal estates such as Pisac, Machu Picchu, and Quispiguanca were extravagant gestures of modified terrain in combination with exceptional masonry. If there is an element that defined the various constructions as Inca, it lay in the combination of masonry techniques and the use of architectural motifs such as trapezoidal doorways, niches, and windows. Despite the great distances within the empire, these architectural markers were readily identifiable even in far-flung outposts and left no confusion as to whom the settlement belonged.

Street Grid: Orthogonal and Radial Planning

The ubiquitous grid plan laid out by Spanish colonialists following the conquest of the Americas differs from street plans native to the Incas. The Spanish colonial grid plan is, in general, a system of streets meeting at right angles, at the center of which lies the *plaza central*, or central square, with church, government, and administrative buildings on its edges. Grid plans are simple to lay out and make efficient use of space. The plaza was certainly utilized by the Incas, but rarely did streets unfold in the rigorous alignment favored by the Spanish.

The Inca orthogonal plan is characterized by streets that cross perpendicularly or nearly so. They may be parallel but typically are not. Plazas in the orthogonal plan, unlike the Spanish plan, are set off at one end or on the side. The result is often one of blocks or units that are slightly rhomboid in shape. Blocks are typically defined by one or several *canchas*, the walled-in habitation compounds. The distribution of the orthogonal plan is limited, with examples found in Ollantaytambo, Chinchero, and central Cuzco and at slightly more distant settlements such as Hatuncolla and Chucuito near Lake Titicaca.

Radial layouts in Inca settlements are more widespread than the orthogonal plan. In radial planning, streets radiate outward from a central point, much in the same way that the *ceque* lines radiate from the Coricancha. As with grids, radial plans may define the entire site or only a portion of the whole. At Cuzco the central orthogonal core becomes a radial pattern at the outskirts. At Huánuco Pampa the street plan radiates outward from the *usnu* platform in the center of its large central plaza, subdividing the city into a number of units on the plaza's four sides. At Incahuasi, a garrison in Peru's Cañete Valley, the radial plan is used only in a part of the site. At many sites the radial plan appears to be an easy accommodation to landscape.

PLAZAS

A large open plaza formed the central core of Cuzco, as well as of most provincial centers. Cuzco's plaza, facing southwest, was called Huacaypata, meaning "terrace of repose," and it was mirrored by another plaza named Cusipata, meaning "fortunate terrace." The Huatanay River separated the two plazas. Huacaypata served as a setting for ceremonies and other displays. The Sapa Inca would have stood atop an *usnu*, or platform, in the middle of the plaza. The plaza also served as a hub for the four principal roads that divided the empire into its quadripartite divisions. Compounds surrounding the Huacaypata, many of whose walls are still visible, include the Hatuncancha, the *acllahuasi*, and the Cassana, which may have served as the 11th ruler Huayna Cápac's compound. In one of the most interesting gestures of spatial unification, as well being a demonstration of power, the plaza was filled with sand from the Pacific coast to a depth reportedly two and a half palms thick, into which gold and silver figurines were interred. Perhaps even more intriguing is that this sand was later used in the construction of the colonial cathedral, providing a complex layer of syncretism to contemporary understandings of the overall urban fabric.

LANDSCAPE ARCHITECTURE

Landscape architecture is less commented on than architecture itself despite numerous examples of sites where it was necessary for the Incas to remodel the earth, in one manner or another, to facilitate the desired design. It is not clear in all instances whether or not, or to what extent, the landscape was modified, but certain modifications are clear. Perhaps the clearest and most common example is Inca terracing. Terracing was used not simply for agricultural purposes, such as the dramatic examples at Pisac, Machu Picchu, and Wiñay Wina, or for purposes of aesthetic display, as was reported by the Spanish at Ollantaytambo, but also to level a site in preparation for construction of architectural and urban forms. In agricultural terracing the modified landscape is a clear functional expression that neatly conflates with ideas of power and control. In nonagricultural instances, excavations such as at Huánuco Pampa's plaza have uncovered terracing that suggests the eastern side of the plaza was leveled by earth fill in order to create a level field. Similarly, at Machu Picchu several terraces were used to level the main plaza.

Cuzco

In terms of landscape modified for urban construction, Cuzco is the exemplary case. Traditional accounts depict Pachacuti razing the entire village and reconstructing it from the ground up, which included the rerouting and channeling of its major rivers—perhaps in an effort to shape the metaphorical scheme of the city into a puma. Early imperial Inca landscape architecture often took form as a direct reflection of sacred geography; that is, it incorporated important ceremonial elements of the landscape into built form. This is most apparent in shrines. For instance, the shrine at Kenka near Cuzco, listed as a *huaca* in Cobo's list of *ceque* system shrines, incorporates a naturally occurring rock outcrop into a modified plan, sculpting a natural feature of the landscape into an elaborate, modeled form that is both ceremonially and ritually significant. The plan included sculpting a cave into the rock itself, creating an amphitheater-like space around a massive upright monolith, and carving numerous abstract forms such as zigzags, steps, and abstracted animal forms directly into the rock.

Urubamba Valley

By comparison, in later imperial architecture, most notably that built by the 11th ruler Huayna Cápac at his estates in the Urubamba Valley, the relation between the landscape and built form was turned on its head. The architectural historian Susan Niles has worked at Huayna Cápac's estates and is a leading scholar on Inca architecture. She suggests that the plans of Yucay, his estates in the Urubamba Valley, follow a different aesthetic, effectively inverting the basic principles of other estates and constructions. For example, framing is a common Inca architectural motif. At the valley sites of Pisac, Machu Picchu, and Ollantaytambo, this means that the Incas consciously constructed frames through which to view specific points in the landscape, such as distant mountain peaks, a particular rock or boulder, or a waterfall or other natural feature, all of which would have been considered sacred. This also means that the view was designed to engage outward across the broader landscape. At the two estates of Huayna Cápac mentioned above, this paradigm was inverted. Here, the architecture seems to reflect an inward turn, expressing a kind of introspection, and the framed views favor internal features, such as those of the palace itself, rather than the natural landscape. It is not certain why the estate was designed this way.

Machu Picchu

Machu Picchu, though known to local inhabitants, was "rediscovered" in 1911 by Yale historian Hiram Bingham and deserves special attention. Its fame, justifiably earned, is a result of its exemplifying many of the Incas' essential architectural expressions. Built by Pachacuti as a royal estate, Machu Picchu synthesizes a dramatic mountaintop setting

9.9 Aerial view of Machu Picchu (Ananda Cohen Suarez)

with the finest dressed-stone masonry, agricultural terracing, expertly crafted domestic architecture, discrete compounds, broad and complicated landscaping of the physical shape of the mountain itself, division of social space into *hanan* and *hurin* elements, use of architecture to frame and emphasize sight lines to sacred or important views, conscious management of access to processional space when moving in and around the site, and sculpting of sacred rock forms in the empire. Furthermore, the location itself marks the site as a sacred space or as a sacred artifact. Far below the mountaintop the Urubamba River practically encircles the site in its horseshoe meandering. Since the Urubamba's water originates in the sacred mountains of the Vilcabamba range, it is thus embedded with the symbolism of the act of creation, further reinforcing the site's sacredness by enveloping it in Inca mythology and cosmology.

READING

Stonemasonry

Carolyn Dean. *A Culture of Stone: Inka Perspectives on Rock* (Durham, N.C.: Duke University Press, 2010).

Graziano Gasparini and Louise Margolies, *Inca Architecture.* Translated by Patricia Lyons (Bloomington: Indiana University Press, 1980).

Stella E. Nair, *Stone against Stone: An Investigation into the Use of Stone Tools at Tiahuanaco.* M.A. diss., University of California, Berkeley, May 1997.

César Paternosto, *The Stone and the Thread: Andean Roots of Abstract Art* (Austin: University of Texas Press, 1989).

Jean-Pierre Protzen, *Inca Architecture and Construction at Ollantaytambo* (London: Oxford University Press, 1993).

———, "Inca Stonemasonry," *Scientific American* 254, no. 2 (1986): 94–105.

Jean-Pierre Protzen and Stella Nair, "Who Taught the Inca Stonemasons Their Skills? A Comparison of Tihuanaco and Inca Cut-Stone Masonry,"

Journal of the Society of Architectural Historians 56 (1997): 146–167.

Margaret Young-Sanchez et al., *Tiwanaku: Ancestors of the Inca* (Denver, Colo.: Denver Art Museum, 2004).

Masonry Architecture

D. Y. Arnold, "The House of Earth-Bricks and Inka-Stones: Gender, Memory, and Cosmos in Qakachaka," *Journal of Latin American Lore* 17 (1991): 3–69.

Juan de Betanzos, *Narrative of the Incas.* Translated and edited by Roland Hamilton and Dana Buchanan (Austin: University of Texas Press, 1996).

Jean-Francois Bouchard, *Contribution á l'étude de l'architecture Inca: Établisements de la vallée du Rio Vilcanota-Urubamba* (Paris: Éditions de la Maison des Sciences de l'Homme, 1983).

Carolyn S. Dean, "Creating a Ruin in Colonial Cusco: Sacsayhuamán and What Was Made of It," *Andean Past* 5 (1998): 161–183.

Javier F. Escalante Moscoso, *Arquitectura prehispánica en los Andes bolivianos* (La Paz, Bolivia: CIMA, 1993).

Valerie Fraser, *The Architecture of Conquest: Building in the Viceroyalty of Peru, 1535–1635.* (Cambridge: Cambridge University Press, 1990).

———, "Art and Architecture in Latin America." In *The Cambridge Companion to Modern Latin American Culture,* edited by John King, 202–235 (Cambridge: Cambridge University Press, 2004).

Teresa Gisbert and José de Mesa. *Arquitectura andina, 1530–1830* (La Paz: Embajada de España en Bolivia, 1997).

John Hemming and Edward Ranney, *Monuments of the Inca* (Albuquerque: University of New Mexico Press, 1992).

Federico Kauffman Doig, *Influencias "inca" en la arquitectura peruana del virreinato: "El fenómeno huamanquino"* (Lima, Peru: Universidad Nacional Mayor de San Marcos, 1965).

Ann Kendall, *Aspects of Inca Architecture: Description, Function, and Chronology.* Bar International Series 242, 2 vols. (Oxford: B.A.R., 1985).

George Kubler, *The Art and Architecture of Ancient America: The Mexican, Maya, and Andean Peoples* (Harmondsworth, U.K.: Penguin Books, 1975).

Stella Elise Nair, *Of Remembering and Forgetting: The Architecture of Chinchero, Peru from Thupa 'Inka to the Spanish Occupation.* Ph.D. diss., University of California, Berkeley, Spring 2003.

———, "Witnessing the Invisibility of Inca Architecture in Colonial Peru," *Building and Landscapes* 14 (2007): 50–65.

Esther Pasztory, "Andean Aesthetics." In *The Spirit of Ancient Peru: Treasures from the Museo Arqueológico Rafael Larco Herrera*, edited by Kathleen Berrin, 61–69 (London: Thames & Hudson, 1997).

Jean-Pierre Protzen, "Inca Architecture." In *The Inca World: The Development of Pre-Columbian Peru, A.D. 1000–1534*, edited by Laura Laurencich Minelli, 193–217 (Norman: University of Oklahoma Press, 1992).

———, *Inca Architecture and Construction at Ollantaytambo* (London: Oxford University Press, 1993).

Building Functions

Brian S. Bauer and David S. P. Dearborn, *Astronomy and Empire in the Ancient Andes* (Austin: University of Texas Press, 1995).

———, *The Development of the Inca State* (Austin: University of Texas Press, 1992).

Terence D'Altroy, *The Incas* (London: Blackwell, 2002).

Garcilaso de la Vega, El Inca, *Royal Commentaries of the Inca and General History of Peru.* Translated by Harold V. Livermore. (Austin: University of Texas Press, 1966).

Felipe Guamán Poma de Ayala, *El primer nueva corónica y buen gobierno.* Edited by John Murra and Rolena Adorno. 3 vols. (Mexico: Siglo Veintiuno, 1992).

———, *Letter to a King: A Picture History of the Inca Civilisation.* Translated and edited by Christopher Dilke (London: George Allen & Unwin, 1978).

Alexander von Humboldt, *Vues des cordillères et monuments des peuples indigènes de l'Amérique* (Paris: Legrand, Pomey et Cruzet, 1813).

Gordon F. McEwan, "Investigations at the Pikillacta Site: A Provincial Huari Center in the Valley of Cuzco." In *Huari Administrative Structure: Prehistoric Monumental Architecture and State Government*, edited by William H. Isbell and Gordon McEwan, 93–119 (Washington, D.C.: Dumbarton Oaks, 1991).

Jerry D. Moore, "The Archaeology of Plazas and the Proxemics of Ritual: Three Andean Traditions," *American Anthropologist* 98, no. 4 (1996): 789–802.

Elisabeth L. Moorehead, "Highland Inca Architecture in Adobe," *Ñawpa Pacha* 16 (1982): 65–94.

Craig Morris, "The Infrastructure of Inka Control in the Peruvian Central Highlands." In *The Inca and Aztec States, 1400–1800: Anthropology and History*, edited by George A. Collier, Renato I. Rosaldo, and John D. Wirth, 153–171 (New York: Academic Press, 1982).

———, "Inka Strategies of Incorporation and Governance." In *Archaic States*, edited by Gary M. Feinman and Joyce Marcus, 293–309 (Santa Fe, N.Mex.: School of American Research Press, 1998).

———, "Master Design of the Inca," *Natural History* 85, no. 10 (1976): 58–67.

———, "State Settlements in Tawantinsuyu: A Strategy of Compulsory Urbanism." In *Contemporary Archaeology: A Guide to Theory and Contributions*, edited by Mark P. Leone, 393–401 (Carbondale: Southern Illinois University Press, 1972).

Susan A. Niles, "Inca Architecture and the Sacred Landscape." In *The Ancient Americas: Art from the Sacred Landscapes*, edited by Richard Townsend, 347–357 (Chicago: Art Institute of Chicago, 1992).

———, "The Nature of Inca Royal Estates." In *Machu Picchu: Unveiling the Mystery of the Incas*, edited by Richard L. Burger and Lucy C. Salazar, 49–70 (New Haven, Conn.: Yale University Press, 2004).

———, "The Provinces in the Heartland: Stylistic Variation and Architectural Innovation Near Cuzco." In *Provincial Inca: Archaeological and Ethnohistorical Assessment of the Impact of the Inca State*, edited by Michael A. Malpass, 146–176 (Iowa City: University of Iowa Press, 1993).

———, *The Shape of Inca History* (Iowa City: University of Iowa Press, 1999).

Pedro Pizarro, *Relation of the Discovery and Conquest of the Kingdoms of Peru*. Translated and edited by Philip Ainsworth Means (New York: Cortes Society, 1921).

Urban/Site Planning

Brian S. Bauer, *Ancient Cuzco: Heartland of the Inca* (Austin: University of Texas Press, 2004).

———, *The Sacred Landscape of the Inca: The Cusco Ceque System* (Austin: University of Texas Press, 1998)

Hiram Bingham, "The Discovery of Machu Picchu," *Harper's Magazine*, April 1913.

———, *Inca Land: Explorations in the Highlands of Peru*. 1912. Reprint, (New York: Houghton Mifflin, 1922).

———, *Lost City of the Incas: The Story of Machu Picchu and Its Builders* (New York: Atheneum, 1948).

———, *Machu Picchu: A Citadel of the Incas* (New Haven, Conn.: Yale University Press, 1930).

———, "Preliminary Report of the Yale Peruvian Expedition," *Bulletin of the American Geographical Society* 44, no. 1 (1912): 20–26.

Richard L. Burger and Lucy C. Salazar, *Machu Picchu: Unveiling the Mystery of the Incas* (New Haven, Conn.: Yale University Press, 2004).

R. Alan Covey, *How the Incas Built Their Heartland* (Ann Arbor: University of Michigan Press, 2005).

Tom Cummins, "A Tale of Two Cities: Cuzco, Lima, and the Construction of Colonial Representation." In *Converging Cultures: Art and Identity in Spanish America*, edited by Diane Fane, 157–170 (New York: Brooklyn Museum/Harry Abrams, Inc., 1996).

Ian S. Farrington, "Ritual Geography, Settlement Patterns and the Characterization of the Provinces of the Inka Heartland," *World Archaeology* 23 (1992): 368–385.

Jonathan Haas et al., eds., *The Origins and Development of the Andean State* (Cambridge: Cambridge University Press, 1987).

Adriana von Hagen and Craig Morris, *The Cities of the Ancient Andes* (London: Thames & Hudson, 1998).

Emilio Harth-Terré, "Fundación de la ciudad incaica," *Revista Histórica* (Lima) 16, nos. 1–2 (1943): 98–123.

John Hemming, *The Conquest of the Incas* (London: MacMillan, 1970).

Jay Kinsbruner, *The Colonial Spanish-American City: Urban Life in the Age of Atlantic Capitalism* (Austin: University of Texas Press, 2005).

Colin McEwan and Maarten van de Guchte, "Ancestral Time and Sacred Space in Inca State Ritual." In *The Ancient Americas: Art from Sacred Landscapes*, edited by Richard F. Townshend, 359–373 (Chicago: Art Institute of Chicago, 1992).

Jerry D. Moore, *Architecture and Power in the Ancient Andes* (Cambridge: Cambridge University Press, 2005).

Craig Morris and Adriana von Hagen, *The Inka Empire and Its Andean Origins* (New York: Abbeville Press, 1993).

Craig Morris and Donald E. Thompson, *Huanuco Pampa: An Inca City and Its Hinterland* (London: Thames & Hudson, 1985).

Michael Moseley, "Chan Chan: Andean Alternative to the Pre-Industrial City," *Science* 187 (1975): 219–225.

John Rowe, "Inca Culture at the Time of the Spanish Conquest." In *Handbook of South American Indians*. Vol. 2, *The American Civilizations*, edited by Julian H. Steward. Bureau of American Ethnology, Bulletin no. 143, 183–330 (Washington, D.C.: Smithsonian Institution, 1946).

———, *An Introduction to the Archaeology of Cuzco* 27, no. 2 (Cambridge: Peabody Museum of American Archaeology and Ethnology, 1944).

———, "What Kind of Settlement Was Inca Cuzco?" *Ñawpa Pacha* 5 (1982): 59–77.

Kenneth R. Wright and Alfredo Valecia Z., *Machu Picchu: A Civil Engineering Marvel* (Reston, Va.: American Society of Civil Engineers, 2000).

Landscape Architecture

Margaret MacLean, *Sacred Land, Sacred Water: Inca Landscape Planning in the Cuzco Area*. Ph.D. diss., Department of Anthropology, University of California, Berkeley, 1986.

Jerry D. Moore, *Cultural Landscapes in the Ancient Andes* (Gainesville: University Press of Florida, 2005).

Johan Reinhard, *Machu Picchu: The Sacred Center* (Lima, Peru: Nuevas Imágenes, 1991).

Jeanette E. Sherbondy, *The Canal System of Hanan Cuzco.* Ph.D. diss., University of Illinois, Urbana, 1982.

———, "Water Ideology in Inca Ethnogenesis." In *Andean Cosmologies through Time: Persistence and Emergence*, edited by Robert V. H. Dover, Katherine Seibold, and John McDowell, 46–66 (Bloomington: Indiana University Press, 1992).

Rebecca Stone-Miller, *Art of the Andes.* 2nd ed. (London: Thames & Hudson, 2002).

Maarten van de Guchte, *"Carving the World": Inca Monumental Sculpture and Landscape.* Ph.D. diss., Department of Anthropology, University of Illinois, Urbana-Champaign (Ann Arbor, Mich.: University Microfilms, 1990).

10

THE CALENDAR, ASTRONOMY, AND MATHEMATICS

Inca cosmology—their understanding of the universe, its origins, and its structures—developed in relation to similar, long-held Andean physical and metaphysical traditions. Grounded in a sense of communication with the natural environment, especially the heavens above, Inca belief placed paramount importance on the Sun and Moon. Sun and Moon worship antedates the Incas and in highland Peru finds potential correlates in the earlier Wari and Tiwanaku civilizations, which were centered in the central Peruvian highlands and at Lake Titicaca, respectively. These civilizations had long disappeared (ca. 1000–1100) by the time the Incas began their imperial phase, but some of their traditions seem to have survived. Though more work needs to be done to determine which Inca cosmological traditions were borrowed and to what extent they were implemented, it seems likely that touches of these early states influenced the Incas. For example, pre-Inca sacrificial material excavated from Lake Titicaca's Islands of the Sun and Moon suggests a long history of Sun and Moon worship. Further evidence of the importance of the Sun and Moon in Inca traditions is located in certain versions of their origin stories, some of which discuss the origin of the Sun and Moon, and the origin of the first Inca peoples, occurring at Lake Titicaca.

By the time the Incas conquered these regions, the Sapa Inca (Inca king) was believed to be the son of the Sun and his wife a descendant of the Moon; thus, imperial power and origin and creation myths were inextricably tied to solar and lunar observation. Suffice it to say that Inca astronomical observation and calendrics are significant strings of thought intricately woven into the larger fabric of Inca imperial power manipulations. With the development of Inca state religion dedicated to the Sun, the insinuation of heavenly observation into the daily lives of Inca subjects only solidified.

In addition to the relationship of astronomy and calendrics to Inca power and religious structures, it is important to note that both are equally invested in—indeed, inextricable from—Inca agricultural practice. The following descriptions highlight that information specific to astronomy, and it will be clear that all descriptions of astronomy are couched in a discussion of agricultural practice. That the Incas used their knowledge of astronomy and calendars to facilitate scheduled, efficient planting and harvesting practices should come as no surprise; what may be surprising is how intertwined, how inseparable, all the factors become. Furthermore, reconstructing Inca astronomical practice is complicated, as is everything else, by the lack of an indigenous writing system. To rectify this the modern researcher must often combine historical evidence with astronomical knowledge and in turn combine that with archaeological, architectural, and topographic data to get at an understanding of what the Incas were doing when they were looking at the sky.

Of particular import are the ethnohistoric records of Spanish and Quechua chroniclers who noted that the Incas were stargazing and measuring heavenly movements. These sources are complemented by recent archaeological and archaeoastronomical investigations in order to ascertain a broad perspective on what the Incas were looking at when they gazed toward the sky. It should be considered, however, that Spaniards who recorded astronomical information themselves had little training or understanding in the intricate workings of celestial objects, although some would have been familiar with them from a navigational perspective (coming across the Atlantic on ships, a few would have been familiar with maritime reliance on stars and planets). The Incas had a complex interpretation of the sciences, and it is important to understand how it affected the structure of their calendar, the various astronomical occurrences as observed by the Incas, the literature relevant to Inca astronomy, the Cuzco *ceque* system specific to its astronomical correspondence, Inca mathematics, and the development of the *quipu* in its functions as a mnemonic recording device relevant to counting and statistics.

CALENDAR

The term *calendar* has at least two meanings: a conceptual scheduling system and the symbolic representation of that system. There are numerous references to Inca calendrics in colonial-era sources, though few are in complete accord as to how the

Incas managed either the conceptual or symbolic framework. One major point of conflict is whether the Inca calendar followed lunar months, solar months, or a combination of the two. In general, the Inca calendar was a mechanism to regulate social activities in time and space. Because the sources disagree on the use of solar and lunar calendars, both will be discussed in brief below.

The Calendar According to Betanzos

Juan de Betanzos's *Narrative of the Incas*, finished in 1557, provides a detailed account of the creation of the Inca calendar. According to Betanzos, the Inca calendar was created by the ninth ruler on the traditional king lists, Pachacuti, whose name translates as "upheaval" or "world reversal." The annual calendar, laid out in months that Pachacuti had imagined, consisted of 12 months of 30 days each for a total cycle of 360 days. This calendar is inseparable from the Inca festival or ceremonial calendar, much of which was marked by sacrifices. The annual calendar was established in accord with solar cycles, while the ritual calendar largely referenced lunar cycles. Discrepancies between the two could have been remedied by adding short intercalation periods, meaning they added leap days or weeks, to bring the calendars into synchrony. At the same time that Pachacuti created the calendar, he also created what was called the *pacha unan changa*. This was a type of clock that helped keep track of the calendar and, specifically, when to sow and prepare the fields for agriculture. The calendar, with its complementary overlay of rituals and feasts, is thus very closely tied to the agricultural cycle. As managers and readers of the "clocks," the Incas became associated with the passage of time itself, further legitimating the state and its rulers.

Pachacuti established his clocks, according to Betanzos's narration, by watching the Sun every morning and afternoon of every month of the year while taking note of the times to plant and harvest. When the Sun went down, Pachacuti made note of the Moon according to when it was new, full, and waning. The clock itself was apparently made of cut stone placed on top of the highest hills set in line with where the Sun rose and where it went down. Similarly, Pachacuti constructed eight sets of stone pillars, set side by side in pairs, and placed these at certain visible points on high, distant hills. On certain days the Sun would rise or set between a specific pair and would thereby mark the progress and movement of the Sun during the year. The days most likely marked by these pillars are the June solstice and a specific sunset in August, which would have marked the day to initiate the planting season. Commoners would then be able to calculate the appropriate time for planting. The point of observation for these calculations would most likely have been from a point in Cuzco on the Huacaypata, the central plaza in the city.

Lunar Calendar

A lunar calendar divides the year according to the phases of the Moon. This is a common occurrence in many ancient societies with established calendars. Lunar cycles are either sidereal or synodic. Sidereal is understood to be the Moon's revolution in the sky in relation to a star's position, or 27.3 days; synodic is understood as months based on the phases of the Moon, or 29.5 days. Thirteen sidereal months would equal a 354.9-day year, and 12 synodic months would equal 354 days, neither of which, of course, correlates with the 365¼-day solar year, making the intercalation of a short "month" necessary. If the calibration is not done, the correlation of the annual calendar and the ritual calendar would very rapidly cease to overlap, and planting correlates would soon occur in winter.

LUNAR SYMBOLISM

In the Andes the Moon is associated with the feminine. The most common name for the Moon is *quilla* ("moon" or "month"), though it is sometimes called Mama Quilla (Mother Moon), Warmi Mayor (Principal Wife), or Coya Cápac (Noble Queen). The Moon is typically thought of as the female counterpart to the masculine Sun and therefore assumes the roles of the mother, the wife, and the queen.

10.1 An Inca coat of arms depicting the Sun, Moon, stars, and Pacariqtambo, the sacred cave featured in the culture's origin myths (Felipe Guamán Poma de Ayala)

Biological Metaphor It has also been suggested that the phases of the Moon were understood in reference to a biological metaphor. In this context the full moon *(pura)* corresponds with the "adult," the half moon *(malqo)* with the "adolescent," a quarter moon *(huahua)* with the "baby," and a crescent moon *(uña paqarin)* with "just born" or the "infant."

Cápac Raymi The Inca annual calendar was closely calibrated to a ritual and festival calendar. Cápac Raymi, which took place before, during, and after the full moon following the first new moon after the December solstice, was perhaps the most important festival. During this ritual members from the 10 *panaqas*, or kin groups, of Cuzco came together and sacrificed 10 llamas of different colors

to the health of the king. Later, each *panaqa* burned a tunic dedicated to a particular deity.

Solar Calendar

The solar year is demarcated by the return of the Sun to its specific solstice point every 365¼ days. At these points the Sun in effect turns back on itself and reverses its direction north to south or south to north. At the solstice the Sun is at its greatest distance from the equator. The disparity between the solar calendar and the lunar calendar noted above is the cause of some confusion. For the Incas it meant recalibrating their "clocks" or their understanding of the movement of time, by adding "months" to keep the annual and ritual calendars in line.

As mentioned above in the section on Betanzos, the Incas constructed stone pillars on the hills above Cuzco in order to keep track of the Sun's movements. At least some of these pillars survived the Spanish conquest by a hundred years, so they are mentioned in sources other than Betanzos. Subsequent accounts confirm their existence but muddy their understanding, calling into question their number, spacing, and location. For example, Betanzos and the chroniclers Ondegardo and Cobo indicate that there may have been 14 pillars in total, whereas El Inca Garcilaso mentions a total of 16. Lacking both unanimity in the sources and solid archaeological data limits the conclusions that can be drawn, yet it is most likely that the pillars functioned as recorders of the solstices. Whether they recorded the movement of other celestial bodies, such as the Pleiades (an easily visible star cluster on the constellation Taurus), or marked the equinoxes or the August planting ritual is a little more speculative.

SOLAR OBSERVATION AND THE CALENDAR

Solar observations were marked against the horizon. They were probably watched from a central point in Cuzco, the most likely location being the *usnu* (stone platform) in the central plaza. Observing and marking both solstices and equinoxes were important ritual considerations in relation to the festival and agricultural calendars, although there is some discrepancy in the chronicles as to whether they were strictly observed. Solar observation could also have made use of shadow casting or light casting by gnomons or in certain openings such as windows or even in caves. The position of the shadow cast would thus be indicative of the day, similar to a sundial.

Measuring Time   The Incas had names for the year *(huata)*, month *(quilla)*, and day *(punchao)*. *Quilla* is the same word used for Moon, and *punchao* is the same word used for the golden Sun idol stored in the Coricancha. The Incas did not have words to distinguish the days of the week, and whether they adhered to the idea of the "week" is debated. Beyond Cuzco there is some possibility that the concept of the "week" registered generally, as there is mention of a 10-day week in some parts of the Andes, but nothing similar in the Cuzco region. Time was not recollected according to hours and minutes and divided incrementally against the markings of a clock. Rather, the Incas judged time by the duration of an event or the interval of a common task. Thus, an amount of time might be expressed as the time it takes to walk to the next village or, commonly, the time it takes to boil water.

Sarmiento on Measuring Time   There is a passage in the writings of Pedro Sarmiento de Gamboa that is reminiscent of descriptions of the horizon pillars, although his description references the casting of light instead of the casting of shadow. He describes four poles separated from one another by two sticks on a hill to the east of Cuzco. Holes in the top of each allowed the Sun to shine through; marking and following the advance of the Sun as it shone through the holes allowed the Incas to measure time with specific regard to seasonal planting and harvesting. Sarmiento says these sticks were later replaced by stone.

The Horizon Pillars above Cuzco   According to the eyewitness accounts of an unknown Spaniard referred to as either the Anonymous Chronicler or the Anonymous Conqueror, there were four solar pillars on the horizon above Cuzco. He indicates that two outer pillars were 200 paces apart, while two inner pillars were 50 paces apart. According to this

anonymous source, the pillars were used to delineate the agricultural season: The Sun passing the first pillar indicated that it was time to plant vegetables at the highest altitudes. When the Sun first entered the space between the two inner pillars, which always corresponded with August, it was time to plant in Cuzco. Then, he says, when the Sun was in the middle of the two inner pillars, as seen from the *usnu* in the middle of Huacaypata plaza, this indicated it was time to plant in the valleys adjoining Cuzco. Recent archaeoastronomical research, which is the study of astronomy in ancient cultures, suggests that the distance of "200 paces" between the two outside pillars in their presumed locations on the horizon, coordinated with the distance to the viewing space in the plaza, translates into a time span of 15 days for the sunset to migrate across the distance. This would have been a reasonable delay in staggering the planting periods at the various altitudes.

SOLAR SYMBOLISM

The most common name for the Sun is Inti, and the Spanish word for the Sun, *sol*, is also very common in the literature. Just as the Moon is associated with the feminine, the Sun is associated with the masculine. Various scholars have recorded names that equate the Sun with Nuestro Dios (Our Lord), Jesús Cristo (Jesus Christ), Huayna Cápac (the 11th Inca king), and Manco Cápac (the first Inca king). In a day-to-day sense perhaps the most relevant solar connection was between the Sun and the Sapa Inca, who was considered to be the son of the Sun. Another significant manifestation of solar symbolism took physical form in the shape of a golden disk, referred to as *punchao*, that was stored at the Coricancha and displayed during the day and "put to sleep" at night.

ASTRONOMY

Aside from solar and lunar observation, the Incas paid attention to and built an elaborate mythology around the movement of numerous other celestial phenomena. For instance, they took special note of

Venus, a collection of stars known as Pleiades, both the Milky Way and the dark spaces in the Milky Way, and other stars, which they used for both secular and religious purposes.

Astronomy in the *Huarochirí Manuscript*

The *Huarochirí Manuscript* is an important colonial-era document for three reasons: It was written by an indigenous author, it records pre-Hispanic Andean religious traditions, and it is written in Quechua, the language of the Incas. It reflects the broad history of a territory not too distant from the Inca capital of Cuzco that was folded into the Inca Empire. Its 31 chapters recount a remote, mythical age; detail the Andean relationship to *huacas*, or sacred places or things; and tell of both Inca and Spanish imperial aggression. For the purposes here the information specific to astronomy is outlined below.

The *Huarochirí Manuscript* suggests that Andeans saw patterns in both positive and negative space; that is, observation accounted for the forms of stars and star clusters as well as the dark space between visible light. According to the manuscript, at least some of these dark spaces contained the power of animation. The Inca scholar Gary Urton has referred to these as "dark cloud constellations." Elsewhere it is suggested that the Incas believed that all the animals and birds on Earth had their counterparts, or likenesses, in the heavens; it was the responsibility of these celestial likenesses to procreate and augment their earthly counterparts. The name given in the manuscript for this "animator" is *yacana*.

The manuscript also accounts for the presence of the Milky Way and the Pleiades in the Inca cosmological system. The *yacana*, mentioned above, resides within the Milky Way. Although the Incas did not refer to it as the "Milky Way," they conceived of it as a cosmic river through which water circulates back into the atmosphere after having run down to the sea. The *yacana* is also linked metaphorically to llamas. The manuscript says that it descends at night, when no one is looking, and drinks all the water out of the ocean. This might refer to the period of the year that coincides with the dry season, when the dark cloud constellation is below the horizon and thus not visible. According to the scholar Frank Salomon, it may also refer metaphorically to the way llamas descend from higher slopes to drink water from lower-lying water holes.

The manuscript discusses the Pleiades in reference to agricultural forecasting, suggesting that when the constellation is visibly at its largest, crops will be "plenty," but that at its smallest, the people are in "for a hard time." Although the *Huarochirí Manuscript* offers a limited amount of information regarding astronomy, it is important in that what is offered is done so in an Andean voice. Similarly important is that the observations are strategically integrated into earthbound cycles specific to survival, such as agriculture, ones that are simultaneously routine and necessary. In this sense the appearance and movement of the stars and constellations is tangibly understood in relation to agriculture and survival as well as metaphorically understood in relation to systems of meaning in their immediate environment.

"ASTRONOMERS" IN THE *HUAROCHIRÍ MANUSCRIPT*

Elsewhere the *Huarochirí Manuscript* validates the claim that the Incas dedicated and trained specific individuals to observe the movements of the Sun and Moon. The manuscript refers to these individuals as *yanca*, which might be casually translated as "astronomer." (Guamán Poma de Ayala called them "astrologers.") The manuscript suggests that these persons watched shadows cast by gnomons. It says, "This man observes the course of the Sun from a wall constructed with perfect alignment. When the rays of the Sun touch this calibrated wall, he [proclaimed] to the people, 'Now we must go'; or if they don't he'd say 'Tomorrow is the time.'" It should be noted that the wall would have been built specifically for use in measuring time and that the time measured, here the departure, would have been in relation to the planting of crops. It should also be noted that the manuscript suggests that these persons were present in all the villages, not simply in Cuzco or other important centers. By closely

10.2 *A drawing of an astrologer. The movements of the Sun, Moon, and other celestial bodies were closely observed.* (Felipe Guamán Poma de Ayala)

watching the movement of celestial bodies, these persons were therefore accountable for the temporal maintenance of the ritual and festival calendar.

Zenith/Antizenith Passages of the Sun

The zenith passage is the point where the Sun passes directly overhead. The day on which this occurs varies depending on where the viewer is in relation to the equator. Unlike many Inca celestial observations, the notation of a zenith passage is not a horizon phenomenon, meaning that it is not an occurrence that could be marked on the landscape; rather, it is an occurrence marked by the absence of cast shadow. Zenith events get little mention in the

sources; thus, there is little known for certain about their importance to the Incas.

The antizenith is the moment when the Sun passes directly underfoot. While it is not an observable phenomenon, its timing can be calculated by noting the day when the Sun rises or sets 180 degrees from the position where it rose or set on the zenith. There has been much recent speculation on the prevalence of antizenith markings because its dates fall somewhat close to important Inca planting and festival dates. More research is needed, however, to clarify the extent and limits of these hypotheses.

EL INCA GARCILASO ON ZENITH PASSAGE

A passage in the chronicle of Garcilaso de la Vega provides documentation on the practice of observing the zenith passage. Describing Inca equinox observation, Garcilaso notes that the Incas verified the equinox through the observation of the Sun acting against richly decorated columns in the plazas or patios of the temples of the Sun. Priests monitored every day the position of the shadow cast by the Sun in relation to the pillar. A circle was drawn around the pillar, and a string was used to draw a line through the circle to bisect it along an east-west axis. Points were plotted along the line indicating certain days. As the shadow advanced along the line, the priests knew the equinox was approaching. When the Sun cast no shadow over the line at noon, they knew that it was the equinox. Knowledge of the equinox was then coordinated with ritual, festival, and agricultural necessities.

Houses of the Sun

As inveterate Sun worshippers the Incas made sure the Sun and the movement of the Sun were worshipped in numerous ways. Many *huacas* in the *ceque* system are referred to as "houses of the Sun." Pillars were built to monitor the Sun's progression in order to mark the periods for sowing and harvesting. Golden icons were fabricated to reflect its importance. Temples were built in its honor. Another significant manifestation of the Incas' relation to the Sun is encoded in the construction of these temples. They were temples in name only and were constructed to, in a sense, engage in the process of the Sun. Through alignment and through internalized features, such as windows and doorways that align with solstitial observation, these structures embodied the idea of the Sun. Two significant examples are mentioned below.

SOLSTITIAL OBSERVATIONS FROM THE CORICANCHA

The chronicles mention that the Sapa Inca worshipped the Sun from the Coricancha. It makes sense, then, that some physical infrastructure was devised for such an event. Recent research suggests that alignments taken from the Coricancha from a position where it is believed the Sapa Inca would have made any astronomical observations correspond to a date that is one lunar month before the June solstice, around May 25, when a new crescent moon rises and when some chroniclers claimed the Incas celebrated their new year. The alignment also correlates closely with where the star group Pleiades rises. These alignments were made in reference to extant walls that, perhaps curiously, are not placed at 90 degrees to each other but slightly askew, raising the question of why the Incas would create an obvious asymmetry.

There is also some indication that the direction the Coricancha faces, together with this particular alignment, also coincides with the direction of a *ceque* line that was believed to point close to where the Pleiades rose. While all the calculations together are somewhat arcane, they suggest that the if the Inca king saw the first crescent moon after May 25, he would know that the first full moon after first seeing the Pleiades rise will always define the month that includes the June solstice. In effect, this system acts as a timekeeping device by which the Sun, Moon, and stars are incorporated into the design of the royal building. Understanding and even anticipating these events could then be used as a demonstration of both knowledge and power.

MACHU PICCHU: THE TORREÓN

The Torreón (also referred to as the Observatory) at Machu Picchu, an estate associated with the ninth Inca ruler, Pachacuti, is a rock outcropping that includes superb examples of Inca masonry, with an interior space dominated by a large altar carved from the stone prominence itself. A cut into the altar aligns precisely with the June solstice sunrise. A masonry wall with windows encircles the stone altar. It has been calculated that light entering through the window will strike the cut in the altar for a period of two months. As the Sun advanced along the cut, the Incas were able to monitor time. A similar Torreón-like altar structure is found at Pisac, an estate also associated with Pachacuti, though the walls are too degraded to know if windows were present.

Zenith Passage Observation There are two windows in the curved wall of the Torreón. The first, mentioned above, admits light over the altar rock only around the solstice, whereas sunlight enters through the other window for most of the year. However, only for a brief period does sunlight enter both windows, around the zenith passage, strongly suggesting that the Incas were marking that phenomenon.

Stellar Observation

While solar observation is well covered in colonial-era sources, especially as it coincides with ritual and ceremonial obligations, accounts of stellar observation, though numerous, are less thorough. Most of the standard chronicles make at least passing reference to stellar observation. The most frequently cited sources are Ondegardo's 1585 abstract for the now-lost *Tratado y averiguación sobre los errores y supersticiones de los indios* and Cobo's 1653 *Historia del Nuevo Mundo*. It is important to consider, when consulting these Spanish documents, that the 16th- and 17th-century Spaniard had a particular understanding of the cosmos, which inevitably influenced the perception, naming, and structuring of their Inca sources. For example, the typical Spaniard of the day believed that stars were in a sense globally inclusive, meaning that they understood the stars to rotate on the outermost sphere of the universe. By definition, then, the Spaniard understood the universe to be both limited and enclosed. It is also important to note that the Incas did not distinguish between stars and planets. In Quechua, the lingua franca of the empire, both the brightest stars and planets are called by the same name—*chasca*, meaning "shaggy hair."

STELLAR OBSERVATION IN ONDEGARDO

According to Juan Polo de Ondegardo, stars were venerated because they held power and could be of assistance to those in need. When reading Ondegardo, it quickly becomes apparent that there is a particularly important relationship between stars and animals. For example, Ondegardo mentions that herders worshipped and sacrificed to a star they called Urcuchillay, which the Spanish called Lyra. The Incas said it was a llama and was related to the conservation of the herd. Ondegardo also mentions that people who reside in the forests "worship another star they call Chuquichinchay, which they say is a jaguar in whose charge are the jaguars, bears, and pumas. . . ," and "they also worship another star which they call Ancochinchay, which protects other animals." Ondegardo also mentions that the Incas worshipped a star named Machacuay, said to be in charge of snakes and serpents, to avoid harm from the animals. He goes on to say that the Incas "in general . . . believed that for each [kind of] animal and bird on earth there was a similar one in the sky who was in charge of its procreation and increase." In other words, according to the Spaniard, these stellar animal referents acted as both doubles and agents responsible for the continued reproduction of the earthly beasts.

STELLAR OBSERVATION IN COBO

Father Bernabé Cobo was aware of, and probably had a copy of, Ondegardo's original manuscript. Accordingly, many details of stellar observation not present in Ondegardo's abstract are reiterated in Cobo's text. Like Ondegardo, Cobo relates that the veneration of stars was as a result of the Inca belief in their agency for animal life on earth. Cobo refers to this as a "second cause" and was meant "to look after the preservation of each kind of thing." Also like Ondegardo, Cobo places much of this power in the Pleiades star cluster, but he goes further and says the Pleiades was referred to as "mother" and was considered a major *huaca*, or sacred thing, in all the provinces. Cobo, like Ondegardo, also mentions the worship of Urcuchillay, Chuquichinchay, and Machacuay in the same context. Cobo mentions a number of other stars or clusters but does not offer additional information to clarify what those stars are or what they might reference.

ASTRONOMY AND STELLAR CONNECTION IN PACHACUTI YAMQUI

Juan de Santacruz Pachacuti Yamqui Salcamaygua, like Felipe Guamán Poma de Ayala and the unknown author of the *Huarochirí Manuscript*, was an indigenous author sympathetic to the native Andean in the postconquest period. Writing in the early 17th century, Pachacuti Yamqui recorded indigenous beliefs, including information specific to astronomy that is not recorded in the Spanish chronicles. Pachacuti Yamqui is perhaps best known for a drawing that is said to represent a wall of the Coricancha, the sacred temple of the Incas, located in Cuzco. This drawing (see figure 6.7, page 141) is typically referred to as a cosmological representation of the Inca universe; eight figures in the drawing appear to be astronomical references.

The overall design of the drawing is contained within an outline that is similar in shape to the facade of a gabled house. At the top of this field, above an empty oval that represents the creator god Viracocha, is a cross of five stars. The cross is made up of three vertical stars attached by a line with one star on either side of the central star. These stars are thought to represent the stars in Orion.

Beneath the five-star construction and to the left of the empty oval is an image of the Sun. To the right of the oval is an image of the Moon. In Inca cosmology the Sun is a masculine deity/principle, and the Moon is a feminine deity/principle. These images thus establish a binary reading of masculine and feminine division: The images that lie below the image of the Sun are masculine, while the images that fall below the image of the Moon are considered feminine. On the right side, beneath the Moon, there is an image of an evening star called Chuquechinchay, which elsewhere Pachacuti

Yamqui describes as "an animal of many colors which is said to be the lord of the Otorongos [large cats]." Similar to the descriptions in Ondegardo and Cobo mentioned above, the relation between animals on Earth and animals in the sky is made concrete. The image of the cat may be a reference to a dark cloud constellation. Beneath the Sun, on the left side, is a morning star, a cluster of summer stars, and one other isolated star. The evening and morning stars might be Venus, and the star cluster might refer to the Pleiades.

Finally, beneath the oval is a group of five stars, four of which are in the shape of an X, while the fifth is located just above the group. It is not known whether this group refers specifically to the star group known as the Southern Cross or to celestial crosses in general. Furthermore, recent literature suggests that the vertical cleaving representing the masculine-feminine division is complemented by a horizontal division into three parts representing the heavens (top), the earth (middle), and the underworld (bottom).

CUZCO *CEQUE* SYSTEM: ASTRONOMICAL AFFILIATION

The Cuzco *ceque* system is a network of shrines, or *huacas*, linked across the landscape by *ceques* (lines) and radiating outward from a central point located in or near the Coricancha, the sacred temple in Cuzco. The Jesuit chronicler Cobo provided the most extensive accounting of the *ceques* in *Inca Religion and Customs*. It is generally believed that Cobo's account is based on the now-lost text written by Ondegardo. In his work Cobo catalogs at least 328 *huacas*, including each one's physical description, location, social affiliations, mythical history, and the sacrifices practiced at each. In this respect the *ceque* system is an elaborate ritual complex tying together social, imperial, and cosmic elements. The system, too, has numerous astronomical and calen-

drical associations, though this is still debated in the literature.

The *huacas* take numerous forms. Cobo lists springs, stones, hills, mountaintops, palaces, temples, fields, tombs, ravines, caves, quarries, stone seats, sunset markers, trees, and roads as being *huacas*. The two most important *huacas* were the Coricancha and Huanacauri, the latter an uncarved stone that was a symbol of Inca mythohistory. To best visualize the *huacas* as they relate to each other it is perhaps best to imagine a pinwheel whose center is the Coricancha and whose spokes (*ceques*), radiating outward, are punctuated by the *huacas*. Most *ceques* ran from five to 11 kilometers (3–7 mi.) long and contained between three and 15 shrines. It is important to note, however, that not all of the *ceques* were straight; in fact, there is much debate regarding their true orientation.

The scholar R. T. Zuidema, who has done extensive fieldwork and writing on the *ceque* system, has proposed that many of the *ceques* formed straight lines and that some of them are astronomically aligned. According to this model, the *ceques* radiate outward from the Coricancha in straight lines to mark certain points on the Cuzco horizon, which then align to specific star rises and sets. By contrast, the scholars Brian Bauer and Susan Niles have proposed that many of the *ceques* did not form straight lines and are thus much less likely to be astronomically aligned.

Ceque System: Astronomy and Myth

Celestially related narratives and stories evolved into myths that referred indirectly to the movements of celestial bodies. One such story refers to the appearance and movements of the star group Pleiades. The story then overlaps and is partially defined by the *ceque* system. The story has to do with Huáscar's coronation (Huáscar succeeded Huayna Cápac as ruler, then later lost a dynastic war to his brother Atahualpa), at which he was given a gift, referred to as the Golden Star (Cori Collyur). The Golden Star walked along a certain road though frequently stopped to rest. It has been suggested that these stops refer to *huacas*, and the road refers to a specific *ceque* line. Information for the *ceque* line indicates that it is related to wives of the creator god Viracocha, who had been out walking at night when they transformed into stone. It is also known that this *ceque* is aligned to the disappearance of the Pleiades in April, during the period when the harvest began. Thus Cori Collyur, by walking the same line as the wives of Viracocha that references the rise of the Pleiades, comes to represent the Pleiades. Narratives like this suggest the close affinity between the landscape, the *ceque* system, and the stars.

Ceque System as Calendar

Whether the *ceque* system functioned as a calendar remains a point of disagreement among scholars. One argument in favor of this idea theorizes that each of the *huacas* represents one day. As there are only 328 *huacas*, a certain amount of days are left unaccounted for. Perhaps explaining this discrepancy, the Incas counted a period known as "dead time," which corresponds with the disappearance of the Pleiades—lasting 37 days—when the fields lay fallow. The *"huaca"* days plus the "dead time" equals 365 days, thereby closely approximating the solar year.

CEQUE SYSTEM AS QUIPU CALENDAR

It is worth mentioning that it has been proposed that the *ceque* system could have functioned as a quipu calendar, meaning that it could have been used to count days and nights. Whereas knots on a quipu record information, it has been proposed that *huacas* on *ceque* lines analogously record information, although in this case the information is specific to astronomical cycles. This model remains problematic for many scholars, as the sources are at best vague on this point.

Ceque System as Solstitial Marker

As the Sun approaches each respective solstice, it appears to slow in its trajectory until it seems to be "standing still" on the day of the solstice itself. These days are therefore marked as important tem-

poral signatures. There is some indication in Cobo's text that certain *ceques* combined with certain *huacas* to act as solstitial markers. Referring to a *ceque-huaca* point in Chinchaysuyu, Cobo indicates that on a hill called Quiangalla there were located two monuments that marked the beginning of summer. In another passage Cobo refers to large hill in the direction of Cuntisuyu where two other monuments stood indicating that when the Sun arrived there, it was time to sow the fields.

Ceque System: *Huacas* Related to Horizon Observation

Huacas effected a participatory aspect separate from their maintenance and upkeep. While their maintenance required proper offerings and sacrifices and were attended to by a specifically assigned *panaqa*, some *huacas*, especially those dedicated to astronomical and/or solar phenomena, seem to have accommodated group activities. The ethnohistorical accounts are unequivocal in mentioning that at least some of the *huacas* were used to observe the Sun's movement. Some of these *huacas* seem to indicate a possible overlap with solar markers mentioned elsewhere, or at the least, they indicate an analogous function. For example, the *huaca* referred to as Quiangalla, in the Chinchaysuyu zone, is a hill on which there were two markers that when the Sun reached them it marked the beginning of summer. Similarly, a *huaca* referred to as Sucanca, also in Chinchaysuyu and also a hill, was described as having two markers that, when the Sun arrived at their location, indicated it was time to plant maize. At these times the appropriate sacrifices and offerings were made to the Sun; that sacrifices were made here indicates this particular *huaca's* significance, as not all *huacas* received sacrifices.

Ceque Stellar Alignment?

There is some disagreement and confusion among the recent literature as to whether the *ceque* lines themselves were aligned with particular stellar phenomena. On the surface it seems reasonable to consider their alignment feasible, especially given the Inca tendency to overlap multiple phenomena, such as *huaca* worship, the festival calendar, and solar observance. It is known that stars were important, and it is known that they were observed, so why would the *ceque* system—so fundamental to the heartland workings—*not* contain a system of alignments? The bulk of the confusion lies in whether or not and to what degree the *ceque* lines were straight. Not all sources agree.

Zuidema has taken the lead on *ceque* alignment research. He has proposed a list of eight alignments oriented toward the Pleiades rise and set, Beta Centauri rise, Betelgeuse rise and set, Vega set, December solstice set, and North. Yet, because there is no historical documentation that confirms these alignments, the issue remains open to the possibility that his alignments occurred as a result of chance. Eight alignments from a series of the original 41 possibilities leaves plenty of room for question. For example, statistical analysis has in part determined that the probability of attaining eight or more alignments within two degrees from the 41 possibilities suggests that the alignments would occur about 40 percent of the time even if the builders did not intentionally mean to align the *ceques* to astronomical events.

Zuidema, however, has also suggested another interesting possibility regarding alignments that accounts, in part, for those *ceques* that do not run straight. He has suggested that some alignments may occur along the lines between *huacas*, rather than along the line from the center. Research in this area is ongoing.

Other Celestial Phenomena

MILKY WAY

The Incas conceived of the Milky Way (Mayu) as a river of recirculating water, in no small part because it appears as a broad band of stars flowing across the night sky. They believed the Milky Way drew moisture into the atmosphere, which was then carried to the cosmic sea believed to circle the Earth. In some regions of Peru today the Milky Way is equated

with the Vilcanota River. Because of its position overhead and because it is especially vivid, it figures more prominently in the sky above Peru than it does in Northern Hemisphere skies.

Dark Cloud Constellation The Incas observed not only the stars themselves but the effects of interstellar clouds in the Milky Way. By blocking light and darkening patches of the sky—taking on a form similar to that of negative space, in this case, the absence of stars—shapes are created in the sky to which the Incas paid heed. In this sense dark cloud constellations have an in-between quality unlike that of star-to-star constellations, whose general outline is understood in connect-the-dots fashion. Mentioned above as "dark cloud constellations," these figures often took on the appearance, for the Inca observer, of animals. The most common reference was that of a llama with a suckling ewe. Other references include the condor, partridge, toad, serpent, and fox. Cobo noted that the celestial river was utilized by the thunder god, who controlled the rain, indicating that the Incas believed he drew water from the Milky Way and let it fall over the earth. The *yacana* spirit-animator mentioned in the *Huarochirí Manuscript* and that resided in the dark cloud constellation takes the form of a llama and takes the stars Alpha and Beta Centauri as its eyes.

ECLIPSES

The appearance of comets and the effects of eclipses were causes of great fear among the Incas. Given that the Sun was accepted as a major deity throughout the Andes and provided the energy to grow crops, its disappearance during a solar eclipse was understandably seen as an event that threatened the existence of the world. Many Spanish chroniclers, including Ondegardo, Cobo, and El Inca Garcilaso, were firsthand witnesses to the Inca reaction during such events. Garcilaso recounts the Inca reaction to a lunar eclipse in the following way: "They observed eclipses of the sun and moon, but without understanding their causes. When there was a solar eclipse, they said the sun was angry at some offense committed against him, since his face appeared disturbed like that of an angry man, and they foretold, as astrologers do, the approach of some grave punishment. When the moon was eclipsed, they said she was ill as she grew dark, and thought that if she disappeared altogether, she would die and the sky would fall in and crush them all, and that the end of the world would come. When a lunar eclipse began, they were seized with fear and sounded trumpets, bugles, horns, drums, and all the instruments they could find for making a noise. They tied up their dogs, large and small, and beat them with many blows and made them howl and call the moon back." Garcilaso's account, like the others, recounts the general fear and trepidation caused by the events, which were seen as representing the near death of the objects.

COMETS

The irregular appearance of comets was read as an augury of ominous events. The Spanish record tended to associate the appearance of comets with major occurrences, the most important being the death of Atahualpa, one of the sons of Huayna Cápac who had fought against his brother Huáscar in the dynastic war of succession that followed their father's untimely death. Atahualpa was taken prisoner by Francisco Pizarro, who held him captive from November 1532 until July 1533. According to Cieza de León, while Atahualpa was being held prisoner a comet passed through the sky, "a green sign as thick as an arm and the length of a lancet." Atahualpa heard about it and asked to be allowed to see it. When he did "a great sadness came over him which lasted all the next day. And when the governor, Don Francisco Pizarro, asked him why he was so sad, he answered, 'I have seen the sign in the sky, and when my father Huayna Capac died, a similar sign was seen.'"

MATHEMATICS AND THE QUIPU

The Incas used the quipu as a device for recording numbers and other information. A quipu is a length of cord from which a series of strings were suspended. Knots on the strings represented informa-

tion. The quipu was ill suited for calculations, however, and the chronicles make clear that calculations were done using seeds or pebbles moved into piles. The Incas were organizers, and the decimal organization of their society necessitated a functional accounting system. Making use of a base-10 number system, they methodically accounted for the entire empire by grouping people in 10s, 100s, 1,000s, and 10,000s. In addition to the base-10 number system, it is believed that at a minimum the Incas knew addition, division, multiplication, fractions, and proportions.

The quipu was most often associated with accounting. It was used to record a wide variety of numerical data such as census records, storage contents, tax obligations, military organization, calendrical information, and land measurements. It was not an original Inca invention but stretched back as much as 1,000 years. The quipu is a length of main string from which a series of pendant cords are suspended. The pendant cords were twisted in specific manners and knotted in various ways, each slight perturbation indicating a unit of information. They were dyed in many colors, and each color indicated a specific context. The combinations of color, position, order, location, and shape offer an almost infinite number of possibilities for recording information.

The earliest information ascertained from the quipus, and perhaps the easiest to discern, was the numbers 1 through 9. Zero was also known and rendered. The numbers 1–9 rendered in knots are

10.3 A quipu consists of knotted strings used to record data. (John Bigelow Taylor/The Library/American Museum of Natural History)

both elegant and simple. The pendant cord is wrapped around itself; the number of loops, easily read, is the number it signifies. The absence of a knot in a certain position indicates 0. The quipu's primary use in this function appears to have been the recording of census data. As discussed elsewhere, the Inca social hierarchy was organized into decimal units of 1, 10, 100, 1,000, etc. The census numbers were transferred to the quipu, in this way quite simply recording the information. In effect, it meant the same thing as writing the number 1,000 on a piece of paper today, thus recording numerical data. In this simple manner the Incas were able to keep surprisingly accurate census records. The same method was used to record other vital statistics as well.

The degree to which the quipu records information beyond accounting is widely debated. Similarly, the degree to which it is solely a mnemonic device, that is, a prompt to trigger memory, is also debated. There are suggestions in the chronicles and in the images created by Guamán Poma of the quipu's use as a letter. One image in particular shows an Inca *chasqui*, or relay runner, holding in his right hand a quipu, to which Guamán Poma has attached a verbal signifier with the word *carta*, meaning "letter" in Spanish. Given Guamán Poma's overall reliability as a purveyor of accurate visual information, some scholars feel that this suggests the possibility that the quipu, in fact, held narrative content. Another of Guamán Poma's images is even more enticing. This image shows a native official holding in one hand a quipu and in the other a book, perhaps suggesting an equivalence, again, of the type of information each signifies. Yet, with the holders of the quipu, those who were responsible for handling and reading them, being long deceased, it is impossible to know at this point if the quipus' secrets will ever be fully unlocked. Their ability to hold "language" remains highly debatable.

The *quipucamayos* were the individuals responsible for the constructing, keeping, and reading of quipus. They were, in effect, record keepers. *Quipucamayos* functioned at both a state and local level. At the state level the *quipucamayo* was a professional position and was organized in a hierarchical ranking according to the type of information each was responsible for. At the local level *quipucamayos* kept

track of such things as community herds. The position itself was passed down from father to son, along with the oral information or directions that were necessary for an accurate reading. After the conquest the Spanish found the quipus and the *quipucamayos*, their keepers, to be so reliable for recording data that they allowed testimony read from quipus into court records.

READING

Calendar

José de Acosta, *Natural and Moral History of the Indies.* Edited by Jane E. Mangan and translated by Frances López-Morillas (Durham, N.C.: Duke University Press, 2002).

Martha B. Anders, *Dual Organization and Calendars Inferred from the Site Plan of Azángaro* (Ann Arbor, Mich.: University Microfilm, 1986).

Anonymous, "Discurso de la sucesión y gobierno de los yngas." In *Juicio de límites entre el Perú y Bolivia; Prueba peruana presentada al gobierno de la República Argentina*, vol. 8, edited by Victor M. Martúa, 149–165 (Madrid: Tipografía de los hijos de M. G. Hernandez, 1906).

Juan de Betanzos, *Narrative of the Incas.* Translated and edited by Roland Hamilton and Dana Buchanan (Austin: University of Texas Press, 1996).

Pedro de Cieza de León, *The Incas of Pedro de Cieza de León.* Translated by Harriet de Onis and edited by Victor W. von Hagen (Norman: University of Oklahoma Press, 1959).

Garcilaso de la Vega, El Inca, *Royal Commentaries of the Inca and General History of Peru* (Austin: University of Texas Press, 1987).

Martin de Murúa, *Historia del origen y genealogía real de los reyes incas del Perú.* Introduction and notes by Constantino Bayle. Biblioteca "Missionalis Hispánica," vol. 2. 1615. Reprint (Madrid: Instituto Santo Toribio de Mogrovego, 1946).

Robert M. Sadowski, "A Few Remarks on the Astronomy of R. T. Zuidema's 'Quipu-Calendar.'"

In *Time and Calendars in the Inca Empire*, edited by Marius S. Ziólkowski and Robert M. Sadowski, BAR International Series 479, 209–213 (Oxford: British Archaeological Reports, 1989).

———, "The Sky above the Incas: An Abridged Astronomical Calendar for the 16th Century." In *Time and Calendars in the Inca Empire*, edited by Mariusz S. Ziólkowski and Robert M. Sadowski, BAR International Series 479, 75–106 (Oxford: British Archaeological Reports, 1989).

Pedro Sarmiento de Gamboa, *History of the Incas*. Translated and edited by Clements Markham. 1907. Reprint (Mineola, N.Y.: Dover Publications, 1999).

Mariusz S. Ziólkowski, "Knots and Oddities: The Quipu-Calendar or Supposed Luni-Sidereal Calendar." In *Time and Calendars in the Inca Empire*, edited by Mariusz S. Ziólkowski and Robert M. Sadowski, BAR International Series 479, 197–208 (Oxford: British Archaeological Reports, 1989).

R. Tom Zuidema, "The Inca Calendar." In *Native American Astronomy*, edited by Anthony F. Aveni, 219–259 (Austin: University of Texas Press, 1997).

———. "Towards a General Star Calendar in Ancient Peru." In *Calendars in Mesoamerica and Peru: Native American Computations of Time*, edited by Anthony F. Aveni and Gordon Brotherston, BAR International Series 174, Proceedings of the 44th International Congress of Americanists, 235–262 (Oxford: British Archaeological Reports, 1983).

Astronomy

Anthony Aveni, "Astronomy and the Ceque System," *Journal of the Steward Anthropological Society* 24, nos. 1–2 (1996): 157–172.

———, "Horizon Astronomy in Incaic Cuzco." In *Archaeoastronomy in the Americas*, edited by Ray A. Williamson, 305–318 (Los Altos, Calif.: Balleana Press, 1981).

———, *Skywatchers*. Rev. ed. (Austin: University of Texas Press, 2001).

———, *Stairways to the Stars: Skywatching in Three Ancient Cultures* (New York: John Wiley & Sons, 1997).

———, ed, *World Archaeoastronomy* (Cambridge: Cambridge University Press, 1989).

Brian S. Bauer and David S. P. Dearborn, *Astronomy and Empire in the Ancient Andes* (Austin: University of Texas Press, 1995).

David S. P. Dearborn and Katherine J. Schreiber, "Houses of the Rising Sun." In *Time and Calendars in the Inca Empire*, edited by Mariusz S. Ziólkowski and Robert M. Sadowski, BAR International Series 479, 49–74 (Oxford: British Archaeological Reports, 1989).

David S. P. Dearborn, Katherine J. Schreiber, and Raymond E. White, "Intimachay, a December Solstice Observatory," *American Antiquity* 52, no. 2 (1987): 346–352.

David S. P. Dearborn, M. Seddon, and B. Bauer, "The Sanctuary of Titicaca: Where the Sun Returns to Earth," *Latin American Antiquity* 9 (1998): 240–258.

David S. P. Dearborn and Raymond E. White, "Inca Observatories: Their Relation to Calendar and Ritual." In *World Archaeoastronomy*, edited by Anthony Aveni, 462–469 (Cambridge: Cambridge University Press, 1989).

———, "The 'Torreón' at Machu Picchu as an Observatory," *Archaeoastronomy* 5 (1983): 37–49.

The Huarochirí Manuscript: A Testament of Ancient and Colonial Andean Religion. Translated by Frank Solomon and George L. Urioste (Austin: University of Texas Press, 1991).

John Hyslop, *Inka Settlement Planning* (Austin: University of Texas Press, 1990).

Erland Nordensköld, "Calculations with Years and Months in the Peruvian Quipus," *Comparative Ethnographical Studies* 6, no. 2 (Göteburg, Sweden: Elanders Boktyckeri Akjebolag, 1925).

Juan Polo de Ondegardo, *On the Errors and Superstitions of the Indians, Taken from the Treatise and Investigation Done by Linentiate Polo*. Translated by A. Brunel, John Murra, and Sidney Muirden (New Haven, Conn.: Human Relations Files, 1965).

Juan de Santacruz Pachacuti Yamqui Salcamaygua, *Relación de antigüedades deste reyno del Peru*. Biblioteca de Autores Españoles, vol. 209. 1613. Reprint (Madrid: Ediciones Atlas, 1968).

Robert Randall, "Qoyllur Rit'I, an Inca Fiesta of the Pleiades: Reflections on Time and Space in the Andean World," *Bulletin de l'Institut Françias d'Études Andines* 11, nos. 1–2 (1982): 37–81.

William Sullivan, *The Secret of the Incas: Myth, Astronomy, and the War against Time* (New York: Crown Publishers, 1996).

Gary Urton, *At the Crossroads of the Earth and the Sky: An Andean Cosmology* (Austin: University of Texas Press, 1981).

———, "Astronomy and Calendrics on the Coast of Peru." In *Ethnoastronomy and Archaeoastronomy in the American Tropics*. Vol. 385, edited by Anthony F. Aveni and Gary Urton, 231–259 (New York: Annals of the New York Academy of Sciences, 1982).

———, "Orientation in Quechua and Incaic Astronomy," *Ethnology* 17 (1978): 157–167.

Mariusz S. Ziólkowski and Robert M. Sadowski, "The Astronomical Data in Fernando Montesinos' Peruvian Chronicle: The Comets of Qhapaq Yupanqui," *Archaeoastronomy* 3, no. 2 (1980): 22–26.

R. Tom Zuidema, "Anthropology and Archaeoastronomy." In *Archaeoastronomy in the Americas*, edited by Ray A. Williamson, 29–31 (Los Altos, Calif.: Balleana Press, 1981).

———, "The Inca Calendar." In *Native American Astronomy*, edited by Anthony F. Aveni, 219–259 (Austin: University of Texas Press, 1977).

———, "Inca Observations of the Solar and Lunar Passages through Zenith and Anti-Zenith at Cuzco." In *Archaeoastronomy in the Americas*, edited by Ray A. Williamson, 419–458 (Los Altos, Calif.: Balleana Press, 1981).

———, "The Pillars of Cuzco: Which Two Dates of Sunset Did They Define?" In *New Directions in American Archaeoastronomy*, edited by Anthony Aveni, BAR International Series 454, 143–169 (Oxford: British Archaeological Reports, 1988).

Cuzco *Ceque* System: Astronomical Affiliation

Brian S. Bauer, *Ancient Cuzco: Heartland of the Inca* (Austin: University of Texas Press, 2004).

———, *The Development of the Inca State* (Austin: University of Texas Press, 1992).

———, "Ritual Pathways of the Inca: An Analysis of the Collasuyu Ceques in Cuzco," *Latin American Antiquity* 3, no. 3 (1992): 7–26.

———, *The Sacred Landscape of the Inca: The Cusco Ceque System* (Austin: University of Texas Press, 1998).

Bernabé Cobo, *Inca Religion and Customs*. Translated and edited by Roland Hamilton (Austin: University of Texas Press, 1990).

———, "Relación de las guacas del Cuzco." In "An Account of the Shrines of Ancient Cuzco," translated and edited by John H. Rowe, *Ñawpa Pacha* 17 (1979): 2–80.

Ian Farrington, "Ritual Geography, Settlement Patterns and the Characterization of the Provinces of the Inka Heartland," *World Archaeology* 23 (1992): 368–385.

Graziano Gasparini and Louise Margolies, *Inca Architecture*. Translated by Patricia Lyons (Bloomington: Indiana University Press, 1980).

Felipe Guamán Poma de Ayala, *El primer nueva corónica y buen gobierno*. Edited by John Murra and Rolena Adorno. 3 vols. (Mexico: Siglo Veintiuno, 1992).

———, *Letter to a King: A Picture History of the Inca Civilisation*. Edited and translated by Christopher Dilke (London: George Allen & Unwin, 1978).

John H. Rowe, "Inca Culture at the Time of the Spanish Conquest." In *Handbook of South American Indians*, edited by Julian Steward, Bureau of American Ethnology, Bulletin 143, no. 2, 183–330 (Washington, D.C.: Smithsonian Institution, 1946).

R. Tom Zuidema, *The Ceque System of Cuzco: The Social Organization of the Capital of the Inca*. Translated by Eva M. Hooykaas, International Archives of Ethnography, supplement to vol. 50 (Leiden, Netherlands: E. J. Brill, 1964).

———, "Hierarchy and Space in Incaic Social Organization," *Ethnohistory* 30 (1983): 49–75.

———, *Inca Civilization in Cuzco*. Translated by Jean-Jacques Decoster (Austin: University of Texas Press, 1990).

Mathematics and the Quipu

Marcia Ascher and Robert Ascher, *Code of the Quipu* (Ann Arbor: University of Michigan Press, 2002).

———, *Mathematics of the Incas: Codes of the Quipu* (Mineola, N.Y.: Dover Publications, 1997).

———. "Numbers and Relations from Ancient Andean Quipus." *Archives for the History of Exact Sciences* 8 (1972): 288–320.

Robert Ascher, "Inka Writing." In *Narrative Threads,* edited by Jeffrey Quilter and Gary Urton, 103–115 (Austin: University of Texas Press, 2002).

William Conklin, "The Information System of Middle Horizon Quipus." In *Ethnoastronomy and Archaeoastronomy in the American Tropics.* Vol. 385, edited by Anthony Aveni and Gary Urton, 261–282 (New York: Annals of the New York Academy of Science, 1982).

Leland L. Locke, *The Ancient Quipu or Peruvian Knot Record* (New York: American Museum of Natural History, 1923).

———, "Supplementary Notes on the Quipus in the American Museum of Natural History." In *Anthropological Papers of the American Museum of Natural History* 30, no. 2 (1928): 37–71.

Fernando de Montesinos, *Memorias antiguas historiales del Perú.* Edited by Philip Ainsworth Means, with introduction by Clements R. Markham (London: Hakluyt Society, 1920).

Jeffrey Quilter and Gary Urton, eds., *Narrative Threads: Accounting and Recounting in Andean Khipu* (Austin: University of Texas Press, 2002).

Gary Urton, "Astronomy and Calendrics on the Coast of Peru." In *Ethnoastronomy and Archaeoastronomy in the American Tropics.* Vol. 385, edited by Anthony F. Aveni and Gary Urton, 231–259 (New York: Annals of the New York Academy of Sciences, 1982).

———. "From Knots to Narratives: Reconstructing the Art of Historical Record Keeping in the Andes from Spanish Transcriptions of Inka Khipus," *Ethnohistory* 45, no. 3 (1998): 409–438.

———, "A New Twist in an Old Yarn: Variation in Knot Directionality in the Inka Khipus," *Baessler-Archiv n.F. Band* 42 (1995): 271–305.

———. "Recording Signs in Narrative-Accounting Khipu." In *Narrative Threads,* edited by Jeffrey Quilter and Gary Urton, 171–196 (Austin: University of Texas Press, 2002).

———, *Signs of the Inca Khipu* (Austin: University of Texas Press, 2003).

Blas Valera, "De las costumbres antiguas de los naturales del Pirú." In *Tres relaciones de antigüedades peruanas,* edited by M. Jimenez de la Espada, 135–203 (Asunción, Paraguay: Editorial Guatanía, 1950).

11

ECONOMY, INDUSTRY, AND TRADE

The Inca economy bore very little resemblance to the monetary-based, free-market economies found in most countries today. The central government controlled almost all the economic activity that took place throughout the empire, including the production, circulation, and consumption of goods. No form of currency existed among the Incas, nor was there a concept of purchasing or ownership of commodities. Instead, government-controlled allocation and redistribution of resources constituted the primary means by which people received their basic necessities. Agriculture served as the backbone of the Inca economy, whose surpluses were crucial for supporting the empire's immense population in times of need. Herding, hunting, and fishing were also important food aquisitional activities. The production of crafts such as ceramics, textiles, and metalwork were carried out both by individual households and by artisans organized into guilds. Public works projects such as the building of dams, canals, roads, and major buildings were made possible through the *mita*, or rotational labor tax. The movement of foodstuffs, water, trade goods, and other important items throughout the 5,470-kilometer-long (3,400-mi.-long) empire was facilitated by both long-distance traders and relay runners known as *chasquis*. The state also provided the necessary infrastructure for easy travel and transport through the extensive road system, way stations known as *tambos*, and provincial centers en route to and from the imperial capital at Cuzco. Government-controlled storage facilities called *colcas* contained stockpiles of food, goods, and weapons to protect from unpredictable harvests or political unrest. All of the goods produced and tracts of land parceled out by the Incas were standardized according to a system of measurements. Moreover, the census kept track of population growth and provided an accurate mechanism for holding households accountable to tribute obligations.

AGRICULTURE

A necessary precondition for empire, agricultural products and surpluses were the lifeblood of the Incas. The extreme verticality of the Andean terrain necessitated the use of several different strategies for the extraction of food resources. Agriculture was the principal means by which the empire's inhabitants fed themselves and made a living. Agriculture was practiced in every altitude zone that supported plant life (up to 4,000 meters [13,123 ft.] above sea level), but the greatest crop diversity could be found in the river valleys along the coast, in the temperate low slopes of the Andes, known as the *yunga* and *quechua* zones, and in the fertile valley bottoms of the highlands.

Agriculture, which had been practiced throughout the Andes since 3000 B.C.E. and in the coastal areas since about 1800 B.C.E., reached unprecedented levels of productivity under the Incas. This was achieved through the construction of canals and agricultural terraces, diverting of rivers, and draining of swamplands to create optimal conditions for agriculture. Tending the fields required relatively little technology. The *taclla*, or foot plow, was a wooden rod with a curved top and a foot rest toward the bottom for plunging the pointed end into the ground to break up the soil. Hoes and clod breakers, made from stone and wood, were also important implements in the farmer's toolkit.

Crops

The carbohydric staples of the Incas were maize and potatoes, but they also grew tomatoes, chili peppers, gourds, fruits such as avocados, cherimoya, and *lúcuma*, chenopods such as quinoa and *tarwi*, and several varieties of tubers including *ulluco*, oca, and *mashua*. Each crop can only be grown under certain climatic and altitudinal conditions. Maize, cotton, chili peppers, coca, peanuts, beans, tomatoes, sweet potatoes, and avocados all thrive in warm climates at altitudes of less than 914 meters (3,000 ft.) above sea level. In the puna only potatoes, oca, and *ulluco* survive. Maize, a more sensitive crop that typically only survives in warm, low-altitude regions, required extensive modification of the landscape to survive in the colder climates of the Andes. Two important technologies—terracing and irrigation—were the primary means by which the Incas ensured agricultural success.

Terracing

The extreme verticality of the Andean landscape, which had often presented an obstacle to cultivation, became an asset to Inca farmers. Terracing consisted of leveling a mountainside adjacent to the valley floor into a series of "steps." Each step could hold as little as a few rows of crops up to hundreds of rows, depending on its size. Some terraces even stretched across 1,524 meters (5,000 ft.) of land. Terracing optimized land use by literally carving otherwise unproductive mountain slopes into flat, fertile areas for crop growth. It also cut down on soil erosion caused by winds, rain, and snow. Moreover, terracing maximized the amount of direct sun exposure to crops and thus created warmer microenvironments in which crops usually unsuitable for mountain environments, such as maize, could thrive. Retaining walls made of cut stone or dry masonry held the terraces in place. Gravel and stones were embedded into the soil to allow for drainage. Canals on the sides of the terraces permitted the steady flow of rainwater, which could be collected and stored. Terracing dramatically altered the landscape, creating a distinctive rippling effect on the terrain that surely awed contemporaries.

Terracing was practiced as early as 2500 B.C.E., used primarily for ceremonial purposes, but it achieved the highest level of grandeur and sophistication under the Incas. Spaniards marveled at the Inca terraces, calling them *escalones de piedras*, or "stairways of stone." Inca kings, notably Huayna Cápac, who was responsible for the expansion of Cuzco and for commissioning important building projects throughout the realm, were celebrated for their terracing projects. At the site of Moray in the Sacred Valley, sinkholes (natural circular

11.1 Agricultural terraces at the site of Pisac in the Sacred Valley. Terraces helped maximize the amount of arable land in unfavorable terrain. (Eloise Quiñones Keber)

depressions in the landscape) were terraced for purely aesthetic purposes to produce a breathtaking visual effect. The terraces at Ollantaytambo and Pisac in the Sacred Valley were both functional and picturesque, undulating to follow the natural contours of the land. These terraces yielded bountiful crops, among other products; according to Spanish chroniclers, some of the terraces at Ollantaytambo were filled with flowers.

Sunken Gardens

Coastal peoples as well as the inhabitants of the Altiplano near Lake Titicaca planted sunken gardens as an alternative to traditional agriculture. Sunken gardens were referred to by a variety of terms by different ethnic groups. The Aymara-speaking peoples of the Lake Titicaca region referred to them as *cochas*, peoples of the Virú Valley on the north coast called them *pukio*, and the inhabitants of Chan Chan, the capital of the Chimú Empire, which fell to the Incas in 1470, called them *huachaque*. Still practiced by some communities today, it involves digging a hole in the ground close to the water table and planting crops inside. They were particularly valuable for inhabitants of very dry environments with little surface water as well as of cold regions prone to frost of the topsoil. Sunken gardens were typically used to cultivate maize, which was one of the principal crops of the Incas. Archaeological evidence and historical sources tell us that sunken gardens were planted near Lake Titicaca in the Altiplano region; in the Virú, Chilca, Chincha, Ica, and Nazca Valleys of the Pacific coast; and at the site of Chan Chan. With the exception of Chan Chan, sunken gardens were primarily a rural phenomenon; more urbanized settlements depended on larger-scale irrigation systems to support a large population. The earliest historical reference to sunken gardens comes from the chronicler Cieza de León in 1550, who described these in Chilca in great detail. He noted that they were fertilized with the heads of sardines, which enriched the soil for abundant harvests. At other sites farmers used the leaves of the native *guarango* tree as fertilizer.

ROLE OF ANIMALS

Herding

Herding took place primarily in the puna and altiplano, the natural habitats for llamas and alpacas. They grazed on what are known as "dwarf" grasses typical to high-altitude tundra regions. Unlike herding practices in other parts of the world, no additional fodder was given to the llamas. Herders allowed the camelids to graze in a particular area until the grass was depleted and then moved on to the next stretch of pasture. Adolescent boys and girls often herded to fulfill their familial responsibilities. Although the official property of the government, llamas were tended to and controlled by the communities to which the herders belonged, and their by-products were submitted to the capital as tribute. The Inca government ordered that shepherds would each be accountable for a group of 500 llamas.

Llamas were used for a variety of purposes among the Incas. Their most important economic asset was their fur; only cloth woven from camelid fiber could protect one from the harsh climate of the Andes. Llamas also provided one of the only sources of protein for the highland Inca diet, as few edible domesticated animals existed in the Americas before the European invasion. Moreover, the fur and meat of the llama were prized commodities; the possession of cloth woven from vicuña (the finest fiber from an undomesticated member of the camelid family) and the consumption of llama meat were privileges reserved for the nobility. Llama hides were used to make shoes; the characteristic Inca sandals worn by men that are drawn and described in colonial historical accounts were fashioned from this very material. Llama dung provided a good source of cooking fuel and was regularly collected by young girls to assist their mothers in household chores. The tallow of the llama served an important function as a lubricant. And finally, llamas served as pack animals and were in fact the only beasts of burden in all of the Americas. They could not carry as much as horses, which were not introduced to South America until the arrival of Europeans. Llamas can carry about 100 pounds of weight. Although strong, several chroniclers have commented on the finicky nature of llamas, which would lie down in the middle of the road, refusing to work if the burden was too heavy or the journey too arduous.

Hunting

Hunting grounds were located throughout the Inca Empire but were reserved for use by Inca kings and elites. Most game preserves were in high-altitude regions, the natural environment of Andean game. As in most premodern cultures, hunting was considered a prestigious activity imbued with ritual significance. Royal hunts occurred periodically, once the game populations had regenerated from the previous one. From the few written documents that mention hunting activities, it can be discerned that large public hunts organized by the Inca king involved hundreds of participants, who would create human concentric circles that eventually trapped the animals into a sufficiently small space for killing effectively and swiftly at high volumes. In fact, during one documented royal hunt in 1536 (four years after the arrival of the Spanish), more than 11,000 animals were killed. Their meat would be used for royal feasts as well as for redistribution among members of society. Wild deer and the guanaco, a member of the deer family, were the animals most commonly hunted for their meat. The viscacha, a rodent that has been described as a cross between a rabbit and a squirrel, was also hunted both for its meat and its highly prized fur, which was woven into fine textiles for elites.

Hunting implements took on a variety of forms. Slings that catapulted round stones were useful for killing small animals. *Bolas*, or balls connected to string tied onto a wooden shaft, were used to hunt birds. A wide net attached to long poles on either side could also serve in capturing birds in flight. Snares, clubs, and nooses ranked as important animal hunting tools among the Incas. Stalking and driving were the principal methods for killing animals.

Fishing

Fishing was an essential economic activity among the empire's coastal inhabitants, where only about 10 percent of the land was suitable for agriculture.

Marine life along the Pacific coast was (and still is) very abundant, with an enormous diversity of fish, mollusks, and vegetation. Aquatic resources are so bountiful that fishermen can produce yields 280 days out of the year; the Incas had a comparable, if not superior success rate. Fishermen rode in narrow reed boats with pointed upturned ends on either side, which are still used today in the north coast region of Peru. Some fish were caught in lakes and rivers of the highlands, although yields were much lower and only a few varieties survived high-altitude marine environments. Fish and other aquatic resources were captured with woven nets that were cast into the sea and pulled up once a sufficient amount had been caught. Nets could range in size from relatively small for individual use to large-scale ones attached to poles for use by two individuals or more. The Incas also caught fish using copper hooks attached to fishing lines or rods and fish spears made from thorns.

Fish provided a crucial source of protein for the coastal Inca diet, which consisted mostly of grains, tubers, and fruit. As a lower-ranked food product, fish fed a diverse cross-section of Inca society; hunted meat was primarily reserved for the upper classes. Although marine products mostly formed a staple of coastal cuisine, they reached the highlands in considerable quantities via long-distance traders. In fact, it was often stated that the Sapa Inca could dine on fresh fish caught in the morning on the coast and delivered to the northern highland site of Cajamarca in time for dinner. Moreover, fishermen in the Lake Titicaca region provided fish to the Inca state as tribute. Fishermen salted and dried fish for highland trade, which could survive longer transport time for delivery to nonelites.

Fishermen along the coast formed a distinct social group, complete with their own dialects and customs. In fact, the children of fisher families married among one another to maintain the tradition over generations. These families held fishing rites over expanses of coastal land and served as intermediaries in the exchange of marine products among both local and distant groups.

AQUATIC RESOURCES

In addition to fish the Pacific Ocean yielded a number of aquatic resources for consumption. Salt, an essential source of iodine and sodium for human survival, was collected in salt pans near the shore. Lizards and shellfish also provided an important source of protein for coastal peoples. The Spanish chronicler Pedro Pizarro, half brother of Francisco, claimed to have seen a *colca*, or storehouse, filled entirely with dried lizards that were to be sent to Cuzco as tribute payment. The Incas also collected algae and seaweed that grew in the coastal waters along the Pacific coast. Referred to as *cochayuyo*, algae were a source of food for coastal peoples. It was also dried and transported to the highlands.

Gathering Food

Although the Incas were primarily agriculturalists, they also gathered wild plants and insects for both dietary and medicinal purposes. Some wild plants collected by the Incas included *oca-oca*, whose leaves were chewed to stave off thirst; the *acopa*, or century plant, used for its fiber to weave baskets and nets; and the fruits of the tuna cactus. Several varieties of wild plants were boiled, eaten raw, or used for special teas. The Incas also collected and consumed some types of insects, such as caterpillars, ants, and beetles, which were eaten raw or roasted.

Household Domesticates

Inca households kept domesticated guinea pigs, known as *cuy*. Given its abundance and easy upkeep, *cuy* was a primary source of meat among commoners living in the highlands. These small rodents, who scavenge insects and other small creatures, were also kept around households to eliminate pests. Dogs were another household domesticate but seen more as pets, and at times as nuisances, rather than as a source of food.

WATER

Water management differed across the empire, depending on its level of scarcity. In the highlands water was relatively abundant, but its unpredictability and the erratic runoff into the valleys required the development of irrigation systems. Drainage of water, a necessary measure to prevent flooding in the highlands, also required a great deal of labor and technology.

Irrigation

Irrigation was another critical component to successful crop growth throughout the entire Inca realm. Control over water resources was the key to imperial expansion throughout Peru beginning in the first millennium up through the time of the Incas. The coastal civilizations beginning with the Moche state (1–700 C.E.) to the Chimú Empire (1000–1470) had developed sophisticated systems that diverted water from the highlands into the coastal valleys. Under the Incas irrigation had reached unprecedented levels of technological sophistication; irrigation ditches that ran for several kilometers allowed for the maintenance of agricultural fields in previously uncultivable land.

Drainage

Archaeological evidence of drainage systems in the highlands have been found in the Inca road system. Drains were placed in the center of the road to prevent flooding. They have also been excavated along the perimeters of buildings to catch rain falling from the roof, such as at Tumipampa, located in modern-day Ecuador. Open drainage channels are also found at buildings, ceremonial platforms, and plazas. They are usually cut directly into the stone foundations of the structures, with little effort taken to hide them from view. In Cuzco, drains spanned great distances for both utilitarian and ceremonial purposes. One canal stretched from the central plaza, Huacaypata, to the Coricancha.

MINES AND MINING

The Andes are rich in mineral resources, with numerous mines that were exploited by the Incas. The most abundant ores found in the Andean region are copper, tin, silver, and gold. The Incas divided their mineral resources into two major categories: local community mines and major state mines. Community mines were worked by local laborers in the service of their *kuraka* (local leaders). They would provide the *kuraka* with the precious metals extracted from the mine in exchange for basic necessities. These mines were small in size and did not yield major quantities of metals. State mines were controlled by local government officials who would report to the royal administration. Upon unification of the empire the state gained control of all high-yield mines throughout the realm.

The vast majority of ores are located in the southern region of the empire, which the Incas referred to as Collasuyu. This includes parts of modern-day Bolivia, Chile, and northwest Argentina. In fact, archaeologists have estimated that more than 75 percent of Inca settlements in Colla-

suyu were dedicated to the mining and processing of ores. Some sites focused exclusively on smelting of ores, while others housed workshops for melting the ores into ingots for transportation to northern workshops.

Major gold deposits were located at Carabaya (to the northwest of Lake Titicaca), Chumbivilcas, Huánuco, Andahuaylas, and Quito. Silver was found in vast quantities at Potosí (present-day Bolivia), and smaller amounts were located at mines in the Chuquiabo region (present-day La Paz, Bolivia). Copper abounded in Chile and northwest Argentina. Tin was found in western Bolivia, northern Chile, and northwest Argentina. In addition to gold, silver, tin, and copper deposits, minor minerals such as zinc and galena were also concentrated in Collasuyu.

Given the high status accorded to precious metals, mining was a heavily regulated affair. Guards were stationed at all times to monitor the workers

11.2 The mines at Potosí. Silver has been mined at this site from the time of the Incas through the present day.
(Eloise Quiñones Keber)

and to ensure that no materials left the site unauthorized. Miners, accompanied by government officials, would transport the extracted metal to Cuzco metallurgy workshops. Both men and women worked in the mines on a rotational basis as part of their *mita* labor obligations. If located in a temperate region, mines were worked year round; those located in excessively cold regions were only worked during the rainy season, when the climate was more temperate.

AN EMPIRE CONNECTED

In an environment full of variation in terrain, climate, and altitude, each yielding a limited number of crops and resources, trade networks were essential for circulating goods among the different regions of the empire. For example, lowland crops, such as maize, coca, and *ají* (chili peppers) were exchanged for goods from the highlands, such as potatoes and *charqui* (beef jerky). The practice of exchanging goods from a variety of altitudinal zones is known by what the archaeologist John Murra termed the *strategy of verticality*. Given the unpredictable ecological character of highland environments, the redistribution of resources from different zones to communities residing along so-called vertical archipelagos prevented shortages and famines. Local and regional trade was facilitated by family members within an *ayllu*, or by *kurakas*, who would distribute foreign products among his populace.

Large-scale trade, however, was controlled by the state. The Incas traded for exotic goods from the tropical lowlands along the eastern slopes of the Andes, such as bird feathers, gold, coca leaf, and honey. Guano (bat dung) from the south coast was used as crop fertilizer. Many of the goods exchanged across long distances were submitted to the state by conquered territories as a form of tribute. Goods from the north coast were obtained by the Inca government through lords residing in coastal valleys who acted as intermediaries in the exchange of highland and coastal goods. These lords, who remained relatively autonomous despite the imposition of Inca rule, traded cotton, beans, *chaquiras*

(shell beads), and salt for goods from the highlands such as wool, potatoes, and other items. They also facilitated trade between Ecuador and the highlands, satiating Inca desires for the coveted *Spondylus* shells (known as *mullu* used in ceremonies to bring rain), fish, and other aquatic resources. The Inca road system, relay runners *(chasquis)*, and way stations *(tambos)* were essential for the movement of goods over vast distances.

The Inca Road System

The Inca road system was a true engineering feat, stretching over nearly 4,000 kilometers (2,485 mi.) of terrain from north to south and totaling 25,000–30,000 kilometers (15,534–18,641 mi.) of roadway. The system consisted of two major trunk roads, or *cápac ñan:* One traversed the highlands, and a second road ran along the coast. The highland road ran from Quito, Ecuador, to Mendoza, Argentina. The coastal road ran from the Inca outpost of Tumbes in Ecuador all the way south to Chile. Although roads had long existed, the Incas were the first to develop a road system that linked major cities and provincial centers of the highlands and coastal areas over nearly the entire expanse of the Andes and Pacific coast of South America.

The full extent of the Inca road system may never be known because many portions of the road have disappeared. The Spanish marveled at the ingenuity and labor investment involved in its construction. The chronicler Cieza de León described them as follows:

> . . . through deep valleys, and over mountains, through piles of snow, quagmires, living rock, along turbulent rivers; in some places . . . smooth and paved, carefully laid out; in others over the sierras, cut through the rock, with walls skirting the rivers, and steps and rests through the snow; everywhere . . . clean swept and kept free of rubbish, with lodgings, storehouses, temples to the sun, and posts along the way.

The grandest highways were paved with cobbles or flagstone, though much of the surface used combinations of dirt, sand, grass, and other natural surfaces.

The highland road was narrow and frequently irregular due to the rocky, uneven terrain typical of mountainous areas. Drainage canals permitted use even during the rainy season. In more favorable highland terrain roads were paved with flat stones and lined with stone retaining walls. The coastal road was lined with adobe walls and decorated with painted motifs on either side, while in other areas it consisted of little more than a rock-lined path. The road ranged in width from about one meter (3 ft.) at its narrowest, to five meters (16 ft.) in favorable terrain.

Roads were constructed and repaired by *mita* laborers. Given the fact that carriages, wagons, and other wheeled vehicles did not exist in the pre-Columbian Andes, consistent paving or a minimum width were unnecessary. The roads rather supported human traffic as well as llamas bearing loads of goods. However, only authorized personnel were permitted to use the roads. This included royalty and their retainers, soldiers, long-distance trainers, and relay runners (*chasquis*).

The road facilitated communication throughout the empire, allowed for the transportation of goods, and made possible the rapid deployment of military forces or forced labor brigades. Parallel infrastructure supported the construction and maintenance of the road network. Channels and culverts drained water alongside or under the roads. Buttressing walls were built along insecure stretches in alpine regions, and causeways were built over wetlands. Rest stops (*tambos*), storehouses, and *chasqui* posts were built along the road at regular intervals. In building the road network the Incas augmented already existing roadbeds, many of which included infrastructure stemming from the Wari Empire, which had ruled the southern and central highlands of Peru from ca. 540 to 1000. Where necessary the Incas created new roads—often paved in stone and sometimes carved straight through rock. Along certain portions of the highway, especially near estates or sacred places, access was severely restricted. The presence of structures inferred to be gatehouses and limited entryways indicates highly restricted use. Altogether the highway system was the key link between peripheral administrative centers and the Inca heartland.

Land Transportation

Overland transportation throughout the Inca realm was carried out by foot. Commoners walked to their desired destinations. Some rode on the backs of men, and members of the nobility were typically carried on litters. Men would hoist individuals on their backs in fulfillment of *mita* labor obligations owed to the state. This system was especially useful for the crippled or infirm who were no longer able to handle steep, uneven terrain on foot. Royal litters, painstakingly depicted in an illustration by the 17th-century chronicler Guamán Poma, could hold up to two people at once. They consisted of two long poles upon which a roofed seating area was attached. Four load bearers were required to hold up the litter, with one man stationed at each end of the poles, although some documents cite up to 80 litter bearers for a single imperial envoy. The interior and exterior of the litter was posh, bedecked with textiles, feathers, and silver or gold detailing. The most well-known provinces to produce litter bearers for the king included Rucanas, Callahuaya, and the Camana Valley, all located in southern Peru.

Llamas were integral as pack animals for long-distance travel. With the capacity to carry approximately 100-pound loads, they were unsuitable for transporting humans. They would travel in packs, each carrying goods in evenly weighted woolen pouches hung across their backs.

Chasquis

The delivery of messages and packages was facilitated by trained Inca runners known as *chasquis*. Operating on a relay system, *chasquis* would run for a prescribed distance with oral messages, goods, and quipus (a system of multicolored knotted strings used to encode information) then pass them along to the next runner, who would continue the journey.

Chasquis worked approximately 15-day shifts, residing in small huts known as *chasquihuasi* set up along the road that were separated at equally spaced intervals. The swift, well-trained runners would deliver messages from one hut to another, with the subsequent runner starting off at a slow jog as the *chasqui* approached him in order to expedite the hand-off process. On average they were able to collectively cover nearly 250 kilometers (155 mi.) a day, making the system even more efficient than the horseback-driven postal system established by the Spaniards in the colonial period. Archaeologists have estimated that the delivery of a message from the second capital of Quito in the north down to Cuzco, a distance of more than 1,500 kilometers (932 mi.), involved about 375 *chasquis* and took one week. In addition to the main Inca roads, *chasquis* also traveled along special *chasqui* roads, usually footpaths that provided shortcuts to the desired destination.

Tambos

Tambos were way stations, or rest stops, for designated personnel, located at strategic points along the road system. Similar to caravan stops along Asia's Silk Road, *tambos* provided food and temporary respite during long journeys. They were intended for use among traveling armies and long-distance travelers and traders. More than 2,000 *tambos* were set up throughout the Inca Empire, spaced out at intervals of approximately 20 kilometers (12 mi.). *Tambos* ranged from simple inns to full-fledged multipurpose cities that provided temporary residences for travelers. Although they varied in layout and size, all *tambos* had housing barracks, storage, and cooking facilities. Their associated buildings were constructed using local materials and techniques, giving each *tambo* a distinctive local character.

The largest and most lavishly accommodated *tambos* were reserved for use by the Sapa Inca during his military campaigns and en route to his royal estates. Unlike the smaller way stations, these major *tambos* doubled as administrative centers and regional capitals with large settlements. They often contained compounds for *chicha*-brewing specialists, weavers, and potters. Archaeological evidence suggests that administrative and ceremonial activities also took place at the larger *tambos*. More modest *tambos* were used by *kurakas*, administrators, and other bureaucrats during their travels. The simplest and smallest *tambos* were reserved for *chasquis*.

Maritime Transportation

Transportation by sea was not as systematized as the Inca road system, since the empire was a con-

11.3 The site of Tambo Machay, located outside Cuzco. It served as a way station for travelers along the royal highway. (Eloise Quiñones Keber)

11.4 Modern-day Aymara peoples using totora *reed boats on Lake Titicaca. These boats are very similar to the ones used in Inca times.* (J. J. George)

tiguous expanse of land that did not require maritime conquests. Boat making was an ancient craft in the coastal region, essential for fishing. Coastal *balsas* (rafts) were made from reeds woven together into small vessels with pointed ends to maintain balance. Canes were used as paddles. They were used principally for fishing and not for transport.

In the warmer equatorial waters off the shore of modern-day Ecuador, more sophisticated boats were constructed for the purposes of exploration and transporting cargo along the coast. These *balsas*, with platforms and storage areas, could hold up to 50 people.

Similar boats were used in bodies of water located in the interior of the empire, such as on Lake Titicaca. The lake's giant *totoras*, or bulrushes that grow up to 3.6 meters (12 ft.) tall, provided the raw materials for *balsa* construction.

Crossing Rivers and Canyons

The Incas had numerous methods for crossing rivers and canyons in the empire. *Oroyas* were large baskets that transported humans and animals across distances by a system of ropes and pulleys. Floating bridges made from *totora* reeds tied to ropes allowed traffic across Lake Titicaca and its nearby rivers, while rafts were used for smaller rivers and marshy areas.

Two types of bridges connected roadways separated by treacherous mountain passes or natural obstructions: bridges constructed from logs and rope suspension bridges. Log bridges connected shorter distances, while the famous suspension bridges allowed for the crossing of rivers and gorges.

and three of them were again braided to make a still larger rope, and so on. The thick cables were pulled across the river with small ropes and attached to stone abutments on each side.

Marketplace Trade

Inca markets bore little resemblance to their Aztec counterparts, which the conquistador Hernán Cortés described as a feast for the eyes. Given that all goods were technically the property of the Inca state, most citizens did not own many surplus items for trade. Nevertheless, some documentation exists of markets at the local level, in which women traded household surpluses such as textiles, foods, and other crafts. Some archaeologists have hypothesized that the *kallanka*, a ubiquitous Inca architectural form consisting of a long rectangular-shaped hall, may have been used to house markets, in addition to other administrative functions.

11.5 Drawing of an Inca suspension bridge. Such bridges were ubiquitous throughout the Inca Empire. (Felipe Guamán Poma de Ayala)

Suspension bridges were familiar and vital links along the highway system. The rugged Andean terrain was in places cut through by deep river canyons. Using fibers from cotton, grasses, saplings, and llama and alpaca wool, the Incas constructed rope bridges that spanned at least as much as 50 meters (165 ft.)—a longer span than any European bridge at the time. The 19th-century American traveler Ephraim Squier wrote about and illustrated one of the largest and elaborately constructed Inca suspension bridges, located at the Apurímac River to the west of Cuzco.

Garcilasco de la Vega, in 1604, reported on the cable-making techniques for these bridges. The fibers, he wrote, were braided into ropes of the length necessary for the bridge. Three of these ropes were woven together to make a larger rope,

DIVISION OF LABOR

Labor was tightly regulated by the central government, which had devised an ingenious system for organizing workers and circulating the fruits of their labor across a continually expanding empire. The *mita*, as well as other overlapping organizational systems, facilitated high economic productivity. A system of checks and balances also existed to retain fairness and accuracy. The governor, or *tucuy ricu*, of each provincial capital was responsible for keeping track of the fulfillment of labor obligations within the jurisdiction. Aside from the *mita*, there were divisions of workers that belonged to other labor systems and thus provided service to the state under different auspices. These included *yanakuna*, *mitmaqkuna*, and members of specialized labor groups. A select group of women known as *acllas* (*acllacuna*, or "chosen women") were selected to provide services to the king and his family.

The *Mita*

The *mita* was a rotational labor system that required heads of households to contribute to state projects. Their required tasks could include construction of buildings, dams, bridges, or roads; mining; military service; personal service to nobles; or the production of crafts such as textiles, ceramics, or metallurgy. The *kurakas*, or local officials, would assign a certain number of men from the community for the *mita* periodically, depending on the needs stipulated by the central government. Men were required to provide their service once a year on projects that were often located outside their home communities and could last for several months at a time. While they were gone, other members of his *ayllu*, or kin group, were expected to compensate for his absence. Every male head of household in the empire was required to participate in the *mita* unless he was exempted by virtue of royal status, old age, or disability.

Yanakuna

The *yanakuna* (*yanaconas*) were men permanently relocated from their home communities to work full time in the service of the Sapa Inca, bureaucrats, or *kurakas* as attendants. They essentially worked as servants to the elites. They usually came from small, minor settlements and were sent to provincial centers, royal estates, or Cuzco itself. The *yanakuna* were exempt from paying taxes through the *mita*. They fulfilled any number of responsibilities from meeting the personal needs of the ruler to working in royal agricultural fields or presiding over the care of royal mummies. A single ruler or high elite could have dozens to hundreds of *yanakuna* in his service. Evidence suggests that they also served *coyas*, or queens. This position was inherited from the parents.

Camayos

The *camayos* were skilled laborers who worked full time in a designated area of specialization for the ruler or as government bureaucrats. The *camayos* included the sons of local elites who were sent to Cuzco for training in a special four-year school; accountants known as *quipucamayos* trained to read

the quipu; tapestry weavers known as *cumbicamayos;* stonemasons known as *pirkacamayos;* coca producers called *cocacamayos;* dye specialists called *tanti camayos;* silversmiths; potters; and *kerocamayos* dedicated to making *keros* (ritual drinking vessels). The majority of *camayos* were permanently relocated to Cuzco or to major provincial centers, although some managed to remain in their home territory. In the highlands *camayos* were almost entirely self-sufficient; in addition to working in their specialty, they also farmed small plots of land for subsistence. On the coast *camayos* acquired basic necessities by bartering the goods they produced, allowing them to work exclusively on their craft. The skill and position were hereditary and usually passed down from father to son.

Mitmaqkuna

The *mitmaqkuna* (*mitmacuna, mitimaes*) were individuals relocated from their home communities to work in foreign lands. The term is often translated to "colonist," but this designation does not fully capture the myriad of activities associated with them. Like foreigners who visited Cuzco, the *mitmaqkuna* were required to wear the dress of their homeland so they could be easily distinguished from those who were indigenous to the area. Some *mitmaqkuna* were also *yanakuna*, and some were also *camayos*; these categories were not mutually exclusive.

The *mitmaqkuna* were used for two specific purposes. The first were those forcibly resettled for economic purposes. For example, an entire community could be moved to another province or a different ecological zone in order to produce different crops, such as maize, for tribute. It was common, in fact, for the government to move communities southward into eco-zones more conducive to agriculture for intensified crop production. This was practiced so that the government could acquire the highest volume and quality of tribute goods. *Mitmaqkuna* benefited as well, receiving exemption from tribute payment by the government upon completion of their service.

The second were those moved to new lands for the purposes of quelling potential conflict among communities newly introduced into the empire. These *mitmaqkuna* typically were accorded high social status and were given gifts of women and special titles by the government for exemplary work. As the military continued to conquer new lands and bring them under Inca rule, previously autonomous communities had to conform to new obligations and ways of life. The clashes between newly conquered groups and ethnic Incas often erupted in violence, necessitating built-in mechanisms for establishing order. The arrival of *mitmaqkuna* into new territory, often regarded by the locals as spies, signaled an imposition of centralized authority. *Mitmaqkuna* fulfilled the task of spreading Inca ideologies by introducing Quechua, the common language of the empire, and by abiding by Inca law to set an example to others for proper behavior. Moreover, the mixing of peoples from different backgrounds decreased the possibility of unified revolt against Inca rule.

Acllas

The *acllas* (*acllacuna*), or "chosen women," served an important role in the Inca division of labor. All of the *acllas* worked in the service of the Sapa Inca and his family, primarily weaving the finest cloth, known as *cumbi*, and brewing *chicha* (maize beer) for royal consumption and ritual. As full-time specialists, they were exempt from tribute obligations. The highest-ranked *acllas* worked in full service of the sun god, Inti, and became known as "virgins of the Sun." These women, known as *mamakuna*, never married and, as they grew older, became the overseers of incoming *acllas*. The next group below in the hierarchy included women who would become the secondary wives of the Sapa Inca or the primary wives of elites and government officials. The lowest-ranking group was composed of the remaining women who did not qualify for the more prestigious positions and worked as servants within the *acllahuasi* (house of the chosen women) or the royal quarters.

CRAFT PRODUCTION

Crafts were produced both locally and at the state level by children, women, men, and specialists and nonspecialists alike. Crafts produced under the Incas included textiles for clothing, bedding, and ritual use; household implements, such as ceramics and cooking and serving utensils; and tools and ornaments crafted out of stone and metal. At the local level, crafts tended to be produced by the family unit, which produced the appropriate quantity of goods necessary for household consumption. Division of labor tended to fall along gender lines; women were the primary weavers and men focused on the making of tools and other implements. At the state level, crafts were more specialized, and workshops were organized by the type of medium used. Objects produced under the auspices of the empire had to conform to certain standardized sizes, methods of manufacture, and decoration. Craft production of the coast took on a different character than that of the highlands, given the differences in the types of materials available in that geographical region. On the coast, craftsmen and -women were expert gourd carvers and ceramicists, whose skills were highly enviable to the Incas. Indeed, a great number of artisans working for the capitulated Chimú Empire (ca. 900–1470 C.E.) were relocated to the new imperial capital of Cuzco.

Household Craft Production

All items necessary for survival were produced by members of the household unit. Household crafts included stone, wood, and bone tools; textiles and weaving implements; and ceramic cooking and serving wares. Tools of various materials were created generally by men and were used for hunting, fishing, cutting, and preparing hides. Weaving was practiced almost exclusively by women, who participated in every part of its production, from spinning cotton and camelid fibers into thread to weaving on a loom. Cloth produced by females of the household was used for clothing and bedding and had a thick, coarse quality, known by the Incas as *chusi*. Both men and women produced ceramics, depending on the region. Household craft production was not specialized and centered on utilitarian items, a fact corroborated both by documentary and archaeological evidence. Household crafts varied according to local production techniques and materials and usually followed centuries-old traditions that remained relatively unchanged over time.

State-Level Craft Production

The production and distribution of specialized crafts were controlled by the state. Still subject to tribute obligations, artisans generally worked part time on their craft. Workshops were medium specific, meaning that each focused on the production of objects out of a single material; this included textiles, clay, metallurgy, stone, and feathers. Workshops were generally located in isolated areas and could house hundreds of artisans working together. Despite their separation according to the type of material manufactured, crafts regulated by the state maintained uniformity by conforming to a specific set of criteria. For example, the same types of geometric motifs, such as crisscrossed lines, stylized plants, stepped frets, and quadripartite (four-part) designs are found on Inca imperial crafts across almost all media. Archaeologists have identified this as the Cuzco style.

TEXTILES AND CLOTH

The most highly prized commodity in the Inca realm, textiles were produced in enormous quantities as clothing, gifts, and offerings to the gods. Textile production outside the domestic sphere was heavily regulated by the government. State-mandated textiles were produced by master weavers throughout the empire. Certain communities were designated as cloth producers; aside from tribute obligations, this would be the principal economic activity of every household in the entire town or hamlet. Each member of the community would be involved in the process. Herders were responsible for shearing llamas of their wool, which was the first step of the complex and involved process of producing cloth among the Incas. People living in lower-altitude regions produced textiles from cotton and local fibers, such as *cabuya*, an agave. Girls were taught how to spin fiber into thread as early as the age of four. They were also in charge of collecting natural dyes that endowed Inca textiles with a colorful vibrancy. Dye specialists, known as *tanticamayos*,

extracted dyes from plants for textiles. Even the old and infirm could participate by picking dirt and extraneous materials out of the unprocessed clods of fiber. Textiles were produced on backstrap looms for smaller pieces and on upright looms for larger ones. Textile-producing communities existed throughout the realm, both in the Inca heartland around Cuzco as well as in the coastal areas and even as far away as present-day Argentina.

By the time of the Incas weaving had become a state-controlled enterprise; each household unit was required to provide tribute payment to the state, which often entailed cloth production. Every household had access to locally grown fibers for communal use. Weaving was typically a female activity, passed down from mother to daughter, though all members of society were involved in different parts of the production process.

Women known as *acllas* ("chosen woman") were handpicked from their respective communities to live in a cloistered communal space with other women to weave the highest-quality *cumbi* for elites. The finest *cumbi* was often interwoven with threads of gold and silver, *spondylus* shell imported from Ecuador, or other precious materials. The *acllas* were believed to be working in the service of Inti, the sun god, producing fine textiles not only for royal use but as cosmological sustenance to honor and regenerate the Sun. The second-highest level of weavers were the *cumbicamayos*, who were highly specialized men who produced *cumbi* as tribute to the state. Moreover, weavers and other artisans from various regions under Inca jurisdiction were sent to Cuzco to participate in the *mitmaqkuna* program for the production of high-status state-mandated textiles. One of the most well-preserved textile production centers was housed at Huánuco Pampa, whose excavations by archaeologist Craig Morris and others have yielded a great deal of information on cloth production in its economic and organizational context. Morris and his colleagues discovered more than 50 enclosed structures dedicated to the production of textiles and inferred that they probably housed *acllas*.

METALLURGY

Given the high value of copper, silver, and gold among the Incas, the crafting of precious metals into objects was an activity restricted to the most skilled metallurgists. Silver and gold objects were accessible only to the nobility. Mining took place throughout the empire. Some of the most plentiful mines offered silver at Potosí, gold at Chuquiabo, and a variety of ores near Samaipata, all located in modern-day Bolivia. Although a few surviving objects, such as miniature llama and human effigies, give us a taste for the sophistication of Inca metalwork, most knowledge of the tradition is lost because precious metals were melted down into currency by the Spaniards. Most information on metallurgy comes from Spanish eyewitness descriptions from the 16th century as well as legal documents describing the Inca gold and silver objects sent to Spain.

The Incas were expert metallurgists, most notably because they imported thousands of artisans to Cuzco from the Chimú Empire stationed in its capital of Chan Chan on the north coast after it was conquered in 1470. These transplanted artisans worked at metallurgy workshops in Cuzco, which would receive ores excavated from various sites for fabrication into vessels, utilitarian and decorative objects, and works of art. Transplanted metalsmiths also were brought to Cuzco from the coastal settlements of Ica, Chincha, and Pachacamac. Metallurgy was what the archaeologist Heather Lechtman has coined a "three-component system," meaning that the main elemental components were gold, silver, and copper. This system was inherited by traditions set in coastal societies in the Intermediate Period.

In addition to precious objects metallurgists also crafted weapons for use by the Inca armies. Tin bronze, created by alloying copper and tin, was used to create weapons and utilitarian objects because it was the strongest metal available to the Incas. The use of tin bronze was inherited by Tiwanaku metallurgists. Tin ore was extracted from mines in Bolivia, Chile, and northwestern Argentina and then distributed in its alloyed bronze form to artisan workshops in Cuzco and provincial cities. Bronze circulated much more freely in the Inca Empire than gold and silver, because it was considered a raw material to create tools such as axes, tweezers, pins, and needles rather than a source of wealth or a luxury good.

Metalsmiths used flattened stones as anvils and different sized copper hammers to produce the desired shape. They worked sitting down on the floor, in groups. Like the practices of Chimú metalsmiths, it can be assumed that Inca production also took on an assembly-line quality, in which one group would hammer sheets of silver and gold, and another would cut, mold, and solder the flattened sheets into objects.

CERAMICS

Many ceramic traditions throughout Inca territory remained relatively unchanged as continuations of local practice established millennia prior. An exception is an Inca pottery style that developed in Cuzco with a specific set of forms, color schemes, and decorative motifs. Inca-style pottery was both exported from the capital as prestige items and imitated by potters throughout the realm. The most distinctive Inca ceramic ware is the *urpu*, aryballoid-shaped jar with a pointed bottom, a restricted flared neck, and handles on each side through which rope could be strung for easy transport. The *urpu* varied in size from about 25 centimeters (10 in.) up to 100 centimeters (39 in.) in height. Other types of pottery forms included pitchers, plates, bowls, jars, and dishes. Inca pottery was often polychromed with various earth tones, applied with slips (natural pigments mixed with water to create a paintlike solution) that acquired a bright, luminous quality after firing at high temperature. All Inca pottery was made from terracotta, abundant dark-colored clay with high levels of iron. Decorative motifs typically found on Inca pottery include triangles, diamonds, stylized plants and animals, hatched and cross-hatched lines, and zigzags.

Ceramic workshops were located throughout the empire. Tools included the turntable, paddle (*paleta*), and anvil. Turntables, used in the Andes since 500 B.C.E., allowed potters to create smooth, even surfaces as the pot rotated on a flat, platelike disc. The paddle, usually made of wood, was slapped along the exterior of the vessel wall to model the clay, while the circular stone anvil was placed inside to maintain its shape. Ceramic production did not achieve as high a level of specialization as textiles and metalwork, given its lower status. Ceramic specialists handcrafted vessels and used molds for rapid mass production, depending on the type of object and need of the patron.

Some Chimú ceramicists were transported to Cuzco, creating the distinctive black wares of the north coast for Inca consumption. They were generally made from two-piece molds in the form of an animal, vegetable, or human, with double and single spouts and a black, heavily burnished surface. These vessels and those produced in former Chimú territory are known as Chimú-Inca. All Inca ceramicists working for the state created vessels that were both decorative and functional, with generally secular themes.

STONEWORK

Stonework required the most manpower of all of the state-mandated crafts, involving the participation of up to thousands of men at a time. Inca stonemasons, conscripted through the *mita* rotational obligation required of most male heads of households, worked on building projects undertaken by various kings at Cuzco and provincial cities. Stones were dragged from quarries to their appropriate sites by the use of ropes. They were partially modified at the quarries and then further adjusted on-site. Stonemasons worked in groups to cut the stones into their distinctive Inca shape—irregular and often multipointed, with beveled edges that cause them to look "pillowed out." They were then fitted together and modified to produce the tightest bind. Stones had to be cut with great precision, as no major buildings were constructed using mortar.

OTHER SPECIALIZED CRAFT PRODUCTION

Featherworking, woodworking, and the creation of military armor were also important crafts among the Incas based on its occasional mention in historical documents and archaeological remains found in storehouses. However, little is known about the specifics of their production.

Craft Specialization on the North Coast

The north coast presents a relatively different scenario from other parts of the empire. While each household in the highlands produced all of the necessary crafts for its survival, for example, on the coast each household could specialize in a separate craft. For instance, one household might produce ceramics, and another, weave textiles, while another might manufacture *chicha*. Specifically coastal crafts such as *mates* (pyro-engraved gourds for serving and drinking *chicha*) and painted textiles were also integral components of specialized craft production in this region. Trade networks along the coast, together with the possible existence of a form of currency (still debated by archaeologists), allowed for the exchange of these goods among communities. Coastal artisans, particularly metalsmiths and potters, were transported to new territories for production in the service of Inca elites. In fact, documentation exists of hundreds of potters from the north coast relocated to the northern highland provincial center of Cajamarca. An even more famous example involves the forced relocation of Chimú metalsmiths to Cuzco after they were conquered in 1470.

MEASUREMENT

Unlike standardized measurement systems based on a fixed unit, such as the metric system or the International System of Units, many Inca measurements were established according to relative proportions. Small measurements were calculated according to the body and its movements. For example, the smallest unit of measurement, known as the *rocana*, was the length of a finger. The next largest unit was the distance between an outstretched thumb and index finger, called the *yuku*. The following measurement was the *capa*, which was about the distance between the thumb and pinkie stretched apart (approximately 20 centimeters [7.8 in.]). After that was the *khococ*, the distance from the elbow to the tip of the hand (about 45 centimeters [17.7 in.]), followed by the *sikya*, which was half of a man's arm span, approximating 81 centimeters (31.8 in.). The largest bodily unit was the *rikra*, which corresponded to the distance between an average man's outstretched hands (about 162 centimeters [63.7 in.]). It served as the base unit for many major architectural constructions in Cuzco and royal estates in its environs.

Relative measurements were also used for measuring distances. The *thatqui* was the distance of a pace, or a full step using each foot, approximating 130 centimeters (51.1 in.). The *tupu* (the same name for women's garment pins), a unit for measuring land of approximately 6,000 paces, or six to nine kilometers (3.7–5.6 mi.), was also an approximate one, which varied according to the topography and ecology of the land. The *huamani*, which also refers to an administrative unit, equaled 30 *tupus*, or about 234 kilometers (145 mi.).

Liquid measure may have been registered according to a dry grain measure called a *collo*, which equaled about 3.8 liters. Maize, quinoa, and other Inca agricultural staples were evenly parceled out through the use of large gourds with a volume of about 28 liters. There was no standard system of weights, but the Incas did use a pan balance called an *aysana*.

STORAGE

The production of agricultural and craft surpluses, a prerequisite for sustaining the empire, required a reliable storage system to protect the populace in times of drought, famine, and environmental catastrophe. Storage facilities were located throughout the empire that contained surplus agricultural products and goods. Known as *colcas*, these buildings contained important surpluses that could be used in times of need, including maize, potatoes, grains, clothing, blankets, tools, weaponry, armor, and even sandals. *Colcas* were crucial for protection against unpredictable harvests and natural disasters and to support the army during military campaigns. Despite the use of terracing and irrigation technology to improve crop productivity, the region encompassed by the Inca Empire was, and still is, environmentally unpredictable. In the highlands earthquakes wrought havoc on settlements, buildings, and fields. Moreover, the constant threat of

11.6 Colcas *were storehouses used for stockpiling agricultural surpluses, textiles, weaponry, and other goods produced for the state.* (Felipe Guamán Poma de Ayala)

frost, drought, and hail meant that successful harvests usually did not come annually. *Colcas* offered some stability by storing basic necessities for potential redistribution among society members in need.

Inca storage systems also had a secondary function of housing gifts used in diplomatic transactions as well as items used for royal feasts and ceremonies. Aside from basic necessities and military equipment, *colcas* also contained enormous amounts of sumptuous *cumbi* cloths, thousands of dried birds whose feathers would be used for mantles and tunics, ornaments crafted out of precious metals, and jugs of *chicha*. These items were critical for such events, which allowed Cuzco elites to forge alliances with foreign leaders and secure power as the empire continued to expand.

Colcas were either round or rectangular with thatched roofs, arranged in rows or clusters. They were entered through a small doorway at the bottom, and archaeologists have discovered that some were built with complex ventilation and drainage systems for the long-term preservation of foodstuffs. *Colcas* were isolated from other buildings and settlements and typically located prominently on a hill at the juncture of important trade routes. Their placement in cool, open-aired locations had a practical function; these areas provided optimal preservation conditions. In fact, maize, potatoes, quinoa, and other stored foods could last for a couple of years without perishing because of the strategic construction and placement of *colcas*.

Chroniclers estimated as many as 700 *colcas* at a single site, although archaeological evidence tells us that certain sites far exceeded this number. At Hatun Xauxa, a provincial center in the central highlands, 2,700 *colcas* were excavated, and even as far south as Argentina archaeologists discovered a site with 1,600 *colcas* in the northwest region of the country. Very little evidence exists of *colcas* in the coastal areas, suggesting that state storage was most heavily concentrated in the highlands. The most likely explanation for the lack of state storage on the coast is because regional systems of exchange maintained by the newly conquered Chimú Empire remained intact even after Inca domination. Some archaeologists have also argued that *colcas* may not have been distributed within former Chimú territory because the surplus goods could have provided the necessary means to overthrow Inca power.

Reading

Agriculture

Brian S. Bauer, "Legitimization of the State in Inca Myth and Ritual," *American Anthropologist* 98, no. 2 (1996): 327–337.

Sophie D. Coe, *America's First Cuisines* (Austin: University of Texas Press, 1994).

R. Alan Covey, *How the Incas Built Their Heartland: State Formation and the Innovation of Imperial Strategies in the Sacred Valley, Peru* (Ann Arbor: University of Michigan Press, 2006).

John Murra, "Rite and Crop in the Inca State." In *Culture in History*, edited by S. Diamond (New York: Columbia University Press, 1960).

Role of Animals

David Browman, "Pastoral Nomadism in the Andes," *Current Anthropology* 15, no. 2 (1974): 188–196.

Frank Salomon, "Vertical Politics on the Inka Frontier." In *Anthropological History of Andean Polities*, edited by John V. Murra, Nathan Wachtel, and Jacques Revel, 89–118 (Cambridge: Cambridge University Press, 1986).

Water

David Brown, "Water and Power in the Provinces: Water Management in Inka Centers of the Central Highlands of Peru," *Tawantinsuyu* 5 (1998): 23–36.

Ian S. Farrington, "Prehistoric Intensive Agriculture: Preliminary Notes on River Canalization in the Sacred Valley of the Incas." In *Drained Field Agriculture in Central and South America*, edited by John Darch, BAR International Series 189, 221–235 (Oxford: British Archaeological Reports, 1983).

Margaret MacLean, *Sacred Land, Sacred Water: Inca Landscape Planning in the Cuzco Area*, Ph.D. diss., Department of Anthropology, University of California, Berkeley, 1986.

Jeanette Sherbondy, "Water Ideology in Inca Ethnogenesis." In *Andean Cosmologies through Time*, edited by Robert H. Dover, Katharine E. Seibold, and John H. McDowell, 46–66 (Bloomington: Indiana University Press, 1992).

Mines and Mining

Jean Berthelot, "The Extraction of Precious Metals at the Time of the Inka." In *Anthropological History of Andean Polities*, edited by John V. Murra, Nathan Wachtel, and Jacques Revel, 69–88 (Cambridge: Cambridge University Press, 1986).

Heather Lechtman, "The Inka, and Andean Metallurgical Tradition." In *Expressions of Inka Power*, edited by Richard L. Burger, Craig Morris, and Ramiro Matos Mendieta, 313–356 (Washington, D.C.: Dumbarton Oaks, 2008).

An Empire Connected

John Hyslop, "Factors Influencing the Transmission and Distribution of Inka Cultural Materials throughout Tawantinsuyu." In *Latin American Horizons*, edited by Don S. Rice, 337–356 (Washington, D.C.: Dumbarton Oaks, 1993).

———, *The Inka Road System* (New York: Academic Press, 1984).

Craig Morris, "The Archaeological Study of Andean Exchange Systems." In *Social Archaeology: Beyond Subsistence and Dating*, edited by C. Redman et al., 135–327 (New York: Academic Press, 1978).

María Rostworowski de Diez Canseco, *History of the Inca Realm.* Translated by Harry B. Iceland (Cambridge: Cambridge University Press, 1999).

John Howland Rowe, "Inca Policies and Institutions Relating to the Cultural Unification of the Empire." In *The Inca and Aztec States, 1400–1800*, edited by George A. Collier, Renato I. Rosaldo, and John D. Wirth, 93–118 (New York: Academic Press, 1982).

Donald E. Thompson and John V. Murra, "The Inca Bridges of the Huanuco Region," *American Antiquity* 31, no. 5 (1966): 632–639.

Irene Silverblatt, "Andean Women in the Inca Empire," *Feminist Studies* 4, no. 3 (October 1978): 36–61.

Tom Zuidema, "Bureaucracy and Systematic Knowledge in Andean Civilization." In *The Inca and Aztec States, 1400–1800: Anthropology and History*, edited by George A. Collier, Renato I. Rosaldo, and John D. Wirth, 419–458 (New York: Academic Press, 1982).

Division of Labor

Timothy K. Earle and Terence N. D'Altroy, "The Political Economy of the Inka Empire: The Archaeology of Power and Finance." In *Archaeological Thought in America*, edited by Carl C.

Lamberg-Karlovsky, 183–204 (Cambridge: Cambridge University Press, 1989).

Catherine J. Julien, "How Inca Decimal Administration Worked," *Ethnohistory* 35, no. 3 (Summer 1988): 257–279.

Floyd G. Lounsbury, "Some Aspects of the Inka Kinship System." In *Anthropological History of Andean Polities*, edited by John V. Murra, Nathan Wachtel, and Jacques Revel, 121–136 (Cambridge: Cambridge University Press, 1986).

John Murra, *The Economic Organization of the Inka State* (Greenwich, Conn.: JAI Press, 1980).

María Rostworowski de Diez Canseco, "The Incas." In *The Inca World: The Development of Pre-Columbian Peru, A.D. 1000–1534*, edited by Laura Laurencich Minelli, 143–187 (Norman: University of Oklahoma Press, 2000).

John Howland Rowe, "Inca Policies and Institutions Relating to Cultural Unification." In *The Inca and Aztec States, 1400–1800: Anthropology and History*, edited by George A. Collier, Renato I. Rosaldo, and John D. Wirth, 93–118 (New York: Academic Press, 1982).

Craft Production

Tamara Bray, "Inka Pottery as Culinary Equipment: Food, Feasting, and Gender in Imperial State Design," *American Antiquity* 14, no. 1 (March 2003): 3–28.

Craig Morris and Adriana von Hagen, *The Inka Empire and Its Andean Origins* (New York: Abbeville Press, 1993).

John V. Murra, "Cloth and Its Functions in the Inca State," *American Anthropologist* 64 (1962): 710–728.

María Rostworowski de Diez Canseco, *Costa peruana prehispánica* (Lima: Instituto de Estudios Peruanos, 1989).

Rebecca Stone-Miller, *To Weave for the Sun: Andean Textiles in the Museum of Fine Arts* (Boston: Museum of Fine Arts, 1992).

Measurement

Bernabé Cobo, *Inca Religion and Customs.* Translated by Roland Hamilton (Austin: Texas University Press, 1990).

Terence N. D'Altroy, *The Incas* (London: Blackwell, 2002).

Garcilaso de la Vega, El Inca, *Royal Commentaries of the Incas and General History of Peru, Parts 1 and 2.* Translated by H. V. Livermore (Austin: University of Texas Press, 1966).

John H. Rowe, "Inca Culture at the Time of the Spanish Conquest." In *Handbook of South American Indians.* Vol. 2, edited by Julian H. Steward, 183–330 (Washington, D.C.: Smithsonian Institution, 1946).

Storage

Terence N. D'Altroy and Timothy K. Earle, "Staple Finance, Wealth Finance, and Storage in the Inka Political Economy." In *Inka Storage Systems*, edited by Terry Y. LeVine, 31–61 (Norman: University of Oklahoma Press, 1992).

Timothy K. Earle, "Storage and the Inka Imperial Economy: Archaeological Research." In *Inka Storage Systems*, edited by Terry Y. LeVine, 327–342 (Norman: University of Oklahoma Press, 1992).

Craig Morris, "Huánuco Pampa and Tunsukancha: Major and Minor Nodes in the Inka Storage Network." In *Inka Storage Systems*, edited by Terry Y. LeVine, 151–175 (Norman: University of Oklahoma Press, 1992).

———, "Storage, Supply, and Redistribution in the Economy of the Inka State." In *Anthropological History of Andean Polities*, edited by John V. Murra, Nathan Wachtel, and Jacques Revel, 59–68 (Cambridge: Cambridge University Press, 1986).

———, "The Technology of Highland Inka Food Storage." In *Inka Storage Systems*, edited by Terry Y. LeVine, 237–258 (Norman: University of Oklahoma Press, 1992).

James E. Snead, "Imperial Infrastructure and the Inka State Storage System." In *Inka Storage Systems*, edited by Terry Y. LeVine, 62–106 (Norman: University of Oklahoma Press, 1992).

12

DAILY LIFE

Knowledge of daily life among the inhabitants of the Inca Empire remains relatively limited due to its scarcity in the historical and archaeological record. Artifacts associated with everyday life, such as household items, games, wedding paraphernalia, children's possessions, and medicine, rarely survive the test of time. Moreover, the ephemeral aspects of day-to-day existence—conversation, music and dance, social relations, and the routine processes of cooking, cleaning, or venerating gods—can never be fully reconstructed. Written sources from the colonial period provide a glimpse of these nonmaterial correlates of daily life, but not without their setbacks. Some aspects of Inca daily life failed to catch the attention of Spanish chroniclers, who were primarily interested in describing the history of Inca imperial expansion, religion, cosmology, and the conquest. As Christians, they viewed many Inca customs as heathen, placing a negative spin on subjects such as religion and medicinal practices, which inevitably obscured their original significance. Finally, much of what the chroniclers wrote only applied to Cuzco and its immediate environs, thus ignoring the diversity of experience among subjects of the Incas across the 2,500-mile stretch of empire.

Nevertheless, the historical record provides some valuable insights into the Incas' marriage customs, family life, daily chores, recreation, education, personal appearance, medicinal practices, and more. Although scholars must keep in mind the limitations of colonial documents to provide a completely unbiased, all-inclusive account of Inca customs, much can still be learned from some key sources. Two 17th-century documents, El Inca Garcilaso de la Vega's *Royal Commentaries of the Incas and General History of Peru* (1609) and the Spanish Jesuit Bernabé Cobo's *Inca Religion and Customs* (1653), serve as the most important foundational texts for reconstructing daily life among the Incas. Garcilaso, a mestizo of Spanish and royal Inca descent, provides a description of daily life that is nestled within a larger narrative about the history of the Inca Empire and the Spanish conquest. Cobo's account makes up part of a full-length book on Inca cosmology and cultural traditions, although some parts have been lost. What differentiates these authors from other historians of the 16th and 17th centuries is their interest in the everyday social realities of the commoner class in the Inca realm. Their works represent years of research to obtain information on many aspects of everyday life, from naming ceremonies to footwear. Despite the fact that these publications postdate the Inca period, both Cobo and Garcilaso took great pains to ensure accuracy through extensive interviews with descendants of the Incas and consultation of existing written sources. This chapter draws heavily from the information provided by these primary sources as well as the current archaeological literature that explores themes of everyday life.

FAMILY

Inca families were relatively large; children were considered assets because they could provide needed labor in the field and the household. This held particularly true for families living in areas where farming was the primary means of subsistence. In fact, Spanish observers often remarked that large families were "rich" families. Because the smallest tribute-paying unit was set at the level of the household, not the individual, larger families could perform labor obligations to the state more quickly and efficiently than smaller ones. The household usually contained the mother, father, children, and unmarried or widowed relatives. The vast majority of men in the Inca realm were commoners and thus only had one wife. Elite men, including *kurakas* (local leaders) and members of the royal Inca lineage, could have a principal wife and several secondary wives. The principal wife was the only wife accorded with any real sense of legitimacy; she was officially recognized as a "true" wife and the inheritor of her husband's estate upon his death. Unlike the secondary wives, the principal wife enjoyed an official marriage ceremony with her husband. Secondary wives for the king were chosen from the *acllahuasi*, or "house of the chosen women," which was a cloister of celibate women dedicated to weaving for the royal family and providing sacrificial offerings to the sun god, Inti.

The Incas employed a complex set of terms for identifying family members, which varied according to the sex of the speaker and his or her familial relationship to the individual in question. The male patriarch possessed two separate labels for *father* (*yaya*) and *husband* (*qosa*), but the matriarch was simply referred to as *mother* (*mama*) or *woman* (*warmi*). A father could call his children by the separate terms for *daughter* (*ususi*) and *son* (*churi*), but the mother referred to all of her children by a singular term, *wawa*, which does not distinguish age or sex. Grandparents also only used one term, *haway*, to refer to their grandchildren. Male and female siblings referred to one another by four different names: *Wawqi* was used among brothers and *ñaña* among sisters; a brother referred to a sister as *pana*, and a sister called her brother *tura*. These labels reveal the rigidity of social categories among the Incas, as well as the extent to which individual identity guided familial relations, all the way from the household to the state level.

Lineage and Descent

Inca notions of cosmic time allowed for the "invention" of ancestors and family histories. The Incas saw themselves as descendants of the founding member of their particular kin group, who could take the form of a mythical human ancestor, a *huaca* (sacred place or shrine), or a sacred animal. The founding ancestor, in whichever form it took, provided a source for group identity among all members of the lineage. This collective of individuals who traced common descent to an ancient ancestor was known as an *ayllu*.

The founding ancestor of the *ayllu*, whether considered human or mythical, produced a male and female heir who, in turn, gave rise to two separate lineages known as moieties. The first two descendants of the original moiety founders settled each of the four parts, known as *suyus*, of the Inca Empire: Antisuyu, Chinchaysuyu, Cuntisuyu, and Collasuyu. Every member of an *ayllu* married a member of the opposite moiety, meaning that the two lineages and lands associated with each would be unified through bonds of marriage. Individual families were split along lines of parallel descent, a

concept known as ambilineality. In other words, males understood themselves as descended from a lineage of men, and females saw themselves as the progeny of a female line. Principles of ambilineality guided Inca social structure, gender relations, and even economic activities.

In addition to organizing families and individuals into cohesive units, the *ayllu* and moiety structures also served practical functions. An *ayllu* doubled as a self-sufficient economic entity. In accordance with Inca notions of balance and reciprocity, *ayllu* members distributed among the four *suyus* exchanged goods and resources within the group. In each zone an *ayllu* held rights to certain natural resources, whether farmland, herding grounds, or water. Because the *suyus* cover all of the empire's different ecological zones, each household was allocated a variety of products, from maize, which thrives in the hot lowlands, to potatoes that can only be grown in the cold, high-altitude Andes.

Marriage

Given that families supported themselves through the bonds of kinship-based reciprocity, it was essential to marry within one's own *ayllu*. Individuals tended to marry within their own towns and villages. Incest among commoners was strictly prohibited and was punishable by death. Brothers and sisters were forbidden from marriage, as were uncles and aunts and direct descendants and ancestors. The closest familial relation permissible for marriage among commoners was between first cousins, but only under the condition that both husband and wife properly revered their mutual grandfather once deceased. Among elites marriage between a brother and his half sister was allowed, presumably because of the limited pool of eligible partners. The king was actually encouraged to marry his sister toward the later Inca period because a royal union between brother and sister of Inca blood was considered the purest of all.

Weddings typically occurred after the month of June, which marked the collection of the harvest. The young men and women of the provinces were brought together by the *kuraka* (local leader), who would select wives for each of the men. Following this matchmaking event the marriage ceremony would commence. The bride was handed over to the groom by her father in front of the groom's family, at which point she would receive a special marriage sandal. The sandal, worn on the right foot, was made of llama wool if she was a virgin, and of *ichu*, a type of grass from the highlands, if she was not. After arriving at the house of the groom, the wife-to-be would publicly present him with an offering of clothing that included a wool *uncu* (tunic), a *llauto* (headband), and other fine accessories. The groom then put on the new clothing after which the bride and groom received gifts from both families. These could include spindles for weaving, seeds that were symbolic of a good harvest and served as a metaphor for reproduction, and ceramic pots. Wedding rituals varied across regions. For example, in some areas the process of gift giving was more elaborate or the ceremonial exchanges between the two families took place over a period of several days. In the hot, dry coastal areas, it can be assumed that the gifts exchanged conformed to typical clothing and adornment practices of the region. Although the documentary record reveals little about elite marriage ceremonies, it can be assumed that they were elaborate and well-attended affairs that included sumptuous feasts, celebrations, and gift giving.

Houses

Inca houses, or *huasi*, were constructed out of a variety of materials depending on climate and geography. In the highlands houses were often made out of stone. There is also archaeological evidence of houses in Cuzco made from sod blocks and adobe. In the tropical zones homes were constructed from wood, and in the dry coastal areas they were made from adobe (dried mud brick) or wattle and daub.

Houses were detached from one another and clustered into towns *(llactas)* in random formation, usually in accordance with the layout of the terrain. *Llactas* were quite small with an average of 100 residents, and houses tended to be far apart so as not to encroach on the plot of land owned by a neighboring family. The wooden houses of the tropical lowlands tended to be more spacious than their highland and coastal counterparts, containing an entire extended family unit of up to a dozen individuals. The adobe and wattle-and-daub houses of the highlands were smaller and square shaped with flat roofs. Stone households in the highlands were a far cry from the majestic stone administrative and religious buildings made of coursed ashlar masonry (masonry that has the appearance of straight rows). The stones were not specially cut but instead stuck together haphazardly with a mud mortar. They were windowless and squat with flat roofs made from *ichu* grass.

The majority of the houses in Cuzco were rectangular in shape, although round ones were common among the ethnic Aymara people. (Round houses conserve heat better; a necessity in the frigid, high-altitude environments that the Aymaras settled in what is now Bolivia.) Doors were made from woven cane that could be rolled up and down. All houses were one-room structures, with no distinction between living, sleeping, and cooking areas. Husband, wife, and children all slept together in the same area. Generally, the houses of the *kurakas* and other important members of society were larger and of finer construction across all regions.

The interiors of commoner houses tended to be quite plain, containing only the essential furnishings and tools and with little to no extraneous decorations. All households, whether elite or commoner, possessed the following amenities: a ceramic stove designed with several holes onto which cooking pots were placed; grinding stones for producing maize flour; ceramic cookware and serving dishes; storage bins for food, drink, and cloth; weaving implements; and bedding. The Incas did not have furniture such as tables and chairs with the exception of elites, who sometimes possessed special ceremonial seats made of wood. The Incas did not have frames or mattresses for their beds but rather slept on top of thick blankets woven out of llama wool, referred to as *chusi*. In the lowlands people slept in hammocks (*puñuna*) made from cotton or plant fibers woven into loose netting.

Stages of Life

Unlike Western societies that measure a person's age and maturity by years, the Incas measured age more loosely, taking into account a person's physical development as well as other factors to determine his or her position within the life cycle. There existed 12 separate stages of life among the Incas, conceived of as roads; each carried a specific set of characterizations. Interestingly, the roads were not ordered according to relative age but by level of contribution to society. Although these life-cycle divisions probably existed in the Andes before the Incas, it was under the Inca Empire that they became systematized for the purpose of census collecting and labor extraction by the central government.

EARLY CHILDHOOD

Babies were cared for by their mothers and occasionally by older siblings. According to Inca law and custom, the mother assumed full responsibility for her newborn, with the exception of twins, whose care was divided between the mother and father for a period of two years. The first major ceremony marking a child's entry into the world was the hair-cutting and naming ceremony known as *rutuchicoy*. This took place once a child was weaned from breast-feeding, usually around two years of age. It commenced with great festivity and was celebrated by family members and friends. The child's most revered uncle would cut his or her hair and fingernails with a flint knife for the first time and save the clippings as sacred heirlooms. It was at this point that the child was officially named and received gifts of cloth, llamas, and maize from family members. Some scholars have postulated high infant mortality rates among the Incas as one reason for waiting two years to name a child and conduct such a ceremony. The delay might also relate to Andean concepts of the soul and the age at which it was thought to be fully formed.

Both boys and girls were put to work as soon as they possessed the required cognitive and physical capabilities, usually by age four or five. They helped care for younger siblings when the mother and father were unavailable. They helped in the fields by pulling weeds and gathering plants. They also tended to the domesticated animals that a family might have in its possession, such as dogs, *cuy* (guinea pigs), and llamas. Some participated in making *chicha*, or maize beer. As the children got older, their duties became more gender specific. Girls began to perform female chores such as spinning fibers into thread, cooking, and assisting in the maintenance of the household. Girls also helped pick flowers whose pigments were utilized for dyeing textiles. Boys began to learn the crafts of their fathers such as hunting, fishing, and toolmaking. They began to hone their skills in hunting by starting with small birds, which they captured with traps. Both boys and girls were taught pottery manufacture and weaving, along with various region-specific duties.

PUBERTY

Both boys and girls underwent initiation ceremonies at about age 14. At the boy's ceremony, known as *huarachicoy*, he would receive his official name as well as a special breechcloth *(huara)*. The name accorded him at *rutuchicoy* would now be replaced with the name that he would use for the rest of his life. A girl experienced a similar rite of passage known as *quicuchicuy* after her first menstruation. This ceremony required her to fast for several days, subsisting on nothing but raw corn, which would not be administered until the third day. During the entire process the girl was locked up in her house without access to the outside world. On the fourth day, if she survived the test, the girl would be cared for by her mother, who cleaned her up and washed and braided her hair. Wearing special clothing and white woolen sandals, she visited with relatives who came to celebrate. The celebrations associated with *quicuchicuy* lasted several days, after which the girl would receive her permanent name given by an important uncle. Both boys and girls would receive names that reflected their personal character—something that presumably was not fully developed until puberty. Their names often referred to an animal, an abstract concept, a feature of the natural landscape, or a fantastical creature. Common boys' names included *amaru* (snake), *pacakoti* (cataclysm), *poma* (puma), *condor*, *qispi* (crystal), or *sinchi* (powerful). Female names tended to carry more serene, peaceful connotations; among the most widely used were *ronto* (egg), *qori* (gold), *ocllo* (pure), and *cuyllor* (star).

Adolescents also began to take on more specialized household duties. Boys were responsible for tending llama herds and hunting. By this time they would have acquired expertise in different hunting techniques. Girls were expected to tend to household duties such as cooking and cleaning.

ADULTHOOD

Adulthood commenced with marriage, which occurred around a woman's late teens and a man's early 20s. It ranked first among the Incas' 12 stages, or "roads," of life, because it marks the period when men and women alike are the most economically productive; they are the greatest asset to the Inca state. The husband and wife received a plot of land inherited from their respective families and were assigned tribute obligations by the state. The husband was now responsible for carrying out his obligations toward the *mita* rotational labor system that required participation in large-scale public projects throughout the empire. Finally, adulthood went hand in hand with producing offspring to assist in day-to-day survival as well as to perpetuate both the male and female lineages.

Unmarried adults led lives that significantly differed from those of their married counterparts. Women and men that did not receive marriage partners continued to live in the household of their parents. Although they did not personally owe tribute to the state, they still assisted in labor obligations for their household of residence. Other types of unmarried adults included men and women shamans, who interacted with the supernatural world through the consumption of hallucinogenic drugs; *acllas*, or cloistered "chosen women," who served the Inca monarch through the production of fine cloth and *chicha*; women prostitutes; and male religious specialists.

OLD AGE

The elderly, sick, and crippled were exempted from tribute obligations to the state unless they retained dexterity in their hands or the ability to move freely. Women continued to weave far past their prime. Men tended to small animals or cultivated small gardens. Once they were physically unable to perform such duties, these men and women were cared for full time by family members. The deceased were treated with the highest dignity and respect, as ancestor worship was integral to Inca religious practice. The body would be carefully mummified by the family and continually cared for with prayers and offerings of food, clothing, drink, and precious objects by the succeeding generations.

WOMEN

Women played an important role in Inca life, not only within the domestic sphere, but in the imperial realm. Royal Inca women, known as *coyas*, exerted considerable political influence, often acting as counsels to the ruler. Female figures also featured heavily in Inca cosmology and religion. Women actively contributed to the maintenance and the perpetuation of important cultural traditions. They were instrumental in organizing and running the household, child rearing, producing cloth at both the local and state level, and participating in agricultural activities. Women bore many responsibilities toward their families and the empire from childhood to adulthood, with each new phase in the life cycle marked by special ceremony or rite of passage. While the Incas conceived of themselves as belonging to separate but parallel female and male lines, they also thought in terms of gender complementarity. Men and women, in other words, were understood to embody different qualities that when brought together created profound balance and unity. The Incas believed that women had a unique ability to transform unprocessed organic materials into finished products; for example, raw food became edible through the acts of preparation and cooking; fibers became thread through spinning, and threads became a finished garment through weaving; and perhaps most fundamentally, the female body was the vehicle for producing human life. Women in the Inca Empire fell under three major status categories: commoner women, chosen women (*acllas*), and elite women, each with a different set of obligations to the state.

Commoner Women

When the Spaniards wrote about the role of women in Inca society, they were appalled by the amount of labor they performed both inside and outside the home. Unlike most women in 16th-century Spain, who remained at home, Inca women were able to operate within both the private and public spheres with relative ease. The female head of household was in charge of rearing her children, cooking, cleaning, weaving and other crafts, and agricultural activities, in addition to participating in religious practices such as venerating *huacas* and gods of the Inca pantheon.

CHILDBIRTH AND REARING

According to chroniclers, mothers-to-be continued working in the fields and performing their duties up until the day they went into labor. Women typically gave birth alone, without a midwife (a woman who assists in childbirth). Childbirth was a no-frills affair; women returned to work shortly thereafter, and no elaborate ceremonies followed the event. Naming ceremonies did not occur until after the child had been weaned, at approximately two years after birth.

Child rearing was the sole province of the mother, who was responsible for all aspects of natal care (with the exception of the birth of twins). Mothers tended to operate out of pragmatism, taking the necessary steps to prepare their child for a life of hard work. According to Garcilaso, mothers only nursed their children three times a day at allotted intervals rather than at the child's whim, even if it cried. They also practiced abstinence during this time, believing that sexual intercourse would reduce the quality of the breast milk. Mothers carried their child on their back, using a cradle-type device known as a *quirau* made out of bendable poles. A blanket was placed between the frame and the baby, who would be tied to the entire structure to ensure safety. Women would wear the cradle with a blanket tied around it to cover the baby and crossed the ends of it around her shoulders in a tight knot. The mother would thus continue with her everyday duties while still caring for her child.

12.1 A baby bound in a quirau, *or a portable cradle* (Felipe Guamán Poma de Ayala)

Babies often underwent cranial deformation, a practice that is evident from both written descriptions and the archaeological record. Cranial deformation involves molding a baby's skull into a particular shape through the use of cradle boards that press the head or tightly wound bandages. This was done for both cultural and aesthetic reasons. According to Cobo, the Incas believed that a pointed head provided health benefits and instilled good qualities in a person. Moreover, the shape accommodated the pointed brimless knit caps, called *chucos*, worn by Inca men.

SPINNING AND WEAVING

Peru's archaeological and documentary records attest to the overwhelming importance of weaving and spinning in the daily lives of women from all age groups and social classes. Although textiles

12.2 A modern Andean woman weaves on a horizontal loom using ancient techniques. (Eloise Quiñones Keber)

preserve poorly in mountainous regions, the survival of tools made of more durable materials of bone and clay provide a relatively accurate picture of the ubiquity of this craft within the domestic sphere. Vast quantities of spinning and weaving implements abound at archaeological sites, such as wooden distaffs or spindles (pointed sticks for rotating the thread), spindle whorls (round ceramic counterweights for spinning), bone heddles (devices for separating the horizontal warp threads on the loom), separators (bone tools for separating groups of warp threads), shuttles (tools for passing threads back and forth across the loom), and small ceramic plates used to hold the spindle in place. These tools are usually found in household trash deposits, signifying their frequent use in the home. Among commoner households women generally created basic cotton and alpaca wool textiles for their family's use as clothing and bedding. More elaborate textile forms such as specialized costumes or cloth made from the precious vicuña fur using a complex tapestry weave were reserved for the state and used only by nobles.

Nearly every observer of the lives of native Andean women in the 16th and 17th centuries commented on their penchant for spinning and weaving. They spun while caring for their children, while conversing, and even while traveling. Any moment of idle time was usually occupied by an activity associated with textile production, whether it was cleaning fibers, spinning fiber into thread, twisting threads together, preparing the loom, or actually engaging in the act of weaving. Women set up their looms near the home in an open-air area. They were relatively easy to set up and could be taken down and reconstructed at any given moment. Backstrap looms and vertical looms were preferred by most weavers in the Inca realm, although horizontal looms were common in the Aymara region (the Aymaras are a major ethnic group that dominates

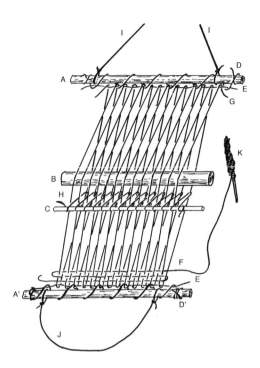

12.3 Diagram of a backstrap loom (Drawing courtesy Michel Besson)

the Southern Andes). Females performed these activities not only out of economic necessity but also because they were considered an intrinsic quality of womanhood. In fact, the act of weaving was often likened to reproduction; the distaff became "impregnated" with thread, which was subsequently "birthed" onto the loom as a finished piece of cloth.

COOKING

Women cooked inside or near the house. All cooking among the Incas required a specific set of utensils and dishes used by women of all social classes. These included stone slabs for grinding maize and other grains into flour, bowls and jugs made of clay earthenware for storing food and drink, stone mortar and pestle, tripod (three-legged) ceramic serving vessels, perforated casserole dishes for toasting maize, and large cooking jars with pointed bases that were set into holes on the stove. Grinding was

performed by leaning all of one's weight on the grinding stone and rocking it back and forth on the grain until flour was produced. A clay oven was located in the house for cooking, which the chroniclers have noted was very fuel efficient. It was fired by llama manure, which provided a good source of fuel, along with small amounts of firewood, both of which were collected by women. Cooking mostly consisted of boiling, stewing, and roasting vegetables, meats, and grains. Women stored maize, potatoes, and quinoa in mud-plastered jars fashioned out of cornstalks that would be placed either in a designated spot within the house or outdoors in special storage bins designed to withstand the elements.

OTHER ACTIVITIES

Women also participated in the local economy through barter and trade of household surplus goods. A household surplus could be anything from extra cloth to additional foodstuffs. Barter and trade occurred informally among different households and at local markets, where women could bring in their goods and wares.

Women performed agricultural labor alongside men and were particularly valued for their ability to select seeds for planting. This was undoubtedly related to the perception of women as strongly connected to the earth and as human embodiments of Pachamama, the earth goddess. In addition to farming activities, women also collected undomesticated plants in the wild for consumption and for their healing properties.

Acllas

The *acllas (acllacuna)*, or "chosen women," were a group of cloistered women handpicked from their communities as adolescents to work in the service of the Inca monarch. Considered the most beautiful women with the most admirable qualities, chosen women were accorded a position of very high esteem. The women also had to be of "pure" blood so that they could produce a royal heir untainted by the bloodline of so-called foreigners and barbarians. This meant that in addition to possessing great beauty, they had to be ethnically Inca and preferably

12.4 Drawing of the acllas (acllacuna). *These "chosen women" worked in the service of the Sapa Inca, weaving fine textiles, brewing* chicha, *and conducting religious rituals.* (Felipe Guamán Poma de Ayala)

the daughter of a *kuraka*. The *acllas* were all housed in the *acllahuasi* (house of the chosen women). The *acllahuasi* in Cuzco, located near the Huacaypata, or central plaza, was famed for having the "purest" and most beautiful women of the entire Inca realm. There were several *acllahuasi* throughout the realm, such as at the pilgrimage center of Pachacamac near present-day Lima and the Chincha polity in the central coast, although the largest and most well-documented one is that of Cuzco. Chroniclers have estimated that there were more than 1,500 *acllas* housed in Cuzco's *acllahuasi* at one time. They underwent extreme seclusion, forbidden to see or speak to anyone from the outside world. Any transgression of this law on the part of ill-intentioned men would result in severe repercussions. The *mamakuna (mamacuna)* were older *acllas* who had

spent their lives in the *acllahuasi* and were in charge of training and caring for the younger women.

The *acllas* remained virgins—in fact, they were regarded as "wives of the Sun"—until placed into concubinage. The *acllas* were considered the "purest" women of the entire empire for their abstinence and fervent religiosity and indeed served as the moral backbone of Inca society. Women of humbler backgrounds would become secondary wives of lesser officials or provincial elites. Sometimes they were offered as gifts to foreign leaders as a way of sealing political partnerships. Women taken from elite families were the only ones eligible to become secondary wives of the Sapa Inca. Because the king was seen as a direct descendant of the sun god, Inti, the transition from wife of the Sun to wife of the Inca was seamless.

The primary duties of the *acllas* consisted of producing large quantities of *chicha*, cooking, maintaining the temple, and weaving elegant *cumbi* (the highest-quality textiles of the Incas) for the royal family. *Cumbi* was woven on large four-pole upright looms specially reserved for its production. They were made from only the softest cotton and the treasured vicuña fur (a member of the camelid family) employing a fine tapestry weave. Feathers imported from the tropical lowlands and threads made of gold and silver were woven into the *cumbi* to give it a dazzling effect.

These activities were all performed to honor Inti. *Cumbi* was woven not only for use by the Sapa Inca and his *coya* (principal wife, also the queen) but also for ritual sacrifice. The *acllas* burned offerings of *cumbi* on a daily basis as a gift to Inti. In addition to serving Inti, the *acllas* worshipped Viracocha, the creator god, and Inti-Illapa, the thunder god, by maintaining altars dedicated to their cult and supplying them with offerings. The most devout women became priestesses of the temples dedicated to these state gods. Lower-ranked women of the *acllahuasi* devoted their lives to the maintenance of minor religious cults.

Elite Women

Women of the elite classes—queens (*coyas*), wives of *kurakas*, and other types of high-standing women—

occupied a more privileged social role than commoner women. There is even documentary evidence of some women serving as *kurakas* themselves. Elite women often held claims to land, which was rare, if existent at all, among women of the lower classes. The *coya* was considered part of the choicest stock; in order to be even considered for marriage to the king, she had to be an ethnic Inca and of close familial relationship, either as first cousin or sister. Serving as the principal wife to the Sapa Inca, the *coya* enjoyed many privileges. She was the only wife who received an official and lavish wedding ceremony. She also held authority over the secondary wives of the king and the *yanakuna*, who served as her attendants. Her household role consisted of delegating tasks to others rather than actually carrying them out. In addition, she played a fundamental role in producing a successor to the throne. *Coyas* had the ability to intervene in the selection process and thus participate in the political sphere by vouching for a favored son or, conversely, by preventing another's rise to power. The *coya* wore the finest clothing, woven out of soft vicuña fur, and elegant *tupus* (garment pins) and jewelry of silver and gold. Elite women were not subject to the same household chores and tribute obligations of their lower-status counterparts. Nevertheless, they performed certain tasks universal to all women of the Inca Empire, such as spinning and weaving cloth.

Women in Inca Cosmology and Religion

Women not only played a fundamental role in the household and, for the higher classes, in the realm of courtly life, they also figured heavily in the origin myths and cosmological beliefs of the Incas. Mama Huaco, one of the early founders of the Inca Empire whose identity straddles the fine line between myth and history, was famously remembered for plunging a golden staff into the earth at the site of Cuzco, which confirmed her convictions of their divine right to found the capital in this area. She was also considered a warrior, and during the siege of Cuzco she brutally killed one of the Guallas peoples, the original inhabitants of the region.

Upon the Guallas's death Mama Huaco extracted his lungs and blew into them, which frightened the rest of the Guallas so profoundly that they immediately fled from the area and thus ceded the site to the Incas. There is also ample evidence in the chronicles of other women warriors who equaled, if not surpassed, their male counterparts in strength, ferocity, and power.

Elements of Inca religion and cosmology are endowed with strong feminine aspects. For example, the two complementary forces of *hanan* and *hurin* that divide Cuzco and many other important cities into two parts incorporate female associations into their meaning. *Hurin*, or the lower aspect, was considered feminine, weaker, and subordinate and was connected to the Moon and silver, both associated with women. There were also several goddesses worshipped alongside male gods. Deities specifically associated with women and with strong women followers of their cult included Mama Quilla, the moon goddess; Pachamama, the earth mother; and Mamacocha, the sea goddess.

AGRICULTURE AND RITUAL

Nearly all able-bodied individuals participated in farming activities, which was the backbone of Andean existence. Even people in other professions would only perform their craft part time because of tribute obligations to the state and because farming was an essential component of Inca systems of reciprocal exchange. Members of the same *ayllu* pooled agricultural resources together from different ecological zones so that each family would have equal shares of a great variety of foods. Moreover, farming was not considered a burden because it was carried out in the context of ceremony, feasting, and drinking.

The plowing festival, called Chacra Yapuy Quilla, serves as an illustrative example. It occurred in August to commemorate the beginning of the planting season. As illustrated by the 17th-century indigenous chronicler Guamán Poma, men would

AGOSTO
CHACRA·IA·PVI
quilla

tienpo de labransa - hayllinmi ynca

12.5 Chacra Yapuy Quilla, or the plowing festival, which took place in August (Felipe Guamán Poma de Ayala)

line up with their digging sticks in a designated area according to their districts. Each man faced his wife, who knelt in front of him and broke up the mounds of dirt picked up by the digging stick with a wooden tool known as an *atuna*. As is the case with most agricultural festivals and rituals, this was all performed while chanting a special song dedicated to the event. Chroniclers have documented that the song was also performed upon military defeat over a rival group, which underscores the connections between agriculture, warfare, and ritual practice. *Chicha* was sprinkled on the ground as an offering to Pachamama, or Mother Earth, who was associated with agricultural bounty.

Much of Inca life corresponded to the rhythms of the agricultural cycle, with each season inaugurating a new flurry of activity dedicated to bringing

the highest yields possible. During the rainy season, which lasted from December to May in the Central Andes, care was taken to prevent animals from destroying the crops. This was actively facilitated by the *arariwa*, or "guardian of the fields," who would dress up in ceremonial costume and make noises to scare them off. In the event that the rainy season came late, communities would make offerings to Inti-Illapa, the thunder god, to bring rain. They did so by dressing in all black and starving black llamas and dogs so they would wail to him in anguish. Harvesting took place during the month of June, which was also accompanied with great festivity. According to Cobo, young men who had just completed the *huarachicoy* initiation rite would commence the harvesting festival. Individuals would select deformed and odd-looking ears of corn, which were known as *saramama*, or "corn mothers," to be placed together in a small storage bin. They would be wrapped in a *lliclla*, or woman's shawl, and even some were fully clothed in female dress, replete with a miniature *tupu*. A member of the community would assess the storage bin after three days to ensure that the *saramama* were appropriately selected. If the community member approved them, the *saramama* would be continually worshipped until the sowing season, at which point their seeds would be planted.

FOOD AND DRINK

Culinary Staples

Inca culinary traditions were diverse, with a great deal of regional variation in flavor and preferred ingredients. Several dishes were nevertheless enjoyed by all members of the Inca Empire, with a culinary legacy that lives on into the present day.

The staple crops of the Incas were maize (corn), quinoa, *tarwi*, and *cañihua*. Maize was incorporated into a variety of Inca dishes. Small corncakes served as sustenance for travelers because of their portability. The Incas also enjoyed popcorn, known as *cancha*. *Mote*, or boiled corn, was a staple that was sometimes cooked with chili peppers and other condiments to add flavor. *Chochoca* was a maize dish made by boiling the kernels and then leaving them out in the sun to dry. *Humitas*, or stuffed steamed corncakes, were another favored culinary fare. Maize was also used for the creation of beverages, serving as the main ingredient of *chicha*. Quinoa, a grain that the Spaniards referred to as "little rice," was used in a variety of dishes as a stew thickener or on its own. Its leaves were also boiled or stewed, and its seeds, ground to produce flours for breads. It was cooked with peppers and herbs to create a stew called *pisqui*. *Tarwi* is a legume grown high in the Andes, used for both its leaves and seeds. The seeds would be boiled and soaked before consumption to rid them of bitterness and toxicity. *Cañihua* was cultivated for its seeds and edible shoots. It was boiled or stewed or its seeds ground into flour for breads.

The Incas also grew and consumed tubers such as oca, *mashua* (also known as *añu*), and *ulluco*. Oca was consumed in an assortment of ways. The sweet variety could be eaten raw or cooked. The bitter variety was freeze-dried to create *ckaya*, which was believed among the Incas to be an aphrodisiac. *Mashua*, on the other hand, only had one variety, which required boiling to eliminate its natural bitterness. *Ulluco* is a tuber with high starch content. It was boiled, fermented, or freeze-dried. Coastal peoples consumed a tuber called *racacha (Arracacia xanthorhiza)* that was purplish in color and had about the same consistency as a potato.

The vegetables of the Incas included the potato, squash, four types of chili pepper, peanut, beans, and manioc (cassava), among others. They also consumed tomato and avocado, two fruits native to the Americas. Fruits such as guava, *lúcuma*, and cherimoya were also widely consumed. All of these vegetables and fruits were grown in the lowlands and would have been distributed in the Andes in exchange for highland crops such as the potato and various Andean tubers and grains. The potato was of particular significance for the Incas, who managed to cultivate 3,000 different varieties. Potatoes freeze-dried in the cold, high-altitude regions and stored for times of need were known as *chuño*.

The Incas also ate meat, but among commoners it was typically consumed during special occasions due to its relative scarcity and amount of time invested in its procurement. Among members of the elite, however, meat was frequently incorporated into their meals. The Incas ate wild animals such as fish, viscacha (a member of the rodent family), and white-tailed and *huemul* deer, as well as domesticated animals, including *cuy* (guinea pig), llama, and the Muscovy duck. Meat was typically stewed, roasted, or barbecued. Both historical evidence and modern-day practice confirm that *cuy* was prepared by gutting the guinea pig and filling the stomach cavity with small heated stones and chilies to cook it from the inside out. Meat was dried to produce *charqui*, which is where the word and concept of *jerky* comes from. More hearty dishes included *locro*, a stew consisting of fish or meat, *chuño*, vegetables, potatoes, and chili peppers.

Culinary Specialties

In addition to the typical dishes of the Inca diet, there were several specialty foods that Incas ate on occasion, whether as delicacies or in times of agricultural shortages. These were commented on by the Spanish chroniclers likely for their astonishment at the diversity and strangeness of the Inca palate from a European perspective. There are documented cases of the consumption of mayfly larvae, which were eaten raw, or toasted and ground up for later use. In an environment with scarce meat sources insects such as ants, caterpillars, and beetles were consumed as a source of protein. Almonds were a specialty cultigen of the Inca settlement of Chachapoyas in the northern highlands. The Incas also consumed special types of clay, called *pasa*, which was dissolved with water and mixed with salt to create a sauce that was eaten with potatoes.

Royal Culinary Fare

Members of the Inca nobility or royalty dined on many of the same culinary staples as their commoner counterparts but with the inclusion of restricted or less readily available ingredients. Royal feasts and banquets were executed with great pomp and circumstance, involving many different courses, and the use of only the finest serving ware crafted from gold and silver. Sumptuary laws restricted commoners from using gold and silver or from feasting on copious amounts of food as did the elites and royals.

Feasts and banquets occurred in the central plaza, found in all major Inca cities. They involved large quantities of food such as stewed and roasted meats, vegetables, and maize dishes. *Chicha* was almost always a central component of feasting, consumed in ritual fashion after all of the food had been eaten. Ceremonial drunkenness was almost mandatory for Inca lords.

Beverages

CHICHA

Chicha, a fermented corn drink, was the primary beverage of the Incas and continues to be widely consumed throughout Peru, Bolivia, Ecuador, and parts of Colombia, Venezuela, and Chile. In very high-altitude regions that do not support corn, *chicha* was brewed with quinoa, using similar techniques. In the highland regions it was generally produced by women, while on the north coast it was produced by men. The first step in making *chicha* required chewing the corn and spitting it out once it was mashed up to the right consistency. Human saliva releases an enzyme that allows for the maize to be converted into a sugar. It was then poured into pots, where it would ferment anywhere from several days to several weeks. After fermentation the *chicha* would be poured into an *urpu*, or storage vessel with a pointed base and restricted flared neck. Another method for making *chicha* involved soaking the corn kernels for a period of a few days until they began to sprout. Then the sprouted corn would be laid out in the sun to dry and subsequently mixed with water and left to ferment. During the fermentation process the alcoholic content of the *chicha* increased, and it developed a more full-bodied flavor. Each household would have several jars of *chicha* in its possession for the family's consumption. *Chicha* was a specialty of the *acllas*, who produced the beverage for the royal family and for religious rituals. *Chicha* was an integral element in state-

sponsored feasts and ceremonies, consumed out of special drinking vessels called *keros (qeros)* and *aquillas*.

Chicha could take on a variety of colors and flavors depending on the type of maize used and the amount of time allotted in the fermenting process. It was also made from quinoa and occasionally manioc in lowland areas. The shorter the fermentation, the sweeter the beverage; the longer it ferments, the more tart and pungent the flavor. *Chicha* could be different shades of yellow, white, purple, red, and gray. *Chicha morada*, made from purple corn, is not fermented but is instead simply boiled and subsequently mixed with flavors and sweeteners.

OTHER BEVERAGES

Another beverage consumed by the Incas was a concoction made from the pepper tree *Schinus molle*, referred to in Quechua as *mulli*. This drink was sometimes referred to as another variety of *chicha*. The fruits yielded from the tree were soaked in hot water for long enough to release their sweet properties, but if left too long the bitter inner cavity of the fruit would ruin the drink. After a few days the beverage would be ready for consumption. *Mulli* was also used for its medicinal properties. Meanwhile, the consumption of plain water was considered an unthinkable act—an aversion that shocked the Spaniards upon their arrival—and was only practiced in dire circumstances.

Royal *Chicha* Consumption

Chicha drinking was a highly regulated and ritualized affair among Inca nobles. Toasting with *chicha* was common and could be conducted among the living and the dead; it was commonplace for an Inca to toast and consume *chicha* with the mummy of a royal ancestor. Cobo describes toasting rituals among the Incas: "The man proposing a toast to another would get up from his place and go toward him with two tumblers of *chicha* in his hands. He would give the other man one of the tumblers while keeping the other for himself. They would both drink together." *Chicha* was typically served and drunk out of *aquillas* and *keros*, or flared-rim drinking vessels crafted out of wood with painted, silver, or gold decorations. *Chicha* was also consumed after military victories. It was even common practice to drink the alcoholic beverage out of the skulls of the vanquished.

Dining Customs

The Incas ate twice a day, once around eight or nine in the morning and again a few hours before sunset. Serving dishes were made of earthenware and were purely utilitarian, although the Inca nobility ate on gold and silver dishes. Serving ware included jugs for liquids such as *chicha*, small plates, and pots. In the coastal regions food and *chicha* was served in bowls and cups carved out of gourds, known as *mates*, since this material was more widely accessible in the area. Eating was performed sitting on the ground and was typically a family affair. Chroniclers have noted that the entire household ate together with the husband and wife traditionally sitting back to back.

EDUCATION

Education as conceived by the vast majority of the empire's inhabitants consisted of effectively training young boys and girls to perform the duties of their fathers and mothers. A structured education administered in a classroom setting was completely foreign to most members of Inca society.

Only boys of the elite class were allowed a formal education. Sons of *kurakas* were sent from all reaches of the empire to a school in Cuzco known as the *yachayhuasi*, or "house of learning." The boys entered at around 10 years of age and finished in time for the hair-cutting ritual of *huarachicoy* at puberty. They were trained by *amautas*, or "wise men," in a specialized four-year program. During the first year students studied the Quechua lan-

guage; in the second year they studied Inca religion; the third year they studied quipus, the knotted cord device used for storing information; and in the fourth year they studied Inca history. Poetry and history were the specialty of the *amautas*, who recited verses about the admirable deeds of a bygone ruler, about love, or any number of topics. Boys learned from their teachers through the process of oral recitation and repetition. Although history and knowledge were not transcribed into a formal written language, devices such as stylized poetry and quipus tabulated knowledge into kinetic, aural, and visual form. This type of education was intended to train young men to become future political leaders, accountants, and bureaucrats.

MEDICINE AND SHAMANISM

Unfortunately, Spanish colonial accounts tend to omit important elements of Inca medicinal practices because of its perceived associations with idolatry. Moreover, the accounts that do exist of Inca medicine and shamanism are permeated with a strong negative bias, criticizing Inca practices as barbarous and motivated by the devil. A careful reading of historical texts can nonetheless reveal important aspects of healing rituals as well as the extent to which medicine operated within the sphere of ritual and religion. Inca systems of medical treatment were based on specifically Andean understandings of the body and its various functions.

Herbs and Plants

Herbs and other substances were not solely administered for their curative properties but also for their preventative ones. Herbs were a central feature of Inca medicine; they could be ingested, used as an ointment, or turned into a balm. Often, they were consumed to induce vomiting, which was believed to rid the body of harmful elements.

The coca leaf was an important element of Inca medicinal practice. With such wide-ranging healing properties it was considered one of the most sacred natural elements of the Inca realm. The leaf could be chewed to ward off the side effects of high altitude, such as muscle weakness, fever, and headache, or to stave off hunger so that people could work all day farming or mining without respite. Coca leaf could also be made into a tea, called *mate de coca*, for the same purposes.

An herb known as *matecllu* was pounded into a liquid and applied to the eyes to cure various ailments. Tobacco, known in Quechua as *sairi*, was smoked to relax the body and mind. The *chillca* herb from the *mulli* tree was known for its ability to ease achy joints. The leaves of the *Schinus molle* tree were boiled to produce a liquid, *mulli*, used for cleaning the body and eliminating skin rashes.

The maguey plant (known by the Incas as *chuchau*) held a variety of uses for the Incas, just as it did for the indigenous cultures of Mesoamerica. This agave cactus, which only flourishes in dry regions, was used for its durable fibers to weave baskets and nets, for the juice it produced as a beverage, and for its medicinal qualities. The liquid extracted from the maguey leaf was applied to sores and wounds as a salve. No part of the plant was wasted; even the roots were crushed and formed into bars of soap for women's hair care. Like the coca leaf, the maguey was highly revered by the Incas and incorporated into many ritual and ceremonial practices.

Bloodletting and Trepanation

Bloodletting served as a painkiller for the Incas. A person's veins were cut in the closest proximity to the source of pain, and blood was allowed to pour out to relieve tension or discomfort. This was performed with an instrument specifically designed for the practice: a stick with a sharpened flint hafted onto the end.

Similarly, a technique called trepanation, or the practice of drilling a hole into the skull, was common among the Incas. Although the documentary record remains mute on the subject, ample archaeological evidence from human burials supports its prevalence. It was commonly believed that creating an opening in the skull would relieve pain. There may have also been a spiritual or cosmological dimension to Inca trepanation, but this information has been lost.

Shamanism

Inca shamans were men and often women known as *soncoyoc* or *camasca*. The Spaniards mistakenly referred to them by the pejorative terms *sorcerers* or *witch doctors* in colonial-period accounts of Inca customs. People consulted shamans for any number of reasons, whether for healing, assistance with amorous pursuits, or religious guidance, as human physiological imbalance was understood as directly correlated with a person's spiritual imbalance. Illness (known as *onqoy*) was cured by reckoning with the supernatural world in order to deflect negative forces or quell angry gods that interfere with an individual's well-being.

Shamans were thought to have special healing powers because of their contacts with the spiritual world. These contacts were forged through a variety of different ways, such as dreams or special cosmic journeys, and were facilitated by the consumption of hallucinogenic substances. The San Pedro cactus and the vine of the *ayahuasca* plant were the most widely consumed hallucinogens by shamans in the Andes. Brewed into a liquid, drinking these substances resulted in immediate physical reactions including sharp pains and vomiting, followed by intense visions that would leave shamans in a trance for several hours or even days at a time. Their spiritual journeys were also aided by the use of talismans, or objects from the natural and human-made world imbued with magical powers, whether a lock of hair, a tooth, fingernails, shells, small animals trapped in jars, votive figurines, or ceramic vessels filled with special substances.

Cobo recounts the practice of curing in a specially prepared room. Handfuls of black-colored maize would be used to scrub the inside of the room from top to bottom. Once the room was thoroughly cleaned, the shaman would ritually burn it. The same was repeated with white-colored maize, after which the entire room would be covered with a substance made of water and maize. The patient would then be brought into the room and instructed to lie flat on his or her back. Once the patient had fallen unconscious with the aid of a ritual drink, the shaman would perform rites on the patient's body.

The Spanish sources reveal other varieties of shamanism as well. There were men who were thought to possess the ability of flight but transformed into other beings such as animals or spirits to obscure their true form while in this omnipotent state. Some served as messengers for admirers wishing to know the whereabouts of the object of their affection. They were aided by a different type of talisman, known as a *huacanqui*, usually consisting of a bodily element of the person seeking help. This could include a fingernail, toenail, piece of hair, or a piece of clothing that had touched his or her body. In some cases these shamans would participate in negative divinatory practices, causing ill will on others. There were also shamans that took on more of a medical role, creating herbal remedies that were specially tailored to the needs of the patient. At a general level shamans removed harmful essences from the body through various healing methods, whether the literal extraction of organs and blood or the metaphysical journey into the spiritual world to seek help from supernaturals.

Animal Augury

The *callpa* was a specialist who could predict the future by looking at the insides of sacrificed llamas. This sometimes required extracting the beating heart of a llama, from which the *callpa* could "read" the prognostications it held for the future. The *callpa* also examined the lungs of sacrificed llamas. He would remove the lungs and blow into them until they were inflated with air. The *callpa* would then examine the appearance of the veins on the

12.6 *A* callpa *conducts an augury. The Incas believed this specialist could predict the future by examining the internal organs of a sacrificed llama.* (Felipe Guamán Poma de Ayala)

inflated lung in order to make predictions. The *hamurpa* studied the entrails of sacrificed animals to similar ends.

The *pacharicuc*, meanwhile, was a specialist who could "read" from spiders. They kept a collection of spiders stored inside hollow human bones or jars until the moment of divination. When an individual came in for a consultation, the *pacharicuc* would drop the spiders and examine the way that they fell to the ground. Correct interpretation of the spider's fall would result in an increased awareness of future events. In other accounts, it is believed that the *pacharicuc* would prod the spider with a stick and, depending on how many of its legs fell off, would make the appropriate prognostications.

Games and Recreation

The Incas participated in a number of games and recreational activities throughout the empire. Dances and musical performances were a vital element of Inca life, both at the imperial and the local level. Music and dance varied dramatically across regions but retained several fundamental qualities throughout the empire, such as the interplay between the drum and the flute. Although we will never be able to fully reconstruct Inca musical and dance traditions, both artifacts of musical instruments and modern-day performances can provide clues as to ancient Inca practices. Surviving artifacts such as spin tops, balls, and broken pieces of pottery modified into flat circles and squares provide clues about the nature of recreation in the Inca Empire. Moreover, Spanish reports from the 16th and 17th centuries contain descriptions of several kinds of games practiced by children and adults. Some games involved gambling, but most were played for pure entertainment. All of the games incorporated such elements of the natural world as dried beans and stones as game pieces.

Games

Pichca was the Inca equivalent to games of dice, involving the use of a five-sided wooden die. *Chuncara* used the same type of five-sided die in conjunction with colored beans. Depending on the number of moves one got from rolling the die, the player would advance the beans through a series of holes until the winner's beans made it to the final goal. The game *tacanaco* was a variation of *chuncara*, using the same types of gaming pieces. These advanced games were more commonly played by adults, who may have received prizes for excellent performance. One game with considerably high stakes was called *aylloscas*, which involved the gambling of lands and estates among members of the elite. A spin top known as *piscoynu* was popular among children. Aside from these kinds of "board games" involving the use of gaming pieces, children certainly would have also participated in races, ball-throwing games, and role-playing games.

Music and Dance

Music was another important aspect of both recreation and ceremony among the Incas. The performance of song and dance was incorporated into many aspects of life, from agricultural festivals to weddings, puberty ceremonies, military battles, and funerals. Musical performance was a communal affair, bringing diverse members of society together. Music was thought to have the transcendent quality of communicating with ancestor spirits and gods and thus was thought of as a sacred activity.

MUSICAL INSTRUMENTS

Almost all musical instruments of the Incas drew from traditions initiated almost 4,000 years before in the Andean highlands. Many instruments were finely carved and decorated with geometric and animal motifs. Drums and wind instruments served as the base ingredients of all Andean music. The drum (*huancar*) was constructed from a hollowed-out timber base with dried llama skin stretched tightly across. Drums were produced in a variety of sizes to produce different sounds. Wind instruments included the *quena*, a flute made from cane; the *quepa*, a small, elongated trumpet fashioned from a hollowed-out gourd; and the *ocarina*, or whistle. The most distinctive and elaborately constructed musical instrument was the *ayarichic*, or panpipe. It was composed of seven flutes arranged in descending order. The musician would blow across the top of the opening, with each flute producing a distinct sound. Instruments such as the *huancar tinya*, a type of tambourine, and bells served as accompaniment. Bells made of copper and silver, known as *chanrara*, were worn on the body of dancers, who would create music through their movements. The Incas also made bells from cheaper materials such as shell and dried beans, known, respectively, as *churu* and *zacapa*. All layered on top of one another, the distinct sounds of each instrument formed the essence of Andean music, which has been described as rhythmic and cyclical with a distinctive dynamic created between the high-pitched wind instruments that produced the melody and the heavy, primordial sounds of the drums.

DANCE

Dance formed a critical component of musical performance; one did not exist without the other. Dances were performed by men, women, the young, and the old. *Taqi* was the general term for dance, although different varieties had their own names. A royal dance called the *guayyaya* was well documented by chroniclers, who were undoubtedly impressed by the amount of pomp and circumstance that went into the performance. It involved dancing in lines, which were sometimes sex-segregated depending on the occasion, to the beat of a single drum. The dancers, moving in linear fashion with slow, deliberate steps, approached the king, who was seated prominently as the focal point of the spectacle. Another royal dance described in great detail consisted of three participants—the king and two female escorts—who danced with hands interlocked the entire time, moving in sweeps and turns in step to the musical accompaniment. Dances among commoners varied widely across regions. They often involved the use of costumes and body paint to represent different animals or gods.

Personal Appearance and Attire

Men and women of the common classes dressed simply and placed sufficient but minimal attention on personal appearance for day-to-day purposes. Much greater care was taken in personal appearances for festivals, rituals, and ceremonies.

Hair

The maintenance of one's hair was regarded as one of the most important elements of personal care. Members of both sexes took pains to ensure their hair was clean and kempt. As mentioned earlier, women washed their hair with soap made from the roots of the maguey plant. They detangled their hair, which was kept long, each morning with a comb made out of thorns. Girls and women wore their hair loose or neatly braided and usually wore some sort of head adornment, whether it was a *vincha* (headband) tied around the forehead or a headdress made of folded cloth. Men wore their hair cut short and blunt above the ears with bangs that hung to the center of their forehead. They often wore a thick wool band around their heads called a *llauto*. Hair was cut using obsidian blades, which produces the sharpest edge of all stones. Haircutting was an important occasion that occurred in a ceremony known as *rutuchicoy*, when a child was weaned from beast-feeding, and later during boys' and girls' puberty ceremonies. The Incas considered their hair a prized possession, and it was thus a great humiliation to have one's hair forcibly cut, punishment reserved for grave offenses. The only time, aside from *rutuchicoy* and puberty, when hair was willingly cut was when women went into mourning.

Commoner Clothing

Both men and women wore garments composed of a single piece of untailored cloth that was wrapped around or draped on the body. Women wore a floor-length garment wrapped around the torso and over the shoulder, called an *anacu*, which was held in place with a *chumpi* (sash) around the waist. A long metal pin called a *tupu* was pierced diagonally across the *anacu* to hold it in place. The *anacu* was open on the sides to allow for easy movement, as women did a great deal of manual labor in the fields and household. A shawl called a *lliclla* was worn over the dress, and a shorter metal pin called a *ttipqui* was pierced horizontally through the *lliclla* to keep it closed. Common women wore *tupus* fashioned out of copper and other lower-quality metals. One end of the *tupu* terminated in a sharp point to pierce through many layers of fabric while the head was hammered into a flat disc or half-disc with sharpened edges so that it could double as a knife, or occasionally into anthropomorphic and zoomorphic designs.

Men wore sleeveless tunics called *uncus*, which came down to the knees. A breechcloth made from a simple strip of cloth would be worn underneath. Sometimes they wore a cloak over the tunic, known as a *yacolla*, which would be draped over the shoulders or tied across the chest. Men and women wore the same type of sandal-like shoes made from llama hide for the soles and fiber cords dyed with a variety of bright colors and twisted into decorative designs for the top part. The loose cords were tied around the ankle for a snug fit. Men also often wore *chuspas*, or small bags that contained coca leaf and other personal objects, between the *uncu* and the *yacolla*.

Every region had a unique style of dress that corresponded to cultural tradition and climate. Rather than suppress this regional variation, the state government actually required that non-Incas wear the appropriate clothing of their region or ethnic group so that they would be easily distinguishable as foreigners when they entered the Cuzco heartland.

Royal Clothing

Because their social status and wealth permitted it, men of the nobility wore finer tunics of vicuña fur or soft cotton; commoners wore clothing of rougher alpaca threads. Nobles' *uncus* and dresses, moreover, were more sumptuous, decorated with elaborate design schemes and interlaced with imported *Spondylus* shells, feathers, threads of gold and silver, and even mirrors. While the *uncus* of commoner men only featured one *tocapu* (a design element consisting of a square inscribed with a particular symbolic pattern), those of elite men often featured rows of them, and even one surviving example features *tocapus* covering the entire piece of cloth. Although their exact meaning remains unclear, *tocapus* probably represented the emblem of a particular ethnic group or settlement; therefore, an individual who wore a piece of clothing that featured many of them suggests that he held domination over a large expanse of territory.

The Sapa Inca, meanwhile, not only wore *uncus* decorated with multiple *tocapus*, but also was bedecked with a number of accessories, including the *mascapaycha* (Inca royal crown with a red fringe that hangs over the forehead), *cápac uncu tarco huallca* (royal tunic), and *huallca* (feather necklace). He also held in his hands any combination of the following objects: the *suntur paucar* (scepter), the *tupa yauri* (battle ax), and the *tupa cusi* (golden beaker).

Royal women wore the same floor-length garment with a *chumpi* and *lliclla* as commoner women, but theirs were woven out of finer wools and decorated with elaborate patterning and multicolored dyes. Royal women wore clothing of red, purple, yellow, and other rich colors, each of which was imbued with special significance and symbolism. They were often interwoven with decorative bands running across the garment or along the openings. The *tupus* of elite women were fashioned out of silver and gold and often encrusted with jewels and hammered into elaborate designs on the head.

Jewelry

On special occasions men and women adorned themselves with additional jewelry and accessories. Necklaces strung with *chaquiras* (shell beads) were popular among women, as were feather headdresses called *pilcocata*. Women and men wore bracelets of gold and silver for special ceremonies. Earspools served as status markers and could only be worn by men of the nobility. They were inserted into the ear by a thick post attached to the circular disc and were made of precious metals and polished stone. Almost as large as an entire ear, they were eye-catching enough for the Spanish chroniclers to refer to such men as *"orejones,"* or "big ears."

CRIME AND PUNISHMENT

Inca law became codified under the reign of Topa Inca, the 10th ruler, although general codes of conduct were observed and regulated in the early days of the Inca Empire. Laws were enforced by regional governors known as *tocricoc*. A justice system also existed among the Incas, somewhat analogous to courts of law.

Inca Law

Given that the Incas lacked an alphabetic writing system, there did not exist an actual document with a list of laws or legal codes like the Hammurabi Code in Egypt. Instead, these laws were transmitted orally and through the quipu. Knowledge of Inca law comes from 16th- and 17th-century sources that attempt to reconstruct Inca culture before the conquest. Some of the most significant Inca laws, enumerated by the 17th-century chronicler Guamán Poma in *The First New Chronicle and Good Government* are as follows:

Those who disobey the orders of a royal Inca are put to death, along with their families. Their homes will be burned and their fields covered with salt to prevent cultivation.

No person can speak negatively about the principal Inca gods, *huacas*, or Inca nobles; violation of this law is punishable by death.

Women and property owners are prohibited from serving as witnesses in the court of law; the former are considered untrustworthy and the latter are susceptible to bribery.

One cannot cut down a tree without permission from the proper authorities; this is also punishable by death or other form of retribution.

Guanacoes, *vicuñas*, wild cats, and foxes are off-limits for hunting.

A widowed woman must remain in the home for the first six months after her husband's death. She must wear mourning clothing for an entire year and cannot have any relations with another man for the remainder of her lifetime.

Children must obey their parents; failure to do so will result in beating for the first offense. Upon second offense, they will be banished to work in the silver or gold mines.

Those who steal or kidnap are punishable by 500 lashes upon first offense. On the second offense, they will be stoned to death and bodies left in the open so they can be devoured by wild animals.

No person can place a death curse or poison another to death. If convicted, this person will be thrown from a cliff and their bodies severed into pieces. If such an act is committed on a royal or noble Inca, their skins will be made into drums, their bones into flutes, their teeth into necklaces, and their skulls into *keros* (vessels for drinking *chicha*, or maize beer). This punishment will be carried out in public.

No woman can enter a sacred temple or visit a *huaca* during her menstrual period.

Committing an act of rape on a woman is punishable by death.

No individual can commit an act of incest (defined as relations up to the first cousin). Such an offense results in gouging the person's eyes out, killed, and his/her body severed into several pieces and left out in the open. Only royal Incas can marry their sisters.

Punishment

Transgression of the law was a major offense, resulting in punishments that were often brutal, even for petty crimes. Types of punishment included banishment, physical torture such as beating or pelting with stones, the termination of one's political position, or death. Some offenders were sent to "prison" in Cuzco, which consisted of an underground lair filled with serpents and wild animals in which few survived. Elite members of society typically received sentences of public humiliation because it was believed that it would be the worst type of punishment since much of their success hinged on public reputation.

Inca courts were administered by local administrators, who would consider the testimony provided by the prosecutor, defendant, and witnesses. They would determine the appropriate form of punishment, which was understood to be final; no appeals were permitted in the Inca justice system. The most serious cases were brought to the *tocricoc* or the Sapa Inca, who were the only ones allowed to administer the death penalty.

READING

Family

Bernabé Cobo, *Inca Religion and Customs*. Translated by Roland Hamilton (Austin: Texas University Press, 1990).

Garcilaso de la Vega, El Inca, *Royal Commentaries of the Incas and General History of Peru, Parts 1 and 2*. Translated by H. V. Livermore (Austin: University of Texas Press, 1966).

Women

Bernabé Cobo, *Inca Religion and Customs*. Translated by Roland Hamilton (Austin: Texas University Press, 1990).

Cathy Lynne Costin, "Housewives, Chosen Women, and Skilled Men: Cloth Production and Social Identity in the Late Pre-Hispanic Andes." In *Craft and Social Identity*. Archaeological Papers of the American Anthropological Association 8, edited by Cathy Costin and Rita Wright, 123–141 (Arlington, Va.: American Anthropological Association, 1998).

Irene Silverblatt, "Andean Women in the Inca Empire," *Feminist Studies* 4, no. 3 (October 1978): 36–61.

Agriculture and Ritual

Brian S. Bauer, "Legitimization of the State in Inca Myth and Ritual," *American Anthropologist* 98, no. 2 (June 1996): 327–337.

Food and Drink

Bernabé Cobo, *Inca Religion and Customs*. Translated by Roland Hamilton (Austin: Texas University Press, 1990).

Sophie Coe, *America's First Cuisines* (Austin: University of Texas Press, 1994).

John H. Rowe, "Inca Culture at the Time of the Spanish Conquest." In *Handbook of South American Indians*. Vol. 2, edited by Julian H. Steward, 183–330 (Washington, D.C.: Smithsonian Institution, 1946).

Education

Bernabé Cobo, *Inca Religion and Customs*. Translated by Roland Hamilton (Austin: Texas University Press, 1990).

John H. Rowe, "Inca Culture at the Time of the Spanish Conquest." In *Handbook of South American Indians*. Vol. 2, edited by Julian H. Steward, 183–330 (Washington, D.C.: Smithsonian Institution, 1946).

Medicine and Shamanism

Constance Classen, *Inca Cosmology and the Human Body* (Salt Lake City: University of Utah Press, 1993).

Bernabé Cobo, *Inca Religion and Customs*. Translated by Roland Hamilton (Austin: Texas University Press, 1990).

Games and Recreation

Bernabé Cobo, *Inca Religion and Customs*. Translated by Roland Hamilton (Austin: Texas University Press, 1990).

Michael Malpass, *Daily Life in the Inca Empire* (Westport, Conn.: Greenwood Press, 1996).

Craig Morris and Adriana von Hagen, *The Inka Empire and Its Andean Origins* (New York: Abbeville Press, 1993).

John H. Rowe, "Inca Culture at the Time of the Spanish Conquest." In *Handbook of South American Indians*. Vol. 2, edited by Julian H. Steward, 183–330 (Washington, D.C.: Smithsonian Institution, 1946).

Personal Appearance and Attire

Constance Classen, *Inca Cosmology and the Human Body* (Salt Lake City: University of Utah Press, 1993).

Kenneth Mills and William B. Taylor, "The Inka's Tunics (Fifteenth to Sixteenth Centuries)." In *Colonial Spanish America: A Documentary History*, 14–18 (Wilmington, Del.: Scholarly Resources, 1998).

Elena Phipps, "Garments and Identity in the Colonial Andes." In *The Colonial Andes: Tapestries and Silverwork, 1530–1830*, edited by Elena Phipps,

Johanna Hecht, and Cristina Esteras Martín, 16–41 (New York: Metropolitan Museum of Art, 2004).

Tom Zuidema, "Guamán Poma and the Art of Empire: Toward an Iconography of Inca Royal Dress." In *Transatlantic Encounters: Europeans and Andeans in the Sixteenth Century*, edited by Kenneth J. Andrien and Rolena Adorno, 151–202 (Berkeley: University of California Press, 1991).

Crime and Punishment

Felipe Guamán Poma de Ayala, *Letter to a King: A Picture-History of the Inca Civilisation by Huamán Poma (Don Felipe Huamán Poma de Ayala)*. Translated by Christopher Dilke (London: George Allen & Unwin, 1978).

John H. Rowe, "Inca Culture at the Time of the Spanish Conquest." In *Handbook of South American Indians*. Vol. 2, edited by Julian H. Steward, 183–330 (Washington, D.C.: Smithsonian Institution, 1946).

13

THE CONQUEST AND THE POSTCONQUEST WORLD

The conquest of Peru by Francisco Pizarro essentially marked the termination of the Inca Empire and the beginning of Spanish colonial rule. This did not, however, signify the cultural death of its descendants in any way. Despite the destructive forces of conquest, many vital aspects of Inca lifeways survived throughout the colonial period and even into the present day. Cultural expressions such as music and the visual and performing arts persisted after the conquest and often helped indigenous communities maintain cohesion in the face of oppressive social conditions. Moreover, Franciscan, Dominican, and Jesuit missionaries often accommodated the needs of its subject populations in their conversion to Catholicism by permitting the integration of Andean ceremonial practices into worship. Schools of art in the colonial period, most notably the Cuzco school, consciously mixed local symbols and cultural references into Spanish-style religious painting to create an entirely new, hybrid genre of religious art. In the world of literature several indigenous authors sought to reconstruct Inca history from the perspective of the vanquished but written in the language of the colonizer. Their testimonies provide critical insights on facets of the Incas and their descendants that their Spanish counterparts fail to address. The mixing of Spanish and indigenous cultures is a process known as *mestizaje*, which began in Peru from the moment of contact and has continued through the present day. Indigenous populations suffered numerous abuses under colonialism, which acted primarily out of a self-interested desire to gain a profit through the economic exploitation of native Andeans. Nevertheless, many aspects of Inca culture have survived, whether in its original form or manifested in newer traditions developed in the colonial period.

THE CONQUEST OF THE INCAS

Early Encounters

The conquest of Peru in 1532 was spearheaded by Francisco Pizarro, who was the second cousin of Mexico's conquistador Hernán Cortés. Pizarro came from rather humble beginnings as an illiterate and illegitimate son of a colonel from Trujillo in Extremadura, Spain. He traveled to the Americas in search of wealth and a better life and remained in the New World until his murder in 1541. He was living in Panama when he learned of Cortés's successes in Mexico; he decided to travel down the South American coastline. Accompanied by Diego de Almagro and a priest named Hernando de Luque, Pizarro attempted an expedition in 1524, but it was thwarted by a series of logistical mishaps and their failure to discover any riches. On their second expedition, in 1526, the same group approached the northern limits of Inca territory at Tumbes in present-day Ecuador, where they got a taste for the grandiosity of an enormous empire that awaited them farther south. Pizarro briefly returned to Spain to request support from King Charles V, then embarked on his third expedition in 1530.

Accompanied again by Almagro and this time by his half brothers, Juan, Hernando, and Gonzalo, along with about 150 soldiers, Pizarro returned to Tumbes and subsequently headed south along the coast of Peru. Pizarro and his soldiers were notified by Native informants that the Inca military had set up camp in the highland city of Cajamarca. Heading inland from the coast, they finally reached Cajamarca, where Pizarro and his men encountered an empire in turmoil. A round of violent succession wars between the two eldest sons of Sapa Inca Huayna Cápac, Atahualpa and Huáscar, had just ended. Huayna Cápac's sudden death in 1524, probably from smallpox, which began to spread through the New World as soon as the first European invaders arrived, had thrown the Inca royal administration into a tailspin.

Huáscar had been crowned successor upon his father's death and dominated the Inca capital of Cuzco and its environs. His half brother Atahualpa governed the imperial army in the northern reaches of the empire, including the Inca outpost at Quito. He was involved in military campaigns to expand the northern part of the Inca Empire to include the territory of tribes living in present-day Colombia. Although the chroniclers remain divided on the details of the brothers' struggle, all are consistent in the fact that within the span of a few years, a conflict between Huáscar and Atahualpa had erupted into civil war. Ultimately, Atahualpa usurped the throne, and Huáscar was taken prisoner.

Atahualpa received word soon thereafter about a group of strange, light-skinned, bearded men heading inland from the coast. He quickly consulted with his military and political advisers but decided to wait for them to arrive to Cajamarca rather than attack them en route. Furthermore, Atahualpa felt that he had little to fear against a band of about 160 men. He sent a group of messengers to Pizarro's traveling army, bearing gifts of food, which were received favorably by the Spaniards. With the help of Pizarro's interpreter, Felipillo, the two groups agreed that Pizarro's army would have a diplomatic meeting in Cajamarca when they arrived. In preparation, Atahualpa amassed a defensive army of about 6,000 men and assembled them in tents along the outskirts of the city so that they could surround the Spaniards for an easy victory. Upon reaching the Cajamarca, Pizarro's army camped out on the city's main square in Cajamarca, awaiting their encounter with the Inca king. Atahualpa sent word to the Spanish contingent that he would agree to meet them the following day. In the meantime, Pizarro ordered his second-in-command, Hernando de Soto, to survey the city and find the Inca army's encampments. Hernando de Soto, along with Hernando Pizarro, Francisco's brother, observed the Inca army stationed in tents. It was at this moment that the differences between the Spanish and Inca armies became clear. The Spaniards, riding on horseback, were able to clear streams and marshes in a single leap, and were protected with metal armor and wielded swords and arquebuses (long-barreled guns). The Incas, on the other hand, possessed bows and arrows, slings, stones, and clubs; did not bear metal armor (instead, they wore breastplates of knotted palm fronts); and lacked the aid of powerful animals.

The Conquest

On November 16, 1532, at around nightfall, Pizarro awaited his first face-to-face encounter with Ata-

13.1 *The encounter of Inca ruler Atahualpa and Francisco Pizarro, with the priest Vicente Valverde presenting the breviary* (Felipe Guamán Poma de Ayala)

hualpa. The Inca king arrived with great fanfare, seated on a palanquin and accompanied by dozens of lavishly outfitted royal retainers. It was on the main square that the famous episode between Atahualpa and the Dominican friar Vicente Valverde ensued. The friar issued the standard *requerimiento*, or "royal requirement," to Atahualpa. This verbal proclamation asserted authority over a given territory as a means of circumventing violent conflict. Atahualpa, no doubt bewildered by this unfamiliar Spanish legal ritual, was far from convinced. Valverde then offered the Inca king a breviary (a book of prayers and religious texts), telling him that it spoke the word of God. Atahualpa inspected it, flipping through the pages before throwing it to the ground in frustration. Some accounts claim that he actually held it up to his ear, waiting for the book to "speak" to him, although the historical veracity of this detail remains unconfirmed. In any event, the Spaniards were severely offended by what they interpreted as Atahualpa's rejection of both the authority of the written word and the sanctity of God. This event marked the beginning of a series of bloody conflicts that would soon bring the Inca Empire to its inevitable end.

Pizarro had hidden men and horses in the principal houses of Cajamarca. After the breviary episode, he ordered the army to attack, and the men charged on horseback toward the Inca army with great noise and fanfare. Perhaps frightened by the deafening sounds of arquebuses, the shouts and trumpets of the Spanish soldiers, and the stampede of horses—all of which would have been completely foreign to the Inca warriors—Atahualpa's army attempted to flee rather than fight. Their weapons of stone and wood were no match for the Spaniard's

13.2 Sapa Inca Atahualpa in his ransom room, watched by a guard (Felipe Guamán Poma de Ayala)

metal swords and guns. Moreover, Inca military tactics differed dramatically from those of the Spanish: The Incas had the intention of injuring the Spaniards and rendering them slaves, while the Spaniards were clearly interested in territorial control through unmitigated slaughter. With fewer than 200 armed soldiers, the outnumbered Spanish attacked and were able to defeat the Inca army without suffering a single casualty. The fighting lasted through the night, and by morning all 6,000 men of Atahualpa's soldiers were slaughtered.

The next morning Pizarro held Atahualpa hostage. In an effort to compromise with the Spanish, Atahualpa sought to ransom himself. In exchange for his release, he promised Pizarro to fill with gold an entire room that measured about 6.7 meters (22 ft.) long, 5.17 meters (17 ft.) wide, and 2.45 meters (8 ft.) high. Atahualpa obtained thousands of dishes, goblets, jars, and basins over the course of the next two months. Still not able to reach his goal, however, he grudgingly entrusted the Spanish to travel with his generals Challcuchima and Quisquis to Cuzco to obtain the remainder of the ransom. Challcuchima, engaged in quelling a pro-Huáscar resistance in Jauja, inexplicably left his post to accompany Pizarro, further exacerbating the empire's internal divisions. Once in Cuzco, Pizarro's forces removed all of the gold that had once sheathed the exterior of the Coricancha, along with many other precious objects, for shipment to Cajamarca. Much to the Incas' dismay, Pizarro's forces melted down the pieces into gold and silver ingots to be used as currency for distribution among the conquistadores and for the royal fifth to be sent to the Spanish Crown. While in captivity, Atahualpa continued to rule the empire, albeit under very compromising conditions. It was then that he ordered the assassination of Huáscar, a tactical blunder that would seal the fate of the Incas. Atahualpa's success in obtaining the ransom apparently was not sufficient for the Spaniards, who left him in captivity and eventually murdered him on dubious charges of treason and for causing the death of Huáscar. Atahualpa was publicly garroted on July 26, 1533, in Cajamarca's main square.

Throughout the tumultuous conquest period, violence ensued not only between Incas and Spaniards but among the conquistadores. The invaders eventually split into two factions over division of the spoils of war. Those who sided with Almagro felt cheated out of their share of the ransom and conquered territory and thus bitterly despised the Pizarro men and their supporters. These tensions broke out into a full-scale factional war on April 26, 1538, known as the Battle of Las Salinas. Pizarro and Almagro's men fought over control of the city of Cuzco, to which both factions laid claim. Pizarro's forces won the battle within an hour of combat, leading to the capture and eventual execution of Almagro in July of 1538. Although the Battle of Las Salinas resulted in a decisive victory for Pizarro's forces, the tensions between the two factions continued. On June 26, 1541, in the newly established capital of Lima, Francisco Pizarro was assassinated by Almagro supporters intent on seeking revenge and appointing Almagro's son governor of Peru. Pizarro's remains can be found today in the Lima Cathedral.

The Neo-Inca State

In 1533 Pizarro appointed Atahualpa's younger brother Manco Inca as the new ruler of the transitional empire following the Spanish takeover of the Inca capital at Cuzco. Despite his official status as "Sapa Inca," Manco Inca (Manco Cápac II) and those under his jurisdiction soon realized that this was not an arrangement among equals. In a last-ditch effort to reclaim power he led a simultaneous attack on Cuzco and Lima that resulted in many casualties but failed to overthrow Spanish rule. The Spaniards' strategic alliances with the Cañari and Huanca groups, both of whom had resisted Inca rule, helped secure their power during this precarious period. In 1537 Manco Inca fled first to Ollantaytambo, then to Vilcabamba (about 130 kilometers [81 mi.] west of Cuzco in dense forest) to establish a neo-Inca state that lasted more than 30 years. Manco Inca's fate did not last as long; he was assassinated by traitorous Spaniards seeking refuge at Vilcabamba in 1544.

TITU CUSI YUPANQUI

After Manco Inca's death his son Sayri Túpac governed the neo-Inca state until 1560, when he renounced his imperial claim after negotiations with the Spanish viceroy. Titu Cusi Yupanqui, another son of Manco Inca, next was at the helm of Inca resistance. Titu Cusi Yupanqui (under the name Don Diego de Castro Titu Cusi Yupanqui) is famed for his written account of the conquest of Peru from an Inca perspective, an English translation of which is entitled *An Inca Account of the Conquest of Peru by Titu Cusi Yupanqui.* He ruled from Vilcabamba for a little over a decade and died from an illness of unknown causes in 1571.

TÚPAC AMARU

Túpac Amaru, yet another son of Manco Inca, was the next and last ruler of the neo-Inca state. The newly appointed viceroy Francisco de Toledo, apprised of the turmoil following the conquest of Peru, became determined to weed out indigenous defiance to colonial rule and reinstate Spanish authority with an iron fist. His forces headed toward Vilcabamba to dismantle Túpac Amaru's state. Túpac Amaru went into hiding in the dense forests to the east of Vilcabamba but was eventually captured by Toledo's forces. The neo-Inca state ended with his execution in 1572: He was publicly beheaded in Cuzco, thus ending three decades of Inca political resistance.

Later Inca-Inspired Rebellions

Despite the technological and tactical superiority of the Spanish forces over Inca ones, the conquest of Peru was met with an enormous amount of resistance. In addition to the neo-Inca state established at Vilcabamba, several rebellions throughout the colonial period continued to test the limits of Spanish control. Even as late as 1781, a mestizo named José Gabriel Condorcanqui, who claimed direct descent from Túpac Amaru and even renamed himself after the Inca, led what came to be called the Túpac Amaru II Rebellion. The rebellion was violent and short-lived. It began in November 1780 in the small town of Tinta, where the local Spanish leader was murdered for his mistreatment of the native population. This action led to a domino effect of fighting between Spaniards and indigenous people that quickly spread through a huge expanse of Andean South America and eventually ended in the capture and execution of Túpac Amaru II in May 1781. The rebellion produced a great deal of collateral damage. Private estates were destroyed, fields were burned, and factories were leveled. The rebellion was largely unsuccessful due to the conflicting interests of the various factions. Nevertheless, it demonstrates the extent to which the historical memory of Inca rule persevered, even more than 200 years after the fall of Cuzco.

Demographic Collapse

It is difficult to calculate the death toll of the conquest with exactitude, because historical accounts remain vague and contradictory. Scholars have estimated the preconquest population of the Inca realm to be anywhere from 4 to 15 million. The proportion that died as a result of warfare and disease brought by the conquest has been postulated as high as 50 percent. The first accurate census counts were not made until 1570 under the newly arrived viceroy Francisco de Toledo and served as the basis from which scholars made their estimates for the extent of demographic change.

Aside from casualties brought on directly by warfare, the major killer was disease. The arrival to the Americas of Old World pathogens such as smallpox, measles, malaria, and typhus had a devastating effect on indigenous populations. While Europeans had developed natural defenses to these diseases, which had inhabited the Eurasian continent for centuries, Amerindians were biologically vulnerable to them, dying in droves when the epidemic reached new territory. The spread of Old World diseases actually preceded the invading conquerors, reaching Inca communities, for example, before the Spanish had even set foot in the Andes. The resiliency of airborne diseases in highly susceptible regions, in fact, allowed for their rapid dissemination throughout the Americas dating back even to European explorers traveling in the late 15th and early 16th centuries. For example, the father of Atahualpa and Huáscar, Huayna Cápac, probably died from smallpox in 1524—eight years

before the encounter of the Spanish conquistadores with Atahualpa in Cajamarca. The number of casualties was not evenly distributed across the former Inca heartland, however. Populations in the coastal areas were more susceptible to epidemics, as the pathogens contaminated water supplies and throve in the hot coastal climate. On the other hand, the high-altitude Andean regions were very susceptible to smallpox, which survives best in cool, dry air. Generally speaking, however, these places provided more protection from foreign disease than their lowland counterparts, where the death toll in some areas reached as high as 95 percent.

COLONIAL TRANSITION AND IDENTITY

Immediately following conquest the Spaniards initiated the process of settling and colonizing Inca territory as well as the rest of the Spanish-speaking region known today as Latin America. Within the span of mere decades Spanish systems of governance, religion, and social organization overtook their Inca antecedents. The colonial administration was structured on two primary objectives: the extraction of wealth through exploitation of natural resources and the mass conversion of indigenous communities to Catholicism. These aims were accomplished through the imposition of colonial institutions that were intended to transform the native peoples into ideal Christian citizens from a European point of view. Despite these efforts Inca ways of life persisted due to the tenacity of indigenous Andeans even in the most formidable circumstances and thanks to the efforts of sympathetic Spaniards who negotiated with indigenous communities to keep their cultural traditions alive.

New Identities

Given the volatile conditions under which the Spanish took control of Inca territory, alliances with members of the newly toppled indigenous aristocracy were essential. Conquistadores and prominent Spanish families often intermarried with Inca royalty to establish political legitimacy. The Incas also benefited from the practice, because it put them in favor with the new ruling class. Strategic intermarriage contributed to the myth that the Spanish invasion was nothing more than a seamless exchange of power, which is best captured in a famous 18th-century genealogical painting that contains the portraits of all of the Inca rulers beginning with the founding brother-sister couple, Manco Cápac and Mama Ocllo, and ending with portraits of the first nine Spanish monarchs of the Viceroyalty of Peru.

The positioning of the Spanish as legitimate heirs to the Inca Empire was facilitated primarily through the marriages of *ñustas* (Inca noblewomen) to high-standing Spanish men. Their offspring, inheriting both Spanish and royal Inca bloodlines, were in a privileged position to negotiate between the two groups for recognition and power. In this case the mestizo and mestiza (mixed-race offspring) lost their association with bastardry because of the prestige associated with both groups. The more typical case of *mestizaje*, however, occurred between low-caste Spaniards and Indians, producing a growing class of mixed-race individuals, who today make up the second-highest proportion of Peru's population after indigenous Andeans.

The arrival of enslaved Africans in Peru shortly after the conquest further diversified a burgeoning colonial population. Slavery in Peru was primarily urban based, with the greatest proportion residing in the newly established capital of Lima. By the end of the 16th century blacks made up nearly 50 percent of Peru's population. Slaves were also sent to the southern coastal areas to work on sugar plantations. Some opportunity existed for manumission, which contributed to a growing class of free blacks, known as *pardos libres*. Blacks often intermarried with other racial groups, creating new *castas* (castes), each with its own group identities and cultural allegiances. Blacks mixed with whites were called *mulatos*, and the products of intermarriage between blacks and Indians were called *zambos*.

The Colonial Economy

ENCOMIENDA

The *encomienda* system was established throughout Spanish America as a major building block of the colonial economy. It consisted of a tract of land that relied on the exploitation of native labor headed by an overseer known as an *encomendero*. Laborers were promised military protection and religious training as rewards for their services. Indigenous Andeans were told that they were working in order to save their souls, which the Spanish perceived as heathen and cursed by the devil. They were essentially farming without pay, but from the point of view of the Spaniards the spiritual reward of Catholicism was a form of pay in itself. The first *encomiendas*, located in the most fertile and accessible lands, were parceled out to the conquistadores as compensation for their participation in the conquest. Lower-ranked soldiers and more recent arrivals from Spain tended to receive less desirable *encomiendas*, which contributed to a growing rift between the original conquistadores and later Spanish immigrants.

Many of the same products were produced as they had been in pre-Hispanic times, such as potatoes, corn, tomatoes, and coca. After the European invasion native people also farmed wheat and barley, along with sugar and olive trees in the lowlands. *Encomiendas* were not limited to agricultural production, however. Some involved the herding of Old World domesticates, such as cattle, sheep, and pigs, or the mining of gold, silver, and mercury.

The *encomienda* in the Andes was different from its Mexican and Caribbean counterparts. For example, Inca labor systems remained relatively intact, although they lost their redistributive element in the colonial period. The Inca *mita* had been a rotational labor system that granted *ayllus* (kin groups) equal access to a variety of goods from different eco-zones. The activities of *mitayos* (*mita* laborers) during Inca times were not limited to labor; festivities and visits to shrines and *tambos* (way stations along the Inca highway) en route to a work site were integral elements of the *mita*. After the conquest the *mita* was transformed into a forced rotational labor draft that retained its name and general structure but was manipulated to serve the needs of the Spanish and select indigenous leaders. During the colonial period, for example, most *mitayos* worked in building and mining activities.

As more Spaniards settled in Peru to try to make their fortunes, the availability of potentially profitable *encomiendas* began to dwindle. Productivity also started to decrease as native Andeans, increasingly discontented by the institution, revolted or fled. Much of this was precipitated not only by direct exploitation under the Spanish but also by abused of power by native *kurakas* over their relatively powerless subject populations. Given that the *kurakas* no longer ruled under the pretext of reciprocity but rather within a system of mercantilism, their loyalties often shifted away from their constituencies in the name of personal gain. The system of *encomienda* began to break down toward the second half of the 16th century largely due to the effects of Viceroy Toledo's economic reforms of the 1570s. These reforms reconstituted the organization of indigenous labor, shifting to the use of labor contracts that offered monetary wages. Although many native people were now working for pay, they were in essence trading one exploitative policy for another. They were still expected to pay tribute; the only difference was that it took the form of money instead of a product. Andeans were now enlisted en masse to work for the new money-making machines of the late 16th and early 17th centuries: mines.

MINING

The Spanish discovery of silver at Carabaya in 1542, Potosí in 1545, Chachapoyas in 1550, and mercury deposits at Huancavelica in 1564 led to a mining boom in the Andes that quickly transformed the Viceroyalty of Peru into the wealthiest colony in the Americas. The Incas had been mining from Potosí and other sources since their rise to power but using different techniques. The greatest distinction between Andean and European mining practices was in the refining process. In the former furnaces known as *huairas* were used for smelting the silver ores, fueled by either llama manure or grass. Indigenous techniques were used in the early phases of colonial mining enterprises throughout the Americas but transitioned in the 1570s in the Andes with German advances in amalgamation techniques. The new process required mixing finely processed silver ores with mercury for the industrial-scale produc-

tion of silver. Unlike smelting, amalgamation could refine low-quality ores after the overexploitation of mines began to deplete the higher-quality ores. Because of the great output generated through amalgamation, this energy-intensive technology necessitated the construction of water-powered amalgamation plants known as *ingenios*. This shift ultimately contributed to both the increased profit of European entrepreneurs and the disempowerment of native Andean miners, whose expertise in native smelting techniques were no longer needed. They still continued to mine but as laborers in amalgamation plants using foreign technologies.

Considering that European currency was set to the silver standard, money was essentially being directly extracted right out of the Potosí mines. One-fifth of the amount extracted went directly to the Spanish Crown, known as the "royal fifth," while the rest was used in exchange for goods. Located in present-day Bolivia, Potosí's mine was known as Cerro Rico, or "Rich Hill." Almost 14,000 *mita* laborers were sent here and to other mines on a yearly rotational basis to produce tribute payment from their towns. Miners worked under dangerous conditions, and many died as the result of respiratory illness or collapsed mine shafts. Potosí became part of the seasonal trade routes that exchanged goods between Europe, Asia, and the Americas. Silver mined from the Andes was exchanged for Chinese silk and other Asian goods that had become popular among members of the upper class. Within a few years Potosí transformed from a small Andean town into a major commercial center that attracted fortune seekers from all over South America and Europe. The population exploded to well over 100,000 by 1600. The late 16th century marked the peak of productivity for mining in the Andes, with Potosí alone producing half of all the silver in the Spanish colonies. By the 17th century, however, its resources began to dwindle, and people began to search for business prospects elsewhere.

Urban Planning and Settlement

The Spanish quickly embarked on city-building campaigns in the aftermath of conquest. Some cities were literally built on top of Inca ruins, endowing them with a hybrid character. A classic example is Cuzco, whose Inca structures literally serve as the foundations for Spanish ones. Other cities, such as Lima and Trujillo, are located near pre-Hispanic ruins but were not founded until the colonial period. Whether a particular city had a more indigenous or Spanish character, however, its initial construction depended almost entirely on native labor. Indians were involved in many aspects of urban development, including the construction and elaboration of colonial churches, cathedrals, estates, and administrative buildings. Using traditional construction and design techniques, native artisans left a distinctively Andean mark on the colonial built environment.

THE COLONIAL CITY

Colonial cities were founded throughout the area once dominated by the Incas. The first city founded by the Spanish was the northern coastal city of Piura in 1532, followed by Quito and Cuzco in 1534 and Lima in 1535. The dominant feature of all colonial cities is the central plaza, or main square. The plaza was the location of all political, social, and economic transactions. In every colonial city in Peru, whether large or small, a church, jail, and municipal buildings surrounded the central plaza. At the square people gathered and public events such as religious processions and ceremonies took place. The plaza was the center from which the major streets emanated, forming a grid pattern that was easily mapped and navigable. Cities were primarily the residence of Spaniards, who settled the areas closest to the central plaza (although Cuzco presents a unique counter-example). Native Andeans typically lived on the outskirts of the city or were resettled into nucleated towns in the countryside *(reducciones)*.

CUZCO

Founded by Pizarro as a "Christian republic" on March 23, 1534, colonial Cuzco was a unique case in

13.3 The Plaza de Armas, Cuzco's main square (Ananda Cohen Suarez)

the urban development of Peru. Because it coincidentally possessed many of the same features of Spanish cities, such as well-constructed buildings, a road system, and plazas, much of its structural integrity was left intact. Instead of razing the city to the ground the Spaniards manipulated the built environment of Cuzco to meet the needs of an entirely new social and political order. Two factors played a role in this decision. First, the Spaniards recognized its importance as a sacred center for people throughout the empire. By building churches on top of Inca religious buildings, the Spanish were overtaking the old city both literally and ideologically. In addition, the use of Inca buildings and the recycling of construction materials were economically advantageous; the Spanish did not have to bear the cost of imported materials. The double plaza of Inca Cuzco (the Huacaypata) was retained but made smaller and renamed the Plaza de Armas. The Cuzco cathedral was built atop the ruins of Inca Viracocha's palace. The Coricancha (Temple of the Sun), perhaps the most sacred building in the Inca realm, subsequently served as the foundation for the Church of Santo Domingo. Even today the remains of the pre-Hispanic city are quite visible: Toppled Inca buildings serve as the foundations for colonial-era ones; Inca stone walls line the streets; and the ruins of Inca structures such as the fortress of Sacsayhuamán lie just beyond the city limits.

Given its earlier role as the capital of the Inca Empire, Cuzco managed to maintain a distinctly Andean flavor into the colonial period. Aside from physical appearance, its populace was overwhelmingly Indian; Spaniards made up only about a quarter of the city's inhabitants in the 17th century. Descendants of the Inca elite resided in Cuzco and played an integral role in the maintenance of Inca cultural traditions after the conquest. Many of them were given land grants by the Spaniards in choice locations as a means of appeasing the former ruling class, who, if provoked, could have easily mobilized an indigenous rebellion. Many Cuzco cultural practices persisted, including textile manufacture, culinary traditions, and the celebration of agricultural festivals.

LIMA

The city of Lima was originally founded at Jauja, a town closer to Cuzco, but was relocated in 1534 to its present location because of the area's natural resources and proximity to the river Rímac and the Pacific Ocean. Although Lima was originally an indigenous settlement featuring the sacred site of Huaca Pucllana and nearby the administrative and ceremonial center of Pachacamac, located 30 kilometers (19 mi.) south, it had never even come near the architectural grandeur of Cuzco. The Spanish city, built from scratch, giving it a strong Spanish character, was named capital of the Viceroyalty of Peru in 1543. Lima was situated at the crossroads of all commercial and political activity of the colony and managed international trade between South America, Asia, and Europe at the famous adjoining port of Callao. The city's physical distance from the Inca heartland rendered it almost totally psychologically and geographically divorced from the Andean world.

Lima was the most racially diverse city in the viceroyalty, boasting a population of Europeans, Indians, Africans, and their various admixtures. In contrast to Cuzco, descendants of the Inca elite did not occupy a privileged place in Lima society. Rather, the growing *criollo* class—individuals born in the Americas of Spanish descent—gained ascendancy within Lima's power structure. The *criollos* were constantly at odds with the *peninsulares* (individuals born in Spain who immigrated to the Americas), who considered themselves socially superior to their American-born counterparts. A population of mestizos and *mulatos* also began to develop in Lima, whose members typically occupied the lower rungs of Lima's class hierarchy. African slaves figured at the bottom of the social order, although a significant number achieved manumission and became property owners or opened businesses. The Inca past did not figure strongly into the identity of the city, which looked more toward Spain as its civic model. In fact, even Indians and racially mixed inhabitants of Lima often took on the mannerisms and dress of their European counterparts for acceptance into mainstream society.

REDUCCIONES

The arrival of Viceroy Francisco de Toledo in Peru in 1569 brought momentous changes to the colony, particularly in its policy toward the native populations. He is most famously credited with the imposition of *reducciones* throughout the Peruvian countryside. *Reducciones* were nucleated villages for indigenous-only residents designed to concentrate native populations by replacing the more numerous and smaller traditional Andean *llacta* (town or hamlet). They were also known as *pueblos de indios,* or Indian towns. The development of *reducciones* entailed the forced resettlement of indigenous communities into Spanish-style towns. These towns began to dominate the countryside, and most small towns of modern-day Peru were founded as *reducciones.* The process of resettlement inevitably split kin groups and ancestral units, thus eroding Andean systems of social sustainability. Dislocated from their original natural and built environments, indigenous communities became even more susceptible to exploitation by the Spanish and their respective *kurakas.* Each *reducción* contained a central plaza surrounded by a church, jail, priest's house, administrative buildings and had a gridded road system. They were specifically designed under Toledo to facilitate religious conversion and economic exploitation. Another objective of the plan was to distance native peoples from the *huacas* that their ancestors would have venerated, along with other local sacred monuments that linked them to the Inca—and in the Spaniards' eyes, idolatrous—past. The deterritorialization suffered by the Indians (principally native Andeans) through the new system of *reducciones,* along with Toledo's decision to reduce the power of local *kurakas,* painted a bleak picture for Peru's indigenous population in the late 16th century. Finally, the construction of *reducciones* also allowed the Spanish to maintain their ideal of separate spheres for Spaniards and Indians. This separation existed more as an ideal than a reality, however, particularly as the groups began to intermarry and produce a growing mestizo population.

Transition to Writing

Inca systems of encoding knowledge lost their legitimacy with the arrival of the Spaniards, who championed alphabetic literacy and the written word. The quipu, a series of knotted strings used for census counts, tabulating tribute, and perhaps even recording histories, were abandoned after the 17th century. Oral tradition persevered through the colonial period and up to the present day, but the Spanish considered this type of history inferior to that which was written down.

Many scholars continue to debate the thorny issue of literacy in the Americas. If the Incas did not write down their histories with a formal written language does this imply that the society was "preliterate"? Or, is there such a thing as "alternative" literacies? Many scholars agree with the latter point, convincingly arguing that other methods for transcribing words and concepts should not be discredited simply because they do not conform to European models.

Oral Tradition

Oral tradition serves as the primary mechanism for disseminating information in a society that possesses no written documents. The Incas made little or no distinction between myth and history, given that the particular details or sequence of events varied depending on who was telling the story. They conceived of history as existing in a series of different interlocked levels—cosmological, royal, or familial. Because the Incas had no concept of linear history that could be ordered into a singular grand narrative as the Europeans did, many of their histories seem to contradict each other. However, this perceived contradiction only appears as such if oral traditions of the Incas are evaluated through European concepts of time and history.

Oral tradition was often communicated through song, dance, ritual, theatrical performance, or procession. Inca strategies for storing and preserving social memory were also quite distinct from those of Europeans. The quipu held quantifiable information through complex patterns of knotted strings. The practice of pilgrimage to *huacas* preserved religious knowledge and belief through the practice of repeated ritual. Inca male poets, known as *amautas,* recited royal histories in ballad form in front of captive audiences. All Inca origin myths and historical accounts were thus preserved orally through a variety of cognitive practices and only later transcribed in the 16th century into Spanish or Quechua. The Spanish shunned the maintenance of any oral tradition that possessed a religious component in their quest to eliminate everything they perceived as "idolatry."

Many origin myths and oral histories relating to the rise of Inca power survived through the colonial period because they were written down at that time. The linguist and friar Domingo de Santo Tomás is credited with the transcription of Quechua into written form, publishing the first Quechua grammar book, *Gramática, o arte de la lengua general de los indios de los reynos del Peru* (Grammar, or art of the language of the Indians of the kingdoms of Peru), in 1560. A system of transcription allowed for the publication of the Bible, catechisms, and historical texts into a language familiar to the indigenous peoples. The step was especially useful in the process of conversion, since it put the material into familiar terms. Moreover, it was easier for missionaries to teach natives to read their own language as opposed to a foreign one.

The 16th-century chroniclers Betanzos and Cieza de León are the most widely credited for transcribing Inca history into written Spanish. The transfer of history and myth from an oral medium to a written one inevitably altered its form as well as the possible interpretations one could draw from it. In many cases aspects of oral tradition manifested themselves in the writings of indigenous authors, given its primacy throughout the pre-Columbian period. For example, in legal documents and literature the events are repeated several times, imitating the way that a storyteller would perform a story. When Spanish speakers transcribed oral histories to written ones, they were engaging in an act of double translation. Despite the advantages of preserving Inca histories that otherwise might have been lost, an inevitable consequence of this practice is that the story becomes filtered through the biases and worldviews of a foreigner to the indigenous cultures of the former Inca Empire. In addition, the use of the written word in the Western literary tradition presupposes a linear concept of time and history, which was often irreconcilable with Andean categories of thought. Moreover, the replacement of Quechua terms with Spanish ones inevitably altered their original meanings and cultural references. For these reasons the Inca histories recorded by a variety of individuals during the colonial period often differed from one another in historical detail and sequence of events.

The Quipu in the Colonial Period

The quipu, a mnemonic device for recording information through a series of multicolored knotted strings, had been used throughout the Inca realm for a variety of purposes. Spanish contemporaries commented that they were used for census taking, for the tabulation of tribute payment, and perhaps even for recording histories and poetry during the Inca period. The 16th-century chroniclers most concerned with describing the quipu and following its history were Sarmiento de Gamboa, writing in 1572, and the mestizo historian El Inca Garcilaso de la Vega, writing in 1609. The color of the individual strings and the size and position of the knots each had a specific significance that could be easily read and interpreted by trained *quipucamayos* (quipu readers). In rare cases quipus continued to be used into the early colonial period. *Quipucamayos* who had managed to maintain their practice after the conquest were instrumental in the colonial court system. Native Andeans often used their services to present information contained in quipus as a form of legal evidence. Quipus and their users avoided the radar of idolatry extirpation campaigns until 1583, when the passing of a new law demanded their condemnation by the Third Council of Lima. But by then most knowledge of their original function was lost. The role of the *quipucamayo* in colonial society increasingly diminished as indigenous scribes, proficient in both Spanish and Quechua, began to take their place.

THE SPREAD OF CHRISTIANITY

Missionaries

The first missionaries in Peru were the Franciscans, who arrived as a group of 12 in honor of the Twelve

Apostles. They were followed by the Dominicans, the Mercedarians, and finally the Jesuits. Although the religious orders differed in ideology, and their missionaries, in their interactions with Indians, they all shared the basic motivation of converting as many nonbelievers as possible to the Christian faith. The first step of the conversion process entailed the destruction of all Inca temples and religious objects, which they saw as the work of the devil. Once the material destruction of pre-Hispanic religion was complete, missionaries then embarked on church-building campaigns and conversion activities in an effort to transplant Catholicism onto new soil.

What ensued was perhaps not what the missionaries had envisioned: A dynamic interplay evolved between Christian and native religious practices and symbols. The missionaries, particularly the Franciscans and the Jesuits, quickly realized that the only way to succeed in the missionizing process was through the negotiation of Catholicism with indigenous belief systems. This was accomplished through a variety of strategies that actively engaged Indian congregations through analogies and associations between the new religion and past Inca practices.

Andean Catholicism

Christian saints often became hybrids, embodying aspects of Andean gods. For example, the Virgin Mary was commonly conflated with the earth goddess, Pachamama. As they both shared characteristics of mother figures, it facilitated the transition to Christianity from the perspective of the missionaries. From an indigenous perspective it allowed the maintenance of old religious traditions albeit in a more covert form. Other popular Andean saints, such as the Virgin of Cocharcas, venerated in the Cuzco area, were not necessarily directly related to a pre-Hispanic god but to the sacred earth. *Huacas* were often converted to Christian shrines because missionaries recognized their sacred importance. While a *huaca* could not be emptied of its significance, its sanctity could be superimposed onto a new set of beliefs. In fact, throughout the Andes churches usually occupied the same spaces as *hua-*

cas, whether they were built literally on top of them or within their vicinity.

Preconquest ritual also manifested itself in colonial-period religious practice. For example, the practice of parading saints through the streets during certain religious festivals shared affinities with the Inca tradition of parading mummies. Andean Catholicism, developed under the conditions of mass conversion, began to acquire an identity that was neither fully Catholic nor fully Inca but a mixture of both.

Religious Resistance

Although the Viceroyalty of Peru boasted an overwhelming number of native converts to the Catholic faith, the process was far from smooth or uninterrupted. Many indigenous people refused to give up their religion and openly defied this new, imposed faith, while others formally converted but continued to practice their religion in secret. The phenomenon of Andean Catholicism accommodated the interpenetration of Christian and Andean belief systems but only to a certain point. Catholic dogma continued to reign supreme as the final authority in the lives of Andeans.

One response to Spanish intolerance of Andean religion culminated in a millenarian movement known as Taki Onqoy, which translates to "dancing sickness." This movement began around 1560 in the Huamanga region of the Central Andes (present-day Ayacucho), making its way toward Lima to the north and Cuzco to the east before being crushed by the Spanish a few years later. Headed by a group of visionaries known as *taquiongos* believed to have been possessed by vengeful *huacas*, its goal was to eliminate any trace of European culture in the Andes. These visionaries, the majority of whom were women, were allegedly told by the gods that they must purge themselves of foreign influence so that order and prosperity would return. The principles behind Taki Onqoy called for a return to a purely Andean, pre-Hispanic way of life. The *taquiongos* would engage in dances and chants and in their possessed state would relay messages from the *huacas* to the populace. Their performative preaching managed to win over the loyalties of many native Andeans who were increasingly disillusioned by Spanish colonial rule and the restrictions it imposed on their cultural practices. While Taki Onqoy gained a substantial amount of converts, its success was short-lived due to internal divisions and aggressive extirpation campaigns by the Spanish in the 1560s. Although this particular movement ultimately failed, it did not signal the total disintegration of all preconquest religious practice.

Although the Spanish worked hard to stamp out all remnants of native Andean religion, many continued to worship *huacas* and use talismans and divinatory figurines through the 17th century. And, while indigenous rebellions against Christianity and Spanish hegemony were always short-lived, many managed to practice their religion in secret. Communities in the isolated high-altitude regions still recognized Inti, the sun god, Pachamama, the earth goddess, and Mama Quilla, the moon goddess, as their principal deities. It has also been well documented that throughout the colonial period native Andeans would often secretly dig up the body of a deceased relative that was buried Christian style and rebury it at a venerated *huaca* and engage in dancing, feasting, and *chicha* drinking—all typical funerary practice in the pre-Columbian era. Human and llama sacrifice also continued after the conquest, although to a lesser degree. Much of this information is available to us because of several treatises written in the 17th century by Spaniards on the "idolatry" of Indian communities. Despite conversion efforts, it came to the attention of religious officials that native Andeans had not completely renounced their original faith. Campaigns to extirpate idolatry became a linchpin of religious reform in this period, which entailed the destruction of all native religious objects (which the Spaniards called "idols") and the public condemnation of idolaters in a ceremony known as an *auto de fe* (act of faith).

COLONIAL ART

After the conquest the visual arts of the Inca regions changed dramatically to accommodate the needs of new, incoming populations of Spaniards and as an integral component of the Indian conversion process. Many different artistic styles and forms coexisted, signaling the vast diversity of artists, artisans, craftsmen and -women, and patrons of the arts in colonial society. The mixture of Andean visual traditions with European ones can also be seen as a form of *mestizaje*; in fact, many scholars have referred to colonial art of the Andes as "mestizo baroque." Some Inca art forms continued to be produced in the colonial period, such as *keros* (flared-mouth drinking vessels) and textiles. Most Inca art did not survive the conquest, however, given its religious associations. Instead, techniques such as stonecutting, weaving, and metalworking were rerouted into new artistic and architectural ventures, typically in the service of the Catholic Church and for wealthy patrons. But, even if executed in a European style, works of art often carried an Andean flavor because of the use of local materials. To cite one example, local pigments imbued paintings and sculpture with a luminescent quality not typically found in Spanish art. Finally, colonial Andean art incorporated Andean styles and design elements—some specifically Inca and others not—found in a range of media, including painting, sculpture, architecture, and manuscript illustrations.

Colonial Artistic Production

Artists and artisans produced work through a variety of venues, whether within a formal workshop, independently in the household, or as part of a guild. Immediately following the conquest artistic production was not very standardized; art producers tended to work on a part-time basis for supplementary income. Spaniards initially depended almost exclusively on native artistry because of the low cost and high availability of Indian labor. Native peoples built the churches and cathedrals of the conquered Inca Empire, typically as a form of tribute payment. The importation of European craft technologies such as tempera and oil paint, glazes, canvas, looms, and the potter's wheel dramatically altered the artistic process, to which native artists adapted quickly and adeptly. Moreover, religious prints from Flanders and Italy served as study aids for aspiring artists and as prototypes for paintings.

The production of Andean crafts, particularly those with utilitarian value, such as textiles, *mates* (hollowed-out gourd containers) for drinking *chicha*, and masks, among others, survived the colonial period relatively unscathed because they existed beyond the boundaries of formal categories of art imposed by Europeans. The new types of art that were valued by the conquerors were religious painting, sculpture, *retablos* (altarpieces), and the decorative arts. Due to the instability brought on by civil wars and earthquakes, formal schools of art did not develop in Peru until the 17th century.

Artists of the Colonial Andes

BERNARDO BITTI (1548–1610)

The first European artists and architects of Peru, who trained Indian artists through a system of apprenticeship, did not arrive until the late 16th century. The most famous European artist to work in Peru was the Jesuit Bernardo Bitti, an Italian painter who arrived in Lima in 1574 and worked in different cities of Peru until his death in 1610. Trained in Rome in the mannerist style that dominated European painting and sculpture after the Renaissance, Bitti's paintings were distinctive for their elongated human proportions and pastel color palette. He introduced mannerism to Andean artists, who adapted it to their own paintings, but not without personal modification and innovation. Religious themes dominated his work and, indeed, the vast majority of all paintings produced in the colonial period. Some of the common subjects found in Bitti's work include scenes from the life of Christ, portraits of the Virgin Mary, and portraits of angels. His work seems to have exerted the most visible influence on subsequent painters throughout the Andes than any other colonial artist, European or otherwise.

DIEGO QUISPE TITO (1611–1681)

Diego Quispe Tito, a painter of royal Inca descent, produced an immense body of work for various religious orders, churches, and wealthy patrons of Cuzco. He achieved the highest status of painting as master, probably at least in part due to his royal heritage. His work is known for its graceful naturalism and imaginative landscapes, which he passed on to numerous native Cuzco artists in his workshop. His best-known painting is the *Signs of the Zodiac* (1681) located in the Cuzco cathedral. Copied from a Flemish engraving, the work illustrates 12 different scenes from the life of Christ, corresponding with each sign of the zodiac. This work, along with others from the colonial period, had a special resonance with native Andeans, many of whom recognized links between the celestial bodies represented by the zodiac and the celestial deities that the Incas and their ancestors once worshipped.

Quispe Tito allegedly traveled to Europe to receive training, but this detail of his life remains unconfirmed. He was familiar with the work of Bitti and his followers, which resided in churches and residences throughout Cuzco. Nevertheless, Quispe Tito's expertise derived from his deft integration of subject matter taken from Flemish engravings into Andean works of art. Although engravings executed in a naturalistic northern European style served as prototypes for his paintings, Quispe Tito was far from a slavish copyist. His ability to weave together European print sources, Inca iconography, and local references into his paintings was highly admired by contemporaries and kicked off a specifically Andean approach to painting that would serve as the inspiration for artists in the subsequent decades of the 17th century.

BASILIO DE SANTA CRUZ PUMAQALLO (1661–1699)

Basilio de Santa Cruz Pumaqallo was also an indigenous artist working in Cuzco and was probably the second best-known native artist of the region after Quispe Tito. Like his predecessor, he ran a large painting workshop that trained numerous native Andean artists and produced an enormous output of work. Santa Cruz Pumaqallo is best known for his large-scale paintings in the Cuzco cathedral, the Church of La Merced, and the monastery of San Francisco.

The Cuzco School

The Cuzco school was founded during the latter part of the 17th century by a group of indigenous artists who wished to escape the exclusionary and abusive policies of mainstream art guilds. Despite the seemingly harmonious exchange between European and Andean visual traditions seen in earlier colonial art, the historical record tells a different story. Many Spanish and *criollo* artists mistreated native Andean artists through exploitation, failure to recognize their achievements, or refusal to promote talented artists to the prestigious status of master artist. After years of protest culminating in legal action, the indigenous artists were allowed to form their own workshops, whose collective output of iconographically and stylistically distinct religious artworks fall under the label "Cuzco school of painting." The Cuzco school produced a massive number of works,

13.4 A painting of the Cuzco school entitled Saint Joseph and the Christ Child *(Courtesy the Brooklyn Museum)*

likely owing to an assembly-line style of production, with different apprentices specializing in one feature, such as drapery or hair. This piecemeal method of painting lent an almost mechanical feel to the works of art, although this by no means discredits their uniqueness and immediacy.

Dissatisfied with the prevailing European styles of austere naturalism, members of the Cuzco school sought to produce work that resonated with the predominantly indigenous population of Cuzco. The style has been referred to by art historians as the "Cuzco popular style" or "mestizo baroque." References to Andean foodstuffs such as *cuy* (guinea pig), cherimoya (an Andean fruit), and corn endowed paintings with a local, familiar flavor. Saints and angels tended to be represented as Indians and mestizos, rather than as fair Europeans. Another identifying feature of art from the Cuzco school is the use of gold filigree as a decorative feature. While the European prototypes from which religious art in the Andes was derived often contained gold accents, the native artists turned gold into a dominant feature in their paintings. Intricate gold patterning, often applied by the use of stamps, overlay almost all paintings from the Cuzco school, endowing them with an illuminated, glittery effect. Some scholars have argued that the excess of gold appealed to Andean sensibilities, given the importance of gold in Inca cosmology, as a direct reference to the sun god, Inti. Finally, the most distinctive category of paintings within the Cuzco school is an enigmatic collection of portraits featuring apocryphal angels holding arquebuses. Representations of angels were wildly popular in the Andean region because they served as stand-ins for celestial deities revered by the Incas less than two centuries prior. Art historians have discovered that the weaponry was copied almost directly from an early 17th-century military manual published in Holland and France that somehow made its way to Peru. The exact significance of the weapon-bearing angels, however, remains a mystery.

THE INCA WORLD TODAY

Although the Incas were conquered more than 450 years ago, they reside in the collective memory of

READING

13.5 This monumental statue of a contemporary Andean male, holding a coca leaf, executed in 2007, is intended to promote Machu Picchu as one of the New Seven Wonders of the World. (Ananda Cohen Suarez)

many Andeans today. The survival of an indigenous—and often, specifically Inca—identity is manifested in many cultural practices such as the yearly Inti Raymi festival celebrated each year at Sacsayhuamán in Cuzco. The Incas have figured in Peruvian and Bolivian literature, popular culture, and even politics. The worldwide interest in the archaeological and cultural patrimony of the Andes has also resulted in outside funding for the maintenance of sites, although this always comes with a double-edged sword, since the rapidly increasing value of Inca and other Andean artifacts intensifies looting and underhanded black-market deals. Nevertheless, Inca culture and identity, many of it mixed with a wealth of local and Spanish tradition, remains strong and makes the Andes one of the most distinctive and fascinating places on Earth.

The Conquest of the Incas

John Hemming, *The Conquest of the Incas* (New York: Harcourt Brace Jovanovich, 1970).

Pedro Pizarro, *Relation of the Discovery and Conquest of the Kingdoms of Peru*. Translated by Philip Ainsworth Means (New York: Cortés Society, 1921).

William H. Prescott, *History of the Conquest of Peru*. 2 vols. (New York: Harper & Brothers Publishers, 1847).

Patricia Seed, "Conquest of the Americas, 1500–1650." In *Cambridge Illustrated History of Warfare: The Triumph of the West*, edited by Geoffrey Parker, 350–517 (Cambridge: Cambridge University Press, 1999).

Ward Stavig, *The World of Tupac Amaru: Conflict, Community, and Identity in Colonial Peru* (Lincoln: University of Nebraska Press, 1999).

Nathan Wachtel, *The Vision of the Vanquished: The Spanish Conquest of Peru through Indian Eyes, 1530–1570*. Translated by Ben and Siân Reynolds (Sussex, U.K.: Harvester Press, 1977).

Colonial Transition and Identity

Rolena Adorno, *Guamán Poma: Writing and Resistance in Colonial Peru*. 2nd ed. (Austin: University of Texas Press, 1986).

Kenneth J. Andrien and Rolena Adorno, eds., *Transatlantic Encounters: Europeans and Andeans in the Sixteenth Century* (Berkeley: University of California Press, 1991).

Noble David Cook, *Demographic Collapse: Indian Peru, 1520–1620* (Cambridge: Cambridge University Press, 1982).

Alfred W. Crosby, *The Columbian Exchange: Biological and Cultural Consequences of 1492* (Westport, Conn.: Greenwood Press, 1972).

Tom Cummins, "A Tale of Two Cities: Cuzco, Lima, and the Construction of Colonial Representation." In *Converging Cultures: Art and Identity in Spanish America*, edited by Diane Fane, 157–170 (New York: Harry Abrams, 1996).

Valerie Fraser, *The Architecture of Conquest: Building in the Viceroyalty of Peru, 1535–1635* (Cambridge: Cambridge University Press, 1990).

Richard L. Kagan, *Urban Images of the Hispanic World, 1493–1793* (New Haven, Conn.: Yale University Press, 2000).

Jay Kinsbruner, *The Colonial Spanish-American City: Urban Life in the Age of Atlantic Capitalism* (Austin: University of Texas Press, 2005).

James Lockhart, *Spanish Peru 1532–1560: A Social History.* 2nd ed. by (Madison: University of Wisconsin Press, 1994).

———, "Three Experiences of Culture Contact: Nahua, Maya, and Quechua." In *Native Traditions in the Postconquest World*, edited by Elizabeth Hill Boone and Tom Cummins, 31–54 (Washington, D.C.: Dumbarton Oaks, 1998).

Susan Elizabeth Ramírez, *The World Upside Down: Cross-Cultural Contact and Conflict in Sixteenth-Century Peru* (Stanford, Calif.: Stanford University Press, 1996).

Irene Silverblatt, *Moon, Sun, and Witches: Gender Ideologies and Class in Inca and Colonial Peru* (Princeton, N.J.: Princeton University Press, 1987).

Transition to Writing

Robert Ascher, "Inka Writing." In *Narrative Threads: Accounting and Recounting in Andean Khipu*, edited by Jeffrey Quilter and Gary Urton, 103–115 (Austin: University of Texas Press, 2002).

Tom Cummins, "Representation in the Sixteenth Century and the Colonial Image of the Inca." In *Writing without Words: Alternative Literacies in Mesoamerica and the Andes*, edited by Elizabeth Hill Boone and Walter D. Mignolo, 188–219 (Durham, N.C.: Duke University Press, 1994).

Joanne Rappaport, "Object and Alphabet: Andean Indians and Documents in the Colonial Period." In *Writing without Words: Alternative Literacies in Mesoamerica and the Andes*, edited by Elizabeth Hill Boone and Walter D. Mignolo, 271–291 (Durham, N.C.: Duke University Press, 1994).

The Spread of Christianity

Carolyn Dean, *Inka Bodies and the Body of Christ: Corpus Christi in Colonial Cuzco, Peru* (Durham, N.C.: Duke University Press, 1999).

Sabine MacCormack, "Pachacuti: Miracles, Punishments, and Last Judgment: Visionary Past and Prophetic Future in Early Colonial Peru," *American Historical Review* 93, no. 4 (October 1988): 960–1,006.

———, *Religion in the Andes: Vision and Imagination in Early Colonial Peru* (Princeton, N.J.: Princeton University Press, 1991).

Kenneth Mills, *Idolatry and Its Enemies: Colonial Andean Religion and Extirpation, 1640–1750* (Princeton, N.J.: Princeton University Press, 1997).

Veronica Salles-Resse, *From Viracocha to the Virgin of Copacabana: Representations of the Sacred at Lake Titicaca* (Austin: University of Texas Press, 1997).

Steve J. Stern, *Peru's Indian Peoples and the Challenge of Spanish Conquest: Huamanga to 1640* (Madison: University of Wisconsin Press, 1982).

Colonial Art

Gauvin Alexander Bailey, *Art of Colonial Latin America* (London: Phaidon Press, 2005).

Carolyn Dean, *Inka Bodies and the Body of Christ: Corpus Christi in Colonial Cuzco, Peru* (Durham, N.C.: Duke University Press, 1999).

George Kubler, *Art and Architecture in Spain and Portugal and Their American Dominions, 1500–1800* (Baltimore, Md.: Penguin Books, 1959).

Ramón Mujica Pinilla et al., *El barroco peruano.* Vols. 1 and 2 (Lima, Peru: Banco de Crédito, 2002).

Suzanne Stratton-Pruit, ed., *The Virgin, Saints, and Angels: South American Paintings, 1600–1825, from the Thoma Collection* (Milan, Italy: Skira, 2006).

The Inca World Today

Thomas A. Abercrombie, *Pathways of Memory and Power: Ethnography and History among an Andean People* (Madison: University of Wisconsin Press, 1998).

John E. Kicza, ed., *The Indian in Latin American History: Resistance, Resilience, and Acculturation* (Wilmington, Del.: Scholarly Resources, 1993).

GLOSSARY

Note: (Q) = Quechua word
      (S) = Spanish word

acllacuna (Q) chosen women; young women chosen by the state to fulfill obligations for the royal family including weaving and *chicha* production

acllahuasi (Q) house of the chosen women; place where ACLLACUNA and MAMAKUNA were housed

acllas (Q) Hispanicized form of ACLLACUNA

aguilla (Q) gold and silver drinking vessel

altiplano high plateau, especially of the Lake Titicaca region

amauta (Q) philosopher

apu (Q) lord

apusquipay (Q) commander of an Inca field army

apusquipratin (Q) deputy commander

aucun runa (Q) warlike people; those who populated Guamán Poma's fourth world age

axis mundi sacred center of the universe

Ayarmarka (Q) November festival in preparation for Cápac Raymi

ayllu (Q) kinship group united by shared descent from a real or mythical ancestor

Aymara language of the Aymara peoples who inhabit parts of southern Peru and Bolivia

Aymoray (Q) festival meaning "great cultivation" that took place during May, during which a ritual harvest of sacred maize fields took place

Ayriwa (Q) ritual festival corresponding to April honoring royal insignia

camasca (Q) man or woman who practiced a form of medicine not unlike shamanistic practice

Camay (Q) period of time corresponding with January in the ritual festival calendar

cancha (Q) enclosed building or group of buildings; basic Inca architectural unit

cápac (Q) term for person of high status

Cápac Hucha (Cápacocha) (Q) royal obligation; state-sanctioned child sacrifice

Cápac Ñan (Q) main Inca royal highway

Cápac Raymi (Q) magnificent festival; celebrated in Cuzco around the first full moon following the December solstice

cay pacha (Q) this world; the Inca name for the terrestrial plane

ceque (Q) imaginary ray or line connecting HUACAS

Chahua Huarquis (Q) festival corresponding to July honoring a specific water source

chasqui (Q) runner who was employed by the central government to deliver messages in a system analogous to a premodern postal service

chicha (Q) maize beer

ciudadela (S) citadel, or "little city"

cocha (Q) any of agricultural works including ridged fields and shallow ponds

colca (Q) storage unit

corporate organized or unified

Coya Raymi (Q) queen's festival, corresponding with September, celebrating the rainy season and to prevent sickness

cumbi (Q) fine cloth

curaca see *KURAKA*

geoglyph earthwork or earth drawing

hañuc pacha (Q) world above; the Inca term for the heavens

harauicu (Q) poet

Hatun Puquy (Q) ritual festival held in February honoring the Sun

hatun runa (Q) adult male

hatun uillca (Q) priest who functioned like a bishop beneath the high priest

huaca (Q) any natural or human-made feature of the environment that is endowed with sacred power

Inti (Q) sun god, the supreme deity of the Incas

Intihuatana (Q) *HUACA* stone that translates to the "hitching post of the Sun," or the "place to which the Sun was tied"

Inti-Illapa (Q) thunder god

Inti Raymi (Q) celebrated in June, this festival included the June winter solstice and a great festival in honor of the sun god, Inti

Itu (Q) special festival held whenever a god's help was deemed necessary

kallanka (Q) large rectangular building with niched walls and multiple doors

K'antaray (Q) festival corresponding with October focused on ensuring sufficient water supplies

kero (Q) ceramic or wood drinking vessel

kuraka (curaca) (Q) local ruler

llacta (Q) town or settlement

Lupaca (Lupaqa) (Q) peoples of Lake Titicaca region

mallqui (Q) a mummified royal ancestor, maintained by a *mallquipavillac*

mamakuna (Q) chosen women of high position who trained the *ACLLACUNA*

Mamasara (Q) festival in which unusually shaped ears of corn, *SARAMAMA*, are wrapped in fine textiles

mascaypacha (Q) woven headdress/crown worn by the Sapa Inca

mestizo person of both Spanish and indigenous ancestry

mita (Q) state tax in the form of labor service

mitimaes Hispanicized form of *MITMAQKUNA*

mitmaqkuna (Q) families removed by the state from their place of origin and sent to fulfill specific tasks or missions

moiety form of social division based on equal halves

ñusta (Q) princess

orejones (S) "big ears"; Spanish term for the Inca king's royal guards and the Inca nobility

Pacariqtambo (Q) cave from which the first Incas emerged according to origin myths

pacha (Q) earth; time; space

Pachacamac (Q) deity and oracle located near modern-day Lima

Pachacuti (Q) meaning "revolution," "turning over/around," or "world reversal," the name of the ninth Inca king

Pachamama (Q) female earth deity; Mother Earth

panaqa (panaca) (Q) royal kin group

pata (Q) terrace or platform

paucar huaray (Q) meaning "earth ripening," the ceremony that corresponds with March in the festival calendar

pukara (purcará) (Q) fortress

puna (Q) high-altitude grasslands above the treeline

punchao (Q) golden disc for the sun god, Inti

Purun Runa (Q) "wild men"; those who populated Guamán Poma's third world age

pururauca (Q) one of many stones that became animated and helped defeat the Chancas according to Inca origin myths

Quechua (Q) lingua franca of the Inca Empire, still spoken today in Peru and parts of Bolivia

quipu (Q) device consisting of knotted strings used for encoding information

runasimi (Q) meaning "human speech," the Inca name for the *QUECHUA* language

Sapa Inca (Q) "unique Inca"; king

saramama (Q) specially chosen corncob wrapped in textiles for use in the *MAMASARA* festival

sinchi (Q) preimperial war leader; also name of Manco Cápac's son

soncoyoc (Q) man or woman who practiced a form of medicine not unlike shamanistic practice

stela large carved stone

suyu (Q) territorial division; each *suyu* was a "quarter" of the Inca Empire, although they were not uniform in shape or size. The four *suyus* were Cuntisuyu, Collasuyu, Chinchaysuyu, and Antisuyu.

tambo (Q) way station, inn, or any small rest stop along the Inca highway system

Tawantinsuyu (Tahuantinsuyo) (Q) the Inca Empire, literally meaning in QUECHUA "four parts together," which refers to the four *SUYUS* that made up the whole: Cuntisuyu, Collasuyu, Chinchaysuyu, and Antisuyu

tumi (Q) ceremonial knives with curved, crescent blades

tupu (Q) shawl pin; also measurement of land

Ucu Pacha (Q) world below; Inca name for the underworld

Uillac Uma (Q) high priest in Cuzco

Wari Runa (Q) those who populated Guamán Poma's second world age

Wari Wiracocharuna (Q) those who populated Guamán Poma's first world age

waru-waru (Q) raised-field agriculture common at Tiwanaku

yanakuna (Q) special class of retainers who served the Inca king and his court

Yana Uillca (Q) ordinary priest

Yapaquis (Q) festival corresponding to August honoring rain and fair weather for planting

BIBLIOGRAPHY

Adorno, Rolena. *Guamán Poma: Writing and Resistance in Colonial Peru.* Austin: University of Texas Press, 1986.

Allen, Catherine. "Body and Soul in Quechua Thought." *Journal of Latin American Lore* 8, no. 2 (1982): 179–186.

———. "Enfolding Oppositions: Structure and Practice in a Quechua Story." *Journal of the Steward Anthropological Society* 25, nos. 1–2 (1997): 9–27.

———. "The Incas Have Gone Inside: Pattern and Persistence in Andean Iconography." *RES: Anthropology and Aesthetics* 42 (2002): 180–203.

———. "Patterned Time: The Mythic History of a Peruvian Community." *Journal of Latin American Lore* 10, no. 2 (1984): 151–173.

———. "Time, Place, and Narrative in an Andean Community." *Bulletin de la Société Suisse sus Américanistes* 57–58 (1993–94): 89–95.

———. "When Utensils Revolt: Mind, Matter, and Models of Being in the Pre-Columbian Andes." *RES: Anthropology and Aesthetics* 33 (Spring 1998): 19–27.

Alva, Walter, and Christopher Donnan. *Royal Tombs of Sipán.* Los Angeles: Fowler Museum, 1993.

Anders, Martha B. *Dual Organization and Calendars Inferred from the Site Plan of Azángaro.* Ann Arbor, Mich.: University Microfilm, 1986.

Andrien, Kenneth J., and Rolena Adorno. *Transatlantic Encounters: Europeans and Andeans in the Six-teenth Century.* Berkeley: University of California Press, 1991.

Anonymous. "Discurso de la sucesión y gobierno de los yngas." In *Juicio de limites entre el Perú y Bolivia; Prueba peruana presentada al gobierno de la República Argentina,* edited by Victor M. Martúa, vol. 8, 149–165. Madrid: Tipografía de los hijos de M. G. Hernandez, 1906.

Arnold, D. Y. "The House of Earth-Bricks and Inka-Stones: Gender, Memory, and Cosmos in Qakachaka." *Journal of Latin American Lore* 17 (1991): 3–69.

Arriaga, Pablo Joseph de. *The Extirpation of Idolatry in Peru.* Translated and edited by L. Clark Keating. Lexington: University of Kentucky Press, 1968.

Ascher, Marcia, and Robert Ascher. *Code of the Quipu.* Ann Arbor: University of Michigan Press, 2002.

———. *Mathematics of the Incas: Codes of the Quipu.* Mineola, N.Y.: Dover Publications, 1997.

———. "Numbers and Relations from Ancient Andean Quipus." *Archives for the History of Exact Sciences* 8 (1972): 288–320.

Ascher, Robert. "Inka Writing." In *Narrative Threads,* edited by Jeffrey Quilter and Gary Urton, 103–115. Austin: University of Texas Press, 2002.

Aveni, Anthony F. "Astronomy and the Ceque System." *Journal of the Steward Anthropological Society* 24, nos. 1–2 (1996): 157–172.

―――. *Between the Lines: The Mystery of the Giant Ground Drawings of Ancient Nasca*. Austin: University of Texas Press, 2000.

―――. "Horizon Astronomy in Incaic Cuzco." In *Archaeoastronomy in the Americas*, edited by Ray A. Williamson, 305–318. Los Altos, Calif.: Balleana Press, 1981.

―――, ed. *The Lines of Nasca*. Philadelphia: American Philosophical Society, 1990.

―――. *Skywatchers.* Rev. ed. of *Skywatchers of Ancient Mexico*. Austin: University of Texas Press, 2001.

―――. *Stairways to the Stars: Skywatching in Three Ancient Cultures*. New York: John Wiley & Sons, 1997.

―――, ed. *World Archaeoastronomy*. Cambridge: Cambridge University Press, 1989.

Aveni, Anthony F., and Gordon Brotherston, eds. *Calendars in Mesoamerica and Peru: Native American Computations of Time*. BAR International Series 174, Proceedings of the 44th International Congress of Americanists, 235–262. Oxford: British Archaeological Reports, 1983.

Bandelier, Adolph F. *The Islands of Titicaca and Koati*. New York: Hispanic Society of America, 1910.

―――. "On the Relative Antiquity of Ancient Peruvian Burials." *Bulletin of the American Museum of Natural History* 20 (1904): 217–226.

Bauer, Brian S. *Ancient Cuzco: Heartland of the Inca*. Austin: University of Texas Press, 2004.

―――. *The Development of the Inca State*. Austin: University of Texas Press, 1992.

―――. "The Legitimization of the Inca State in Myth and Ritual." *American Anthropologist* 98, no. 2 (1996): 327–337.

―――. "Ritual Pathways of the Inca: An Analysis of the Collasuyu Ceques in Cuzco." *Latin American Antiquity* 3, no. 3 (1992): 7–26.

―――. *The Sacred Landscape of the Inca: The Cusco Ceque System*. Austin: University of Texas Press, 1998.

Bauer, Brian S., and David S. P. Dearborn. *Astronomy and Empire in the Ancient Andes*. Austin: University of Texas Press, 1995.

Bauer, Brian S., and Charles Stanish. *Ritual and Pilgrimage in the Andes*. Austin: University of Texas Press, 2001.

Bauer, Ralph, ed. *An Inca Account of the Conquest of Peru by Titu Cusi Yupanqui*. Boulder: Colorado University Press, 2005.

Bawden, G. L. *Galindo and the Nature of the Middle Horizon in Northern Coastal Peru*. Ph.D. diss., Harvard University, 1977.

―――. "Galindo: A Study in Cultural Transition during the Middle Horizon." In *Chan Chan, Andean Desert City*, edited by Michael Moseley and K. C. Day, 285–320. Albuquerque: University of New Mexico Press, 1982.

Bennett, Wendell. "The Archaeology of the Central Andes." In *Handbook of South American Indians*, vol. 2: *The American Civilizations*, edited by Julian H. Steward, Bureau of American Ethnology, Bulletin no. 143, 61–148. Washington, D.C.: Smithsonian Institution, 1946.

―――. "Excavations at Tihuanaco." *Anthropological Papers of the American Museum of Natural History*, 34, no. 3 (1934).

―――. "Excavations in Bolivia." *Anthropological Papers of the American Museum of Natural History* 35 (1936): 331–505.

―――. *A Reappraisal of Peruvian Archaeology*. Menasha, Wisc.: Society for American Archaeology, 1948.

Bennett, Wendell, and Junius Bird. *Andean Cultural History*. 2nd rev. ed. Handbook Series, 15. New York: American Museum of Natural History, 1960.

Berrin, Kathleen, ed. *The Spirit of Ancient Peru*. London: Thames & Hudson, 1998.

Betanzos, Juan de. *Narrative of the Incas*. Translated and edited by Roland Hamilton and Dana Buchanan. Austin: University of Texas Press, 1996.

Bingham, Hiram. "The Discovery of Machu Picchu." *Harper's Magazine* (April 1913), 709–719.

―――. *Inca Land: Explorations in the Highlands of Peru*. 1912. Reprint, New York: Houghton Mifflin Company, 1922.

―――. *Lost City of the Incas: The Story of Machu Picchu and Its Builders*. New York: Atheneum, 1948.

―――. *Machu Picchu: A Citadel of the Incas*. New Haven, Conn.: Yale University Press, 1930.

―――. "Preliminary Report of the Yale Peruvian Expedition." *Bulletin of the American Geographical Society* 44, no. 1 (1912): 20–26.

Bonavia, Duccio. *Mural Painting in Ancient Peru*. Translated by Patricia Lyons. Bloomington: Indiana University Press, 1985.

Boone, Elizabeth H., ed. *Andean Art at Dumbarton Oaks.* 2 vols. Washington, D.C.: Dumbarton Oaks, 1996.

Boone, Elizabeth Hill, and W. D. Mignolo, eds. *Writing without Words: Alternative Literacies in Mesoamerica and the Andes.* Durham, N.C.: Duke University Press, 1994.

Bouchard, Jean-François. *Contribution á l'étude de l'architecture inca: Établisements de la vallée du Rio Vilcanota-Urubamba.* Paris: Éditions de la Maison des Sciences de l'Homme, 1983.

Bourget, Steve. *Sex, Death, and Sacrifice in Moche Religion.* Austin: University of Texas Press, 2006.

Bram, Joseph. *An Analysis of Inca Militarism.* Seattle: University of Washington Press, 1944.

Browman, David L. "Tiwanaku Expansion and Altiplano Economic Patterns." In *Estudios Arquelógicos 5,* 107–120. Antofagasta: Universidad de Chile, 1980.

———. "Toward the Development of the Tiahuanaco (Tiwanaku) State." In *Advances in Andean Archaeology,* edited by D. L. Browman, 327–349. The Hague, Netherlands: Mouton, 1978.

Brundage, Burr C. *Empire of the Inca.* Norman: University of Oklahoma Press, 1963.

———. *Lords of Cuzco: A History and Description of the Inca People in Their Final Days.* Norman: University of Oklahoma Press, 1967.

———. *Two Earths, Two Heavens: An Essay Contrasting the Aztecs and the Incas.* Albuquerque: University of New Mexico Press, 1975.

Brush, Stephen B. *Mountain, Field, and Family: The Economy and Human Ecology of an Andean Valley.* Philadelphia: University of Pennsylvania Press, 1977.

Burger, Richard L. *Chavín and the Origins of Andean Civilization.* London: Thames & Hudson, 1992.

———. *The Occupation of Chavin, Ancash, in the Initial Period and Early Horizon.* Ph.D. diss., Department of Anthropology, University of California, Berkeley, 1978.

———. "An Overview of Peruvian Archaeology (1976–1986)." *Annual Review of Anthropology* 18 (1989): 37–46.

———. "The Radiocarbon Evidence for the Temporal Priority of Chavín de Huantar." *American Antiquity* 46 (1981): 592–602.

———. "The Sacred Center of Chavín de Huantar." In *The Ancient Americas: Art from the Sacred Landscape,* edited by Richard F. Townsend, 265–277. Chicago: Art Institute of Chicago, 1992.

———. "Unity and Heterogeneity within the Chavín Horizon." In *Peruvian Prehistory: An Overview of Pre-Inca and Inca Society,* edited by Richard W. Keatinge, 99–144. Cambridge: Cambridge University Press, 1988.

Burger, Richard L., and Lucy C. Salazar. *Machu Picchu: Unveiling the Mystery of the Incas.* New Haven, Conn.: Yale University Press, 2004.

Carrasco, Pedro. "The Political Economy of the Aztec and Inca States." In *The Inca and Aztec States, 1400–1800: Anthropology and History,* edited by George A. Collier, Renato I. Rosaldo, and John D. Wirth, 23–40. New York: Academic Press, 1982.

Chauchat, Claude, "Early Hunter-Gatherers on the Peruvian Coast." In *Peruvian Prehistory: An Overview of Pre-Inca Society,* edited by Richard W. Keatinge, 41–66. Cambridge: Cambridge University Press, 1988.

Cieza de León, Pedro. *The Discovery and Conquest of Peru.* Durham, N.C.: Duke University Press, 1998.

Classen, Constance. *Inca Cosmology and the Human Body.* Salt Lake City: Utah University Press, 1993.

Cobo, Bernabé. *History of the Inca Empire.* Translated and edited by Roland Hamilton. Austin: University of Texas Press, 1979.

———. *Inca Religions and Customs.* Translated and edited by Roland Hamilton. Austin: University of Texas Press, 1990.

———. "Relación de las guacas del Cuzco." In "An Account of the Shrines of Ancient Cuzco," translated and edited by John H. Rowe. *Ñawpa Pacha* 17 (1979): 2–80.

Collier, George A., Renato I. Rosaldo, and John D. Wirth, eds. *The Inca and Aztec States, 1400–1800.* New York: Academic Press, 1982.

Conklin, William. "The Information System of Middle Horizon Quipus." In *Ethnoastronomy and Archaeoastronomy in the American Tropics,* edited by Anthony Aveni and Gary Urton, 261–282. New York: New York Academy of Sciences, 1982.

Conrad, Geoffrey W. "Cultural Materialism, Split Inheritance, and the Expansion of Ancient Peruvian Empires." *American Antiquity* 46 (1981): 3–26.

Cook, David Noble. *Born to Die: Disease and New World Conquest, 1492–1650.* Cambridge: Cambridge University Press, 1998.

———. *Demographic Collapse: Indian Peru, 1520–1620.* Cambridge: Cambridge University Press, 1981.

Covey, R. Alan. *How the Incas Built Their Heartland.* Ann Arbor: University of Michigan Press, 2005.

Cummins, Tom. "A Tale of Two Cities: Cuzco, Lima, and the Construction of Colonial Representation." In *Converging Cultures: Art and Identity in Spanish America*, edited by Diane Fane, 157–170. New York: Harry Abrams, Inc., 1996.

D'Altroy, Terence N. *The Incas.* London: Blackwell, 2002.

———. *Political and Domestic Economy in the Inka Empire.* Columbia-NYU Latin American, Caribbean, and Iberian Occasional Papers, no. 3. New York: Consortium of Columbia University Institute of Latin American and Iberian Studies and New York University Center for Latin American and Caribbean Studies, 1988.

———. *Provincial Power in the Inka Empire.* Washington, D.C.: Smithsonian Institution, 1992.

———. "Transitions in Power: Centralization of Wanka Political Organization under Inka Rule." *Ethnohistory* 34, no. 1 (1987): 78–102.

D'Altoy Terence, and Christine Ann Hastorf. *Empire and Domestic Economy.* Interdisciplinary Contributions to Archaeology. New York: Kluwer Academic, 2001.

Davies, Nigel. *The Incas.* Niwot: University Press of Colorado, 1995.

Dean, Carolyn S. "Creating a Ruin in Colonial Cusco: Sacsayhuamán and What Was Made of It." *Andean Past* 5 (1998): 161–183.

Dearborn, David S. P., and Katherine J. Schreiber. "Houses of the Rising Sun." In *Time and Calendars in the Inca Empire.* BAR International Series, no. 479, edited by Mariusz S. Ziólkowski and Robert M. Sadowski, 49–74. Oxford: British Archaeological Reports, 1989.

Dearborn, David S. P., M. Seddon, and B. Bauer. "The Sanctuary of Titicaca: Where the Sun Returns to Earth." *Latin American Antiquity* 9 (1998): 240–258.

Dearborn, David S. P., and Raymond E. White. "Intimachay, a December Solstice Observatory." *America Antiquity* 52 (1987): 346–352.

———. "The 'Torreón' at Machu Picchu as an Observatory." *Archaeoastronomy* 5 (1983): 37–49.

———. "Inca Observatories: Their Relation to Calendar and Ritual." In *World Archaeoastronomy*, edited by Anthony Aveni. 462–469. Cambridge: Cambridge University Press, 1989.

Demarest, Arthur Andrew. *Viracocha: The Nature and Antiquity of the Andean High God.* Peabody Museum Monographs 6. Cambridge, Mass.: Harvard University, Peabody Museum of Archaeology and Ethnology, 1984.

Dillehay, Tom D., ed. *Tombs for the Living: Andean Mortuary Practices.* Washington, D.C.: Dumbarton Oaks Research Library and Collection, 1995.

Donnan, Christopher B. *Ceramics of Ancient Peru.* Los Angeles: Fowler Museum, UCLA, 1992.

———. *Early Ceremonial Architecture in the Andes.* Washington, D.C.: Dumbarton Oaks, 1986.

———. *Moche Fineline Painting: Its Evolution and Its Artists.* Los Angeles: Fowler Museum, UCLA, 1999.

Dover, Robert V., Katherine E. Seibold, and John H. McDowell, eds. *Andean Cosmologies through Time.* Bloomington: Indiana University Press, 1992.

Earle, Timothy K., and Terence N. D'Altroy. "The Political Economy of the Inka Empire: The Archaeology of Power and Finance." In *Archaeological Thought in America*, edited by Carl C. Lamberg-Karlovsky, 183–204. Cambridge: Cambridge University Press, 1989.

Escalante Moscoso, Javier F. *Arquitectura prehispánica en los Andes bolivianos.* La Paz, Bolivia: CIMA, 1993.

Farrington, Ian S. "Prehistoric Intensive Agriculture: Preliminary Notes on River Canalization in the Sacred Valley of the Incas." In *Drained Field Agriculture in Central and South America.* BAR International Series, no. 189, edited by John Darch, 221–235. Oxford: British Archaeological Reports, 1983.

———. "Ritual Geography, Settlement Patterns and the Characterization of the Provinces of the Inka Heartland." *World Archaeology* 23 (1992): 368–385.

Fraser, Valerie. *The Architecture of Conquest: Building in the Viceroyalty of Peru, 1535–1635*. Cambridge: Cambridge University Press, 1990.

———. "Art and Architecture in Latin America." In *The Cambridge Companion to Modern Latin American Culture*, edited by John King, 202–235. Cambridge: Cambridge University Press, 2004.

Gade, Daniel W. "Lightning in the Folklife and Religion of the Central Andes." *International Review of Ethnology and Linguistics* 78 (1980): 770–788.

Garcilaso de la Vega, El Inca. *Royal Commentaries of the Inca and General History of Peru*. Austin: University of Texas Press, 1987.

Gasparini, Graziano, and Louise Margolies. *Inca Architecture*. Translated by Patricia Lyons. Bloomington: Indiana University Press, 1980.

Gelles, Paul H. "Equilibrium and Extraction: Dual Organization in the Andes." *American Ethnologist* 22, no. 4 (1995): 710–742.

Gisbert, Teresa, and José de Mesa. *Arquitectura andina, 1530–1830*. La Paz: Embajada de España en Bolivia, 1997.

Gonçález Holguín, Diego. *Vocabulario de la lengua general de todo el Perú llamada lengua Quichua od del Inca*. Edited by Ramiro Matos Mendieta, with a prologue by Raúl Porras Barrenechea. Lima: Universidad National Mayor de San Marcos, Editorial de la Universidad, 1989.

Guamán Poma de Ayala, Felipe. *El primer nueva corónica y buen gobierno*. Edited by John Murra and Rolena Adorno. 3 vols. Mexico: Siglo Veintiuno, 1992.

———. *Letter to a King: A Picture History of the Inca Civilisation*. Edited and translated by Christopher Dilke. London: George Allen & Unwin, 1978.

The Guamán Poma Web site. Available online. URL: http://www.kb.dk/permalink/2006/poma/info/en/frontpage.htm. Accessed June 12, 2008.

Guilmartin, John F., Jr. "The Cutting Edge: An Analysis of the Spanish Invasion and Overthrow of the Inca Empire, 1532–1539." In *Transatlantic Encounters: Europeans and Andeans in the Sixteenth Century*, edited by Kenneth J. Andrien and Rolena Adorno, Berkeley. University of California Press, 1991.

Haas, Jonathan, et al., eds. *The Origins and Development of the Andean State*. Cambridge: Cambridge University Press, 1987.

Harth-Terré, Emilio. "Fundación de la ciudad incaica." *Revista Histórica* (Lima) 16, nos. 1–2 (1943): 98–123.

Heath, Ian. *The Armies of the Aztec and Inca Empires, Other Native Peoples of the Americas, and the Conquistadors, 1450–1608*. Vol. 2: *Armies of the Sixteenth Century*. Guernsey, U.K.: Foundry, 1999.

Hemming, John. *The Conquest of the Incas*. London: MacMillan, 1970.

Hemming, John, and Edward Ranney. *Monuments of the Inca*. Albuquerque: University of New Mexico Press, 1992.

Hennesey, Alistair. "The Nature and Conquest of the Conquistadores." In *The Meeting of Two Worlds: Europe and the Americas, 1492–1650*, edited by Warwick Bray, 5–36. Oxford: Oxford University Press, 1993.

Humboldt, Alexander von. *Vues des cordillères et monuments des peuples indigènes de l'Amérique*. Paris: Legrand, Pomey et Cruzet, libraries-éditeurs, 1813.

Hyland, Sabine P. "The Royal Khipu of Blas Valera." In *Narrative Threads*, edited by Jeffrey Quilter and Gary Urton, 151–170. Austin: University of Texas Press, 2002.

Hyslop, John. *An Archaeological Investigation of the Lupaca Kingdom and Its Origins*. Ph.D. diss., Columbia University, New York, 1976.

———. *The Inka Road System*. Orlando, Fla.: Academic Press, 1984.

———. *Inka Settlement Planning*. Austin: University of Texas Press, 1990.

———. *Inkawasi: The New Cusco, Cañate, Junahuaná, Peru*. BAR International Series 234. Oxford: British Archaeological Papers, 1985.

Israel, Fred L. *The Ancient Incas: Chronicles from National Geographic*. Philadelphia: Chelsea House, 1999.

Jones, Julie, and Heidi King. *Gold of the Americas*. New York: Metropolitan Museum of Art, 2002.

Julien, Catherine. *Inca Administration in the Titicaca Basin as Reflected at the Provincial Capital of Hatunqolla*. Ph.D. diss., Department of Anthropology, University of California, Berkeley, 1978.

———. "Inca Decimal Administration in the Lake Titicaca Region." In *The Inca and Aztec States, 1400–1800*, edited by George A. Collier, Renato I. Rosaldo, and John D. Wirth, 119–152. New York: Academic Press, 1982.

———. *Reading Inca History.* Iowa City: Iowa University Press, 2002.

Kauffman Doig, Federico. *Influencias "inca" en la arquitectura peruana del virreinato: "El fenómeno huamanquino."* Lima, Peru: Universidad Nacional Mayor de San Marcos, 1965.

Keatinge, Richard W., ed. *Peruvian Prehistory.* Cambridge: Cambridge University Press, 1998.

Kendall, Ann. *Aspects of Inca Architecture: Description, Function, and Chronology.* BAR International Series 242, 2 vols. Oxford: British Archaeological Report, 1985.

King, Heidi, et al. *Rain of the Moon: Silver in Ancient Peru.* New Haven, Conn.: Yale University Press, 2001.

Kinsbruner, Jay. *The Colonial Spanish-American City: Urban Life in the Age of Atlantic Capitalism.* Austin: University of Texas Press, 2005.

Kirchoff, Paul. "The Social and Political Organization of the Andean Peoples." In *Handbook of South American Indians.* Vol. 5: *The Comparative Ethnology of South American Indians,* edited by Julian H. Steward, Bureau of American Ethnology Bulletin, no. 143, 293–311. Washington, D.C.: Smithsonian Institution, 1946.

Kolata, Alan L. *The Tiwanaku: Portrait of an Andean Civilization.* London: Blackwell, 1993.

Kubler, George. *The Art and Architecture of Ancient America: The Mexican, Maya, and Andean Peoples.* Harmondsworth, U.K.: Penguin Books, 1975.

———. "The Behavior of Atahualpa, 1531–1533." *Hispanic American Historical Review* 25, no. 4 (November 1945): 413–427.

———. "The Neo-Inca State (1537–1572)." *Hispanic American Review* 27, no. 2 (May 1947): 189–203.

———. "A Peruvian Chief of State: Manco Inca (1515–1545)." *Hispanic American Historical Review* 24, no. 2 (May 1944): 253–276.

———. "The Quechua in the Colonial World." In *Handbook of South American Indians.* Vol. 2: *The American Civilizations, Bureau of American Ethnology Bulletin,* no. 143, edited by Julian Steward, 331–410. Washington, D.C.: Smithsonian Institution, 1946.

Labbe, Armand J. *Shamans, Gods, and Mythic Beasts: Colombian Gold and Ceramics in Antiquity.* Seattle: University of Washington Press, 1999.

Lee, Vincent. "The Building of Sacsayhuaman." *Ñawpa Pacha* 24 (1990): 49–60.

———. *Design by Numbers: Architectural Order among the Inca.* Wilson, Wyo.: self-published, 1992.

———. *The Lost Half of Inca Architecture.* Wilson, Wyo.: self-published, 1988.

———. "Reconstructing the Great Hall at Inkallacta." In *Investigations in Bolivia,* 35–71. Wilson, Wyo.: self-published, 1992.

Lewis, Henri S. "Warfare and the Origin of the State: Another Formulation." In *The Study of the State,* edited by Henri J. M. Classen and Peter Skalnik, 201–221. The Hague, Netherlands: Mouton, 1981.

Locke, Leland L. *The Ancient Quipu or Peruvian Knot Record.* New York: American Museum of Natural History, 1923.

———. "Supplementary Notes on the Quipus in the American Museum of Natural History." In *Anthropological Papers of the American Museum of Natural History* 30, no. 2 (1928): 37–71.

Lumbreras, Luis G. *The Peoples and Cultures of Ancient Peru.* Translated by Betty J. Meggers. Washington, D.C.: Smithsonian Institution Press, 1989.

MacCormack, Sabine. "Children of the Sun and Reason of State Myths, Ceremonies and Conflicts in Inca Peru." *Discovering the Americas:* 1992 Lecture Series. Working Papers no. 6. Department of Spanish and Portuguese, University of Maryland, College Park, 1990.

———. *On the Wings of Time: Rome, the Incas, Spain, and Peru.* Princeton, N.J.: Princeton University Press, 2006.

———. "Pachacuti: Miracles, Punishments, and Last Judgment. Visionary Past and Prophetic Future in Early Colonial Peru." *American Historical Review* 93, no. 4 (October 1988): 960–1,006.

———. *Religion in the Andes: Vision and Imagination in Early Colonial Peru.* Princeton, N.J.: Princeton University Press, 1991.

MacLean, Margaret. *Sacred Land, Sacred Water: Inca Landscape Planning in the Cuzco Area.* Ph.D. diss., Department of Anthropology, University of California, Berkeley, 1986.

Malpass, Michael A. *Daily Life in the Inca Empire.* Westport, Conn.: Greenwood Press, 1996.

Markham, Clements Robert. *Cuzco: A Journey to the Ancient Capital of Peru*. London: Chapman & Hall, 1856.

McEwan, Colin. *Pre-Columbian Gold: Technology, Style, and Iconography*. London: British Museum, 2000.

McEwan, Colin, and Maarten van de Guchte. "Ancestral Time and Sacred Space in Inca State Ritual." In *The Ancient Americas: Art from Sacred Landscapes*, edited by Richard F. Townshend, 359–373. Chicago: Art Institute of Chicago, 1992.

McEwan, Gordon F. *The Incas: New Perspectives*. Santa Barbara, Calif.: ABC-CLIO, 2006.

———. "Investigations at the Pikillacta Site: A Provincial Huari Center in the Valley of Cuzco." In *Huari Administrative Structure: Prehistoric Monumental Architecture and State Government*, edited by William H. Isbell and Gordon F. McEwan, 93–119. Washington, D.C.: Dumbarton Oaks, 1991.

———. *The Middle Horizon in the Valley of Cuzco, Peru: The Impact of the Wari Occupation of Pikillacta in the Lucre Basin*. BAR International Series, S-372. Oxford: British Archaeological Reports, 1987.

Menzel, Dorothy. *Pottery Style and Society in Ancient Peru: Art as a Mirror of History in the Ica Valley, 1350–1470*. Berkeley: University of California Press, 1976.

Mills, Kenneth. *Idolatry and Its Enemies: Colonial Andean Religion and Extirpation, 1640–1750*. Princeton, N.J.: Princeton University Press, 1992.

Montesinos, Fernando de. *Memorias antiguas historiales del Perú*. Translated and edited by Philip Ainsworth Means. Introduction by Clements R. Markham. London: Hakluyt Society, 1920.

Moore, Jerry D. "The Archaeology of Plazas and the Proxemics of Ritual: Three Andean Traditions." *American Anthropologist* 98, no. 4 (1996): 789–802.

———. *Architecture and Power in the Ancient Andes*. Cambridge: Cambridge University Press, 2005.

———. *Cultural Landscapes in the Ancient Andes*. Gainesville: University Press of Florida, 2005.

Moorehead, Elisabeth L. "Highland Inca Architecture in Adobe." *Ñawpa Pacha* 16 (1982): 65–94.

Morris, Craig. "The Archaeological Study of Andean Exchange Systems." In *Social Archaeology: Beyond Subsistence and Dating*, edited by C. Redman, 315–327. New York: Academic Press, 1978.

———. "The Infrastructure of Inka Control in the Peruvian Central Highlands." In *The Inca and Aztec States, 1400–1800: Anthropology and History*, edited by George A. Collier, Renato I. Rosaldo, and John D. Wirth, 153–171. New York: Academic Press, 1982.

———. "Inka Strategies of Incorporation and Governance." In *Archaic States*, edited by Gary M. Feinman and Joyce Marcus, 293–309. Santa Fe, N.Mex.: School of American Research Press, 1998.

———. "Master Design of the Inca." *Natural History* 85, no. 10 (1976): 58–67.

———. "Reconstructing Patterns of Non-Agricultural Production in the Inca Economy: Archaeology and Ethnohistory in Institutional Analysis." In *The Reconstruction of Complex Societies*, edited by C. Moore, 49–60. Philadelphia: American Schools of Oriental Research, 1974.

———. "Signs of Division, Symbols of Unity: Art in the Inka Empire." In *Circa 1492: Art in the Age of Exploration*, edited by Jay A. Levenson, 521–528. Washington, D.C.: National Gallery of Art, 1991.

———. "State Settlements in Tawantinsuyu: A Strategy of Compulsory Urbanism." In *Contemporary Archaeology: A Guide to Theory and Contributions*, edited by Mark P. Leone, 393–401. Carbondale: Southern Illinois University Press, 1972.

———. "Symbols to Power: Styles and Media in the Inka State." In *Style, Society, and Person: Archaeological and Ethnological Perspectives*, edited by Christopher Carr and Jill E. Neitzel, 419–433. New York: Plenum Press, 1995.

Morris, Craig, and Adriana von Hagen. *The Inka Empire and Its Andean Origins*. New York: Abbeville Press, 1993.

Morris, Craig, and Donald E. Thompson. *Huanuco Pampa: An Inca City and Its Hinterland*. London: Thames & Hudson, 1985.

Moseley, Michael. "The Archaeological Study of Andean Exchange Systems." In *Social Archaeology: Beyond Subsistence and Dating*, edited by C. Redman et al., 135–327. New York: Academic Press, 1978.

———. "Chan Chan: Andean Alternative to the Pre-Industrial City." *Science* 187 (1975): 219–225.

———. "The Evolution of Andean Society." In *Ancient Native Americans*, edited by J. D. Jennings, 491–541. San Francisco: W. H. Freeman, 1978.

———. *The Incas and Their Ancestors*. Rev. ed. New York: Thames & Hudson, 2001.

———. *The Maritime Foundations of Andean Civilization*. Menlo Park, Calif.: Cummings, 1975.

———. *Peru's Golden Treasure*. Chicago: Field Museum of Natural History, 1979.

———. "Subsistence and Demography: An Example of Interaction from Prehistoric Peru." *Southwestern Journal of Anthropology* 28 (1972): 25–49.

Moseley, Michael, and K. C. Day, eds. *Chan Chan: Andean Desert City*. Albuquerque: University of New Mexico Press, 1982.

Murra, John. "An Aymara Kingdom in 1567." *Ethnohistory* 15 (1968): 115–151.

———. "Cloth and Its Functions in the Inca State." *American Anthropologist* 64 (1962): 710–728.

———. *The Economic Organization of the Inca State*. Greenwich, Conn.: JAI Press, 1980.

———. "The Expansion of the Inka State: Armies, War, and Rebellions." In *Anthropological History of Andean Polities*, edited by John V. Murra et al., 49–59. Cambridge: Cambridge University Press, 1986.

———. "La guerre et les rebellions dans l'expansion de l'État inca." In *Annales Economies, Sociétés, Civilisations* 34, nos. 5–6, *Anthropologie historique des sociétés andines* (1978): 927–935.

———. "The Mit'a Obligations of Ethnic Groups to the Inka State." In *The Inca and Aztec States, 1400–1800*, edited by George A. Collier, Renato I. Rosaldo, and John D. Wirth, 237–262. New York: Academic Press, 1982.

———. *New Data on Retainer and Servile Populations in Tawantinsuyu*. Congreso Internacional de Americanistas, Spain, 1964. *Actas y Memorias*, vol. 2, nos. 35–45. Seville, Spain: 1943.

———. "Rite and Crop in the Inca State." In *Culture in History*, edited by S. Dimond, New York: Columbia University Press, 1960.

Murra, John, and Craig Morris. "Dynastic Oral Tradition, Administrative Records and Archaeology in the Andes." *World Archaeology* 7, no. 3 (1976): 259–279.

Murúa, Martín de. *Historia del origen y genealogía real de los reyes incas del Perú*. Introduction and notes by Constantino Bayle. Biblioteca "Missionalis Hispánica," vol. 2. 1615. Reprint, Madrid: Instituto Santo Toribio de Mogrovego, 1946.

Nair, Stella Elise. *Of Remembering and Forgetting: The Architecture of Chinchero, Peru from Thupa 'Inka to the Spanish Occupation*. Ph.D. diss., University of California, Berkeley, 2003.

———. *Stone against Stone: An Investigation into the Use of Stone Tools at Tiahuanaco*. M.A. diss., University of California, Berkeley, 1997.

———. "Witnessing the Invisibility of Inca Architecture in Colonial Peru." *Building and Landscapes* 14 (2007): 50–65.

Niles, Susan A. *Callachaca: Style and Status in an Inca Community*. Iowa City: University of Iowa Press, 1987.

———. "Inca Architecture and the Sacred Landscape." In *The Ancient Americas: Art from the Sacred Landscapes*, edited by Richard Townsend, 347–357. Chicago: Art Institute of Chicago, 1992.

———. "Looking for 'Lost' Inca Palaces." *Expedition* 30, no. 3 (1988): 56–64.

———. "The Nature of Inca Royal Estates." In *Machu Picchu: Unveiling the Mystery of the Incas*, edited by Richard L. Burger and Lucy C. Salazar, 49–70. New Haven, Conn.: Yale University Press, 2004.

———. "The Provinces in the Heartland: Stylistic Variation and Architectural Innovation Near Cuzco." In *Provincial Inca: Archaeological and Ethnohistorical Assessment of the Impact of the Inca State*, 146–176. Iowa City: University of Iowa Press, 1993.

———. *The Shape of Inca History*. Iowa City: University of Iowa Press, 1999.

Nordensköld, Erland. *Calculations with Years and Months in the Peruvian Quipus*. Göteburg, Sweden: Elanders Boktyckeri Akjebolag, 1925.

Pachacuti Yamqui, Juan de Santa Cruz. *An Account of the Antiquities of Peru*. Translated by Clements R. Markham. Boston: Massachusetts Historical Society, 1916.

Parker, Geoffrey, ed. *Cambridge Illustrated History of Warfare: The Triumph of the West*. Cambridge: Cambridge University Press, 1995.

Pasztory, Esther. "Andean Aesthetics." In *The Spirit of Ancient Peru: Treasures from the Museo Arqueológico Rafael Larco Herrera*, edited by Kathleen

Berrin, 61–69. London: Thames & Hudson, 1997.

Paternosto, César. *The Stone and the Thread: Andean Roots of Abstract Art.* Austin: University of Texas Press, 1989.

Patterson, Thomas C. "The Huaca La Florida, Rimac Valley, Peru." In *Early Ceremonial Architecture in the Andes,* edited by Christopher B. Donnan, 59–70. Washington, D.C.: Dumbarton Oaks, 1985.

———. *The Inca Empire: The Formation and Disintegration of a Pre-Capitalist State.* New York: St. Martin's Press, 1991.

Paul, Anne. *Paracas Art and Architecture.* Iowa City: University of Iowa Press, 1991.

———. *Paracas Ritual Attire.* Oklahoma City: Oklahoma University Press, 1990.

Pease, Franklin G. Y. "The Formation of Tawantinsuyu: Mechanisms of Colonization and Relationship with Ethnic Groups." In *The Inca and Aztec States, 1400–1800,* edited by George A. Collier, Renato I. Rosaldo, and John D. Wirth, 173–198. New York: Academic Press, 1982.

Pillsbury, Joanne, ed. *Moche Art and Archaeology in Ancient Peru.* New Haven, Conn.: Yale University Press, 2001.

Pineda, Rosa Fung. "The Late Preceramic and Initial Periods." In *Peruvian Prehistory: An Overview of Pre-Inca Society,* edited by Richard W. Keatinge, 67–98. Cambridge: Cambridge University Press, 1988.

Pizarro, Pedro. *Relation of the Discovery and Conquest of the Kingdoms of Peru.* Translated and edited by Philip Ainsworth Means. New York: Cortés Society, 1921.

Polo de Ondegardo, Juan. *Instruction against the Ceremonies and Rites That the Indians Practice in Conformance with the Stage of their Infidelity.* Translated by A. Brunel, John Murra, and Sidney Muirden. New Haven, Conn.: Human Relations Files, 1965.

———. *On the Errors and Superstitions of the Indians, Taken from the Treatise and Investigation Done by Licentiate Polo.* Translated by A. Brunel, John Murra, and Sidney Muirden. New Haven, Conn.: Human Relations Files, 1965.

———. *A Report on the Basic Principles Explaining the Serious Harm Which Follows When the Traditional Rights of the Indians Are Not Respected.* Translated by A. Brunel, John Murra, and Sidney Muirden, 53–196. New Haven, Conn.: Human Relations Files, 1965.

———. *Superstitions of the Indians, Taken from the Second Provincial Council of Lima.* Translated by A. Brunel, John Murra, and Sidney Muirden. New Haven, Conn.: Human Relations Files, 1965.

Prescott, William Hickling. *History of the Conquest of Peru.* 2 vols. New York: Harper & Brothers Publishers, 1847.

Protzen, Jean-Pierre. "Inca Architecture." In *The Inca World: The Development of Pre-Columbian Peru, A.D. 1000–1534,* edited by Laura Laurencich-Minelli, 193–217. Norman: University of Oklahoma Press, 1992.

———. *Inca Architecture and Construction at Ollantaytambo.* London: Oxford University Press, 1993.

———. "Inca Stonemasonry." *Scientific American* 254, no. 2 (1986): 94–105.

Protzen, Jean-Pierre, and Stella Nair. "Who Taught the Inca Stonemasons Their Skills? A Comparison of Tihuanaco and Inca Cut-Stone Masonry." *Journal of the Society of Architectural Historians* 56 (1997): 146–167.

Proulx, Donald. *A Sourcebook of Nasca Ceramic Iconography.* Iowa City: University of Iowa Press, 2006.

Quilter, Jeffrey. *Treasures of the Andes.* London: Duncan Baird Publishers, 2005.

Quilter, Jeffrey, and Gary Urton, eds. *Narrative Threads.* Austin: University of Texas Press, 2002.

Raaflaub, Kurt A. *War and Peace in the Ancient World.* The Ancient World—Comparative Histories. Malden, Mass.: Blackwell Publishing, 2007.

Randall, Robert. "Qoyllur Rit'I, an Inca Fiesta of the Pleiades: Reflections on Time and Space in the Andean World." *Bulletin de l'Institut Français d'Études Andines* 11, nos. 1–2 (1982): 37–81.

Reinhard, Johan. *Machu Picchu: The Sacred Center.* Lima, Peru: Nuevas Imágenes, 1991.

Rodman, Amy Oakland, and Vicki Cassman. "Andean Tapestry: Structure Informs the Surface." *Art Journal* 54 (1995): 33–39.

Rostworowski de Diez Canseco, María. *History of the Inca Realm.* Translated by Harry B. Iceland. Cambridge: Cambridge University Press, 1999.

Rowe, Ann. "Inca Weaving and Costume." *Textile Museum Journal* 34–35 (1997): 5–54.

———. "Technical Features of Inca Tapestry Tunics." *Textile Museum Journal* 17 (1978): 5–28.

Rowe, John H. "Absolute Chronology in the Andean Area." *American Antiquity*, 10, no. 3 (1945): 265–284.

———. "How Did the Inca Say 'Sacsayhuamán' in the Sixteenth Century?" *Ñawpa Pacha* 25–27 (2004): 151–153.

———. "Inca Culture at the Time of the Spanish Conquest." In *Handbook of South American Indians*. Vol. 2: *The American Civilizations*, edited by Julian H. Steward, Bureau of American Ethnology Bulletin 143, 183–330. Washington, D.C.: Smithsonian Institution, 1946.

———. "Inca Policies and Institutions Relating to the Cultural Unification of the Empire." In *The Inca and Aztec States, 1400–1800*, edited by George A. Collier, Renato I. Rosaldo, and John D. Wirth, 93–118. New York: Academic Press, 1982.

———. "The Incas under Spanish Colonial Institutions." *Hispanic American Review* 37, no. 2 (May 1957): 155–199.

———. *An Introduction to the Archaeology of Cuzco*. Cambridge, Mass.: Peabody Museum of American Archaeology and Ethnology, 1944.

———. "The Kingdom of Chimor." *Acta Americana*, Mexico (January–February 1948): 26–59.

———. "What Kind of Settlement Was Inca Cuzco?" *Ñawpa Pacha* 5 (1982): 59–77.

Sadowski, Robert M. "A Few Remarks on the Astronomy of R. T. Zuidema's 'Quipu-Calendar.'" In *Time and Calendars in the Inca Empire*, edited by Marius S. Ziólkowski and Robert M. Sadowski, BAR International Series 479, 75–106. Oxford: British Archaeological Reports, 1989.

———. "The Sky above the Incas: An Abridged Astronomical Calendar for the 16th Century." In *Time and Calendars in the Inca Empire*, edited by Mariusz S. Ziólkowski and Robert M. Sadowski, BAR International Series 479, 75–106. Oxford: British Archaeological Reports, 1989.

Salles-Reese, Veronica. *From Viracocha to the Virgin of Copacabana: Representations of the Sacred at Lake Titicaca*. Austin: University of Texas Press, 1997.

Sallnow, Robert J. *Pilgrims of the Andes: Regional Cults in Cuzco*. Washington, D.C.: Smithsonian Institution Press, 1987.

Salomon, Frank. "'The Beautiful Grandparents': Andean Ancestor Shrines and Mortuary Ritual as Seen through Colonial Records." In *Tombs for the Living: Andean Mortuary Practices*, edited by Tom D. Dillehay, 315–353. Washington, D.C.: Dumbarton Oaks Research Library and Collection, 1995.

Salomon, Frank, and Stuart B. Schwartz, eds. *Cambridge History of the Native Peoples of the Americas*. Vol. 3. Cambridge: Cambridge University Press, 1999.

Sarmiento de Gamboa, Pedro. *Historia índica*. Biblioteca de Autores Españoles, vol. 135. 1572. Reprint, Madrid: Ediciones Atlas, 1960.

Schaedel, Richard P. "Early State of the Incas." In *The Early State*, edited by Henri Claessen and Peter Skalnick, 289–320. The Hague, Netherlands: Mouton, 1978.

Schreiber, Katharina J. *Wari Imperialism in Middle Horizon Peru*. Anthropological Papers 87. Ann Arbor: University of Michigan, Museum of Anthropology, 1992.

Seed, Patricia. "Conquest of the Americas, 1500–1650." In *Cambridge Illustrated History of Warfare: The Triumph of the West*, edited by Geoffrey Parker, 132–154. Cambridge: Cambridge University Press, 1995.

Shimada, Izumi. "Evolution of Andean Diversity (500 B.C.E.–C.E. 600)." In *The Cambridge History of the Native Peoples of the Americas*. Vol. 3: *South America*, edited by Frank Salomon and Stuart B. Schwartz, 350–517. Cambridge: Cambridge University Press, 1999.

Silverblatt, Irene. "Andean Women in the Inca Empire." *Feminist Studies* 4, no. 3 (1978): 37–61.

———, *Moon, Sun, and Witches: Gender Ideologies and Class in Inca and Colonial Peru*. Princeton, N.J.: Princeton University Press, 1987.

Silverman, Helaine. "The Archaeological Identification of an Ancient Peruvian Pilgrimage Center." *World Archaeology* 26, no. 1 (1994): 1–18.

Silverman, Helaine, and Donald Proulx. *The Nasca*. London: Blackwell, 2002.

Sherbondy, Jeanette E. *The Canal System of Hanan Cuzco*. Ph.D. diss., University of Illinois, Urbana, 1982.

———. "Water Ideology in Inca Ethnogenesis." In *Andean Cosmologies through Time: Persistence and Emergence*, edited by Robert V. H. Dover, Katherine Seibold, and John McDowell, 46–66. Bloomington: Indiana University Press, 1992.

Spalding, Karen. "Invaded Societies: Andean Area (1500–1580)." In *Cambridge History of the Native Peoples of the Americas*. Vol. 3: *South America*, edited by Frank Salomon and Stuart B. Schwartz, 904–972. Cambridge: Cambridge University Press, 1999.

Squier, George. *Incidents of Travel and Exploration in the Land of the Incas*. London: Macmillan, 1877.

Steele, Paul. *Handbook of Inca Mythology*. Santa Barbara, Calif.: ABC-CLIO, 2004.

Stern, S. J. *Peru's Indian Peoples and the Challenge of the Spanish Conquest: Huamanga to 1640*. 2nd ed. Madison: University of Wisconsin Press, 1993.

Stone-Miller, Rebecca. *Art of the Andes*. 2nd ed. London: Thames & Hudson, 2002.

———. *To Weave for the Sun*. London: Thames & Hudson, 1992.

Sullivan, William. *The Secret of the Incas: Myth, Astronomy, and the War against Time*. New York: Crown Publishers, 1996.

Thompson, Donald E., and John V. Murra. "The Inca Bridges of the Huanuco Region." *American Antiquity* 31, no. 5 (1966): 632–639.

Uhle, Max. "Explorations at Chincha." *University of California Publications in Archaeology and Ethnology* 21, no. 2 (1924): 55–94.

———. *Pachacamac. Report of the William Pepper, M.D., LL.D. Peruvian Expedition of 1896*. Philadelphia: Department of Archaeology, University of Pennsylvania, 1903.

Urton, Gary. "Astronomy and Calendrics on the Coast of Peru." In *Ethnoastronomy and Archaeoastronomy in the American Tropics*, vol. 385, edited by Anthony F. Aveni and Gary Urton, 231–247. New York: Annals of the New York Academy of Sciences, 1982.

———. *At the Crossroads of the Earth and the Sky: An Andean Cosmology*. Austin: University of Texas Press, 1981.

———. "From Knots to Narratives: Reconstructing the Art of Historical Record Keeping in the Andes from Spanish Transcriptions of Inka Khipus." *Ethnohistory* 45, no. 3 (1998): 409–438.

———. *The History of a Myth: Pacariqtambo and the Origin of the Inkas*. Austin: University of Texas Press, 1990.

———. *Inca Myths*. 1st University of Texas Press edition. Austin: University of Texas Press, 1999.

———. "A New Twist in an Old Yarn: Variation in Knot Directionality in the Inka Khipus." *Baessler-Archiv n.F. Band* 42 (1995): 271–305.

———. "Orientation in Quechua and Incaic Astronomy." *Ethnology* 17 (1978): 157–167.

———. "Recording Signs in Narrative-Accounting Khipu." In *Narrative Threads*, edited by Jeffrey Quilter and Gary Urton, 171–196. Austin: University of Texas Press, 2002.

Valera, Blas. "De las costumbres antiguas de los naturales del Pirú." In *Tres relaciones de antigüedades peruanas*, edited by M. Jimenez de la Espada, 135–203. Asunción, Paraguay: Editorial Guatanía, 1950.

Van Buren, Mary. "Rethinking the Vertical Archipelago: Ethnicity, Exchange, and History in the South Central Andes." *American Anthropologist*, New Series 98, no. 2 (1996): 338–351.

van de Guchte, Maarten. *"Carving the World": Inca Monumental Sculpture and Landscape*. Ph.D. diss., Department of Anthropology, University of Ilinois at Urbana-Champaign. Ann Arbor, Mich.: University Microfilms, 1990.

von Hagen, Adriana, and Craig Morris. *The Cities of the Ancient Andes*. London: Thames & Hudson, 1998.

Wachtel, Nathan. "The *Mitimas* of the Cochabamba Valley: The Colonization Policy of Huayna Cápac." In *The Inca and Aztec States, 1400–1800*, edited by George A. Collier, Renato I. Rosaldo, and John D. Wirth, 199–235. New York: Academic Press, 1982.

Willey, Gordon. "Functional Analysis of 'Horizon Styles' in Peruvian Archaeology." In *A Reappraisal of Peruvian Archaeology*, vol. 4, edited by Wendell C. Bennett, 8–15. Menasha, Wisc.: Society for American Archaeology Memoir, 1948.

Wright, Kenneth R., and Alfredo Valecia Z. *Machu Picchu: A Civil Engineering Marvel*. Reston, Va.: American Society of Civil Engineers, 2000.

Young-Sanchez, Margaret, et al. *Tiwanaku: Ancestors of the Inca*. Denver, Colo.: Denver Art Museum, 2004.

Ziólkowski, Mariusz S. "Knots and Oddities: The Quipu-Calendar or Supposed Luni-Sidereal Calendar." In *Time and Calendars in the Inca Empire*, edited by Mariusz S. Ziólkowski and Robert M.

Sadowski, BAR International Series 479, 197–208. Oxford: British Archaeological Reports, 1989.

Ziólkowski, Mariusz S., and Robert M. Sadowski. "The Astronomical Data in Fernando Montesinos' Peruvian Chronicle: The Comets of Qhapaq Yupanqui." *Archaeoastronomy* 3, no. 2 (1980): 22–26.

———, eds. *Time and Calendars in the Inca Empire.* BAR International Series 479. Oxford: British Archaeological Reports, 1989.

Zuidema, R. Tom. "Anthropology and Archaeoastronomy." In *Archaeoastronomy in the Americas*, edited by Ray A. Williamson, 29–31. Los Altos, Calif.: Balleana Press, 1981.

———. *The Ceque System of Cuzco: The Social Organization of the Capital of the Inca.* Translated by Eva M. Hooykaas. International Archives of Ethnography, supplement to vol. 50. Leiden, Netherlands: E. J. Brill, 1964.

———. "Guamán Poma and the Art of Empire: Toward an Iconography of Inca Royal Dress." In *Transatlantic Encounters: Europeans and Andeans in the Sixteenth Centuries*, edited by K. J. Andrien and Rolena Adorno, 151–275. Berkeley: University of California Press, 1991.

———. "Hierarchy and Space in Incaic Social Organization." *Ethnohistory* 30 (1983): 49–75.

———. "The Inca Calendar." In *Native American Astronomy*, edited by Anthony F. Aveni, 219–259. Austin: University of Texas Press, 1977.

———. *Inca Civilization in Cuzco.* Translated by Jean-Jacques Decoster. Austin: University of Texas Press, 1990.

———. "The Inca Kinship System: A New Theoretical View." In *Andean Kinship and Marriage*, no. 7, edited by Ralph Bolton and Enrique Mayer, 240–281. Washington, D.C.: American Anthropological Association Special Publication, 1977.

———. "Inca Observations of the Solar and Lunar Passages through Zenith and Anti-Zenith at Cuzco." In *Archaeoastronomy in the Americas*, edited by Ray A. Williamson, 419–458. Los Altos, Calif.: Balleana Press, 1981.

———. "Myth and History in Ancient Peru." In *The Logic of Culture*, edited by I. Rossi, 150–175. South Hadley, Mass.: Bergin, 1982.

———. "The Pillars of Cuzco: Which Two Dates of Sunset Did They Define?" In *New Directions in American Archaeoastronomy*, edited by Anthony Aveni, 143–169. BAR International Series 454. Oxford: British Archaeological Reports, 1988.

———. "Towards a General Star Calendar in Ancient Peru." In *Calendars in Mesoamerica and Peru: Native American Computations of Time*, edited by Anthony F. Aveni and Gordon Brotherston, 235–262. BAR International Series 174, Proceedings of the 44th International Congress of Americanists. Oxford: British Archaeological Reports, 1983.

INDEX

hunter-gatherers
    Archaic Period 61
    Early Archaic Period 26–27
    Guitarrero cave 26
    Late Pleistocene/Paleo-
       Indian Period 24–26
hunting **235**
hunu kuraka 101
hurin **75**
    cosmology 142
    Cuntisuyu 64
    Cuzco division 65. *See also*
       Hurin Cuzco
    Early Inca 44
    military organization 101
    urban planning 202, 204
Hurin Cuzco 65, 76*m*, 81, 137,
    144*m*, 204
Hurin Pacha 151

I
Ice Maiden **158–159**
ichu 54–55, 256
identity. *See* national identity
An Inca Account (Castro) 281
Inca conquests **113–117**, 115*m*,
    117
    in *Relación de Chincha* 13
    strategies of 107–109
"Inca Culture at the Time of the
    Spanish Conquest" (Rowe) 6
Inca decimal administration. *See*
    civil administration
Inca Empire **63–70**, 66*m*,
    85–93, 115*m*
    administration. *See* civil
       administration
    barriers to unity 93
    beginnings of 83–85
    building campaigns 92–93
    Cajamarca 67
    Caranqui 65–66
    Catarpe 69
    ceramics 173, *173*
    Chachapoyas 67
    Chanca War 84–85
    Chincha 68

Cochabamba 69
crime and punishment 273
Cuzco 64–65
decline of xi
demographic collapse 282
ecological zones 50*m*
expansion **85–86**
expansion myth 138–139
highway system 92*m*. *See also*
    roads
Huamachuco 67–68
huamani 64
Huánuco Pampa 68
infrastructure 91–93, 201–
    202
modern life 292–293
Pumpu 69
Quito 66
reciprocity 108
Relación de Chincha 13
Samaipata 69
split inheritance 113
stone and origin myth 164
stonework and beginning
    myths 164
suyus 63–64, 64*m*
territorial acquisition by
    rulers 85–86
at time of arrival of Spanish
    xi
Tucumán 70
Tumbes 65
Tumipampa 66–67
types of conquest 107–109
unification strategies 86–89
Vilcashuamán 68–69
incahuasi 202
Incallacta **107**, 196
Inca Religion and Customs (Cobo)
    222, 254
Inca Roca **81**
Incas by privilege **76–77**, 81
Incawasi **107**
indio ladino 16
industry **242–247**
    craft production 244–247
    labor division 242–244

maritime transportation
    240–242, *241*, *242*
    trade networks 247
ingenios 284
Initial Period (ca. 1800–1300
    B.C.E.) **29–31**
    Alto Sechín complex 30–31
    Caballo Muerto 31
    Chiripa 31
    Cuzco Basin 31
    Huaca La Florida 30
intermarriage 283
intermediate periods 7. *See also*
    Early Intermediate Period;
    Late Intermediate Period
Inti 86–87, 127, 128, **129**
Intihuatana *168*, **168–169**, 197
Inti-Illapa **130**
    acllas and 262
    and Coricancha 198
    and *huacas* 125
    and rainy season 264
    sacrifices to 127
    Viracocha and 128
Inti Raymi **132**
*Introduction to the Archaeology of
    Cuzco* (Rowe) 6
irrigation **236**
    and agriculture 232
    in the Andes 57
    and Chahua Huarquis 132
    in Cordillera Oriental 59
    in Early Intermediate Period
       38
    and expansion of Inca Empire
       51
    in Inca Cuzco 63
    in Initial Period 30
    in Late Intermediate Period
       41, 42
    in Middle Horizon Period 40
    and sunken gardens 234
    and terraces 170
    Wari 40
Island of the Sun/Island of the
    Moon 199
Itu ceremony 109, 133–134

F
3429
.S93
2011